The Magnificent '60s

ALSO BY BRIAN HANNAN AND FROM MCFARLAND

*The Gunslingers of '69: Western
Movies' Greatest Year* (2019)

*In Theaters Everywhere: A History of the Hollywood
Wide Release, 1913–2017* (2019)

*Coming Back to a Theater Near You: A History
of Hollywood Reissues, 1914–2014* (2016)

The Making of The Magnificent Seven: *Behind
the Scenes of the Pivotal Western* (2015)

The Magnificent '60s

*The 100 Most Popular Films
of a Revolutionary Decade*

BRIAN HANNAN

McFarland & Company, Inc., Publishers
Jefferson, North Carolina

ISBN (print) 978-1-4766-8723-0
ISBN (ebook) 978-1-4766-4506-3

LIBRARY OF CONGRESS AND BRITISH LIBRARY
CATALOGUING DATA ARE AVAILABLE

Library of Congress Control Number 2022017330

© 2022 Brian Hannan. All rights reserved

*No part of this book may be reproduced or transmitted in any form
or by any means, electronic or mechanical, including photocopying
or recording, or by any information storage and retrieval system,
without permission in writing from the publisher.*

Front cover image © 2022 DGIM studio/Shutterstock

Printed in the United States of America

*McFarland & Company, Inc., Publishers
Box 611, Jefferson, North Carolina 28640
www.mcfarlandpub.com*

To Anne Marie. As always. For always.

Table of Contents

Preface
1

Introduction
3

The Films
13

Conclusion
197

Appendix: Oscar Alignment
201

Chapter Notes
205

*Bibliography: Sources and Books
for Further Reading*
255

Index
259

Preface

My formative years in terms of movies coincided with the rise of the critic and the auteur theory, invented by Andrew Sarris,[1] which valued directors far more highly than actors, dramatically changing the status quo. Critics like Sarris developed their own pantheon of artists who could be considered great and routinely ridiculed those actors or directors who did not come up to the mark or whose works occasionally fell short of the lofty standards thus set.[2] Critics liked nothing better than to hail a new, unknown talent—and be the first to do so—and regularly found fault with films that had big budgets.[3] In short, they set out to pulverize popularity. In a separate endeavor, academics found a new way of looking at films, deciphering in movies previously unforeseen aspects, epitomized by Peter Wollen's seminal *Signs and Meaning in the Cinema* (1969).[4] If ever a small picture turned into a big hit, it was always, it was claimed, down to the efforts of critics who championed the movie. More importantly, critics were a law unto themselves.[5] Movies the public loved were often the very ones that critics and academics disdained. As a consequence, the universal question on critical lips was: How could the public be so foolish and so gullible?

That meant I was often a puzzle to myself. How could I enjoy a picture that apparently lacked critical merit? Or had no redeemable features according to those who knew best? It was a paradox that I have pondered to this day. I am not talking here of films "so bad they're good," a category invented to accommodate a particular guilty pleasure such as the Ed Wood portfolio, or of films deemed "camp classics" like *Valley of the Dolls* (1967). In fact, *Valley of the Dolls* is a good place to start in the critic vs. public divide. Here was a film based on a novel which the literary critics of the period derided (although more recently its merits have been reassessed) and turned into a big-budget film with an Oscar-nominated director whom the film critics of the period also vilified. The book was a bestseller and the movie a huge hit. Public and critics were at an impasse. Was the public duped into devouring book and movie? When I wrote my book on the making of *The Magnificent Seven* (1960 version), I discovered that that movie had not been generally well received either by the critics or the public but that it had turned into the most popular Western of all time, courtesy of endless repeats on television and a considerable number of reissues. Other movies in the genre termed classics fell far short of such universal appeal and adoration—except as far as critics and academics were concerned.

Some time ago, I started investigating this question of popularity and looked back at how movies of the 1950s were perceived by the general public. That small-scale experiment became a small-scale book (*Paisley at the Pictures 1950*) and I discovered, through dialogue with people who had lived through that era, that the general moviegoer had little truck with the views of the critics and depended far more on opinion collated from friends, family, colleagues and neighbors. So when I came to look at the best films of the 1960s—a period of which I am inordinately fond—I decided I would in a sense ask the public. After all, box office is nothing more than a public thumbs-up or thumbs-down. My concept would mean cutting out the middle man.

I would be going straight to the public vote, determining popularity from box office receipts. We are not talking here about people who watched a movie for free on television years after it debuted and saw a version reduced in size, scale and sound and which in some cases had been trimmed for censorship reasons or to make room for commercials. Instead, I am referring to this decade's moviegoers willing to slap down their hard-earned bucks, take time out of their schedule, their effort maybe involving hiring babysitters or shelling out for transportation and parking and whatever.

In a sense, there is something supremely egalitarian in that approach in that the people who pay to see movies are the ones whose box office dollar ends up funding new pictures; without them, there would be neither popular not unpopular films. So this assessment of the Top 100 Movies of the 1960s is based purely on the public's response to a given film through the simple act of paying to go and see it. That act turns into the movie's box office and that underpins this book.

So there are bound to be a few surprises, a few of your favorite pictures turning out to be a lot less popular than you thought or, going the other way, more successful. In fact, I can guarantee there will be surprises.

Introduction

This was the decade of legend. It spawned many of the greatest films ever made. Movie companies made more money than ever before,[1] budgets ballooned[2] and stars received record sums.[3] As the auteur theory grew in influence, directors were feted.[4] Business-wise, it bridged the old studio system where high numbers of movies were cranked out every year and the new approach where production was reduced[5] in the expectation of creating the equivalent of today's "tentpoles." Films made on a scope not conceived since *Gone with the Wind* (1939) became routine, arriving in theaters nearly every month, some so spectacularly successful they set the template for the future blockbuster. New genres such as the spy picture, driven by the James Bond phenomenon, came out of nowhere. Other moribund genres, previously restricted to low-budget or B-picture status, such as horror and sci-fi, reached new heights thanks to bigger budgets and top-name directors. While every genre thrived, the decade will be remembered particularly for musicals like *The Sound of Music* (1965) and historical epics like *Lawrence of Arabia* (1962) and an explosion of British movies. It was also the era of "the little films that could," low-budget pictures such as *Lilies of the Field* (1963) and *Charly* (1968) whose success far exceeded expectation. This epoch of dramatic change saw the industry embrace different attitudes to sexuality, violence and racism, adopt alternative release strategies[6] and reassess movies' ancillary value.

A new generation of stars emerged. Steve McQueen, Sidney Poitier, Jane Fonda, Barbra Streisand, Sean Connery, Peter O'Toole, Natalie Wood, Faye Dunaway, Peter Sellers, Clint Eastwood, Julie Christie, Dustin Hoffman, Warren Beatty, Michael Caine, Raquel Welch, Omar Sharif and Lee Marvin formed the new elite.[7] But that was not at the expense of existing stars. The postwar and 1950s generation retained—and in some instances expanded—their appeal. Into that category fell Elizabeth Taylor, Burt Lancaster, Audrey Hepburn, Doris Day, Richard Burton, Sophia Loren, Rock Hudson, Tony Curtis, Charlton Heston and Frank Sinatra. And although Gary Cooper and Clark Gable died early in the decade,[8] studios still counted on the box office prowess of prewar contemporaries like John Wayne, Bette Davis, James Stewart, Joan Crawford, Spencer Tracy, Henry Fonda, Katharine Hepburn and, until his retirement in 1966, Cary Grant. However, the "star system" had vanished and studios no longer invested millions annually on training new talent. Although in the 1950s Yul Brynner, Audrey Hepburn, Tony Curtis and Rock Hudson had graduated from smaller-scale new-talent programs, by the 1960s those programs were largely defunct (although occasional attempts were made to revive the concept[9]). Occasionally, television might throw up a new prospect—a Steve McQueen or James Garner—but most new stars, as far as the public was concerned, came from nowhere. One minute you had never heard of them, the next they

3

were everywhere, Sean Connery in particular falling into this category. Where the previous system had relied on steady grooming, now stars were born in an instant. One picture was all it took.

Behind the camera was a parallel situation. The old-stagers like John Ford, Howard Hawks, Henry Hathaway, Fred Zinnemann, Billy Wilder, William Wyler, David Lean and Carol Reed were joined by postwar debutantes Robert Aldrich, Robert Wise, Stanley Kramer and Stanley Kubrick. The newer crop graduating from television included John Frankenheimer, Robert Mulligan, Sam Peckinpah, George Roy Hill, Franklin J. Schaffner, Sidney Lumet, Arthur Penn, Norman Jewison and Sydney Pollack. They were augmented by the British New Wave of Karel Reisz, Tony Richardson, John Schlesinger

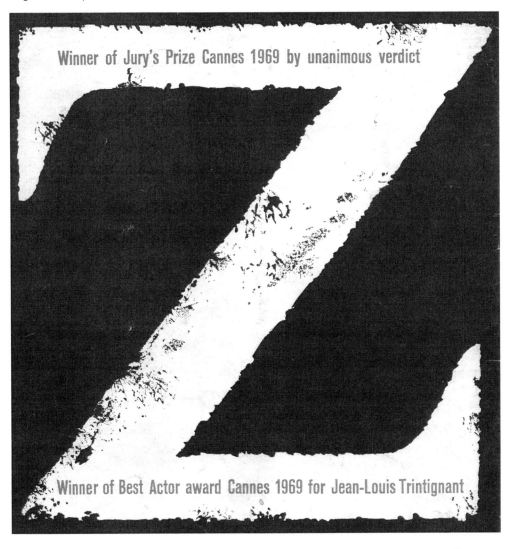

Where the bulk of foreign movies making a big box office splash in the 1960s—and prior—had relied on sex as the main selling ingredient, *Z* was a political picture released in the U.S. by Cinema V. A double winner at Cannes, Oscar-nominated for Best Film and Best Foreign Language Film (which it won), the thriller directed by Costa-Gavras saw Yves Montand investigating a cover-up (press advertisement, *Films and Filming*, June 1970, 23).

Introduction
5

and Lindsay Anderson. European directors welcomed into the Hollywood mainstream included Michelangelo Antonioni (*Blow Up,* 1966) and Roman Polanski (*Rosemary's Baby,* 1968). Foreign-made pictures like Federico Fellini's *La Dolce Vita* (1960) and Costa-Gavras' *Z* (1969) made massive inroads into the box office and helped create a different artistic sensibility. While French New Wave films were mostly confined to arthouses, many of their techniques in storytelling and especially editing were embraced by Hollywood directors.

Studios began the decade in financial turmoil, MGM and Twentieth Century–Fox on the verge of bankruptcy. Movie theater attendance was in terminal decline. As had occurred at the start of the 1950s, studios gambled on a bigger throw of the dice, this time the 70mm big-budget roadshow,[10] movies that paid little heed to budget strictures. The roadshow aimed to woo audiences away from the encroaching maw of television, to give small-screen viewers something that small-screen producers could not match, and at the same time reinvigorate the moviegoing experience. First-run big-city theaters already generated far greater revenues than cinemas further down the food chain and now movie companies intended increasing the box office take further by hiking prices. Big city center cinemas would offer an experience unparalleled in the modern cinema-going age.[11] Roadshows were shown in the separate program format so you could not just slip in and out to suit yourself. And the movie started with a fanfare, an overture that could last up to ten minutes, giving you time to take your seat, and there was an intermission to let you stretch your legs, use the facilities or refuel. The whole experience, what with souvenir programs on sale and babysitters to be hired, and maybe cocktails or dinner beforehand, was an event. And movies had never been events of any regularity. The prior moviegoing ethos was that it was a habitual part of your life. You popped into your neighborhood theater as you might go bowling or visit a bar. There was nothing fancy about it. It was just what everybody did. Or had done—until TV became the way you spent your evenings, staring at a tiny box in the corner which lacked widescreen, color, 3D and all the other gimmicks that for a time in the 1950s stopped the decline in theater attendance.

Ben-Hur (1959) was the gamble that paid off not just for MGM but for the industry. Rolled out in the normal fashion, it would certainly have played for months at a city center theater but instead was launched as a big-ticket roadshow, restricted to a limited number of cinemas where it would run as long as it pulled in the crowds rather than being quickly shunted into a general release to feed the distribution chain. In a sense, roadshow became a showcase in the old-fashioned term (the term "showcase" soon usurped to mean restricted wide release). The longer-running roadshow whetted exhibitor appetite as competition ensued to be the first to show it outside the roadshow. By the time it appeared in a neighborhood theater, it was re-marketed all over again as being available at "normal prices." There was a subtle psychology at play, suggesting that audiences were getting a bargain since they need not stump up for inflated roadshow tickets. That they would not be enjoying the full roadshow experience (local theaters were not equipped with 70mm projectors) was never mentioned. The 70mm enterprise continued in historical epic vein on through *Exodus* (1960), *El Cid* (1961), *Cleopatra* (1963) and *Lawrence of Arabia* before ceding the box office high ground to the musical trio *Mary Poppins* (1964), *My Fair Lady* (1964) and *The Sound of Music*. Others contributing to the great roadshow bonanza included the war film *The Longest Day* (1962) and the Western *How the West Was Won* (1963). Roadshows accounted for the biggest percentage of

6   **Introduction**

pictures that brought in the greatest receipts. By 1967, 17 of the 25 films whose gross (not rental) topped $25 million were roadshows.[12]

But the roadshow created as many problems as it solved. The exhibition system was not prepared to have four or five of the biggest cinemas in every major city tied up for months—sometimes years—at a time to show these behemoths. With non-roadshow major releases also requiring lengthy playing time, the lack of available theaters meant that city center sites were booked solid. Arthouses offered some relief, sometimes day-dating a more commercial picture, in other circumstances providing venues where a smaller movie might play untroubled for months on end. However, whichever way you cut it, there was an exhibition logjam.[13] That created an opening for independent companies like American International which dashed out low-budget horror shockers and, in complete contrast, family-friendly beach-themed movies before adding biker pictures to the mix. Exhibitors were so short of product that they even invested in movies off their own bat, Motion Picture Investors being involved in such schemes in the early 1960s.[14] In addition, exhibitors headed down the multiplex route—often in shopping malls[15] where there were no parking problems—once they realized that the logjam was restricting potential hits to one-week runs.

Even though roadshows ate up a lot of the box office juice, the movie industry did not stay still for long, and when a new phenomenon—the James Bond glossy action thriller—entered the fray, studios and exhibitors were quick to respond. Until now, the series film—Sherlock Holmes, Tarzan, etc.—had been a low-budget enterprise. Although the public turned out for stars who were effectively repeating themselves by remaining in the same genre—John Wayne and James Stewart in Westerns, for example, or Doris Day comedies—there was no sense that audiences wanted to see major stars playing the same character over and over again.[16] The Bond pictures were the first instance of what has today become a studio essential: an ongoing movie universe or multiverse as exemplified by the Marvel and DC comic adaptations—and were planned ahead with the end of each movie bearing an announcement of the title of the sequel. The first Bond venture, *Dr. No* (1962) was not a huge hit in America, in part because it was denied major first-run playing time and in part because Britain was not a proven source of box office hits. However, *From Russia with Love* (1963) doubled its predecessor's box office take. For a package with across-the-board appeal, the Bond template comprised handsome male star, beautiful female star, action, gadgets, fast cars and a splash of humor; and outside of the Disney franchise, no movie had mined so much ancillary gold. By the time *Goldfinger* (1964) appeared, the entire industry was primed for a box office explosion and an even bigger one the following year with *Thunderball* (1965). The Bonds took Hollywood into an entirely new genre—spy films—before being a sub-genre of a sub-genre, rarely involving a decent budget unless, perchance, a big star was involved. Not only did other studios start up their own franchises—Columbia with the Matt Helm series and Twentieth Century–Fox with Derek Flint[17]—but the Bonds kicked off a reappraisal of the reissue market. In the earlier part of the decade, reissues had fallen spectacularly out of fashion despite major attempts to revitalize their potential.[18] After *Goldfinger*, the first two Bonds were doubled up and made a fortune, introducing the notion of speedy reissues that resonated throughout the decade and beyond.

The Bonds were part of another new sub-genre: the successful British film. Although academics like to tell you of major British successes in Hollywood over the previous three decades, in reality there had not been a single one with the exception

Introduction
7

of *Pygmalion* and that had been in 1938. Sure, films like *Great Expectations* (1946), *The Red Shoes* (1948), *The Third Man* (1949) and some of the Ealing comedies had attracted critical attention but they did not actually have audiences lining up in droves. And while British stars like Richard Burton, Jean Simmons and Deborah Kerr had headlined big-budget Hollywood pictures, the stars left behind did not feature in the kind of British-made pictures likely to make a small town operator in Ohio hold his breath. The initial movies that emerged from the British New Wave were mostly U.S. arthouse hits[19] and even with commercial crossover did not register big results. *Tom Jones* (1963) changed all that and, coupled with Beatlemania and the Swinging London fashion scene, British films and British stars entered the Hollywood mainstream as never before. Even so, the Bonds and *Tom Jones* apart, few British films managed to establish themselves at the box office—even the big-budget *Zulu* (1963) backed by marketing genius Joseph E. Levine flopped in America.

The British films that did succeed were part of another sub-genre—what I have called "the little films that could." In general terms, low-budget films almost never achieved big-budget success. The closest any came was *Marty* (1955), which had been boosted by Oscar recognition. There was an obvious reason for this. The big films were placed in the biggest cinemas which meant, courtesy of substantial seating capacity, they would generate the biggest grosses. Smaller films had to fight to find a venue in first run. Arthouses had always been one option—a route taken by *Lili* (1953), for example. But although that ran for a record 93 weeks in the Trans-Lux on 52nd Street in New York, it was categorized as arthouse and therefore did not break out. So, much as arthouses were an opportunity, they were also, given smaller seating capacities, an inbuilt restriction to box office potential.

That changed somewhat in the 1960s when the role of arthouses in the release pattern altered and they became an accepted outlet for commercial movies when bigger cinemas were snapped up. As mentioned above, *Lilies of the Field* (1963) was the first of the smaller films to exploit this potential and, once Oscar nominations and a win for the star gave it a marketing boost, revenues soared. The British films *Georgy Girl* (1965) and *Alfie* (1965) went down the same route, both assisted by the commercial kudos that Oscar coverage could bring. American films like *The Pawnbroker* (1964) took advantage of this commercial loophole and, of course, at the end of the decade, *Easy Rider* (1969) set a new mark for this kind of limited arthouse-based release.

The Pawnbroker was significant for another reason: the assault on the Production Code, the self-regulated censorship in force since the 1930s. Foreign film producers could sidestep the Code—only American studios were obliged to be signatories. Foreign films offering a freer attitude to sex simply did not apply to have their movies passed by the Code, with subsequent outcries or local censorship merely generating media attention and increased revenue. While Ingmar Bergman films from Sweden demonstrated artistic merit, the vast majority of foreign pictures did not. Sophia Loren and Brigitte Bardot were introduced to American audiences as sex goddesses, the Frenchwoman's physical attributes in … *And God Created Woman* (1956) turning it into the biggest foreign film at the U.S. box office. The censor took the view that Fellini's *La Dolce Vita* (1960), which otherwise set a new mark for moral outrage, was sufficiently artistic to be shown as long as the movie was dubbed in the belief that customers interested only in the film's salacious elements would not be willing to sit through three hours of subtitles. Domestic filmmakers disadvantaged by toeing the Code line planned assaults on

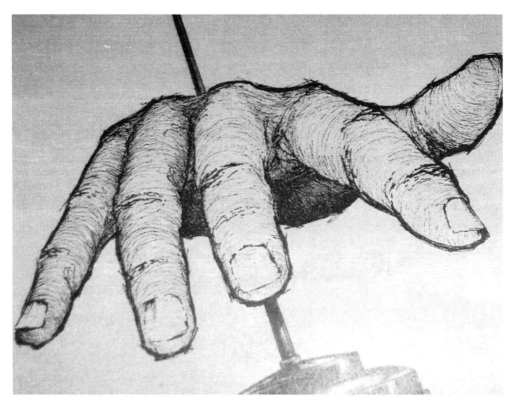

This startling image from the pressbook of *The Pawnbroker* (Allied Artists, 1964) encapsulates one of the striking moments of the film. Although not presented in the grandeur of 70mm, *The Pawnbroker* played as a roadshow on its British debut, with separate performances and advance booking (pressbook).

the historically impregnable censorship wall under the cover of artistic validity. *The Pawnbroker* with naked breasts proved the breakthrough[20] and it was only a matter of time before other directors rode roughshod over the existing censorship rules: *Blow Up* (1966)[21] the first to show pubic hair, a same-sex relationship the theme of *The Fox* (1967), *Bonnie and Clyde* (1967) battering into submission preconceptions about acceptable levels of violence. The whole censorship system underwent a revolution.

Racism was also tackled in a variety of genres: drama (*Guess Who's Coming to Dinner*, 1967), crime (*In the Heat of the Night*, 1967) and the Western (*100 Rifles*, 1969). Sidney Poitier became the first African American superstar, Jim Brown the first action star and Gordon Parks the first African American to direct a mainstream film.[22]

As mentioned above, historical epics and musicals became synonymous with the decade, but every genre had its standout commercial success. Drama flourished from *BUtterfield 8* (1960) through *A Man for All Seasons* (1966) and *Midnight Cowboy* (1969). Comedy kings included *That Touch of Mink* (1962), *The Graduate* (1967) and *The Odd Couple* (1968). It was a golden era for Westerns ranging from *How the West Was Won* (1963) and *Shenandoah* (1965) to *True Grit* (1969). Science fiction fans could count on *2001: A Space Odyssey* (1968) and *Planet of the Apes* (1968). Horror was given a shake-up through *Psycho* (1960) and *Rosemary's Baby* (1968). *Bonnie and Clyde* (1967) and *Bullitt* (1968) led a new crime spree and the private eye returned in the guise of Paul Newman *as Harper* (aka *The Moving Target*, 1966) and Frank Sinatra as *Tony Rome* (1967). And there was romance a-plenty from David Lean's *Doctor Zhivago* (1965) to *Romeo and Juliet* (1968).

Although this book highlights the most popular films of the decade, perhaps it is surprising how often the public and critics met along the Oscar fault lines. Many of the biggest hits were covered in Oscar glory (see Appendix). In a few cases, *Lilies of the Field* and *Charly* for example, Oscar recognition proved the difference between so-so box office and big bucks, but for other pictures like *Tom Jones* the Oscars were icing on the commercial cake. During the 1960s, critics let off steam about the way Hollywood was run and in defending the director often launched corresponding attacks on what was seen as the establishment. And while the critics might also espouse particular favorites on annual 10 Best Lists, it was surprising how often there was a general consensus about what made a good picture, and how often the public, so often maligned, agreed.

One curious element connected the most successful pictures. They were rarely original works. In the main, they had already been bestsellers and hit Broadway musicals or plays. Among the top films of the decade, only about one-fifth were original screenplays. Hollywood had been harvesting bestsellers and successful shows for decades since they came with an inbuilt readership or audience and offered opportunities for cross-promotion marketing.

A significant new revenue stream was developed through the soundtrack. In the past, musicals apart, few hit singles derived from movies, the theme from *High Noon* (1952) a classic exception. In general, movies did not spawn hit singles or albums. That changed at the start of the decade when the themes from *Never on Sunday* (1960), *The Alamo* (1960) and *Exodus* (1960) all became bestselling singles. Record retailers entered the marketing equation. As the decade wore on and the public became attuned to a hit single from a Bond movie and "Lara's Theme" from *Doctor Zhivago*, sales of movie-related recordings became a massive ancillary boon for studios, and composers like John Barry and Maurice Jarre achieved stardom in their own right. Later in the decade, *The Graduate* and *Easy Rider* ushered in the era of rock- and pop-oriented soundtracks while the likes of *Interlude* (1968) and *2001: A Space Odyssey* plundered the works of classical composers.

In addition, fashion formed a major bulwark of marketing campaigns. In the past, stars had created demand for certain styles: Lana Turner with her turtleneck sweater, Greta Garbo's pillbox hat, Marlene Dietrich in pants. But these tended to be one-offs. In 1960, Sindlinger carried out market research for Universal that concluded that women made up the majority of the audience for the majority of the current top ten movies. Consequently, the studio made fashion core to its marketing strategy, the first beneficiary being *Midnight Lace* (1960).[23] Audrey Hepburn's outfits in *Breakfast at Tiffany's* galvanized the public and from then on, fashion was at the heart of the promotions for several films. Cecil Beaton's costumes for *My Fair Lady* (1964) provided an editorial bonanza for fashion editors, both sexes took to dressing Russian-style following *Doctor Zhivago* and in imitation of *Bonnie and Clyde*, while legendary designers such as Dior and Yves St. Laurent were brought in to design outfits for stars.[24] Even films as male-oriented as *Seven Days in May* (1964) and *Point Blank* (1967) devised fashion marketing hooks.[25]

There was a dramatic shift in movie companies and their ownership. Before the Second World War, studios had broken down into the Big Six (MGM, Paramount,

Warner Brothers, RKO, Universal and Twentieth Century–Fox) and the Little Three (Disney, Columbia and United Artists), the division not so much to do with output and type of product but that most of the top half-dozen owned substantial cinema chains, giving them proportionately higher incomes. RKO dropped out of the equation in the 1950s thanks to the reckless financial management of Howard Hughes. In the 1960s, the smaller studios upped their game. Columbia invested in big blockbusters like *Lawrence of Arabia*, and United Artists became the go-to studio for talent seeking creative control, like Netflix today happy to accommodate big names as a short-cut to building audiences. Disney built on its "family" brand by increasing output and making films with wider appeal than feature-length cartoons or TV spin-offs. Until the 1960s, movie companies had been primarily run by individuals, some, like Darryl F. Zanuck at Twentieth Century–Fox and Jack Warner of Warners, holding top posts for decades. But the success of the business in the 1960s made studios prey for bigger companies. When Gulf & Western took over Paramount, it substantially altered the way the business was run. Only two of the big studios survived the decade without a takeover or a merger.[26] Bigger companies had different priorities and the pressure to continually increase share prices and return dividend to shareholders changed forever the way studios were run.

The top 100 films of the 1960s accounted for just under $1.4 billion (equivalent to $9.97 billion today).[27] United Artists led the way with $298 million ($2.21 billion equivalent) amassed from 21 titles. Next was Twentieth Century–Fox with $223 million ($1.58 billion) for a dozen pictures. MGM, from one fewer picture, was third with $202 million ($1.43 billion). Columbia came fourth after its 13 entries knocked up a total of $162 million ($1.15 billion). Warner Brothers generated $144 million ($1.02 billion) from 11 pictures. Outside the top five were: Paramount $130 million ($926 million) from 11 films, Disney $120 million from nine ($855 million) and Universal $68 million ($484 million) from seven. Five minor studios contributed $48 million ($342 million) from one movie each—Dino De Laurentiis leading the charge with $15 million ($106 million), followed by Allied Artists $12 million ($85 million), Astor $7.5 million ($53 million), ABC $7.26 million ($51 million) and Janus Films/Grove Press $6.6 million ($47 million).

Many academics are divided on the issue of what constitutes an epoch. While the idea of examining cinema decade by decade is my preference and that of the seminal *History of the American Cinema* series, others believe it is better to go from mid-decade to mid-decade. Gerald Mast, for example, asserts that one defining period covers 1946–1965 and another 1965–1976. Thomas Schatz breaks down this period from 1946 to 1975 into three separate eras: 1946–1955, 1956–1965 and 1966–1975. David A. Cook argues that the seminal period is 1962–1975.[28] Of course, depending on your point of view, you could choose to follow any of these ways of dividing cinema history. However, I am firmly of the belief that a decade from start to finish is the best way to define a particular era. This one, from 1960 to 1969, of course, did not end well, out-of-control budgets pushing most studios into financial quagmires, from which a couple, namely MGM and United Artists, emerged as smaller production units. The wholesale embracing at the end of the decade of the youth culture, as epitomized by *Easy Rider*, proved to be a massive misstep: The bulk of the movies targeting this audience proved to be flops, although the trend towards making films for a younger audience continued in the 1970s.

As well as recognizing the particular financial success of certain pictures, this book also seeks to put those movies into context. Most obviously, that might be in regards to sexuality, violence and racism. But it also takes into account developments in particular

Introduction 11

genres and the arrival of a new star or director or the consolidation or revival of an existing reputation. In addition, attention is paid to the inner workings of the industry (changes in release strategy, for example) and the abandonment of the Production Code.

How the Movies for This Book Were Chosen

As mentioned above motion pictures have qualified for entry in this book by means of their box office status. The figures I used are based on rentals rather than grosses. Rental is what the studio makes after the movie theaters have taken their cut. In the 1960s, it was impossible to get hold of grosses on any consistent basis, but once a year the studios would 'fess up and tell trade magazine *Variety* how much each film took in in rentals.[29] *Variety* set up its own parameters: The magazine only included in its year-end report those films which had rentals of at least $1 million. Qualification for entry has nothing to do with a film's profit or loss since that often depends on a movie's budget whereas box office simply denotes attendance. If a film with a big budget and a film with a small budget generate the same rental income, the standard rule-of-thumb is that the former is a flop and the latter a hit. In reality, both have achieved exactly the same level of popularity. So in this regard, box office and rentals are seen as the true measure of public acceptance. From time to time, *Variety* would upgrade or downgrade these rental figures and I have accommodated such changes.[30] In addition, I drew from the appendices in Audrey Solomon's history of Twentieth Century–Fox and biographies[31] and studio records such as those kept at the University of Wisconsin for United Artists.

This book relates only to box office in the 1960s so some movies released in 1969 which earned the vast majority of their income in future years have been excluded or limited only to the amount earned before the end of the decade. For example, *Cactus Flower* was released in December 1969 so very little of its box office was achieved in that year; and although critics would refer to it as a 1969 movie, for the vast majority of the general public it was a picture they saw in 1970. *Easy Rider* and *Butch Cassidy and the Sundance Kid* (1969) also earned the much larger share of their box office in the years after 1969[32] so only the amount relating to this decade is included. You might also be surprised to find *Ben-Hur* included in this volume, but again, for only a tiny fraction of its overall audience was it a film of 1959—the vast majority of its immense audience viewed it in 1960 or 1961 or on reissue later in the decade. Some pictures, most obviously the James Bond series, earned extra revenue after initial release through reissue and that is included in the total sum, as long as, again, such sums were confined to this particular decade. To put this exercise in some kind of perspective, a total of 762 movies produced rentals of $1 million or more in the 1960s and probably at least the same number did not get near that income figure. So, we start, as is normal in these kinds of proceedings, in reverse order. If you want to find what was the number one movie of the decade, of course you can just skip to the end.

A note on numbering: There are multiple ties among the 100 movies that follow, and consequently the list is not a consecutive one through one hundred, but skips the next number following a tie. As an example, there are two films in the 98th position, so the numbering then skips 99 and goes to 100 (the two 98s, taken together and interchangeable, making up the 98th and 99th entries in the series of 100 films).

The Films

100: *Where Eagles Dare*

Starring Richard Burton and Clint Eastwood; directed by Brian G. Hutton; screenplay, Alistair MacLean; music, Ron Goodwin; producer, Elliott Kastner. MGM. Released on January 22, 1969 (London), March 12, 1969 (U.S.).[1]

As much as the 1960s introduced new stars and directors, it was also a decade that saw a new breed of producer emerge. Former agent Elliott Kastner[2] packaged films, tying up screenplay and star before turning to a major studio, in this case MGM, for financing. Unlike previous independent producers like Sam Spiegel[3] (*Lawrence of Arabia*, 1962), he did not seek a long-term alliance with one particular company. *Bus Riley's Back in Town* (1965) was made for Universal, the Paul Newman shamus picture *Harper* (1966) for Warner Brothers, and the thriller *Sol Madrid* (1968) for MGM.[4]

By the time *Where Eagles Dare* premiered, Alistair MacLean's novel was riding high on the bestseller charts; but the book was in fact a novelization of an original screenplay[5] by the author, responding to a request from Kastner for a World War II mission picture along the lines of MacLean's *The Guns of Navarone* (1961).[6] Kastner considered Marlon Brando and Michael Caine[7] for the leading role of Major Smith, finally played by Richard Burton for a fee of $750,000[8] plus ten percent of the gross. Clint Eastwood[9] was not first choice either. Others in the running were Rod Taylor (*Dark of the Sun*, 1968), Richard Boone (*Hombre*, 1967), Richard Egan (*Chubasco*, 1968), Nicol Williamson (*The Bofors Gun*, 1968) and Robert Webber (*Harper*, 1966).[10] Burton pushed for Leslie Caron (*Father Goose*, 1964) for the female lead but happily settled for Mary Ure (*Custer of the West*, 1967), with whom he had worked on *Look Back in Anger* (1959).[11] It was a significant change of pace—and a gamble—for Burton, who was more readily associated with Oscar nominated dramas[12] than action. Kastner handed the directorial reins to school friend Brian G. Hutton,[13] whose portfolio boasted three flops: the low-budget indie *Wild Seed* (1965), a comedy with a no-name cast, *The Pad* (1966), and the aforementioned *Sol Madrid*. But Kastner was very much a hands-on producer, overseeing the entire project from start to finish.

In the 1960s, the bulk of big-budget war films had been serious affairs focusing on real events: *The Longest Day* (1962), *Battle of the Bulge* (1965), *Operation Crossbow* (1965) and *In Harm's Way* (1965). Or they had the action angle leavened by questions about the nature of war (*The Guns of Navarone*) or the rehabilitation of a bunch of murderers (*The Dirty Dozen*, 1967). *Where Eagles Dare* was a more old-fashioned shoot-'em-up and while it had an espionage core, it was more dependent on genuine thrills and derring-do. A massive input by stuntmen was key to the proceedings which, in the days before CGI,

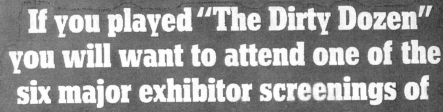

involved incredible feats atop cable cars. Would an American audience, by now divided over the Vietnam War, welcome such a popcorn confection?

A crack commando team is parachuted into the wintry Alps to rescue a captured American brigadier-general from an impenetrable castle before he can divulge the secrets of D-Day. At least that's the upfront storyline. In reality, the infiltrators are intent on uncovering a traitor. Awaiting Burton is MI6 agent Mary Ure, to whom he is romantically attached, and another top agent, busty Ingrid Pitt, in disguise as a barmaid. Meanwhile, members of the covert force are being mysteriously murdered and the Germans are aware of the mission. Burton and Eastwood hitch a lift to the castle via the cable car. Once inside, there's nothing but twists and turns as Burton attempts to sniff out the traitor and, as with the best war pictures, does so with a clever ruse. Thereafter, escaping with traitors in tow involves more cable car hijinks, a bucketful of explosions, and battering through the enemy forces with a snowplow to a final revelation on board the waiting plane. Double-dealing ensures tension is kept up, with more than enough action to satisfy thrill-seeking audiences.

Burton is chillingly ruthless and Eastwood reveals that, outside the Western, he packs a mean dramatic punch. There is sterling support from Ure, Pitt[14] and British character actors Patrick Wymark (*Operation Crossbow*), Michael Hordern (*Khartoum*, 1966) and Donald Houston (*The Blue Lagoon*, 1949) and, representing the younger generation, Derren Nesbitt (*The Naked Runner*, 1967) in his now-familiar alter ego as a German. Hutton stepped up to the big-budget plate in sensational fashion, handling both drama and action with aplomb, and the end result is less a glorification of war than a tale of courage. The icing on the cake was the score by Ron Goodwin (*633 Squadron*, 1964) which, from the steady drums of the opening sequence, built up into a crescendo, in keeping with the vertigo-inducing stunts.

Critical reception: "Both absurd and entertaining" (*New York Times*); "rarely lets down for a moment" (*Variety*); "ultimate action picture overflowing with mayhem" (*Box Office*).[15]

Rentals: $6.56 million[16] (equivalent to $46.7 million today)

98 (tie): *A Shot in the Dark*

Starring Peter Sellers and Elke Sommer; directed and produced by Blake Edwards; screenplay, Edwards and William Peter Blatty, based on the Harry Kurnitz adaptation of the Marcel Achard play *L'Idiote*; music, Henry Mancini. United Artists. June 23, 1964.

For most of 1964, until *Goldfinger* exploded onto U.S. screens, if you asked American moviegoers to name the most successful British actor, they would have pointed to Richard Burton (*Cleopatra*, 1963) or Peter Sellers. Sellers was, for a time, a respectable

---

Opposite: **Initially seen as an all-out action movie, MGM's *Where Eagles Dare* was reassessed by Mark Allison in *Little White Lies* magazine in 2018 as marking a "turning point for Hollywood action ... perfectly pitched for the counter-culture generation ... serves as a bridge between two eras of American action cinema—the bloodless fun of *The Guns of Navarone* and the unflinching brutality of *Dirty Harry*."* That year Penguin published a scene-by-scene analysis *Broadsword Calling Danny Boy* by *The Guardian* critic Geoff Dyer. Trade press advertisement (*Box Office*, November 11, 1968).**

**Little White Lies*, September 22, 2018.

16 The Films

American arthouse draw in British films such as *Two-Way Stretch* (1960)[17]; his attempts to win a larger audience in *The Millionairess* (1960) and *Lolita* (1962) had failed. He had returned home for *The Wrong Arm of the Law* (1963) and *Heavens Above* (1963) before, by chance, Peter Ustinov dropped out of *The Pink Panther* (1963).[18] Sellers' role as the bumbling French detective was expanded to the detriment of top-billed David Niven, as director Blake Edwards[19] explored Sellers' comic genius.[20] Although United Artists would soon become synonymous with sequel exploitation, *A Shot in the Dark* was speedy even by their standards, turning up barely three months after the original. By then, Sellers' anarchic comedy *Dr. Strangelove* (1964) had also hit home.[21] There was also Sellers' *The World of Henry Orient* (1964). Four films in six months[22] was a superstar-making gusher.

If the loss of two leading players—Ava Gardner[23] as well as Ustinov—in *The Pink Panther* was not bad enough, the sequel had to recast after Sophia Loren,[24] Walter Matthau[25] and director Anatole Litvak[26] dropped out. The initial script by Alec Coppel and Norman Krasna was also discarded. *A Shot in the Dark* was based on a hit Broadway play[27] and, while it involved murder, the investigating officer did not go by the name of Inspector Clouseau. When Blake Edwards replaced Litvak, it was his idea to change the entire concept, open up the play and reprise the character Sellers had so brilliantly created. Such drastic script changes saw Matthau quit along with Loren's replacement, Austrian actress Romy Schneider (*The Cardinal*, 1963).[28] German Elke Sommer, fresh from *The Prize* (1963), was brought in. Apart from the initial set-up of murder in a millionaire's chateau, Edwards and co-writer William Peter Blatty[29] rewrote the entire script, letting Clouseau loose in a nudist camp and Parisian nightclubs. Herbert Lom is unveiled as Clouseau's boss, whose frustration with his underling leads to a nervous breakdown and to making several attempts on his life. Burt Kwouk debuts as Cato, the detective's servant, who has legitimate reason to attack his master when least expected since that is part of his duties. More importantly, Clouseau's demented French accent, one of the hallmarks of the actor's characterization, makes its first appearance. Chambermaid Elke, found with the gun that killed the chauffeur, is the chief suspect. Further murders implicate the maid but Sellers, convinced of her innocence and madly attracted to her, seeks to clear her name. It is really an excuse to indulge in Edwards' love of slapstick and Sellers' greatest character impersonation. The plot gets crazier but that's part of the fun.

As if in keeping with the picture's tortuous beginnings, there was at least as bizarre a denouement. Sellers hated the movie so much he proposed buying it if production company Mirisch agreed to put it into cold storage.[30] Although this offer was refused, the relationship between Edwards and Sellers was by now so tainted that they refused to work together again,[31] a situation reversed in the 1970s when the character returned to revive both ailing careers. However, since *A Shot in the Dark* produced bigger box office than *The Pink Panther*, and a boost to burgeoning ancillary music[32] and cartoon[33] income, Mirisch succumbed to the temptation to give the character another outing in the guise of Alan Arkin as *Inspector Clouseau* (1968)—without success. Even had there been no future sequels, *A Shot in the Dark* deserves recognition as one of the great comedies of the decade with Sellers' quintessential comic creation on a par with Charlie Chaplin and Buster Keaton.

Critical reception: "Brimful of slapstick" (*Variety*); "enough is enough already" (*Los Angeles Times*); "the real fun comes from sight gags" (*Washington Post*); "extremely jolly" (*New Yorker*).[34]

Rentals: $6.6 million (equivalent to $47 million today)

98 (tie): *I Am Curious (Yellow)*

Starring Lena Nyman and Vilgot Sjoman; directed and written by Sjoman; producer, Lena Malmsjo; music, Bengt Emryd. Janus Films-Grove Press. March 1969.[35]

Previous attempts to break down the barriers of the outdated Production Code had usually come bolstered by critical approval and/or a sympathetic ear from Geoffrey Shurlock, the high priest of the self-regulated censorship system. Recognition of merit had ushered *The Pawnbroker* (1964) and *Who's Afraid of Virginia Woolf?* (1966) through these tricky currents. Had one picture, ultimately, been responsible for busting the Code wide open, the industry would rather it had been a film with more artistic credentials than *I Am Curious (Yellow)*. Most imports likely to cause offense were trimmed before they reached U.S. shores, edited after consultation with the authorities or, on occasion, granted special dispensation. Distributors were generally unwilling to incur the costs required to fight a court case which, while generating publicity, might return an unfavorable verdict. Nor were many films released without the Production Code Seal of Approval.[36] While the burden of restraint regarding dubious imports fell to U.S. Customs, they were rarely called upon.[37] However, there was growing external pressure to introduce tougher, legally enforced classification, with many states threatening to pass their own laws.[38]

Of course, in the 1960s the country was in state of turmoil and change. As well as the Civil Rights movement and unrest over Vietnam, there was increasing liberality in attitudes toward—and exploitation of—sex. Following the Las Vegas example, strip shows were booming.[39] By the late 1960s, after a flurry of pictures stretching existing parameters covering sex and violence, Hollywood recognized the need for a complete overhaul of the existing Code. A new classification scheme was introduced[40]—including, for the first time, an "X" category—in November 1968. Jack Valenti, president of the Motion Picture Association of America (MPAA), insisted that the new scheme was for children. "We do not censor films and we do not ban films," he contended. "We inform parents."[41] While he appeared on television to expound on these points,[42] the networks introduced their own code, forcing commercials advertising movies to contain their classification letters.[43] Into this mix came a case that would test the Code and the industry.

The controversial Swedish film *I Am Curious (Yellow)*, which had scenes of sex and fellatio, was playing uncensored to packed houses in Germany, Sweden, Norway and Denmark[44] but cut by 14 minutes in France.[45] Grove Press, which had successfully challenged American law over publishing *Lady Chatterley's Lover* and Henry Miller's *Tropic of Cancer*,[46] was an unexpected purchaser of the property, paying $100,000 for the rights and planning to spend the same amount on promotion.[47] *I Am Curious (Yellow)* was held up for a year by U.S. Customs. In challenging this ruling in court, Grove Press argued that the film was "not obscene by dint of redeeming social value,"[48] and industry observers made a distinction between "pornographic" and "explicit."[49] A May 1968 jury deliberated for just three hours and declared it obscene.[50] On November 26, 1968, the U.S. Circuit Court of Appeal, in a two-to-one verdict, ruled that the film "was entitled to protection under the First Amendment."[51] It was launched in February 1969 at the Evergreen and Cinema Rendezvous theaters in New York.[52] With an unprecedented wave of publicity, the Rendezvous, with screenings from 10 a.m. to 2 a.m., boasted not just a record gross but the biggest sum ever taken by an arthouse.[53] The film also set new highs in Los Angeles and Chicago.[54]

18 The Films

However, even after clearing New York hurdles, *I Am Curious (Yellow)* was denied exhibition in Maryland,[55] Boston,[56] Houston,[57] Kansas,[58] Illinois[59] and Youngstown, Ohio.[60] While attempts were foiled elsewhere,[61] anti-obscenity bills were considered in over a dozen states[62] and arthouse owners, normally susceptible to such fare, refused to book it.[63] Other films were caught up in the aftermath: The American-made *Fanny Hill Meets Dr. Erotico* (1967) incurred the wrath of the Boston authorities,[64] *Therese and Isabelle* (1968)[65] was impounded in Pittsburgh, *Starlet* (1969) was confiscated in Memphis. States planned to tax theaters for screening risqué pictures.[66] Meanwhile, contrary to expectations, U.S. Customs remained active, seizing the British film *Pattern of Evil*[67] and the German-Swiss-Italian co-production *Venus in Furs* (1969).[68]

Despite the furor over *I Am Curious (Yellow)* and heavy-handed attempts to prevent the spread of salacious material, other pictures took advantage of the marketing opportunity opened up by the new "X" certificate. Enjoying commercial success were Russ Meyer's *Vixen* (1968),[69] the country's first X-rated movie, *Inga* (1968),[70] *The Libertine* (1968),[71] *Karla* (1969),[72] *The Taming* (1968)[73] and a Swedish version of *Fanny Hill* (1968).[74] Their box office seduced exhibitors who might have steered shy of *I Am Curious (Yellow)*. A March 1969 survey determined that a quarter of the New York first-run theaters were showing sexy fare.[75] Towards year-end, *I Am Curious (Yellow)* broke out of the arthouse straitjacket and was pitched into a New York showcase release with around 40 houses agreeing to a four-week minimum booking in the expectation of a million-dollar gross.[76]

So what was the fuss all about? It's primarily a film about social issues. The heroine Lena (Lena Nyman), passionate about social justice, interviews people about society and gender equality and pickets travel agents offering holidays in Spain, then under the dictatorship of General Franco. Although promiscuous herself, she has a difficult relationship with a new lover after discovering he has other women. Without the sex (tame by modern standards), it is doubtful that this movie would have been seen outside Sweden, except for arthouses interested in its political aspects. There's neither enough political nor emotional context to engage the viewer and it remains an oddity.

Critical reception: "Good, serious movie" (*New York Times*); "a real dog" (*Chicago Sun-Times*); "episodic and overlong" (*Box Office*); "mostly rather boring" (*Variety*)[77]; "blue, boring and botched" (*Boston Globe*),[78] "an exercise in tedium" (*New York Daily News*).[79]

Rentals: $6.6 million[80] ($47 million today)

97: *The Apartment*

Starring Jack Lemmon, Shirley MacLaine and Fred MacMurray; directed and produced by Billy Wilder; screenplay, Wilder and I.A.L. Diamond; music, Adolph Deutsch. United Artists. June 30, 1960.

One of the most astonishing aspects in the astonishing career of seven-time Oscar-nominated director Billy Wilder was that after a decade of turning out some of the most intense and provocative dramas in the history of the industry—*Double Indemnity* (1944), *The Lost Weekend* (1945), *Sunset Blvd.* (1950), *Ace in the Hole* (1951) and *Stalag 17* (1953)—he discovered a talent for comedy that expressed itself in *The Seven Year Itch* (1955) and *Some Like It Hot* (1959). For most of the 1950s, according to the annual

Top 20 box office charts, audiences responded best to dramas, adventure and musicals. But towards the end of the decade, a comedy boom took shape. There were outright laffers like the adaptation of Ira Levin's Broadway hit *No Time for Sergeants* (1958), Disney's *The Shaggy Dog* (1959), Jerry Lewis in *The Sad Sack* (1957) and *Don't Give Up the Ship* (1959), and *Some Like It Hot*. There was a romantic comedy cycle: Glenn Ford and Gia Scala in *Don't Go Near the Water* (1957), Cary Grant and Sophia Loren in *Houseboat* (1958), Frank Sinatra and Eleanor Parker in *A Hole in the Head* (1959), and the first Rock Hudson–Doris Day confection, *Pillow Talk* (1959). The next decade began in similar fashion: Doris Day and David Niven in *Please Don't Eat the Daisies* (1960), Curtis, Dean Martin and Janet Leigh in *Who Was That Lady?* (1960), etc.

The comedy default was frivolity, narrative driven by misunderstandings, miscalculations and unusual situations with the sex element treated purely for laughs. In other words, no matter how immoral character intent, they still held to a moral code, or one that fitted in with the social conventions of the time and, in movie industry terms, adhered to the restraints of the Production Code. *The Apartment* swept all that aside. Every character acts immorally. Office drone Jack Lemmon[81] lends out his apartment to senior colleagues for sexual trysts in the hope of promotion. Locked out of his own apartment in the evenings, Lemmon has nothing else to do but work harder. He has his eyes on spunky elevator girl Shirley MacLaine. But when Lemmon receives his promotion on condition that he add the company's personnel director Fred MacMurray to his list of apartment users, he does not realize that she is his lover. On discovering that she is the latest in a long line of his discarded mistresses, she attempts to commit suicide. Lemmon nurses her back to health. Although nothing untoward occurs between the pair, and she continues the affair, Lemmon becomes the victim of office gossip and attracts the violent attentions of MacLaine's brother-in-law. Eventually, everyone receives their comeuppance and MacLaine realizes Lemmon is her true love.

There are plenty of laughs and great lines and Lemmon is the kind of actor who will always elicit sympathy from an audience; but even he strains that relationship to the limit by rationalizing his immoral behavior. The outcome is a savage indictment of modern mores and of a system that prompts people towards the unethical. Wilder shot the film in black-and-white to concentrate on the core dilemmas and not distract audiences with colorful costumes and sets. Wilder and I.A.L. Diamond[82] wrote the picture with Lemmon in mind and although the actor had been gradually climbing the Hollywood tree, this was a star-making vehicle. The gamine appeal of MacLaine in an era of more straightforward beauties was showcased and soon she, too, stepped up to top billing. Both actors were Oscar-nominated and Wilder picked up the Best Director award as well as sharing the Best Writing award, while the movie was named Best Picture.[83] Far more than any other film beyond foreign imports, its financial and artistic success opened the industry up to more challenging examinations of sexual behavior.

Critical reception: "High in comedy, wide in warmth" (*Variety*); "gleeful, tender and even sentimental" (*New York Times*); "every inch an exceptional film and certainly the equal of anything that Wilder has previously given us" (*Films and Filming*).[84]

Rentals: $6.65 million[85] (including 1961 post–Oscar reissue double bill with *Elmer Gantry*) ($47.3 million equivalent)

Author Donn Pearce was a high-school dropout and safecracker. After a two-year stretch on a Florida chain gang, he based *Cool Hand Luke* on a real prisoner killed during this period. The book was purchased after a mention in a publishing trade paper, not, as was more usual, from being touted around in pre-publication galley proofs* (Hannan Collection).

*Frederick, Robert B., "Donn Pearce: Chain Gang Antecedents Into Novel Sold to Jack Lemmon," *Variety*, September 15, 1965, 2.

96: *A Patch of Blue*

Starring Sidney Poitier, Shelley Winters and Elizabeth Hartman; directed by Guy Green[86]; screenplay, Green, based on the novel *Be Ready with Bells and Drums* by Elizabeth Kata; producers, Green and Pandro Berman[87]; music, Jerry Goldsmith. MGM. December 10, 1965.

If anything summed up Hollywood's attitude to race, it was the industry attitude to Sidney Poitier. While hiding behind a screen of Oscar acceptance—Best Actor nomination for *The Defiant Ones* (1958), Best Actor winner for *Lilies of the Field* (1963), in both cases the first African American to achieve that distinction—studios steadfastly refused to offer him top billing except in movies that called for someone of his heritage. Several times in his decade-long career, Poitier appeared on the cusp of stardom but every time he was top-billed for one, invariably low-budget, picture, he dropped down the credits for anything requiring larger financial investment. He was the denoted star of *Porgy and Bess* (1959), *A Raisin in the Sun* (1961), *Pressure Point* (1962) and *Lilies of the Field* (1963). But you were as likely to find him playing second fiddle to Paul Newman in *Paris*

Blues (1961) and Richard Widmark in both *The Long Ships* (1964) and *The Bedford Incident* (1965). For many years, he was the only African American actor with any significant leverage[88] in Hollywood, and only on account of his Oscar.[89]

A Patch of Blue was ostensibly about the relationship between a young white blind uneducated woman (Elizabeth Hartman) and a compassionate man (Poitier) whom she meets by accident in the park; she is unaware that he is African American. As their romance grows, tension builds over both her potential discovery of this fact and her reaction. But there was a lot more to it than that. Poitier is her guide to a world she cannot see and she must overcome her inhibitions and her repressive alcoholic mother in order to take charge of her life. In addition, Hartman was already being touted as a "Star of the Future,"[90] snapped up on a Warner Brothers contract. Before *A Patch of Blue* premiered, she had dumped WB in favor of MGM,[91] shot her next picture *The Group* (1966) for United Artists, and lined up her first starring role in Seven Arts' *You're a Big Boy Now* (1966). She was as hot as they come and the industry and the public, softened up by a wave of publicity, were eager to see whether she would deliver on her promise, given she would be a few days shy of her twenty-second birthday when the film appeared. Added to the mix was an incendiary performance by Oscar-winner[92] Shelley Winters as Hartman's vicious, alcoholic sex-worker mother, responsible for the girl's physical incapacity. Her performance and that of veteran Wallace Ford as her grandfather grounded what could otherwise have been an over-sentimental picture. Winters seeks no audience sympathy, her relentless, self-centered brutality taking center stage as she grooms her daughter for prostitution. The ending is optimistic but open. Both Hartman and Poitier deliver tender performances, but the script is weighted in favor of Hartman and Winters.

A Patch of Blue was another low-cost picture, brought in five days under schedule with $65,000 shaved off its original $1.2 million budget.[93] Completed in May 1965, its low budget suggested a film that would zip through post-production. Yet it sat on the shelf until the end of the year. On the face of it, MGM adopted the *Lilies of the Field* template in marketing the picture. That film had tripled its gross after the star collected the Oscar.[94] So although *A Patch of Blue* opened in Los Angeles[95] and New York in December 1965, no other bookings were scheduled until late February 1966 when Oscar nominations were announced. But, in reality, the two approaches could not have been more different. *Lilies of the Field* had been extensively seen before Oscar appreciation. For *A Patch of Blue*, MGM did not risk a general release until the film proved its artistic mettle.[96] The December launch date was selected three months before[97] and *Variety* detected an "Oscar Shadow" in the studio's marketing strategy.[98] In September, it was screened at the annual Aspen Film Festival.[99] Considerable effort went into targeting the youth market[100] and a "soft-sell pitch."[101] As expected, the film opened to record box office in L.A. At the Oscars, Shelley Winters was named Best Supporting Actress and Hartman the youngest-ever nominee for Best Actress.[102] In the Oscar run-up, Poitier was hampered by the release, five days after *A Patch of Blue*, of another low-budget Oscar contender, *The Slender Thread*.[103] Although *A Patch of Blue* encountered some hostility in the South,[104] that did not deter moviegoers and it broke records in Atlanta and Charlotte.[105]

Critical reception: "Genuine warmth and credibility" (*Box Office*); "touching contemporary melodrama" (*Variety*)[106]; "astonishing" (*Los Angeles Times*); "deeply moving drama" (*New York Post*).[107]

Rentals: $6.8 million ($48.4 million equivalent)

22　The Films

95: *Cool Hand Luke*

Starring Paul Newman, George Kennedy and Strother Martin; directed by Stuart Rosenberg; screenplay, Frank Pierson, based on the book by Donn Pearce; producer, Gordon Carroll; music, Lalo Schifrin. Warner Brothers. November 1, 1967.

Cool Hand Luke resulted from collaboration between Jack Lemmon and Paul Newman. The stars were among the best known of a new breed, the actor-producer. In the 1950s, stars[108] had entered production as a means of funding vanity projects, gaining a slice of profits or reducing tax bills.[109] The most prominent were Burt Lancaster, John Wayne and Kirk Douglas. Too many flops capsized Hill-Hecht-Lancaster, and Wayne's Batjac foundered after *The Alamo* (1960). Douglas' Bryna brought *Paths of Glory* (1957), *The Vikings* (1958) and *Spartacus* (1960) to the screen.[110] Most wannabe actor-producers soon realized risk was greater than reward. Sitting in the producer's chair meant rarely receiving your full salary, settling for a nominal fee in the hope of a bigger backend; a hit made you a bundle, a flop left you penniless. Production also limited the time available for other films so most actors gave up.

Lemmon and Newman were exceptions. Having bought his way out of his Warner Brothers contract, Newman set up his own company to ensure that he worked on quality projects. He entered into a partnership with Martin Ritt,[111] who had directed Newman in *The Long, Hot Summer* (1958), *Paris Blues* (1961) and *Hemingway's Adventures of a Young Man* (1962). Their production debut *Hud* (1963) was followed by *The Outrage* (1964) and *Hombre* (1967). Like Newman, Lemmon[112] established Jalem to develop his career to suit his talents. In keeping with most comedians, there was a serious man behind the comic face. *Days of Wine and Roses* (1962) had started life as a television play with Charles Bickford in the title role. Lemmon was not the obvious choice until, wearing his producer's hat, he was the only choice.

After acquiring *Cool Hand Luke*, Lemmon recognized he lacked the physical authority for the part and stepped aside in favor of Newman while retaining ownership. *Cool Hand Luke* was the last of the quartet of pictures—the others being *Harper* (1966), *Torn Curtain* (1966) and *Hombre* (1967)—that make up Paul Newman's mid–60s halcyon period. A box office heavyweight with fees to match, he hankered after another iconic role in the vein of *The Hustler* (1961) and *Hud*. Reportedly, Telly Savalas was in pole position to play Lucas Jackson, the cool character of the title, but was delayed returning from filming *The Dirty Dozen* (1967) in England.[113] The script was knocked into shape by Frank Pierson (*Cat Ballou*, 1965). There were no other stars[114] and a first-time director in Stuart Rosenberg,[115] who had helmed the television pilot for *The Name of the Game* (1966) and the TV movie *A Small Rebellion* (1966) for which Simone Signoret won an Emmy. There was strong support from George Kennedy (*The Dirty Dozen*, 1967) as Dragline and Dennis Hopper (*The Trip*, 1967) while Strother Martin as the warden would spout one of the movie's classic lines: "What we've got here is a failure to communicate."

This meditation on martyrdom remains an iconic curiosity. Luke's hatred of authority puts him in prison in the first place and his refusal to buckle keeps him there. In a prison movie, where the narrative thrust is escape, Luke is as much trying to escape from himself. This is a world reduced to a single common denominator: brutality. For a man who loathes rules, it is hell. At first he makes an enemy of the other prisoners since, lacking a criminal background, he is almost there on a whim. But his determination not to back down—even when thumped senseless by Dragline—wins them over and sets the scene for confrontations with the warden and escape attempts. He becomes a motivational figure, cementing legendary status in a classic sequence by eating 50 hard-boiled eggs in one hour. Escapes are punished so harshly it appears his spirit is broken—but that is a ruse for a future breakout. His final getaway ends in death, but one with Christlike symbolism.

Outside of Butch Cassidy, a more amiable criminal you would struggle to find. He defies authority with a smirk but with none of the truculence of the ordinary rebel. This is probably Newman's best role, the character suiting both his acting style and his screen charisma. But where Hud Bannon and *The Hustler*'s Fast Eddie Felsom have inherent meanness, this is a good-ol'-boy somewhat perplexed by life. It is ironic that a man going nowhere finds salvation in the pit of prison. But the movie also examines the universal need for hero worship, Dragline's bewilderment when Luke eventually fails to live up to expectations is affecting. With every prisoner in the same uniform and the countryside bleak and undistinguished, Conrad Hall's cinematography is miraculous and Lalo Schifrin's simple, wonderfully evocative score continuously inventive. It proved as definitive an examination of the outsider as the later *Easy Rider*.

The screenplay was nominated for an Oscar, Newman received his fourth nomination, composer Schifrin and George Kennedy their first. Only the latter (Best Supporting Actor) went home victorious.

Critical reception: "Succeeds as a ... deeply dramatic study ... and as an allegory" (*Hollywood Reporter*); "a tough, honest film with backbone" (Roger Ebert); "Newman gives an excellent performance ... [The film] maintains interest throughout rambling exposition to a downbeat climax" (*Variety*).[116]

Rentals: $6.8 million[117] (including 1968 post–Oscar reissue double bill with *Wait Until Dark*) ($48.4 million equivalent)

94: *The Greatest Story Ever Told*

Starring Max von Sydow; directed and produced by George Stevens; screenplay, Stevens and James Lee Barrett, based on the book by Fulton Oursler, with input from Henry Denker[118] and Carl Sandburg; music, Alfred Newman. United Artists roadshow. February 15, 1965.

The source material to which filmmakers most often returned was the Bible.[119] With rare exceptions, such films seethed with spectacle, often of the lurid kind, rather than reverence. The highlights of *Ben-Hur*, for example, were a sea battle and a pulsating chariot race while *Solomon and Sheba* (1960) and *Sodom and Gomorrah* (1962) concentrated more on seduction and violence than faith. George Stevens was Hollywood royalty, one of *the* most acclaimed and commercially successful directors. Three times he ascended the Oscar podium, for *A Place in the Sun* (1951) and *Giant* (1956) and to receive the Irving G. Thalberg Memorial Award (for lifetime achievement).[120] For United Artists, his hiring was a coup.

But Stevens had drastically reduced his output. From 11 features in the 1930s, including *Swing Time* (1936) and *Gunga Din* (1939), six in the 1940s, and five in the 1950s, Stevens had not managed a single picture in the 1960s until this one, an ambitious near-four-hour[121] depiction of the life of Christ.[122]

John Wayne was the first star to be announced followed by Sidney Poitier* in a projected all-star cast of 80. Although shown in close-up in the advert, in the film Wayne's features are obscured. Both were originally signed up when Twentieth Century–Fox planned the production and remained loyal to the project when it shifted to United Artists. Trade press advertisement (*Box Office*, October 17, 1960, 10).

*Archer, Eugene, "John Wayne Joins *Greatest Story*," *New York Times*, Sep 14, 1960, 51; advert, *Variety*, Oct 19, 1960, 10.

Stevens wanted a relative unknown for the lead. Although an arthouse star thanks to Ingmar Bergman's *The Seventh Seal* (1957), Max von Sydow was making his Hollywood debut.[123] While Hollywood had welcomed European females in abundance, the same did not apply to males. Frenchmen Maurice Chevalier and Charles Boyer had been swoon kings in the Hollywood Golden Age,[124] but opportunities for foreigners in 1960s Hollywood were limited, Hardy Kruger and Maximilian Schell primarily supporting actors; the biggest domestic stars of Italy (Marcello Mastroianni) and France (Jean-Paul Belmondo and Alain Delon with the occasional exception of Yves Montand) were bypassed. Stevens collected an all-star cast in smaller roles as back-up for von Sydow, Oscar recognition the common denominator. Charlton Heston had been named Best Actor for *Ben-Hur,* Jose Ferrer for *Cyrano de Bergerac* (1950) and Sidney Poitier for *Lilies of the Field*. Claude Rains had four Best Actor nominations and even John Wayne had one. Best Actress nominees included Carroll Baker (*Baby Doll*, 1956) and Dorothy McGuire (*Gentleman's Agreement*, 1947). Shelley Winters had won Best Supporting Actress for Stevens' previous *The Diary of Anne Frank* (1959). Van Heflin had picked up Best Supporting Actor for *Johnny Eager* (1941). Big stars in small roles were a marketing ploy, filling out the credits, inviting audiences to play Spot the Star, and a way of hedging one's bets.

Hollywood often gave name directors carte blanche. When budgets soared due to directorial intransigence or extravagance, it proved impossible except in rare circumstances for studios to limit the damage, extricate themselves from the project or get rid of the director. United Artists parted ways with Fred Zinnemann over his concept for *Hawaii*, for example, but stuck with Stevens all through *The Greatest Story Ever Told* even though his perfectionism delayed the film's release for two years. The film did not premiere until Easter 1965, in part because editing took over a year and in part for marketing reasons. Easter was the only possible date for releasing a film about the Son of God where crucifixion was the climax. But that did provide plenty of time to activate group sales among churchgoers.

The original intention was to shoot the film in three-strip Cinerama, but that quickly changed to Ultra Panavision 70. While the landscape scenes were shot in-camera, most city scenes were created using matte paintings, the special-effects technique used before CGI. A trio of matte experts—Matthew Yuricich (*Ben-Hur*), Jan Domela (*Vertigo*) and Albert Maxwell Simpson (*King Kong*)—pulled off the visual magic. In the bird's-eye view of the entire walled city of Jerusalem, only the soldiers at the center of the composition are real.[125]

There is no questioning the power of the cinematography or the music (both Oscar-nominated), and the film certainly captures a great deal of the aura of the man. In some scenes, von Sydow invests the character with great authority. But like many religious films, it is reverential rather than powerful and in the end did not justify the budget. If ever a director deserved to be called an auteur, it was Stevens over this five-year project. He said,

> The basic theme of the story is one which, unfortunately, has not always been associated with it in the past. It relates to the universality of men and how they must learn to live together. I think it is a theme of great earnestness and utmost simplicity and I think all the usual trappings connected with Biblical productions ... are in alarming disagreement with this simple theme. We tried ... to think the story out anew and present it as living literature rather than something archaic.[126]

26   The Films

Rarely re-evaluated, the movie is at its best when set against naturalistic backgrounds, at its worst when utilizing painted backdrops and heavenly choruses. But it remains a bold cinematic telling of the most famous story ever written.

Critical reception: "Stevens' masterpiece" (*New York Daily News*); "stunningly rendered" (*Good Housekeeping*)[127]; "the sum of its merits is impressive, the residue of its defects unimportant" (*Variety*)[128]; "does not succeed ultimately in elevating its theme visually or intellectually much beyond dime-story-holy-pictures-Sunday school primer level" (*Tribune*); "four hours is much too long to devote to a far-from-complete dramatization ... but Mr. Stevens has done it in a generous and often stunning style (*New York Times*)."[129]

Rentals: $6.9 million.[130] ($49.1 million equivalent)

92 (tie): *Hatari!*

Starring John Wayne, Hardy Kruger and Elsa Martinelli; directed and produced by Howard Hawks; screenplay, Leigh Brackett,[131] story, Harry Kurnitz; music, Henry Mancini. Paramount. June 19, 1962.

Howard Hawks was the biggest beneficiary of the reassessment of American directors stimulated by the auteur theory,[132] but he was slowing down. From 13 movies in the 1930s and nine in the 1940s, his output dropped to six in the next decade. The monumental flop *Land of the Pharaohs* (1955) explained the long gap before *Rio Bravo* (1959) restored his standing.

Hawks received $300,000 for directing and producing *Hatari!* plus 50 percent of the profits—in comparison, John Ford was paid $250,000 for *The Horse Soldiers* (1959). But Paramount balked at $1.5 million plus percentages to pair Clark Gable and John Wayne. For a rewritten Gable part, Hawks considered Yves Montand, Peter Ustinov, Peter Sellers and Leo McKern before settling on Hardy Kruger. Initially, Claudia Cardinale was in pole position for the female lead, then it was Antonella Lualdi (*The Mongols*, 1961) and finally Elsa Martinelli.[133] While currently behind Cardinale, Sophia Loren and Gina Lollobrigida in the Italian star-stakes, Martinelli had been first to win a major Hollywood role when recruited by Kirk Douglas for *The Indian Fighter* (1955) after he spotted her photograph in *Vogue*.[134] Although *Rice Girl* (1956) brought her art-house notoriety and she was one of Universal's *Four Girls in Town* (1957), pulling out of a long-term contract with Douglas[135] meant it was another 13 pictures before she re-entered the Hollywood mainstream. Hawks saw her in Roger Vadim's *Blood and Roses* (1960).

This was still an era when exotic locales could pull in audiences: Though movies had been made about explorers and big-game hunters, none had covered quite what Hawks had in mind. The animals would be trapped rather than killed, and sold to zoos. Wayne's team included Kruger, Red Buttons and Frenchman Gerard Blain with the lithe Martinelli[136] as a wildlife photographer providing unlikely romantic interest (she was 29, Wayne 55). Martinelli arrived on set a month before the other stars, just when the baby elephants were born, and involvement in their feeding created the rapport seen on film.[137] The wilder and more unpredictable the creatures, the wilder the excitement, so that meant rhinos and elephants and anything that had a mind of its own. It turned out to be a very realistic shoot, the camera tracking at speed, vehicles threatening to

The Films   27

overturn at any moment chasing animals across the plains. Most of the actors spurned stunt doubles, Wayne riding on the outside of the pursuit vehicle.

Hawks combines his two most common themes: a group of men stuck together facing an unusual task and a battle of the sexes. But without the tension of an upcoming gunfight (*Rio Bravo*) or bizarre romantic comedy set-up (*Bringing Up Baby*), it falls short of the director's highest standards. But as he set such high standards, virtually anything would. It remains a highly entertaining and a thrilling ride, vehicles bouncing, swerving and twisting, the thunder of hooves, confrontations with dangerous animals making up for other deficiencies. Martinelli lacks the zap of a Hepburn or Monroe but does well as the photographer infiltrating a male enclave. A pet leopard also provides a decent riff on the girl-in-the-bath number. Plot lines are worked in to give actors of the caliber of Hardy Kruger something to do and stretch the likes of Red Buttons.

In quite a different role, Wayne, for once not called upon to save the day, gives a good performance. Not only do they not make them like that any more, they wouldn't be allowed to make them like that these days, notions about working with animals (though none were harmed) much changed. The picture has an appealing exuberance, improvisation[138] adding to the excitement, like the chariot race in *Ben-Hur* except with animals. (Wayne would have preferred more variety in the catching methods.[139]) While not a classic in the mold of *The Big Sleep* (1946) or *Red River* (1948) (never enough conflict or sexual tension for that), it was surprisingly likable, with some affecting scenes involving the baby elephant which produced an unexpected hit for composer Henry Mancini's "Baby Elephant Walk" theme. While it might be blasphemous to suggest Hawks was taking a walk on the Udult side (see below, *Son of Flubber*), Paramount cited the combination of "cleanliness and commerce" that worked so well for Disney, and believed that the film's lack of objectionable material would set the box office alight.[140]

Critical reception: "There is a complete lack of nuance or development of character ... constant switching from leopards to love and back again verges on tedium" (*New York Times*); "elaborately produced if dramatically negligent and overlong" (*Variety*); "never much more than a fitfully rousing entertainment" (*Films and Filming*).[141] *Cahiers du Cinema* called it the third-best film of 1962.[142]

Rentals: $7 million[143] ($49.8 million equivalent)

92 (tie): *Chitty Chitty Bang Bang*

Starring Dick Van Dyke and Sally Ann Howes; directed by Ken Hughes; screenplay, Roald Dahl and Hughes, from the Ian Fleming novel; producer, Albert R. Broccoli; music, Richard M. Sherman and Robert B. Sherman. United Artists roadshow. December 12, 1968 (London); December 18, 1968 (U.S.).

Possibly if the book on which this musical was based had been written by anyone other than James Bond creator Ian Fleming, it would never have been greenlit. But Disney had proved there was a strong market for movies that, while ostensibly aimed at children, could hold adult interest; and, of course, this was the boom era for musicals. Bond co-producer Albert "Cubby" Broccoli envisioned the kind of picture that would return grosses in the *Mary Poppins* (1964) range. To achieve that, he planned to re-team Julie Andrews and Dick Van Dyke, but Andrews passed and only hefty financial inducement convinced Van Dyke. Continuing the *Mary Poppins* connection, Broccoli brought in songwriters Robert B. Sherman and Richard M. Sherman, who had won Oscars for that film. British director Ken Hughes had been making features since 1954 including *Of Human Bondage* (1964) and, for Broccoli, *The Trials of Oscar Wilde* (1960). One scene from the latter (the playwright telling his children a fairy story) inspired the producer to re-hire the director.[144]

Roald Dahl—his children's books *James and the Giant Peach* (1961) and *Charlie and the Chocolate Factory* (1964) nowhere near their later levels of fame—was hired to write the screenplay. Although he had some television experience, and had just come off writing *You Only Live Twice* (1967), his only other picture was *36 Hours* (1964) starring James Garner, which derived from his own short story. Dahl upped the story's tempo, introducing fantastic villains (including Gert Frobe of *Goldfinger* fame), changing the plot to focus on creepy child-catchers, creating Vulgaria and inventing leading lady Truly Scrumptious (a name with more than a hint of a Bond femme fatale). Initially, Hughes and Dahl collaborated on the script but with production pressing and Dahl's output too slow, Hughes took over. "What upset me was Dahl thought I had engineered the whole thing and I had nothing whatsoever to do with it," said Hughes. In fact, Hughes "called in British comedian Benny Hill to tweak the script...."[145]

Although still a marquee name for family-friendly movies, Van Dyke had diversified into adult roles such as in Bud Yorkin's *Divorce American Style* (1967) but he was the ideal actor to bring inventor Caractacus Potts to life. Van Dyke wisely decided to play him as an American rather than deploy the British accent much-derided in *Mary Poppins*. On the strength of having taken over from Julie Andrews in the Broadway production of *My Fair Lady* in the late 1950s, and without a movie role in a decade, British former child actor Sally Ann Howes (36 at the time) came on board as Truly Scrumptious and brought a decided Englishness to the proceedings. British character actor Lionel Jeffries (a year younger than Van Dyke) plays the grandfather whose kidnapping kicks off the plot. Prior to that, the first third of the film introduces the characters, including two children played by Heather Ripley and Adrian Hall in the cute Disney tradition. Ripley undertook elocution lessons to lose her Scottish accent.[146] From the title sequence, which got kids in a sing-along mood, it's pretty inventive stuff, the flying car, colorful costumes, zany characters including Benny Hill as the Toymaker, and especially the villains' lair, inspired by the Castle of Bavaria. Robert Helpmann (who wore six false noses as the Child Catcher) is one of the creepiest characters ever put on celluloid, never mind that this is a film aimed at children. Baron Bomburst and his wife are outsize villains when they are not being entertaining and there are many jokes at their expense.

Unusually, for a musical, one of the film's centerpieces was the car itself, in Fleming's book an amalgam of two 1920s vehicles he had owned, the Standard Tourer and a racing car based on the Mercedes chassis. Production designer Ken Adam, who had overseen all the Bonds including the vast volcano for *You Only Live Twice*, was tasked with creating the titular car. ("I liked the idea of a body like a boat and the bonnet of a Bugatti.") Ford's director of racing Alan Mann "constructed the vehicle, which, while resembling a car from the 1920s, had a 1960s Ford V6 engine and automatic transmission. Brass fittings were obtained from Edwardian wrecks, the wheels molded in alloy to replicate the timber wheels of the period and the dashboard plate came from a World War I fighter plane."[147] The Sherman Brothers, given special dispensation by Walt Disney, put together a pretty good score, the standouts being the title song "Posh" (sung by

Lionel Jeffries), "Hushabye Mountain" and "Me Ol' Bamboo." Van Dyke's dance numbers have flair and energy. Naturally, the dance numbers took the longest to rehearse and film, "Toots Sweet" involving 38 dancers, 40 singers and 85 musicians. "Me Ol' Bamboo" required two weeks of rehearsal, four days of shooting and 23 takes.[148] It was Van Dyke who suggested he perform like a puppet. Howes had a terrific concerto voice, like Julie Andrews "both right on pitch—you could key pianos to their voices," commented Van Dyke, "so I was constantly straining to get up there and not be flat."[149]

The movie was shot at Pinewood and on location at Ibstone Mill, Turville, in England, St. Tropez and Neuschwanstein Castle in Bavaria and Rothenberg on the river Tauber. Although considered overlong by some, at 144 minutes, it was only a few minutes longer than *Mary Poppins*. In the Disney fashion, the opening was heralded by a host of merchandising.

Critical reception: "Warmth, wit and imagination ... a virtual bonanza for youthful audiences" (*Box Office*); "a picture for the ages—the ages between five and twelve" (*Time*); "fast, dense, trendy, children's musical" (*New York Times*); "about the best two-hour children's musical you could hope for with a marvelous magic auto and lots of adventure" (*Chicago Sun-Times*).[150]

Rentals: $7 million[151] ($49.8 million equivalent)

90 (tie): *Son of Flubber*

Starring Fred MacMurray and Nancy Olson; directed by Robert Stevenson; screenplay, Bill Walsh and Don DaGradi, from a Samuel L. Taylor story based on the "Danny Dunn" books by Ray Ashley and Jay Williams; producer, Walt Disney; music, George Brun. Disney. January 16, 1963.

Disney was the decade's surprise package, reinvented as a box office frontrunner whose hits pre-empted the "high concept" picture. A Hollywood anomaly, the company had never made enough movies, too dependent on a new or revived animated feature. Without a regular supply line, distribution[152] was a thorny issue. Its 1950s output mixed nature documentaries like *The African Lion* (1955), adventure pictures made in Britain (*The Story of Robin Hood and His Merrie Men*, 1952), just one big-budget venture (*20,000 Leagues Under the Sea*, 1954), live-action family pictures (*Old Yeller*, 1957) and features cannibalized from television (*Davy Crockett and the River Pirates*, 1956). Other studios had a "secret fear of family films," believing that TV had corralled that particular market.[153] Disney was the exception. To reconstitute itself as a Hollywood powerbase, Disney embarked on a new concept called "Udult." Disney defined Udult as "U" pictures with adult appeal. Focusing on comedy, fantasy and adventure, Disney set out to make movies aimed at both adults and children. Long before the all-star cast became an essential roadshow ingredient, Disney adopted a similar formula, hiring older Oscar winners like Donald Crisp[154] and nominees and current stars like Maureen O'Hara (to bring in the adult audience) with child stars like Hayley Mills (appealing to all age groups).[155] And it worked. In 1961, Disney produced three of the top five films at the box office and thereafter enjoyed sustained commercial success.

During the decade, Disney drew on three main male stars: Fred MacMurray, previously a big Hollywood star, TV star Dick Van Dyke, and Dean Jones, who had no pedigree in either medium. MacMurray (*Double Indemnity*, 1944) was critical to the

The Films

WHAT ARE 'UDULT' PICTURES ?

Disney's original "Udult" schedule comprised *Swiss Family Robinson* (1960), *Pollyanna* (1960), *The Parent Trap* (1961), *The Absent-Minded Professor* (1961), *Greyfriars Bobby* (1961) and *101 Dalmatians* (1961) (Hannan Collection).

development of the Udult concept. Although he had in both 1943 and 1944 been the biggest single earner of either gender in Hollywood—taking home over $800,000 in total during the two years[156]—he had lost his box office cachet in the 1950s, third-billed, for example, in *The Rains of Ranchipur* (1955) and by decade's end more likely to be found in television. However, that meant he was affordable and with comedy in his repertoire—*Never a Dull Moment* (1950) and *The Egg and I* (1947)—he played the lead in *The Shaggy Dog* (1959). For both actor and studio, it was a gamble. But it paid off. The film was the second-highest performer at the U.S. box office that year, beating *Some Like It Hot*, *North by Northwest* and *Rio Bravo* as well as Disney's own *Sleeping Beauty*. The fact that it outscored the animated feature, traditionally Disney's highest earners, gave the studio the courage to embark on the Udult initiative. Its success allowed Disney to carve out a niche for broad comedies with MacMurray, five collaborations in the 1960s. His female equivalent was 1950s star Nancy Olson,[157] who appeared in three.

Son of Flubber was a sequel to the Disney hit *The Absent Minded Professor* (1961) starring MacMurray and Olson. He reprises the character of Professor Brainard, now struggling to make money from his discovery of the substance Flubber. He creates an alternative—Flubbergas—which can alter the weather. The ensuing shenanigans are undercut by marital woes as wife Olson files for divorce and attracts the attention of a suitor while Brainard becomes involved with an old girlfriend. It's all very silly but great fun. Five of the

The Films   31

top six films in 1963 were big-budget roadshows, the outlier being *Irma La Douce* in third spot. Behind them, though, in seventh spot, was *Son of Flubber*. It was impossible to place so highly on the annual box office charts with a picture just aimed at kids. Prices for matinees were lower and there were just not enough showings, even were a film to prove a hit with children, for a picture to achieve such elevated heights unless applying the Udult formula.

Critical reception: "Old-fashioned sight-gag slapstick farce but it is fun" (*New York Times*); "doesn't fill its father's footprints" (*Variety*); "hilarious follow-up ... delightfully wacky characterizations" (*Box Office*).[158]

Rentals: $7.1 million.[159] ($50.6 million equivalent)

90 (tie): *To Kill a Mockingbird*

Starring Gregory Peck, Mary Badham and Brock Peters; produced and directed by Robert Mulligan; screenplay, Horton Foote, from the book by Harper Lee; music, Elmer Bernstein. Universal. December 25, 1962.[160]

Studios used to buy bestsellers by the ton. They would take out full-page advertisements in the trade press, listing all their purchases, sometimes with stars or directors attached but most often not, as a promise to exhibitors of future quality product. Bestsellers were highly valued as pre-sold commodities, widely reviewed, widely seen in bookshop displays, and with an inbuilt audience of readers. The film version triggered a movie tie-in edition, further bookshop promotion, and coverage comparing book to film. Seven of the top ten bestsellers in 1962, for example, would be turned into movies.

But there was little interest in Harper Lee's bestseller *To Kill a Mockingbird* (third on the *Publisher's Weekly* annual rankings for 1961) because nobody thought a tale of rape and racism told from the perspective of a six-year-old girl was filmable. Producer Alan J. Pakula and directing partner Robert Mulligan took the opposite view. At that time, Mulligan was best known for comedy—*The Rat Race* (1960), *The Great Imposter* (1960) and *Come September* (1961). The exotic drama *The Spiral Road* (1962) did not seem to automatically lead to a movie as potentially inflammatory as *To Kill a Mockingbird*, whose subject matter could not be handled, like comedy, in broad strokes, but would require delicacy and nuance.

Issues of racism were only beginning to surface in the Hollywood mainstream. Woody Strode as *Sergeant Rutledge* (1960) is charged with the rape and murder of a white girl. *West Side Story* (1961) concerns racism towards Puerto Ricans. *Bridge to the Sun* (1961) focuses on hostility towards the interracial marriage between an American woman and a Japanese man. *Paris Blues* (1961) contrasts Parisian acceptance of African-Americans with that of America. The British film *Flame in the Streets* (1961) examined racial tensions afflicting the West Indian community in London. In *A Raisin in the Sun* (1961), an African American family is offered money to stay away from a prosperous white community. Roger Corman's *The Intruder* (1962) focused on a racist in a small town. But *To Kill a Mockingbird* was the most explosive of all: again an African American accused of the rape of a white woman in the Deep South, but this time defended by an upstanding white attorney.

Star Gregory Peck preferred filmed literary works—*The Keys of the Kingdom* (1944), *The Yearling* (1946), *Gentleman's Agreement* (1947), *Captain Horatio Hornblower R.N.* (1951), *The Snows of Kilimanjaro* (1952), *The Million Pound Note* (1954), *The Purple Plain*

32 The Films

(1954), *The Man in the Gray Flannel Suit* (1956) and *Moby Dick* (1956).[161] His previous five movies were based on books: *Pork Chop Hill* (1959), *Beloved Infidel* (1959), *On the Beach* (1959), *The Guns of Navarone* (1961) and *Cape Fear* (1962).[162] Peck had also turned producer, but the Western *The Big Country* (1958) under-achieved and *Pork Chop Hill* flopped. His involvement on *To Kill a Mockingbird*, through his Brentwood Productions, was a paper exercise, merely a tax-saving device.

But Atticus Finch was a role that brought out Peck at his best: upright, quiet, commanding, tolerant, unwilling to let injustice lie, and his six-minute speech during the trial had Oscar nomination written all over it. Screenwriter Horton Foote, until now, apart from one movie excursion (*Storm Fear*, 1955) working exclusively for TV, had managed to combine the enticing style of the novel with dramatic intensity. While retaining the child's point of view, Mulligan helped give it an adult slant by filming in black-and-white, to prevent the glorious colors of the Deep South acting as a distraction. The young heroine retained her childlike innocence while adult rigor was applied, preserving the spirit of the novel while turning it into a special movie in its own right, a plea for tolerance, for true justice for all.

The film's stance against racism as much as its directorial brilliance and acting pushed it into the potential Oscar class. For Best Picture it was up against *The Longest Day*, *The Music Man*, *Mutiny on the Bounty* and *Lawrence of Arabia* (the winner). Mulligan lost out to David Lean for Best Director. This was Peck's fifth tilt at the Best Actor Oscar after *The Keys of the Kingdom*, *The Yearling*, *Gentleman's Agreement* and *Twelve O'Clock High* (1949). Also in contention were Peter O'Toole (*Lawrence of Arabia*), Burt Lancaster (*Birdman of Alcatraz*), Jack Lemmon (*Days of Wine and Roses*) and Marcello Mastroianni (*Divorce, Italian Style*). Peck's victory rounded off a night that saw *To Kill a Mockingbird* collect another two statuettes, for Best Screenplay and for Best Art Direction-Set Decoration. Mary Badham, making her debut as Finch's daughter Scout, was nominated for Best Supporting Actress, Mulligan for Best Film and Elmer Bernstein for the score.

Getting the young cast members (Jem was played by Philip Alford) to work together and endure the boredom of a movie set was one of the director's biggest problems. The two children did not get along and Mulligan found it best to settle for early takes of scenes.[163] Brock Peters, who plays the accused, went on to essay the first gay African American in *The Pawnbroker* (1964) and had roles in *Major Dundee* (1965) and *The Incident* (1967).

Critical reception: "A major film achievement" (*Variety*); "not much of a movie by formal standards" (*Village Voice*); "expresses the liberal pieties of a more liberal time, the early 1960s, and goes very easy on the realities of small-town Alabama in the 1930s" (*Chicago Sun-Times*); "powerful picturization … fine example of thought-provoking fare" (*Box Office*)[164]; "Gregory Peck's pious Lincoln impersonation" (*New Republic*).[165]

Rentals: $7.1 million[166] ($50.6 million equivalent)

88 (tie): *Our Man Flint*

Starring James Coburn, Lee J. Cobb and Gila Golan; directed by Daniel Mann; screenplay, Hal Finberg and Ben Starr; producer, Saul David; music, Jerry Goldsmith. Twentieth Century–Fox. January 16, 1966.

Hollywood could not resist a trend—a "cycle" in industry parlance. After the first flush of late 1940s Westerns, it seemed every studio was cashing in; and in the 1950s, MGM and Twentieth Century–Fox went head to head in the musical genre. The spy film was

JET-PROPELLED TOURS TO BLAST OFF "FLINT" OPENINGS!

JAMES COBURN—FLINT HIMSELF— TAKES TO THE AIR IN HIS PRIVATE, 6 PASSENGER LEAR JET

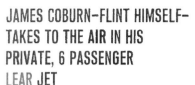

on a whirlwind coast-to-coast tour that covers New York, Boston, Pittsburgh, Cleveland, Cincinnati, Detroit, Chicago, St. Louis, Kansas City, Dallas, Denver, Salt Lake City, San Francisco!

A SUREFIRE PUBLICITY BREAK MAKER AS HE TAKES PRESS AND OPINION-MAKERS UP 40,000 FEET IN THE AIR FOR HIGH-FLYING COVERAGE OF 20TH'S HIGH-FLYING HERO!

FLINT'S GIRL— GILA GOLAN— DELTA JETS OUT TO MEET THE PRESS

in New Orleans, St. Louis, Memphis, Birmingham, Atlanta, Miami, Washington, Baltimore, Philadelphia, New York!

AND JUST WATCH THE COVERAGE WHEN SHE STARTS GIVING THE INSIDE SCOOP ON "OUR MAN" AND HIS GIRLS!

IT'S DOUBLE-BARRELLED ACTION FROM 20th—TO MAKE "OUR MAN" YOUR MAN FOR JANUARY!!

"James Bond may have met his match in Derek Flint" — *Variety*

Polish-born fashion model and "Miss World" runner-up (representing Israel) Gila Golan had one of the shortest movie careers on record, just another five pictures following debut *Ship of Fools* (1965). The female lead here was her peak. Fourth-billed in the Jerry Lewis comedy *Three on a Couch* (1966), she went into Italian picture *Catch as Catch Can* (1967), then the female lead in the low-budget prehistoric adventure *The Valley of Gwangi* (1969) and lastly a bit part in comedy *L'Allentore nel Pallone* (1984). Trade press advertisement (*Box Office*, January 24, 1966).

34 The Films

never even a genre. At best, it fitted into a larger genre like film noir or thriller, but nobody could point to a major success. When United Artists slipped in the slick, violent, sexy *Dr. No* (1962), studio heads were not particularly impressed; its box office reception was better than expected but not a major hit in America. *From Russia with Love* (1963) did better— cracking the annual top 20—but not enough to elicit copycat mania. Nobody could ignore *Goldfinger* (1964). British company Rank had a head start with *The Ipcress File* (1965),[167] MGM dabbled in films based on its *Man from U.N.C.L.E* TV series[168] and made a stab at creating a series based on John Gardner books beginning with *The Liquidator* (1965). Paramount took the realistic spy route, trussing Richard Burton up as John le Carré's dour *The Spy Who Came In from the Cold* (1965). Spoofs went by the name of *The 2nd Best Secret Agent in the World* (1965) and *Dr. Goldfoot and the Bikini Machine* (1965). Fox and Columbia separately came to the conclusion that an ersatz Bond with high production values and star quality might have legs. Fox was first out of the gate with *Our Man Flint*.

Normally stars emerge from successes. Rarely did they come out of a flop like *The Magnificent Seven* (1960). But the Western had already furnished Hollywood with one bona fide star in Steve McQueen, and another with breakout potential in Horst Buchholz (*Nine Hours to Rama*, 1963). Robert Vaughn was a small-screen heartthrob courtesy of *The Man from U.N.C.L.E.* James Coburn, *The Magnificent Seven*'s knife-thrower, was moving haltingly towards stardom after a featured role in *The Great Escape* (1963), fourth billing in *Charade* (1963) and *Major Dundee* (1965), escalated to second-billing in *A High Wind in Jamaica* (1965). He had a lanky, effortless screen presence and a distinctive delivery even if the plot of *Our Man Flint* verged on the preposterous: mad scientists controlling the weather.

Coburn played wealthy super-spy Derek Flint, with playmates on tap, and not having to deal with the British bureaucrats who always seemed determined to prevent Bond having a good time. The studio took the Bond formula and yanked it up to 11 in all directions: girls, gadgets and violence. Acronyms abounded (Flint works for ZOWIE), there were references to SPECTRE, Agent 008 and a Walther PPK. The $3.5 million budget[169] was more than *Batman* (1966) and *Modesty Blaise* (1966)—a less successful attempt to cash in on the spy boom. Director Daniel Mann was first-rate, having helmed *The Teahouse of the August Moon* (1956) and *BUtterfield 8* (1960). But most of all, *Our Man Flint* had an actor who fitted the role. Coburn's athleticism, wide smile, debonair appearance, laconic attitude and super-confidence carried the whole endeavor. It was an infectious concoction—even the ads were a spoof[170]—and critics and audiences responded. It turned Coburn into a star. Fox repeated the formula again for *In Like Flint* (1967) but Coburn, fearing being typecast like Sean Connery, wisely pulled back from committing himself to further outings and went on to have a long career.

Critical reception: "Action-jammed swashbuckling spoof" (*Variety*); "inferior burlesque of Bond" (*New York Times*), "fast moving and good fun" (*Box Office*).[171]

Rentals: $7.2 million ($51.3 million equivalent)

88 (tie): *Easy Rider*

Starring Peter Fonda, Dennis Hopper and Jack Nicholson; directed and produced by Hopper; screenplay, Fonda, Hopper and Terry Southern.[172] Columbia. May 12, 1969 (Cannes Film Festival); U.S.: July 14, 1969.

In Britain, rejected by the Odeon circuit, which feared its nationwide unsuitability, *Easy Rider* opened at the 270-seat Classic Piccadilly on the periphery of the main West End hub where Leicester Square boasted five theaters with a combined seating capacity of nearly 7,000. Columbia chose the tiny venue, complete with round-the-clock showings, as a way of making a splash. Trade press advertisement (*Kine Weekly*, September 20, 1969, 15).

Easy Rider—costing $501,000[173]—fell into the "little films that could" category that had provided the industry with previous sleepers like *Alfie* (1965) and *To Sir, with Love* (1967). The movie was a little slow perhaps, but the sex-drugs-violence storyline was a natural fit for the AIP biker strand[174]—especially as stars Peter Fonda (*Wild Angels*, 1966), Dennis Hopper (*The Glory Stompers*, 1967) and Jack Nicholson (*Hell's Angels on Wheels*, 1967)[175] had form in that genre. And a quick saturation release[176] would probably make a profit.

36   The Films

The alternative was trickier. Arthouse pictures usually meant restricted distribution, unless they came with built-in critical raves. Festival acceptance was the best way to garner that. The world's most famous film festival Cannes had provided the publicity lift-off and commercial crossover in the U.S. for previous winners *La Dolce Vita*, *The Leopard* (1963), the French romance *A Man and a Woman* (1966) and the controversial *Blow Up* (1966). Although taking the smallest of three main prizes in 1969—the Palme D'Or went to Lindsay Anderson's *If...* and the Jury Prize to *Z*—*Easy Rider* (named best first film) proved the bigger sensation,[177] primarily because the makers hijacked all the publicity available. This ran counter to normal procedure, by which *If...* should have received the marketing bounty.[178] The French seal of approval[179] was intended to shield it from domestic critical hostility, but it snagged superlative reviews from influential critics Richard Schickel (*Life*), Judith Crist (*New York*) and Andrew Sarris (*Village Voice*). It opened at the Beekman[180] in New York in July 1969, its 538 seats[181] representing a third or quarter of the capacity of the more commercial theaters and one-tenth of the audience crammed into Radio City Music Hall. Its second week of $46,609, improving upon a record-breaking debut,[182] was a prelude to box office success.[183]

Initially, the combination of director-cum-star Hopper, co-star Fonda[184] and supporting actor Nicholson did not appear to contain the alchemy required to move them up the Hollywood food chain. They were movie veterans, appearing in plenty of pictures, albeit not always good ones, without coming close to the kind of status that would consistently pay the rent. Fonda was the best known, in part due to father Henry and sister Jane, with top billing in *The Young Lovers* (1964), *The Wild Angels* (1966) and *The Trip* (1967). Hopper had made his movie debut in *Rebel Without a Cause* (1955), Nicholson in *The Cry Baby Killer* (1958) and he, too, had been top-billed, in Monte Hellman's *Ride in the Whirlwind* (1966).

You could be forgiven for thinking that *Easy Rider*'s main influences were the early Cinerama pictures that focused on extensive tracking shots of scenery (in this case, the open road) and unusual customs (here: alternative lifestyles and dope), but it also drew on the assumption, as did Hitchcock's *Vertigo* (1958) and Kubrick's *2001: A Space Odyssey*, that a camera doing nothing can be hypnotic. Message pictures were the remit of older directors like Stanley Kramer and Martin Ritt while films that had something to say about the human condition generally emanated from Europe, not mining the low-budget Hollywood seam. *Easy Rider* has a European sensibility and random unconnected episodes. The plot is incredibly slight, two mild-manned dudes heading for the Mardi Gras. Road trips were not particularly unusual in American cinema but previous locomotion was horse-related—Westerns—although the journey, physically or figuratively, had been a central theme to movies. It's an 80-minute picture masquerading as a 95-minute one, a good 15 minutes taken up with endless shots of Fonda and Hopper biking through the landscape, the contemporary soundtrack offering comment. This is also a hymn to ancient values, prayers at mealtimes, a marching band, and more prayers in the cemetery.

What marks the film out stylistically, perhaps enforced by the lean financing, is the sparing way it is told. The most dramatic scenes—the three murders—are filmed in shockingly simple fashion. The few stylistic flourishes—long pans along groups of characters and flash-cut flash-forward edits—add little to what is otherwise a very reflective film. The cinematography by Laszlo Kovacs and the contemporary music soundtrack (the unforgettable "Born to Be Wild" leading the charge) are equally inventive. Inspired

The Films   37

use is made of natural sound, the muffled thumping of oil derricks at the cemetery, one death confined to the battering of unseen clubs by unseen assailants. The dialogue could have been written by Tarantino, none of the confrontation or angst that drives most films, but odd musings that bring characters to life.

At the beginning of the trip, Hopper and Fonda are welcomed wherever they go but towards the end they are resented, treated as itinerant aliens. They entrance young girls but are vilified by authority, jailed for no reason except the threat to traditional values they represent. Nicholson's character attempts to explain this conundrum. Elements not discussed at time of release make this more rounded than you would imagine. The excitable Hopper, a nerd in hippie disguise, is driven by the American dream of making money. The more reflective Fonda senses something is not only missing from his life but has been lost forever. He has the rare stillness of a top actor, face reflecting unspoken inner turmoil.

It remains an extraordinary film, a series of accumulated incidentals holding up a mirror to an America nobody wanted to acknowledge and a brutal climax. Critical raves did not translate into Oscar recognition, just nominations for Nicholson as Best Supporting Actor and for the script.

Although *The Graduate* (1967) lit the touch paper that sent the film-scoring business down a new route, *Easy Rider* fanned the flames. Artists like Steppenwolf, Jimi Hendrix, the Band and the Byrds represented a different culture to the more mainstream Simon and Garfunkel. It heralded a shift away from traditionally composed soundtracks. *Easy Rider* was also credited with creating the "youthquake" that suggested audiences pictures targeting the older crowd were liable to failure. But, in fact, other youth-slanted films appeared at approximately the same time including *Last Summer*, *Putney Swope*, *Goodbye, Columbus* and *Midnight Cowboy*. Interestingly enough, the industry had already identified "young film buffs" responding to *If...*, *Goodbye, Columbus* and *Romeo and Juliet*.[185] That hidden counter-culture surfaced, not just in *Easy Rider* but the hordes of pot-smokers making up its audience. While massive financial success was the best thing that could happen to *Easy Rider*, it proved to be the worst possible development for Hollywood, as the film that changed Hollywood initially changed it for the worse, letting loose a host of box office bombs aimed at the youth market.

Critical reception: "Major youth attraction ... significant and frightening sub-surface" (*Box Office*); "a frightening view of America today as seen through youthful eyes and brilliant camerawork" (*International Motion Picture Exhibitor*); "an historic movie" (*Life*); "eloquent, important" (*Newsweek*); "the impact is devastating" (*New York*); "rousing, rhythmic, splendid" (*Village Voice*).[186]

Rentals: $7.2 million[187] ($51.3 million equivalent)

87: *The Blue Max*

Starring George Peppard, James Mason and Ursula Andress; directed by John Guillermin; screenplay, David Pursell, Jack Seddon and Gerald Hanley, based on the book by Jack D. Hunter; producer, Christian Ferry; music, Jerry Goldsmith. Twentieth Century–Fox roadshow. June 21, 1966.

The World War I action picture *The Blue Max*[188] was blown up—like *Doctor Zhivago*—to 70mm to qualify as a roadshow,[189] though director John Guillermin was not in the league of compatriot David Lean, being better known for *Tarzan's Greatest*

38 The Films

Adventure (1959) and *Tarzan Goes to India* (1962). But Fox head honcho Darryl F. Zanuck had been impressed by his war drama *Guns at Batasi* (1964).

Given that the *Blue Max* characters were German, it was a risky project. Throw in some amazing aerial footage and stunts with genuine aircraft (no CGI here), an illicit love story featuring Ursula Andress (*Dr. No*, 1962) and a working class guy taking on the establishment and the dice might easily roll in its favor. However, George Peppard (playing Lt. Bruno Stachel) still fell into the category of rising star, *Breakfast at Tiffany's* (1961) belonging to Audrey Hepburn, *How the West Was Won* (1962) and *The Victors* (1963) ensemble efforts, and *The Carpetbaggers* (1964) owing much to the scandalous source material; the World War II film *Operation Crossbow* (1965) had been headlined by Sophia Loren. *The Third Day* (1965), Peppard's only true starring role, flopped. British actor James Mason (as General Count von Klugerman) had been playing Germans for over a decade, in *The Desert Fox* (1951), *Five Fingers* (1952) and *The Desert Rats* (1953). Andress remained one of the top foreign female stars after Elvis' *Fun in Acapulco* (1963), the Rat Pack comedy *4 for Texas* (1963) and the title role in *She* (1965).

The Blue Max is the highest German award for gallantry. Peppard, a corporal in the army, determines to become a pilot and win it. When he joins the flying corps at the tail end of the war, he makes an enemy of Mason's nephew (Jeremy Kemp), his rival for glory who wins the Blue Max first. After Peppard saves the life of Baron von Richtofen, Germany's top flying ace, Mason builds him up as a public hero. Peppard seduces Andress, for once given the chance to act. Kemp dies after engaging in aerial devilry with Peppard. Determined to notch up enough kills to gain his medal, Peppard, with a full arsenal of attitude, continues to challenge authority, clashes with colleagues who retain fanciful notions of chivalry in a conflict notorious for mass slaughter, and finally wins the medal. In the end, to get him out of the way, Mason asks him to fly a new type of plane, which crashes.

The biplanes are both balletic and deadly, seemingly held together by straw, slower than World War II fighters, and the aerial scenes, where you can see your opposite number's face, are riveting. When the studio failed to rent original World War I flying craft, it converted Tiger Moths and Stampe SV4s and added Fokkers built to order. Irish Air Corps pilots were involved in the dogfights. A civilian pilot undertook the flight under the bridge—with only four feet clearance on either side. Other scenes were shot in an aerodrome outside Dublin, in many historic buildings in Dublin, and in County Wicklow. Guillermin makes the shift from small British films to a full-blown Hollywood epic with ease. His camera tracks and pans and zooms to capture emotion and other times is perfectly still. The action sequences are brilliantly constructed and one battle involving planes and the military is a masterpiece of cinematic orchestration, contrasting raw hand-to-hand combat on the ground with aerial skirmishes. Guillermin takes a classical approach to widescreen with action often taking place in long shot with the compositional clarity of a John Ford Western. Peppard hits the bull's-eye as a man whose chip on one shoulder is neatly balanced by arrogance on the other, but the stiff chin and blazing eyes are not tempered enough with other emotion. Mason is at his suave best and, as previously noted, Andress does more than just swan around.

Critical reception: "Exciting aerial sequences" (*Variety*); "aerial dogfights have thrilling impact" (*Los Angeles Times*); "flight sequences and fantastically frail-looking planes run away with the picture" (*Washington Post*); "the plot never gets in the way of the spectacle" (*Films and Filming*).[190]

Rentals: $7.25[191] ($51.6 million equivalent)

86: *Charly*

Starring Cliff Robertson and Claire Bloom; directed and produced by Ralph Nelson; screenplay, Stirling Silliphant, from the novel by Daniel Keyes; music, Ravi Shankar. ABC/Cinerama Releasing Corporation. June 1968 (Berlin Film Festival); U.S.: September 23, 1968.

Television had been considered the enemy of Hollywood since the 1940s so it was something of a shock when the networks decided to join the movie business. While studios cried foul, exhibitors, struggling for product, put out the welcome mat.[192] ABC Television launched its moviemaking arm in 1965 but the first movie did not appear until two years later, the British comedy *Smashing Time* with Lynn Redgrave and Rita Tushingham. Neither that nor the next two pictures did much business but the fourth was *For Love of Ivy* (1968) with Sidney Poitier, then well into his box office stride. The fifth was *Charly,* based on the 1958 science fiction short story "Flowers for Algernon" by Daniel Keyes. After Keyes transformed it into the CBS program *The Two Worlds of Charlie Gordon* (1961), he turned it into a novel under the original title which became a surprise bestseller in 1966.

Actor Cliff Robertson, who starred in the telecast, bought the movie rights to avoid losing the role to an actor with a bigger box office name, as had previously occurred with *Days of Wine and Roses.*

Robertson had funded the initial screenplay by William Goldman.[193] "He knocked it off very quickly," said Robertson, "but he missed it. He's a hell of a writer but he just didn't have it."[194] Robertson's low marquee standing accounted for the long delay in making the transition to movie. Although he debuted in *Picnic* (1955) and was second-billed in *The Naked and the Dead* (1958), his career had been patchy, as likely to end up in the undemanding *Gidget* (1959) as Sam Fuller's *Underworld U.S.A.* (1961), with television filling the gaps. The starring role in *PT 109* (1963), about John F. Kennedy's war career, led to a similar credit in *633 Squadron* (1964) and the thriller *Masquerade* (1965). But when the budgets got bigger or he came up against a bigger star, his name dropped down lower on the credits, second-billed to Lana Turner in *Love Has Many Faces* (1965), to Rex Harrison in *The Honey Pot* (1967) and to William Holden in *The Devil's Brigade* (1968).

Robertson owned the rights to Keyes' story and, as Katharine Hepburn had done when buying *The Philadelphia Story* which she had essayed on Broadway, and Jack Lemmon with *Days of Wine and Roses*, the picture would not get made without his participation. Newcomer ABC did not object, especially as Robertson's acting fee was only $25,000. Although it later became common for stars to take on assignments where they play characters facing physical or mental challenges (Dustin Hoffman in *Rain Man*, 1988, Daniel Day-Lewis in *My Left Foot*, 1989), it was rare in the 1960s. More likely, the star would help the afflicted person (Anne Bancroft in *The Miracle Worker*, 1962, Warren Beatty in *Lilith*, 1964). So the role was a considerable gamble for a young actor. "No leading young man would play a retarded guy," said Robertson.[195]

Ralph Nelson, who had steered home another difficult project, *Lilies of the Field* (1963), was handed the directorial reins. He had been interested in the project for some years.[196] Stirling Silliphant rewrote the screenplay, though Robertson claimed he contributed the second act of the picture, uncredited.[197] But there was no money available for a name co-star. British actress Claire Bloom, married to Rod Steiger, had not appeared on screen since *The Spy Who Came In from the Cold* (1965).

40   **The Films**

The story is simple but affecting: Charly, a janitor with cognitive impairment, struggling to read and write, baited by work colleagues, takes part in a clinical study, competing with a mouse called Algernon to solve mazes. The mouse, subject of an experiment to improve intelligence, wins. Undergoing similar treatment turns Charly into a genius and he begins a relationship with his teacher (Bloom). Eventually he reverts to his original state.

The movie reflects on anguish suffered by those with mental health stigma. Nelson's split-screen effects were scarcely required for this touching drama. Robertson is superb. Oscar voters thought so too. Robertson was up against Peter O'Toole in *The Lion in Winter*, Alan Arkin in *The Heart Is a Lonely Hunter*, Ron Moody in *Oliver!* and Alan Bates in *The Fixer*.[198] He was the surprise winner. Just as surprising was its box office momentum. It was a word-of-mouth sleeper, another "little film that could."

Critical reception: "Done with a dash of whimsy" (*Time*); "self-conscious contemporary drama" (*New York Times*); "pyrotechnics of the camera … jarringly out of place" (*Life*); "a warm and rewarding film" (*Chicago Sun Times*).[199]

Rentals: $7.26 million[200] ($51.7 million equivalent)

85: *The Silencers*

Starring Dean Martin, Stella Stevens, Daliah Lavi and Victor Buono; directed by Phil Karlson; screenplay, Oscar Saul, based on Donald Hamilton's novel; producer, Irving Allen; music, Elmer Bernstein. Columbia. February 18, 1966.

The other contender for the James Bond crown starred Dean Martin in the first of four movies loosely based on the Matt Helm book series and an outlay on a par with *Our Man Flint*. The plot was just as outlandish: The villainous organization BIG O (Bureau for International Government and Order) intends to blow up a nuclear bomb test site as a way of triggering World War III. Helm works for ICE (Intelligence and Counter Espionage), there are gadgets galore and the "Slaygirls" are equivalent to the Bond beauties. While Columbia followed Bond in employing rising stars like Daliah Lavi (*Lord Jim*, 1965), it recruited more accomplished leading ladies such as Stella Stevens, Elvis Presley's co-star in *Girls! Girls! Girls!* (1962), second-billed to Jerry Lewis in *The Nutty Professor* (1963) and to Glenn Ford in *Advance to the Rear* (1964). She had the acting chops to play a spoof of the hero's sidekick as the accident-prone Gail Hendricks. Sharon Tate would play a similar klutz in *The Wrecking Crew* (1968).[201] But the whole enterprise revolves around Dean Martin, who pretty much plays himself, or the persona he invented for *The Dean Martin Show*, launched on television in 1965 and a massive hit. It made him Mr. Cool.

Martin had been a bigger movie star in the 1950s, as the straight half of the Martin and Lewis combo. Having begun as a singer, now he was in a position to capitalize. "That's Amore" appeared in 1953, "Memories Are Made of This" in 1956 and "Volare" in 1958. His solo movie career started with a serious role in *Some Came Running* (1958) and as the alcoholic in Howard Hawks' Western *Rio Bravo* (1959). As well as being the number two attraction to Frank Sinatra in the Rat Pack outings *Ocean's 11* (1960) and *4 for Texas* (1963), he was the star of such films as *Toys in the Attic* (1963) and *Kiss Me, Stupid* (1964).

But you would not pick him, as a middle-aged man (48 when *The Silencers* was released), to star in an action thriller, no matter how spoofed-up. Which was just as well,

Producer Irving Allen might have felt a certain satisfaction in making *The Silencers* because earlier in his career he had partnered Bond supremo Albert R. Broccoli in Warwick Films. The pair separated in part because Allen believed the Bond novels were not good enough screen material. From a British base the duo made *Hell Below Zero* (1954) with Alan Ladd and *Fire Down Below* (1957) with Robert Mitchum. As a sole operator, Allen produced *Genghis Khan* (1965). Trade press advertisement (*Box Office*, February 14, 1966, 17).

then, that he chose himself, for it was his company Meadway-Claude Productions that set the movie up. And, presumably, he decided that, rather than attempting any reinvention, the role should be played in his inimitable style. Still, he is plausible as the good guy beating various bad guys and the movie works for the quips being intentional rather than the throwaway style of the Bonds. The over-the-top, suave playboy has a definite charm, the action scenes work, and the premise, while a shade too spoofy, pulled in

42   The Films

audiences.[202] Taking a leaf out of the Bond playbook, the films were reissued as double bills as soon as possible.

Critical reception: "Packed with gorgeous dames, electrifying moments and imaginative plottage" (*Variety*); "most amusing spy spoof.... Martin is at his urbane, witty, best ... deadly gadgets galore" (*Box Office*); "loud, fast, obvious and occasionally funny" (*New York Times*).[203]

Rentals: $7.35 million (including reissues) ($52.3 million equivalent)

84: *Mutiny on the Bounty*

Starring Marlon Brando, Trevor Howard and Richard Harris; directed by Lewis Milestone; screenplay, Charles Lederer, based on the book by Charles Nordhoff and James Norman Hall; producer, Aaron Rosenberg; music, Bronislau Kaper. MGM roadshow. November 8, 1962.

The prospect of stratospheric profits of the *Ben-Hur* kind inclined studios to take greater risks,[204] none more so than the $19 million gambled on *Mutiny on the Bounty*,[205] a remake of the 1935 classic starring Clark Gable and Charles Laughton. The new version had Marlon Brando—he turned down *Lawrence of Arabia* to go to Tahiti[206]—and, as director, Carol Reed (*The Third Man*, 1949). But whereas *Ben-Hur*, *The Alamo* (1960) and *West Side Story* (1961) had relied on studio sets and *How the West Was Won* (1962) was filmed on very familiar locations, *Mutiny on the Bounty* would have the most spectacular backdrop, glorious authentic Polynesian scenery with a depth of vibrant color never before brought to the screen.

Brando received $500,000 and a percentage plus $5000 a day if production exceeded its six-month schedule.[207] But thriller writer Eric Ambler's script did not pass muster[208] and it went through many hands before finally being credited to veteran Charles Lederer (*His Girl Friday*, 1940).[209] Brando fell out with co-stars Trevor Howard[210] (*Sons and Lovers*, 1960) and Richard Harris (*The Guns of Navarone*, 1961), and his fights with Reed caused his replacement[211] by double–Oscar winner Lewis Milestone, whose career spanned *All Quiet on the Western Front* (1930) and *Ocean's 11* (1960). Even he gave up at the end, the last few scenes shot (uncredited) by Billy Wilder.[212]

Storms disrupted shooting. The ship, built to order at a cost of $750,000[213] and sailed 7000 miles to the location,[214] turned up three months late. Thousands of extras— paid $3 a day[215]—vanished at will. Love interest Tarita (whom Brando later married) could not remember her lines.[216] It was a walking advertisement for Murphy's Law. Costs for costumes, sets and the ship ballooned. As shooting went on and on, the overruns were mountainous (the media blamed Brando),[217] leaving the movie requiring revenues close to those of *Ben-Hur* just to break even.

It would be a shame to judge this picture by its budgetary excess. For it pretty much delivered what it promised: sumptuous photography by Robert Surtees, the first to use the Ultra Panavision extremely wide ratio of 2.76:1 to take in the idyllic scenery and fabulous kaleidoscope of color that provided the background to a riveting tale of adventure, mutiny and murder.

The narrative is straightforward: Strict disciplinarian Captain Bligh (Howard) takes H.M.S. *Bounty* to Tahiti to collect breadfruit. Once there, the sailors, including ordinary seaman Mills (Richard Harris), think they have landed in paradise. On the

The 118-foot ship was built from scratch based on copies of the original plans at the British Admiralty Museum. Ten miles of rope were used, along with 400,000 feet of oak from New Jersey. It was several feet wider than the original to accommodate cameras, and also fitted with two diesel engines. Intended to be burned at the end of filming, it was reprieved and it went on to feature in *Yellowbeard* (1983), *Treasure Island* (1990) and *Pirates of the Caribbean: Dead Man's Chest* (2006).* Trade press advertisement (*Kine Weekly*, November 7, 1963, 1).

*Cook, Peter, "Recreating the Bounty," *Cinema Retro* Special Edition, 13.

return voyage, perhaps indulged by island life, they refuse to accept Bligh's ruthless discipline: Led by aristocratic officer Fletcher Christian (Brando), they rebel, take over the ship and dispatch Bligh and others over the side in a longboat.

With a three-hour playing time, the film easily divides into the classic three acts. The opening section sets the scene, establishes the main characters, shows the terrible living conditions aboard ship, and a voyage featuring barbaric action by the captain. The

44 **The Films**

central section is devoted to the island's temptations, Christian romancing a chieftain's daughter, others finding compliant lovers. The final act covers mutiny and consequence, Bligh by this point enraged by delayed departure and attempted desertion. When water rations are cut and the death toll mounts, Christian, confronting Bligh, strikes his superior, a hanging offense. Christian is spurred into mutiny. Bligh reaches safety and is exonerated at a court martial, while the mutineers are cast ashore at Pitcairn Island where Christian dies.

While his accent occasionally falters, Brando is solid, perfectly believable as a dandy with ideas above his station. The three principals are forceful screen personalities, Howard at his blustering best, Harris never one to back down, while Brando's humanity is often overridden by a classic case of self-entitlement. The superb supporting cast includes Oscar winner Hugh Griffith, Scotsman Gordon Jackson and Australian Chips Rafferty. While the screenplay suffers from poor structure and too many hands, the dialogue is still taut and Milestone handles the material and the actors very well. It is an excellent movie, cinematography and authenticity an added bonus.

Critical reception: "Unquestionably handsome spectacular" (*Washington Post*); "Brando is in many ways giving the greatest performance of his career" (*Variety*); "eye-filling and gripping as pure spectacle" (*New York Times*).[218]

Rentals: $7.4[219] ($52.7 million equivalent)

82 (tie): *The World of Suzie Wong*

Starring William Holden and Nancy Kwan; directed by Richard Quine[220]; screenplay, John Patrick, adapted by Paul Osborn from the novel by Richard Mason; producer, Hugh Perceval; music, George Duning. Paramount. November 10, 1960.

If you had told star William Holden, or anyone in Hollywood for that matter, that this would be his last hit until *The Wild Bunch* (1969), they would probably have laughed in your face. Holden was as big as they came, an Oscar winner for Billy Wilder's prisoner-of-war drama *Stalag 17* (1953), star of the blockbuster *The Bridge on the River Kwai* (1957); he had the power to choose his projects,[221] currently in the $750,000-per-picture-plus-percentage bracket.[222] For tax reasons—Switzerland being his official residence—Holden wanted to make movies outside America. He had investments in Africa and Hong Kong.

Holden's *Love Is a Many-Splendored Thing* (1955) and *The World of Suzie Wong* follow a similar trajectory: American businessman falling in love with a native. But in the first movie, the woman was a middle-class professional and played by Hollywood star Jennifer Jones. In *The World of Suzie Wong*, Holden's artist-wannabe Robert Lomax romances prostitute Mei Li (Hong Kong–born Nancy Kwan, who replaced the original choice, French-Vietnamese France Nuyen[223]). The original book by Richard Mason[224] owes much to Somerset Maugham, whose novel *Of Human Bondage* covers a similar theme while the hero of *The Moon and Sixpence* goes from stockbroker to painter. The location shots, on which such exotic movies rely, paint a time capsule picture of a vibrant city trying to shake off its British colonial roots.

Initially, Lomax is respectful, hiring Mei Li as a model, but events soon progress, though he cannot afford to keep her to himself. Both characters change, Lomax from idealistic and naïve, Mei Li from a woman with a psychological screen to prevent her true self toppling into the fantasy she invents for her customers. Lomax attracts the attention of a banker's daughter (British actress Sylvia Syms) in whose upper-class society Mei Li is not accepted. When Mei Li reveals she has a child, Lomax has to set aside his selfish nature to accommodate the boy. There are plenty of clichés here, especially some of the bar's raucous customers, but Holden's world-weariness is played to good effect and he manages to infuse the relationship with real feeling. Mei Li is a character with genuine spark, as shown when out of mischief she nearly has Lomax arrested.

Given endemic attitudes to racism, Hollywood's approach to romance between Americans and Asians fell into a separate, and sympathetic, category. As well as *Love Is a Many-Splendored Thing*, American audiences had lapped up *Sayonara* (1957) which concerned interracial marriage. Hollywood extended a bigger welcome to actors of Asian origin than those of African American heritage. Although most people recall Japanese-born Sessue Hayakawa as the camp commander in *The Bridge on the River Kwai*, he had been Hollywood's first Asian male star, a romantic idol in the silent era,[225] with second generation Chinese-American Anna May Wong flourishing during the talkies.[226]

But while Miyoshi Umeki won the Best Supporting Actress for *Sayonara*, it was not until the 1960s that Asian actresses attained popularity.[227] Nancy Kwan[228] starred in Twentieth Century–Fox's big-budget Rodgers and Hammerstein musical *Flower Drum Song* (1961), *Tamahine* (1963) and *The Wild Affair* (1965), and had the female lead in *Lt. Robin Crusoe, U.S.N.* (1966). France Nuyen was the female lead opposite Holden in *Satan Never Sleeps* (1962), *A Girl Named Tamiko* (1962) and *Man in the Middle* (1964). But the trend for Asian actresses in big roles mostly died out mid-decade.

Critical reception: "Holden gives a first-class performance, restrained and sincere" (*Variety*); "best movie in ages," (*Journal-American*); "beguiling, enchanting, exquisite" (*World Telegraph and Sun*) "the image of Hong Kong is brilliantly and sensuously conveyed" (*New York Times*).[229]

Rentals: $7.5 million ($53.4 million equivalent)

82 (tie): *La Dolce Vita*

Starring Marcello Mastroianni, Anita Ekberg and Anouk Aimée; directed by Federico Fellini; screenplay, Fellini, Ennio Flaiano, Tullio Pinelli and Brunello Rondo; producer, Giuseppe Amato; music, Nino Rota. Riama Film, Cinecittà, Pathé Consortium/U.S. distributor: Astor Pictures. February 3, 1960 (Rome); U.S.: April 19, 1961.

Foreign films held a distinct advantage over Hollywood movies: They could ignore the Production Code, the industry's self-regulating censorship system. That allowed foreign directors to include more risqué material and nudity. Foreign movies had been punching a hole in the U.S. distribution pattern since the late 1940s with pictures like the Italian *Bitter Rice* (1949), and while featuring statuesque women they were sold as arthouse product. Italians Silvana Mangano, Sophia Loren, Gina Lollobrigida and Frenchwoman Brigitte Bardot came to American attention in this fashion, Bardot the ruling foreign sex kitten in America thanks to *…And God Created Woman* (1956), the top foreign picture at the box office.[230]

Even so, such imports were risky. Few hit the $1 million mark in rentals; and although rights could be acquired for reasonable sums, considerably more was required for marketing.

Joe Levine, who knew a thing or two about importing Italian pictures after the whopping success of *Hercules* (1958), believed he had the rights tied up. So, too, did the Ohmat Corporation. Both believed they had made a "handshake" deal to win the rights. In its previous life, Astor Pictures, under the guidance of Robert Savini, had been a reissue specialist (Hannan Collection).

Although director Federico Fellini initially struggled for funding,[231] he was now a major arthouse name in the U.S. (directors more marketable to that audience than stars), winning back-to-back Oscars for Best Foreign Film with *La Strada* (1954) and *Nights of Cabiria* (1957). But neither burst open the American box office. *La Dolce Vita* was a different story. The Catholic Church in Italy was outraged—always a good publicity hook—and the movie became a hit, turning into, by some margin, the biggest Italian film of the year. Columbia bought the British rights but assumed the combustible material would never pass muster with the Production Code. When the American

The Films

rights went to auction, independent Astor Pictures paid $625,000 and committed $400,000 to marketing,[232] sums requiring a $2.5 million gross to turn profit—impossible on arthouse release alone. While ignoring the Production Code, Astor wooed the Legion of Decency, which agreed to give the movie a separate classification on the grounds of artistic integrity, effectively granting it a seal of approval.[233] Further publicity came from an unlikely source: critic Bosley Crowther started a campaign against subtitles at a time when most people preferred them to the usual atrocious dubbing.[234] Astor released the picture as a roadshow in a specially converted stage outlet, the Henry Miller Theater.[235] Publicity included a book and a record of the theme tune. Critics praised it to high heaven and Astor embarked on a clever distribution strategy: limiting access, making exhibitors bid against each other. It was a massive hit. Six years later, it was bought by AIP, who relaunched it in a dubbed version. Those extra revenues coupled with the original grosses turned it into the biggest foreign film of all time.

And that was some doing for a three-hour black-and-white picture. It's an extraordinary artistic achievement, not least because no character exhibits a redemptive streak, all, at the very least, shallow, but mostly stupid, naïve, self-indulgent and rich. In stitching together a variety of episodes encompassing extravagant wealth and unbelievable poverty, Fellini creates quite a different tapestry. By today's standards, the sexuality is minimal, sex implied between a couple on a bed, a striptease towards the end, and an orgy that looks more like minor frolics. Far more memorable are the image of Anita Ekberg in the Trevi Fountain and the statue of Christ being helicoptered over Rome. This was the film that introduced the paparazzi, the photographers dogging every celebrity.

Various American stars were considered, including Paul Newman, Burt Lancaster, Henry Fonda and Barbara Stanwyck. In the end, the cast was cosmopolitan enough: Italian Marcello Mastroianni as the gossip journalist, Swede Anita Ekberg plus, from France, Anouk Aimée, Alain Cuny and Yvonne Furneaux. There's not much to the story although it begins in dramatic enough fashion with Mastroianni bedding an heiress (Aimée) and finding his fiancée (Furneaux) has taken an overdose. But mostly he wanders round Rome, partly in the company of a famous actress (Ekberg), and interacts in episodic fashion with different characters and situations. There is a purported sighting of the Madonna by some children, intellectual discussion, Mastroianni's father's heart attack, a suicide and murder, the discovery of a leviathan on the beach. What seems leisurely is anything but; and as one sequence leads to another, a different picture builds up of a man suffering internal conflict amid a world of inexplicable behavior.

Fellini won the Palme D'Or at the Cannes Film Festival and was nominated as Best Director (in the main, not Foreign Film, category) at the Oscars as well as two other nominations. As far as the foreign film market went, it was by far the most influential picture of the 1960s, since its unique marketing opened it up to audiences that rarely attended this kind of movie.

Critical reception: "Matured talent of poetic stature … honors the Italian film industry" (*Variety*); "an allegory, a cautionary tale of a man without a center" (Roger Ebert)[236]; "the most exciting film of the year" (*New York Herald Tribune*); "an awesome picture" (*New York Times*) "a masterpiece of movie-making" (*New York Daily Mirror*)[237]. *Cahiers du Cinema* ranked it seventeenth for the year.[238]

Rentals: $7.5 million.[239] (including 1966 reissue) ($53.4 million equivalent)

81: *BUtterfield 8*

Starring Elizabeth Taylor and Laurence Harvey; directed by Daniel Mann; screenplay, Charles Schnee and John Michael Hayes, from the novel by John O'Hara; producer, Pandro S. Berman; music, Bronislau Kaper. MGM. November 4, 1960.

Elizabeth Taylor called *BUtterfield 8* "the most pornographic script I ever read."[240] Twentieth Century–Fox had offered her a million dollars for *Cleopatra*, double her normal salary, but MGM refused to release her until she made this film.[241] The hot streak of *Giant* (1956), *Raintree County* (1957), *Cat on a Hot Tin Roof* (1958) and *Suddenly Last Summer* (1959) had made her the biggest female star in the world. With her million-dollar payday hanging in the balance, she gave in but insisted the screenwriter "clean up her character" so that instead of being a high-class call girl, Gloria Wandrous turned into a nymphomaniac alcoholic model. Her deal also ensured $100,000 for Taylor's real-life lover, crooner Eddie Fisher, in a supporting role. First choice director Richard Brooks, who had helmed *Cat on a Hot Tin Roof*, was unavailable so MGM turned to Daniel Mann,[242] like Taylor a former child actor, known as a woman's director, wringing Oscar-winning performances from Shirley Booth in *Come Back Little Sheba* (1952) and Anna Magnani in *The Rose Tattoo* (1955) and an Oscar-nominated one from Susan Hayward in *I'll Cry Tomorrow* (1955). Laurence Harvey (*The Alamo*, 1960) signed for the role of Gloria's lover Weston Liggett. The script was revised by Charles Schnee (*Red River, The Bad and the Beautiful*) and John Michael Hayes (*Rear Window, Peyton Place*). The actors' strike of 1960 interrupted production, only a month's work in the can before shooting temporarily stopped.[243]

The film opens audaciously with a ten-minute (nearly ten percent of the movie) virtually silent sequence. The camera pans from a telephone off the hook and a full ashtray to Taylor waking up just as Harvey has departed. The camera follows her languorously wrapped in a bed sheet and then a white slip through her opulent flat where she is furious to find $250 in her purse. In an instant, the film's core drama is silently played out. The audience knows she's a courtesan even if she refuses money. Who's she fooling? Only herself. And that is the movie's tragic nub. But she is also sending another message: this is a different sex worker from any previously seen on screen. She's neither cliché: hooker with heart of gold, nor sad sack. Her vivacity and intensity light up the screen with a lust for life and the fine things that money can buy. Childhood friend Steve (Fisher), a musician who holds a torch for her, acts as her conscience. Harvey has a lovely home, money, wife, good job. He glosses over the money, explaining it was for her torn dress, and they continue to meet. She does work as a model. He soon gets it: "You pick the man, he doesn't pick you." She refuses to return to his apartment but they end up in a motel and her ferocious independence softens. Both are intent on change, Harvey asks for his old job back, Taylor quits her psychiatrist. And those two life-changing actions might have resolved all the issues. But Harvey's domestic crisis sends him out drinking in bars where Taylor is only too well known. "Catnip to every cat in town," quips one barman. Taylor and Harvey make up, they fight. She tells Fisher she was molested in her childhood by a man who taught her "more about evil than any 13-year-old should know." Harvey demands a divorce from his wife. Taylor determines to get an ordinary job. He asks her to marry him. Although eventually agreeing, she drives off without him and crashes into a roadblock, killing herself.

Sure, it's a film with flaws. The screenplay tells us more often than necessary that

Taylor was brought up fatherless and that Harvey is emasculated by his wife's wealth. While the result is a bit stagey, Mann creates intimacy with the camera: characters are bound in tight two-shots or head-on confrontations or in small rooms. The writing is barbed, and although Harvey does not reveal true depth, Taylor conveys anguish with simple looks or raw emotion, as illuminated by joy as downcast by depression. Taylor appealed, in a sense, to the inherent envy in female cinemagoers. For every woman appalled, there would be another who wondered just what you had to do to live such a fine, lazy, opulent life. Taylor was dressed sumptuously. Her torn dress was a luxurious metallic silk brocade with matching heels. In a bar she wears a black chiffon dress with pearl necklace and black gloves. Shopping on Fifth Avenue finds her in a brown-belted fur-trimmed tweed with luxurious accessories, alligator purse and leather gloves, surrounded by top-of-the-range leather bags.[244] Every outfit seduces the audience. As one commentator observed of Taylor: Every man wanted to bed her, every woman wanted to be her. And no wonder.

For the third year in a row, Taylor was nominated for Best Actress, up against Greer Garson (*Sunrise at Campobello*), Deborah Kerr (*The Sundowners*), Melina Mercouri (*Never on Sunday*) and Shirley MacLaine (*The Apartment*). Mercouri was the odds-on favorite according to *Variety*, pointing out that five of the last nine winners had been foreign. On March 4, Taylor was rushed from the Dorchester Hotel in London to hospital for an emergency tracheotomy after being diagnosed with pneumonia with heavy lung congestion. She nearly died, but recovered sufficiently to collect the Oscar.

Critical reception: "By the odds it should be a bomb, but a bomb it is not" (*New York Times*); "daring, brilliant performance" (*Los Angeles Times*); "immensely handsome but painfully shallow" (*Washington Post*).[245]

Rentals $7.55 million[246] (including 1966 reissue)[247] ($53.8 million equivalent)

79 (tie): *Georgy Girl*

Starring James Mason, Alan Bates and Lynn Redgrave; directed by Silvio Narrizano; screenplay, Peter Nichols, from the Margaret Forster novel; producers, Robert A. Goldston and Otto A. Plaschkes; music, Alexander Faris. Columbia. October 17, 1966.

James Bond, the miniskirt and the Beatles helped turn Britain into the hub of the Swinging Sixties. Everyone wanted to join in but not everyone could. Georgy Girl was one such. The main character (Lynn Redgrave) is more homely than beautiful, a virgin pursued by her father's middle-aged employer (James Mason). She envies the life of her beautiful roommate (Charlotte Rampling) who has a handsome young boyfriend (Alan Bates) and already two abortions. It is a pretty stunning cast, with the exception of Mason all young stars on the cusp. Best of all, for the producers, it was low-budget, certainly by Hollywood standards. Redgrave, about the same age as her character, was the daughter of British acting legend Michael Redgrave and sister of Vanessa Redgrave. She had a small part in *Tom Jones* (1963) and billed third in romantic drama *Girl with Green Eyes* (1964). Mason was the reason the movie got made, backing a financially a risky project. A huge British star in the 1940s, and still with considerable marquee pull, he alternated leading roles (*Lolita*, 1962) with supporting roles in blockbusters like *Lord Jim* (1965) and *The Blue Max* (1966). Bates was the most established of the young stars, with starring roles in *A Kind of Loving* (1962) and *Nothing But the Best* (1964) and as

50 **The Films**

the Englishman bowled over by *Zorba the Greek* (1964). Model-turned-actress Charlotte Rampling had a blink-and-you-miss-it role in *The Knack* (1965) before winning her leading lady spurs in the Boulting Brothers crime comedy *Rotten to the Core* (1965). It was the sophomore outing for Canadian director Silvio Narizzano, previously of horror film *Die! Die! My Darling!* (1965) with Hollywood legend Tallulah Bankhead.

Redgrave is completely engaging as the innocent in changing times, wanting to be part of the fashionable set but too often making a fool of herself. When she does change hairstyle, clothes and attitude, life improves. Bates can get away with wearing the trendy clothes, but his girlfriend Rampling is in the self-centered mold of *Darling* (1965), submitting all to her will and whims. The businessman in Mason goes so far as offering Georgy a contract to become his mistress, in return for a life of luxury. When Rampling becomes pregnant with Bates' child, they get married for no other reason really than that she is bored. Bates moves in with the two girls but falls in love with Redgrave. When Rampling gives up her child for adoption, the maternal Redgrave marries Mason so they can adopt the child. Told baldly, the story sounds very kitchen-sink drama, but the performances are superb. Redgrave was nominated for a Best Actress Oscar, Mason for Supporting Actor, and the film was nominated for its cinematography. The nominated theme song was also a chart hit.

This was the "little film that could." Any film made in Britain, apart from the Bonds, was almost by definition a low-budget item compared to the standard Hollywood product. Prior to the 1960s, very few small films broke out of their budget category to hit the box office bull's-eye. The way the business was constructed in the 1940s and 1950s ensured that the biggest films received the biggest exposure in terms of hullabaloo and bookings. Only a handful of small pictures did substantially better than expected: *Marty* (1955), primarily thanks to Oscar wins, ...*And God Created Woman* (1956) because of Brigitte Bardot and the sex angle, movies built around pop stars like Pat Boone ($4 million in rentals for *April Love*, 1957) and Elvis Presley (the same the same year for *Jailhouse Rock*), a few Disney pictures (*Old Yeller*, 1957, $6 million) and the occasional exploitationer (*The Bad Seed*, 1956, $4.1 million). As *La Dolce Vita* had shown, a combination of sex and art often did the trick. But art was often not enough. A British picture like *The Red Shoes* (1948) did exceptionally well in arthouse situations but struggled when attempting any wider reach. What made the difference for the small movie in the 1960s was the ability of the big city center cinema to hold on to the picture for months on end, sometimes with the prospect of an Oscar nod at the end of it to provide the necessary marketing oxygen, so that it could make a decent pile regardless of its performance in the sticks. But generally speaking, big box office coin required a movie with wide appeal.

Redgrave chanced upon something universal in her character, the ugly duckling transformed, with enough reality to keep it from turning into a popcorn fairy story. This was not an arthouse picture in the general sense, although the performances stacked up, but it proved that audiences were willing to look way outside the norm for satisfying entertainment.

Critical reception: "Constantly funny" (*Newsweek*); "new star of the first magnitude" (*Vogue*)[248]; "fleet-footed, zany-surfaced, farcical frolic" (*Films and Filming*); "every girl whose mother has assured her she is a 'late bloomer' will love this movie and delight in seeing a girl with no waist and no style marry well" (*The Harvard Crimson*).[249]

Rentals: $7.6 million ($54.1 million equivalent)

79 (tie): *Lover Come Back*

Starring Doris Day and Rock Hudson; directed by Delbert Mann; screenplay, Stanley Shapiro and Paul Henning; producers, Shapiro and Martin Melcher; music, Frank De Vol. Universal. December 20, 1961.

Four times between 1960 and 1964 (inclusive), Doris Day was voted the #1 box office star in America primarily due to sophisticated comedies. Sometimes her co-star was Rock Hudson, on other occasions rising stars James Garner (*The Thrill of It All*, 1963, and *Move Over Darling*, 1963) and Rod Taylor (*Do Not Disturb*, 1965, and *The Glass Bottom Boat*, 1966). *Pillow Talk* (1959) with Hudson had created this romantic comedy template. Despite Day's smash hit *Calamity Jane* (1953), in big-budget efforts she was usually female lead rather than top-billed star: to Frank Sinatra in *Young at Heart* (1954), James Stewart in Hitchcock's *The Man Who Knew Too Much* (1956) and Clark Gable in *Teacher's Pet* (1958). In smaller films, she won top billing: above James Cagney in *Love Me or Leave Me* (1955), Richard Widmark in *Tunnel of Love* (1958) and Jack Lemmon in *It Happened to Jane* (1959). She was versatile (comedy, drama, thrillers, musicals) and had a separate career as a top recording artist.

Day's production company Arwin was involved in *Lover Come Back*. Hudson had spent the first half of the 1950s in Westerns and action pictures and the second half in big-budget dramas like *Written on the Wind* (1956), *Giant* (1956), *A Farewell to Arms* (1957) and *This Earth Is Mine* (1959). The discovery that he had a knack for comedy came as a welcome surprise.[250]

Although Rock Hudson-Doris Day became an extremely marketable commodity, in fact they only made three movies together, *Lover Come Back* being the second. They play advertising rivals nettling each other, enduring a series of comic mishaps and falling in love. Co-writer Stanley Shapiro proved a natural with this kind of material, honing his skills in television sitcoms *Hey Jeannie* and *Where's Raymond*.

Apart from the initial flashpoint—Day attempting to get Hudson thrown out of the business because he bribes clients with alcohol and women—the storyline relies on misunderstanding. To avoid being barred Hudson has to create a commercial for a product that does not exist and, when that arouses public interest, find a way of making it. Day mistakes Hudson for its inventor as she invests in the wining, dining and seducing required to win the account. When she discovers the truth, she again attempts to get Hudson disbarred but by this time he has managed to get a product made, one that has unforeseen intoxicating effects, which leads the pair to bed on the back of a speedy marriage license (so as not to offend audience sensibilities). Afterwards, she annuls the marriage but is pregnant. Hudson redeems himself by getting rid of the product and giving Day a big share of his company's advertising and marries her just before she gives birth. The two stars are at the top of their game and there are plenty of genuine laughs, often fueled by Day's outrage or naiveté. The advertising background gives it an element of satire which helped pacify critics. But the script zips along, building up the farce and loading the laughs.

Critical reception: "Extremely funny" (*New Yorker*); "engaging, smartly-produced show" (*New York Times*); "farcical mix-up, double entendres and all" (*Los Angeles Times*); "funny and worldly from start to finish." (*Washington Post*).[251]

Rentals: $7.6 million[252] ($54.1 million equivalent)

78: *Von Ryan's Express*

Starring Frank Sinatra and Trevor Howard; directed by Mark Robson; screenplay Wendell Mayes, from the book by David Westheimer; producer, Saul David; music, Jerry Goldsmith. Twentieth Century–Fox. June 23, 1965.

It was a wonder Frank Sinatra could spare the time for acting since he was a major recording artist (sometimes as many as five albums a year), performed in Las Vegas, and at the start of the '60s ran record label Reprise before selling it to Capitol. Except for *The Devil at Four O'Clock* (1961), *The Manchurian Candidate* (1962) and his directorial debut *None But the Brave* (1965), Sinatra had coasted during the 1960s, drifting between romantic comedies and Rat Pack movies.

But this was a different Sinatra. He had nearly drowned while filming *None But the Brave* in Hawaii and whether it was that incident or after-hours revels on the island, the man who for two decades had been defined as "skinny" now put on weight, enough to change the shape of his face, "more spherical and bull-necked."[253] Whether audiences would react to the unexpected new look was just one of the worries facing producers.

Von Ryan's Express was based on the bestseller by David Westheimer (purchased for $125,000)[254] in the vein of *The Great Escape*, with prisoners of war held in Italy, the escapees planning to hijack a train. Part of the screenplay by Wendell Mayes (*In Harm's Way*, 1965) was rewritten by Joseph Landon to turn Sinatra's character from an upright West Point–trained officer to the flippant man more suited to the actor's screen persona. Sinatra, sensitive to the treatment of Italians in movies, was also responsible for ensuring that Italians were not seen to be aligned with Germans.[255] He also resisted the studio's notion of changing the ending, denying it the opportunity for a sequel.[256]

The movie was shot in northern Italy with a couple of locations in Spain for the railway section at the end.[257] For most of the film, the engine used was an Italian ALCO-built class 735 but for the climax filmed in Spain, this was switched to a Franco-Crosti class 743. A miniature was employed for the sequence when the train was hit by British bombers at night. Most sequences were filmed on the state railroad, which still used steam engines; the Santa Maria Novella station in Florence played a major role.[258] A 40,000-square-foot set for the P.O.W. camp was built on the Fox back lot.[259] As was standard at the time, vintage airplanes and trains were used since much of this materiel was still around.[260] When the movie shifted to Fox, Mia Farrow, shooting the TV series *Peyton Place* there, happened to wander by and a Frank-Mia romance began to ferment.[261]

British actor Trevor Howard, a long way from his heyday as a matinee idol and now mostly second-billed, co-starred as Major Fincham, a role turned down by Peter Finch and Jack Hawkins; Sinatra had lobbied Richard Burton to play it. Sinatra's pal Brad Dexter, who had saved him from drowning in Hawaii, had a featured role. Italian actress Rafaella Carra has the only meaningful female part.

Action was an odd choice for director Mark Robson, Oscar-nominated in successive years for *Peyton Place* (1957) and *Inn of the Sixth Happiness* (1958) with a couple of highly regarded early pictures—1949's *Champion* and *Home of the Brave*—in his canon. Although he was most at home with drama, *From the Terrace* (1960) and *The Prize* (1963) both with Paul Newman among his recent forays, he had also turned in the Alan Ladd actioner *Hell Below Zero* (1954) and the William Holden-starrer *The Bridges at Toko-Ri* (1954). In any case, as with *The Great Escape*, the bulk of the picture is drama, internal conflict between the inmates, culture clashes and jockeying for power. As if there was

Sinatra, grouchy at the best of times on a movie set, was heavily pampered here, yacht and helicopter at his disposal. The studio put him up in an 18-bedroom villa outside Rome with two swimming pools and a helipad* (Hannan Collection).

*Kaplan, *Sinatra*, 602.

not enough drama on the picture itself, there was immediate confrontation between star and director. Bringing together the methodical Robson with one-take Sinatra, ever eager to work through his scenes at top speed, was a recipe for trouble. With little regard for production logistics or cost, Sinatra demanded his scenes be filmed consecutively.[262] The more old-fashioned Robson preferred multiple takes of key scenes and expected his star to be on hand for retakes.[263] The four-month shoot cost $5.7 million.[264]

When Sinatra, an airman, arrives at the camp, he assumes command since he has

54   The Films

the senior rank, much to the irritation of Howard, previously in charge. Howard is on a par with the stuffy Brits in *The Great Escape* but without their inventiveness. Howard has no truck with escape since he reckons, with the Italians close to surrender, there is no need. When this does occur, they still have to make a move or will be attacked by Germans. They escape but are recaptured and put on a train where Sinatra hatches a daring plan to take control. There are enough twists and tension to fuel the picture; the train takeover and action sequences are well done. There are a couple of standout dramatic episodes, such as the camp on naked parade after being double-crossed by the commander. Also, after the Italian surrender, Sinatra orders the commander, on trial as a war criminal, put in the sweat box, this camp's version of the cooler in *The Great Escape*. Sinatra gets the name "von Ryan" when the commander sides with the Germans who shoot sick prisoners. The dramatic highlight, of course, is when Sinatra, having engineered the escape, fails to make it. Sinatra's performance was definitely one of his better ones, and along with *The Manchurian Candidate*, his best of the decade. The movie appeared with one of the most intriguing taglines ever: "Why did 600 Allied prisoners hate the man they called Von Ryan?" As it happened, there was a competing World War II picture also featuring a train, called simply *The Train* (1965), but *Von Ryan's Express* beat that on the box office tracks and whistled past all Sinatra's other films of the decade.

Critical reception: "hard-hitting action and sharply-drawn performances" (*Variety*); "such inspired casting" (*Films and Filming*); "one of the season's finest suspense-thrillers" (*Box Office*).[265]

Rentals: $7.7 million ($54.8 million equivalent)

77: *Shenandoah*

Starring James Stewart and Doug McClure; directed by Andrew V. McLaglen; screenplay, James Lee Barrett; producer, Robert Arthur; music, Frank Skinner. Universal. June 3, 965.

Since 1961, James Stewart had been alternating Westerns—*The Man Who Shot Liberty Valance* (1962), *How the West Was Won* (1962) and *Cheyenne Autumn* (1964)—with a string of comedies in the vein of *Mr. Hobbs Takes a Vacation* (1962) and *Dear Brigitte* (1965). Although it would be easy to lump *Shenandoah* in with the other Westerns, as good as they are, in reality, it was much more than that. It's unusually anti-war for a Western and unusually humanitarian. It prefigured many of the debates about the escalating Vietnam War that would soon split families down the middle.

Stewart plays a widowed Virginia farmer with seven children, six boys and one girl, doing his best to stay out of the Civil War, which he has managed right up to 1864. Even when his daughter (Rosemary Forsyth in her debut) marries a soldier, he insists on remaining neutral. After one son is mistaken for a Confederate and taken prisoner by Union soldiers, he sets his beliefs to one side. Though Stewart appears a good, law-abiding citizen—despite living in Virginia, he has no slaves—there's more than a touch of the bitterness he expressed in *It's a Wonderful Life* rather than the common man of so many other films in his output. Theoretically God-fearing, he blames God for taking away his wife and he's a nuisance at church, always turning up late. Once he sets off after his missing son, his farm is raided, leaving dead one son and his daughter-in-law (Katharine Ross, also in her debut). On Stewart's way home, another son is killed. Stewart plans

To promote the film James Stewart was inveigled into cutting a record, released on the Decca label, with special lyrics put to the famous song. He was entering a crowded market, 30 other versions already being available including four by Harry Belafonte and three by Jimmie Rodgers. With no expectation of great sales, the single was a marketing device, achieving airplay and record store window displays* (pressbook).

*Pressbook, *Shenandoah*.

to strangle the killer but stops on learning the shooter is only 16. Back home, he ruminates on the destruction of his family. Cigar butt in mouth, a grizzled Stewart, the harder-edged character formed in the Anthony Mann Westerns of the 1950s, carries the film, not just weighted down with many wise speeches, but delivering a riveting performance that is up there with his best. When he was playing the man next door in 1940s pictures, the growl and grouchiness in his trademark drawl were generally ignored, but here are ramped up several levels. Doug McClure from the TV series *The Virginian* took second billing and there was a spot for Patrick Wayne, Duke's son, and a cameo by George Kennedy as a Confederate colonel. Action and emotion combine in equal measure and the sentimentality seems justified as Stewart finds both comfort and desolation in the home.

This was an original screenplay by James Lee Barrett (*The Greatest Story Ever Told*), who went on to write others for Stewart including *Bandolero!* (1968) and for John Wayne. Director Andrew V. McLaglen, son of John Ford stock company actor Victor McLaglen, was a veteran of a host of TV shows when he took the helm for only his second big-budget picture (he made four low-budget ones first) after *McLintock* (1963). McLaglen is routinely considered a journeyman director but that's not the case here nor in another picture that touches on similar themes, *The Undefeated* (1969). Not only are the battle sequences deftly handled—amazingly well done considering this was the director's first action film—with an unusual grasp of the detail of war, but the underlying emotion and the general theme of the stupidity of war are equally well-treated. The picture refuses to take sides but sadness is a constant refrain.

The Academy, in handing out Oscar nominations or the statuette itself, did not usually take to Westerns, unless by a director with a "serious" reputation such as George Stevens (*Shane*, 1953) or William Wyler (*Friendly Persuasion*, 1956), and had generally passed over most John Ford classics although looking kindly on John Wayne's *The Alamo* (1960). Equally, the genre had been blessed by so many stylists (add Howard Hawks and Anthony Mann to the above list) that critics tended to dismiss the efforts of directors considered not in their league, such as McLaglen. And it was rare for an acting performance to be singled out in a movie that lacked Oscar credibility, which may account for Stewart's turn being overlooked. McLaglen reckoned Stewart's "was one of the most underrated performances ever. It was a *tour de force*."[266] The traditional folk song "Shenandoah," essentially expressing longing, with its hymn-like choral qualities, was used extensively to considerable effect during the film. Even so, it was a surprise that a decade later, a musical based on the film was launched on Broadway and probably just as surprising that it ran for over 1000 performances and was nominated for a Tony.[267]

Critical reception: "Engrossing film with lots of heart and even a soul" (*Washington Post*); "pretty good Civil War drama [but] too long" (New *York Times*); "Stewart … creates an unique character" (*Los Angeles Times*); "packs drama, excitement and an emotional quality" (*Variety*).[268]

Rentals: $7.75 million ($55.2 million equivalent)

75 (tie): *Lt. Robin Crusoe, U.S.N.*

Starring Dick Van Dyke and Nancy Kwan; directed by Byron Paul; screenplay, Don DaGradi and Bill Walsh, from the Daniel Defoe novel; producers, Ron Miller and Walsh; music, Bob Brunner. Disney. June 29, 1966.

Disney films were sometimes an event *à la Mary Poppins* (1964), but often, while being no such thing, proved very welcome as audiences grappled with the gradual mid–1960s influx of sex and violence. It came to a point when any decent Disney picture with a halfway reasonable star and an interesting concept could easily compete with bigger-budgeted or more controversial mainstream fare.

Lt. Robin Crusoe, U.S.N. was a good example of the Disney magic at the box office, finishing joint fifth in 1966, ahead of *The Silencers*, Hitchcock's *Torn Curtain*, *Our Man Flint*, Paul Newman as *Harper*, Steve McQueen as *Nevada Smith* and the all-star-cast of *Battle of the Bulge*. For that to occur, something mighty strange must have happened or the world was going to Hell in a handcart. Disney had achieved something that studios had been trying to do for nigh on half a century: build a brand that delivered consistent promise.[269] Every studio under the sun believed that its logo at the front of the credits was enough to have audiences standing in line. MGM truly believed that MGM meant something. So did Twentieth Century–Fox. So did all the rest. But the productions that appeared were such a mishmash, high-budget, low-budget, everything in between, you could not believe they had emanated from the same studio.

Disney was different. Holding true to the "Udult" concept introduced at the start of the decade, it delivered high concept movies with stars. Regardless of budget, Disney provided family entertainment. The public believed the Disney logo stood for something they could believe in. That was a real brand.

Hollywood had stopped looking to TV as a source of new stars. The last of the great grooming projects of the 1950s had created a few stars but the vast majority ended up in TV or nowhere. Steve McQueen was the most famous star to emerge from television—his CBS series *Wanted: Dead or Alive* running for three seasons from 1958 to 1961. Clint Eastwood from *Rawhide* would later rival him for popularity but the "Dollar" westerns had to wait until 1967 for U.S. release. James Garner, the small screen's *Maverick* (1957–1962), had not established himself as a genuine star—only *The Great Escape* (1963) and *The Art of Love* (1965) actually hitting the mark. Lucille Ball moved in and out of TV with ease, but she had been a sometime Hollywood star since the 1940s. Apart from McQueen, the only true crossover star was Dick Van Dyke thanks to *The Dick Van Dyke Show* (1961–1966), the kind of innocuous comedy material that could have fitted the Disney brand, its standards consistently high to win 15 Emmy Awards, including three for the star. On the big screen, he made his debut as the star of the musical *Bye Bye Birdie* (1963), following his appearance in the Broadway show; and despite his dodgy Cockney accent, he proved a key element in the colossal success *Mary Poppins* (1964). He was a larger-than-life screen character with limbs that appeared capable of going in several directions at once and a likable presence.

Disney's fancy for desert islands was reflected in *Swiss Family Robinson* (1960) and *In Search of the Castaways* (1962). This one updates Daniel Defoe's classic *Robinson Crusoe* with Van Dyke as a Navy pilot who ditches his plane in the ocean. He helps himself to gadgets from an abandoned submarine and befriends a chimp who belonged to the U.S. space program. Instead of Friday, there is Girl Wednesday played by Nancy Kwan[270] who, as mentioned before, had reasonable marquee credentials. The story requires the star to spend a good proportion of the film in solitude, so you need an actor an audience is going to warm to. Unable to leap into a song-and-dance routine to while away the time, this was a pretty good test of his acting skills. Male-female dynamics lead Girl Wednesday to believe Crusoe is going to marry her according to tribal tradition. When that does not occur, cue chaos and Crusoe's escape. It was certainly a warm-hearted, harmless comedy with enough laughs to keep an adult audience entertained as well as the kids, thus fulfilling the "Udult" criteria. Judging from the box office, it seemed that Disney had a better finger on the pulse of the times than a whole load of pictures with more adult themes.

Critical reception: "Recommended, with reservations, only for the very young" (*New York Times*); "sophisticated parents might want to stay away" (*Los Angeles Times*); "cheerfully foolish comedy" (*Washington Post*); "Van Dyke ... carries the whole thing off effortlessly" (*Films and Filming*).[271]

Rentals: $7.8 million[272] ($55.5 million equivalent)

75 (tie): *Wait Until Dark*

Starring Audrey Hepburn and Alan Arkin; directed by Terence Young; screenplay, Robert Carrington and Jane-Howard Carrington, based on the Frederick

Knott play; producer, Mel Ferrer; music, Henry Mancini. Warner Brothers. October 26, 1967.

If you told anyone in Hollywood after the success of *Wait Until Dark* that Audrey Hepburn would be off-screen for the best part of a decade, nobody would have believed that.[273] There was scarcely a more iconic figure during the 1960s than Hepburn after her turn as Holly Golightly in *Breakfast at Tiffany's* (1961). Although for sure Elizabeth Taylor had more headlines and more column inches, Hepburn had fashion editors eating out of her hand. But despite the success of *My Fair Lady* (1964), her box office in the 1960s was patchy. Apart from William Wyler's *The Children's Hour* (1961), studio bosses

Director Terence Young had been wounded during the Battle of Arnhem in World War II. He was treated in a Dutch hospital, partly staffed by volunteer nurses, one of whom was 16-year-old Audrey Hepburn. Trade press advertisement (*Kine Weekly*, June 8, 1968, 1).

teamed her up with a top male star. That worked singularly well for the thriller *Charade* (1963) with Cary Grant but less so for the romantic comedy *Paris When It Sizzles* (1964) with William Holden, the crime caper *How to Steal a Million* (1966) with Peter O'Toole, and *Two for the Road* (1967) with Albert Finney. Nonetheless, she commanded a million dollar fee.[274]

Wait Until Dark was a complete departure. For a start, there was no glossy male co-star. The budget was low, just $3 million, the same as Peter Sellers' comedy *The Bobo* (1967).[275] And it was not just a thriller but at times so terrifying it bordered on horror. Based on a play by Frederick Knott (*Dial M for Murder*), the story concerns a blind woman terrorized by thugs searching for a doll stuffed with heroin. Alan Arkin,[276] Richard Crenna and Jack Weston play the villains[277] with Arkin particularly malevolent. In a clever twist, Hepburn unwittingly cooperates with the search, believing she is assisting a murder investigation. Most of the tension comes from the audience being able to see what she cannot. British director Terence Young (*Dr. No*, 1962) produced one of his most effective movies, using considerable discretion compared to the boom and blast of his Bond pictures. Lee Remick had played the blind woman on stage but although nominated for a Tony could not compete with Hepburn's box office clout. Hepburn's performance turned into a *tour de force*. She had immersed herself in the role, spending several days at clinics and institutes for the visually impaired and wearing contact lenses to simulate blindness. Without sight, she had to rely on sound to give her clues about what was going on and clearly she could neither fight off her antagonists nor easily escape. She received her fifth Oscar nomination for her performance.[278]

However, as was often the case in Hollywood, professional triumph disguised personal despair. Hepburn's marriage to Mel Ferrer, the film's producer, was in such trouble that, to counteract rumors of an affair with Albert Finney, she held a press conference at her home prior to filming to "prove" that the couple was still very much in love. The trauma of the role as much as the tensions in her private life caused her to lose weight, dropping nearly 14 pounds, until she resembled an "emaciated grasshopper." But it was one thing to keep up a pretense on a movie set when all concentration was focused on production, and another to dive into the whirlwind of media interviews that heralded its release. And so her separation from Ferrer was announced before the movie hit the screens. Hollywood marriages rarely worked and theirs had lasted more than most, 14 years. The days were long gone of studio moguls concealing from the press indiscretions and marital breakdowns but nobody believed that the grieving process would last so long.

Critical reception: "Barefaced melodrama without character revelation of any sort" (*New York Times*); "story is as full of holes as a kitchen colander" (*Time*); "some nice, juicy passages of terror" (*Chicago Sun-Times*).[279]

Rentals: $7.8 million[280] (including 1968 post–Oscar reissue double bill with *Cool Hand Luke*) ($55.5 million equivalent)

73 (tie): *The Alamo*

Starring John Wayne, Richard Widmark and Laurence Harvey; directed by Wayne; screenplay, James Edward Grant; producer, Wayne; music Dimitri Tiomkin. Batjac–United Artists roadshow. October 24, 1960.

The Mission that Became a Fortress –
The Fortress that Became a Shrine

Wayne was furious that in the 1950s Republic refused to back *The Alamo*, especially as he had given up profit percentages—worth in the end about $700,000—in order for the studio to be able to afford *Rio Grande* and *The Quiet Man*.* Republic filmed the story anyway as the low-budget *The Last Command* (Hannan Collection).

*Eyman, John Wayne, 216.

    John Wayne had been attempting to make *The Alamo* for 15 years beginning with hiring scriptwriter James Edward Grant, then with a $500 advance from Republic in 1947 scouting locations and a year later generating an outline and first draft script from Pat Ford (son of John) with a further bout of location hunting in 1949. By 1951, a budget of $1.2 million—increased a year later by $300,000—was on offer from Republic, to whom Wayne owed three pictures. When Republic exited negotiations, Wayne had $2.5 million on the table from United Artists in 1956 for half the projected cost.[281] John Ford advised it was too complicated a movie for a first-time director,[282] but Raoul Walsh, who had directed Wayne in *The Big Trail* (1930), was rooting for him.[283] But even $5 million was too little and eventually another $1.5 million was procured from businessman Clint Murchison. Wayne added $1.2 million from his own pocket.[284] That—and further sums later added—was not enough. By the time shooting finished, in order to break even it would have to become one of the top 15 grossers ever made.

Wayne planned to shoot in Durango, Mexico, but settled instead for Brackett-ville, Texas, where set construction began in February 1958. Frank Sinatra would have played Lieutenant Colonel Travis if production could be postponed for a year. Instead the part went to Englishman Laurence Harvey (*BUtterfield 8*, 1960), with Richard Widmark (*Panic in the Streets*, 1950) as Jim Bowie.[285] A few days into filming, Widmark tried to quit and later fell out with Wayne. Pop star Frankie Avalon came on board as the Alamo's youngest defender. Wayne himself, who initially wanted to play the smaller part of Sam Houston so as to concentrate on the direction, ended up, at the behest of investors, taking on the role of Davy Crockett. John Ford lent a hand, expecting to play a major part in direction; to avoid interference, Wayne instead sent him to man a second unit. He told cast and crew to oblige Ford in all his requests but had already made up his mind that nothing the famous director shot would appear in the picture. "All they have to do is find out in Hollywood that Old Man Ford shot a scene or something and they'll say... 'Well, he shot *The Alamo.*' And this is not going to happen!"[286] Wayne did not doubt his own skill, and his abilities were apparent to others. Assistant producer Robert Rel-yea, whose career would encompass work with William Wyler and John Sturges, commented: "Technically, Wayne was the best director I ever worked with. He understood cameras, he understood editing, he understood lenses."[287]

Principal photography took 83 days, 17 more than originally planned, with another few weeks set aside for battle close-ups. Over 500,000 feet of film had been used and Wayne lost over 20 pounds. Post-production lasted ten months.[288] The Dimitri Tiomkin score produced two hit singles, "The Green Leaves of Summer" and "The Ballad of the Alamo." The movie, shot in 70mm and 192 minutes long, was at the extreme end of road-show requirements, although length itself was not necessarily detrimental. But it was soon apparent that Wayne's regular audience was not happy at the prospect of shelling out more bucks than usual and so within a few months it was whipped out of roadshow, chopped by 30 minutes, and rammed into regular cinemas. Oscar nominations—seven including Best Picture—did not help, many commentators feeling they were unjustified.

The story is part history and part drama. The set-up is straightforward: On learning that Mexican general Santa Anna (Ruben Padilla) is coming north, Sam Houston (Richard Boone) tasks Travis to defend the Alamo, a former mission in San Antonio, Texas. Bowie and Crockett arrive with reinforcements. They believe a larger force is on its way to relieve them. Most of the first half of the film is taken up with conflict among the leaders, romance between Crockett and a woman (Linda Cristal) he saves from a forced marriage, and the usual brawls. Before the start of the battle proper, the defenders take the offensive by sabotaging the enemy's biggest cannon in a daring nighttime assault. When battle is joined, the Mexicans suffer the heavier losses, but the 200 defenders are badly depleted and Bowie wounded. They discover the relief expedition has been ambushed and destroyed. Offered the chance to leave, Crockett and Bowie decide to do so until convinced to stay—for a fight to the death. The siege lasts 13 days. In the last all-out attack by the Mexicans, Travis is killed. Crockett begins a rearguard action but dies blowing up the powder magazine while Bowie bows out, fighting to the last, on his sickbed.

There are some surprisingly effective emotional moments—an African American given his freedom decides to stay and fight, the blind wife (Veda Ann Borg) standing alongside her man with the beleaguered fort as a backdrop, and certainly the deaths of the major players drape the whole episode in a swath of patriotism. The battle scenes are superb—panoramic views of the Mexicans readying the attack, their red-coated battalions, blue-coated cavalry and white-coated infantrymen observed from the walls of the Alamo; hand-to-hand combat; fusillades of cannon fire; walls exploding; invaders pouring through; smoke- and dust-clouded desperation; fighters literally throwing themselves against walls.

The problem with *The Alamo* was not that it cost too much or that the roadshow idea was ill-conceived but that it was just too talky for a John Wayne picture. There is way too much exposition and, once the movie gets going, way too much general speechifying. First half dull, second half terrific. Everyone who advised Wayne against the project was proven right. It did cost too much and it cost him his shirt. It was reissued in 1967 in a shortened version, but by that time Wayne no longer had a financial interest. By the time it was sold to television a couple of years later, it officially went into profit. But Wayne thought it was worth it. As Scott Eyman, Wayne's biographer, put it: "*The Alamo* was a film that was born only because of John Wayne's total dedication and will. But it fought him every inch of the way."[289]

Critical reception: "Action scenes are usually vivid … talk scenes … long and unusually dull" (*New York Times*); "as flat as Texas" (*Time*); "a magnificent job" (*Herald Tribune*); "Wayne has spread his talents too thin for best results" (*Variety*).[290]

Rentals: $7.9 million,[291] including 1967 reissue ($56.3 million equivalent)

73 (tie): *That Touch of Mink*

Starring Cary Grant and Doris Day; directed by Delbert Mann; screenplay, Stanley Shapiro and Nate Monaster; producers, Shapiro, Martin Melcher and Robert Arthur; music, George Duning. Universal. June 14, 1962.

Rock Hudson was surprised to learn he was not so essential to the Doris Day comedy, director Delbert Mann preferring Cary Grant. Cary was 20 years older than Doris Day but she was at least a dozen years older than her character. Now celebrating three decades in the business, Grant was enjoying a golden twilight with the romantic comedy *Houseboat* (1958) opposite Sophia Loren, the Hitchcock thriller *North by Northwest* (1959) and the Blake Edwards war comedy *Operation Petticoat* (1959). *That Touch of Mink* was another original screenplay by Stanley Shapiro, with some assistance from Nate Monaster, another refugee from TV sitcoms. This is a very neat concept: Attracted to each other, Grant envisages an affair, while Day hears wedding bells. The meet-cute sets up their differing circumstances, his Rolls-Royce splashes her with mud and she rages at him until they meet. He is suave and polished and she is innocent and honest. She is the type of woman who would not ordinarily interest him. He is the kind of man she would ordinarily run a mile from.

Grant wines and dines her but when they go to a baseball game (filmed at Yankee Stadium) she is ejected for her complaints about the umpire in earshot of the likes of Mickey Mantle and Yogi Berra. Grant begins to think he is being over-zealous, which increases Day's interest, but when they go to Bermuda (actually, the Miramar Hotel on Wilshire Boulevard), she breaks out in a rash due to her anxieties over the sexual implications of the trip. Calming her nerves with alcohol, she over-indulges and tumbles from the balcony. To make Grant jealous, she dates someone else. The plan works and Grant gives in and marries her only to discover on their honeymoon that he's the one with the nervous laugh. This kind of role is a stroll in the park for Grant, and Day has perfected her part by now; even so, it is a sophisticated effort. A subplot in which Grant is believed by his therapist to be homosexual moves things along.

As previously mentioned, Jack Lemmon and Paul Newman had piled into the production business in order to control their careers, but neither was involved in green-lighting as many pictures in the 1950s and 1960s as Day. A dozen films bore the imprimatur of Arwin Productions, beginning with *Young at Heart* (1954) and moving through *Julie* (1956), *The Tunnel of Love* (1958), *It Happened to Jane* (1959) and *Pillow Talk*. Naturally, she received top billing in all these films, which, in consequence, helped the public accept her as star rather than leading lady. She was the most successful of the actor-producers because, with rare exceptions, the bulk of her output hit it big. Of her 1960s contingent, as well as the two films making it into this volume, Arwin was behind *Midnight Lace* (1960), *Billy Rose's Jumbo* (1962), *The Thrill of It All* (1963), *The Glass Bottom Boat* (1966) and *With Six You Get Eggroll* (1968). She lost box office appeal towards the end of the decade because she was disinclined to pay hefty sums for co-stars.

Critical reception: "Glittering verbal wit … pin-point precision in timing sight gags" (*New York Times*); "the gloss … doesn't obscure the essentially threadbare lining" (*Variety*)[292]

Rentals: $7.9 million[293] ($56.3 million equivalent)

72: *The Boston Strangler*

Starring Henry Fonda and Tony Curtis; directed by Richard Fleischer; screenplay, Edward Anhalt, based on the Gerold Frank book; producers, James Cresson and Robert Fryer; music, Lionel Newman. Twentieth Century–Fox. October 16, 1968.

As a commercial enterprise, *The Boston Strangler* was dodgy, possibly the only marketable aspect being the title, based on serial killer Albert DeSalvo, who terrorized Boston in the early 1960s. The three principals—Tony Curtis, Henry Fonda and director Richard Fleischer—were poor box office prospects. Fleischer had overseen the calamitous musical *Doctor Dolittle* (1967)—budget $17 million, U.S. rentals $6 million. Curtis had not had a hit since *The Great Race* (1965) and was on *Variety*'s list of least bankable performers.[294] Except for the unlikely success of the comedy *Yours, Mine and Ours* (1968) and the thriller *Madigan* (1968),[295] Fonda had not starred in a hit for at least a decade, success in the former owing more to Lucille Ball and in the latter to Richard Widmark. However, for Twentieth Century–Fox, which spent $250,000 on acquiring the rights, crime pictures were a decent bet after the success of its own *Tony Rome* (1967) and *The Detective* (1968), both starring Frank Sinatra, complemented by the Oscar-winning *In the Heat of the Night* (1967) and *Bonnie and Clyde* (1967).

Casting DeSalvo was always going to be difficult. As he does not appear until the last hour, it was logical to cast a character actor. The studio did not think Curtis would cut it. But Curtis worked putty into the bridge of his nose to make it look broken, mussed his hair and put dark makeup around his eyes, then took a photo of himself as if a police mug shot. Not recognizing Curtis, producer Richard Zanuck hired him. After getting the part, Curtis put on 15 pounds and used ankle weights to alter his walk.[296] There was always the hope that a part like this would at the very least revitalize his career and at best put him in the frame for an Oscar. An initial script by English playwright Terence

Unusually, the film's advertising campaign concentrated on the above image, rather than, as was normal, offering exhibitors a diverse choice. What changed was the tagline. "Why did 13 women open their doors to The Boston Strangler? This is a true and remarkable motion picture." Another took a different approach. "By his own admission, Albert DeSalvo is the Boston Strangler. Why has he never been brought to trial?"* Trade press advertisement (*Box Office*, September 30, 1968).

*Pressbook, *The Boston Strangler*.

Rattigan (*The VIPs*, 1963) was dumped in favor of a new approach by Edward Anhalt,[297] double–Oscar winner for *Panic in the Streets* (1950) and *Becket* (1964). What was in effect on the screen a dogged piece of detective work was enlivened by Fleischer's use of the split screen process—as many as seven areas of action shown at one time—used to such great effect in *Grand Prix* (1966) and *Charly* (1968). Fonda plays John S. Bottomly, who heads up a "Strangler" bureau.

Various suspects are investigated. As the body count mounts, a psychic finds a potential candidate but a murder is committed while he is under observation. Then we see a DeSalvo murder attempt thwarted when the potential victim bites him. After entering another apartment, he is arrested. But it is only when Bottomly by coincidence sees DeSalvo in an elevator and spots his wound that he becomes a suspect. DeSalvo's split personality hinders the investigation until under interrogation it is revealed and the killer recoils from his other self in shock.

Budgeted at $4.1 million,[298] the movie is gripping as a straightforward narrative—the detection work, the investigative failures, the mounting paranoia—but also unusual in examining the murderer, especially one with mental illness, although the movie was tainted with accusations of bogus psychology. An Oscar nomination eluded Curtis though he was nominated for a Golden Globe.

Critical reception: "Essentially a work of fiction based on real events … should not have been made at all" (*Chicago Sun-Times*); "represents an incredible collapse of taste, judgment, decency … [It] pretends to report the story of a living man who was neither convicted nor indicted for his crimes"[299] (*New York Times*).[300]

Rentals: $8 million[301] ($57 million equivalent)

71: *The Music Man*

Starring Robert Preston and Shirley Jones; directed and produced by Morton DaCosta; screenplay, Marion Hargrove, based on the musical by Meredith Willson; music and lyrics, Willson. Warner Brothers. June 19, 1962.

Even if you've never heard of composer Meredith Willson, there's a fair chance you will be familiar with his songs "Seventy-Six Trombones" and "Till There Was You." The latter became such a standard, it was sung by the Beatles on their *Ed Sullivan Show* debut. The former was the standout of *The Music Man*, a Tony-winning Broadway musical from 1957.[302] Willson also wrote *The Unsinkable Molly Brown*, which made its Broadway debut in 1960 and was filmed four years with Debbie Reynolds.

Sixty when *The Music Man* was filmed, Willson was a Hollywood veteran, composing music for *The King of Kings* (1927), *All Quiet on the Western Front* (1930), *The Great Dictator* (1940) and *The Little Foxes* (1941); he was nominated for Oscars for the latter two. But mostly he was a songwriter, only turning his hand to a musical when prompted by a couple of producers in the early 1950s to create a work based on his Iowa upbringing.

The Music Man is a curious story for a musical. In the early twentieth century, con man Harold Hill (Robert Preston) travels the Midwest masquerading as a professor of music, forming marching boy-bands as a way of, theoretically, alleviating juvenile problems. He absconds with the money raised for instruments and uniforms. His routine involves seducing the local music teacher but this time she (Shirley Jones) is more than his match.

Preston had an inconsequential movie career, able to steal scenes but not prop up an entire picture. He had supporting parts in the Cecil B. DeMille productions *Union Pacific* (1939), *North West Mounted Police* (1940) and *Reap the Wild Wind* (1942) and the second male lead in *This Gun for Hire* (1942), *The Macomber Affair* (1947) and *Blood on the Moon* (1948). Starring roles only came in smaller films like *Parachute Battalion* (1941) and *Cloudburst* (1951). For most of the 1950s, he alternated between TV and Broadway, playing the lead in the original production of *The Music Man*. It was not unusual at that time for the star of the Broadway show to fail to win the movie role; Mary Martin lost out on *South Pacific* (1958), Audrey Hepburn on *Gigi* (1958), Julie Andrews on *My Fair Lady* (1964). Warner Brothers had similar misgivings and offered the Harold Hill role to Frank Sinatra and Cary Grant, who, instead, lobbied for Preston to be given the role. On the other hand, Shirley Jones was a stage and movie musical star, graduating from the Broadway version of *South Pacific* to the film version of *Oklahoma!* (1955) and leading lady of *Carousel* (1956), *April Love* (1957) and *Never Steal Anything Small* (1959). A complete change of direction saw her win the Best Supporting Actress Oscar for *Elmer Gantry* (1960) and she was the leading lady in the John Ford Western *Two Rode Together* (1961). In consequence, she was more bankable than Barbara Cook, who had played the part on Broadway. Also in the cast were comic Buddy Hackett, Hermione Gingold (*Gigi*) and future director Ron Howard. Morton DaCosta (*Auntie Mame*, 1958's #1 film), who had helmed the Broadway show, took the directorial reins.

The twist in the story is that the con man falls in love with the woman he is trying to con while she, despite being aware of his deceit, falls in love with him. The songs are well-directed but the picture, while lacking the verve of a Robert Wise or George Cukor, captures the vibrancy of the stage show and both leads give excellent performances.

Despite its 151-minute running time, it was not released as a roadshow.

Critical reception: "Made rounder and richer through the magnitude of film" (*New York Times*); "a triumph, perhaps a classic, of corn" (*Variety*).[303]

Rentals: $8.1 million ($57.7 million equivalent)

69 (tie): *The Professionals*

Starring Burt Lancaster, Lee Marvin and Claudia Cardinale[304]; directed and produced by Richard Brooks; screenplay Brooks,[305] based on the novel *A Mule for the Marquesa* by Frank O'Rourke; music, Maurice Jarre. Columbia. November 2, 1966.

Columbia originally intended this tale of a band of mercenaries sent to Mexico in 1913 to rescue the kidnapped wife of a millionaire to star Gregory Peck, Frank Sinatra and Robert Mitchum.[306] When this proved too expensive, the property was shelved. It seemed an unlikely project for Richard Brooks, whose forte was meaty drama: *Cat on a Hot Tin Roof* (1958), *Elmer Gantry* (1960) and *Lord Jim* (1965). But after so many complex, time-consuming pictures, he wanted something simpler. Burt Lancaster signed on as the lead, after his flops *The Train* (1964) and *The Hallelujah Trail* (1965). He needed the money, being paid a mere $150,000 for his last four pictures to pay off debts[307] from his production company.[308] By the time *The Professionals* started in October 1965, he had been out of work for a year. The Western was not in great shape either—every *Shenandoah* was matched by high-priced flops *The Hallelujah Trail, Cheyenne Autumn* (1964) and *Major Dundee* (1965).

The Films

67

Summer 1965 was Lee Marvin's breakthrough in, of all things, the comedy Western *Cat Ballou* (1965). Marvin's career had been one of dashed promise, a decade toiling in the lower echelons, surfacing once in a while as a notable heavy, rarely rising up the billing. Mainstream recognition failed to arise either from his TV series *M Squad* (1957–1960) or his Emmy nomination for *People Need People* (1962) with only roles in *The Comancheros* (1961), *The Man Who Shot Liberty Valance* (1962) and *Donovan's Reef* (1963) as respite. Then NBC released their made-for-TV movie *The Killers* (1964) theatrically, and its success brought him *Ship of Fools* (1965) and a memorable drunk scene which catapulted him into *Cat Ballou* and an unexpected Best Actor Oscar. *The Professionals* was the first in a Columbia four-picture deal. Already on board were Woody Strode, Robert Ryan and Jack Palance as Mexican revolutionary Jesus Raza. The kidnap victim was Tunisian actress Claudia Cardinale[309] on a three-picture Columbia contract following roles opposite Lancaster in Visconti's *The Leopard* (1963), Peter Sellers in *The Pink Panther* (1963) and John Wayne in *Circus World* (1964). It was a tough shoot, Lancaster suffering the aftereffects of a knee injury, the script unfinished, murderous desert sun turning into flash floods, and Marvin's drinking bringing him close to being fired.[310]

The film is complex and different. For a start, the violence is very realistic and was cited along with *A Fistful of Dollars*[311] as starting that trend. The men have genuine codes of honor and as likely to outwit the enemy by tactics as force. Marvin is quiet and calculating. Ryan plays against type, more out of his depth as the film progresses. Raza, personally executing prisoners, appears barbaric until we learn that the government once killed 2000 townspeople, Marvin's wife among them. Reaching the Mexican stronghold, they create a diversion by blowing up the water tower, dynamite hitting the target via Woody Strode's arrows. When Marvin and Lancaster reach Cardinale, they realize that she is not a kidnap victim, but Palance's lover. Aware they have been duped, they take her anyway and Marvin prevents Lancaster from killing Palance. They battle their way out, escaping on a train. Now the mercenaries are the kidnappers. In the mountains, when Cardinale attempts escape, explosions bar her way. Open desert is not freedom either. Hit by a fierce sandstorm, they are reduced to walking, Mexicans still in pursuit. Cardinale turns into their conscience, shifting antipathy from her husband (Ralph Bellamy). She tries to seduce Lancaster, but he is ready for her, pressing the pistol she seeks to her throat. Lancaster tries to talk Marvin out of taking her back. The Mexicans catch up. Lancaster risks his life to save the others, sending them on ahead, holing up in a ravine, taking on the pursuers on his own, picking them off. The dogfight lasts six terse minutes. Both Lancaster and Palance are wounded but in the end it is just the two of them plus Chiquita (Maria Gomez), another revolutionary, previously Lancaster's lover. Palance can no longer fight. Gomez tricks Lancaster but when she attempts to shoot him, she has no bullets left. Up ahead, the kidnappers reach their destination. Lancaster arrives with the wounded Palance, whom the mercenaries prevent Bellamy from killing. As Bellamy slaps Cardinale to the ground, Marvin intervenes, informing the husband: "We made a contract to save a lady from a nasty old kidnapper who turns out to be you." The mercenaries plan to return Palance and Cardinale to Mexico. "You bastard," shouts Bellamy. "In my case an accident of birth," says Marvin, saddling up, "But you, sir, you're a self-made man." A classic last line for a classic Western.

Brooks became only the fifth person in history, following John Ford for *Stagecoach* (1939), Fred Zinnemann for *High Noon* (1952), George Stevens for *Shane* (1953) and William Wyler for *Friendly Persuasion* (1956), to receive a Best Director nomination for

68   The Films

a Western. He was in another select band: In being also nominated for Best Adapted Screenplay, he was one of only five writers receiving that distinction in the genre.

Critical reception: "Exciting, occasionally hackneyed, Western" (*Films and Filming*); "hell-for-leather action and raw adventure" (*New York Times*); "exciting explosive sequences, good overall pacing and acting overcome a sometimes thin script" (*Variety*); "top action fare" (*Box Office*).[312]

Rentals: $8.3 million ($59.1 million equivalent)

69 (tie): *Exodus*

Starring Paul Newman and Eva Marie Saint; directed and produced by Otto Preminger; screenplay, Dalton Trumbo, based on the book by Leon Uris; music, Ernest Gold. United Artists roadshow. December 15, 1960.

MGM commissioned Leon Uris in 1955 to write the book *Exodus*,[313] the biggest bestseller after *Gone with the Wind*,[314] covering research costs before acquiring the movie rights.[315] After publication, a new management team sold the rights for $75,000 to independent producer-director Otto Preminger.[316] He had burned through three careers thus far, from big-budget dramas like *Forever Amber* (1947) for Twentieth Century–Fox in the 1940s to a spell as a key innovator of film noir—*Fallen Angel* (1945), *Whirlpool* (1950), *Angel Face* (1953), *et al.*—and finally, as his own boss, mixing controversy (*The Man with the Golden Arm*, 1955, *Anatomy of a Murder*, 1959) and musicals (*Carmen Jones*, 1954, *Porgy and Bess*, 1959) with more intimate productions like *Bonjour Tristesse* (1958).

Although Frank Sinatra was interested,[317] Paul Newman was recruited at a cost of $200,000[318] with Eva Marie Saint the top-billed female. Newman was not quite the fully rounded star, every success like *From the Terrace* (1960) twinned with a poor performer such as *The Young Philadelphians* (1959). Even after winning the Best Supporting Actress Oscar for *On the Waterfront* (1954), Eva Marie Saint was not in huge demand until Hitchcock's thriller *North by Northwest* (1959) put her firmly back in the box office shop window. Ralph Richardson, Lee J. Cobb, Peter Lawford and Sal Mineo completed the all-star cast.

Cutting the massive book down to a workable film even with a three-and-a-half-hour running time was a massive undertaking. After rejecting a first draft by blacklisted Albert Maltz, Preminger hired another blacklistee, Dalton Trumbo,[319] and then openly advertised the fact. A front page *New York Times* story[320] was one of the reasons why the blacklist[321] was soon lifted. Compressing the story while retaining the dramatic ingredients, including romance and betrayal, at the same time as maintaining the political background, ensuring historical accuracy and being even-handed to real-life participants meant the movie was in turns stagey, emotionally solid and action-filled. It was filmed in 70mm in Israel and Cyprus. Ernest Gold provided a stirring score which won him an Oscar, and the poster by Saul Bass proved memorable.

Newman, who constantly clashed with Preminger,[322] plays Ari Ben Canaan, one of the leaders of the movement trying to establish the state of Israel, while Saint is Kitty Fremont, nurse at a Cyprus internment camp. The first section focuses on the hunger strike organized by Newman for refugees smuggled aboard a ship called *Exodus* but detained in Cyprus by British blockade. Saint has befriended a young Jewish girl (newcomer Jill Haworth) seeking her lost father and goes with her to Palestine where her romance with Newman blooms until she finds she cannot compete with a previous love tortured and killed by Arabs. When Haworth finds her father, he does not recognize her. Newman's uncle leads the bombing of the King David Hotel and is arrested but during his rescue, organized by Newman, he is killed. Newman is badly wounded and only Saint's intervention saves his life. Meanwhile, Haworth, after proclaiming her love for a young terrorist, dies in an ambush. There is no celebration of an independent Israel at the end, just Newman and Saint setting off for further battle.

Excluding stars, the initial budget was $1.75 million,[323] but the total figure climbed to $3.7 million.[324] Preminger earned more than Newman, $160,000 up front, the first $250,000 of profits and 75 percent of profits thereafter,[325] to most observers quite a lopsided deal.[326] It produced a record roadshow advance of $1 million.[327] Although critics railed at Preminger for cramming too much incident into the film while also stuffing it full of too much talk, it's actually a very decent stab at telling a true story in dramatic fictional fashion. Each of the protagonists loses someone they love, the locations are superb, the battle for survival intense and the explanations, long though they were, served to keep the film on an even historical keel. The main romance is subject to the realities of living with a terrorist, and life in the kibbutz, the internment camp and on board ship is well drawn. Newman tones down the theatrics and Saint plays a very human being caught up in a situation not of her making, her first instinct maternal rather than selfish. According to Oscar voters, Sal Mineo was the standout performer, winning Best Supporting Actor.

Overlong for general release, it was heavily cut after roadshow.

Critical reception: "Awesome talkfest" (*New Yorker*); "of incalculable influence in reaching those unfamiliar with the background" (*Washington Post*); "kaleidoscopic yet memorable impression of highlights from the long-time best-seller" (*Los Angeles Times*); "dazzling, eye-filling, nerve-tingling display" (*New York Times*).[328] Ranked twelfth on the *Cahiers du Cinema* annual list.[329]

Rentals: $8.3 million[330] ($59.1 million equivalent)

68: *What's New Pussycat*

Starring Peter Sellers, Peter O'Toole, Woody Allen, Capucine and Ursula Andress; directed by Clive Donner; screenplay, Allen; producer, Charles K. Feldman; music, Burt Bacharach. United Artists. June 22, 1965.

Who better to play a playboy than Warren Beatty? At least, that was the initial plan. Striking a somewhat autobiographical note, Beatty wanted to do a comedy about "the plight of a compulsive Don Juan."[331] The film was developed by the star as a vehicle to re-start his career after the commercial disappointment of *Lilith* (1964). Funding came from producer Charles K. Feldman (*North to Alaska*, 1960), the title a phrase Beatty coined.

Woody Allen, then a stand-up comedian, wrote the screenplay for $30,000 on condition he was given a part, his first.[332] Beatty demanded Allen be fired when the latter's role grew at the former's expense.[333] Feldman, realizing Beatty was not the draw he had once been,[334] backed Allen. When Beatty walked away, it opened the door for Peter O'Toole, seeking relief from heavyweight roles. Peter Sellers, elevated to stardom after

70   The Films

the surprise success of the two *Pink Panther* movies, co-starred as a psychoanalyst. The leading ladies were like a casting call for a more sophisticated Bond picture: French actress Capucine[335] (*The Pink Panther*, 1963), Paula Prentiss (*Man's Favorite Sport*, 1964), Viennese Romy Schneider (*Good Neighbor Sam*, 1964), beauties all, plus original Swiss-born Bond girl Ursula Andress (*Dr. No*, 1962). Apart from *How the West Was Won*, this was probably the only film in the 1960s that truly qualified as an "all-star" cast. British director Clive Donner, fresh off *Nothing But the Best* (1964), took the helm. Tom Jones turned the Burt Bucharach-Hal David theme tune into a hit single. Other curios included a poster by fantasy illustrator Frank Frazetta and a tie-in novelization by Marvin H. Albert, who wrote the *Tony Rome* series.

The set-up is farce. Playboy O'Toole wishes to mend his ways and settle down with Scheider. To get him jealous, she makes a play for O'Toole's friend Woody Allen. Sellers hopes to bed patient Capucine, who eyes O'Toole, who attracts interest from exotic dancer Prentiss and parachutist Andress. The fun begins when the main characters shack up for the weekend in a French chateau. The end result is a mixture of slapstick and funny lines with anything serious to be said about sex addiction turned into a joke. Once the ball starts rolling on this kind of film, it's hard to make it stop and the secret is to try and prevent it getting out of control. Donner achieves that well enough. Some of the material was pretty tasteless, but as long as it got laughs, then who cared? There were plenty of those but in the future Woody Allen would pay more attention to structure. According to Peter Biskind, this experience was critical to the development of Beatty as an instigator of projects. First of all, he realized how much money he had thrown away by quitting the movie, and, secondly, next time he set up a film, he was determined to retain complete control.[336]

Critical reception: "It has been attacked as tasteless yet I have never seen a more tasteful movie" (*Village Voice*); "outrageously cluttered and campy" (*New York Times*); "marriage of sophisticated comedy and crazy humor" (*Films and Filming*); "star-filled expensive non-movie" (*Time*).[337]

Rentals: "$8.4 million[338] ($59.8 million equivalent)

67: *Alfie*[339]

Starring Michael Caine and Shelley Winters; directed and produced by Lewis Gilbert; screenplay, Bill Naughton, based on his play; music, Sonny Rollins. Paramount. March 24, 1966 (London); U.S.: August 24, 1966.

Asides to the audience—in vogue through *Deadpool* (2016) and TV's *House of Cards* (2013) and *Fleabag* (2016)—were a rarely used Hollywood device except by Bob Hope or the Marx Brothers. *Alfie* fitted into the category of the breakout small film, preceding *Georgy Girl*. Michael Caine's historical action picture *Zulu* (1964) had flopped in the U.S.[340] but by the time *Alfie* premiered in America, the spy thriller *The Ipcress File* (1965) and the comedy *The Wrong Box* (1966) had been released to surprisingly good reviews and box office. Caine was not first choice.[341] Original producer John Woolf (*Room at the Top*, 1958) wanted that film's star Laurence Harvey.[342] When he dropped out, British director Lewis Gilbert favored Terence Stamp from William Wyler's *The Collector* (1965), but his Broadway performance in *Alfie* was a disaster, with the show closing after 21 performances.[343] Gilbert's son informed him of Caine's performance in

The extent to which music played a major role in marketing was demonstrated by *Alfie*, the theme song of which was recorded by nine artists. The idea was to suit a variety of tastes, rather than assign the song to one singing star as occurred with the James Bond films. Cilla Black's rendition, which under composer Burt Bacharach's direction took nearly 30 takes,* was a big hit in Britain. Dionne Warwick sang the song at the Oscars. Trade press advertisement (*Box Office*, August 15, 1966, 80).

*Bacharach Burt with Greenfield, Robner, *Anyone Who Had a Heart, My Life in Music* (New York: Harper 2013), 118.

the forthcoming *The Ipcress File*, and that film's editor Peter Hunt allowed Gilbert a sneak preview.[344] Paramount had already agreed to fund the picture for $800,000, a miserable amount by Hollywood standards. On being hired, Caine found a tailor who made the sharp suits the actor envisaged, and he gave the character a jaunty walk to demonstrate his self-confidence. Gilbert, famous for the British war films *Carve Her Name with*

72   The Films

Pride (1958) and *Sink the Bismarck!* (1960), was about to enter his third decade as a director. His most recent picture was *The 7th Dawn* (1964) starring William Holden, but he was perceived as a journeyman not an artist, nor in the commercial league of compatriots David Lean or Carol Reed.

Despite his charm, Alfie is essentially a predator, who sees women only as seduction material, objectifying them as "birds" (a British colloquial term) or "it." His attitude avoids any necessity to love or care for them. His women range from doormats to tougher cookies. Shelley Winters (*A Patch of Blue*, 1965) signed up to play the toughest, Ruby. Jane Asher, then Paul McCartney's girlfriend, plays a sweet country girl, Shirley Anne Field a nurse in the hospital where he is recovering from tuberculosis. Vivien Merchant (Mrs. Harold Pinter), the wife of another hospital patient, ends up pregnant. Alfie calls in an abortionist (illegal at the time).[345] When he leaves, Merchant convulses with pain and he slaps her to prevent her screaming. But that proves the character's wake-up call. Seeing the aborted fetus, he realizes that sex is about more than his pleasure. The first gesture of atonement, humanity, call it what you will, comes when Alfie picks up a stray dog with the clear intention of adopting it.

The film presents an alternative version of swinging London. Less Carnaby Street and more seedy reality—Bayswater, Whitechapel, King's Cross and Notting Hill (then not a gentrified part of the city). Transport cafés rather than fashionable eateries, although fashion remains an element with Caine as its male epitome. It was a standout performance from Caine, especially compared with the dour persona of Harry Palmer in *The Ipcress File,* and it opened the door for his Hollywood career. Although his cocksure attitude was at the root of the film's success, Caine's best scene was an emotional one, when he describes the fetus to a friend. Gilbert's direction was also a revelation: the confidence to include the asides and not to succumb to the temptation to make the character more likable, to retain the vibrant patois, and to avoid a Hollywood version of London. Jazz saxophonist Sonny Rollins, in residence at Ronnie Scott's Club in London, fashioned the score.[346] The theme song "Alfie" by Burt Bacharach and Hal David, and sung by Cher, was added to the American version but in a speedy British reissue was sung by Cilla Black.

Alfie was always going to have trouble with the censor, especially in America where the Production Code forbade mention of abortion. However, impressed British censor John Trevelyan contacted American counterpart Geoffrey Shurlock, who realized the film's merits outweighed the old-fashioned censorship guidelines and set about rewriting the Code to permit the film's release.[347] For American audiences, Paramount wanted dubbing to erase the Cockney accents.[348] When that was resisted[349] the film received a platform release, meaning it was restricted to a couple cinemas until—and if—it caught on; failure to find an audience would end its run. The *New York Times* published a glossary of rhyming slang.[350] While it performed well in New York, exhibitors elsewhere predicted disaster,[351] instead of which, it received a warm critical reception, handsome box office and five Oscar nominations including Best Picture and Best Actor.

Critical reception: "There is a zing in the language and a zip in the pace" (*Life*); "bubbles with impudent humor and ripe modern wit" (*New York Times*); "unreels more like a score card than a scenario" (*Time*); "presented in the best of humor with complete frankness" (*New York Post*).[352]

Rentals: $8.5 million ($60.5 million equivalent)

66: *The Fox*

Starring Sandy Dennis, Anne Heywood and Keir Dullea; directed by Mark Rydell; screenplay, Lewis John Carlino and Howard Koch, based on the book by D.H. Lawrence; producer, Raymond Stross; music, Lalo Schifrin. Warner Brothers. December 13, 1967.

Repressive attitudes about sexuality and the all-powerful Production Code had limited discussion of lesbianism in mainstream Hollywood pictures. Even William Wyler's *These Three* (1936) starring Miriam Hopkins and Merle Oberon, an adaptation of the Lillian Hellman play *The Children's Hour*, was not permitted to mention the word, and the original storyline was altered. When Wyler remade the picture as *The Children's Hour* (1961) with Audrey Hepburn and Shirley MacLaine, sufficient development in Hollywood permitted mention of this plot point whereby two spinster schoolteachers are accused of being lesbians. The anticipated ending of the Production Code, as prefigured by *Alfie* (1966) and other films, had led to a disregard for the existing system and the beginnings of a greater examination of sexuality. *The Fox* was based on a short story by D.H. Lawrence. Although he was the most famous literary figure in the world at the start of the 1960s courtesy of the British obscenity trial over *Lady Chatterley's Lover*, no filmmaker had cashed in, *Sons and Lovers* (1960) having preceded the trial.

The Fox was a Canadian example of the "little film that could." Relocated to Canada, it marked the debut of Mark Rydell and was the sophomore screenplay of Lewis John Carlino (co-written with Howard Koch) after the John Frankenheimer thriller *Seconds* (1966). Originally, Alan Bates (*Georgy Girl*, 1966), Patricia Neal (*Hud*, 1963) and Vivien Merchant (*Alfie*, 1966) were in the frame for the three roles. Of replacements Sandy Dennis, Keir Dullea and Anne Heywood, the male was the biggest name after the mental health drama *David and Lisa* (1962), *The Thin Red Line* (1964) and *Bunny Lake Is Missing* (1965). But since the last two had flopped, more was riding on Sandy Dennis, Best Supporting Actress Oscar winner for *Who's Afraid of Virginia Woolf?* (1966) and star of the high school drama *Up the Down Staircase* (1967). Former Miss Great Britain Anne Heywood[353] had been a Rank starlet[354] until marriage to English producer Raymond Stross provided a career upgrade, to female lead in *The Night Fighters* (1960) starring Robert Mitchum. But top billing in the sci-fi film *The Brain* (1962) and the thriller *90 Degrees in the Shade* (1965) did not set Hollywood alight and she was already in her mid–30s, too old for traditional Hollywood stardom, when *The Fox* began.

Dennis and Heywood play spinsters running a chicken farm in rural Canada, Dennis introspective and content, Heywood self-sufficient but sexually frustrated. Merchant seaman Dullea (the symbolic fox in the hencoop) visits, romancing Heywood, proposing marriage. He kills a real fox which had been eating their chickens. When Dullea temporarily leaves, Dennis confesses her feelings for Heywood and they make love. Dullea returns and, following an incident chopping down a tree, Dennis is crushed to death. Heywood sells the farm and leaves with Dullea, although it is clear her loss mitigates against finding true happiness.

Rydell displays considerable confidence in his material, emphasizing the natural backdrop, early morning sunrises and a chill in the air adding a certain tone, with the isolation providing a thematic template. The tiny cast creates a sense of intimacy as well as tension and the acting is uniformly good. There is no sense of lust, just a gradual materialization of submerged emotion. Tackling such a bold theme would have brought the movie some attention anyway, but nudity, masturbation and sex brought

74   The Films

much more. That scenes were filmed in good taste impressed critics but hardly deterred the salacious-minded. The nervy, whiny Dennis has the showiest role but Heywood, trapped by her conflicting sexual needs, is the central figure. George Roy Hill might well have purloined his freeze-frame ending in *Butch Cassidy and the Sundance Kid* from an idea Rydell employs here, one of two effective stylistic devices in an otherwise highly controlled piece. The only directorial downside is the intrusion of some unnecessary melodramatic music when otherwise Lalo Schifrin's gentle theme perfectly expresses the mood.

Reliant entirely on acting and directorial skill, this is one of the decade's low-budget triumphs, not least for its sensitive treatment of its subject matter. Oscar voters showed little interest apart from a nomination for Schifrin, but as a Canadian production it qualified as a foreign film at the Golden Globes where it won that category. Although Hollywood stardom did not come her way, Heywood's British career was revitalized after the movie proved an unexpectedly big hit in her homeland.

Critical reception: "A masterpiece ... do not go to see *The Fox* because of its subject matter and do not stay away for that reason" (*Chicago Sun-Times*); "a brooding sense of something not quite right" (*New York Times*); "if *The Fox* isn't the masterpiece which for a few minutes near the beginning it looked like being, its qualities remain most impressive" (*Films and Filming*).[355]

Rentals: $8.6 million ($61.2 million equivalent)

65: *Operation Petticoat*

Starring Cary Grant and Tony Curtis; directed by Blake Edwards; screenplay Stanley Shapiro and Maurice Richlin; producer Robert Arthur; music David Rose. Universal. December 3, 1959.[356]

It says something for Cary Grant's sense of humor that he was willing to co-star with the man who had impersonated him in *Some Like It Hot* (1959). *Operation Petticoat* was hot off the Stanley Shapiro (*Pillow Talk*, 1959) production line and the writer had already fashioned *The Perfect Furlough* (1958) to suit Curtis' style. For most of the picture, Grant's face is filled with his trademark bafflement as in typical strait-laced fashion he fails to understand the "wiles" of women, in this case a squad of Second World War nurses rescued by the submarine he commands. Universal embarked on the project because Curtis wanted to make a submarine picture with Grant since it was the latter's role as a sub commander in *Destination Tokyo* (1943) that inspired him (Curtis) during the war.[357] As with many Shapiro projects, the concept is ideal and once the set-up is established, you light the touch paper and stand back.

Grant[358] and Curtis were at a commercial peak, the former after *Houseboat* and *North by Northwest* (1959), the latter after *The Perfect Furlough* and *Some Like it Hot*. Director Blake Edwards, better known at the time as the creator of the *Peter Gunn* TV series, had previously helmed *This Happy Feeling* (1958) with Debbie Reynolds and a pair of comedies with singer Frankie Laine, *He Laughed Last* (1956) and *Bring Your Smile Along* (1955). He was familiar with Curtis, having directed him in *Mister Cory* (1957) and *The Perfect Furlough*. Joan O'Brien and Dina Merrill, the most conspicuous of the nurses, were both at the start of their careers, O'Brien in her second picture following the MGM legal drama *Handle with Care* (1958) in which she was second-billed to future

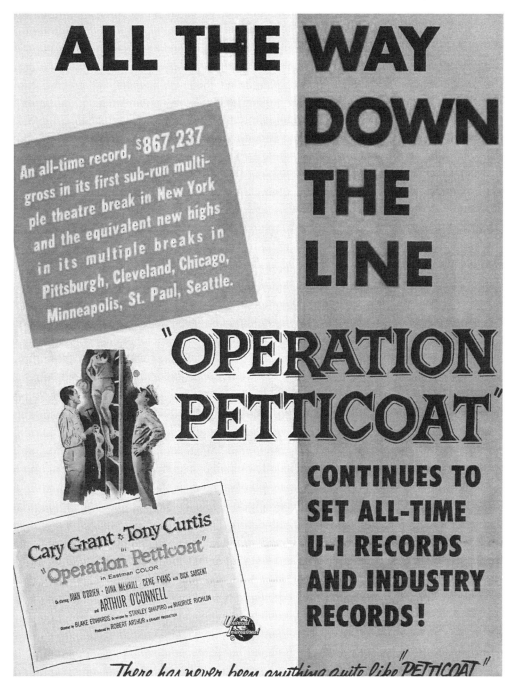

Memories of serving on a submarine prompted Curtis to make this movie, originally to co-star Universal alumnus Jeff Chandler. When Chandler was dropped over a row about billing, Curtis wanted Clark Gable. But Gable had just made a submarine movie. Cary Grant took up the slack. Exteriors were shot off Florida and between takes the pair basked in the sun, with Curtis slightly more active by dipping a fishing line into the water.* Trade press advertisement (*Box Office*, March 7, 1960, 3).

*Munn, Michael, *Tony Curtis, Nobody's Perfect* (London: JR Books, 2011) 164-165.

76 The Films

Disney favorite Dean Jones. Merrill was on her fourth after *Desk Set* (1957), *A Nice Little Bank That Should Be Robbed* (1958) and as leading lady in another maritime comedy, *Don't Give Up the Ship* (1959).

Grant's submarine is sunk by an air raid in the Philippines. Curtis is the scrounger tasked with finding the materials for repairs. They set off with only one functioning engine and a skeleton crew, stopping reluctantly to pick up the nurses. The eventual romantic pairing is Grant-O'Brien and Curtis-Merrill but not before a series of misadventures (firing a torpedo in the wrong direction, setting up a casino, painting the ship pink and being mistaken for the enemy), not to mention the comedy potential mined from physical proximity in cramped quarters. Some of the comedy is a bit sexist, especially given that O'Brien is in the statuesque class, but this proves an ideal vehicle for all concerned. The movie had a more authentic air than such an idea might suggest since some incidents were based on true stories.

As previously mentioned, several actors had branched out into production. Few would do it as successfully as Cary Grant, already the owner of real estate and with interests outside the movies.[359] He launched his production career under the aegis of Granart Productions on this picture. In conjunction with director Stanley Donen, he set up Grandon for his picture *The Grass Is Greener* (1960), and for the rest of his career, few films lacked his involvement on the production side, often with a different company name.[360]

Critical reception: "No more weight than a sackful of feathers but ... a lot of laughs" (*Variety*); "nothing like a dame to occupy the interests of men plagued by the tediousness of war" (*New York Times*)[361]

Rentals: $8.75 million[362] ($62.3 million equivalent)

64: *Barefoot in the Park*

Starring Jane Fonda and Robert Redford; directed by Gene Saks; screenplay, Neil Simon, from his play; producer, Hal B. Wallis; music, Neal Hefti. Paramount. May 25, 1967.

This was intended as the breakout film for rising star Robert Redford. But it didn't work and he had to wait another two years before a better vehicle for his talents came along in *Butch Cassidy and the Sundance Kid*. Co-star Jane Fonda[363] stole the show, which was only fair since she was, after all, by far the bigger star at the time. Redford had already wasted a hatful of chances to establish his name: third-billed in *Inside Daisy Clover* (1965) and *The Chase* (1966) and second-billed behind Natalie Wood in *This Property Is Condemned* (1966), all meaty dramas which should have provided a tilt at stardom.

Jane Fonda, daughter of Henry, was already a bona fide star, second-billed in her debut *Tall Story* (1960)—also Redford's movie debut in a much smaller part. She continuing with that status through dramas like *A Period of Adjustment* (1962) and the romantic comedy *Sunday in New York* (1963). She split to France for the Rene Clement crime drama *Joy House* (1964) and future husband Roger Vadim's *La Ronde* (1964). She came home to a star's welcome, top billing in the comedy Western *Cat Ballou* (1965), only to have her thunder stolen by an Oscar-winning performance by Lee Marvin. As the leading lady in *The Chase* and *Hurry Sundown* (1967), you would have thought she deserved top billing in *Barefoot in the Park*.

TWENTY-FOUR SHEET

Robert Redford had played the part on Broadway opposite a Tony-nominated Elizabeth Ashley. Neil Simon's longest-running Broadway play—and the tenth biggest overall non-musical production—it clocked up 1,530 performances from 1963 to 1967 and was directed on stage by Mike Nichols (pressbook).

After a lawsuit with Warner Brothers,[364] Paramount had paid $450,000[365] for the rights to the play[366] by millionaire playwright Neil Simon.[367] Redford won top billing because his character makes the greater transformation. Had Natalie Wood accepted the female lead in the movie when offered, the billing would have been shifted in her favor. Fonda was not the automatic second choice, media reports at the time linking Yvette Mimieux (*Joy in the Morning*, 1965), Geraldine Chaplin (*Doctor Zhivago*, 1965)[368] and Tuesday Weld (*The Cincinnati Kid*, 1965) with the part. Director Gene Saks was making his movie debut.[369] Simon had previously adapted for the screen his own *After the Fox* (1966) with Peter Sellers.

Redford and Fonda—in her sixth stage adaptation[370]—essay a newly married couple coming to terms with the realities of living in a sixth floor apartment. They are opposites, he a legal stuffed shirt, she an off-the-cuff free spirit. The title refers to her long-standing grievance that his cautious nature prevented him walking barefoot one freezing evening. That's pretty much as far as the movie goes in terms of story. There's a subplot trying to pair her mother with neighbor Charles Boyer. After one difference and row too many, Fonda kicks Redford out. Her drunken husband now runs barefoot through the park. Alcohol alters him. He becomes more fun but also more drunk and the twist is that Fonda now prefers his previous, sober personality. Back at their apartment, he climbs onto the roof but is too scared to come down. Eventually, she persuades him and they make up. It's more charming than hysterically funny. But audiences responded to the author's observational comedy. Fonda comes across as a more attractive screen personality, naturally effervescent, whereas Redford is too reserved to reveal the charm later exhibited in *Butch Cassidy*.

Critical reception: "A funny adaptation by Neil Simon of his funny play" (*New Yorker*); "it is as funny as it ever was" (*Washington Post*); "[the stars] handle themselves with a fine, deft charm" (*Los Angeles Times*); "old-fashioned romantic farce with … snappy verbal gags" (*New York Times*).[371]

Rentals: $9 million ($64.1 million equivalent)

63: *From Russia with Love*

Starring Sean Connery and Robert Shaw; directed by Terence Young; screenplay, Richard Maibaum; producers, Harry Saltzman and Albert R. Broccoli; music, John Barry. United Artists. October 11, 1963 (London); U.S.: May 27, 1964.

This movie created Hollywood history—but not for the reason you imagine. Yes, it did prove that the series film could be revived in a big way. But, more importantly, it taught Hollywood not to cast aside its back catalogue so casually. For in the aftermath of the box office behemoth *Goldfinger* (1964), a revival in 1965 of *From Russia with Love* in a double bill with *Dr. No* (1962) reinvented the reissue business. Both films made more than on their original release[372] and together they made more, far more than any revival program in history[373]: They finished with over $9 million in rentals, outpointing the current standard bearer *Gone with the Wind*,[374] and generating four times as much as the best revival of the 1960s so far, *The Bridge on the River Kwai* (1957), which had raked in $2.13 million in rentals in 1964.[375] The reissue double bill was the fifth biggest earner in 1965, beating *What's New Pussycat?*, *Shenandoah*, *The Sandpiper* and *Von Ryan's Express*. By this point, studios had thrown in the towel in regards to older films, any second release most likely appearing on TV. However, the dualer's success ensured that United Artists initiated a process whereby every new Bond was greeted by two previous ones paired. UA applied the same formula to its *Dollars*[376] and *Magnificent Seven* series. Columbia followed suit with its Matt Helm pictures and Twentieth Century–Fox reissued *Our Man Flint* and *In Like Flint*. But it also speeded up the revival business. A studio with a hit one year looked to bring it back the next. If not part of a series, it was coupled with a likely partner, hence *Wait Until Dark–Cool Hand Luke*[377] and *Bullitt–Bonnie and Clyde*[378] from Warner Brothers, *The Dirty Dozen–Grand Prix* from MGM,[379] and a double bill revolving around stars Sidney Poitier[380] and Elizabeth Taylor[381] or director Alfred Hitchcock.[382]

It also encouraged studios to invest in a series, knowing that reissue provided an extra financial cushion and increased the value to TV. Though mostly B-movies, the series film had once been a Hollywood staple. Exhibitors could count upon a regular supply of westerns (66 Hopalong Cassidy pictures, for example, between 1935 and 1948), crime (47 Charlie Chan mysteries between 1926 and 1949) and comedy (28 from the Blondie camp from 1938 to 1950). But the concept had more or less died out apart from the British-made Edgar Wallace mysteries (30 in three years since 1960), bigger-budgeted Tarzan adventures (still going strong after 25 outings), Margaret Rutherford as Miss Marple (two films in 1961 and 1963) and two sequels over six years to *Tammy and the Bachelor* (1957) plus *Return to Peyton Place* (1961) four years after the original.

However, the idea of setting out to create an annual big-budget series was anathema to the Hollywood movie companies of the 1960s until *Dr. No* proved a smash in Britain and a surprising, though not spectacular, success in the U.S. The follow-up *From Russia with Love* was not quite as eagerly anticipated as historians would like you to believe—an eight-month gap between British and American release scarcely a sign of exhibition zeal. This was not a sequel wherein characters and events had moved on but a series in the old-fashioned sense where nothing much changed. Where *Dr. No* did not rank in the top 40 in the annual box office race, the sequel finished inside the top 20

The Films

Hoping to build up U.S. demand, United Artists set out to tempt exhibitors by listing the movie's British revenues and pointing out it was first film to play four London West End theatres. The first 489 U.K. bookings grossed $2.91m compared to $1.76m for *Dr. No*. In addition, there was a record gross for a London release of $465,267 compared to $323,964 for *Dr. No*.* Trade press advertisement (*Box Office*, April 5, 1965).

*Advert, "Incredible News, Staggering Numbers," *Box Office*, February 18, 1964, 4.

and established Sean Connery as a major star. The template established for *Dr. No*—gadgets, beautiful girls, characters known just as M and Q, outlandish villains, global criminal network SPECTRE, Miss Moneypenny, even director Terence Young—was the same. But the budget doubled to $2 million. Whereas *Dr. No* locations were limited to England and Jamaica, the sequel was filmed in Scotland, Wales, Turkey and Venice as well as England. With Daniela Bianchi taking over the Ursula Andress arm-candy role, the movie featured two legendary opponents, Donald "Red" Grant (Robert Shaw) and Rosa Klebb (Lotte Lenya) of the poison-tipped shoe. The storyline has Bond hunting for a Russian coding machine before it can fall into the hands of SPECTRE. This takes him to Istanbul where he seduces Bianchi and indulges in more actual spying than normal. The climactic hand-to-hand fight on the train with Shaw took three weeks to shoot.

Critical reception: "Smart, shrewdly directed and capably performed" (*Time*); "immoral in every way imaginable" (*The Guardian*); "Sean Connery, who is a master in his own right in the art of sifting into a scene, covertly inflicting a soft dramatic quality inside the external toughness" (*New Republic*).[383]

Rentals: $9.2 million[384] (including 1965 reissues) ($65.5 million equivalent)

62: *Cat Ballou*

Starring Jane Fonda and Lee Marvin; directed by Elliott Silverstein; screenplay, Walter Newman and Frank Pierson, based on the novel *The Ballad of Cat Ballou* by Roy Chanslor; producer, Harold Hecht; music, Frank De Vol, songs, Mack David and Jay Livingston. Columbia. May 7, 1965.

Elliott Silverstein's comedy Western was intended as a star-making vehicle for Jane Fonda, returning to Hollywood after a two-year sojourn in France. Despite a string of medium-budgeted movies from *Tall Story* (1960) to *Sunday in New York* (1963), she had not yet stepped up to top billing. This was meant to be that step. Unfortunately for her, the picture was hijacked by Lee Marvin, who had nothing like her standing in the business and picked up just $30,000 for his dual role of legendary gunfighter Kid Shelleen and his brother, hired killer Tim Strawn. It's a curious hybrid, Nat "King" Cole and Stubby Kaye constantly interrupting the proceedings with songs that act like a Greek chorus commenting on the action, starting out in rite-of-passage format with an innocent Fonda returning home from boarding school. A corporation, seeking to acquire her father's ranch, hires Strawn to kill her father; in retaliation, Fonda recruits Shelleen, who proves a drunken incompetent. The picture is a third of the way through before Marvin turns up and his over-the-top acting completely upends the movie. When her father is killed and the townspeople refuse to bring the killer to justice, Fonda turns outlaw, robbing the payroll, while the good Marvin shapes up and kills the bad Marvin. Impersonating a sex worker, Fonda accidentally kills the corporation boss, is saved from hanging, and escapes to further "the Legend of Cat Ballou."

The source material was a serious Western novel by Roy Chanslor. TV writer Frank Pierson and Walter Newman (*The Magnificent Seven*, 1960) shared the screenplay credit but it took nearly a dozen writers to knock out the mishmash of sight and verbal gags. Fonda's transformation from prim young woman to sexy outlaw would have worked a treat except for the two doses of Marvin that whipped that concept out from under her. What's left is a highly entertaining, definitely original comedy Western with a hit theme tune and a probably undeserved Oscar for Marvin, who won out against a quartet of powerful dramatic performances: Rod Steiger in *The Pawnbroker* (1964), Richard Burton in *The Spy Who Came In from the Cold* (1965), Oskar Werner in *Ship of Fools* (1965) and Laurence Olivier as *Othello* (1965). Elliott Silverstein had spent the last decade in TV dramas like *Naked City*, *The Defenders*, *Dr. Kildare* and *Kraft Suspense Theatre*—and even a short stint on *The Twilight Zone* hardly set him up for a wacky comedy though his

The Films 81

big-screen inexperience might explain why Marvin was given such free rein. It spelled sweet revenge for producer Harold Hecht, who had failed to get it greenlit at Hill-Hecht-Lancaster[385] and now, on dissolution of that outfit, was free to do so, especially as Burt Lancaster (the third of the triumvirate) was having financial issues. But it is another addition to the "little film that could" department: small budget, no big stars, first-time director and screenplay that went through a dozen pairs of hands.

Critical reception: "Lumpy, obvious and coy" (*Film Quarterly*); "springy satire" (*Washington Post*); "breezy little film" (*New York Times*); "better done as a musical" (*Films and Filming*); "small package of enormous delight" (*New York Herald Tribune*).[386]

Rentals: $9.3 million ($66.2 million equivalent)

59 (tie): *Grand Prix*

Starring James Garner, Yves Montand and Eva Marie Saint; directed by John Frankenheimer; screenplay, Robert Alan Aurthur[387]; producer, Edward Lewis; music, Maurice Jarre.[388] MGM roadshow. December 21, 1966.[389]

If ever there was a case to be made for six-track stereophonic sound or, for that matter, split screen, the $10 million *Grand Prix* would serve as best evidence. That it was made in Cinerama[390] 70mm was merely a bonus. Most roadshow movies start with an overture, a ten-minute or so musical introduction that thematically gives the audience some indication of where they are headed. Thrumming and roaring engines formed the montage opening (filmed and edited, incidentally, by George Lucas), a noise that almost shook a cinema to its foundations. Cinerama had been built on its ability to create almost primeval effects. There was always a downward rush, a runaway train, a roller coaster, something to set an audience on the edge of its seat in pure exhilaration. But the visual had nothing on the aural and what set *Grand Prix* apart was danger, that constant thrum of engines rising to impossible crescendos. Split screen allowed the director to tell several stories at once as competitors chased each other around perilous circuits at a time when death was a racing driver's constant companion. (In fact, of 32 professional participants including Graham Hill, Jim Clark and Jack Brabham,[391] five were dead within two years of the movie's completion.) Nobody needed to remind an audience how hazardous the sport was, they could read about the continuous carnage in the newspapers, but what was less easy to convey, although such events were well attended, was the pure thrill of being at a race meeting.

At nearly three hours long, *Grand Prix* had room to tell several stories and in that respect it was more of an ensemble picture than something like *Lawrence of Arabia* (1962) which took even more time to tell just one story. Many of these stories came to an abrupt end as the character died in an accident. Racing aficionados Steve McQueen and Paul Newman would have been the ideal candidates for the leading roles[392] but McQueen had a competing picture on the starting grid.[393] Burt Lancaster and Rock Hudson[394] were also considered before top billing went to James Garner, also a racer who did all his own driving in the film (though not necessarily at the speeds indicated). Motor racing was an international sport so other drivers were played by Frenchman Yves Montand (*The Wages of Fear*, 1953) and Italian Antonio Sabato,[395] with Adolfo Celi (*Thunderball*, 1965) as the Ferrari boss and Toshiro Mifune[396] (*Seven Samurai*, 1954) as a Japanese team owner. Swedish star Harriet Andersson (*Through a Glass Darkly*, 1961) was cast as the

Four actors made their debut in the picture as part of an MGM commitment to developing new talent—Françoise Hardy, Brian Bedford, Jessica Walters and Antonio Sabato, who was signed a six-picture deal (Hannan Collection).

female lead but dropped out in favor of Eva Marie Saint, a role also turned down by Monica Vitti.

Garner and Saint had previously worked together in the thriller *36 Hours* (1964). Although top billed, Garner did not have a consistent track record.[397] Saint's career had been as peripatetic after *Exodus* as before, star of *All Fall Down* (1962) but third-billed in *The Sandpiper* (1965) and second-billed in *The Russians Are Coming, The Russians Are Coming* (1966), the latter pair big hits. Frankenheimer, Saint's *All Fall Down* director, had enjoyed a distinguished career with *Birdman of Alcatraz* (1962), *The Manchurian Candidate* (1962) and *Seven Days in May* (1964) although his commercial reliability was tarnished by *The Train* (1964) and the thriller *Seconds* (1966).[398] *Grand Prix* was not only the biggest film of his career, but also his first in color. The movie was filmed on existing legendary circuits[399] with Formula 3 racing cars adapted to look like Formula 1 and a thousand other incidental details including an appearance by a Shelby Mustang (with Carroll Shelby as technical adviser)[400] that presented an accurate depiction of the sport. A total of 22 electronically controlled cameras were used to film the races.[401]

The narrative arc follows the Grand Prix season against a background of emotional turmoil wreaked on drivers and the wives and girlfriends living in the shadow of death. Garner, too reckless for the top spot in a racing team, bids for redemption by signing for a new company. Former world champion Montand is at career end. English actor Brian Bedford makes his mainstream movie debut as a driver recovering after a horrific crash caused by Garner. Subplots include Garner's affair with Bedford's wife (Jessica Walter), Montand's affair with journalist Saint and French actress Françoise Hardy (better known as a chanteuse) involved with Sabato. In addition, there are some telling sequences in which the drivers unload about their fears. Frankenheimer does a terrific job in marshaling all the effects and the minute details, and the fact that there is no big star in the mix makes the battles between the characters more realistic.

Critical reception: "Roaring, suspenseful, tremendous thrilling drama" (*Box Office*); "action-rammed adventure ... interesting cast of characters" (*Variety*); "the new, definitive film about auto racing" (*Washington Post*); "interest-arresting potential through the visual" (*Los Angeles Times*).[402]

Rentals: $9.5 million[403] (includes 1968 reissue) ($67.7 million equivalent)

59 (tie): *The Green Berets*

Starring John Wayne and David Janssen[404]; directed by John Wayne; screenplay, James Lee Barrett, from the book by Robin Moore; producer, Michael Wayne[405]; music, Miklos Rosza. Warner Brothers-Seven Arts. June 19, 1968.

As if John Wayne had not endured enough directing *The Alamo* (1960), he took on an even weightier task with this Vietnam War picture, which, from the start, was likely to receive a critical roasting given the actor's well-known stance on the conflict. Wayne had enjoyed a charmed life at the box office with three successive hit Westerns, *The Sons of Katie Elder* (1965) with Dean Martin, *The War Wagon* (1967) with Kirk Douglas and *El Dorado* (1967) with Robert Mitchum. Universal had originally agreed to fund *The Green Berets* and when they backed out, it shifted to Warner Brothers.[406] And as if not having learned anything from *The Alamo*, it was initially greenlit with an inappropriate budget of $5.1 million[407]—he was paid $120,000 for directing and his normal $750,000 plus percentage for acting, and co-director Ray Kellogg collected $40,000[408]—the final cost touching $7 million.[409]

Concerned that the picture was falling behind schedule, Warner Brothers drafted in veteran director Mervyn Leroy (*Little Caesar*, 1931) who had over 40 years in the business; his most recent picture was the thriller *Moment to Moment* (1966).[410] But exactly what he contributed over nearly six months on set was open to question. Some reports had him directing the scenes involving the star; others held that he was on hand to offer advice.[411] Even with his presence, the film came in 18 days over schedule—25 percent longer than planned.[412] It had been filmed in Georgia on five acres of government land around Fort Benning, and Wayne lost 15 pounds due to the pressure.[413] But the oppressive heat and weather of that location was nothing compared to the reviews. It was slated by the critics, with Wayne's age for an active commander called into question, never mind the parachuting, the gung-ho approach and the dalliance in nightclubs. "In terms of Wayne's directorial career," wrote biographer Scott Eyman, "*The Alamo* has many defenders, *The Green Berets* has none."[414] That assessment, of course, would be to ignore the global moviegoers who bought the tickets and put the picture into reasonable profit. Wayne was clear in his own mind about the kind of movie he was making—"about good against bad"[415]—and accommodated neither gray areas nor current attitudes to the war reflected in nationwide demonstrations.

It is virtually impossible to examine a movie like this without taking a political stance. Other war movies had been allowed considerable leeway regarding authenticity, audiences and critics alike appearing to understand that creating watchable drama often took precedence over facts. Both *The Deer Hunter* (1978) and *Apocalypse Now* (1979), considered the best of this small sub-genre, were criticized for venturing away from strict reality. With half a century to distance a contemporary viewer from those inflammatory times, it's worth a reappraisal. The film still divides critics and audiences. Although Rotten Tomatoes deems it an "exciting war film," the critics on this website gave it a 23 percent score against 61 percent from the audience. That contrasts, for example, with a more even split for *Exodus*—63 percent from critics and 69 percent from audiences. However, interestingly, *The Green Berets* attracted twice as much interest, totaling over 9000 votes compared to under-4300 for *Exodus*.

After this, Wayne's price went up to a million a picture—"he wasn't a guarantee of success, he was a guarantee against failure," said son Michael Wayne.[416] At this point in his career, he was gold-plated. Where other stars in his commercial league suffered the occasional box office lapse, Wayne did not.[417]

Critical reception: "Immoral" (*Glamour*); "rip-roaring Vietnam battle story ... but certainly not an intellectual piece" (*Motion Picture Exhibitor*); "cliché-ridden throwback" (*Hollywood Reporter*); "a filmmaker of truly monstrous ineptitude" (*New York Times*).[418]

Rentals: $9.5 million[419] ($67.7 million equivalent)

59 (tie): *That Darn Cat!*

Starring Hayley Mills and Dean Jones; directed by Robert Stevenson; screenplay, Gordon Gordon and Mildred Gordon; producers, Walt Disney, Bill Walsh and Ron W. Miller; music, Robert F. Brunner. Disney. December 2, 1965.

This marked the end of an era. It was the last hurrah (in a family film) for British child star Hayley Mills and it would be another quarter of a century before Hollywood produced another moppet with genuine box office appeal in Macauley Culkin.[420] Mills, on the cusp of adulthood, was something of a Disney mascot. Although the era of the child star in the Shirley Temple-Mickey Rooney-Margaret O'Brien vein was long gone, Mills enjoyed considerable success with *Pollyanna* (1960), *The Parent Trap* (1961), *In Search of the Castaways* (1962) and *Summer Magic* (1963). Her next three outings had involved more grown-up material: the drama *The Chalk Garden* (1964), the mystery *The Moon-Spinners* (1964) and the adventure *The Truth About Spring* (1965)—and there a was sense that her "cute" screen persona was coming to the end of its sell-by date. *That Darn Cat!* was the final burst of cuteness before taking off for more adult fare (and nudity) in *The Family Way* (1967). *That Darn Cat!* marked the Disney debut of actor Dean Jones who would become a Disney standby for the next few years.

When Walt Disney had problems attracting worthwhile stars to his movies in the 1950s, he turned to animals. At first he was content to observe, turning out nature documentaries like *The Living Desert* (1953) and *The African Lion* (1955) which, surprisingly, struck a box office chord. It did not take long for the producer to realize that a

The Films   85

live-action movie about an animal would not be so much more expensive. When *Old Yeller* (1957) proved a surprise box office hit, it provided the company with another template, admittedly heavy on sentiment, leading to *Greyfriars Bobby* (1961) and *Savage Sam* (1963).[421] The animal lead in these pictures had been dogs, but for *The Incredible Journey* (1963) Disney introduced a cat to the dog mix followed by a solo cat adventure, *The Three Lives of Thomasina* (1963).[422] *That Darn Cat!* was almost a merger of two successful Disney cycles: the child star and the feline movie.

The story is typically odd, matching a clever and appealing animal with a clever and appealing juvenile. The cat in question is Siamese and one night it returns with what Mills believes is a clue to a robbery-kidnapping. She informs the F.B.I. and agent Jones decides to track the cat to find the hostage while Mills determines to play her part, unintentionally getting in the way of the investigation. This triggers a whole set of misunderstandings and situational comedy while the sinuous cat acts like a lure for the audience. In true Disney style, it's pretty inventive stuff, built on a wild concept, with some comedy targets too obvious to miss (Jones is allergic to cats). Mills, as ever, is watchable throughout. It's not hilarious and it's not particularly tense but following the cat sets some kind of hypnotic tone. As a barometer of public taste in comedies, it is worthwhile pointing out that in the annual box office rankings, it finished higher than *The Russians Are Coming* and *Lt. Robin Crusoe, U.S.N.* as well as the more expensive spy spoofs *The Silencers* and *Our Man Flint*.

Critical reception: "A typical product of the giant Disney flapdoodle factory" (*New Yorker*); "an entertaining picture" (*New York Times*); "dandy Christmas present" (*Washington Post*); "content to settle for a series of gags" (*Los Angeles Times*).[423]

Rentals: $9.5 million[424] ($67.7 million equivalent)

58: *The Russians Are Coming, The Russians Are Coming*

Starring Carl Reiner, Eva Marie Saint and Alan Arkin; directed and produced by Norman Jewison; screenplay, William Rose, from novel *The Off-Islanders* by Nathaniel Benchley; music, Johnny Mandel. United Artists. May 25, 1966.

Before he pulled out plums like the Oscar-nominated *In the Heat of the Night* (1967), the slick thriller *The Thomas Crown Affair* (1968) and the musical *Fiddler on the Roof* (1971), Canadian director Norman Jewison seemed stuck in a comedy rut. After a decade in TV, first at the Canadian Broadcast Commission and then in America, he made his movie debut with *40 Pounds of Trouble* (1962) starring Tony Curtis in typical lightweight form and followed up with a Doris Day double, *The Thrill of It All* (1963) with James Garner and her final pairing with Rock Hudson in *Send Me No Flowers* (1964)—plus another dalliance with Garner in *The Art of Love* (1965). The Steve McQueen starrer *The Cincinnati Kid* (1965)[425] might have indicated he had other genres in mind, but *The Russians Are Coming, The Russians Are Coming* immediately refuted that notion. Based on Nathaniel Benchley's 1961 novel *The Off-Islanders*, the movie took four years to reach the screen as producer Walter Mirisch waited for a break in Jewison's busy schedule.[426] The delay turned to the film's advantage because by that time, the Cold War was at its peak. The story concerns a Russian submarine[427] that accidentally goes aground off New England, sparking a hostile reaction. In the same way as *In the Heat of the Night* is more than a murder mystery, so *The Russians Are Coming, The Russians Are Coming* is as much social comment as comedy.

The movie did not ignite Arkin's career. He said, "I received five or six offers ... mostly what I'd call Jack Lemmon rejects"* (Hannan Collection).

*Austen, David, "After Alan Arkin," *Films and Filming*, November 1967, 4-7.

The Films   87

Perhaps as unusual as the film's approach was the casting: comedian Carl Reiner in his first starring role and movie debuts for Alan Arkin and John Phillip Law. That there was any marquee name in the cast only came about because Felicia Farr (wife of Jack Lemmon) dropped out and was replaced by Eva Marie Saint.[428] Despite being a mainstay of innovative TV comedy via *Your Show of Shows* and the "2000 Year Old Man" routine with Mel Brooks, Reiner was nobody's idea of a leading man. When he created what was to become *The Dick Van Dyke Show*, it was with the intention of being its star, but CBS rejected the notion.

On the basis of a supporting role in *The Art of Love*, Reiner was selected to play the top-billed part of the writer at whose house the Russians, led by Arkin, unexpectedly arrive. Arkin had made some impact on Broadway. Comedy was a departure for Saint, better known for *On the Waterfront* (1954), *North by Northwest* (1959), *Exodus* (1960) and *The Sandpiper* (1965).

The Russians take Reiner and family hostage but are spotted stealing a car. Before long, wild rumors depict them as an invasion force. Misunderstandings propel the rest of the plot until finally there is a standoff between the submarine and the islanders, resolved when foreigners and locals unite to rescue a small child. After the situation has been sorted out, the Air Force arrives, but the submariners are saved by being surrounded by a flotilla of small boats. The Russians are revealed as human, wishing to avoid conflict, with similar outlooks on life, with love (Law falling for Reiner's daughter) filling any other gaps. Reiner and Arkin deliver sparkling performances, the latter's baffling accent a piece of comedy in itself. Screenwriter William Rose was responsible for *It's a Mad Mad Mad Mad World* (1963) and repeats that slapstick formula with the addition of quips and barbs. Never were so many laughs derived from community outrage. The political message is dated now, but the comedy is everlasting.

Critical reception: "Refreshingly witty comedy" (*Washington Post*); "astonishingly inventive" (*Los Angeles Times*); "rousingly funny and perceptive" (*New York Times*); "an unfunny big farce" (*New Yorker*).[429]

Rentals: $9.775 million[430] ($69.6 million equivalent)

57: *Casino Royale*[431]

Starring Peter Sellers, David Niven, Orson Welles and Woody Allen; directed by John Huston, Ken Hughes, Robert Parrish, Val Guest and Joe McGrath[432]; screenplay, Wolf Mankowitz, John Law and Michael Sayers, based (loosely) on the novel by Ian Fleming; producer, Charles K. Feldman[433]; music, Burt Bacharach. Columbia. April 13, 1967 (London); U.S.: April 28, 1967.

It was not so much interlopers like Derek Flint and Matt Helm who rained on the James Bond box office parade, but the spy spoof *Casino Royale*, released two months before *You Only Live Twice*. The budget exceeded that of any Bond, it spawned two hit singles,[434] accommodated five directors,[435] seven Bonds including four females, and around a dozen writers. And in an era when an all-star cast usually meant a couple of top names and others well past their sell-by date, *Casino Royale* has a cast to die for.[436] It was only confusing if you took it seriously. Former agent turned producer Charles K. Feldman, who had struck gold with *What's New Pussycat?* by taking the oddball approach to comedy, was convinced he could repeat a winning formula.

88　　　　　　　　　　　　　　The Films

The plot was as outlandish as any in the real series. David Niven as the original Bond comes out of retirement to combat SMERSH, whose female agents line up to seduce him. Promoted to M, Niven comes up with the diabolical scheme of renaming all his agents "James Bond" in order to confuse the enemy and sets up a training program to prevent them being seduced. The usual Bond elements—biological warfare, casino, gadgets, underground headquarters, imminent atom bomb explosion—are given comic twists. Bad guys have good gadgets, the usually decorative Bond girls now mostly all have serious intent while the villains provide the arm candy (including Alexandra Bastedo, Angela Scoular and Gabriella Lucidi). Le Chiffre (Orson Welles) steals from his own organization, whose deadly mission is to make all women beautiful and kill tall men, and the countdown to Armageddon is accompanied by hiccups. Almost all producer Feldman retained from the novel are characters such as Le Chiffre and Vesper Lynd while the screenwriters conjured up the likes of Mata Bond, daughter of Mata Hari.

Where Flint and Helm were more in the way of imitators, this was a serious send-up of the Bond malarkey, tempting audiences to enjoy a farrago of in-jokes. Despite the overload, it pretty much works once you get into the swing of it, and very much these days verges on the cult. On the other hand, if you wanted to take it apart, that was also easily accomplished. After Niven, the other pseudo–Bonds are Peter Sellers as an ace baccarat player, Woody Allen (secretly the head of SMERSH), British actor Terence Cooper,[437] Barbara Bouchet[438] (aka Miss Moneypenny), Ursula Andress,[439] Joanna Pettet (Mata Bond) and Daliah Lavi. Deborah Kerr and Jacqueline Bisset are agents on the wrong side and there are cameos by William Holden, Charles Boyer, John Huston, George Raft and Jean-Paul Belmondo.[440] As with *What's New Pussycat?*, Woody Allen tries to steal the picture.

It proved a fair candidate for the most chaotic picture ever made. Sellers—on a $750,000 salary—insisted his friend Joe McGrath direct. But when their relationship ended in a fistfight, McGrath quit.[441] Feldman replaced him, more or less, with everyone who was available, so that different directors were filming different segments on the insane assumption that their portions could all be edited together. They couldn't, at least initially, the studio hacking Feldman's first cut by 50 minutes.[442] The original script was by Hollywood veteran Ben Hecht, but he died before filming started. Sellers called in Terry Southern (*Dr. Strangelove*, 1964) to rewrite his dialogue.[443] Then it turned into a screenwriting free-for-all.[444] There was even an extra producer, Jerry Bresler, appearing out of the blue. Who did what[445] and how much each director contributed[446] became an aficionado's parlor game.

Columbia expected the worst and there were no advance press screenings. Reviews appeared regardless. Audiences ignored disparaging reviews to the extent that *Casino Royale* finished third in the annual box office race, beaten only by *You Only Live Twice* and *The Dirty Dozen*. But the very presence of *Casino Royale* clearly impacted on the Bond film's revenues.

Critical reception: "Reckless, disconnected nonsense" (*New York Times*); "an incoherent and vulgar vaudeville" (*Time*); "possibly the most indulgent film ever made" (*Chicago Sun-Times*).[447]

Rentals: $10.2 million ($72.7 equivalent)

55 (tie): *Oliver!*

Starring Ron Moody, Oliver Reed and Mark Lester; directed by Carol Reed; screenplay, Vernon Harris, based on the musical by Lionel Bart and *Oliver Twist* by Charles Dickens; producer, John Woolf; music and lyrics, Lionel Bart. Columbia roadshow. September 26, 1968 (London); U.S.: December 11, 1968.

After the double whammy of *My Fair Lady* (1964) and *The Sound of Music* (1965), the 70mm roadshow musical was pronounced a potential gold mine, studios pumping tens of millions of dollars into follow-ups. But that only lasted until the fall-out from disasters like Twentieth Century–Fox's *Doctor Dolittle* (1967), Disney's *The Happiest Millionaire* (1967) and Paramount's *Half a Sixpence* (1967). Columbia had other reasons to worry about its forthcoming *Oliver!* For a start, it was British and, as proven by *Half a Sixpence*,[448] the British could not make commercial musicals. The biggest film musicals had effectively auditioned on Broadway, length of run an accurate gauge to screen success. The dozen musicals clocking up 1000-plus performances on Broadway did not include *Oliver!* Despite a record seven-year run in London,[449] on Broadway *Oliver!* enjoyed half the run of *The Sound of Music* and a quarter of *My Fair Lady*.[450] And there was no recognizable star. Columbia reportedly pursued Peter Sellers, Peter O'Toole, Richard Burton, Elizabeth Taylor[451] and Julie Andrews without success.[452] On the other hand, the fact that the production was being filmed in Britain without a major name in the cast kept the budget down to a tolerable $10 million.

Ron Moody was cast as Fagin. He had played the role in London's West End so was held in some esteem by British musical aficionados but not on Broadway, so he was an unknown to American audiences. Oliver Reed as Bill Sykes was at the start of his mainstream career and was, coincidentally, the nephew of director Carol Reed. The rest of the cast members were unknowns: Mark Lester as Oliver Twist, Jack Wild as the Artful Dodger and Shani Wallis[453] as Nancy. Oscar winner Hugh Griffith had a small part; singer-comedian Harry Secombe, who played a supporting role, was a well-known British celebrity.

Carol Reed was not first choice. Lewis Gilbert (*Alfie*, 1966) had begun writing the screenplay with Vernon Harris, working on the project for several years before being blocked by Paramount, with whom he had signed a new contract,[454] and which had assigned him Harold Robbins' *The Adventurers*.[455] Gilbert had been involved in the sets, choreography, musical arrangements and casting so that another director could logically step in, advising the producers to look no further than Carol Reed. When eventually Reed came on board, Gilbert had to sign an agreement removing his name from the screenplay.[456] Reed had no background in musicals and a bad experience of big-budget roadshows—sacked from *Mutiny on the Bounty* (1962) and unable to turn *The Agony and the Ecstasy* (1965) into a commercial prospect. However, *Oliver!* was in more than capable hands. Producer John Woolf's output included *The African Queen* (1951), *Room at the Top* (1958), *The L-Shaped Room* (1962) and *Life at the Top* (1965).

The story follows the original Charles Dickens template with songs thrown in at intervals. Orphan Oliver Twist runs away from the man who has purchased him from the workhouse and ends up with gang of pickpockets. Wrongly accused of stealing a wallet, he is taken in by his accuser and enjoys a better life before being snatched back by the gang and rescued again. The film worked because the director paid as much attention to the drama as the songs. Lester is both believable and cute as the orphan, Moody

In the U.S. the soundtrack was certified gold and sold 140,000 copies in Britain. A glossy color souvenir program sold in the thousands to people attending the roadshow. In addition, there was a coffee table book, a 189-page hardback novelization, not of the original Dickens novel, but of the screenplay, and packed with photographs.* Trade press advertisement (*Kine Weekly*, April 19, 1969, 11).

*Holston, *Movie Roadshows*, 229-230.

creepy, and Oliver Reed exudes a sense of menace. But it is as feel-good a movie as *The Sound of Music*, charming and exhilarating, a genuine film for all the family at a time when Hollywood was moving in other directions. It also had instantly hummable songs ("Food, Glorious, Food," "Consider Yourself," "You've Got to Pick a Pocket or Two") and some terrific choreography such as that accompanying "Who Will Buy?" as a whole street bursts into early morning life. You would have to be extremely churlish not to warm to it. Nominated for 11 Oscars, it collected six including Best Picture and Best Director and a rare Honorary Award recognizing the choreographic achievement of Onna White.

Critical reception: "Nearly universal entertainment" (*Chicago Sun-Times*); "tuneful, joyous heart-tugging entertainment" (*International Motion Picture Exhibitor*); "they'll want more of *Oliver!*" (*Daily Mail*); "a film you'll want to see twice" (*Sunday Mirror*); "much much more than a musical" (*Guardian*).[457]

Rentals: $10.5 million[458] ($74.8 million equivalent)

55 (tie): *Goodbye, Columbus*

Starring Richard Benjamin and Ali MacGraw; director Larry Peerce; screenplay, Arnold Schulman, from the novella by Philip Roth; producer, Stanley R. Jaffe; music, Charles Fox. Paramount. April 3, 1969.

The traditional young-love, rite-of-passage picture was given a twist by arriving in the middle of Hollywood's reaction to the lifting of the Production Code, allowing greater sexual expression. That *Goodbye, Columbus'* two main characters inhabited different sides of the class divide permitted the kind of social commentary much beloved at that time. Setting those two elements aside, it was an old-fashioned love story introducing two new stars to the Hollywood firmament, even though neither was that young: She was 30, he a year older. A late developer as a model, Ali MacGraw was given a leg up in the movie world by her romance with Robert Evans, then heading Paramount. Richard Benjamin's background was television and had just completed a starring role with wife Paula Prentiss in the TV series *He & She* (1967–1968), for which both were Emmy-nominated.

The biggest initial marketing tool for the movie was the source material: a novella by Philip Roth, then the most controversial literary figure in America after publishing earlier in the year the #1 bestseller *Portnoy's Complaint*, whose main theme was sexuality. However, once the producers saw what they had captured on film, the marketeers subverted contractual agreements by plastering MacGraw's face across the advertising posters with a photo of top-billed Benjamin crammed into a postage-stamp space.

Benjamin plays a Jewish librarian who meets upper-class Jewish university graduate MacGraw at a country club where her family enjoys membership while he is a guest. Their sexual relationship is complicated by her feelings of entitlement, her ignorance of birth control, resistance by her parents, and their different outlooks on life. What begins as sweet romance soon turns sour and when she returns to college, they split up. The book was essentially a satire of the rich family but in the movie it turns into a clash of lifestyles, traditional working-class vs. the pretensions of the *nouveau riche*. Sometimes the humor is biting and other times softer, more observant. While covering similar territory to *The Graduate* (1967), it is often funnier since it ventures further into family relationships and parental expectation than the Mike Nichols film. In keeping with the times, there was fleeting nudity which also, in keeping with the times, tended to encourage ticket sales. While Benjamin lacks the acting ability and appeal of Dustin Hoffman, MacGraw possesses a far more accessible screen persona than Katharine Ross. This was an era that gave birth to a number of new stars and few so instantly lit up the screen as MacGraw while Benjamin, somewhat in the nerdy Hoffman mold, had plenty to offer. MacGraw, especially, had a freshness that came as much as anything from not spending her early life beating down the doors of Hollywood.

The two stars apart, *Goodbye, Columbus* certainly rode the zeitgeist and, perhaps as much as *Easy Rider* (1969), proved that a low-budget film[459] with attractive characters could hit it big. It was certainly, and remains so, perfectly likable. The movie only received one Oscar nomination, for the Arnold Schulman screenplay, but it was no surprise that MacGraw won the Golden Globe Award for the Most Promising Newcomer. Director Larry Peerce's previous three films could not have more varied content: the art-house drama *One Potato, Two Potato* (1964), the concert film *The Big TNT Show* (1966) and the low-budget thriller *The Incident* (1967).

Critical reception: "A thing of real and unusual pleasure" (*New York Times*); "cast-wise the feature excels" (*Variety*); "a pastiche of all the trends that run rampart in film-making today" (*Films and Filming*).[460]

Rentals: $10.5 million ($74.8 million equivalent)

54: *The Great Race*

Starring Jack Lemmon, Tony Curtis and Natalie Wood; directed by Blake Edwards; screenplay, Arthur A. Ross; producer, Martin Jurow; music, Henry Mancini. Warner Brothers roadshow. July 1, 1965.

Where trends go, Hollywood follows. The colossal success of Stanley Kramer's *It's a Mad Mad Mad Mad World* (1963) sent studios looking for a me-too version of madcap comedy on a roadshow scale. Most comedies came in 90- or 120-minute packages, but Kramer's was a whopping three hours–plus and apart from 1960's *Pepe*, which was more of a comedy-musical, none of them ended up in roadshow. Screenwriter Arthur A. Ross (*Creature from the Black Lagoon*, 1954) had spent most of the 1960s in television: *Dr. Kildare, The Alfred Hitchcock Hour,* etc. But he also wrote the Harold Lloyd movie compilation *World of Comedy* (1962); and when he came up with the idea of revisiting slapstick on the big screen with a tale that hung on old motor cars, it ended up in the hands of Laurel and Hardy fan Blake Edwards. Edwards was the king of comedy after the Inspector Clouseau pair *The Pink Panther* and *A Shot in the Dark*.[461] United Artists, which had made both, believed Edwards the "spiritual heir to Billy Wilder."[462] When the budget topped $6 million, UA pulled out in favor of Warner Brothers.[463] Possibly if WB had realized the budget would double, they might also have passed. Instead, they reunited *Some Like It Hot* pair Tony Curtis and Jack Lemmon and teamed them with Natalie Wood, who had a brief affair on set with Curtis.[464] Lemmon had greater box office traction, his last five films grossing over $60 million (gross, not rentals).[465] Edwards had directed Curtis in *Operation Petticoat* and Lemmon in *Days of Wine and Roses* (1962) and had a production deal with Lemmon.[466] Wood and Curtis starred in *Sex and the Single Girl* (1964). Wood had been the decade's first proper new star following an

The Films 93

Initially, Curtis was paid $125,000 while Lemmon and Wood earned $100,000 but agent "Swifty" Lazar argued this was unfair, and the other two in the end received the same as Curtis.* (Hannan Collection)

*Curtis, *American Prince*, 249-250.

Oscar-nominated performance in *Splendor in the Grass* (1961), after which she was topbilled in the musicals *West Side Story* (1961) and *Gypsy* (1962) and above Steve McQueen in *Love with the Proper Stranger* (1963). But she had had her fill of comedies and musicals and wanted to continue doing drama,[467] so she was enticed into *The Great Race* with the promise of *Inside Daisy Clover* (1965).[468] The ever-increasing budget—first to $8 million, then $10 million,[469] topping out at $12 million[470]—caused Edwards to be fired and then reinstated.[471]

Nominally, the story concerned a road race from New York to Paris (emulating a real one in 1908) with the competitors, obviously, in antique cars, but in reality it was an excuse to create the biggest-ever slapstick extravaganza, clocking in at two hours and 40 minutes. The competitors are melodrama surrogates, the bad guy Professor Fate (Lemmon) dressed in black complete with black mustache, sidekick Maximilian (Peter Falk) just as nasty. The good guy, "The Great Leslie" (Curtis), sports an all-white ensemble. Wood is a photojournalist driving a car entered by a newspaper. Along the way, Curtis and Wood become romantically embroiled. But primarily it is an excuse for over-the-top set pieces including a spectacular four-minute pie fight involving 4000 pies, a barroom brawl and scenes set in a sheik's tent and a mad scientist's laboratory, plus a bunch of sight gags with further humor deriving from double entendres.

Since the movie had nothing to offer in the way of social comment and, worse, was attempting to emulate the sacred cows of the silent era, critics gave it a hard time, but audiences came out in droves. However, it had a rival in the comedy race department, the antique airplane spectacular roadshow *Those Magnificent Men in Their Flying Machines* (1965), which had appeared six months earlier and took a chunk out of its box office potential and perhaps to an extent sated audience interest in this mini-genre. There is no question that Edwards achieved what he set out to do and the slapstick is truly breathtaking while the whole enterprise works a treat.

Critical reception: "Bumps along very pleasantly for the most part" (*Life*); "frequently garners belly laughs" (*Variety*); "one of the zaniest and most thrilling comedies of all time" (*Box Office*).[472]

Rentals: $10.8 million[473] ($76.9 million equivalent)

53: *In the Heat of the Night*

Starring Rod Steiger and Sidney Poitier; directed by Norman Jewison; screenplay, Stirling Silliphant, based on the novel by John Ball[474]; producer, Walter Mirisch; music, Quincy Jones. United Artists. August 2, 1967.

The success of *Lilies of the Field* and *A Patch of Blue* did not result in studios rushing to offer Sidney Poitier top-billing in major, big-budget pictures even though the latter commercially overshadowed anything in the last three years from the more highly remunerated Steve McQueen, Cary Grant, Jack Lemmon, Peter Sellers, Burt Lancaster and Kirk Douglas. The best that could be said about Poitier's "progress" in the industry was that he had been given a role in *Duel at Diablo* (1966) originally intended for a white man, but even then was second-billed to James Garner, who he outranked at the box office. He was forced to go to Britain for his next starring role and that had been in the cards for two years.[475] What exactly Hollywood was missing was spelled out in no uncertain terms during his 1967 "annus mirabilis" of *To Sir, with Love, In the Heat of the Night* and *Guess Who's Coming to Dinner,* all dealing with issues of race and tearing the box office apart.

Poitier had brought the John Ball novel *In the Heat of the Night* to the attention of producer Walter Mirisch,[476] one of Hollywood's biggest independents.[477] The bulk of Poitier's top-billed experiences had been low-budget and that remained surprisingly true of *In the Heat of the Night*. Even with director Norman Jewison, hot after *The Russians Are Coming, The Russians Are Coming*, a top producer in Mirisch (*Hawaii*, 1966), and backed by United Artists, the budget was just $2.09 million,[478] with a 41-day schedule on the grounds that the subject would restrict bookings in the Deep South, thus limiting box office potential.[479] Poitier received $200,000 plus a hefty 20 percent of profits.[480]

Poitier's biggest-ever payday. He had earned $200,000 from *The Bedford Incident* (1965), plus another $200,000 in deferred profits; $80,000 plus 10 percent of the profits from *A Patch of Blue* (1965); and was offered $250,000 for a role in *Doctor Dolittle*, in which he never appeared.* Trade press advertisement *(Box Office,* February 5, 1968, 70).

*Harris, Mark, *Scenes from a Revolution,* 81, 158, 159.

George C. Scott was lined up to play redneck Sheriff Bill Gillespie until he opted instead for Broadway.[481] Rod Steiger, largely disdained by mainstream Hollywood,[482] primarily a supporting actor (*Doctor Zhivago*, 1965) except for *The Pawnbroker* (1964) and the Pope biopic *A Man Called John* (1965), stepped in. Enticed away by *Grand Prix*, screenwriter Robert Alan Aurthur handed over to Stirling Silliphant (*The Slender Thread*),[483] the most prolific writer in the industry, though mostly, at that point, for television, from which he had become a millionaire.[484] Warren Oates and blacklisted Lee Grant had supporting roles.[485] Quincy Jones (*The Pawnbroker*) composed the score.

Several aspects of the novel were tweaked. For a start, in the original, Tibbs was "a polite, chatty Pasadena police officer who passes through a town ... and stays to help solve the crime."[486] The murder victim, originally a musician, became a factory developer, thus creating a conflict between conservative forces and economically empowered progressives inclined to push for racial equality. The setting shifted from South Carolina to Mississippi. Tibbs no longer hailed from Arizona but Philadelphia.[487] The town changed from Wells to Sparta.[488] Instead of Ball's tall, lean sheriff,[489] the shorter Steiger bulked out his shape by 20 pounds. The script also eliminated much institutional bigotry.[490] "We didn't want our movie to seem like a polemic," said Mirisch.[491] For the sake of authenticity, the director wanted to shoot in the South, but Poitier refused, anticipating a repeat of the harassment he had endured when visiting Mississippi with Harry Belafonte.[492]

Although racism is significant, the story pivots on the constant friction between detective and sheriff. Virgil Tibbs is a suspect because he happens to be in the vicinity. When revealed as a top detective, Gillespie is duty-bound to enlist his help. In a character-driven tale, Tibbs and Gillespie develop respect for each other. Poitier has such a screen authority that it takes huge acting effort from Steiger to match him. But the screenplay also shows Gillespie as put-upon, wifeless, childless and lonely. And there is enough classic detection to ensure the mystery is more than a prop to highlight racial inequality. Tibbs establishes crucial clues to the murderer's identity. In the dynamic scene where Tibbs slaps back an irate racist plantation owner, it is the sheriff who comes to the rescue, as he does later in the picture when Tibbs is surrounded by a mob. Despite endless examples of incipient and obvious racism, it is ironic that the murder is committed for the oldest of sins, getting a girl pregnant and needing to steal money for an abortion.

Poitier and Steiger are both superb, the latter perhaps getting the edge because his character undergoes more change. Jewison shows a remarkable dramatic dexterity given that the bulk of his work up to this point had been comedy and Silliphant, stripping everything away to the bone,[493] devised a lean screenplay. While it was never a candidate for roadshow, the producers gave it an almighty splash by opening at New York's 1500-seat Capitol. Nominated for seven Oscars, it won five including Best Picture, Rod Steiger as Best Actor and Best Editing by future director Hal Ashby (*Harold and Maude*, 1971). In a decade where politics reached a new public crescendo, this was one of the best adverts for the role Hollywood could play in bringing issues to the forefront while at the same time not denying audiences dramatic entertainment.

Critical reception: "Poitier ... gets a rare opportunity to demonstrate the full sweep of his power" (*Newsweek*); "fantasy of racial reconciliation" (*Village Voice*); "spurious air of concern" (*New Yorker*); "an excellent Sidney Poitier performance and an outstanding one by Rod Steiger overcome some noteworthy flaws" (*Variety*).[494]

Rentals: $10.9 million[495] ($77.6 million equivalent)

52: *Midnight Cowboy*

Starring Dustin Hoffman and Jon Voight; directed by John Schlesinger; screenplay, Waldo Salt, from the novel by James Leo Herlihy; producer, Jerome Hellman; music, John Barry.[496] United Artists. May 25, 1969.

When a new Production Code[497] was introduced on November 1, 1968,[498] Hollywood studios decided that the "R" for 16-year-olds accompanied by an adult was the

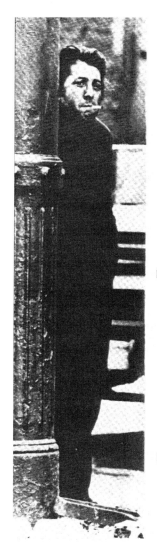

"Certain themes attract me and solitude is certainly one of them," said Schlesinger. "In the case of Joe Buck we are asking an audience to identify with a character in search of his particular ill-founded fantasy ... into the underbelly of New York with all its horrors."* Trade press advertisement (*Kine Weekly*, October 11, 1969, 2).

*Gow, Gordon, "A Buck for Joe," *Films and Filming*, November 1969, 4-8.

acceptable limit, avoiding like the plague the more stringent "X." That category was for peddlers of pornography[499] or used as a marketing device for arthouse imports like *I Am Curious (Yellow)*. The main obstacles to wider acceptance of the "X" were the ordinary exhibitor who rejected these films outright, local censors[500] and newspapers which refused to carry advertising for such films.[501] With its lesbian theme, Robert Aldrich's *The Killing of Sister George* (1968) was the first mainstream Hollywood picture to run afoul of the new regulations,[502] being censored locally and damaging the box office.[503] Even so, United Artists refused to cut *Midnight Cowboy* to achieve an "R."[504] Although the company later claimed the "X" was self-imposed to ensure nobody was misled, that was not what was reported at the time. The makers had expected to be awarded an "R" but when the ratings board classified it "X,"[505] United Artists refused to cut it.[506]

In some respects, it could afford to. Costs had been kept down to $3.2 million so if denied wider release it might, given the ensuing controversy and publicity barrage, play long enough in arthouses to make a profit. UA gambled that a movie by Oscar-nominated director John Schlesinger, featuring *The Graduate* (1967) star Dustin Hoffman and distributed by a respectable company, could beat the odds. After all, during the current decade, UA epitomized quality, attaining the height of artistic achievement as judged by its peers with four Best Picture Awards: *The Apartment* (1960), *West Side Story* (1961), *Tom Jones* (1963) and *In the Heat of the Night* (1967)[507]—more than any other studio. UA embarked on a risky strategy of early previews for critics; if it backfired, moral outrage could dent the movie's prospects. The mostly positive critical reaction prompted journalists to take the ratings system to task in bracketing *Midnight Cowboy* with "a tasteless piece of filmed trash."[508]

Following the template set down by other small films seeking a commercial breakout, *Midnight Cowboy* was launched at the 598-seat semi-arthouse Coronet in New York (but on the East Side, not Broadway), where "house full" notices could be more easily achieved. After the requisite lines around the block indicating record business,[509] the next concern was whether the box office would grow beyond the sophisticated market into provincial cities.[510] So the studio simply delayed release until "feed-out" (reviews) could reach the sticks and exhibitors could salivate over New York's record grosses.[511] In July, it launched in a further seven cities to fulsome reviews and by August, now in 49 venues, racked up terrific grosses.[512] Even the feared National Catholic Office for Motion Pictures considered that mature audiences would find it "a rewarding experience."[513] Many pictures had centered around sad sacks—Jerry Lewis made a career out of them— but none with the intense realism displayed here in which "pathetic Texas boob" (Jon Voight) joins forces with a "lower depths hustler" (Dustin Hoffman).[514] Each is ruthlessly exploitative without realizing how exploited both are. It is the American Dream turned desperately upside down with no safety net and spiraling out of control.

British director Schlesinger, originally specializing in documentaries, came to prominence in his homeland with the dramas *A Kind of Loving* (1962) and *Billy Liar* (1963) before turning out a coruscating analysis of "Swinging London" with his box office hit *Darling* (1965), which won an Oscar for Julie Christie and a nomination for himself. The follow-up literary adaptation *Far from the Madding Crowd* (1967),[515] also with Christie, did not fly. So it was a surprise when he resurfaced two years later intent on tackling a different slice of life in *Midnight Cowboy*. It was as much a surprise to find Hoffman as its star. He had struggled to find another fit after *The Graduate*, considered a one-hit wonder by Hollywood, with only the Italian crime comedy *Madigan's Million* (1968)[516] and a supporting role in one episode of a TV series to show for his endeavor. He had to audition for *Midnight Cowboy* with Mike Nichols advising him against the role. Jon Voight had no movie credibility, just second billing in the low-budget flop *Fearless Frank* (1967), a bit part in *Hour of the Gun* (1967) and a leading role in the unreleased *Out of It* (1969).[517] James Leo Herlihy's[518] 1965 novel was considered too controversial for Hollywood. Screenwriter Waldo Salt (*The Flame and the Arrow*, 1950) had been blacklisted, not resuming duties until *Taras Bulba* (1962).

The story is deceptively slight, exploring previously unforeseen lifestyles but, like *In the Heat of the Night*, essentially a study of two characters who come to respect each other. Schlesinger set out to make a film "about loneliness and elusion; it is about the emergence of some sort of human dignity from degradation." Voight is the cocky Texan wannabe gigolo who ends up as bait for the opposite gender. Although starving and living rough, Hoffman presents himself as street smart and cons his new acquaintance. As Voight fails at his chosen occupation, he accepts Hoffman's offer to live in a condemned building and their co-dependent relationship grows. Voight experiments with drugs and attends a wild society party. As Hoffman's health declines, Voight steals to buy tickets to take him to Florida but Hoffman dies on the bus. Improvisation helped the two actors find their characters.[519] In other hands, it would have been mawkishly sentimental. Schlesinger turns it into an exploration of an unforgiving disintegrating society with a rawer attitude to sexuality than hitherto. The two actors are quite extraordinary, Voight's cocksure exterior vanishing as he discovers the loser inside, the crippled Hoffman pulling the audience into a terrible world where despite abject poverty, he still has principles, refusing to work as a shoeshine boy, refusing medical help and in one glorious scene demanding dignity from his fellow man: *I'm walkin' here!*" he rages when a cab nearly mows him down crossing a street. It's possibly the most beautifully played picture about human degradation ever put on the screen.

It won Best Picture with Schlesinger named Best Director. Salt picked up Best Screenplay. The two principals were nominated for Best Actor and Sylvia Miles in the Supporting Actress category. The ratings board re-rated the film in 1971 as "R."

Critical reception: "Compassionate brutally touching love story about two men" (*Box Office*); "brilliant, uncompromising and shocking because it has the ring of truth" (*International Motion Picture Exhibitor*)[520]; "ultimately moving experience" (*New York Times*); "a masterpiece" (*New York Post*).[521]

Rentals: $11 million[522] ($78.4 million equivalent)

51: *The Absent Minded Professor*

Starring Fred MacMurray and Nancy Olson; directed by Robert Stevenson; screenplay, Bill Walsh, based on the novel "A Situation of Gravity" by Samuel W. Taylor; producers, Walt Disney and Bill Walsh; music, George Bruns. Disney. March 16, 1961.

It's probably escaped most people's notice that Walt Disney was a master of comedy. If you remember him for *Snow White and the Seven Dwarfs* (1937) and *Fantasia* (1940), you will see him as a conjurer of fabulous animated fantasy. But actually for most of his four decades as a producer, his forte was comedy. He called humor his "sixth sense." "What I've learned about the nature of fun," he said, "has come largely from the adventures of Mickey Mouse, Donald Duck, Pluto, Goofy and other members of our cartoon family and how their antics have been received by audiences."[523] He learned about comedy, too, from observing animals in the *True-Life Adventure* series, an early example of fly-on-the-wall reality documentary.

Disney came to reinvent his company with the "Udult" concept in the early 1960s; he relied in the main on comedy. *The Absent Minded Professor* was the first of the live-action pictures that went out under that brand at the start of the decade.

Definition of absent-minded: a professor who forgets to attend his own wedding—for the third time. There was no reason for audiences to suddenly take to innocuous single-concept comedies like this except that hitherto Disney had not made them.

Walt Disney called humor his sixth sense. "I'm presumed to know a lot about humor," he commented, "because I've been dealing it out in one form or another over a quarter of a century. The live animals in our 'True-Life Adventure' films have added much to our lore of laughter. For the need to clown seems to permeate all nature"* (pressbook).

*Disney, Walt, "Humour: My Sixth Sense," *Films and Filming*, November 1966, 8.

Most Hollywood comedies were about (mostly romantic) relationships whereas Disney tended to take a single outlandish idea and run with it. And it is generally forgotten that in order for films like this to generate such large box office, they had to win the approval of adults (not just parents) as well as children. Even with the encroachment of TV, movies were still mass entertainment at this point in the decade, not split by age or class. It is highly likely that this film commanded the same audience as those who rushed out to see the more sophisticated *Some Like It Hot* and *The Apartment* despite later historians deciding they should be more discerning.

Fred MacMurray was the unlikeliest of the previous Hollywood A-team to take the Disney coin but his career was drifting; and continuing with the likes of his offensive supporting role in *The Apartment* could damage his burgeoning TV career. The tale's origins date back to a 1943 sci-fi short story by Samuel L. Taylor. Disney was not expecting a financial bonanza, so it was filmed in black-and-white at a time when color dominated. Professor Brainard (MacMurray) invents flying rubber (Flubber) and the audience sits back and enjoys the consequences and that's as far as the central plank of the story goes. The results of his experiment include a car that flies, shoes for basketball players that allow them to out-jump opponents and balls that disappear out of sight. Brainard's excitement at his invention pushes his fiancée (Nancy Olson) to the back of his mind, leaving her prey to others. Enemies want to steal his invention which has potential as a weapon.

For once, critics were kind, with *Variety* spot-on with its assessment of the film's "infectious absurdity." That it was a one-joke picture did not deter the public and it was the second most popular film of its year and spawned sequel *Son of Flubber* two years later.

Critical reception: "Directed in a broad Mack Sennett–like fashion which will have audiences howling" (*Box Office*); "persuades fantasy and familiarity to add up" (*Films and Filming*).[524]

Rentals: $11.1 million (including 1967 reissue) ($79.1 million equivalent)

50: *Psycho*

Starring Anthony Perkins, Janet Leigh and Vera Miles; directed and produced by Alfred Hitchcock; screenplay, Joseph Stefano, based on the novel by Robert Bloch[525]; music, Bernard Herrmann. Paramount. June 16, 1960.

Even though *Psycho* was critically reviled at the time,[526] Hitchcock blasted wide open the doors to what would be deemed acceptable in modern American cinema. Made on a low budget in black-and-white following the sumptuous color of *North by Northwest*, it seemed a perverse choice. No studio wanted it. Hitchcock had to fund it himself, with Paramount only involved as distributor. Based on a real-life case,[527] it was certainly an unappealing prospect: leading actress murdered halfway through by a maniac with a predilection for dressing up as his mother. Using the crew from his TV series,[528] Hitchcock made it quickly for just over $800,000,[529] a quarter of the cost of *North by Northwest*. An initial stab at the script from James Cavanaugh was discarded[530]; working with Joseph Stefano (*The Black Orchid*, 1958), Hitchcock shifted the focus of the novel. Instead of a fat, middle-aged alcoholic, Norman Bates would become young and attractive like the character from the French thriller *Les Diaboliques* (1955). The story itself changed from "Norman and the role Marion plays in his life…[to] the redemptive but ultimately tragic role Norman plays in her life."[531]

Although Hitchcock openly claimed he detested filming, having already worked out the entire shoot in his head, this was never entirely true. Some ideas just did not work. In *Psycho*, for example, the director had planned a helicopter shot tracking into

Marion and Sam's hotel room but "high winds kept jiggling the camera" and it was changed to three separate shots.[532] Also, by using two cameras, he allowed the opportunity to choose a different shot than originally imagined and, in a change from the shooting script, the post-shower focus changed from Sam to Lila, making her the focus of the film's final section where she confronts the killer.[533]

Marion Crane (Janet Leigh) is not a typical Hitchcock villain. She is not cut out for the work. Alone in his repertoire, she regrets her action, tortured by, not so much her conscience, as the thought of getting caught. Having stolen $40,000, she is so jittery she turns a harmless highway cop suspicious. Once more, Hitchcock has us rooting for the bad guy or, in this case, the bad girl. In *Vertigo* (1958), the drive is silent, but here the silence is punctuated by Marion imagining what people are saying about her, knowing pursuit is inevitable. By the time she reaches the Bates Motel, she is repentant, planning to return and face the music: "I stepped in a private trap back there and I'd like to go back and pull myself out of it." Unfortunately for her, Norman Bates (Perkins) has other plans. Although Bates is presented as fighting his demons, he always gives in, while Crane never hears a voice urging her on, telling her she will get away with it. Crane has a working conscience, Bates a defunct one.

Bernard Herrmann's strings-only score behind the jarring opening credits is only the first in a series of taboos broken. In the opening scene, beefcake Sam Loomis (John Gavin) is shirtless, nothing unusual there for a male star, but to show an actress three times in her underwear and more flesh glimpsed in the shower is new. Killing her off is, obviously, not the done thing either, that scene a colossal shock at the time. Effectively, she is the bait, the sexiest MacGuffin ever, leading us to the mystery of Bates. There are many brilliant scenes: Crane's car sinking in the swamp, the murder of private detective Arbogast (Martin Balsam), the shrieking music as the strings hit their topmost register, the discovery by Crane's sister Lila (Vera Miles) of the corpse of Bates' mother, the motel's neon sign flickering in the dark, the spectral house behind the motel filled with strange voices and, of course, the enigmatic Bates, alternating eager smile with defensive reaction. There are a host of great lines: "The first customer of the day is always trouble," says the salesman; "We're quickest to doubt people who have a reputation of being honest," says Arbogast; and the immortal, "A boy's best friend is his mother."

On release, the director engineered a publicity coup by insisting nobody be allowed into the theater after the start. This was an illogical demand, for what did it matter if a patron missed the opening 10 or 20 minutes? But it certainly got the public's attention—for a different reason entirely. It was an assault on their basic rights as theatergoers. In those days, people went into a film 30 minutes, 50 minutes after the start and left when the film came full circle.

When *Psycho* opened, long queues outside the box office, the best kind of word of mouth, attracted interest, thus alerting people who might otherwise have simply passed by. Even drive-ins were forced to comply. Trade advertisements showed Hitchcock pointing to his watch, exhorting, "Surely you do not have your meat course after your dessert at dinner?" Exhibitors were promised a special manual, "The Care and Handling of *Psycho*." As well as smashing box office records, it demolished another convention by showing in local New York theaters while still playing at major first run theaters in Manhattan.

The film has enormous visceral power. The shower scene has, rightly, achieved legendary status, every frame dissected by scholars, some images, the curtain wrenched loose, the hand reaching out, the dead eye, the blood draining away, imprinted on the universal brain, and the music unforgettable. The acting from Anthony Perkins and Janet Leigh is excellent, Leigh nominated for a Best Supporting Actress Oscar, Perkins not so lucky, ending up typecast. For collectors of trivia, Hitchcock's daughter, Patricia, plays Marion Crane's office colleague. And for academics, especially those with auteur on their minds, this was a good place to start.[534]

Critical reception: "Up to his clavicle in whimsicality" (*Variety*); "turns something of human consequence into a fairground sideshow" (*Films and Filming*).[535] It placed ninth on the *Cahiers du Cinema* annual hit list.[536]

Rentals: $11.2 million (including reissues in 1965 and 1969)[537] ($79.8 million equivalent)

49: *The Parent Trap*[538]

Starring Hayley Mills, Maureen O'Hara and Brian Keith; screenplay and directed by David Swift, based on *Lottie and Lisa* by Erich Kästner; producer, Walt Disney; music Paul Smith. Disney. June 21, 1961.

Although reliant on misunderstandings and body-swap to fuel the plot, this is quite an adult subject for a safety-first producer like Disney. Most of his movies pivot on zany comedy or adventure, whether starring kids or adults or a mixture of both, but the thrust of this picture is emotional. In times of personal crisis or unwarranted parental punishment, children the world over fantasize about having ended up by mistake in the wrong household. Children the world over believe themselves responsible for parental divorce; if only they had been better behaved, it would not have occurred. So this was somewhat dangerous territory for a lightweight like Disney. And it was promoted as a "sophisticated comedy"[539] in an attempt to overcome the audience resistance that had prevented *Pollyanna* (1960) achieving expectations.[540] Like *The Absent Minded Professor* (1961), the source material was obscure, a book written in German a dozen years before, *Lottie and Lisa* by Erich Kästner. Former animator David Swift, creator of the TV sitcom *Mr. Peepers* (1952), took the helm and wrote the screenplay, as he had done with *Pollyanna*, British actress Hayley Mills' Disney debut.

This was a bigger stretch for Mills, who had signed a five-year deal with Disney the previous summer beginning with *Pollyanna*. That had been more typical Disney fare, about a girl who can do nothing but good in a town where a lot has gone wrong. In *The Parent Trap*, another in the "Udult" brand, Mills plays a double role as a set of twins separated at birth, who meet at summer camp. Initially, the comedy centers on resentment, as each psychologically loses their identity with someone else so obviously identical, and as each tries to gain the upper hand. At last, thrown together, they work out the truth. Their parents have divorced, each taking a child. At first, their motivation is just the thrill of getting to know a long-lost parent but it is a harder slog to get the parents back together again especially as the father is engaged. Naturally, the parents kiss and make up. Originally, Disney's idea had been that they would use a body double for the other twin but Mills was growing at such a rate that they would have to employ several to keep up. Instead, process shots allowed Mills to play both girls in the same scene.

Maureen O'Hara and Brian Keith are the parents. After over two decades, Irish actress O'Hara, with films like Hitchcock's *Jamaica Inn* (1939) and John Ford's *The Quiet Man*

The Films

(1952) to her credit, as well as countless Westerns and swashbucklers, had seen her career dip,[541] with only the spy comedy *Our Man in Havana* (1959) to show for the last three years. Keith was TV's *The Westerner* (1960), created by Sam Peckinpah, and this film marked a considerable step up. Coincidentally, O'Hara and Keith had been working together on Sam Peckinpah's first picture *The Deadly Companions* (1961), and it was released in the same month as *The Parent Trap*. Mostly a TV actress except for bit parts and Jane in *Tarzan, the Ape Man* (1959), Joanna Barnes plays the scheming fiancée who receives her comeuppance.

Mills was a find for Disney, with terrific comedy timing, and enough charm to bring in the audiences without over-cuteness tainting the experience. She was perfectly believable as two characters and despite the subject matter treading on thin emotional ice, the sight gags kept the kids happy and the verbal quips the adults. This was more heart-warming fare than *The Absent Minded Professor* and has a wholesomeness that still appeals.

Critical reception: "Should be most appealing to adults, as well as children" (*New York Times*); "unusually well designed for the entire family" (*Los Angeles Times*); "charmingly lively" (*Washington Post*).[542]

Rentals: $11.3 million.[543] (including 1968 reissue) ($80.5 million equivalent)

47 (tie): *The Jungle Book*

Voices of Phil Harris, George Sanders and Louis Prima; directed by Wolfgang Reitherman; screenplay, Larry Clemmons, Ralph Wright and Ken Anderson, based on the stories of Rudyard Kipling; producer, Walt Disney; music, George Bruns. Disney. October 18, 1967.

Walt Disney's last film (he died in 1966), *The Jungle Book* is a joy from start to finish and practically impossible not to adore even when its old-fashioned animation is set against the modern equivalent.

The Disney animation production line had slowed down in the last decade. From four full-length animated features in five years from 1950 to 1955, *The Jungle Book* was only the third since *Sleeping Beauty* (1959), discounting the cartoon segments of *Mary Poppins* (1964). The gap was in part the result of dispiriting returns for *The Sword in the Stone* (1963) and in part because of the upsurge in live-action films.

To a greater extent, *The Jungle Book* succeeds because it is a film of its time. It is so laid-back. Compared to previous productions, there is virtually no story, just Mowgli happening upon a variety of animals. If there is danger, he is often oblivious, and when occasionally put in harm's way, he slips off unharmed. The only plot lines consist of Bagheera the panther realizing the boy raised by wolves must return to his own kind and of tiger Shere Khan noticing this easy prey. The rest of the time, Mowgli basically just goofs around, only enticed to quit the jungle when entranced by a girl in a village.

The plot is basically irrelevant when the animators have cooked up such brilliant characters as Baloo the Bear, hissing snake Kaa, and Louie, King of the Apes; and the Sherman Brothers have rattled up a fabulous array of songs. "The Bare Necessities" (written by Terry Gilkyson) and "I Wanna Be Like You" are the standouts but supported by "Colonel Hathi's March," the sinuous python's "Trust in Me" and the vulture chorus "That's What Friends Are For." Casting is inspired with Phil Harris as Baloo, plummy-voiced English actor George Sanders as Shere Khan, Sterling Holloway as Kaa and Louis Prima as Louie. The vultures are voiced with deadpan Liverpudlian accents.

The Films
105

Harris, married to film star Alice Faye, was a former bandleader and familiar to American audiences from his radio show. Sanders, an Oscar winner for *All About Eve* (1950), was coming to the end of a 30-year-plus career and had played series characters The Saint and The Falcon and still enjoyed decent supporting roles (*The Quiller Memorandum*, 1966). Holloway had voiced the Cheshire Cat in *Alice in Wonderland* (1951) and had a long-running role in the TV series *The Baileys of Balboa* (1964). Prima was a jazz trumpeter, famed for recording "That Old Black Magic." Unlike now, animated features were a rarity and if Disney was not turning them out, there could be a complete absence. Since audiences had not responded to *The Sword in the Stone*, the studio threw serious money ($4 million) at *The Jungle Book* with a switch away from the anthropomorphic characters of earlier films, substituting them with this cool bunch of happy-go-lucky creatures. At a time when Hollywood was in the midst of change, the unexpected was scoring more highly than the predictable. In this case, the new mix worked. Audiences had the time of their lives and went out humming the tunes.

Critical reception: "Best thing since *Dumbo*" (*Life*); "thoroughly delightful" (*Time*); "really, really good Disney" (*Los Angeles Times*).[544]

Rentals: $11.5 million[545] ($81.9 million equivalent)

47 (tie): *True Grit*

Starring John Wayne, Glen Campbell and Kim Darby; directed by Henry Hathaway; screenplay, Marguerite Roberts, based on the novel by Charles Portis; producer, Hal B. Wallis; music Elmer Bernstein. Paramount. June 12, 1969.

John Wayne reacted to the critical mauling of *The Green Berets* (1968) and audience disinterest in *The Hellfighters* (1968) by jumping back into the saddle as Rooster Cogburn in *True Grit*. The book by Charles Portis, unusually for a Western, spent 22 weeks on the *New York Times* bestseller list, its main attraction a first-person narration by 14-year-old Mattie Ross, her language peppered with colorful phrases, seeking revenge for her father's death. Veteran producer Hal B. Wallis[546] had been responsible for *Casablanca* (1942), *Becket* (1964), *Barefoot in the Park* (1967) and a string of westerns: *Gunfight at the O.K. Corral* (1957), *The Sons of Katie Elder* (1965) and *5 Card Stud* (1968). Mia Farrow turned down the role of Mattie Ross; Sally Field, TV's *The Flying Nun*, was considered before the part went to 21-year-old Kim Darby.[547] Henry Hathaway had directed 60 movies since 1932 including the films noir *The Dark Corner* (1946) and *Kiss of Death* (1947) and two Westerns this decade with Wayne—*North to Alaska* (1960) and *The Sons of Katie Elder*—as well as *Nevada Smith* (1966) and *5 Card Stud*. Screenwriter Marguerite Roberts (*Ivanhoe*, 1952), a blacklist victim for nearly a decade, worked closely with Hathaway to fashion an old-style Western with a modern anti-hero.

Cogburn is as out of place as *The Wild Bunch*, but there is another perspective. Seen through Mattie's eyes, it is essentially a rite-of-passage film and she represents both the old and the new, able to outwit a horse dealer but hankering after a Biblical form of justice. Ideas of fair play vanish when confronted by the unforgiving West. Civilization tolerates her strong will but the wilderness does not. Without intervention, she could twice have been sexually molested, and certainly killed. Ironically, her spunky self-confidence—wrongly assuming she can handle the recoil from a pistol, for example—sends her into harm's way. Two directorial characteristics give the picture an unusual tone.

Hathaway loved panorama as much as John Ford and much of the movie is filmed in long shot, widescreen bracketed above by sky or trees and below by grass or rock. Hathaway is also given to enormous detail, setting out the background of the town of Fort Smith where a hanging takes place as Mattie arrives, while the characters always point out specifically where they are going. Cogburn carefully orchestrates the shoot-outs, two of which are largely in long shot.

Cogburn fully justifies the description "a pitiless man, double tough, fear doesn't enter into his thinking." This is a Wayne transformed, usual slow drawl replaced by a raucous bark, pushing forward with purposeful stride, black eyepatch lending a piratical look, head lurching to one side, arms more mobile than usual. He is not the noble defender of justice of previous films, but a twisty, sly, ruthless killer. Texas Ranger Labeef (Glen Campbell) joins forces with Cogburn. "She reminds me of me," says Cogburn of Mattie. Not enough to prevent endless bickering, but, as the film develops, she takes on the mantle of the daughter he never had, while he comes to represent a tougher paternal figure.

There are two classic shoot-outs and a final confrontation that sees Cogburn taking on the gang alone, charging, reins in teeth, firing two-handed. Trapped under a horse, he is saved by LaBeef. The picture takes a while to wind up, Mattie needing rescue from a snake pit and a climactic race to get medical attention. When finally Cogburn takes his leave, it is with a triumphant leap on horseback over a four-bar fence, waving his hat in the air. It is a wonderful Western, up there with the best of John Ford and Howard Hawks, and owing much to Wayne's performance and Hathaway's direction.

Critics, who had slaughtered *The Green Berets* the previous year, virtually gave Wayne a standing ovation with calls for an Oscar. The movie was boldly launched at Radio City Music Hall in New York, the biggest cinema in America, the first Western so honored, and the actor appeared on the cover of *Time* magazine. At the Oscars, Dustin Hoffman and Jon Voight from *Midnight Cowboy* cancelled each other out voting-wise. Otherwise, the competition comprised Peter O'Toole for the musical *Goodbye Mr. Chips* and Richard Burton in the historical drama *Anne of the Thousand Days* (another Wallis production). Wayne's victory crowned his career.

As with the previous year when it looked like *The Odd Couple* and *Yours, Mine and Ours* were standing up against an onslaught of sex and violence, so *True Grit* (although featuring low-level violence) became a similar bastion. But in the middle of the charge of the new wave films—*Easy Rider, Midnight Cowboy, Last Summer, Goodbye, Columbus*—the Western made a glorious comeback, a fact that seems completely overlooked when historians assess that summer's youthquake, as if, once again, you could split the American audience right down the middle.

Critical reception: "One of the major movies of the year" (*New York Times*); "suspenseful, humorous, action-packed adventure film" (*Saturday Review*); "John Wayne's finest moment" (*New York Daily News*); "*True Grit* is truly great" (*Los Angeles Times*).[548]

Rentals: $11.5 million[549] ($81.9 million equivalent)

46 (tie): *Yours, Mine and Ours*

Starring Lucille Ball and Henry Fonda; directed and written by Melville Shavelson; producer, Robert F. Blumofe; music, Fred Karlin. United Artists. April 24, 1968.

A tale like this—father of ten and mother of eight romantically entwined—must surely be the product of a fevered concept-driven mind. But it wasn't. It was based on the true story of Helen Eileen Beardsley, a widow with eight children who married in 1961 a Navy widower with ten, and they attracted national attention with the largest mass adoption in history as each legally took on the other's offspring. After appearing on *The Johnny Carson Show*, the whole troupe dived into TV commercials and in 1965 she wrote a book, *Who Gets the Drumstick*, which took four screenwriters to transform into a movie.

Stars Lucille Ball and Henry Fonda were pretty much busted flushes in the movie business. Ball's marquee flame had burned out in the early 1950s and her two movie credits this decade, *The Facts of Life* (1960) and *Critic's Choice* (1963), were opposite Bob Hope. On the other hand, she was a huge name in television, through Desilu Productions, initially with husband Desi Arnaz, the biggest independent producer of TV shows in America. She bought him out in 1962 and made it bigger, before selling out for $17 million (equivalent to $121 million today). The company had been responsible for *The Untouchables, Star Trek, Mission: Impossible* and, of course, *I Love Lucy*. And it was Desilu that set up *Yours, Mine and Ours*, having bought the rights to the Beardsley story pre-publication[550] as a big screen vehicle to showcase Ball's talents. But she struggled to raise the finance after the poor showing of *Critic's Choice*. Fonda was either top-billed in movies that scarcely made a dime (*Welcome to Hard Times*, 1967), part of an ensemble cast in big-budget movies (*Battle of the Bulge*, 1965) or second-billed to a bigger male star such as James Stewart (*Firecreek*, 1968) or Richard Widmark (*Madigan*, 1968). He was not first choice either, as James Stewart, Fred MacMurray and even John Wayne were considered. But as Ball was only too aware, comedies about couples depend on chemistry and she had worked previously with Fonda in *The Big Street* (1942). Budget was a mere $2.5 million. Ball was paid $250,000 and 50 percent of the profits.[551]

Ball plays a nurse, Fonda a Navy chief warrant officer, and the first comedic element is the pair trying to keep secret the respective sizes of their families. But as the romance develops, secrets are revealed and the laughs come from the children objecting to impending marriage and to losing their birth names when adoption becomes imminent. But mostly the humor arises from countless incidents relating to a gigantic family. The problem facing the scriptwriters is obvious: how to tone down Ball's TV persona and that show's penchant for slapstick and quick-fire gags in order to create a film that has a more generous atmosphere. Fonda, as ever, is a good foil and generally it works, though the "drunken mother" scene, hilarious though it is, appears a remnant of the TV show. While it is often viewed as a bulwark against the rising tide of modern sexuality, epitomized by that year's top grosser *The Graduate* and fourth-placed *Valley of the Dolls*, it is unlikely that audiences split quite so sharply along those lines, old crowd vs. the young, since the amount of money taken in by all three films required across-the-board acceptance.

Critical reception: "Uncertain, embarrassing, protracted little comedy" (*New York Times*); "series of hilarious situations" (*Box Office*); "marked by uniform excellence, literate scripting, excellent performances" (*Variety*).[552]

Rentals: $11.6 million[553] ($82.6 million equivalent)

45: *Camelot*

Starring Richard Harris and Vanessa Redgrave; directed by Joshua Logan; screenplay, Alan Jay Lerner, based on the musical by Lerner and Loewe and the novel *The Once*

108 The Films

and Future King by T.H. White; producer, Jack L. Warner; music, Alan Jay Lerner and Frederick Loewe. Warner Brothers-Seven Arts roadshow. October 25, 1967.

At one time you had to be actually able to sing to appear in a musical. But few of the people who could sing on stage showed genuine star power. Filling a single Broadway house did not equate to attracting millions of paying customers to thousands of movie theaters. Hollywood had learned this lesson early on, in the 1940s and 1950s, when the likes of Mary Martin, Alfred Drake, Ezio Pinza and Ray Middleton (who had originated characters in musicals such as *Oklahoma!* and *South Pacific*) were considered surplus to requirements. The 1950s musicals like *Annie Get Your Gun* (1950), *Showboat* (1951) and *High Society* (1956) showcased genuine talent of the caliber of Bing Crosby, Frank Sinatra, Betty Hutton, Kathryn Grayson and Howard Keel. The escalating cost of musicals created demand for stars who did not need to sing, audiences duped into thinking they could. *The King and I* was the first to take this route, Marni Nixon the secret voice of Deborah Kerr. Nixon repeated for Natalie Wood in *West Side Story* (1961) and to a great extent for Audrey Hepburn in *My Fair Lady* (1964). It had been accepted practice since Yul Brynner in *The King and I* that a man with a less than outstanding vocal range could pretty much "talk" his way through a song, a technique utilized by Rex Harrison in *My Fair Lady* (1964). Richard Burton, who had originated King Arthur on stage, was too expensive. Peter O'Toole, Marlon Brando and Gregory Peck were in the running before Richard Harris' campaign won over director Joshua Logan.[554] Julie Andrews (Burton's stage partner), Audrey Hepburn, Julie Christie, Polly Bergen and Mitzi Gaynor were in contention before Vanessa Redgrave swooped in.[555]

Lerner and Loewe were different to Rodgers and Hammerstein. Many of their tunes were sung by an ensemble (*Paint Your Wagon*, 1969, a classic example), thus reducing the necessity for a lead male singer. In *Camelot*, King Arthur (Harris) has two solo songs.[556] Director Logan believed their acting skills[557] would compensate for perceived vocal deficiencies[558] and that since *Camelot* was a more heavyweight drama than *The Sound of Music* (1965), it required actors who could meet that challenge.[559] It was a gamble in other ways for neither was a proper star. Although top-billed in the British-made *This Sporting Life* (1963), in Hollywood Harris was strictly second billing, albeit in the big-budget ventures *Mutiny on the Bounty* (1962), *The Heroes of Telemark* (1965) and *Hawaii* (1966). Redgrave was more a prospect than anything else with only an Oscar-nominated performance in the British-made *Morgan!* (1966)[560] and the surprise hit *Blow Up* (1966)[561] to her credit. First choice director Robert Wise (*The Sound of Music*) bowed out.[562] Logan's credentials were never in doubt thanks to *South Pacific* (1958) and three Oscar nominations. To save money, Warner Brothers wanted the entire set built on the back lot, but acceded to the director's demand to shoot some scenes in Spain, with Camelot represented by Castillo de Coca and Lancelot's citadel by the Alcazar castle in Majorca.[563] But the Spanish shoot was hit by unseasonal rain and a 30-day schedule ballooned to 42 days before the production moved back to Hollywood and the biggest set ever constructed so far in Hollywood, designed by Australian John Truscott, responsible for the London stage sets.

Camelot told a darker tale, embracing adultery and betrayal, carrying more baggage than the standard musical. You could argue it was the first adult musical. Unusually, the story is told in flashback, as King Arthur prepares for battle against former friend Lancelot (Franco Nero). Although the Arthur-Guinevere (spelled Guenevere in the film) romance is considered one of history's greatest, it was actually an arranged marriage and initial songs reveal the couple's fears. But it is love at first sight. Their relationship is interrupted by celibate Lancelot, and soon a love triangle is underway. Mordred, the king's bastard son, catches the lovers and a new law sentences her to be burned at the stake. Her rescue by Lancelot ordains battle.

The songs in *Camelot* reflect the inner feelings of characters terrified of consequence, especially after the establishment of the idyllic kingdom. The first songs, Arthur's "I Wonder What the King is Doing Tonight" and Guenevere's "The Simple Joys of Maidenhood," represent characters on the brink of the unknown. "How to Handle a Woman" reveals cracks in the relationship. Lancelot's guilt is the theme of "If Ever I Would Leave You" and forbidden love the subject of "I Loved You Once in Silence." A musical with an unhappy ending was almost a contradiction in terms. Harris and Redgrave both imparted great depth; David Hemmings and Nero were less substantial. Sets and costumes costing $5 million were stunning. Logan was more receptive to ideas than Otto Preminger in *Exodus*.[564] As a musical with a hardline dramatic core, it has few equals. Although lumped in with overpriced 70mm roadshow musicals that sent Hollywood into meltdown, *Camelot* was the fifth most popular musical of the decade. Harris released the hit single "Macarthur Park" and an album the following year and later, having purchased the stage rights, became synonymous with endless tours.

Critical reception: "One of Hollywood's all-time great screen musicals" (*Variety*); "long, leaden and lugubrious" (*Washington Post*); "a very considerable disappointment" (*Los Angeles Times*).[565]

Rentals: $11.9 million[566] ($84.8 million equivalent)

44: *El Cid*

Starring Charlton Heston and Sophia Loren; directed by Anthony Mann; screenplay, Philip Yordan, Fredric M. Frank[567] and Ben Barzman; producer, Samuel Bronston; music, Miklos Rosza. Allied Artists. December 6, 1961.

Samuel Bronston, having laid the groundwork for establishing his Spanish production empire with *King of Kings*, and "determined to take on the mantle of DeMille,"[568] returned to do justice to one of the country's legendary heroes, El Cid, who drove the Moors out of his homeland, achieving his final victory after he was dead. Charlton Heston, offscreen since his Oscar-winning turn as *Ben-Hur*, was the only choice for the title role. Female lead went to Sophia Loren,[569] herself an Oscar winner (*Two Women*, 1960) who had replaced Brigitte Bardot as the biggest foreign import at the box office. She earned $1 million for ten weeks work,[570] far above her going rate, and had extra scenes written to her specifications. Loren had starred opposite Cary Grant in *Houseboat* (1958) and Clark Gable in *It Started in Naples* (1960) and was a major attraction in her own right, top-billed in George Cukor's *Heller in Pink Tights* (1960) and *A Breath of Scandal* (1960). She had an old-fashioned attitude toward work, regularly appearing in three or four films a year. Director Anthony Mann—best known for his hard-hitting Westerns *Winchester '73* (1950) and *The Naked Spur* (1953)—had his fingers burnt on roadshows: *Cimarron* (1960) was a flop and he was fired from *Spartacus* (1960). So this was an opportunity for redemption and he had (uncredited) experience of historical epics after directing some sequences in *Quo Vadis* (1951). However, he did call upon the expertise of Yakima Canutt[571] to orchestrate the battles and individual fight scenes.

The bill for jewelry alone came to $40,000 with $150,000 spent on candelabras, tapestries and artworks. Foundries in Toledo turned out broadswords, scimitars and axes while craftswomen produced 2,000 costumes* (souvenir program).

*Martin, The Magnificent Showman, 81-82.

Although the picture involves court politics, intrigue, vendettas, thrilling battles and a hero's rise and fall, at its heart it is a dramatic tale of tempestuous romance. Heston and Loren are due to be married (arranged, as was the custom) until Heston kills her father in a duel. While he battles to win her hand, she conspires to leave him. On realizing she does not love him, Heston refuses to consummate the marriage and she enters a convent. After offending the king, Heston is banished. Loren realizes that she does love this noble man after all and joins him in exile where he becomes a mercenary. Exile over, Loren is imprisoned though subsequently freed and reunited with Heston. After witnessing her husband wounded in battle in the conflict against the Moors, Loren has to agree to allow him to die in order to send him back into action, ostensibly still the leader, routing the enemy who believe he has risen from the dead. That's only half the story. The other half is, of course, equally dramatic and sumptuous. Fabulous sets, thousands of extras—provided by the Spanish army and mounted police—forming the forces of the invading Moors and the defending Spaniards (and not created by CGI as in later epics like *Gladiator*). The supporting cast included Raf Vallone, Herbert Lom[572] and French actress Genevieve Page. The script was credited to Philip Yordan (an ongoing Bronston accomplice) and Fredric M. Frank but was written by blacklisted Ben Barzman (*Back to Bataan*, 1945) with Bernard Gordon (*The Lawless Breed*, 1952), also blacklisted, supplying the love scenes.[573] The characters spoke in idiom to transport audiences back to medieval times. Miklos Rozsa (*Ben-Hur*) delivered a terrific score.

Part of what makes the film so special is the authenticity. Bronston wanted everything to be real, not just elements appearing in close-up, but the entire background. These were the genuine articles, not standard Hollywood props. The film required

The Films 111

40,000 arrows, 5000 shields, over 1000 harnesses and 500 saddles.[574] Although most of the shooting was done at existing castles, the cathedral at Burgos was reconstructed over a period of 90 days in Seville studios, an absolute match even to the stream running through the original.[575] Audiences who came looking for an epic like *Ben-Hur* got more than they bargained for. The battle scenes and the duels were outstanding and there were clever ploys, the siege of Valencia lifted by lofting bread over the walls by catapults. And this was a film about honor, not glory. El Cid did not wish to become king of Spain but he was desirous of a unified country, ordinary people and royalty uniting to eject the invaders. That theme is universal; a central, believable romance with powerful performances from the principals even more so.

Critical reaction: "Better than any spectacle since *Spartacus*" (*Time*); "Mann at his stylish peak" (*Films and Filming*); "corpse-strewn battle picture" (*Variety*); "as big as *Ben-Hur* if not bigger" (*Los Angeles Times*); "crammed with jousts and battles" (*Newsweek*).[576]

Rentals: $12 million ($85.5 million equivalent)

43: *Irma La Douce*

Starring Jack Lemmon and Shirley MacLaine; directed and produced by Billy Wilder; screenplay, Wilder and I.A.L. Diamond; music, Andre Previn. United Artists. June 5, 1963.

It might seem crazy to buy the rights to a hit stage musical[577] and then release a film minus the songs, but that's exactly what occurred with *Irma La Douce*. The cost of the rights was substantial–$350,000[578] (equivalent to $2.5 million today). Apparently, director Billy Wilder—on a 25 percent profit share[579]—had shot some numbers but the effort reminded him of the previous musical flop *The Emperor Waltz* (1948) with Bing Crosby so took them out. That the subject matter was unsavory, even more so than *The Apartment* (1960), was another sticking point. The main characters were sex workers and pimps. Several movies around that time focused on sex workers: *The World of Suzie Wong* (1960), *BUtterfield 8* (1960) and *Never on Sunday* (1960), for example—but they were not comedies like *Irma La Douce*. Most comedies had shifted away from sleazy subject matter, Doris Day and innocuous Disney fare now leading the way at the box office. Even with Billy Wilder at the helm, it was doubtful it could be made at all. Arthur Krim of United Artists "had misgivings from the beginning ... and [felt] this picture would never be made."[580] Production company Mirisch had to agree to split the cost of the rights purchase. United Artists felt audiences could be swayed.

Star Jack Lemmon had acquired considerable kudos after an Oscar nomination for *Days of Wine and Roses* (1962) so the prospect of reuniting him with *Apartment* co-star Shirley MacLaine, at $350,000 plus a percentage[581] (first choice Marilyn Monroe died before production began), seemed foolproof. MacLaine, by the way, had joined Lemmon in the production business, having put together the comedy *My Geisha* (1962).[582] Not by a long shot was she the first actress to turn producer.[583] In some respects, you could argue that Wilder was the fly in the ointment, his previous picture *One, Two, Three* (1961) a big flop. To tailor the picture for American consumption, Lemmon's role was changed from pimp at the outset to cop, and, in fact, an honest cop, so incorruptible he is discharged from the force. After falling in love with MacLaine, at her behest he agrees to act as her

112 **The Films**

pimp. To save her from a life of debauchery, he pretends to be a rich customer. As if that was not enough to be getting on with, the plot adds a mountain of development until it is essentially a farce, with Lemmon desperately trying to maintain a double identity. This was also to be Wilder's first film in color since *The Seven Year Itch* (1955), black-and-white now indicative of a low budget, an occasional prestige picture like *To Kill a Mockingbird* (1962) or a war film (*The Longest Day*, 1962) intent on incorporating newsreel footage. It was shot on a back lot in Hollywood rather than location.[584] A studio lot, essential to control a musical's costs, detracted from a movie set in Paris, no matter how gloriously imagined by designer Alex Trauner.[585] While high cost went with the territory for a musical, $5 million was a hefty budget for a comedy. United Artists "were very cold" to the finished movie and even asked producer Walter Mirisch to look for another distributor who could return the UA's investment. In the end, worst fears were not realized, and, after flirting with going roadshow,[586] UA opted for straightforward release. It became Wilder's biggest hit, its holdover power demonstrating terrific word of mouth.[587]

While too long at nearly 150 minutes, it is impossible not to be drawn in by the performances of the pair who create another comedy double act *tour de force*, although judging by her Oscar nomination, MacLaine has the upper hand. There is a good supporting performance from Lou Jacobi (Charles Laughton, initially cast,[588] died before filming began) as the proprietor of a local hangout who has quite the knack for improbable stories. Wilder wrote the screenplay with regular collaborator I.A.L. ("Izzy") Diamond. Tunes from the original musical were adapted for the score by Andre Previn, also Oscar-nominated. (Lemmon also released an album.)[589]

Not as zany as *Some Like It Hot* and not quite as considered as *The Apartment*, *Irma La Douce* nonetheless presses all the right comedic buttons.

Critical reception: "Delightfully nonsensical" (*Box Office*); "diverting romp" (*Variety*); "overblown and overlong" (*Washington Post*); "brisk and bubbly" (*New York Times*).[590] Rated thirtieth in the annual Cahier du Cinema list.[591]

Rentals: $12.1 million ($86.2 million equivalent)

42: *A Man for All Seasons*

Starring Paul Scofield and Robert Shaw; directed and produced by Fred Zinnemann; screenplay, Robert Bolt, from his play; music, George Delerue. Columbia roadshow. December 12, 1966.

Where reprising a stage role for the screen had not electrified Robert Redford's career in *Barefoot in the Park* (1967), the opposite held true for British actor Paul Scofield in the historical drama *A Man for All Seasons*. The Robert Bolt[592] play premiered in London in 1960 and ran for a year on Broadway, and Scofield scored a Tony. Although an accepted stage star, he was an unknown screen quantity with only two previous films— *That Lady* (1955) and *Carve Her Name with Pride* (1958)—before John Frankenheimer's *The Train* (1964). *Becket* (1964) had provided a precedent for roadshowing a talk-laden action-lite historical drama but that picture had Richard Burton and Peter O'Toole. Scofield's lack of marquee appeal led producers to envisage Burton or Laurence Olivier as Sir Thomas More and O'Toole as his nemesis King Henry VIII. The miserly budget— under $2 million[593]—probably accounted for Scofield getting the part with Robert Shaw (*From Russia with Love*, 1963) as the king and Orson Welles in the other prominent role of Cardinal Wolseley.[594] Vanessa Redgrave, lined up to play More's daughter, proved unavailable[595] and the role landed in the lap of Susannah York. Director Fred Zinnemann had lost his box office cachet after the big-budget flop *Behold a Pale Horse* (1964) with Gregory Peck and Anthony Quinn. He was dropped from *Hawaii* (1966), and *The Day Custer Fell* was shelved. However, he still negotiated an advantageous back-end deal.[596] His lack of success in the past five years was in startling contrast to his commercial and critical success in the 1950s: —Marlon Brando's screen debut in *The Men* (1950), *High Noon* (1952), *From Here to Eternity* (1953), *Oklahoma!* (1955) and *The Nun's Story* (1959)— plus an Oscar and three nominations. So he was in the market for career redemption.

Bolt's screenplay eliminated the play's Chorus, distributing their lines to various cast members. Zinnemann widened out the play by conspicuous use of historical British locations such as Hampton Court Palace, Beaulieu Abbey and adjacent river, Studley Prior and exteriors in Oxfordshire and Hampshire. The story concerned the clash between two titanic figures, lord chancellor and philosopher Sir Thomas More (he wrote *Utopia*) and Henry VIII. More sticks to a moral principle which costs him his life. The king wanted a male heir but wife Catherine of Aragon failed to deliver. Henry VIII decided to marry someone else (an affair that produced a bastard would result in that succession challenged). With divorce not an option, and wanting the marriage annulled, the king sought More's support. More refused. Although principled, More was not ascetic, enjoying a privileged life. For refusing to back the king's appointment as head of the Church of England, More is imprisoned for treason, brought to trial, found guilty and executed. The bald facts of the story belie the wonderful monologues, verbal duels and array of strategies More employs to challenge the king and escape his fate. The politics of the royal court and the wiles of men seeking advancement are also explored. Usually, in Hollywood when a character faces a moral dilemma, the person is in dire circumstances (financial, emotional, disadvantaged), odds stacked against him, so that his redemption is all the sweeter. But none of those techniques gain traction here. No scripting wiles or camera angles are employed to woo the audience. For moviegoers ignorant of English history, it must have seemed that More was making a stand over nothing much. And that was the clever lure, drawing moviegoers in to understand the nature of a man who would risk his life in such an unfashionable fashion. The movie, like the play, requires a brilliant actor to make the concept work. Scofield rises to the challenge while Shaw delivers a career-best performance.

Columbia was in a quandary over optimum release pattern. It was, in essence, a small film, certainly compared to other prestige projects. In terms of budget there was not a great deal to lose should audiences ignore it. The most obvious route would be arthouse release, a slow opening in select cinemas in the hope of Oscar nominations to boost commercial prospects. At two hours, it was too short for a roadshow; most roadshows clocked in a good 30 minutes longer. So Columbia opened it in the 468-seat Fine Arts arthouse[597] in New York on roadshow terms,[598] that is advance booking, raised prices, and two shows a day plus an extra one on Wednesdays and Saturdays.[599] The smaller seating capacity was crucial to generating sold-out signs. The Oscars did come to the rescue: Eight nominations boosted the box office, with six wins including Best Actor and Best Picture.

Critical reception: "One cannot believe there will be a better picture this year" (*New York Post*); "a film for all time" (*New York Herald Tribune*); "beautiful and faithful transposition to the screen" (*New York Daily News*); "fine job." (*New York Times*).[600]

Rentals: $12.75 million ($90.8 million equivalent)

114 The Films

41: *The Guns of Navarone*

Starring Gregory Peck, David Niven and Anthony Quinn; directed by J. Lee Thompson; written and produced by Carl Foreman, from the novel by Alistair MacLean; music, Dimitri Tiomkin. Columbia. April 27, 1961 (London); U.S.: June 22, 1961.

The commercial and critical success of *The Guns of Navarone* belied its extreme production difficulties. Producer Carl Foreman lost his original screenwriter, initial director, first choice male and female cast, and very nearly one of his actual stars when David Niven came close to death during shooting. Foreman was an Oscar-nominated (*High Noon*, 1952), blacklisted screenwriter who had fled to Britain (albeit with $250,000)[601] and turned British producer (*The Key*, 1958) with funding from Columbia. When the dream team of William Holden,[602] Cary Grant,[603] John Mills and Jack Palance[604]—and then Dean Martin, Richard Burton and Louis Jourdan[605]—failed to commit, Foreman recruited Gregory Peck, David Niven and Anthony Quinn. Thriller writer Eric Ambler failed to knock the script into shape,[606] so Foreman took over those duties and added two female characters not in the original novel. Opera diva Maria Callas[607] was signed to play Peck's love interest. So was Danish newcomer Annette Stroyberg,[608] wife of French director Roger Vadim (*…And God Created Woman*, 1956), but both dropped out, the former replaced by Greek actress Irene Papas, the latter firstly by Ina Balin[609] and then Gia Scala.[610] Director Alexander Mackendrick (*The Ladykillers,* 1955; *The Sweet Smell of Success*, 1957) dropped out after shooting began[611] with British director J. Lee Thompson (*Ice Cold in Alex,* 1958) drafted in, although Foreman envisaged himself in the job.[612]

It was still a killer cast. Four-time Oscar nominee Gregory Peck had enjoyed a long string of hits including Hitchcock's *Spellbound* (1945) and *Roman Holiday* (1953) though *Beloved Infidel* (1959) tanked and he pulled out of *Let's Make Love* (1960)[613] with Marilyn Monroe. David Niven, an Oscar winner for *Separate Tables* (1958), had played opposite Doris Day in the comedy hit *Please Don't Eat the Daisies* (1960). Two-time Oscar winner[614] Anthony Quinn was top-billed in *The Savage Innocents* (1960) and *Barabbas* (1961). The cast also included Anthony Quayle, Stanley Baker and James Darren.[615]

Screenwriter Foreman took further liberties with the book. Changing the sex of two partisans from male to female (Papas and Scala) added sexual tension. Foreman had six men on the mission to the book's five, Major Franklin (Quayle) the new addition, his injury requiring mountaineer Mallory (Peck) to take over leadership. Foreman gave Mallory and Andrea (Quinn) a new back story, creating hostility between the two. Foreman created relationships between the characters which had not previously existed with each character set his/her own personal test. MacLean's sense of place was sketchy but Foreman's was exceptional, taking advantage of historic scenery and inserting a traditional Greek wedding at a crucial point in the proceedings. It was also Foreman who provided the film's anti-war sentiments.[616] It's a mission picture, deadline to beat, blow up the titular guns or thousands will perish. It's typical do-or-die, stakes continually raised by a storm, spies, romance and a running battle with the Germans, first at sea, then land as they are tracked from refuge to refuge. Everywhere are obstacles. Tension mounts. The Germans use a truth serum to extract information from the captured Franklin. An unexpected traitor is uncovered, Miller taking center stage examining the evidence. Subterfuge is even required at the final stage, obliterating the guns.

While the mountaineering required little more than simple technique[617] and most of the picture shot on location on the island of Rhodes, the storm sequence employed the biggest water tank in Europe, at Shepperton Studios. Water tanks are a strange shape, trapezoid, the back wall about twice as wide as the front where the camera usually sits, but the water depth is only about three and a half feet. The set was partly flooded and the storm created by dumping thousands of gallons down giant chutes with wind machines blasting the water in all directions. For long shots, the boat was a miniature but otherwise it was a larger boat on hydraulics. Doubles could not be used so all actors suffered injury, Peck's head being gashed, Quinn damaging his back, Niven reopening war wounds, Darren almost drowning.[618] The gun set was the largest ever built, three stories high, held together with 100 feet of scaffolding. It took five months to build at a cost of £100,000 and another £20,000 to rebuild after it was wrecked by a thunderstorm. Three sets of guns fashioned at different lengths created the necessary scale, their demolition filmed by six cameras. To set the charges, Niven was required to stand chest-deep in water. He contracted septicemia, was rushed to intensive care, and nearly died.[619] Composer Dimitri Tiomkin (*The Alamo*, 1960) earned a record fee of $50,000 for the music,[620] and the score was one of the longest ever, just ten minutes shy of the running time.

Foreman favored the prestige of a roadshow but Columbia wanted its money back quick. It was a smash hit from the start, and the reviews were generous. It was nominated for seven Oscars including Best Picture and Best Director but only won for Special Effects. It is a totally engrossing movie, creating the template for the wartime mission picture, with a brilliantly structured screenplay, excellent direction, thrilling effects and strong acting all-round.

Critical reaction: "Stirring stuff" (*Films and Filming*); "best adventure movie to hit the screen this year" (*Los Angeles Times*); "no less thrilling because ... preposterous" (*New Yorker*); "magnificently detailed cliffhanger" (*Washington Post*).[621]

Rentals: $13 million ($92.6 million equivalent)

40: *The Sand Pebbles*

Starring Steve McQueen, Candice Bergen and Richard Attenborough; directed and produced by Richard Wise; screenplay, Robert Woodruff Anderson, based on the book by Richard McKenna; music, Jerry Goldsmith. Twentieth Century–Fox roadshow. December 20, 1966.

Sometimes it helps to give a struggling actor a leg up. In this case, Robert Wise had cast Steve McQueen in an uncredited role in *Somebody Up There Likes Me* (1956) and now, as director of the uber-hit *The Sound of Music* (1965), he wanted the ultra-macho actor to star in the big-budget adaptation of Richard McKenna's bestseller *The Sand Pebbles* after Paul Newman turned down the role.[622] Although intended as a roadshow set against the political turmoil of Hanoi in the 1920s, the story could be condensed into one man and his machine but instead of the motorbike of *The Great Escape* (1963), the machine in question was the engine of the gunboat U.S.S. *San Pueblo* for which McQueen, a petty officer, takes responsibility. This early in his career, McQueen, paid $300,000 plus points or $650,000,[623] was generally associated with action pictures such as *The Magnificent Seven* (1960) and the John Sturges P.O.W. classic. In reality his films were primarily dramas: *Soldier in the Rain* (1963), the Robert Mulligan duo *Love with the Proper Stranger* (1963) opposite Natalie Wood and *Baby the Rain Must Fall* (1965) with Lee Remick, and Norman Jewison's poker epic *The Cincinnati Kid* (1965). Classy pictures

Finding the right location is not as hard work as transporting staff there. It took three weeks for the production team to airlift 104 actors and crew plus 60 family members to Taipei in Taiwan. The main problem was a lack of available flights, with only three a week in planes limited to a maximum 16 people* (Hannan Collection).

*"Airlift 166 to Taiwan," *Variety*, November 10, 1965, 3.

The Films

all, until he reverted to what was perceived as type with the Henry Hathaway Western *Nevada Smith* (1966), the pick of the bunch in terms of box office.

British actor Richard Attenborough (*Guns at Batasi*, 1964), familiar to McQueen as "Big X" from *The Great Escape*, is a shipmate who falls for Chinese sex worker Emmanuelle Arsan.[624] Richard Crenna, graduating from TV's *Slattery's People* (1964), is the gunboat captain while missionary Candice Bergen (*The Group*, 1966) is McQueen's love interest. Although inevitably drawing comparisons with Vietnam, the book was fictional and, set in 1926–27, not based on a real incident, although the author had served on similar gunboats a decade later. Shot mainly on location, *The Sand Pebbles* went way over budget as the original schedule in Taiwan and Hong Kong of nine weeks more than doubled.[625] The titular boat was built at a cost of $250,000.[626] Other scenes were shot on the U.S.S. *Texas*. After original composer Alex North (*Spartacus*, 1960) fell ill, Jerry Goldsmith (*The Blue Max*, 1966), under contract to Twentieth Century–Fox, was pulled out of a loan deal to MGM for *Grand Prix*.

Like the book, the film is sprawling and without McQueen at its center would have been out of control. The gunboat is rundown when McQueen arrives and knocks the maintenance into shape, earning the enmity of shipmates. He ends up defending the ship's coolies in various situations. Local politics are dicey with the gunboat under strict orders to avoid diplomatic incident. This proves virtually impossible when a coolie is killed, the gunboat marooned and McQueen framed for the murder of Arsan. An attempted rescue of Bergen misfires when she refuses to leave. McQueen remains with Bergen and, after another attempted evacuation, he dies.

The movie's biggest flaw is trying to cram too many episodes into a three-hour running time. McQueen does sterling work as the defender of the underclass and as lover and fighter. But most important is what he doesn't do. His acting is spare, emotions conveyed through a shift of the eyes or a change in his stance. He does not go through the showboating that might result in an Oscar nomination. And yet, strangely enough, for someone seen as more of a star than an actor, he registered his only Oscar nomination. He was up against Richard Burton for *Who's Afraid of Virginia Woolf?* and Paul Scofield for *A Man for All Seasons* so it would have been a major miracle had he won. But it was a minor miracle just to be nominated. Although his acting was primarily viewed as a revelation, it was really the culmination of hard work in the previous half dozen films where his minimal acting style came into its own.

Viewed in hindsight, of course, the political stance is at best patronizing and at worst demoralizing but the film has a decent heart, the battle scenes are superb and the levels of tension stoked up.

Critical reaction: "Beautifully mounted" (*New York Times*); "perfectly suited to Steve McQueen" (*Washington Post*); "molasses-in-January" (*New Yorker*); "scenes are simply too long to hold our interest" (*Films and Filming*).

Rentals: $13.5 million ($96.2 million equivalent)

39: *Those Magnificent Men in Their Flying Machines*

Starring Stuart Whitman, Sarah Miles and James Fox; directed by Ken Annakin; screenplay, Jack Davies; producer, Stan Margulies; music, Ron Goodwin. Twentieth Century–Fox roadshow. June 3, 1965 (London); U.S. June 16, 1965.

118   The Films

The race was on—to find the most profitable race. After the monster hit *It's a Mad Mad Mad Mad World* (1963), movie companies searched for a comedic follow-up, the final contenders being Warner Brothers' *The Great Race* (1965) and Twentieth Century–Fox's *Those Magnificent Men in Their Flying Machines*. Both were set in the early days of machinery, both with international backgrounds, one concerning automobiles, the other airplanes; one with stars, the other doing without. Airplanes of this period (circa 1910) cost little to reproduce since they were not much more than bits of wood, canvas and wire cunningly connected. Authentic materials were used but with more powerful engines. Two monoplanes of genuine vintage did take part, a Deperdussin 1910 and a Blackburn Type D 1912. They were not tough enough to survive very strong winds, so aerial shots were done in the early mornings. The race was from London to Paris.

Director Ken Annakin had been prepping another picture about transatlantic flight, *Flying Crazy*[627] with Peter Sellers[628] or Dick Van Dyke,[629] with different backers, British studio Rank splitting the cost with United Artists.[630] The latter, at that point involved in *The Great Race*, demurred. Twentieth Century–Fox stepped into the breach, pricing the venture at $5 million,[631] small potatoes for a roadshow. Although uncredited, Annakin co-wrote the picture with regular collaborator Jack Davies. After the big-scale Disney adventure *Swiss Family Robinson* (1960), Annakin had been recruited by Fox for part of *The Longest Day* (1962) and had completed, ironically enough, the British vintage sports car comedy *The Fast Lady* (1962)[632] with Leslie Philips. As Fox had discovered from *The Longest Day*, an international cast worked wonders in attracting an international audience. Unlike *The Great Race* which focused on three competitors, there was no requirement for top stars. The American contingent was represented by Oscar-nominated Stuart Whitman (*Rio Conchos*, 1964), the British by Sarah Miles and James Fox (both from *The Servant*, 1963), the German by Gert Frobe (*Goldfinger*, 1964), the Italian by Alberto Sordi (*The Best of Enemies*, 1961), the French by Irina Demick[633] and Jean Pierre Cassel (both from *Male Companion*, 1964) and the Japanese by Yujiro Ishihara (*Escape into Terror*, 1963). In addition, well-known comedians popped up: Red Skelton (in a host of parts) and the British Benny Hill, Tony Hancock and Eric Sykes. Susannah York[634] and Julie Christie[635] were originally eyed for the female lead that finally went to Sarah Miles. Michael Caine failed a screen test[636] for the James Fox character.

National stereotypes engage in centuries-old traditional rivalries and the plot is too ridiculous to condense but it's no less fun for that. Sight gags abound and when one of the highlights is a hot-air balloon duel, you know the kind of viewing to expect. Archetypal upper-class bad guy Terry-Thomas (*The Mouse on the Moon*, 1963) is intent on sabotage. Whitman and Fox are rivals for Miles. Producer Darryl F. Zanuck suggested the running gag in which Demick (his girlfriend) plays a series of flirts.[637] With 14 actual competitors and umpteen subplots in the mix, Annakin had his work cut out to juggle stories and keep the viewer involved, the entire film storyboarded in advance to track every episode. The director's *Longest Day* stint was useful experience in keeping a multi-faceted enterprise zipping along.

The movie begins with a swagger thanks to the memorable theme tune by Ron Goodwin.[638] Unlike the later *The Blue Max*, which was blown up to 70mm, this was filmed with the proper roadshow cameras. Even so, it was an awkward fit for a roadshow, running just 138 minutes and somewhat lacking in "bigness." Not a natural for Broadway's usual roadshow outposts, it was launched at the DeMille arthouse on New York's East Side.

The Films   119

Critical reception: "Funny picture, highly colorful" (*New York Times*); "a piece of clever picture-making" (*Variety*); "what really makes the film a treat are the aerial shots" (*Films and Filming*).[639]

Rentals: $14 million (including reissue) ($99.7 million equivalent)

38: *Swiss Family Robinson*

Starring John Mills and Dorothy McGuire; directed by Ken Annakin; screenplay, Lowell S. Hawley, based on the novel by Johann David Wyss; producer, Walt Disney; music, William Alwyn. Disney. December 21, 1960.

In 1960's *Swiss Family Robinson*, Disney did not use much of Johann David Wyss' original novel. The RKO movie (1940) and the NBC-TV version (1958) were more faithful. The Disney approach left logic out of the equation, putting everything possible on a desert island "no matter how crazy."[640] Hence, pirates, anaconda, swamp, elephant, tiger, ostrich, zebra and others comprise the menagerie.[641] While the novel contained a shipwreck, it was Disney who supplied a desert island and pirate attacks. The novel's woman, shipwrecked separately, became the girl Roberta. The studio learned from *The Shaggy Dog* (1959) the importance of using actors of substance. After *20,000 Leagues Under the Sea* (1954), Disney, financially strapped from investment in the theme park, had abandoned mainstream features, making do with compilations of TV episodes (1955's *Davy Crockett, King of the Wild Frontier*[642]), true-life documentaries (1955's *The African Lion*) and low-budget children's films (1958's *Tonka*). So it brought on board John Mills, father of Disney child sensation Hayley Mills. He was an accomplished British actor who, despite marquee value limited to quintessentially British films like *Ice Cold in Alex* (1958), radiated authority on screen. He was joined by Dorothy McGuire, considerably more familiar to American audiences after being Oscar-nominated for *Gentleman's Agreement* (1947), starring in *The Spiral Staircase* (1946) and Disney's *Old Yeller* (1957) and leading lady in *Three Coins in the Fountain* (1954) and *Friendly Persuasion* (1956). Silent film star Sessue Hayakawa (*The Bridge on the River Kwai*, 1957) is the pirate chief.[643] Disney had learned another lesson from bigger companies: To keep down costs, he groomed his own young stars. James MacArthur had appeared in *The Light in the Forest* (1958), *Third Man on the Mountain* and *Kidnapped* (1959), second-billed in the last two. Janet Munro was the female lead in *Darby O'Gill and the Little People* (1959) and *Third Man on the Mountain*. Tommy Kirk appeared in *Old Yeller* and *The Shaggy Dog*, Kevin Corcoran in *Old Yeller*, *The Shaggy Dog* and *Pollyanna*.

British director Ken Annakin was a Disney veteran, helming *The Story of Robin Hood and His Merrie Men* (1952) and *Third Man on the Mountain* (1959).[644] Annakin spent over a year on the project[645] and after considering Jamaica[646] opted for Tobago, with animals and trainers imported, for "adventures never shown in a picture before."[647] Famed second unit director Yakima Canutt headed a contingent of 14 animal handlers.[648] Three storms affected production and unforeseen technical problems caused lighting issues.[649] Many scenes were dangerous: the raft in a real whirlpool, a shark dragged through the water, hyenas attacking the crew,[650] a tiger leaping out of an 18-foot-deep pit.[651] Not to mention the anacondas. Related Annakin: "Neither of the two boys (James MacArthur and Tommy Kirk) was very happy about having the snake coiled around them but they accepted the word of the snake expert when he said it would always leave go if its head was put under water."[652] It was the studio's biggest live-action gamble since *20,000 Leagues*; the budget increased from \$3.5 million to \$5 million.[653] Despite initial musings about roadshow,[654] it proved difficult to find a Broadway first run operation willing to gamble on a family picture. The 556-seater Embassy in Times Square only occasionally delved into first run and required a \$75,000 upgrade.[655]

A thrilling shipwreck is followed by episodes of inventive comedy, often featuring animals, leading to an equally inventive climactic battle with pirates. The story, however, is intelligent, driven by serious issues. After resourceful Mills, king of the do-it-yourself dads, has knocked up a luxurious tree house complete with waterwheel, the family enjoys an idyllic life, but sons growing up fast will eventually lust after the unmentionable. So the two older boys set off in search of other life, in the process discovering the pirate camp and freeing the captured Roberta (Munro), who begins romancing Fritz (MacArthur). Expecting imminent attack, the family rigs booby traps. Stirring battle commences and naturally it ends happily. All terrific stuff, great effects, Mills at his paternal best, a little bit of young love, plenty of comedy, and a great battle, family not essential to appreciate it.

Critical reception: "Rousing, humorous and gentle-hearted" (*New York Times*); "overstuffed Disney version" (*Variety*); "wonderful to watch, yet dull to hear" (*Films and Filming*).[656]

Rentals: \$14.1 million[657] (including 1969 reissue) (\$100.4 million equivalent)

37: *Who's Afraid of Virginia Woolf?*

Starring Elizabeth Taylor and Richard Burton; directed by Mike Nichols; screenplay, Ernest Lehman, based on the Edward Albee play; producer, Lehman; music, Alex North. Warner Brothers. June 21, 1966.

The most vicious marriage ever committed to screen was a huge risk for Elizabeth Taylor as the vitriolic, foul-mouthed wife. She was the biggest star in the world bar none, far ahead of Newman, Wayne and McQueen on salary alone (she earned \$1.1 million here plus 10 percent[658])—never mind box office pulling power, and she was considered one of the great movie beauties. Taylor would be transformed into a dowdy, frumpy, overweight sight, playing a woman a decade older than her 33 years,[659] far removed from the gloriously photographed classical pictures—"two decades of merchandising her looks"[660]—on which she had built her name. Director Mike Nichols had his doubts: "It's like asking a chocolate milkshake to do the work of a double martini."[661]

The story is slight: inebriated couple, university professor George (Richard Burton) and wife Martha (Taylor), daughter of the university president, invite over a newly arrived professor (George Segal) and his meek wife (Sandy Dennis) for an evening of Hell. Taylor was not first choice, playwright Albee's dream team being Bette Davis and James Mason.[662] Burton—\$750,000 but no points[663]—was far from anybody's idea of a henpecked husband. Jack Lemmon and Glenn Ford turned it down.[664] Directors Fred Zinnemann, Frenchman Henri-George Clouzot (*The Wages of Fear*, 1953) and John Frankenheimer were considered.[665] Mike Nichols was not an obvious choice. Being a three-time Tony winner was some accomplishment but those were comedies; this would be his first stab at drama.

Taylor was at a career peak after scoring box office hoopla and/or acting kudos for *BUtterfield 8* (1960), *Cleopatra* (1963), *The V.I.P.s* (1963) and *The Sandpiper* (1965), all but one co-starring her husband. Burton was similarly at a career high with, apart from the dramatic duets with Taylor, Oscar nominations for *Becket* (1964) and *The Spy Who Came In from the Cold* (1965) plus *The Night of the Iguana* (1964). While not in his wife's league as a box office attraction, he had very much come into his own.

After the chief supporting role was turned down by Robert Redford, whom Nichols had directed on stage in *Barefoot in the Park*, it passed to George Segal, a movie novice with only a role as a vicious P.O.W. in *King Rat* (1965) to suggest he could cope. Discounting a tiny role in *Splendor in the Grass* (1961), this would comprise Tony winner Sandy Dennis' movie debut.[666] Even so, in acting terms, the pair could easily be lambs to the slaughter.

Edward Albee was paid $500,000 for his play,[667] considered the greatest work of the decade. The playwright was viewed as the natural successor to Tennessee Williams and Arthur Miller, and the text regarded as a sacred cow, so untouchable that when screenwriter Ernest Lehman tampered with it, the stars objected. The film ended up close to the original. Boy wonder theater director Nichols—on $250,000[668]—could not have chosen a more difficult assignment or more difficult leading man and lady, both known for their own knockout verbal fisticuffs and alcohol consumption. Although capable of disruptive on-set tantrums, Taylor proved the consummate professional, line perfect, hitting her marks; Nichols was "awed by her technical virtuosity."[669] Cinematographer Harry Stradling was fired for making Taylor look too good and replaced by Haskell Wexler.[670] Exteriors were filmed at Smith College in Northampton, Massachusetts, and Richard Sylbert designed the studio set. Two weeks (unpaid) rehearsal time was allocated to allow the stars, with little direction from Nichols, to find their characters.[671]

Basically, the whole movie is one long argument with little respite, filmed virtually on one set in black-and-white. But it had worked extraordinary well on stage and the movie did not disappoint. The entire acting corps was superb with Taylor a revelation in a role that took some guts to tackle. The movie made history by being Oscar-nominated in every category. Taylor and Dennis walked away with Best Actress and Best Supporting Actress, respectively; there was also prizes for photography, art direction and costume design. But it made history in another way—the final nail in the coffin of the Production Code. Nichols refused to temper the expletive-ridden dialogue.[672] It would open with or without the seal of approval. Warner Brothers imposed an "adults only" contract on exhibitors,[673] the Catholic Office passed it as A-IV ("for adults with reservations") and Geoffrey Shurlock initially withheld Code approval; it then passed upstairs to Jack Valenti, new boss of the MPAA. The original ruling was overturned[674] after two lines were cut.[675] "The Code Is Dead," screamed trade newspaper headlines.[676]

Critical reception: "Taylor … a revelation…. Burton's acting the best of his career" (*Life*); "an ordered mélange with not too many pieces but each of them colliding against its neighbor" (*Saturday Review*); "a cinematic equivalent for the essentially theatrical form of Edward Albee's play" (*Films and Filming*); "outstanding drama" (*Box Office*).[677]

Rentals: $14.2 million ($101.2 million equivalent)

35 (tie): *Romeo and Juliet*

Starring Leonard Whiting and Olivia Hussey; directed by Franco Zeffirelli; screenplay, Franco Busati, based on the play by William Shakespeare; producers, John

122   The Films

Brabourne and Anthony Havelock-Allen; music, Nino Rota. Paramount. March 4, 1968 (London)[678]; U.S.: October 8, 1968.

Shakespeare had not been big box office since Sir Laurence Olivier went into battle with *Henry V* (1944). If Marlon Brando could not tempt audiences, beyond hordes of bored school kids, to watch *Julius Caesar* (1953), and the adulteration of plays as material for musicals *Kiss Me Kate* (1953) and *West Side Story* (1961) did not popularize the works, then the world's most famous writer appeared finished as a source of screenplays. Then the world's most famous movie couple Elizabeth Taylor and Richard Burton stepped into the breach with *The Taming of the Shrew* (1967), directed by Franco Zeffirelli. The duo, fresh from artistic and box office acclaim for *Who's Afraid of Virginia Woolf?* (1966), revived interest in his works. Emboldened, the director hazarded an even more adventurous subject: *Romeo and Juliet*.

There was already a ballet,[679] a possible musical[680] and other versions.[681] Rather than calling on experience, Zeffirelli considered actors closer in age to the play's characters. This thirteenth screen adaptation[682] would include a nude scene. For Leonard Whiting (Romeo), just 17 at the time of its release, this marked his movie debut, while Olivia Hussey (Juliet), a year younger, was only marginally less the screen neophyte with small roles in *The Battle of the Villa Fiorita* (1965) and the British-made *Cup Fever* (1965). Both had more stage experience, Whiting the Artful Dodger in the musical *Oliver!* for 18 months and a stint at the National Theatre, Hussey also on the London stage in *The Prime of Miss Jean Brodie*,[683] where she was spotted by Zeffirelli.[684] Paul McCartney has claimed he was in the running for the role of Romeo[685] and Angelica Huston pulled out of possible involvement when cast in her father's *A Walk with Love and Death*.

Zeffirelli bracketed the young stars with slightly older actors in key parts: John McEnery as Mercutio and Michael York as Tybalt, plus seasoned stage performers Robert Stephens and Milo O'Shea. Olivier[686] read the prologue. To make the film more accessible and to mask the young couple's lack of experience, Zeffirelli eliminated many long speeches and placed greater focus on close-ups as a way of registering romance in visual fashion. To open up a potentially stagey picture, the film was shot in a variety of Italian locations: the balcony scene at Palazzo Borghese in Artena, the church and tomb scenes in Tuscany, and the duel in Gubbio. The Palazzo Piccolomini in Pienza doubled as the Capulet palace. With the budget held down below the million-dollar mark, it was no great financial risk, a greater fear being ridicule for audacity. Although it was given a "critical drubbing" in Britain,[687] where it opened first, Paramount believed its timing was just right, *Bonnie and Clyde* (1967) and especially *The Graduate* (1967) having opened up the prospect of a different audience age-group, the "youth" market. Although at just over 135 minutes it was too short for roadshow, Paramount intended to ape Columbia's *Man for All Seasons* (1966) strategy. This appeared the optimum route because "the cultural trappings would be enhanced by slow playoff on a reserved seat basis at small urban arties." The launch was set for the 568-seat Paris in New York despite "almost no advance sales or theater parties" and the opposition of the director.[688] In the end, market research prevailed and it began with a continuous program policy.[689]

For the first time, viewers came to the heart of a glorious romance without words getting the way. Cutting down the text freed the lovestruck stars to emotionally respond without having to wait for the other to finish a speech and Zeffirelli's focus on faces ensured that rapt listening delivered the goods. Audiences, and not just the young, were enthralled, the world's greatest love story reinvented as a romance for the times. The actors gave highly credible performances, jointly winning a Golden Globe for Most Promising Newcomer. Zeffirelli and the film were Oscar-nominated. Without doubt the director managed to capture young love at its most intense, delivering an engaging picture that does not hang on every Shakespearean word, but lets the camera do the talking.

Critical reception: "The most exciting film of Shakespeare ever made" (*Chicago Sun-Times*); "brash casting experiment hampers classic tale" (*Variety*); "valiant attempt" (*Films and Filming*); "a vibrant electric rendering" (*Box Office*).[690]

Rentals: $14.5 million[691] ($103.3 million equivalent)

35 (tie): *2001: A Space Odyssey*

Starring Keir Dullea and Gary Lockwood; directed and produced by Stanley Kubrick; screenplay, Kubrick and Arthur C. Clarke; music provided by classical composers. MGM roadshow. April 2, 1968.

The youth-oriented audience to which Stanley Kubrick's landmark film most obviously appealed did not come out of nowhere. It had been spawned by *The Graduate* in December 1967, fueled by the stunning 1968 reissue of *Bonnie and Clyde* (1967)[692] and taken to new worlds by the February 1968 release of *Planet of the Apes*. All films were in general release so they swamped the nation rather than trickling out piecemeal, in a sense, priming a new kind of audience, even if it didn't know for what. Nobody knew for what.

2001: A Space Odyssey was a mystery, filmed in great secrecy.[693] At that point, the director was not an enigma; rather, he was well-regarded and decent box office as *Spartacus* (1960), *Lolita* (1962) and *Dr. Strangelove* (1964) attested. But he was close to becoming a liability. The budget had gone from $4.5 million to $10 million. It was the Delay of the Decade: The movie was announced for Christmas 1966, then Easter 1967, then Fall 1967, until it finally appeared at Easter 1968.[694]

There were only two actors of note, Keir Dullea and Gary Lockwood. When production began, Dullea was a promising actor after *David and Lisa* (1962) and when the film launched he was in exactly the same position after Mark Rydell's *The Fox* (1967), a surprise hit. Lockwood was an unknown, having mostly appeared on television. Propping up the marquee should have been E.G. Marshall (of the TV series *The Defenders*) but he pulled out.[695] Canadian actor Douglas Rain had the most memorable role, although unseen, as the voice of HAL. The film was shot in Britain from December 1965, the bulk of the budget spent on groundbreaking special effects with intricate models and rotating sets. Books have been written about the process and I'm not going to attempt to encapsulate that here. Originally, Alex North (*Spartacus*, 1960) was commissioned to write a score but he was dropped in favor of classical music. Kubrick and sci-fi novelist Arthur C. Clarke spent most of 1964 writing the picture, the following year polishing the screenplay and picking the brains of technical experts.[696] But when principal photography finished, there remained the challenge of over 200 special effects.[697]

In the mid–1960s, it looked as if a new sci-fi golden age was on the horizon. Hollywood was entering a fictional space race. Universal was ramping up Ray Bradbury's *The Martian Chronicles* as a 70mm Cinerama roadshow to star Gregory Peck, directed by Robert Mulligan on a $10 million–plus budget.[698] Twentieth Century–Fox released *Fantastic Voyage* (1966) and Universal a different Bradbury project, *Fahrenheit 451* (1966),

Struggling to find excuses for the film's oft-delayed release MGM came up with the notion that (a) its release so close to another Cinerama venture *Grand Prix* would confuse viewers and (b) there were not enough roadshow theaters available.* Trade press advertisement (*Box Office*, January 17, 1966, 2).

*"Metro Delays *2001* for Fall Opening, *Variety*, January 25, 1967, 3; "Release Brake May Stall B.O.," *Variety*, September 13, 1967, 3.

directed by Francois Truffaut. Paramount was readying Roger Vadim's *Barbarella* (1968) with Jane Fonda and Twentieth Century–Fox *Planet of the Apes* (1968). But these all had definable stories and nobody knew what Kubrick had. And while roadshow was a ready-made vehicle for spectacle, it was also a medium that required story. Beyond the special effects, it was clear that whatever plot existed did not kick in until halfway through the picture. The idea of selling a movie as pure experience might work with *Grand Prix* (1966) with its split screens and seismic explosions of noise but that had a strong storyline and stars with some box office credentials. This picture had neither stars nor, as compensation, stars in the making and whatever acting was taking place did not involve romance, thrills, a shootout or even aliens.

However, MGM could not back out of roadshow now, despite an initial advertising campaign under Kubrick's supervision intent on not making it "look like a movie ad."[699] Advance sales, although originally "perky,"[700] fell away once the movie opened and it became clear that its "quasi-hippie" audience was disinclined to book in advance.[701] On the other hand, it was just as well it went into roadshow because exhibitors were committed to a specific length of booking and could not yank it off the screen, giving the movie breathing space. This permitted moviegoers to find it at their leisure. Exhibitors reported an unusual trend, customers not taking a seat but lying down in the aisles. It took a while for staid cinema managers to work out that half the time the audience was stoned. But the kids kept coming and coming until MGM had a hit on its hands.

Never mind the kids, the movie turned into a *cause célèbre*, in part because of the negative reaction of New York critics[702] who saw it first in its full 160-minute glory. Los Angeles and Washington critics were more positive, as were most provincial critics presented with the shortened version, 19 minutes lopped off between the third and fourth public viewings.[703] Andrew Sarris, who should have recognized a true auteur when he saw one, to his shame panned it twice, blaming his dislike on the "generation gap." Other newspapers recanted original views, the *New York Times* assigning William Kloman to give a second opinion—he pronounced it "poetry."[704] Stars, directors and rock royalty—Paul Newman, Mick Jagger, John Schlesinger, Mike Nichols, John Lennon, Henry Fonda, Warren Beatty—came out in public support. Franco Zeffirelli cabled Kubrick: "You made me dream."

In hindsight it became obvious what a monumental movie Kubrick had in mind. Based on the Arthur C. Clarke story "The Sentinel," Kubrick's epic took the audience from a tribe of hominids confronting an alien monolith to a future where a similar artifact is discovered orbiting Jupiter. A malevolent computer attempts to take control. An astronaut is then sucked into a kaleidoscope of mesmeric light and transformed. Kubrick's visual extravaganza is a journey through awe, the stunning monolith, the vast rotating spaceship, vengeful computer HAL and the final burst of effects like an out-of-control aurora borealis. The power of the movie is in equal measure delivered by the earth-shattering special effects and a mystery that appears to move further away the closer we get. For many viewers, it was one giant, stunning visual puzzle; for others, it was boring.

Critical reaction: "An antiseptic adventure in space and suspense, though one is never sure where the suspense is leading" (*International Motion Picture Exhibitor*)[705]; "biggest amateur movie of all time" (*Harpers*)[706]; "unprecedented psychedelic roller coaster of an experience" (*Life*); "breathtaking to watch" (*Saturday Review*); "special effects border on the miraculous" (*Newsweek*); "a milestone, a landmark in the art

126   The Films

of film" (*Los Angeles Times*).[707] In the *Cahiers du Cinema* year-end best list, it ranked thirteenth.[708]

Rentals: $14.5 million[709] ($103.3 million equivalent)

34: *Spartacus*

Starring Kirk Douglas, Tony Curtis and Jean Simmons; directed by Stanley Kubrick; screenplay, Dalton Trumbo, based on the novel by Howard Fast; producer, Edward Lewis; music, Alex North. Universal roadshow. October 6, 1960.

Yul Brynner battled Kirk Douglas to produce the first film about Spartacus. In the late 1950s, Brynner was on the verge of becoming a one-man movie mogul, his deal with United Artists running to 11 pictures,[710] first offering the $5.5 million *Spartacus and the Gladiators* with Brynner as star and Martin Ritt directing.[711] In a clash over title rights, Hollywood's governing body, the MPAA, stepped in and allowed Brynner to retain his title,[712] although it was subsequently renamed *The Gladiators*.[713] Douglas had discovered he was not as big a star as he imagined. Despite three Best Actor Oscar nominations for *Champion* (1949), *The Bad and the Beautiful* (1952) and *Lust for Life* (1956) and hits like *20,000 Leagues Under the Sea* (1954) and *Gunfight at the O.K. Corral* (1957), he struggled to find backing for a multi-million dollar project on the strength of his name alone. When Oscar-winning director David Lean (*The Bridge on the River Kwai*, 1957) turned it down,[714] Douglas pursued another route, the all-star-cast, sending the script to five-time Oscar nominee Laurence Olivier, Oscar winner Charles Laughton and Peter Ustinov[715]—only to discover Brynner had done the same.[716] When all three agreed to Douglas' proposal, he had a movie—Brynner shifting focus to *The Magnificent Seven* (1960)—with Universal putting up the cash for what would become its biggest-ever picture,[717] the budget mushrooming to $12 million.[718] How Tony Curtis, who had worked with Douglas on *The Vikings* (1958), came to be signed was open to dispute. Douglas insisted he created a part for him,[719] Curtis that it was Universal who did the insisting.[720]

Douglas' former protégé Elsa Martinelli would have been ideal for the female lead, but there was too much water under that bridge. Ingrid Bergman turned it down. Douglas nixed Jean Simmons, preferring French actress Jeanne Moreau who was not interested.[721] Douglas instead hired German actress Sabina Bethmann (*Tiger of Bengal*, 1959)[722] but when she proved unacceptable, Simmons was awarded the part.[723] Simmons had successfully made the transition from British films like *The Blue Lagoon* (1949) to Hollywood leading lady opposite Robert Mitchum in Otto Preminger's *Angel Face* (1953), Richard Burton in the Biblical epic *The Robe* (1953), Marlon Brando in *Guys and Dolls* (1955) and Gregory Peck in *The Big Country* (1958). The outstanding supporting cast included John Gavin, Oscar-nominated Nina Foch, Charles McGraw, Herbert Lom and Woody Strode. Douglas openly broadcast the fact that blacklisted writer Dalton Trumbo had written the screenplay.[724] Universal placed Anthony Mann, who had directed many of the studio's biggest films including *Winchester '73* (1950) and *The Glenn Miller Story* (1954), at the helm.[725] The director was sacked early on, Douglas asserting he could not handle the scope of the picture,[726] a rather strange assessment given that Mann went on to make the outstanding *El Cid* (1961). He was replaced by Stanley Kubrick, who had directed Douglas in *Paths of Glory* (1957). Kubrick never quite claimed ownership of the film, complaining of interference by Douglas in his capacity as producer. But it is hard to specifically see the stamp of Douglas, especially compared to the quality of later films he directed, the nondescript *Scalawag* (1973) and *Posse* (1975).

Historical epics are often masterpieces of construction. The three-hour–plus running time provides the opportunity to place intimacy within the broad sweep of history. Individuality is set alongside intrigue, battles, huge sets involving thousands of extras and glorious costumes. Action, drama and romance are easily accommodated. However, some of the best scenes here are the characters' displays of dignity in the face of humiliation. Complex scheming sees Olivier, Laughton and Ustinov conspiring to achieve or retain political power. As with *El Cid*, it is the personal that holds it together. Spartacus, a slave condemned to death, is rescued by Ustinov, who places him in his gladiator school. When offered the servant Simmons as reward for good behavior, he refuses to take her by force and their romance develops. As punishment, Simmons is taken away by Olivier. After Woody Strode has staged an act of defiance in the arena, simmering rebellion produces escape. Spartacus leads the army of revolt and is joined by Simmons. Despite early success, the rebellion is put down. The Romans' attempt to identify the leader results in the famous "I'm Spartacus" scene, but Simmons is imprisoned along with their son. Spartacus is captured and fights a battle to the death against Curtis. Spartacus is crucified but Simmons escapes.

The thematic thrust of the film is about freedom and inhumanity but the core romance exerts a constant grip. Simmons is superb as the chattel finding freedom in love, eventually gaining freedom itself. Top-class actors deliver top-class performances although Ustinov was singled out by Oscar voters in the Supporting Actor category. The same voters disdained Douglas, possibly feeling they had seen this performance before, too much chin and teeth, and the film itself failed to be nominated for Best Picture. Audiences disagreed and it did better commercially than all the other nominated films. This was a movie made for roadshow, crammed with spectacle but full of intelligence, and in its examination of values and power as relevant today as it was then.

Critical reaction: "A spotty, uneven drama" (*New York Times*); "a work of splendid size and substance" (*Films and Filming*); "Kubrick has out–DeMilled the old master" (*Variety*); "lengthy spectacle consistently interesting" (*Washington Post*).[727]

Rentals: $14.6 million (including 1967 reissue) ($104 million equivalent)

33: *Thoroughly Modern Millie*

Starring Julie Andrews and James Fox; directed by George Roy Hill; screenplay, Richard Morris; producer, Ross Hunter; music, Elmer Bernstein.[728] Universal roadshow. March 21, 1967.

The jukebox musical is not a modern invention. A greatest hits package of 1920s songs provided the musical interludes in *Thoroughly Modern Millie*. As far as musicals were concerned, it was downhill after the triple whammy of *My Fair Lady* (1964), *Mary Poppins* (1964) and *The Sound of Music* (1965). It was hard to re-capture their special magic. Nonetheless, movie companies, salivating over the prospect of similar returns, proceeded to throw away more than the cumulative profits of those three in a vain attempt to repeat their success. Otherwise, it is unlikely that *Doctor Dolittle* (1967), *Half a Sixpence* (1967), *The Happiest Millionaire* (1967), *Star!* (1968) and a dozen others would ever have seen the light of day.

Songwriters Jimmy van Heusen and Sammy Cahn had three Best Song Oscars: "All the Way" (*The Joker Is Wild*, 1957), "High Hopes" (*A Hole in the Head*, 1959) and "Call Me Irresponsible" (*Papa's Delicate Condition*, 1963). Others in their portfolio included "Ain't That a Kick in the Head" (*Ocean's 11*, 1960) and "My Kinda Town" (*Robin and the 7 Hoods*, 1964). Trade press advertisement (*Box Office*, January 16, 1967, 7).

The Films   129

One of the few that did not fall by the commercial wayside was *Thoroughly Modern Millie*, conceived when Julie Andrews was still at her peak with *Hawaii* (1966) and Hitchcock's *Torn Curtain* (1966) to add to her previous musical pair. The movie covered similar flapper territory to Sandy Wilson's *The Boyfriend*.[729] While there's way too much plot, there are also plenty of good songs and Andrews shining through. Even though Universal had given musicals a wide berth since *Flower Drum Song's* (1961) so-so returns and avoided roadshows after *Spartacus* (1960), Andrews's name prompted that release format, especially with a relatively low budget of $6 million and a production that encountered no obstacles. The singer was reunited with *Hawaii* director George Roy Hill, singularly lacking in musical experience. British actor James Fox (*Those Magnificent Men in Their Flying Machines*, 1965) was the leading man. Better known, perhaps, to American audiences was Mary Tyler Moore, coming off a five-year stint on TV's *The Dick Van Dyke Show*. Making her movie debut was Carol Channing, Tony winner for *Hello, Dolly!* John Gavin's movie career had wound down after *Back Street* (1961) and he was now more of a TV name (*Destry*, 1964, and *Convoy*, 1965).

It's a slight story unnecessarily complicated. In the 1920s, Andrews plays a "modern" girl who takes Moore under her wing. The modern girl wants a modern job, the old-fashioned girl wants to become an actress. For romance, Andrews targets wealthy boss Gavin, whom she considers more "husband material" than happy-go-lucky salesman Fox. Gavin, meanwhile, fancies Moore. So far, so typically old-fashioned, girl-meets-boy, girl-loses-boy, and then who knows. But suddenly the movie shifts into a different gear. Moore disappears, victim of white slave trader Carol Channing. The rescue descends into farce. It turns out that Andrews is not poor after all and the romances are all straightened out. Luckily, the plot shenanigans fail to unhinge what is otherwise a very sweet picture with Andrews in top form. The Roaring Twenties setting adds a certain something, especially with Andrews as its chief influencer. It also contains the madcap sensibility of *The Great Race* (1965) with stereotypical bad guys (and woman), plot devices such as Fox disguised as a woman and nods to silent movies.

Although Andrews was a lock, any guarantee that she would bring in the audiences still depended on the material. Unusually for a musical, this had no Broadway precedent, so the songs had not been tried out on stage in front of live audiences and polished to perfection before making the leap to the screen. Universal got around that by turning it into a compilation of old songs such as "Baby Face" (1926), "Do It Again" (1922), "Jazz Baby" (1919), "Lookin' at the World Thru Rose Coloured Glasses" (1920s), "Ah Sweet Mystery of Life" (1910), "I Can't Believe That You're in Love with Me" (1926), "Stumbling" (1922), "Poor Butterfly" (1916) and "Rose of Washington Square" (1920)—originally performed by Fanny Brice (subject of the 1967 biopic *Funny Girl*). These were given an updated treatment by Andre Previn. For the theme song, also called "Thoroughly Modern Millie," the director turned to songwriters Jimmy Van Heusen and Sammy Cahn, who also contributed "The Tapioca." Nostalgia was the movie's secret weapon.

Much of the marketing revolved around recreating the fashions and dances of the period. Elmer Bernstein won an Oscar for the music, Channing a Best Supporting Actress nomination. Despite quibbles about the plot and racist stereotypes, it's a decent old-fashioned confection.

Critical reaction: "Swell enchantment" (*Los Angeles Times*); "thoroughly delightful" (*New York Times*); "first half much better than the second" (*Variety*).[730]

Rentals: $14.7 million[731] ($104.7 million equivalent)

130 The Films

28 (tie): *Rosemary's Baby*

Starring Mia Farrow and John Cassavetes; directed by Roman Polanski; screenplay, Polanski, based on the book by Ira Levin; producer, William Castle[732]; music, Krzysztof Komeda. Paramount. June 12, 1968.

Blockbusting books the size of bricks dominated the hardback bestseller lists in the 1960s,[733] novels like *Hawaii* by James Michener, *The Agony and the Ecstasy* by Irving Stone, *Ship of Fools* by Katharine Anne Porter, *Valley of the Dolls* by Jacqueline Susann, all filmed during that decade. Thrillers, on the other hand, barely accounted for ten percent of the annual Top Ten hardback charts—a couple from John le Carré, a brace from Ian Fleming, a pair from Mary Stewart, one from Helen MacInnes—and Ira Levin's *Rosemary's Baby*, the only one not to feature spies. Levin was best known for plays, one every two years, especially the stage comedies *No Time for Sergeants*, made into a hugely successful film two years later, and *Critic's Choice*, which became a Bob Hope movie vehicle. Levin had only one previous novel to his name, the thriller *A Kiss Before Dying* (1953).[734] Its sales did not suggest that *Rosemary's Baby*, published in 1967, would sell four million copies.

The heyday of horror fiction—Mary Shelley, Edgar Allan Poe and Bram Stoker—was long past, apart from Shirley Jackson's *The Haunting of Hill House*[735] and Robert Bloch's *Psycho*; the diabolical was primarily in the hands of Dennis Wheatley. Horror films, churned out by American International and the English outfit Hammer, were strictly B-division. No matter the genre, bestsellers were eagerly snapped up, the prevailing wisdom that they provided a built-in audience and marketing angles.[736]

Rosemary's Baby ended up at Paramount, undergoing a production revolution[737] thanks to a young go-getter called Robert Evans. Not quite the whiz kid he would become, not with Otto Preminger's *Skidoo* (1968) on his slate and *Darling Lili*, still two years away from release, already looking dicey. But he had someone in mind for *Rosemary's Baby*, someone unusual. There *had* been decent horror films made in the 1960s—except they originated from Europe and out of the mind of Polish director and Holocaust survivor Roman Polanski. *Repulsion* (1965) and *Cul de Sac* (1966), more of a thriller, had been two of the most original movies Evans had ever seen. Sure, Polanski then blotted his copybook with *The Fearless Vampire Killers* (1967), a horror spoof. Correctly surmising the last thing Polanski wanted was another horror film, Evans tempted the director, a ski nut, with *Downhill Racer*. But when Polanski took the meeting, Evans owned up to the subterfuge and slipped him a pre-publishing copy of *Rosemary's Baby*. Twenty-four hours later, the director was hooked.[738]

Mia Farrow was far from first choice, Tuesday Weld (*Lord Love a Duck*, 1966) and Polanski's fiancée Sharon Tate (*The Fearless Vampire Killers*) hotter favorites, Patty Duke and Goldie Hawn decent side bets.[739] Farrow was one of a host of stars of TV's *Peyton Place* (1964) but public awareness skewed high through marriage to Frank Sinatra. She had a supporting role in *Guns at Batasi* (1964) but this would be a huge snatch at fame. Robert Redford (*Barefoot in the Park*, 1967) would have been a cinch for the male lead except he was in a legal dispute with the studio.[740] John Cassavetes (*The Dirty Dozen*, 1967) was not first choice[741] either, although he was almost better known as a director (*A Child Is Waiting*, 1963). Also better known in another department was Ruth Gordon, who along with Garson Kanin had scripted the Tracy-Hepburn showcases *Adam's Rib* (1949) and *Pat and Mike* (1952) and had only revived her acting career in 1965 after a 15-year absence. For collectors of trivia, Victoria Vetri, before donning furs and not much else for *When Dinosaurs Ruled the Earth* (1970), had a supporting role.

One of the significant elements of the R-rated film[742] was that it played out in the middle of uptown New York rather than, as in most horror films, a small town or an eerie castle. The setting was chic, mini-skirts, mini-haircuts, the backdrop real rather than contrived, the sleek production designed by Richard Sylbert, Oscar winner for *Who's Afraid of Virginia Woolf?* (1966). The film is a variation on the Faust legend, but instead just selling himself to the Devil, Cassavetes sells his wife and, more importantly, her womb.

The story is from the perspective of Farrow, perfectly cast as an innocent (and even more elfin and slight after her haircut), married to struggling actor John Cassavetes. There is a hint of what is to come when the couple takes an apartment in a building rumored to have a diabolical history. Cassavetes' career is on the upturn after they make the acquaintance of elderly neighbors. Although previously child-averse, he is suddenly in favor. She has a terrifying dream and shortly after becomes pregnant but later, suspicions aroused, fears that her baby will be sacrificed to the Devil. But she is wrong. The narrative is straightforward and Farrow an ideal victim whose increasing worries are dismissed by husband and neighbors. Directorial delivery is perfectly pitched. Cassavetes' creepiness is compensated by an Oscar-winning performance by Ruth Gordon[743] as the apparently harmless, dotty neighbor. The shocks are well-timed and the denouement terrific.

Critical reception: "Extremely implausible" (*New York Times*); "class shocker" (*Box Office*); "several milestones, all but one exhilarating" (*Variety*)[744]; "superb suspense" (*Time*); "masterpiece of suspense and horror" (*Newsday*).[745] It placed 16th on the annual *Cahiers du Cinema* list.[746]

Rentals: $15 million ($106.9 million equivalent)

28 (tie): *Planet of the Apes*

Starring Charlton Heston; directed by Franklin J. Schaffner; screenplay, Michael Wilson and Rod Serling, based on the novel *Monkey Planet* by Pierre Boulle; producer, Arthur P. Jacobs; music, Jerry Goldsmith. Twentieth Century–Fox. February 8, 1968.

J. Lee Thompson (*The Guns of Navarone*, 1961) saw a much-needed boost to a drifting career vanish when he ducked out of this project[747] in favor of *Mackenna's Gold* (1969). Blake Edwards, first director attached, probably also lamented losing out.[748] Producer Arthur P. Jacobs could hardly believe his luck after the calamitous *Doctor Dolittle* (1967)[749] and you could probably say the same for director Franklin J. Schaffner,[750] relegated to television and movie stiffs like *The Double Man* (1967) after the failure of big-budget historical drama *The War Lord* (1965). Charlton Heston was also in dire need of career resuscitation; his past five movies—*Major Dundee* (1965), *The Agony and the Ecstasy* (1965), *The War Lord* (1965), *Khartoum* (1966) and the realistic Western *Will Penny* (1967)—had all tanked.[751] And Warner Brothers regretted letting it go.[752]

Twentieth Century–Fox pictures studio head honcho Darryl F. Zanuck found a part for his daughter-in-law Linda Harrison[753] as Nova, the mute love interest. Former child star Roddy McDowall, Kim Hunter and Maurice Evans flesh out the ape contingent. Source material was the novel *Monkey Planet* by Pierre Boulle, author of the 1952 novel

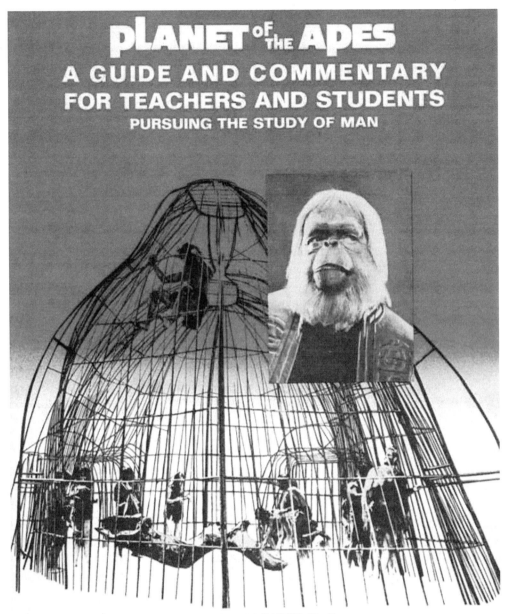

Leader was the author of a college textbook, *Atoms of Galaxies*. He posed questions asking whether man was the most dangerous creature on the planet and whether man's dominance could be overtaken by apes (pressbook).

The Bridge Over the River Kwai. Twilight Zone creator Rod Serling took a year to turn in a viable screenplay and the formerly blacklisted Michael Wilson,[754] whose name had been removed from the credits of *The Bridge on the River Kwai* (1957) and *Lawrence of Arabia* (1962), added the polish.[755]

If you were looking for a sci-fi picture with dramatic heft, decent action, mysterious outcome and an examination of the human condition, this was a more straightforward bet than *2001: A Space Odyssey* (1968). While Fox reckoned its previous sci-fi venture *Fantastic Voyage* (1966) had worked out well, it had reservations about the cost and the possibility of making an ape setting believable. In this case, the special effects conundrum was makeup for the apes. If they just looked like humans wearing monkey suits, the movie would not fly. Faces that could not express emotion and were as stiff as a Botox overdose would invite audience ridicule. In the end, the studio spent a million on pioneering ape renditions by John Chambers.[756] There were almost as many scripts as crew and the changes wrought as the picture moved closer to being greenlit were to switch from a futuristic setting to a primeval one (which, incidentally, saved on costs), covering up the breasts of the female prisoners and inventing the stunning ending. There were three endings, the one shot favored by the star. Heston's hoarse voice was not in the script, but an incidental by-product of him catching the flu. Apart from studio sets, the movie was partly filmed in blistering heat in Arizona. The rocket ship crashed into Lake Powell in Utah. Ape City—modeled on the work of celebrated Spanish architect Gaudi—was constructed on the Fox Ranch in Malibu, and the final scene was filmed on Zuma Beach in Malibu.[757]

The film is already set in the future but as the movie opens it accelerates 1,300 years ahead. Unlike *Fantastic Voyage* which told audiences what the mission was, *Planet of the Apes* opens with mystery. Where are we? What's going wrong? Nonetheless, there is a sense of human supremacy. Space travel is the result of human ingenuity, after all. For about the first quarter of the film, the astronauts stumble about lost. When the apes appear, nothing cute about them, the movie bolts in a different direction where shocks come thick and fast and the film exudes "bitter social comment."[758] Like *Rosemary's Baby*, the movie is viewed through the eyes of an innocent, one who cannot accept his fall down the evolutionary food chain. The casting of Heston dupes the audience into thinking he is somehow going to win, rather than just escape. His escape leads to a final horror. He is an experiment who has wandered into the wrong planet. His world is turned upside down as he is poked, prodded, routinely humiliated and generally treated like an animal while the ruling classes debate whether man is worth anything. The apes are thoroughly convincing, and in their marauding capacity very frightening, herding humans with nets, armed with rifles and fierce on horseback. It is a riveting watch, the audience roots for the Heston of *Ben-Hur*, expecting triumph, not realizing they are watching a chase movie and that there is, ultimately, no escape. The disjointed Jerry Goldsmith score underwrites that concept. A batch of brilliant lines deserves a place in the Screenplay Hall of Fame and there are few films that can top that shock ending.

Critical reception: "An amazing film" (*Variety*); "no good at all, but fun, at moments, to watch" (*New York Times*); "triumph of artistry and imagination" (*Los Angeles Times*); "amusing and unusually engrossing" (*Washington Post*).[759]

Rentals: $15 million ($106.9 million equivalent)

28 (tie): *Lawrence of Arabia*

Starring Peter O'Toole, Omar Sharif, Alec Guinness and Anthony Quinn; directed by David Lean; screenplay, Robert Bolt and Michael Wilson; producer, Sam Spiegel; music, Maurice Jarre. Columbia roadshow. December 10, 1962 (London); U.S.: December 16, 1962.

134 The Films

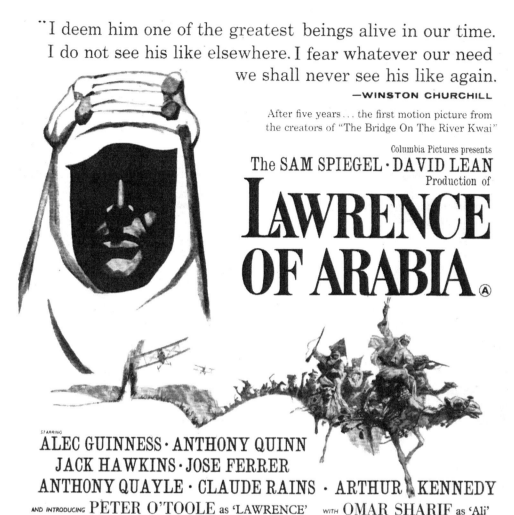

David Lean drove his Rolls-Royce Silver Cloud complete with air conditioning all over the desert during shooting. Rolls-Royce Silver Cloud armored cars, which had originally seen action during World War I, were employed by the production team. To keep them tuned up, mechanics had been shipped over from the company's Crewe factory in Britain* (Hannan Collection).

*Fowlie, *Dedicated Maniac*, 160.

You could have been watching John Wayne striding over those desert sands if an initiative in 1953 by Cinerama had come to fruition.[760] By that point, moviemakers had been trying to bring the legend of Lawrence of Arabia to life for over two decades. British producer Alexander Korda (*The Private Life of Henry VIII*, 1933) came closest[761] and MGM mooted a version with Clark Gable.[762] Also approached: David Lean, who turned it down.[763] In 1958, British studio Rank proposed Dirk Bogarde in the biggest British picture of all time but that never get off the runway either.[764] By the end of the 1950s, Lean came around to Sam Spiegel's version of the project as a follow-up to the pair's Oscar-winning *The Bridge on the River Kwai* (1957), Columbia's record box office grosser. Spiegel announced Marlon Brando in the title role for a million dollar fee,[765] and hired blacklisted writer Michael Wilson. Lean turned to playwright Robert Bolt, whose *A Man for All Seasons* was on its way to becoming a huge stage success.[766]

Brando dropped out, creating a massive opportunity for rising British star Albert Finney (*Saturday Night and Sunday Morning*, 1960). But the offer came with the caveat of a seven-year deal with Spiegel so Finney walked away.[767] That left the door open for unknown Peter O'Toole. Omar Sharif entered the equation only after Lean had considered Horst Buchholz (*The Magnificent Seven*, 1960), Jacques Bergerac (*Gigi*, 1958), Alain Delon (*Rocco and His Brothers*, 1960) and Maurice Ronet (*Purple Noon*, 1960).[768] With two unknowns, the film needed the marquee power of three Oscar winners: Alec Guinness (*The Bridge on the River Kwai*), Anthony Quinn (*Lust for Life*, 1956) and Jose Ferrer (*Cyrano de Bergerac*, 1950). Lean had hopes of William Holden or Gene Kelly[769] for the role finally played by Oscar nominee Arthur Kennedy (*Some Came Running*, 1958). The script was incomplete with Bolt, who compressed several characters into one composite,[770] constantly on call except for his writing being interrupted by a spell in prison, arrested at a CND march.[771] Shooting problems included dysentery, dehydration, swarms of locusts and temperatures over 100 degrees. With the picture 30 percent over budget, filming shifted to Spain[772] where unseasonal flooding caused further delay. Almeria doubled as the desert. Then production transferred to Morocco[773] where they ran out of camels. A few last scenes were shot in Britain.[774] In total, the schedule lasted 313 days.

Columbia oldtimer Morris Stoloff was hired to do the score, then replaced by Richard Rodgers.[775] Maurice Jarre was a last resort. In the run-up to launch, the film looked set for commercial disaster. Advance bookings indicated roadshow box office prospects; *Spartacus* (1960) registered $120,000 prior to opening while *Exodus* (1960) sold $611,000 worth of tickets. *Lawrence of Arabia* had barely $11,000 two months before opening.[776] If that was unexpected, then so was the picture. Nobody had envisaged such grandeur. Locations were stunning, music more evocative than virtually anything heard before from the screen.

The movie depicts the legend's rise and fall, the first half full of bravado and astonishing feats, the second half, as reality strikes, sees the hero's vision dissolve. Two stars are born, O'Toole and Sharif, the Arab's initial enmity giving way to respect. It is full of brilliant scenes: the first sighting of Sharif emerging from the mirage in a shot that lasts 100 seconds, the rescue of his servant Gassim, the blowing-up of trains, O'Toole striding atop a train in white flowing robes, the trek across the desert, Arabs overrunning Turkish guns at Aqaba, O'Toole's torture, and his robes getting thinner and thinner until he looks like a ghost. Running alongside bravura direction is O'Toole's performance as Lawrence on a voyage of self-discovery, from outcast at the beginning, dismissed as naïve by his superiors, to an outcast at the end, abandoned by the Arabs. He is used by political masters, British and Arabs, and never finds peace. Lawrence remains an enigma, his soul camouflaged behind his achievements, and that is perhaps the film's only flaw; it does flag in the second half, dragged down by politics.

It was nominated for ten Oscars, winning Best Picture, Best Director, Best Score and four more but O'Toole (Best Actor) and Sharif (Best Supporting Actor) were overlooked, giving way to Gregory Peck for *To Kill a Mockingbird* (1962) and Ed Begley for *Sweet Bird of Youth* (1962), respectively. It was also applauded by Lean's peers, Fred Zinnemann, Billy Wilder and King Vidor.[777] The movie was cut immediately after opening and again for general release. For later reissues, Lean added and subtracted scenes. Depending on which edit you saw, it lasted 202 minutes (first general release), 222 minutes (premiere) or 228 minutes (restored version). Whatever version you see, it will be worth it. Few films deserve their reputation more.

Critical reception[778]: "In the blockbuster league" (*Variety*); "huge, thundering camel-opera that runs down badly as it rolls on" (*New York Times*); "an epic with intellect behind it" (*London Evening Standard*); "one of the great all-time films" (*New York Post*); "dull ... overlong and impersonal" (*Village Voice*).[779]

Rentals: $15 million[780] ($106.9 million equivalent)

28 (tie): *The Bible*

Starring Richard Harris, George C. Scott and Peter O'Toole; directed by John Huston; screenplay, Christopher Fry; producer, Dino De Laurentiis; music, Toshiro Mayuzumi. Twentieth Century–Fox roadshow. September 8, 1966.

The best bits of the Old Testament had already been taken: *The Ten Commandments* (1956), *Samson and Delilah* (1949), *David and Bathsheba* (1951), *Solomon and Sheba* (1959)—so Italian producer Dino De Laurentiis went back to the beginning. He was also counting on the fact that Old Testament films had done significantly better than New Testament ones. Along with Carlo Ponti (*Doctor Zhivago*, 1965), De Laurentiis, married to Italian star Sylvana Mangano, was the most significant of the Italian producers who worked in conjunction with Hollywood. De Laurentiis announced himself to international audiences with the controversial *Bitter Rice* (1949), won the Best Foreign Language Film Oscar for Federico Fellini's *La Strada* (1954) and hired Kirk Douglas for the more commercial *Ulysses* (1954). He took on Hollywood at its own game with the Paramount co-production *War and Peace* (1956) with Audrey Hepburn and Henry Fonda and thereafter was the driving force behind Hollywood-financed films like *Five Branded Women* (1960) and *Barabbas* (1961).

The Bible was intended to be the first in what would these days be called a "Bible-verse" series. This picture concentrated on certain chapters from Genesis in portmanteau fashion with episodes covering Adam and Eve, Cain and Abel, Abraham, Noah and Lot. Initially conceived as a multi-director vehicle, it eventually ended up the sole preserve of John Huston (*The African Queen*, 1951). Since no character would run through the whole picture, it was presented, in typical roadshow fashion, with an all-star cast, whose marquee pull, it has to be said, was varied. Completed by 1964 but released two years later meant some cast members had now solidified audience appeal such as Richard Harris (*Major Dundee*, 1965), George C. Scott (*Dr. Strangelove*, 1964) and Stephen Boyd (*Genghis Khan*, 1965). Fans of Peter O'Toole would rightly be disgruntled since he has but a cameo of a cameo. On a global scale, Ava Gardner (*The Night of the Iguana*, 1964) was possibly the biggest star. But Michael Parks was an unknown and Swedish actress Ulla Bergryd was making her debut (they played Adam and Eve, respectively). Others were familiar primarily to Italian audiences: Franco Nero (*Django*, 1966), Gabriele Ferzetti (*Three Rooms in Manhattan*, 1965) and Eleonora Rossi Drago (*Behind Closed Shutters*, 1951).

Episodes were chosen for dramatic purposes and, in Cecil B. DeMille fashion, tested censor sensibilities—and attracted newspaper coverage—with nudity in the

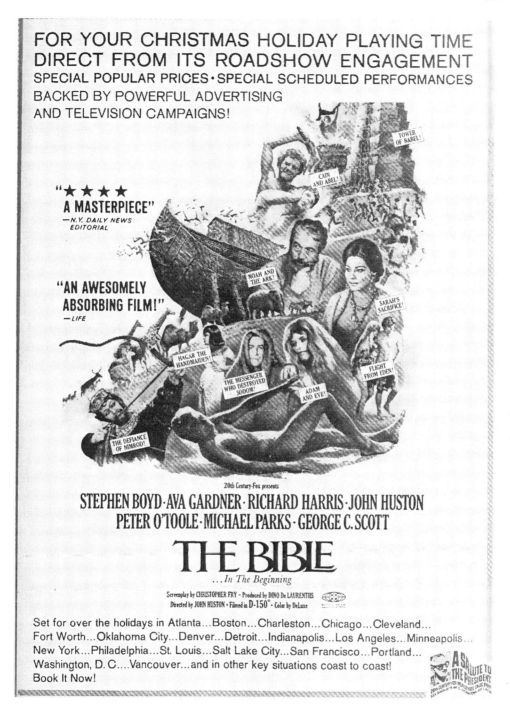

Paul Newman, Richard Burton and Maria Callas were also being sought to appear.* The film faced an Italian rival—San Paulo Film announcing a series of Biblical pictures beginning with *Saul and David,* followed by *The Judges of the Bible* with *Paulus* further along the line.† Trade press advertisement (*Box Office*, November 20, 1967).

*"Casting Bible with Familiar Faces," *Variety*, January 22, 1964, 1.
†Advert, *Variety*, April 29, 1964, 98.

138   The Films

Adam and Eve section, plus a fairly vivid account, for the times, of Sodom and various romantic entanglements; in other words, under the guise of goodness, plenty to sell. Given the odd mixture of talents and the equally unconnected episodes, most of it works well, the irredeemable redeemed by sensitive photography and the best parts, such as Noah (John Huston), delivered with intelligence rather than pontification.

Critical reaction: "Magnificent almost beyond cinematic belief" (*Los Angeles Times*); "impressive in some instances, absurd in others" (*Washington Post*); "no more than a picture book interpretation" (*Films and Filming*).

Rentals: $15 million ($106.9 million equivalent)

28 (tie): *Butch Cassidy and the Sundance Kid*

Starring Paul Newman, Robert Redford and Katharine Ross; directed by George Roy Hill; screenplay, William Goldman; producer, John Foreman; music, Burt Bacharach. Twentieth Century–Fox. September 23, 1969.

That screenwriter William Goldman was paid a record $400,000 was the only momentous element pre-production for *Butch Cassidy and the Sundance Kid*.[781] Hollywood routinely paid much more for bestsellers and musicals; *My Fair Lady* (1964) cost $5.5 million. Goldman, doubling as a novelist,[782] had rewritten *Masquerade* (1965) starring Cliff Robertson, been jettisoned by Robertson from *Charly* (1968) and adapted his own novel *No Way to Treat a Lady* for the 1968 movie. The Hollywood axiom "nobody knows anything," attributed to Goldman,[783] could easily apply to *Butch Cassidy and the Sundance Kid*. There was nothing auspicious about this picture as it entered production apart from the fact that it was ever made at all, after studio Twentieth Century–Fox suffered staggering losses on roadshows *Doctor Dolittle* (1967) and *Star!* (1968). Its $6.8 million budget was lower than the current productions *The Undefeated* (1969) and *Justine* (1969).[784] Sure, when it looked like Steve McQueen[785] might be Paul Newman's foil it attracted publicity but when McQueen was replaced by Robert Redford, media interest diminished. The word on Redford was so poor that Universal had shelved *Tell Them Willie Boy Was Here* (1969).[786] Newman was solid, though, box office hits *Hombre* (1967) and *Cool Hand Luke* (1967) adding to a growing reputation (four Oscar nominations[787] including *Cool Hand Luke*). Katharine Ross (*The Graduate*, 1967, and *The Hellfighters*, 1968) however, was a rising star.

After five years in TV and three on Broadway, director George Roy Hill made his movie debut with *Period of Adjustment* (1962) followed by *Toys in the Attic* (1963), *The World of Henry Orient* (1964) and the Julie Andrews pair *Hawaii* (1966) and *Thoroughly Modern Millie* (1967). Directors making their Western debuts had a habit of turning the genre upside down as witnessed by Howard Hawks' *Red River* (1948) and Fred Zinnemann's *High Noon* (1952)" In *Butch Cassidy and the Sundance Kid*, Hill brought a fresh pair of eyes which resulted in stylistic innovation, not least the musical interludes,[788] the black-and-white opening and ending, the freeze frame climax, and sparked a whole new sub-genre—the "buddy" movie, or what would be called these days a "bromance." Nonetheless, screenplay was key. To circumvent audience expectation, Goldman had to keep one step ahead. He adopted certain traditional Western sequences (a player accused of cheating at cards, a gang leader facing challenge, train robbing and pursuit by a posse), but he did so with a twist. Instead of confrontation at the poker

Butch Cassidy and the Sundance Kid did not open in London until February 1970—five months after the U.S. launch—and then not at one of the big Leicester Square cinemas but in nearby Haymarket at the 1,159-seat Carlton, which suggested less optimism about its release. Trade press advertisement (*Kine Weekly*, February 14, 1970, 2).

140 The Films

game, the heroes try steadfastly to avoid it, the challenge to Butch's leadership is resolved without bloodshed, the robberies are littered with both humanity and humor, and the posse remains a mysterious, distant threat.

The movie comprises, effectively, the classic three acts, each separated by a musical interlude. The relatively small number of sequences quickly pushes the story along as the heroes, if that is what they are, find their world increasingly compromised. The outlaws' camaraderie does not mask bitterness; they are not laden with regret, even if (like Butch) they have abandoned wife and children along the way, nor given to self-pity. Details about their past (real names, birthplace, etc.) are woven into the narrative, sometimes at moments of high drama. (We learn Butch cannot shoot at the one moment when he needs to.) Unusually, too, they are amiable characters for the most part, likable, evoking more audience sympathy than Pike Bishop's gang; Butch generally abhors violence. Like *The Wild Bunch*, this depicts the end of the road for the Western outlaw. The picture is studded with great lines: "You just keep thinking, Butch, that's what you're good at" and "Think you used enough dynamite, there, Butch?" Relentless pursuit had been a theme of the 1969 Westerns (*The Stalking Moon, True Grit,* etc.), but nobody has ever been as relentless as this. The posse always appears in long shot, a threat, but inescapable.

Hill keeps focus on the two main characters, plus Etta Place when they go on the run, the main players rarely seen apart. He only steers away from the Goldman screenplay to maintain tension and emotion. The action scenes are shot with bravura and, except for News Carver, incidental characters appear only to punch up the narrative or let the audience know what Butch and Sundance prefer to avoid. Even the lengthy chase sequence works very well thanks to the interplay between the outlaws, as confidence gives way to fear. Nuggets of humor, character-related rather than situational as in *Support Your Local Sheriff!* (1969), frame hidden feelings. The audience's final memory, rather than Butch's quip or the freeze frame, might well have been the image of them tenderly bandaging each other's wounds. Twentieth Century–Fox was not as confident of the end result as it later claimed, the film originally scheduled to open on Memorial Day (when it would have faced *Winning*, also starring Newman) and then July (up against *The Wild Bunch* and *True Grit*), so ended up in the box office black hole of September. It won four Oscars, for Goldman's screenplay, Bacharach's score, theme song and best sound.

Critical reaction: "Slow and disappointing" (*Chicago Sun-Times*); "directorial *tour de force*" (*International Motion Picture Exhibitor*); "dialog could have been lifted from a *Batman and Robin* episode" (*Time*).

Rentals: $15 million[789] ($106.9 million equivalent)

26 (tie): *The Carpetbaggers*

Starring George Peppard, Carroll Baker and Alan Ladd; directed by Edward Dmytryk; screenplay, John Michael Hayes; producer, Joseph E. Levine; music, Elmer Bernstein. Paramount. April 9, 1964.

Few Hollywood interlopers rose as high as Joseph E. Levine. Beginning, like the bulk of the men who set up Hollywood's initial studios, as an exhibitor, he turned himself into a distributor and from there to producer. Although credited with being the first to use wide release—or "saturation" as it was known then—instead of the long, slow, roll-out traditional in the 1950s and 1960s, he was not. (I wrote a book about the

Canadian director Edward Dymytryk spent a year in Mill Point Federal Prison, West Virginia, after being tried as one of the Hollywood Ten during the anti-communist witch hunt. Blacklisted, he moved to England where he helmed *Obsession* (1949) and *Give Us This Day* (1949) but later managed to resume his Hollywood career. Trade press advertisement (*Box Office*, May 11, 1964, 13).

development of the wide release system, *In Theaters Everywhere*, if you are interested.) But Levine certainly shook up Hollywood when he bought the Italian sword-and-sandals *Hercules* (1958) and spent a fortune releasing it everywhere at once in the same week. (What happens today, but rarely then.) For a good few years that was basically his *modus operandi*, buying someone else's pictures, usually from Italy, and releasing them with a huge marketing bang. He moved into production with *Boys' Night Out* (1962) and *Zulu* (1964)—the latter a hit in Britain but, despite the marketing money he threw at it, a flop in the States—and then set up a huge slate of pictures.[790]

But *The Carpetbaggers* was in a different league. Based on Harold Robbins' big, lusty[791] bestseller, in part about Hollywood,[792] it was sold as a big-budget prestige production when, in fact, its cost was low—just $3.3 million[793]—compared to other big films of the time. But, of course, Levine would shell out another million in marketing,[794] including the infamous

142 The Films

hand-biting advertisements,[795] a fashion show[796] and a tie-in with Coppertone.[797] Negative costs were kept low because, believing the book—and its controversy[798]—would sell the film, and Robbins being more publicity-savvy than other big-name writers, Levine thought he did not need overmuch marquee pull in the way of stars. George Peppard had not capitalized on his splash role in *Breakfast at Tiffany's* (1961), down the pecking order in the ensemble pictures *How the West Was Won* (1962) and *The Victors* (1963). Which suggested that Hollywood did not know how to best use him. But Levine did. Put him front and center. Call him the star and you'll make him the star.[799] To add sensation, bring in Carroll Baker (*Baby Doll*, 1956) in a sensational role. To add a quality, give screen legend Alan Ladd (*Shane*, 1953) his best role in a decade. Then go censor-baiting with glimpses of nudity, passionate sex scenes and sadism, provoking censor Geoffrey Shurlock into considering denying the film a Production Code Seal of Approval.[800] The resulting furor would help sell tickets. Director Edward Dmytryk's career had tailed off since the highs of *Raintree County* (1957) with Elizabeth Taylor and Montgomery Clift and *The Young Lions* (1958) with Marlon Brando and Clift; his latest film had been the little-seen Italian-made *The Reluctant Saint* (1962). But he was a strong director of talent and, although the recipient of only one Oscar nomination himself, many stars in his films had received such accolades.

Peppard plays a tycoon loosely based on Howard Hughes rampaging through Hollywood, Carroll Baker as his gold-digging stepmother, and Alan Ladd as gunslinger-turned-actor Nevada Smith (a role Steve McQueen would reprise a couple years later). The story is soap opera deluxe, a bitter father-son feud, sex with his stepmother, business wheeling-and-dealing and ruthless womanizing. When Peppard makes a film out of Ladd's life story, it turns Baker into a big star and, to get revenge on Peppard, she marries Ladd. And so it goes on—more women, more fights, more movies, and, against all the odds, a happy ending when Peppard turns over a new leaf. In the *Peyton Place* stakes it's not bad at all, the stars sizzle and Ladd pulls out all the stops. Critics, of course, hated it, audiences lapped it up. Ladd's death before the film was completed gave the picture, in callous Hollywood fashion, a marketing bonus. Levine also took advantage of a recent innovation, the New York showcase, a version of wide release-saturation but limited to top cinemas, a distribution ploy that James Bond pictures, for example, had used well. Levine's picture would end up topping the annual New York showcase rankings.[801]

Critical reaction: "Vividly exciting" (*Box Office*); "sickly, sour distillation of Harold Robbins' big-selling novel" (*New York Times*); "trash, but it has the curiosity pull of a trashy novel" (*Los Angeles Times*); "wild, fruity nonsense" (*Washington Post*); "lusty but erratic, sometimes distasteful" (*Variety*).[802]

Rentals: $15.5 million ($110.4 million equivalent)

26 (tie): *Hawaii*

Starring Julie Andrews, Max von Sydow and Richard Harris; directed by George Roy Hill; screenplay, Daniel Taradash and Dalton Trumbo, from the novel by James Michener; producer, Walter Mirisch; music, Elmer Bernstein. United Artists roadshow. October 10, 1966.

The untold story of the 1960s is that moviemakers did not lead the way in terms of the kinds of narratives most likely to keep the public glued to their seats. They just paid for ideas that had already proved winners, either as novels or musicals. Except twice, the number one picture every year during the decade was based either on a bestseller or a Broadway smash. Directors either tried to condense a book or cherry-picked various episodes, the length of the standard roadshow allowing them considerable leeway.

Joseph E. Levine realized there was more than one film in *The Carpetbaggers* (1964) and followed it up with the prequel *Nevada Smith* (1966). Similarly, Oscar winner Fred Zinnemann (*From Here to Eternity*, 1953), the original director of *Hawaii*, believed the James Michener book was too much for one film and proposed making two. Producer Walter Mirisch drafted in Dan Taradash, who had reduced James Jones' lumbering *From Here to Eternity* into an Oscar-winning screenplay. When Taradash was deemed a failure at the task, next came Dalton Trumbo (*Exodus*, 1960).[803] Alec Guinness and Audrey Hepburn would star.[804] When United Artists vetoed the Zinnemann concept, he pulled out—eventually, so did the proposed stars.[805]

Zinnemann was replaced by George Roy Hill, whom Mirisch had worked with on *Toys in the Attic* (1963). British actor Tom Courtenay (*Billy Liar*, 1963)[806] was next up for the lead along with Oscar-winning Julie Andrews, now the biggest star on the planet, looking for dramatic roles similar to *The Americanization of Emily* (1964). Courtenay dropped out and in came Swedish actor Max von Sydow (*The Greatest Story Ever Told*, 1965). Richard Harris (*The Heroes of Telemark*, 1965) was added. Polynesian French-speaking Jocelyn LaGarde with no acting experience and no English was trained up for a crucial part and Gene Hackman (*The French Connection*, 1971) had a supporting role. A budget of $9.9 million[807] was set for a film expected to come in at 150 minutes, although there were still disagreements over the script. Underlying bitterness exploded into outright confrontation over whether a scene would use artificial flowers. Eventually, concerns about the budget and the picture's length led to Hill being fired.[808] Mirisch called in Arthur Hiller (*The Americanization of Emily*).[809] Hawaiian natives playing supporting roles and extras refused to continue unless Hill was reinstated. So he was.[810] Among changes necessitated to reduce the length of the picture were cuts in Harris' role, so he later sued. The film went over budget by $4 million and was nearly 40 minutes longer than envisaged, fine for roadshow but not for general release. Filming was in four phases, beginning in February 1965, the final phase starting in June 1965.[811]

The plot can essentially be condensed to the damage wreaked by overzealous missionaries on the native population of Hawaii. Von Sydow plays a zealot who needs to be married before becoming a missionary. Julie Andrews, duped into thinking whaling captain Richard Harris no longer loves her, becomes his unfortunate bride since von Sydow believes sex is sinful. The voyage to Hawaii is well done, especially sailing round Cape Horn. Initially, their brand of Christianity is welcome in Hawaii, but attempts to cut down on native sexuality backfire. Harris comes back into Andrews' life. Most of the dramatic high points concern conflict over the native way of life—some of which are barbaric but others are not—and von Sydow's folly. Brought to his senses after personal grief, von Sydow becomes more tolerant, turning his self-righteousness on white settlers destroying the land. In Hill's hands, it is an engrossing picture, the clash of cultures given a harder edge than *Mutiny on the Bounty* (1962). Von Sydow delivers a performance of almost Biblical wrath, and Andrews is pretty decent, too.

Critical reception: "Perhaps the biggest empty movie … ever made" (*New Yorker*); "one of the outstanding pictures of 1966" (*Los Angeles Times*); "one comes out of the theater not so much moved as numbed" (*New York Times*).[812]

Rentals: $15.5 million[813] ($110.4 million equivalent)

144 The Films

25: *Bullitt*

Starring Steve McQueen and Robert Vaughn; directed by Peter Yates; screenplay, Alan R. Trustman[814] and Harry Kleiner, based on the novel *Mute Witness* by Robert L. Fish; producer, Philip D'Antoni[815]; music, Lalo Schifrin. Warner Brothers. October 17, 1968.

Mostly cars had been objects for comedy. *It's a Mad Mad Mad Mad World* (1963) and *The Great Race* (1965) used vehicles as the basis for madcap slapstick. Except for Steve McQueen's motorbike escape in *The Great Escape* (1963) and a bunch of Hells Angels B-pictures, speed played little part in screen drama.[816] *Grand Prix* (1966) was the exception, although the high speeds achieved were confined to an enclosed circuit. Even at high speeds, autos were mostly decorative and fun, like the dune buggy sequence in *The Thomas Crown Affair* (1968), until British director Peter Yates staged a scorching car chase through London streets in the crime picture *Robbery* (1967). And that alerted McQueen, who had been trying to finance a racing picture, *Le Mans*. McQueen's production company Solar purchased a crime thriller, *Mute Witness*, inserted a car chase, hired Yates and called the movie *Bullitt*.

McQueen had now come into his own. Early career highlights *The Magnificent Seven* (1960) and *The Great Escape* had been augmented by *The Cincinnati Kid* (1965), the stylish romantic thriller *The Thomas Crown Affair* (1968) and an Oscar nomination for *The Sand Pebbles* (1966). But where he was a debonair criminal millionaire mastermind in the latter, in *Bullitt* he was a down-to-earth cop. Yates was an unexpected choice for *Robbery*, his previous films the insipid musical *Summer Holiday* (1963) with pop singer Cliff Richard and the comedy *One Way Pendulum* (1965) with comedian Eric Sykes. Theoretically, the highlight of *Robbery*[817] was the multi-million–pound theft from a train but it was the car chase that got the pulses going. Robert Vaughn was trying to avoid being typecast as *The Man from U.N.C.L.E*, but he had been trying to escape television ever since emerging with some star quality from *The Magnificent Seven*. Instead, apart from small roles in *The Big Show* (1961) and *The Caretakers* (1963) and top billing in thriller *The Venetian Affair* (1966), he appeared tied by an umbilical cord to the spy series. Second billing as an ambitious politician in *Bullitt* offered a chance to break out. British female lead Jacqueline Bisset was a rising star after *The Detective* (1968) and *The Sweet Ride* (1968). It was the director's idea to shoot *Bullitt* on location.[818]

Bullitt is taut. The plot is simple. McQueen has to look after a witness, hiding from organized crime, over the weekend. When the man is killed, McQueen investigates, but is soon aware he is under surveillance, which triggers the car chase. There is a fair bit of subterfuge and double-dealing before McQueen gets his man. The car chase is, of course, the standout, but that would be to overlook the other elements, the main one being McQueen's performance. He is almost monosyllabic, not a word or gesture wasted. Without doing a thing, he exudes screen charisma. On top of that, he is not the traditional bitter cop, steeped in booze or worse. He lugs the groceries home, for goodness sake. He has a loving relationship with Bisset. And she's not nasty or bitter either but considers that being a cop is not so much dangerous as working in a sewer. An atmospheric score by Lalo Schifrin keeps the chill in the air. Vaughn is brilliant as the smug politician. The direction is as minimalist as the star, dialogue crisp, buttoning down the camera, the opposite of the split-screen exuberance of *The Thomas Crown Affair*. Even without the car chase, it would have been an intriguing picture.

The Films 145

But then there's the car chase, filmed on the steep hills of San Francisco where the vehicles travel half the time in mid-air. McQueen has a cool V8 Ford Mustang GT Fastback with engine modified,[819] and the other car in the chase, a Dodge Charger, had its suspension altered to cope with the hills. When McQueen was photographed, he was in the car doing the driving. Otherwise, it's Carey Loftin, Bud Ekins and Loren Janes.[820] At the wheel of the Dodge is Bill Hickman.[821] The cars hit top speeds of 110 miles per hour. The ten-minute chase took three weeks to shoot. Filming in the heart of San Francisco added excitement.

The only Oscar the film won was for editing, awarded to Frank P. Keller, and that was primarily down to his stunning work on the chases, "the most compelling street footage of 1968," into which he also seeded little snapshots of the city.[822] This chase still stands head and shoulders above every pursuit since.

Critical reception: "Terrific movie" (*New York Times*); "hard, tough, detective drama…. McQueen is no smoothie" (*International Motion Picture Exhibitor*); "for all the brilliance of its technical expertise, it has no heart at all" (*Films and Filming*).[823]

Rentals: $16.4 million[824] (includes reissue double bill with *Bonnie and Clyde*) ($116.8 million equivalent)

24: *Funny Girl*

Starring Barbra Streisand and Omar Sharif; directed by William Wyler; screenplay, Isobel Lennart, based on the musical by Lennart, Jule Styne and Bob Merrill; producer, Ray Stark; music, Styne and Merrill. Columbia roadshow. September 18, 1968.

When you appear on the cover of *Time* magazine (April 10, 1964) before your twenty-second birthday, your career is going only one way: up. By that point,[825] with three Grammy Awards for her first album, Barbra Streisand had made her debut as *Funny Girl* on Broadway. The stage musical began as a movie, a biopic of producer Ray Stark's mother-in-law Fanny Brice.[826] But when the screenplay could not be licked,[827] it morphed into a 1964 stage musical.[828] Initial New York reviews were sniffy,[829] but Streisand shone. Even failing to win a Tony[830] hardly mattered,[831] for Streisand was a phenomenon. The cast album sold 250,000 copies in four months,[832] adding to her existing five gold disks.[833] Promoters charged $5 more for her concerts than for the Beatles[834] and CBS-TV signed her to a $1 million two-year deal in 1965.[835] She was, by some distance, the world's highest-paid singer. Former agent Stark's Seven Arts produced prestige projects like *The Night of the Iguana* (1964), *This Property Is Condemned* (1966) and *Reflections in a Golden Eye* (1967).[836] He set up Rastar Productions specifically to turn Broadway musicals into movies, *Funny Girl* the first.[837] Streisand wanted "a dramatic film with musical numbers"[838] so Stark hired Sidney Lumet (*The Group*, 1966). When that partnership failed,[839] triggering rumors that Columbia wanted to offload the $7 million project,[840] Stark snagged William Wyler. After *Ben-Hur* (1959), Wyler had concentrated on smaller-scale projects *The Children's Hour* (1961), *The Collector* (1965) and *How to Steal a Million* (1966). He was lined up for *Patton*, the first in a four-picture deal with Fox, but script rewrites[841] put things on hold.[842] At the second time of asking,[843] Wyler, who had directed more Oscar-winning performances than any other director, took the *Funny Girl* reins. Streisand earned $500,000 while Stark nabbed 50 percent of the profits.[844]

146 The Films

Getting a name actor to play the male lead was difficult because a top star demanded top billing. For that reason, Marlon Brando and Gregory Peck turned it down. Stark felt Frank Sinatra was too old.[845] Omar Sharif (*Doctor Zhivago*, 1965) proved ideal. His chemistry with Streisand was palpable, and off-screen they had an affair.[846] Veteran Walter Pidgeon (*Mrs. Miniver*, 1942) and Anne Francis (*Forbidden Planet*, 1956) bolstered the supporting cast. There was a trend by now for musicals to be directed by newcomers as per George Roy Hill (*Thoroughly Modern Millie*, 1967) but Stark imported future director Herbert Ross to stage the musical numbers. Reports that Streisand and Wyler did not get along were untrue, she desperate to learn, he happy to teach and, as importantly, listen, adopting some of her ideas.[847] Streisand owned this show on stage and she owned it on screen. Stars who originated a stage character often lost out on the screen role. But there was no question of Streisand being sidelined; her record sales and popularity saw to that. Streisand's connection with the audience was such that in previews she was applauded after every number as if spectators were watching a live show.

The story is straightforward enough and as old as the hills. Fanny Brice from New York's Lower East Side becomes a vaudeville star for legendary impresario Florenz Ziegfeld. She marries a debonair gambler (Sharif) but he is imprisoned for fraud and their love never recovers. But as much as Wyler delivers the required dramatic punch and as much as the romance weaves in and out of will-she, won't-she, it was Streisand whom audiences came to see, and she did not let them down. It is a stunning debut and mostly because Streisand does more than sing: She demonstrates dramatic chops, without which her ugly duckling romance with the incredibly handsome Sharif would have been unbelievable. Standout songs included "People," "Second Hand Rose" and "Don't Rain on My Parade," the last-named most apt because there was little chance of anyone spoiling Streisand's entrance as a major movie star. There were eight Oscar nominations, including Best Picture, but Streisand was the sole winner, sharing Best Actress with Katharine Hepburn in *The Lion in Winter* (1968). Interestingly, the film poster contained the exact same image as had been used to launch the stage show.[848] That was not the only unusual promotional element: The $9 million film,[849] taking bookings 14 months before it opened,[850] broke advance records.[851]

Critical reception: "A vehicle for the exploitation of Barbra Streisand's considerable talents" (*International Motion Picture Exhibitor*); "a long, drippy bore" (*Washington Post*); "charismatic ingredients of a smash musical" (*Variety*); "over-produced, over-photographed and over-long" (*Chicago Sun-Times*).[852]

Rentals: $16.5 million[853] ($117.6 million equivalent)

23: *Tom Jones*

Starring Albert Finney and Susannah York; directed and produced by Tony Richardson; screenplay, John Osborne, from the novel by Henry Fielding; music, John Addison. United Artists.[854] June 26, 1963 (London); U.S. October 6, 1963.

Long before James Bond and the Beatles conquered America, *Tom Jones* ruled the roost. It was the biggest "little film that could" of the decade so far and it followed a release pattern laid down by *La Dolce Vita* (1960): arthouse launch, critical acclaim, then re-marketed to the general public as raunchy rather than artistic. A reality revolution had swept through British movies, a new wave of dynamic writers, actors and

It was the first British film since Laurence Olivier's *Hamlet* (1948), only the second British venture overall, and the first low-budget movie since *Marty* (1955), to be named Best Picture (pressbook).

filmmakers triggering Jack Clayton's *Room at the Top* (1958) starring Laurence Harvey, Karel Reisz's *Saturday Night and Sunday Morning* (1960) starring Albert Finney and Tony Richardson's *The Loneliness of the Long Distance Runner* (1962) with Tom Courtenay. Domestic successes, they made little commercial impact in the U.S. British films were a reasonable investment from the Hollywood perspective because they cost

148   **The Films**

so little.[855] The key players in this homegrown boom were Bryanston and Woodfall.[856] Bryanston linked up with American company Seven Arts (headed by Ray Stark). Their second project was *Tom Jones*, Woodfall's first picture in color, budgeted at just over $1 million, with Columbia co-financing.[857] When the budget increased by half, Columbia pulled out, replaced by United Artists.

Tom Jones was a historical comedy, based on a Henry Fielding novel[858] once considered exceptionally lascivious. Playwright John Osborne wrote the screenplay, Albert Finney, having rejected *Lawrence of Arabia* (1962), was set for the lead, and Tony Richardson would oversee.

Finney was the leader of a new breed of British stars including Courtenay, Richard Harris, Sean Connery and Peter O'Toole. He made his movie debut in Woodfall's *The Entertainer* (1960), directed by Richardson and toplining Laurence Olivier. After *Look Back in Anger* and *The Entertainer*, Richardson had been spirited over to Hollywood for *Sanctuary* (1961) before returning home for *A Taste of Honey* (1961) and *The Loneliness of the Long Distance Runner*. *Tom Jones* gave a push to rising stars Susannah York (*Tunes of Glory*, 1960) and Diane Cilento (*I Thank a Fool*, 1962), and afforded David Warner his debut.

The movie, like its source, is picaresque with Tom Jones (Finney) enjoying bouts of lust and adventure in equal measure. Unfairly banished from home and true love (York), the naïve Tom seeks his way in the cruel world. His money is stolen, he gets into fights. After saving an older woman (Joyce Redman) from danger, he leaps into bed with her and later with a noblewoman (Joan Greenwood). Meanwhile, York has set off to find him. Tom, convicted of robbery and attempted murder, is pardoned. And there is a typical contrived happy ending. It sounds like a bawdy comedy with little arthouse appeal. But arthouses attracted two distinct crowds, film buffs seeking pictures from around the world and those interested in foreign pictures exhibiting a looser approach to sexuality than the Production Code permitted. While fulfilling the second criteria in abundance, *Tom Jones* was also cinematically avant-garde. The opening scene was a pastiche of a silent film with subtitles. An unseen commentator voiced displeasure at the goings-on. Characters broke the fourth wall, acknowledging the camera in various ways or addressing the audience. And there was one extraordinary scene in which seduction takes place during the consumption of food.

On the other hand, the bawdiness, ramped up in the advertising, appealed to a wider audience. But a film that skirted the edge of decency would not have racked up such tremendous receipts without Finney's endearing performance. Comedy was also big box office: Disney fare, Doris Day, *Some Like it Hot* (1959) and *Irma La Douce* (1963). So in one sense, the moviegoer was ripe for something different. Historical movies that had also done big business tended to be serious. This was anything but. Although the movie did well in Britain,[859] United Artists treated its U.S. launch with one eye on the Oscars. It opened in the Cinema One arthouse in New York (on the East Side, not the city center)—to record-breaking business[860]—and the Beverly arthouse in Los Angeles in October 1963 and was deliberately kept out of any other cinema until mid–December. But then it played in only four more theaters[861] and it wasn't until after the February Oscar preliminaries—ten nominations including Best Picture—that it was released anywhere else. By April 17 when the Oscars came around, cinemas were screaming for it. It was the "sleeper of the year," with colossal grosses and running in every cinema for months. The Oscars were the icing on the cake: Clips of the film shown repeatedly during the event sold the movie to a massive TV audience. There was a fashion hook,[862] too, and

The nominations included a record three for Best Supporting Actress, Edith Evans, Cilento and Redman. *Tom Jones* was named Best Picture[864] with Richardson taking the Best Director statuette, and other awards for John Addison's score and adapted screenplay. Profit participation earned Finney over $1 million.[865]

Critical reception: "Wonderful exercise in cinema" (*Time*); "sumptuous satisfying production" (*Saturday Review*)[866]; "one of the wildest, bawdiest and funniest comedies ever" (*New York Times*); "absolute triumph" (*Newsweek*); "most engaging" (*Life*).[867] It ranked 28 for the year in the *Cahiers du Cinema* poll.[868]

Rentals: $16.95 million[869] (including reissues in 1966 and 1969) ($120.8 million equivalent)

22: *The Love Bug*

Starring Dean Jones and Michele Lee; directed by Robert Stevenson; writer-producer, Bill Walsh, based on the novel *Car, Boy, Girl* by Gordon Buford; music, George Bruns. Disney. December 4, 1968.

Disney mixed the speed of *Grand Prix* and *Bullitt* with the decade's earlier automobile comedies to snap out another concept picture. Instead of scientist invents flying rubber (*The Absent Minded Professor*, 1961) and reuniting twins separated at birth (*The Parent Trap*, 1961), it's a car with a mind of its own. Sure, you still needed a few plot twists and to keep the cute-o-meter running, but basically it was all concept. By this point, Dean Jones had replaced Fred MacMurray as the company's go-to star. After small parts in *Jailhouse Rock* (1957) and *Never So Few* (1959), his main beat was television as *Ensign O'Toole* (1962). That led to second billing in the medical drama *The New Interns* (1964) and the horror film *Two on a Guillotine* (1965) but it wasn't until Disney spotted his potential, when he was in his mid–30s, that his movie career took off. He was the star of *The Ugly Dachshund* (1966), co-starred with Maurice Chevalier in *Monkeys Go Home* (1967) and with Peter Ustinov in *Blackbeard's Ghost* (1968) before reclaiming top billing in *The Horse in the Gray Flannel Suit* (1968). No matinee idol, more a grown-up boy-next-door, Jones was basically the straight man for whatever comic tomfoolery Disney threw at him. Playing the love interest in *The Love Bug* was singer Michele Lee (*How to Succeed in Business Without Really Trying*, 1967).[870] British actor David Tomlinson (*Mary Poppins*, 1964) plays Herbie's previous owner. Comic Buddy Hackett (*It's a Mad Mad Mad Mad World*, 1963) is a friend. Screenwriter Bill Walsh was another Team Disney regular, having written *The Shaggy Dog*, *The Absent Minded Professor*, *Mary Poppins* and *That Darn Cat!* The studio remained true to the Udult concept of family films that "contain more adult treatment."[871]

The Love Bug was based on the novel *Car, Boy, Girl* by Gordon Buford, which basically debunks the idea of the car as a lifestyle choice, the grand autos of American vintage replaced by a tiny Volkswagen. But as usual with Disney, the concept required fleshing out. Initially, the Volkswagen was not the specified make. But Disney held a car "audition" and watched the reactions to a variety of vehicles including Toyotas, Volvos and an MG. The Volkswagen passed the cute test, the only car that those passing gave a friendly pat. Despite no official cooperation from Volkswagen, Disney lined up a tie-in with car distributors.[872] Over 20 professional drivers took part including *Bullitt* (1968) stunt drivers Bill Hickman and Bud Ekins.[873] Racetracks used were Riverside, Laguna Seca and Willow Springs.

Over a dozen famous cars were featured, including a 1956 Ferrari 250 GT Berlinetta, a 1963 Shelby Cobra, a 1959 Austin-Healey 3000 and a 1957 Chevrolet Two-Ten 2-Door Sedan. Trade press advertisement (*Box Office*, January 6, 1969, 7).

Struggling sports car racing driver (Jones) comes across a Beetle, "Herbie," that follows him home. Taking the wheel, he finds he is not in control. The car, however, is a speed merchant. After achieving racing success, the car's previous owner demands its return and challenges Jones, only to sabotage Herbie. The heat is on to repair the car before the race begins. In keeping with a car movie, the picture had pace as well as gallons of charm, Herbie holding down a special place in the Cute Hall of Fame. The comedy is inventive and every time the car sprints off on its own, the audience is on its side, another of the Disney pictures that has cleverly assessed its potential market, as enjoyable for adults as kids.

Although released at the end of 1968, it made the vast bulk of its income in 1969. In the year when, purportedly, Hollywood was in the grip of a "youthquake," a revolution driven by *Midnight Cowboy* and *Easy Rider*,[874] *The Love Bug* was the number one picture.

Critical reaction: "Engaging fantasy" (*Variety*); "surefire family comedy" (*Box Office*); "best live-action to come from Disney studios since *The Absent Minded Professor*" (*Films and Filming*); "long, sentimental Volkswagen commercial" (*New York Times*).[875]

Rentals: $17 million[876] ($121.1 million equivalent)

21: *The Longest Day*

Starring John Wayne, Henry Fonda and Robert Mitchum; directed by Ken Annakin, Andrew Marton and Bernard Wicki; screenplay, Cornelius Ryan, James Jones and Romain Gary, based on the book by Ryan; producer, Darryl F. Zanuck; music, Maurice Jarre. Twentieth Century–Fox roadshow. September 25, 1962 (France); U.S. October 4, 1962.

Twentieth Century–Fox was heading for oblivion in 1962. Thanks to the spiraling costs of *Cleopatra* (1963) the company had a loss of $39.8 million, the biggest in its history.[877] Without Darryl F. Zanuck, the studio's biggest shareholder and former boss, riding to the rescue with *The Longest Day*, it would have been curtains.

The Longest Day, in itself, was a massive gamble, a three-hour black-and-white documentary-style picture costing nearly $10 million without a major star. Yes, Zanuck crammed in as many big names as he could get hold of, and many lesser names passed off as stars, but whether the public would pay to see a few minutes here and there of John Wayne (earning $250,000 for ten days' work)[878] and Robert Mitchum ($25,000)[879] and hours of actors they had hardly heard of was almost an act of folly. Other big-budget titles had big-name stars in leading roles, not cameos: Charlton Heston in *Ben-Hur* (1959), Paul Newman in *Exodus* (1960), Gregory Peck in *The Guns of Navarone* (1961).[880]

Based on Cornelius Ryan's non-fiction bestseller, the movie follows in infinite detail the Allied preparation and assault on D-Day, the German defense strategy and the role of the French resistance. Three directors were assigned: Ken Annakin (*Swiss Family Robinson*, 1960) handled the British scenes, Bernard Wicki (*The Bridge*, 1959) the German section and Andrew Marton (*King Solomon's Mines*, 1950) the American parts. Oscar-winning film editor Elmo Williams (*High Noon*, 1952) coordinated battle scenes. As well as supervising production,[881] Zanuck lent a hand at direction.[882] The assembled cast members represented the countries involved. As well as Wayne and Mitchum, the American contingent included Henry Fonda (*12 Angry Men*, 1957), Jeffrey Hunter (*King of Kings*, 1961), Robert Ryan (*The Canadians*, 1961), George Segal (*The Young Doctors*, 1961), Rod Steiger (*Al Capone*, 1959) and Stuart Whitman (*The Comancheros*, 1961). The British element offered Richard Burton (*The Bramble Bush*, 1960), Sean Connery (*Dr. No*, 1962),[883] Kenneth More (*Reach for the Sky*, 1956) and Richard Todd (*D-Day, the Sixth of June*, 1956). In the French quarter were comedian Bourvil, Jean-Louis Barrault (*The

152   The Films

Miracle of the Wolves, 1961), Zanuck's mistress Irina Demick making her Hollywood debut, and Christian Marquand (*Shadows of Adultery*, 1961). The Germans were headed by Curt Jurgens (*I Aim at the Stars*, 1960) and Gert Frobe (*The Terror of Dr. Mabuse*, 1962).

Novelist Ryan also delivered the screenplay with some additional scenes written by French novelist Romain Gary, James Jones (author of *From Here to Eternity*) and the screenwriting team David Pursall and Jack Seddon (*Murder She Said*, 1961). Maurice Jarre devised the music. Actors who had seen action in World War II included British pair Richard Todd and Donald Houston, German Hans Christian Blech (with the scars to prove it) and American Eddie Albert. Most of the actors taking part, however, were much older than their real-life characters. Despite the complicated logistics involved, Zanuck did not play it safe. There were subtitles when foreign actors spoke in their own language. The attack around the casino was shot from a helicopter and lasted eight minutes.[884] Six cameras captured the British landings sequence involving 36 landing craft and 3000 troops.[885] The scene with Lord Lovat (Peter Lawford) leading his commandos ashore with a Highlander playing the bagpipes was accompanied by dive-bombing Stukas and fires raging above on the cliffs.[886] At Studio Boulogne, 47 sets were built for everything from the interior of a glider to a landing craft at sea. The directors generated 360,000 feet—66 hours—of footage.[887]

Inevitably, the movie could not cover all the incidents from the book. Key scenes are all magnificently done—the parachute drop, the landings themselves, the battle for Omaha Beach, the scaling of the cliffs, the blistering German firepower, futile resistance by two German pilots, French sabotage. As well-handled is the tension on both sides of the Channel, Allied concerns about the weather, frustration at the German High Command. As importantly, there are no bad guys. While appearing complacent, German officers are not portrayed as villains. Despite the complexities, the narrative remains clear, each episode standing on its own, the whole well stitched together. Although audiences had a time of it star-spotting, the ensemble casting worked a treat. The gamble paid off both financially and artistically, the end result wholly involving. This was, in the end, a film as much about the pain as the glory and a fitting tribute to the sacrifices made. It was nominated for five Oscars and won two, for Cinematography and Special Effects.

Critical reaction: "Stunning war epic" (*Variety*); "I ended … being bored" (*New Yorker*); "tingling, eye-gripping, fantastic" (*Washington Post*).[888]

Rentals: $17.6 million (including reissues in 1964 and 1969)[889] ($125.4 million equivalent)

20: *You Only Live Twice*

Starring Sean Connery and Akiko Wakabayashi; directed by Lewis Gilbert; screenplay, Roald Dahl, based on the novel by Ian Fleming; producers, Harry Saltzman and Albert R. Broccoli; music, John Barry. United Artists. June 12, 1967 (London); U.S.: June 13, 1967.

An 18-month production gap had allowed Bond's rivals to catch up. By the time the fifth Bond appeared, audiences had been introduced to a number of other spies from James Coburn in *Our Man Flint* (1966) and *In Like Flint* (1967) to Dean Martin as Matt Helm in *The Silencers* (1966) and *Murderers' Row* (1966), via Monica Vitti as *Modesty*

Merchandising included bubblegum cards, Airfix construction kits of the Toyota and Little Nellie, Corgi cars, souvenir brochures, James Bond action figures and a Kissy Suzuki doll, Triang board game and a volcano set, plus non-licensed items like a replica Walther PPK firing blanks* (Hannan Collection).

*Cerulli, Mark, "*You Only Live Twice* At Fifty," *Cinema Retro*, Vol. 13, Issue 39, 24.

154   The Films

Blaise (1966) and the all-star spoof *Casino Royale* (1967) … not to mention a second Harry Palmer installment, *Funeral in Berlin* (1966). All except the last-named had gadgets, guns and girls a-plenty and in the latter department almost out–Bonding Bond, with Senta Berger, Ann-Margret, Camilla Sparv, Stella Stevens, Daliah Lavi and even Ursula Andress. Each successive film in the Bond series had outdone the last, *Thunderball* (1965) the peak, earning ten times as much as *Dr. No* (1962)—plus an explosion of merchandising. Budgets had followed a similar trajectory with *You Only Live Twice* costing $9.5 million, an exceptional amount for a non-roadshow picture.

The Bonds had not been filmed in the same order as the books, *Dr. No*, for example coming after *From Russia with Love* (1963). In the book series, *You Only Live Twice* followed *On Her Majesty's Secret Service*[890] in which Bond had been widowed; much of that plot was scrapped except for the Japanese connection and return of arch-villain Blofeld. Two Oscar-nominated writers had first crack at the screenplay, first Sydney Boehm (*The Big Heat*, 1953),[891] then Harold Jack Bloom[892] (*The Naked Spur*, 1953). The final screenplay was credited to Roald Dahl,[893] who invented the space heist. Scouting by helicopter for new locations in Japan, director Lewis Gilbert and art director Ken Adam spotted an extinct volcano, ideal for an underground lair, so that was built into the screenplay.[894] In addition, Dahl was instructed to provide parts for three Bond girls, two attracted to 007 plus a femme fatale who also succumbs to his charms.[895] Japanese[896] actresses Akiko Wakabayashi and Mie Hama (both in *What's Up, Tiger Lily?*, 1966)[897] played the good girls, German Karin Dor (*Target for Killing*, 1966) the baddie. The Japanese pair could not speak English and even after three months' tuition Hama still struggled, so her part was re-voiced.[898] Dor did her own stunt work when being drowned in the piranha pool.[899] For the first time, Blofeld's face was revealed. The first choice, Czech actor Jan Werich (*The 25th Hour*, 1967), proved unsuitable, opening the door for British actor Donald Pleasence (*Cul-de-sac*, 1966).[900] The gadget jewel in the crown was the autogyro "Little Nellie."[901] Bond drove an Aston Martin DB5 and a Toyota 2000GT, in this version a convertible because otherwise Connery could not fit inside. But the volcanic lair proved to be the *pièce de résistance*.

The opening sequence sets the tone for a different kind of Bond film: A mysterious spacecraft gobbling up an American Gemini capsule while an astronaut is in the middle of a space walk. Bond's death is faked so, along with Japanese secret agent Wakabayashi, he can infiltrate a chemical company with links to an operation in a remote fishing village. He evades death from Dor and while flying the autogyro gets into an aerial dogfight with several helicopters. Bond pretends to marry another agent (Hama) and they access the volcano. Bond confronts Blofeld, who expects America to blame Russia for the space thefts, leading to nuclear war, with SPECTRE picking up the pieces. There is plenty of action, tension and death. Highlights included the space hijack (as awe-inspiring as the Kubrick epic the next year), the autogyro dogfight, Dor's death by piranha and the attack on the volcano. Once again, John Barry supplied the score. The orchestral music accompanying the space capsule seizure is outstanding. Nancy Sinatra sang the theme tune. By this time, of course, Sean Connery was fed up with the role so it was announced that this would be his last. Normally such news would provide a box office spike, but audiences, perhaps suffering spy fatigue, did not respond as readily as to *Thunderball*.

Critical reception: "The formula fails to work its magic" (*Chicago Sun-Times*); "a bag of good Bond fun" (*New York Times*); "compares favorably [to] its predecessors" (*Variety*).[902]

Rentals: $18 million[903] (including 1968 reissue[904]) ($128.2 million equivalent)

19: *To Sir, with Love*

Starring Sidney Poitier; written and directed by James Clavell, based on the book by E.R Braithwaite; producers, Clavell and John R. Sloan; music, Ron Grainer. Columbia. June 14, 1967.

The biggest of the decade's sleepers—the "little films that could"—fell into the feel-good category despite all the social issues it raised. The biggest unresolved question was why it required Sidney Poitier to head to Britain in the first place to make what turned out to be his breakout movie. He should have been coasting to stardom by now. Best Actor for *Lilies of the Field* (1963), enough low-budget sleeper hits—*A Raisin in the Sun* (1961) and *A Patch of Blue* (1965)—to assume that leading man status in bigger Hollywood productions was a foregone conclusion when, in fact, he was generally assigned second billing in any topline production[905] or his films never got off the ground.[906] Australian director Clavell had written the sci-fi film *The Fly* (1958) and the adventure *Watusi* (1959), then made his directorial debut on *Five Gates to Hell* (1959). He wrote the bestseller *King Rat*[907] based on his experiences as a Japanese prisoner of war, and *Tai-Pan*.[908] He directed *The Bitter and the Sweet* (1962)[909] before writing *The Great Escape* (1963), *633 Squadron* (1964) and *The Satan Bug* (1965). E.R. Braithwaite's semi-autobiographical tale of teaching and redemption, *To Sir, with Love*[910] was a minor British bestseller. Clavell cut a writer-producer-director deal with Columbia, even though the studio pressed him to add a harder edge of conflict into what is sometimes a soft-centered story.[911] The budget was tiny, just $640,000, with a short shooting schedule,[912] with Poitier and Clavell taking no fees in return for a percentage.[913] Adding marquee insurance was Scottish pop star Lulu.[914] The remainder of the supporting cast, to keep the budget down, made debuts: Judy Geeson, Christian Roberts and Adrienne Posta as classmates.[915]

Lack of belief in Poitier's star wattage led to Columbia shelving the movie for a year.[916] In fact, Poitier's stock was rising and from an unusual source. Television audiences recognized what Hollywood missed. When *Lilies of the Field* made its small screen premiere early in 1967, it was the top-rated movie of the season, a TV show he hosted was also highly popular, and two networks bid for him to play Othello.[917] While United Artists had signed him for *In the Heat of the Night*, that, too, was low-budget by mainstream standards.[918]

To Sir, with Love was finally launched in America ahead of, and to take advantage of, publicity generated by *In the Heat of the Night*. But still Columbia refused to gamble on a general release and pitched it into an arthouse, which attracted older moviegoers, rather than the younger ones *Variety* reckoned were its best hope.[919] However, as noted earlier, an arthouse could work strategic magic: a couple of sold-out shows in a low-capacity venue, and word could spread.[920] To everyone's astonishment, especially naysayers in the studio, the tiny unwanted movie broke box office records at the 700-seat Cinema One in New York.[921] Two weeks later, in Boston, it did the same.[922] Then Pittsburgh. As exhibitors clamored for the movie, Columbia abandoned arthouses and shifted it into general release. Stumped by its success, Columbia commissioned a survey asking moviegoers what was the big attraction. The answer: Sidney Poitier.

Poitier plays an immigrant[923] unemployed engineer moving into teaching[924] in a school for rejects, kids expelled from elsewhere. The school is in a rough London area, in a building that resembles a prison. His final year class does little but make noise and cause trouble. Poitier is a lonely, friendless character, living in a one-room apartment, spending his spare time applying for engineering jobs. Products of broken homes, the kids take out their frustrations on any authority figure who cannot strike back (the school has no corporal punishment).[925] Christian Roberts is trouble-in-chief, Lulu and Adrienne Posta girl toughies, but Judy Geeson stands out as a swan, giving a very affecting poetry reading, with a crush on the teacher. Initially, Poitier is a poor teacher, making no connection with his unruly class until he realizes it is too late for them to learn the standard rudiments of education. Instead, he proposes supplying the tools they need to face the world when they leave the cocoon of school. He teaches them respect, talks about responsibility, gives them a different perspective. Despite discipline improving, underlying tensions soon explode and he is beaten up by Roberts and loses the kids' trust when he reveals he is considering quitting. The issue of race, which has rarely been mentioned, now comes to the fore, and it is that, in the instance of attending a funeral, that heals the breach with the kids. At the class end-of-year party, Lulu sings "To Sir, with Love." Later, he tears up the job offer.

Despite obvious flaws, this is a very affecting film. It's a different Poitier, more reflective, less aggressive, more emotionally vulnerable. Oscar voters turned a blind eye. Most commentators put its success down to luck, an antidote to the sex and violence filling the screen. But that's a pretty dismissive view. Most feel-good movies consist of characters overcoming adversity and making connections where none previously existed. That's just the format. This is a moving film touching upon social issues with a terrific understated performance from Poitier and, given the budget, well handled by Clavell. But it's also a movie fairy story. "Give the public what they want" is often a Hollywood mantra. In this case, Columbia thought they knew better than the public, as studios so often do, and it was only public reaction that prevented the film being buried.

Critical reception: "Good-humored and unbelievable" (*New York Times*); "well-made, sometimes poignant, drama" (*Variety*); "Poitier … stands out from the rest of the cast" (*Box Office*).[926]

Rentals: $19.1 million[927] (including 1969 reissue[928]) ($136.1 million equivalent)

18: *It's a Mad Mad Mad Mad World*

Starring Spencer Tracy and Phil Silvers; directed and produced by Stanley Kramer; screenplay, William and Tania Rose; music, Ernest Gold. United Artists roadshow. November 7, 1963.

The last person in the world you might choose to make a wild rollicking comedy was Stanley Kramer. He was the king of Serious,[929] spending the last few years worrying about the woes of the world, past, present and future. He had tackled man's origins in *Inherit the Wind* (1960), concentration camps in *Judgment at Nuremberg* (1961) and the end of the world in *On the Beach* (1959). He was best known for well-meaning, high-minded movies that often came across as tracts. This view of Kramer was hardly misplaced. As either director or producer, he had rattled more skeletons in more cupboards than any other filmmaker in America. He had exposed the medical profession in *Not as a Stranger* (1955), racial prejudice in *The Defiant Ones* (1958), boxing malpractice in *Champion* (1949) and the plight of postwar paraplegics in *The Men* (1950). His peers recognized his worth enough to Oscar-nominate him seven times.[930] Humor, you might

The Films   157

think, was not high on his agenda. But you would be wrong. His first film as a producer was a comedy, *So This Is New York* (1948), from a screenplay by Carl Foreman. The plot sounds familiar: A man inherits a fortune. Does that ring a bell? Of course, the basis for all inheritance stories is conflict and greed.

The *Mad Mad World* screenplay, purchased for a record $150,000, was by William Rose (*Genevieve*, 1953) and Tania Rose. He envisaged a monster car chase heavily loaded with visual gags, a loony adjunct to *High Noon*, where as this particular deadline approached every minute of screen time represented two minutes of real time. United Artists conceived it as the biggest budgeted movie for a film with no stars. Most would be drawn from television, Milton Berle the first comic signed, for fees ranging from $50,000 to $150,000.[931] To give the film gravitas, Kramer pulled in Spencer Tracy, star of *Judgment at Nuremberg* and *Inherit the Wind*, for three days' work. The only downside of using stage and TV stars was that most of the time they were too busy working. The peak period for shows and TV work was autumn and spring so that left only the summer free. It would have seemed a completely insane gamble except for two things. *Some Like It Hot* (1959) and *The Apartment* (1960) had led to a rash of comedies while compilations of silent slapstick-oriented comedies such as *When Comedy Was King* (1960) and *Days of Thrills and Laughter* (1961) dominated the reissue market. *Mad Mad World*'s original budget of $6 million mushroomed to $9.6 million.[932]

It was a mammoth shoot lasting 165 days and a boon for stuntmen. Because of a crackdown on TV violence, they were being squeezed out of the business. At one point, 50 were employed during filming of the movie.[933] Filming auto wrecks on a studio back lot was too problematical so, thanks to cooperation from the Bureau of Land Management, public highways were used.[934] The movie drained Los Angeles dry of extras, 2000 required, too many for the Screen Extras Guild to supply so the remainder were commandeered from the California state unemployment office on $10 a day plus lunch.[935] *Mad Mad World* was not originally set for Cinerama and shot for three months on 70mm Panavision; it was switched to that format[936] to launch the new Cinerama Dome[937] in Los Angeles[938] with $400,000 set aside for the press junket.[939]

The final cast was a Who's Who of comedy: Sid Caesar, Jimmy Durante, Buddy Hackett, Phil Silvers, Buster Keaton, Jack Benny, Joe E. Brown, Jerry Lewis, the Three Stooges and from Britain Terry-Thomas. And that's just the start. The roles were all types: hypochondriac, tough guy, young wife of an older husband, swindler, grown-up baby, mother-in-law, etc. Actors were chosen for their ability to fulfill those types. Tracy plays against type, an honest cop taking dishonest action. Singer Ethel Merman, the aforementioned shrewish mother-in-law, is subjected to being turned upside down and dumped in a trash can.

The movie pivots on an age-old plot device, the hunt for buried treasure. With his dying breath, a car crash victim tells gathered motorists of $350,000 buried under a "big W" in Santa Rosita near Mexico. The group sets off in orderly fashion until they break ranks and start competing with each other. Others join in the hunt. The race is on through near-collisions, car crashes, planes coming apart at the seams, the destruction of a filling station, and the collapsing fire escape of a tall building. The gags are non-stop, building on slapstick and chase routines endemic to silent movies including slipping on a banana skin. It's impossible to describe the humor in a movie like this and even though you could argue it goes on too long, it is still wonderfully concentrated as each plot strand and the characters unravel. Kramer still liked to think he had made a film

158   The Films

with a message—i.e., greed is bad—but nobody else cared about the message. They were too busy laughing.

Critical reception: "Out-Sennetts Mack Sennett" (*Box Office*); "spectacular film with some classic comedy sequences" (*Variety*); "never slows below a hell for leather pace" (*Films and Filming*).[940]

Rentals: $19.3 million[941] ($137.5 million equivalent)

17: *West Side Story*

Starring Natalie Wood and George Chakiris; directed by Robert Wise and Jerome Robbins; screenplay, Ernest Lehman, based on the musical by Leonard Bernstein and Arthur Laurents; producer, Walter Mirisch; music, Bernstein and Laurents. United Artists roadshow. October 18, 1961.

Seven years before Franco Zeffirelli insisted on employing actors close to the age of the play's characters for the leading roles in *Romeo and Juliet* (1968), director Robert Wise took the same tack in adapting for the screen the Broadway version of the Shakespeare play for *West Side Story*. Larry Kert and Carol Lawrence, who originated the roles of Tony and Maria on Broadway, at 31 and 29,[942] respectively, were screen-tested; they were a decade too old. That rule did not seem to apply to Audrey Hepburn who would have been 32 (she turned it down)[943] or Elizabeth Taylor, the same age as Lawrence, or Harry Belafonte, three years older than Kert but at least a singer, all of whom were considerations ultimately not pursued.[944] The presence of Hepburn or Taylor would have necessitated a male star of equal magnitude and would have pushed up the budget. It is more likely that while Kert and Lawrence could dominate a stage, their personalities did not translate to the screen. Natalie Wood was closer to the desired age, 23,[945] with considerable movie experience: She had been Oscar-nominated for *Rebel Without a Cause* (1955), notable in *The Searchers* (1956), female lead in *Marjorie Morningstar* (1958), *Kings Go Forth* (1958) and *All the Young Cannibals* (1960) opposite future husband Robert Wagner, top-billed for Elia Kazan in the box office hit *Splendor in the Grass* (1961). Her singing never entered the equation (she would be dubbed), but an actress of her maturity would add dramatic weight to the film.

There was talk, at least rumor, that Elvis Presley was offered the role of Tony.[946] Producer's choice Horst Buchholz (*The Magnificent Seven*, 1960) was tied up with Billy Wilder's *One, Two, Three* (1961). Richard Beymer, the same age as Wood, won the role, his credits supporting roles in *Johnny Tremain* (1957), *The Diary of Anne Frank* (1959) and *High Time* (1960). Russ Tamblyn had been Oscar-nominated for *Peyton Place* (1957), starred in *High School Confidential!* (1958) and *Tom Thumb* (1958), and had a role in the big-budget Western *Cimarron* (1960). Puerto Rican Rita Moreno's portfolio included *The King and I* (1956) and top billing in the teenage gang war drama *This Rebel Breed* (1960). George Chakiris so far was limited to tiny roles.

The stage musical had been a long time brewing. Choreographer-director Jerome Robbins, composer Leonard Bernstein and playwright Arthur Laurents had begun work on turning *Romeo and Juliet* into a musical in 1947, initially as *East Side Story*, pairing a Catholic boy with a Jewish girl.[947] When lyricist Stephen Sondheim became involved, Laurents shifted the focus to Puerto Rican immigrants. Every major producer turned the project down until Hal Prince launched it on Broadway in 1957.[948] It ran for nearly two years and was nominated for six Tonys.[949]

Shooting in an area due for demolition required the restoration of broken or missing windows and installation of shades and curtains. Stores were furnished, signs were painted and fresh fruit was placed on an open sidewalk stand* **(Hannan Collection).**

*"Race Against Raze," *Variety*, August 24, 1961, 16.

For the movie, Robert Wise was brought in to handle the dramatic elements, leaving Jerome Robbins free to work on the choreography. Wise had Oscar nominations in different categories, editing for *Citizen Kane* (1941) and direction for *I Want to Live!* (1958). For Wise, a musical did not appear illogical, his career having spanned horror (*The Body Snatcher*, 1945), Western (*Blood on the Moon*, 1948), film noir (*The House on Telegraph Hill*, 1951), sci-fi (*The Day the Earth Stood Still*, 1951) and war (*Run Silent, Run Deep*, 1958). Ernest Lehman (*North by Northwest*, 1959) penned the script.

Robbins and Wise were soon at odds over the nature of the project, the former favoring a stage-type presentation with stylized sets, the latter seeking something more realistic. Matters quickly came to a head over shooting the prologue. Wise wanted actors dancing in what was recognizably a rundown street. Producer Walter Mirisch found a New York tenement block due for demolition.[950] In the end, Robbins conceded ground and this proved to be a seminal moment for the movie in indicating to the audience

160 The Films

they were in for a different kind of musical. Two-handed direction proved impossible.[951] Every scene, every shot had to be discussed and agreed between the two principals. When this held up shooting, Mirisch dispensed with Robbins. After he departed, possibly *because* he left, the budget continued to rise, up by a third to $6.75 million.[952]

However, the result, without doubt, was dynamic. The songs—"Maria," "America," "Tonight," "I Feel Pretty," "Gee, Officer Krupke," "Somewhere"—held huge appeal,[953] but now they were surrounded by energetic choreography, a kind of dancing never seen on the screen, finger-snapping, the camera in all sorts of angles to capture the raw tension. The realistic background added a new dimension. Wood and Beymer were dubbed by Marni Nixon and Jimmy Bryant, respectively, and Rita Moreno by Betty Wand, but if the actors' singing was not up to scratch, their acting was. As youngsters coming to terms with emotional complication, that, too, carried new power. When lists of great musicals are compiled, this often, rightly, sits on top. Nominated in 11 Oscar categories, it only missed out on one.[954] It was named Best Picture, Wise and Robbins shared Best Director, with George Chakiris Best Supporting Actor and Rita Moreno Best Supporting Actress.

Critical reception: "Five years ahead of its time" (*New York Herald Tribune*); "new high film musical" (*New York Journal American*)[955]; "most advanced movie musical ever made" (*Life*); "nothing short of a cinema masterpiece" (*New York Times*).[956] It was ranked 17th for the year by *Cahiers du Cinema*.[957]

Rentals: $19.4 million[958] (including 1968 reissue) ($138.2 million equivalent)

16: *The Dirty Dozen*

Starring Lee Marvin and Charles Bronson; directed by Robert Aldrich; screenplay, Nunnally Johnson,[959] from the novel by E.M. Nathanson; producer, Kenneth Hyman; music, Frank De Vol. MGM. June 15, 1967.[960]

John Wayne rejected the role of Major Reisman in *The Dirty Dozen*.[961] But he was not first choice. The Perlberg-Seaton[962] outfit bought the rights to E.M. Nathanson's novel[963] with Oscar-nominated Nick Adams in mind, then Glenn Ford.[964] When the project landed[965] on Kenneth Hyman's desk,[966] he passed it to Robert Aldrich—for a hefty profit share.[967] Aldrich had been a big name since the double whammy of *Apache* (1954) and *Vera Cruz* (1954)[968] and more recently *Hush...Hush, Sweet Charlotte* (1964) and *The Flight of the Phoenix* (1965). The budget was set at $3.5 million,[969] Burt Lancaster briefly in the frame[970] prior to Oscar winner Lee Marvin, who had worked with Aldrich on *Attack* (1956). The biggest names in the supporting cast were famous for other reasons: Jim Brown, the legendary Cleveland Browns footballer and publicity magnet,[971] pop star Trini Lopez, the biggest-selling artist in the burgeoning tape cassette medium, and TV's *Cheyenne* Clint Walker.[972] George Kennedy, Ernest Borgnine, Charles Bronson and Richard Jaeckel had worked with Aldrich before.[973] Other roles went to John Cassavetes, Oscar winner Telly Savalas and Robert Ryan plus British actor Al Mancini and Canadian Donald Sutherland.[974] Many would later achieve stardom. Terrible weather across Europe played havoc with the schedule[975] and helped balloon the budget to $5.6 million.[976]

The Dirty Dozen is a classic three-act picture, opening section devoted to Marvin learning about the condemned prisoners, the central sequence training and war games,

The Films 161

The men grew their own beards rather than wearing false ones, resulting in them being unable to film a scene that called for them to be clean shaven when bad weather delayed the completion of the bearded sequence* (pressbook).

*Pressbook, *The Dirty Dozen*.

the final part an attack on a French chateau housing high-ranking German officers just before D-Day. In terms of screen time, the star does not hog the picture. For many key scenes relating to character development, he is absent, as he is for the bulk of the mock exercise. So the audience has the opportunity to get to know other characters: Sutherland painting over someone's hand, Cassavetes pocketing wire cutters, Bronson, Brown and Walker preventing Cassavetes' escape. The prisoners are all shapes, sizes and ethnicities, tall and small, heavyset and skinny, reflecting Army reality. Unlike the normal army, sheer authority will not work, Marvin has to introduce co-dependency. Second World War recruits were thrown together in alien circumstances with complete strangers and yet combat forged them into a band of brothers. In previous films such as *The Magnificent Seven* and *The Great Escape*, characters had not bonded in this fashion.

162   The Films

What makes *The Dirty Dozen* unique is that Marvin is not a leader in the traditional sense. He does not have various bust-ups with individuals, like a star would in previous movies, until, miraculously, they see sense. He does not risk his life for them or feud with them over a woman. Instead, he builds his squad into a team by leaving them to it. Another star would have stolen, and another director surrendered, choice scenes or lines that Aldrich allotted to his dozen, in which, bit by bit, they created the essential camaraderie. Told by the psychiatrist that the men see Marvin as the enemy, he retorts, "It gives them something in common." When the men mutiny and refuse to shave, an officer comments, "Mutiny." Marvin replies, "A team."

The movie could have gone straight from there to planning the raid and missed out entirely the second act. The characters have all been established, Marvin has succeeded in gelling them as a unit, the mission has been revealed, the soubriquet "The Dirty Dozen" applied, the audience rooting for them. Played out in this fashion, the movie would have come in at a trim 100 minutes, the right length for a normal action film, not the 150-minute finished running time.[977] Yet it is the middle section that creates this picture's unique warmth. We learn nothing more about their characters except that Cassavetes requires further education in group ethos and Sutherland is given a chance to shine. Minus Marvin's presence and leadership, the Dozen cheat their way to victory in the war games. This sequence is the reason the movie reverberates so much with the audience: The good guys triumph over bureaucrats and officers on their own side who treat them with scorn.

And then, quickly, the phony war is over and the dangerous mission begins. Tension mounts, Bronson struggling with a grappling iron, the nervous Sutherland waiting outside, sadistic Savalas unable to contain himself, chateau occupants scurrying into the basement where they are trapped. French staff, innocent bystanders, are allowed to escape. The Germans retaliate. Only Marvin, Bronson, Cassavetes and the sergeant escape. The attack and ensuing battle are brutal. Aldrich does not flinch from the raw truth. War is hell. Despite a media storm over violence (with particular outcry over Savalas' savage glee and dousing trapped Germans in petrol), the film is surprisingly bloodless compared to *Bonnie and Clyde* (1967) and *The Wild Bunch* (1969). Thanks to the character development and acting, it is involving. Take out the climactic battle and you still have a pretty decent picture.

Critical reception: "Convincing and exciting" (*Box Office*); "scenes of rousing indiscipline and scrumptious battle" (*Films and Filming*)[978]; "femme audience appeal despite all-male principals" (*Variety*).[979]

Rentals: $19.9 million[980] ($141.8 million equivalent)

14 (tie): *Valley of the Dolls*

Starring Barbara Parkins, Patty Duke and Sharon Tate; directed by Mark Robson; screenplay, Helen Deutsch and Dorothy Kingsley,[981] from the novel by Jacqueline Susann; producer, David Weisbart; music, Andre Previn and John Williams. Twentieth Century–Fox. December 15, 1967.[982]

Half a century after publication, Jacqueline Susann's novel *Valley of the Dolls* has been re-evaluated, reprinted by feminist publisher Virago and considered "brave, bold, angry and, yes, a feminist book." The film by comparison was dumped early on into the "so-bad-it's-good"[983] category and has remained there ever since. A bit-part actress,[984] Susann wrote a novel that became the decade's biggest,[985] at a time when male authors dominated bestseller charts.[986] The book follows three Hollywood actresses: small-town girl Anne, ruthless Neely and sex symbol Jennifer. They love, they lose and come apart at the seams. They lie and cheat and are betrayed in return. Drugs, abortion, sexual experimentation, pornography, plastic surgery, suicide ... few subjects are taboo. A happy ending is never in sight. Offering three plum roles[987] (and a great supporting character in Helen Lawson), it became a priority project for Twentieth Century–Fox[988] on a $4.4 million budget.[989] Candice Bergen,[990] Lee Remick, Jane Fonda, Julie Christie, Raquel Welch, Joanna Pettet and Jean Hale turned down roles while Natalie Wood, Bette Davis, Debbie Reynolds and Kim Novak lobbied for roles.[991] Males screen-tested included Christopher Plummer and James Garner.[992]

Judy Garland[993] (Helen Lawson) was easily the most accomplished but she turned up on the set drunk and was replaced by Oscar-winning Susan Hayward (*Where Love Has Gone*, 1964). Oscar winner[994] Patty Duke (Neely) had just finished a four-year TV stint on *The Patty Duke Show* (1963). Barbara Parkins (Anne) from TV's *Peyton Place*[995] made her debut.[996] Sharon Tate (Jennifer) was a rising star, after supporting roles in *Eye of the Devil* (1966), *Don't Makes Waves* (1967) and *The Fearless Vampire Killers* (1967). The leading male parts went to Paul Burke (TV's *12 O'Clock High*), Martin Milner (TV's long-running *Route 66*) and debutant singer Tony Scotti.[997] Don Siegel (*The Killers*, 1964) was in early discussion to direct until Mark Robson (*Von Ryan's Express*, 1965) suddenly became available.[998] Oscar nominee Robson had been through all this soap opera malarkey before in *Peyton Place* (1957) and had safely steered home the big, unwieldy bestsellers *From the Terrace* (1960) and *The Prize* (1963).

The screen adaptation shifted the book's time-frame to the 1960s and provided an unlikely happy ending, although both screenwriters admitted the work was problematic.[999] The costume budget was $350,000.[1000] Designer William Travilla,[1001] who had set trends designing outfits for Marilyn Monroe, Lauren Bacall and Greer Garson,[1002] was convinced that what he put on the screen would "provide a guide to what the well-dressed woman would wear."[1003] The production could have been a film in itself. Duke suffered from drug and alcohol abuse, mood swings and nervous skin conditions and constantly clashed with the director. Between Duke and Barbara Parkins was "raging professional animosity" akin to Bette Davis and Joan Crawford. Robson filmed with a stopwatch in his hand.[1004] As well as the on-set travails, real-life tragedy struck when producer David Weisbart dropped dead playing golf with the director.[1005] The studio had begun its marketing campaign before filming began,[1006] standard practice for roadshows like *Lawrence of Arabia*, but not for relatively standard items. The novel's continued sales—6.8 million in paperback—meant immense public awareness. Fashion was implemented in the marketing scenario.[1007]

Something curious occurred at the beginning of the film. Before the traditional Fox logo, up popped a disclaimer, either because the producers feared legal action or as a hint to audiences that the tale had fictionalized truth.[1008] While high on drama, the story is less salacious due to restrictions of the Production Code.[1009] Tate delivers the best performance in part because she is the least driven, wanting an ordinary life. As the most driven and devious, Duke, on a knife edge, seems most of the time to be over-acting. Parkins, too, is good but the more experienced Hayward, her character expecting to be usurped by the younger wannabe, steals the show. One of the film's flaws is that the men,

164 **The Films**

all stereotypical, have little to work with. Robson delivered a polished picture and it's hard to see how the so-bad-it's-good simplification applies beyond the obvious limiting soap opera characteristics of the source material.

Critical reception: "Talky, sudsy version of the book, handsome production, otherwise dull" (*Variety*); "soap opera with sex" (*Box Office*)[1010]; "Hollywood once again astounds even its critics and demonstrated just how great are its powers of self-renewal" (*Films and Filming*).[1011]

Rentals: $20 million[1012] ($142.5 million equivalent)

14 (tie): *The Odd Couple*

Starring Jack Lemmon and Walter Matthau; directed by Gene Saks; screenplay, Neil Simon[1013] based on his play; producer, Howard W. Koch[1014]; music, Neal Hefti. Paramount. May 2, 1968.[1015]

This is the "buddy" movie (before *Butch Cassidy and the Sundance Kid* invented the concept) as marriage. Two guys are good friends until they have to live together—that would be "the elevator pitch." That they are chalk and cheese and drive each other crazy is as much plot as the movie musters. It's based on the Neil Simon Broadway hit, which is to say that, except for opening it up a little with scenes outside their apartment building, it's almost an exact replica of the stage production. Simon had already demonstrated his worth, previous adaptations of his Broadway comedies being *Come Blow Your Horn* (1963) and *Barefoot in the Park* (1967). Simon had made his bones in television on the legendary *Your Show of Shows* (1950) followed by *Caesar's Hour* (1954), *The Phil Silvers Show* (1958) and *The Garry Moore Show* (1959). His Broadway debut *Come Blow Your Horn* ran for 678 performances, *The Odd Couple* 699 performances with a Tony to boot and a million-dollar profit.[1016] *The Odd Couple* was based on situations arising out of the divorce of his brother Danny, his sometime television co-writer. He wrote one version with two male leads and a different one based on the men's wives.

Walter Matthau had played the part of Felix the slob on stage with Art Carney as obsessive-compulsive Oscar. Carney lost out to Jack Lemmon, top star for nearly a decade through *Some Like It Hot* (1959), *The Apartment* (1960) and *The Great Race* (1965). His Oscar nomination for *Days of Wine and Roses* (1962) was his fourth. Matthau's comedic talent, on the other hand, was slower to emerge and he had built a reputation as a sterling supporting actor in dramas like *Fail-Safe* (1964) and the thrillers *Charade* (1963) and *Mirage* (1965). When Billy Wilder threw them both into *The Fortune Cookie,* it proved the pivotal moment of Matthau's career and he was top-billed for the first time in his next picture, the hit comedy *A Guide for the Married Man* (1967). Director Gene Saks had made his debut with *Barefoot in the Park*.

The film begins on a somber note, Lemmon contemplating suicide after his wife leaves him. Because the movie starts at such a low point, it gives the characters space to grow. Moving in with fun-loving Matthau initially lifts Lemmon out of his depressed state but gradually he becomes irritated by his friend's bad habits. Meanwhile, Lemmon's exceptionally clean living is driving Matthau and his poker pals crazy. To try and get Lemmon out of himself, Matthau sets up a double date. Lemmon talks to his girl about his ex-wife and Matthau spends all his time complaining about Lemmon to his girl. Infuriated, Matthau tries to be as messy as possible and Lemmon retaliates by being

The Films 165

Unusually, trade journalists were denied a press screening, which was usually enough to set alarm bells ringing since studios only kept a movie away from critics if they were worried about its prospects.* Trade press advertisement (*Box Office*, June 24, 1968).

*"Odd Delay on *Odd Couple*," *Variety*, April 10, 1968, 7.

166   The Films

as tidy as possible, resulting in Lemmon being given his marching orders. Fearing this will trigger another suicide attempt, the guilty Matthau organizes a search party only to discover Lemmon happily ensconced in the apartment of the girl he dated. The friends reconcile.

A simple retelling of the story hardly gets across the magical chemistry of Lemmon and Matthau that carries the picture. Inside the comedy, the feelings they have for each other spill over into "bromance" and Simon never lets the comedy pace slacken, whether it is Lemmon unable to open a window when attempting suicide or cleaning the poker cards or setting fire to dinner. It is also a movie about men without women, about their inability to cope and their problems dealing with their feelings. Having said all that, it is just hilarious, Simon matchless at setting up scenes and delivering punchlines. All the director has to do is make sure the actors hit their marks. As you might expect, the film's title was a gift to the marketing department.[1017]

Critical reception: "Will cause more people to do more laughing than any film you are likely to see all year" (*Los Angeles Times*); "can't imagine anybody not enjoying it" (*Films and Filming*); "in an era where comedies tend to be devastatingly tragic, this one is refreshing" (*International Motion Picture Exhibitor*): "funniest comedy of the year" (*Independent Film Journal*).[1018]

Rentals: $20 million[1019] ($142.5 million equivalent)

13: *Bonnie and Clyde*

Starring Warren Beatty and Faye Dunaway; directed by Arthur Penn; screenplay, Robert Benton and David Newman[1020]; producer, Beatty; music, Charles Strouse. Warner Brothers.[1021] August 4, 1967 (Montreal)[1022]; U.S.: August 13, 1967.

Producer-star Warren Beatty spent a lot of time convincing gullible journalists that the movie's poor performance in initial release was entirely the fault of Warner Brothers. Beatty claimed the movie was inexpensive when in fact the budget was on a par with *Wait Until Dark* (1967) and *Cool Hand Luke* (1967).[1023] Beatty's self-indulgence forced the studio to postpone the premiere, allowing the competing gangster picture *The St. Valentine's Day Massacre* (1967) to steal a box office march. Following a strategy used by films with much lower budgets, Beatty got his way to open the film in arthouses, but the idea of an arty gangster picture confused audiences[1024] when the movie entered general release.[1025] Even though it attracted a heap of publicity when famed critic Joseph Morgenstern of *Newsweek*, who had originally tagged it "a squalid shoot-em-up," changed his mind, it still flopped.[1026] Finally, Beatty claimed the studio resisted the idea of a reissue to take advantage of potential Oscar nominations when those now in charge at Warners had built a massive business on the back of both reissues and Oscars.[1027] The studio re-purposed the advertising campaign, and held the movie steady in a select few houses until grosses started to build; then after Oscar nominations, they let it loose across the country. *Bonnie and Clyde* became one of the all-time great reissue stories, generating eight times as much revenue the second time around.[1028]

Beatty, younger brother of Shirley MacLaine, had squandered the promise of *Splendor in the Grass* (1961). Where he identified as an artist, studio chiefs never saw beyond good looks and charm. His top-billed status added commercial weight to the risky projects *Lilith* (1964) and *Mickey One* (1965). When both flopped, Beatty was forced into

In the U.S it enjoyed an arthouse opening with a sympathetic representation of the characters in advertising and the pressbook. In Britain, they were presented as gun-toting gangsters. This approach did so well it encouraged Warner Brothers to re-release the picture—up to then a flop—in America. Trade press advertisement (*Kine Weekly*, September 2, 1967, 1).

the lightweight comedies *Promise Her Anything* (1966) and *Kaleidoscope* (1966). He saw *Bonnie and Clyde* as the vehicle to restore both his box office luster and artistic credibility. Arthur Penn, too, was in sore need of salvation after being fired from *The Train* (1964), with *The Chase* (1966) missing its box office target. He, too, had squandered early promise: the Western *The Left Handed Gun* (1958) and *The Miracle Worker* (1962) for which he was Oscar nominated.

Esquire journalists Robert Benton and David Newman had started writing the *Bonnie and Clyde* script in 1963, interesting French New Wave directors Francois Truffaut[1029] and Jean-Luc Godard[1030] in the project before Truffaut passed it on to Beatty. Fast-rising star Faye Dunaway is the gangster's moll, with supporting roles filled by relative newcomers Michael J. Pollard (*Caprice*, 1967) and Gene Hackman (*Banning*, 1967). Estelle Parsons came from TV and Gene Wilder was making his debut.

The film is different not just from any previous gangster effort but from most American mainstream product. Not just that it featured a hero troubled by his sexuality and excessive violence, but that its style was more akin to the French New Wave—it popularizing the auteur theory[1031]—a stack of extremely short disconnected shots often making

168 The Films

up a scene.[1032] Most gangster films are more about the gangster than the moll. *Bonnie and Clyde* is about two gangsters who egg each other on with a relationship as much about violence as sex. They are not portrayed as tougher than tough but as human beings with emotional flaws. Bonnie becomes a gangster because she is bored. Beatty is as good in scenes displaying his internal troubles as the gun-toting bank robber. Given the way they are portrayed, it is astonishing that the whole film still manages to cover them in a romantic sheen. They are rebels in the sense that they want to see how much they can get away with, not in the thefts, but the violence which clearly gives them a buzz. Normally, an audience roots for the cops chasing the gangsters, but here the audience is on the side of the bad guys. It is an anti-establishment picture no matter how many innocents they slaughter.

Both Beatty and Dunaway are superb,[1033] switching from the violent to softer emotion with ease, both displaying an internal tenderness that runs counter to what they show the outer world. Pollard and Hackman are excellent. But it is Penn's picture (albeit recognizing Beatty's input), his ability to coax terrific performances from all the cast members coupled with bravura sequences such as, of course, the final shoot-out in which so many bullets were expended you would have thought the cops were trying to rub out the entire Mob. It was up for ten Oscars, all five actors in the running in various categories, plus Best Picture. Parsons came away with the Best Supporting Actress gong and Burnett Guffey for cinematography.

Where establishment figures complained about the violence,[1034] youthful moviegoers pointed to government-endorsed slaughter in Vietnam. These were anti-heroes who would kill anyone who got in their way and didn't care if they died in the process. This was James Dean for a new generation. But as much as moviegoers enjoyed what the picture had to say, they also loved its look. After the reissue, the *Bonnie and Clyde* fashions boomed and identification with gangsters was a simple matter of wearing similar clothes. For wannabe filmmakers, it freed the imagination.

It freed Warren Beatty, too. He had struck a deal for 40 percent of the gross—over $6 million.[1035] He was a rich man.

Critical reception: "Triumph" (*Vogue*); "engrossing, fascinating and magnificently made" (*Newsday*); "an American work of art" (*Cosmopolitan*)[1036]; "a work of truth and brilliance" (*Chicago Sun-Times*); "generating a sadistical feeling in the audience" (*New York Times*).[1037] It placed 20th in the *Cahiers du Cinema* annual round-up.[1038]

Rentals: $20.2 million[1039] (including 1969 reissue in a double bill with *Bullitt*) ($143.9 million equivalent)

12: *How the West Was Won*

Starring John Wayne, James Stewart, Gregory Peck and Debbie Reynolds; directed by Henry Hathaway, John Ford and George Marshall; screenplay, James R. Webb; producer, Bernard Smith; music, Alfred Newman. MGM. November 1, 1962 (London); U.S.: February 20, 1963.

These days, fact-based magazine articles commonly spark movies: *The Fast and the Furious* (2001) inspired by a piece in *Vibe*, *A Beautiful Day in the Neighborhood* (2019) started life in *Esquire*—but it was rare in the 1960s.[1040] However, a series of seven lengthy historical articles in the multi-million-selling *Life* magazine in 1959 about the Wild

West, extensively illustrated with material from the time, captured the attention of the nation. Bing Crosby acquired the rights, not as a potential movie, but for a double album[1041] and a TV special. When this proved too expensive, the rights were sold to MGM to become the first dramatic film in the Cinerama format. Crosby initially remained part of the concept, crooning songs to connect various episodes.[1042] James R. Webb (*The Big Country*, 1958) was entrusted with knocking the unwieldy story into a coherent narrative. His first draft accommodated various montages covering the journey from the Pilgrim Fathers to the building of the Erie Canal and the Civil War. It was only in subsequent drafts that the tale of Linus Rawlings (James Stewart) emerged with surprising focus on female pioneers.[1043]

Given the size of the undertaking, it was initially intended there be five directors but this was reduced to three, John Ford (*The Searchers*, 1956), Henry Hathaway (*North to Alaska*, 1960), and George Marshall (*The Sheepman*, 1958); Hathaway carried the biggest share of the burden. Richard Thorpe (*Ivanhoe*, 1952) handled some transitional historical sequences. For once, this was a genuine all-star cast headed up by actors with more than a passing acquaintance with the Western: John Wayne, Gregory Peck, James Stewart, Richard Widmark and Henry Fonda, with Spencer Tracy as narrator plus George Peppard in his first Western. The two strongest female roles were given to actresses playing against type, Carroll Baker, who normally essayed sexpots, as a homely pioneer and Debbie Reynolds, more at home in musicals and

World premiere at the Casino Theatre in London's West End took a record $500,000 advance. The picture had amassed over 62,000 reservations for groups and parties. Advance bookings guaranteed the picture at least a year's run.* Press advertisement (*Films and Filming*, November 1962, 3).

*"Brilliant World Premiere in London for *West*," *Box Office*, November 12, 1962, 12.

170 The Films

comedies, as her tough daughter. The impressive supporting cast included Lee J. Cobb, Eli Wallach, Walter Brennan, Robert Preston, Carolyn Jones and Karl Malden. Glenn Ford and Burt Lancaster were unavailable.[1044]

Virtually three-quarters of the picture was shot on location to satisfy Cinerama customers accustomed to seeing new vistas and to bring to life the illustrations from the original articles. Backdrops included the Ohio River Valley, Monument Valley, Cave-in-Rock State Park, the Colorado Rockies, the Black Hills of Dakota, Custer State Park and Mackenzie River in Oregon. The directors broke new ground, technically. The cumbersome cameras required peculiar skills to achieve common shots. Directors lay on top of the camera to judge what a close-up looked like. Sets were built to take account of the way dimensions appeared through the lens, camera remaining static to prevent distortion.[1045] The picture, including narration, took over a year. Standard Cinerama sensation was achieved by shooting the rapids, runaway locomotive, buffalo stampede, Indian attack, Civil War battle and cattle drive. Motion was central to Cinerama so journeys were undertaken by raft, wagon, Pony Express, railroad and boat.

It is amazing how well the various sequences fit together and narrative thrust maintained throughout this episodic film. The story covers a 50-year stretch beginning in 1839 with the river sequence bringing together Stewart and Baker. After Stewart is bushwhacked by river pirates, he marries Baker and they set up a homestead. The next section pairs singer Reynolds with gambler Peck whose wagon train is attacked by Indians on the way to San Francisco. Later, Stewart and son Peppard enlist in the Civil War (appearance by Wayne). Stewart dies at the Battle of Shiloh. Peppard joins the cavalry. Later, as an Arizona marshal, he meets Reynolds and prevents a robbery that results in a spectacular train wreck. It took a superb piece of screenwriting to pull the elements together, ensure the characters had just cause to meet and to create solid pace with high drama and action quotient. Alfred Newman provided a thunderous score with a foot-stomping overture. There are solid performances all around and, for once, scenery does not clog a Cinerama picture but opens it up. It was nominated for a Best Picture Oscar and won for the screenplay, sound and editing. It became MGM's biggest hit after *Gone with the Wind* and *Ben-Hur*.

Critical reaction: "The real historical drama of the West … wasted" (*New York Times*); "memorable sequences" (*Variety*); "magnificent production" (*Box Office*).[1046]

Rentals: $20.93 million[1047] ($149.1 million equivalent)

11: *Goldfinger*

Starring Sean Connery and Honor Blackman; directed by Terence Young; screenplay, Richard Maibaum and Paul Dehn, based on the novel by Ian Fleming; producers, Harry Saltzman and Albert R. Broccoli; music, John Barry. United Artists. September 17, 1964 (London); U.S.: December 22, 1964.

This was the film that made Hollywood think again. Up to that point, major studios had believed that big-budget roadshows were the key to financial sustainability. While not quite in the category of the "little films that could," its phenomenal box office performance provided studios with an alternative strategy and started the flood of me-too spy pictures. You could also argue that it gave male stars the green light to be tougher: Paul Newman and Steve McQueen could engage in fisticuffs rather than tough talk. Although

This film spawned a vast merchandising program to rival Disney. The Corgi toy version of the Aston Martin provided an unbelievable sales bonanza and instilled in kids a love of the series. Merchandising and sponsorship tie-ins could often make as much for the producers of a Bond film as the movie itself. Press advertisement (*Films and Filming*, October 1964, 6).

there had been two Bond films so far, *Dr. No* (1962) and *From Russia with Love* (1963), you could make an argument that *Goldfinger* established the quintessential template. This saw the arrival of gadgets and the beginning of the mushrooming budget. From now on, everything would be bigger than ever. There was good reason for the bolder approach, to do with immediate financial satisfaction and sustainability. In America, the second film had taken in twice as much as the first and the producers were hoping the same rule would apply to the third. But more important was longevity. There had been no shortage of series pictures in the past (Charlie Chan, Bulldog Drummond, the Lone Wolf) and some still ongoing via *Sherlock Holmes and the Deadly Necklace* (1962) and *Tarzan's Three Challenges* (1963). But they had all eventually lost their audience because they were the same picture over and over again with lower budgets. To prevent Bond falling into the same trap, the producers had to invent new ideas, new perils, larger-than-life villains. The task set was constant upgrade.

So budgets increased. *Goldfinger* cost $3 million, more than the first two films combined. Much went to accoutrements, top-of-the range Aston Martin DB5 and the gadgets. In the book, the auto had a smoke screen; the movie added revolving license plate, ejector seat and tire-shredding spikes. Weapons were up-scaled, Goldfinger's instrument of choice the laser. Thematically this film was an art director's dream. One character dies after being painted gold. Goldfinger's number plate is AU1, the chemical symbol for gold. He has a golden pistol,[1048] is bound to a gold-plated bench. And if it's not gold, it's near enough. Pussy Galore wears a metallic gold vest. Goldfinger has a yellow Rolls-Royce.[1049] And the plot revolves around stealing gold. *Goldfinger* began the tradition of theme tune sung over title sequence. Location work was more extensive: Florida, Kentucky, Switzerland and around Fort Knox. The villains were also upsized, in personality and physique. Goldfinger was far more dominant than Dr. No (Joseph Wiseman) while the indomitable Oddjob with his steel-brimmed bowler hat—which makes him susceptible to electrocution—has the edge on previous redoubtable adversaries Rosa Klebb and Red Grant. German actor Gert Frobe (*The Longest Day*, 1962) plays Goldfinger and Hawaiian Harold Sakata makes his debut as Oddjob. Honor Blackman, from the English TV series *The Avengers*, plays Pussy Galore, another bad girl charmed into goodness by Bond, while Shirley Eaton (*The Girl Hunters*, 1963) is the girl smothered by paint.

Of course, it's an outlandish plot but it's outrageous in every way, that's the fun of the Bond series. This was one film where nobody cared what the critics said (though, in fact, most liked it) because the audience knew it was in for a great time.

Critical reception: "A thriller exuberantly travestied" (*Time*); "terrifically exciting and elaborately scientific" (*Box Office*); "zestful slice of fantastic hokum" (*Variety*).[1050]

Rentals: $22.5 million[1051] (including 1967 and 1969 reissues in double bills with other Bond titles) ($160.3 million equivalent)

10: *Guess Who's Coming to Dinner*

Starring Spencer Tracy, Sidney Poitier and Katharine Hepburn; directed and produced by Stanley Kramer; screenplay, William Rose; music, Frank De Vol. Columbia. December 11, 1967.

In a decade devoted to ridding the industry of the shackles of the Production Code, one subject remained taboo. Stanley Kramer had explored racism in *Home of the Brave*

(1949), *The Defiant Ones* (1958)[1052] and *Pressure Point* (1962). While *The Defiant Ones* was Oscar-nominated for Best Picture and Best Director, that was as far as Hollywood would go. The idea of a relationship between an African American and a white was beyond comprehension.[1053] Southern exhibitors even took issue with Poitier's appearance as a Moor with a white wife in *The Long Ships* (1964).[1054] After the commercial peak of *It's a Mad Mad Mad Mad World* (1963) and the success of *Ship of Fools* (1965), Kramer suggested setting an idea about interracial marriage, by screenwriter William Rose, in the United States.[1055] This translated into the story of a handsome African American doctor, highly regarded in his field, whose white fiancée takes him to meet her liberal parents. It avoids the bigoted setting of *In the Heat of the Night* (1967) and *Hurry Sundown* (1967). The comedy is gentle, similar to *Father of the Bride* (1950). However, no matter what it was, Hollywood didn't want it. Columbia agreed to a $3 million picture[1056] starring frequent collaborators Spencer Tracy[1057] and Katharine Hepburn, who had not worked together in a decade, Kramer informing studio heads that it was about a marriage, omitting the detail of its interracial nature.[1058]

Tracy, seriously ill, had not worked since his three days on *It's a Mad Mad Mad Mad World*, but Kramer used Hepburn to win him over.[1059] Hepburn's last role had been *Long Day's Journey into Night* (1962) and before that, *Suddenly, Last Summer* (1959). Poitier agreed on the assumption that Tracy and Hepburn were in when they were not.[1060] When Kramer told Columbia the truth, the studio backed out, only reversing their decision on realizing that they were committed to paying Kramer $500,000 anyway.[1061] Columbia pulled out again when Tracy could not get insurance.[1062] No other studio was interested so Kramer and Hepburn put their salaries in escrow.[1063] To accommodate Tracy's physical frailty,[1064] he worked only mornings, Hepburn on set to help with the cosseting. Poitier initially was a bigger problem, overcome by nerves when acting with a legend.[1065] Hepburn's niece Katharine Houghton, limited thus far to TV, was enrolled as Poitier's fiancée. Isabel Sanford debuted as the African American housekeeper. Playing Poitier's parents were Beah Richards, who had small roles in *In the Heat of the Night* and *Hurry Sundown*, and Roy Glenn, a veteran bit-part player going back to *Bomba and the Jungle Girl* (1952). Cecil Kellaway, Oscar-nominated for *The Luck of the Irish* (1948), appeared as a priest. By the time the film opened, Tracy had died of a heart attack.[1066] Devastated, Hepburn never saw the finished picture.[1067] Two days after Tracy's death, the U.S. Supreme Court, in the *Loving vs. Virginia* case, ruled anti-miscegenation marriage laws, still in force in 17 states, unconstitutional.[1068]

The story is classic meet-the-parents. Poitier, a widower, is introduced to Tracy and Hepburn, then Houghton meets Poitier's parents, neither couple initially aware of their child's choice of mate. Tension is supplied by Poitier needing the engagement finalized before jetting off to Switzerland. And there are unexpected twists: Tracy's housekeeper talking against Poitier for "getting uppity." But basically it's all down to reaction. Liberal newspaper publisher Tracy and art gallery owner Hepburn find their convictions tested when racial equality is so close to home, no matter Poitier's impeccable credentials and that he objects to intercourse before marriage. The climax is a dinner party with all the parents and children plus the saving presence of the priest. The issues are hammered out with Tracy giving an emotional six-minute speech.

Whether audiences turned up for the last hurrah of Tracy or that of the Tracy-Hepburn partnership so familiar to generations of moviegoers[1069] or Sidney Poitier, career in the stratosphere after *To Sir, with Love* and *In the Heat of the Night*, or the prospect of

174   The Films

a decent romantic comedy, or the racial issues explored, it did not seem to matter. The movie covered all bases and avoided sex, violence and swearing. The three principals are uniformly excellent, Poitier giving Tracy a run for his money, and the supporting cast works well. The script delivers, the drama punctuated by laughs, and Kramer is efficient behind the camera.

Critics were a bit snippy, most feeling the picture had not gone far enough even though (as Poitier pointed out) this was far as Hollywood was willing to go at the time.[1070] It opened up the industry to a more favorable attitude to African American stars. Critics who sniped at Kramer's direction were bowled over by Tracy and Hepburn. It was nominated for ten Oscars including Best Picture and provided Tracy with his ninth nomination; it was Hepburn who triumphed, her third Best Actress Oscar,[1071] along with screenwriter Rose. Take away the controversial elements, as anyone watching today would do unless pretty familiar with the mood of the times, and it still stands as a quality production with standout performances.[1072]

Critical reception: "Earnestly preaching" (*Life*); "glorious actors playing very good parts" (*Newsweek*); "superior in almost every imaginable way" (*Variety*); "rare specimen of a film from which legends grow" (*Box Office*).[1073]

Rentals: $25.5 million[1074] ($181.7 million equivalent)

9: *Cleopatra*

Starring Elizabeth Taylor, Richard Burton and Rex Harrison; directed by Joseph L. Mankiewicz; screenplay, Ranald MacDougall and Sidney Buchman[1075]; producer, Walter Wanger[1076]; music, Alex North. Twentieth Century–Fox roadshow. June 12, 1963.

It's a wonder there was a halfway decent movie anywhere in sight given the calamitous production travails of *Cleopatra*, not least a budget that set some kind of record for excess in skipping from an initial $2.95 million[1077] to $44 million,[1078] plus expenditure on buying up a rival production,[1079] in the process nearly sending the studio into liquidation.[1080] The film that finally appeared was the second version, the first, directed by veteran Rouben Mamoulian (*The Mark of Zorro*, 1940)[1081] and co-starring Peter Finch (*The Trials of Oscar Wilde*, 1960) and Stephen Boyd (*Ben-Hur*, 1959),[1082] was shut down following Elizabeth Taylor's illness after 16 weeks, ten minutes of film shot and the budget racing past $7 million. The second, directed by another veteran, double–Oscar winner Joseph L. Mankiewicz (*All About Eve*, 1950), personal choice of the star, brought in replacements: Rex Harrison and, after considering Laurence Olivier[1083] and Trevor Howard,[1084] settled on Richard Burton (on $250,000).[1085] It was not long before the scandal of the mushrooming budget was lost in the bigger scandal of the Taylor-Burton affair. Both were married at the time, the actress to crooner Eddie Fisher.[1086] Taylor was not first choice. When the budget was considerably more mundane, Joan Collins,[1087] top-billed in *Sea Wife* (1957) above Richard Burton, was first name in the hat. When she pulled out, Susan Hayward and Audrey Hepburn[1088] were other possibilities until Taylor agreed to do it for a million dollars,[1089] a record fee for an actor of either gender.[1090] MGM, to whom Taylor still owed a picture, held her, as previously mentioned, to ransom, forcing her to make *BUtterfield 8* (1960) before releasing her for *Cleopatra*. Locations shifted from Hollywood,[1091] Pinewood and Shepperton[1092] in Britain, Rome[1093] and Egypt with Spain and Greece[1094] also considered.

CLEOPATRA

The royal barge was built to specifications described by the historian Plutarch. "The barge was rowed by silver-mounted oars. The great purple sails hung idly in the still air of the waning day. On the deck a number of beautiful slave women were grouped, costumed as sea-nymphs and graces"* (souvenir program).

*"The Challenge: Filming *Cleopatra*," Souvenir Program, National Publishers Inc, 1963.

176 The Films

Essentially, the story presents Cleopatra as a woman who seduces the two most powerful Romans of the era, Julius Caesar (Harrison) and Mark Anthony (Burton), in a bid to retain her position as Egypt's queen. This triggers political intrigue, passionate romance and battle. But it is a very literate script, the three principals extremely well-drawn, with many one-liners besides. This Cleopatra is one of the most powerful women ever seen on the screen, able to hold onto her perspective while ostensibly superior men are losing themselves in love. When not charming all in sight, Cleopatra is within inches of a hissy fit. But it is a film of two halves. Despite Burton's undoubted screen presence, Harrison is the more compelling of the two and when he departs halfway through, the picture loses a lot of its dramatic thrust. The second half seems almost preoccupied with the tragic end in sight as the lovers are pursued by a ruthless Octavian (Roddy McDowall). Harrison acts like a king whereas Burton is a madman in love. The elegant duel of wits in the first half between Cleopatra and Caesar descends into melodrama in the second half.

For a movie known for budgetary excess, a surprising amount of the money finds its way onto the screen. The sets are stunning, the costumes designed to the minutest detail and the set pieces quite extraordinary, especially as anybody going into battle is actually an extra and not a figment of a CGI engineer's imagination. Part of the reason for the cost was that Mankiewicz wanted to split the movie in two, with one film each devoted to the separate love stories, both lasting three hours with different narrative arcs. So he was making a six-hour picture. If the Taylor-Burton affair continued with a full head of steam, that would help sell the second part. Having spent so much money—and a full half-century before studios started splitting movies in two—the studio refused to bite. Both original producer Walter Wanger and Mankiewicz were fired,[1095] though the director was reinstated for further filming of "essential bridges and episodes" to make sense of what had been lost in editing, costing another $2 million.[1096] By the time the film appeared, public demand was huge,[1097] not surprising since "no picture including *Gone with the Wind* has ever come to the market so thoroughly presold and marketed."[1098] As well as $500,000 in advance ticket sales, exhibitors shelled out $18 million in guarantees.[1099]

It's far from being a bloated mess but there's no doubt budgetary excess got in the way of critical assessment. The six-hour concept might well have shown the movie in a new light. The four-hour version is a lot better than the one truncated for general release. As it stands, it is an excellent epic, well up to the standards of the best roadshows of the era, with Taylor in commanding form, an intelligent screenplay, and the stunning backdrops recreating history, authenticity the watchword. It received nine Oscar nominations including Best Picture, and won four in minor categories.[1100]

Critical reception: "Something for the mind as well as the eye" (*Variety*); "extraordinary" (*Hollywood Reporter*); "stunning and entertaining" (*New York Times*); "most dazzling screen spectacle ever made" (*Journal-American*).[1101] *Cahiers du Cinema* placed it 19th in its annual list.[1102]

Rentals: $26 million[1103] ($185.3 million equivalent)

8: *Thunderball*

Starring Sean Connery and Claudine Auger; directed by Terence Young; screenplay, Richard Maibaum, John Hopkins and Jack Whittingham, based on the novel by

Producers Harry Saltzman and Albert R. Broccoli vacated their normal position at the top of the credits in favor of Kevin McClory who, with Jack Whittingham, had gained the rights to the novel after suing Ian Fleming. McClory remade the film as *Never Say Never Again* (1983). Press advertisement (*Films and Filming*, September 1965, 2).

Ian Fleming; producer, Kevin McClory; music, John Barry. United Artists. December 9, 1965 (Tokyo); U.S.: December 21, 1965.

James Bond reversed the usual rule of sequels. Until now, in the expectation of declining box office as a series progressed, producers, in particular United Artists, reduced budgets for sequels. Bond took the opposite approach. The trailer screamed: "Here Comes the Biggest Bond of All." Bigger and better than the previous bigger and better *Goldfinger* (1964) in the expectation of bigger and better box office. The plan had worked to perfection so far, box office assisted by a merchandising gold mine. *Thunderball*'s budget touched $9 million. Terence Young, director of the first two adventures, returned after a break making *The Amorous Adventures of Moll Flanders* (1965) with Kim Novak and the spy portmanteau *The Dirty Game* (1965) with Henry Fonda. Screenwriter Richard Maibaum, who had written the first two Bonds, also returned with TV scriptwriter John Hopkins (*Z Cars*, 1962). Italian star Adolfo Celi (*The Agony and the Ecstasy*, 1965) was lined up as the SPECTRE villain. Julie Christie, Raquel Welch, Yvonne Monlaur and Maria Grazia Bucella were considered for the role of Domino.[1104] The part went to Miss World runner-up Claudine Auger (*In the French Style*, 1963) with Luciana Paluzzi (*Muscle Beach Party*, 1964), Martine Beswick (*From Russia with Love*, 1963) and first-timer Molly Peters adding further glamour.

Following the Goldfinger recipe, there were an array of gadgets, ambitious special effects, fast cars, a larger-than-life villain and three women, one good (Beswick), one bad (Paluzzi) and one who switches sides (Auger). The Aston Martin DB5 sports rear water jets and armor plating, Bond is equipped with a rocket belt, underwater infrared camera, flare gun, harpoon gun, scuba jet pack, sky hook and watch Geiger counter, the highlight an underwater battle. Location work took place in Paris and the Bahamas.

Theoretically, the story is as simple as previous affairs. SPECTRE plans to hijack two atomic bombs and hold NATO to ransom. But there are complications. An operative has received plastic surgery to pass for the NATO pilot on the plane carrying the bombs, the pilot turning out to be the brother of Auger. The bombs are delivered off the coast of the Bahamas where Celi has his lair. Bond tracks down Auger, Celi's mistress. Under Celi's yacht, Bond finds an underwater hatch. His colleague Beswick commits suicide when captured. Bond is kidnapped by Paluzzi, only escaping when she is accidentally killed. Auger switches sides, but is tortured by Celi. Following the underwater fracas, the main plot is foiled but Celi escapes. He is hunted by Bond and killed by Auger. Death in this case is the relish. The bad guys not only attempt to eliminate the good guys but also turn on their own men, the pretend pilot left to drown, Paluzzi dispatching one of her colleagues before being accidentally killed by another. Another henchman is thrown to the sharks and Celi harpooned.

It was the longest Bond so far, 15 minutes longer than *From Russia with Love*, for some critics overlong. But the public didn't care what a critic thought about James Bond. Who in their right mind would? The high voltage recipe kept the action at boiling point, the underwater scenes top-notch, Connery and Auger struck sparks, and the Bond-loving public counted themselves lucky. John Stears won the Oscar for Best Visual Effects.

Critical reception: "The same as its predecessors, only more so" (*Los Angeles Times*); "script hasn't a morsel of genuine wit" (*Time*); "blatantly ignores all the basic rules for a good thriller" (*Films and Filming*); "a posh catalogue for licentious living" (*Film Comment*).[1105]

Rentals: $27 million[1106] (including 1968 reissue) ($192.4 million equivalent)

7: *My Fair Lady*

Starring Audrey Hepburn and Rex Harrison; directed by George Cukor; screenplay, Alan Jay Lerner, based on the musical by Lerner and Frederick Loewe and the play *Pygmalion* by George Bernard Shaw; producer, Jack L. Warner; music, Lerner and Loewe. Warner Brothers roadshow. October 21, 1964.

It was the biggest musical of all time—a record seven years and 2717 performances on Broadway,[1107] a global moneymaking machine with $65 million (and counting) in the kitty.[1108] So when Jack L. Warner bid for the *My Fair Lady* movie rights, he expected to be shooting for the moon. Even so, the $5.5 million paid[1109] was about ten times higher than any studio had spent to transfer book, play or musical to the screen. Even bids were delayed five years to permit the musical to complete its various runs. It had the perfect cast: In the original production, Rex Harrison played Professor Higgins and Julie Andrews Eliza Dolittle.[1110] Producer Warner wanted neither.[1111] Elizabeth Taylor had her heart set on the role.[1112] Instead of Andrews *or* Taylor, Warner preferred Audrey Hepburn (*Breakfast at Tiffany's*, 1961). Warner said,

> There was nothing mysterious or complicated about my decision to cast Audrey. With all her charm and ability, Julie Andrews was just a Broadway name, known primarily to those who saw the musical. But in thousands of cities and towns throughout the United States and abroad, you can say "Audrey Hepburn" and people instantly know you're talking about a beautiful and talented star. In my business you have to know what brings people to the box office.[1113]

For being such a star attraction, Hepburn received a million-dollar payout.[1114]

Warner's $17 million budget was a colossal gamble not least because musicals were a hard sell outside America, and postwar they had been in decline. As Hollywood relied more on foreign income, "distributors complained European patrons did not understand American musicals and their songs were difficult to translate."[1115] For the male lead, Warner considered Rock Hudson, Cary Grant and Peter O'Toole, all far better box office prospects than Harrison. After postwar efforts like *Anna and the King of Siam* (1946) and *The Ghost and Mrs. Muir* (1947), Harrison had just three films in six years, the only success, *Midnight Lace* (1960), being put down to the presence of Doris Day.[1116] But O'Toole was too expensive, Hudson turned it down and Grant campaigned for Harrison so Warner signed "Sexy Rexy."[1117]

From the outset, Alan Jay Lerner and Frederick Loewe had wanted an actor, rather than a singer, who would deliver his songs by "talking on pitch." Hepburn wanted to do her own singing and worked hard in practice, but virtually none of her work made it onto the screen; Marni Nixon's voice is the one you hear.[1118] Stanley Holloway repeated his role from the stage version as her father, an impoverished dustman. Director George Cukor (*A Star Is Born*, 1954) invested $1 million in sumptuous sets, $200,000 for the Ascot design alone, with Cecil Beaton, who had won an Oscar for *Gigi*'s (1958) costume design, in charge. The movie was filmed in continuity so that Hepburn's emotional and physical development would be more acute. The entire film was shot in the studio.

Theoretically, the story is standard ugly duckling territory. But, in fact, as you might expect from a piece written by world-famous playwright George Bernard Shaw, from whose play *Pygmalion* this is adapted, it is something else. Normally, movies about characters crossing class or cultural boundaries pivot on romance. But that is not the case here. Aloof and condescending phonetics scholar Professor Higgins takes on flower

As well as the cast album of the movie, eight other "companion albums" were released at the same time. Three were in different languages—Spanish, Italian and Hebrew—the others including cover albums by Andy Williams, Percy Faith and, for dancers, by Sammy Kaye (pressbook).

girl Eliza Dolittle as a pupil simply to prove that he can turn an illiterate and low-class young woman into someone who could pass for a duchess, not taking into account that such improvements would make it difficult for her to fit back into her *previous* life. The movie is mostly about her transition, his reassessment of her character and various trials and tribulations before the more confident woman emerges. "I Could Have Danced All Night," "The Street Where You Live" and "I've Grown Accustomed to Her Face" are the standouts in the song department as well as the more comical "The Rain in Spain" and "A Hymn to Him." The best musicals always have more songs that you come out of the cinema humming and this is one of the very best. Given that Hepburn was most commonly associated in the public mind with the flighty Holly Golightly from *Breakfast at Tiffany's*, it was an achievement that this role quickly supplanted it. Harrison's most celebrated film work won him the Oscar. Nominated in 11 other categories, the movie won eight including Best Picture and Best Director. Just as welcome were album sales.[1119]

Critical reception: "Most all-around entertaining musical of all time" (*Box Office*); "superlative film" (*New York Times*); "a total triumph" (*Los Angeles Times*).[1120] It placed twenty-third on the *Cahiers du Cinema* annual list.[1121]

Rentals: $30 million[1122] ($213.8 million)

6: *Mary Poppins*

Starring Julie Andrews and Dick Van Dyke; directed by Robert Stevenson; screenplay, Bill Walsh and Don DaGradi, based on the books by P.L. Travers; producer, Walt Disney; music, Richard M. Sherman and Robert B. Sherman. Disney. August 27, 1964.

British director Robert Stevenson is rarely mentioned in any assessment of *Mary Poppins* but for the past decade had been a Disney mainstay and one of the unsung Hollywood heroes. He brought films in on time and on budget, could turn his hand to any genre and got the best out of a cast that was usually inexperienced, often actors, like Julie Andrews in this one, making their movie debut. His filmmaking went back 30 years to *Happy Ever After* (1932). Before coming into the Disney orbit, he was responsible for *Back Street* (1941) and *Jane Eyre* (1943). During World War II, he worked in Frank Capra's Army Signal Corps, filming the liberation of Rome. He also helmed the films noir *Dishonored Lady* (1947), *My Forbidden Past* (1951) and *The Las Vegas Story* (1952), before spending half a decade in American television. He initially went to work for Disney for six weeks and stayed 20 years, kicking off his stint with *Johnny Tremain* (1957) and *Old Yeller* (1957). He was soon helming *The Absent Minded Professor* (1961), *In Search of the Castaways* (1962) and *Son of Flubber* (1963).

As luck would have it, in among the dramas, films noir and comedies in his repertoire, Stevenson had turned out the musical *Falling for You* (1933). The *Mary Poppins* $6 million budget was gargantuan compared to anything entrusted to him previously. Of course, he didn't have to direct all the picture, animated sequences falling outside his jurisdiction.

How Disney managed to acquire the rights to the much-loved books by P.L. Travers has been well-documented, not least in the movie *Saving Mr. Banks* (2013) starring Tom Hanks, and perhaps the safer option would have been a straightforward comedy. A full-blown musical appeared quite a stretch for Disney until you considered that his animated features contained musical sequences and hits of the caliber of "When You Wish

In the twentieth century British director Robert Stevenson was considered the "most commercially successful director in the history of films" with 16 films on *Variety*'s all-time rental chart (Hannan Collection).

Upon a Star" and "Whistle While You Work." Songwriters Robert B. Sherman and Richard M. Sherman made their movie musical debut, although they had "You're Sixteen" among their credits and cranked out songs for Disney's TV programs and the score for *In Search of the Castaways*.

It's not often that disappointment in losing out on a major film role transitioned so easily into success but that was the Julie Andrews experience. Jack Warner's rejection of her for *My Fair Lady* (1964) left her free to accept Walt Disney's offer to make her film debut in *Mary Poppins*. Although Disney had purchased the rights to the Travers books, those did not include the illustrations by Mary Shepard, so the character's look was designed from scratch by Andrews' husband Tony Walton. "The costumes helped formulate Mary's character," said Andrews, especially the iconic hat with daisy on top.[1123]

The film was set in the 1910s rather than the book's 1930s to take advantage of richer Edwardian detail. Andrews invented the character's distinctive gait: "I felt she would never stroll leisurely."[1124] The special effects were created using a yellow screen (rather than the traditional blue screen which had been around since the 1930s),[1125] a sodium vapor process. Making a movie debut after thousands of performances on Broadway[1126] would have been difficult enough ("shooting a few lines was like working on a jigsaw puzzle")[1127] without flying through the air on wires. Dick Van Dyke was in the second season of his eponymous television show and appeared in *Bye Bye Birdie* (1963). As was now standard, Disney peopled the picture with older, well-known actors such as Elsa Lanchester and Hermione Baddeley.

Mary Poppins was quite different from other musicals in that, although there is a mild plot, it is primarily a good-natured endeavor with plenty of comedy. As ever, cute children (Karen Dotrice and Matthew Garber) are to the fore but held in rein by the initially stern, finally exhilarating Miss Poppins, with Van Dyke bringing his best worst Cockney accent to town.[1128] With no Broadway antecedents weighing them down, songwriters and director could have fun. The whole thing is utterly infectious from toe-tapping tunes like "A Spoonful of Sugar," "Step in Time" and "Let's Go Fly a Kite" to the more emotionally grounded "Feed the Birds" and the quite daft "Supercalifragilisticexpialidocious." The dancing is energetic and often inspired, especially when bringing Van Dyke's comic instincts to bear. Andrews, having lost out to Audrey Hepburn for *My Fair Lady*, got her "revenge" by winning the Oscar. She is perfectly cast as the English rose with a heart of gold, steely resolve and a voice no one would dare dub.

Critical reception: "Most wonderful, cheering movie" (*New York Times*); "some … sequences have real charm" (*Life*); "scenario witty but impeccably sentimental" (*Variety*).[1129]

Rentals: $31 million[1130] ($220.9 million equivalent)

5: *Ben-Hur*

Starring Charlton Heston, Stephen Boyd and Haya Harareet[1131]; directed by William Wyler; screenplay, Karl Turnberg, based on the book *Ben-Hur: A Tale of the Christ* by General Lew Wallace[1132]; producer, Sam Zimbalist Jr.; music, Miklos Rosza. MGM roadshow. November 18, 1959.

You might well ask what is a 1959 film doing in an assessment of the most popular films of the 1960s. *Ben-Hur* was released in only a handful of U.S. cinemas in November

In New York *Ben-Hur* ran for 75 weeks and grossed $3 million. It clocked up a year or more in Boston, Philadelphia, Los Angeles, Chicago, San Francisco, Detroit, Portland, Oregon, Seattle and Vancouver.* Trade press advertisement (*Box Office*, August 22, 1960, 3).

*"More than 51,000,000 Have Seen *Ben-Hur*," *Box Office*, January 1, 1962, 15.

and December 1959, and by my calculations, allowing some leeway for error, no more than $1 million was taken in rentals during those months. That makes it, to my mind, a film that was primarily seen in 1960. And for most moviegoers, this was where the 1960s started: with a promise of something quite different in the field of movie entertainment, the most expensive film ever made and, until *Gone with the Wind* came out of retirement, poised to become the most successful film ever made, heralding the Golden Age of the Roadshow.[1133]

Two-time Oscar winner William Wyler had all the acclaim a director might need, but signed up for *Ben-Hur* since he was lacking the accompanying financial security. He was tempted with a record $350,000 plus an eight percent share of the gross to sidestep fudging from studio accountants.[1134] But it cost him his reputation. He was "completely written off as a serious director.... I had prostituted myself."[1135] For a studio on the verge of bankruptcy,[1136] it was some gamble.[1137] But the executives knew they could go bust quietly, turning out medium-budget pictures in the hope one would strike gold, or they could go out with a bang, by throwing everything (the initial budget was $9 million)[1138] on one colossal project. As far as producer Sam Zimbalist Jr. was concerned, the much-heralded chariot race would take care of itself but what the film really needed was a director capable of conveying real characters of depth and emotion, who would make relationships come alive, and have audiences rooting for them the way they had for *Mrs. Miniver* in 1942 and the war veterans of *The Best Years of Our Lives* (1946), Wyler's Oscar-winning duo and, notably, the biggest box office successes of their years.

Filmed in 70mm,[1139] *Ben-Hur* was a remake of MGM's $4 million 1924 silent.[1140] Wyler, who had worked with Charlton Heston on his previous film *The Big Country* (1958), was more inclined for the actor to play Messala, the Roman villain.[1141] Initially Marlon Brando, Burt Lancaster, Rock Hudson, Paul Newman and Kirk Douglas appeared preferable,[1142] or possibly an unknown.[1143] The actor's salary was $250,000 but that was for 30 weeks work at a time when most films were shot in half or a third of that.[1144] After Heston the most important recruit was legendary stuntman Yakima Canutt, who would handle the chariot race although Wyler had offered that position to David Lean with the added lure of receiving a screen credit.[1145] Northern Irishman Stephen Boyd, Brigitte Bardot's leading man in *The Night Heaven Fell* (1958), took on the role of Messala while Israeli actress Haya Harareet provided the romantic interest. British actors Jack Hawkins and Hugh Griffith were in the supporting cast. The screenplay went through several extra hands, including Gore Vidal and British playwright Christopher Fry.[1146] As exemplified by the Biblical epic *Quo Vadis* (1951) and the African adventures *King Solomon's Mines* (1950) and *Mogambo* (1953), producer Zimbalist was a master of the behind-the-scenes detail required for big-budget pictures.[1147]

Filmed in Rome, the production required 25,000 extras, 100,000 costumes, over a million props, 50 ships for the naval battle and 60,000 blossoms for the victory parade.[1148] The nine-minute chariot race took three months to shoot at a cost of a million dollars. The set was the biggest ever built, requiring a million pounds of plaster, 250 miles of metal tubing and 40,000 tons of white sand. An identical track was built to train the 82 cart horses and the charioteers.[1149] While Canutt accounted for the choreography, the actual shooting was in the hands of Andrew Marton, the entire race filmed once with doubles, then re-shot with the principals who did everything they are seen on screen to do except for two stunts deemed too dangerous. Initially, on the straights, the horses were faster than the small Italian car carrying the camera so a speedier American vehicle was required. The camera was only a few feet ahead of the horses so a sudden jolt over the hard earth could have spelled disaster.[1150] Final budget for the nine-month shoot tallied an eye-watering $16 million[1151] with another $3 million on marketing.[1152] The most expensive picture of all time would require the biggest grosses of all time just to break even. Although the promotional effort concentrated on the chariot race and the naval battle, the core of the picture remained the drama of friends who become bitter enemies, torn apart by politics and religion. The chariot race was one of the most dramatic examples in Hollywood history of rivalry decided by spectacle. Nominated for 12 Oscars, *Ben-Hur* only missed out on one, named Best Picture and with Wyler winning his third Oscar and Heston his first. The film's colossal financial success, with all the hoopla that represented,[1153] paved the way for the roadshow epidemic of the 1960s.

Critical reception: "Majestic achievement" (*Variety*); "remarkably intelligent and engrossing human drama" (*New York Times*); "magnificent, inspiring, awesome, enthralling" (*Los Angeles Times*).[1154]

Rentals: $35.6 million[1155] (including 1969 reissue) ($253.7 million)

186   The Films

4: *Gone with the Wind*

Starring Clark Gable and Vivien Leigh; directed by Victor Fleming; screenplay, Sidney Howard, based on the novel by Margaret Mitchell; producer, David O. Selznick; music, Max Steiner. MGM. Reissued 1961; 70mm roadshow reissue 1967.

A question similar to that relating to *Ben-Hur* will now arise: What's a film made before America entered the Second World War doing on a list of the most popular films of the 1960s? Well, it's here courtesy of two reissues, one in 1961 and the other in 1967. It was already the Reissue King, a movie that MGM had carefully husbanded over the years, resisting the mating call of television and safeguarding its long-term worth by removing it from circulation for long periods. Each successive reissue had proved the value of this policy: In 1941, it had brought in $4 million in rentals; in 1947, it hit $5 million, and in 1954, totaled $7 million. In 1961, the centenary of the start of the Civil War, it picked up another $6.5 million and could have been reasonably expected to do the same again after another suitable interval.

Come 1967, however, MGM set its sights on a bigger prize. As has been demonstrated in this book, this was the era of the roadshow and MGM, with *Ben-Hur* (1959) and *Doctor Zhivago* (1965) boosting its coffers, believed that *Gone with the Wind* could return in that format. This was something of a risk since two previous attempts at roadshow reissue a few years earlier, for *Around the World in 80 Days* and *The King and I*, had flopped so badly that Columbia prevented their *Bridge on the River Kwai* revival going that route.[1156] And a considerable gamble given that there was a $10 million offer for *Gone with the Wind* on the table from television.[1157] But MGM had something different in mind. Nearly 30 years after its debut, the studio intended to turn *Gone with the Wind* into an event by blowing it up to 70mm. This proved a very cumbersome, time-consuming technical process. The studio spent $40,000 in six months on two 70mm test reels before venturing any further. The original ratio of 1.33 to 1 was converted to the modern widescreen of 2.2 to 1, four different steps employed to reshoot each frame. To simply blow up the old negative would have resulted in the loss of the top or bottom one-third of the picture so a scanning system was employed to ensure that key action was retained. Total refurbishment cost $700,000, about a quarter of the sum set aside for marketing.[1158]

But the movie marketplace had not only changed enormously since *GWTW*'s initial premiere in 1939, the industry had undergone huge change since its previous outing in 1961. It was going to come up against the sex comedy *The Graduate*, the sex drama *Valley of the Dolls*, the violent crime drama *In Cold Blood*, the bloody Western *The Good, the Bad and the Ugly* and thrillers like *Wait Until Dark* and *Billion Dollar Brain* while audiences seeking something less controversial could rely on *The Jungle Book*. Excitement soon reached fever pitch with advances hitting the $1 million mark,[1159] far exceeding *Doctor Zhivago*, prior to the traditional premiere in Atlanta, Georgia. Playing nine or ten performances a week in roadshow in the major cities, it was soon in the phenomenal class, returns increasing by the week, setting box office records in the eighth week in Kansas City, for example, and the twelfth in New York.[1160] By the end of 1967, it had earned $7 million in rentals, enough for twelfth place in the annual box office chart. It steamrolled on through 1968—$23 million in rentals—and on through 35mm general release. Everywhere it went, whether in roadshow or continuous performance, whether at escalated prices or normal prices, it cleaned up.

Whether the success of *Doctor Zhivago* had put audiences in the mood for epic failed romance against turbulent historical background or whether audiences wanted

The Films 187

Gone with the Wind had originally opened in London in 1940 at three theaters—the Empire, Leicester Square, the Palace and the Ritz. It remained at the Ritz for a record-breaking four years and two months (Hannan Collection).

188   The Films

to savor the picture in glorious widescreen and whether the movie simply appealed to those turned off by current Hollywood offerings, it made little difference. The film's sweep and the performances by Clark Gable and Vivien Leigh kept audiences coming back for more, the only blight in the movie's presentation its depiction of African Americans, an issue which had gained substantial ground since initial release. While critic Richard Schickel continued to disdain it, and even questioned its status as popular art,[1161] Andrew Sarris had to admit it was the "single most beloved entertainment ever produced."[1162] It has never lost a place in the heart of the moviegoing public or the industry itself, voted the most popular film ever made by the American Film Institute in 1977 and even in 2016 placing ninth in a poll by the Directors Guild of America.[1163]

Critical reception (in 1967): "Far from merely holding up well it remains a powerful breathtaking spectacle" (*Variety*); "one of the glories of Hollywood filmmaking" (*Box Office*).[1164]

Rentals: $35.9 million.[1165] (1961 and 1967 reissues) ($255.8 million equivalent)

3: *Doctor Zhivago*

Starring Omar Sharif, Julie Christie and Geraldine Chaplin; directed by David Lean; screenplay, Robert Bolt based on the novel by Boris Pasternak[1166]; producer, Carlo Ponti; music, Maurice Jarre. MGM roadshow. December 22, 1965.

That Italian producer Carlo Ponti[1167] owned the rights to Boris Pasternak's worldwide bestseller *Doctor Zhivago* made it easier for David Lean to sever links with Sam Spiegel, producer *of Lawrence of Arabia* and *The Bridge on the River Kwai*. MGM not only gave Lean carte blanche but the biggest salary ever handed a director, plus a generous profit share.[1168] Max von Sydow was Lean's first suggestion for the leading role while MGM wanted Paul Newman and Ponti was keen on Burt Lancaster.[1169] Peter O'Toole reportedly turned it down.[1170] Omar Sharif, lined up to play a smaller part, stepped in.[1171] Marlon Brando and James Mason[1172] were considered for Komarovsky before that went to Rod Steiger. Jeanne Moreau,[1173] Jane Fonda, Yvette Mimieux, Sarah Miles[1174] and Sophia Loren[1175] were in the running for Lara until, at the recommendation of John Ford who had directed Julie Christie in *Young Cassidy* (1965), the part went to that British actress.[1176] Audrey Hepburn was Lean's choice for Tonya until he was bowled over by the screen test made by Geraldine Chaplin, daughter of Charlie Chaplin.[1177] And in the run-up to release, Chaplin received the bulk of the advance publicity.[1178]

Initially, Lean intended to shoot a 70mm production in black-and-white but 70mm equipment was deemed too cumbersome and monochrome too risky for such a big film, so it was made in 35mm with the intention of later blowing it up to the larger format for roadshow release.[1179] Ponti reckoned the movie could be made in Yugoslavia for $5 million. The eventual location, Spain, with some scenes filmed in Finland,[1180] added $2 million. Much of what appeared on screen was illusion. The Red Army charged across an apparently frozen lake in the height of summer, the lake itself non-existent, just a field covered in cement with sheet iron topped with thousands of tons of crushed white marble ironed out by steamrollers so when the horses slid it looked realistic. To complete the picture, a rowing boat was moored at the edge.[1181] Other effects combined directorial genius and practicality. Prior to the scene of the huge field of daffodils, Lean had filmed three minutes of Zhivago and Lara against a freezing background, everything sprayed

Two pieces of glitter were added to the balalaika to enhance the lighting. The face inside the coffin containing Yuri's mother is not that of a model but a waxwork taken from a mold of Omar Sharif's face.* Trade press advertisement (*Box Office*, February 27, 1967, 2).

*Fowlie, *Dedicated Maniac*, 183.

190   **The Films**

gray to remove the last hint of color so that the sudden appearance of the golden flowers cast the spell of spring.[1182] But to prevent the flowers blooming too early, they had been dug up and put in pots to control their growth and replanted when required.[1183] To make snow glisten in another scene, cellophane was spread over wintry bushes and trees.[1184] The sleighs had little wheels fitted to the runners, icicles were made from polystyrene, the balalaika was created by the props team, and the interior of the Ice Palace was made with cellophane crushed into thousands of creases, paraffin wax and salicylic acid powder creating fantastic shapes; the floor was fashioned from a layer of soap flakes.[1185] The aftermath of the dragoon charge down the city streets was seen through the horrified eyes of Zhivago and it was just as well it worked because Lean had filmed no alternative.[1186] The final budget was $11 million and filming lasted just over 33 weeks.[1187]

Although set against the backdrop of the Russian Revolution, it is a simple, classic love story of a man (Sharif) in love with two women (wife Chaplin and mistress Christie) and his battle to fulfill his own potential as a poet. While slow, it is not slow-going, but makes the most of the epic format, with stunning scenery and scenes. While Chaplin is more anemic than helped her acting cause, both Sharif and Christie are believable as the doomed lovers, so much so that it is this movie they will be remembered for.

The film initially struggled to attract public attention despite a $3 million publicity budget. Lean was not marketable like Hitchcock or DeMille. The female leads were unknown, *Darling* (1965) starring Christie[1188] not yet setting the box office buzzing other than in arthouses, Sharif not capitalized on *Lawrence of Arabia*. The famous "Lara's Theme" was not yet in the shops and the designer Phyllis Dalton's furs[1189] were a long way from setting a fashion trend. Advance sales were poor, only $200,000 compared to $600,000 for *Exodus* and $500,000 for *Cleopatra*.[1190] There was even speculation that the Capitol in New York where the film premiered lied about the opening week's figures, Lean going on record as saying that during the first week the cinema was "empty."[1191] However, this kind of conspiracy would have been anathema to the industry and *Variety*, which faithfully listed receipts every week. Historical epics had been going out of fashion, *Lord Jim* (1965) and *The Agony and the Ecstasy* (1965) among the year's casualties, while *The Sound of Music* (1965) by contrast was cleaning up. The biggest factor was that it was going up against *Thunderball*, the fourth Bond, which, true to expectations, demolished records. Lean's hopes of three wins in a row at the Oscars were dashed. Of the actors, only Tom Courtenay was nominated (Best Supporting Actor), although Julie Christie won for *Darling* and Rod Steiger was nominated for *The Pawnbroker*. Robert Bolt won for his screenplay and Jarre for the music[1192] with other wins for cinematography, art direction and costume design.[1193]

Critical reception: "Soaring dramatic intensity" (*Variety*); "ultimately tedious epic-type soap opera" (*New York Herald Tribune*); "haunting emotion-charged drama" (*New York Daily News*); "painfully slow-going and inevitable tedium" (*New York Times*).[1194]

Rentals: $38.2 million[1195] (including 1968 reissue) ($272.2 million equivalent)

2: *The Graduate*

Starring Dustin Hoffman, Anne Bancroft and Katharine Ross; directed by Mike Nichols; screenplay, Buck Henry, based on the novel by Charles Webb; producer,

Lawrence Turman; music, Dave Grusin, with songs by Simon and Garfunkel. Embassy Pictures. December 20, 1967.

If ever a movie befitted the "Nobody Knows Anything" adage ascribed to screenwriter William Goldman, it was *The Graduate*. Nobody wanted the screenwriting job—not even Goldman.[1196] Nobody wanted to back it, nobody wanted to star in it, and for a while it looked like it would never find an audience. Then when it did, no one could imagine it would be on such a scale. Oddly enough, Warren Beatty, a complete physical opposite to Dustin Hoffman, was first to show interest since the novel's hero was a handsome, WASP-type college track star, not an introverted nerd.[1197] Before Beatty could take his interest any further, the rights were purchased for $1000[1198] in 1963 by producer Lawrence Turman (*I Could Go on Singing*, 1963).[1199] He spent $500 on a screenplay by unknown William Hanley.[1200] When Mike Nichols[1201] signed on—not as his movie debut[1202]—and wanted to alter the title[1203] and script, Hanley quit. In 1964, Turman, budgeting the film at a mere $1 million, was turned down by every studio in Hollywood except independent Embassy,[1204] who greenlit it for summer 1965. But then Nichols was hijacked by Warner Brothers to make *Who's Afraid of Virginia Woolf?* (1966). Calder Willingham and another unknown, Peter Nelson, took unsuccessful stabs at the screenplay before Nichols handed it over to TV writer Buck Henry, who used the character's fear of the unknown to make him more sympathetic.[1205] Robert Redford[1206] and Candice Bergen[1207] tested for the main parts. Doris Day,[1208] Ava Gardner and Patricia Neal turned down the part of Mrs. Robinson.[1209]

The prospective movie was no longer in limbo; it was in a hole. Embassy had financial problems and Turman found other movie companies no more interested the second time around.[1210] The turning point was hiring Oscar winner Anne Bancroft (*The Miracle Worker*, 1962)—though Jeanne Moreau had been considered[1211]—for $200,000 to play the part of Mrs. Robinson, "the most interesting person in the picture," according to Nichols.[1212] Charles Grodin, then in television, was the next Benjamin prospect.[1213] Dustin Hoffman was a standard out-of-work actor[1214] until rave reviews for the off-Broadway *Eh?* brought a screen test[1215] with Katharine Ross (Barbara Hershey and Kim Darby were also in the running).[1216] During the test, Nichols recognized "the exact kind of confused, panicky character he wanted."[1217] Just as coincidentally, Nichols was nominated for Best Director for *Who's Afraid of Virginia Woolf?* and that turned him, as far as executive producer Joseph E. Levine was concerned, into an instantly bankable commodity. With two Oscar winners on board, finance was now no object. At this point, Gene Hackman was to play Mrs. Robinson's husband. Both Hoffman and Bancroft, unable to come to terms with their characters, struggled through rehearsals while Hackman was fired.[1218] Actual production was long for a small-budget movie and Levine grew frustrated when it entered its fourth month.[1219] Simon and Garfunkel were paid $25,000 to come up with two songs, one of which, "Mrs. Robinson," made it into the final film, the soundtrack otherwise recycling older works such as "The Sounds of Silence."[1220] The latter, a hit the previous year, had run out of commercial juice; a new song had more chance of airplay.

Levine hated the movie. He had nothing to sell. A past master at selling movies with nothing in them to sell, here he was stymied. In an era of permissiveness, there was no sex and only a fractional glimpse of nudity. He considered dumping it in the arthouses. But that required a favorable pre-release reception, some kind of buzz to attract trendsetters. Those who saw it hated Hoffman. Unveiled with Levine razzamatazz at a preview for celebrities like Gregory Peck, Julie Andrews, Burt Bacharach and Neil Simon, it died

192   The Films

a slow death.[1221] Divided critics did not help.[1222] But the one thing that had changed to the movie's advantage was that while audiences were getting younger, studios only rarely made anything specifically for that market. *The Graduate* became the archetypal "generation gap" picture. (Nichols denied this.[1223])

The Graduate is a hymn to the disaffected, reflected through the eyes of a more normal character than the handsome confident Paul Newman and Warren Beatty, the anti-hero poster boys of *Cool Hand Luke* and *Bonnie and Clyde* out earlier that year.[1224] A young man who has everything but rejects the "gold-plated future" that lies ahead first has a dalliance with Mrs. Robinson before falling in love with her daughter (Katharine Ross), who is planning marriage to somebody else. Its initial success was attributed to the fact that it opened at Christmas when students were on holiday. But when box office increased rather than declined after students returned to college, it turned out that "nobody knows anything" summed it up. Out of seven Oscar nominations, including Hoffman and Bancroft, only Nichols triumphed.

Critical reception: "Delightful, satirical comedy drama" (*Variety*); " the small triumph of *The Graduate* was to have domesticated alienation" (*New Yorker*); "alarmingly derivative" (*Time*); "there is a studied effort to make everyone exotic and nutty, like walking fish tanks" (*Film Comment*).[1225]

Rentals: $43 million[1226] ($306.4 million equivalent)

1: *The Sound of Music*

Starring Julie Andrews and Christopher Plummer; directed and produced by Robert Wise; screenplay, Ernest Lehman, from the Rodgers and Hammerstein musical; music, Richard Rodgers and Oscar Hammerstein II. Twentieth Century–Fox roadshow. March 2, 1965.

The "generation gap" did not exist for *The Sound of Music*. It was not so much that the term had not been invented; the idea itself had existed since the 1950s when pictures like *The Wild One* (1953) and *Jailhouse Rock* (1957) divided audiences by age, but had little relevance here because people of all ages adored it. For many it was simply the ideal picture, so perfect that it was a standard marketing ploy to locate a moviegoer who had seen the movie 50 or 100 times, and millions of people knew every song frontwards and backwards. The picture held a special place in the hearts of Twentieth Century–Fox personnel, for it was the first picture greenlit after the 1962 threat of bankruptcy forced a two-month production shutdown.[1227] Film rights, costing a record $1.25 million, had been purchased in 1960,[1228] at a time when album sales for stage and film productions carrying the Rodgers and Hammerstein brand had passed the $13 million mark.[1229]

Perhaps it helped that Robert Wise was at the helm. He had seen the impact on audiences of a vivid opening, rather than the standard leisurely introductory scenes

---

Opposite: **Although by June 1967, most roadshow engagements had ended, the picture was showing no signs of slowing down. In the first limited release stanza in New York and New Jersey in 26 theaters, its first week pulled in $120,000 (equivalent to $930,000 today). It was still eighteenth in the album charts after 116 weeks.* Trade press advertisement (*Box Office*, August 7, 1967).**

*Advert, *Variety*, June 28, 967, 17; "Album Bestsellers," *Variety*, June 14, 1967, 49.

for a musical, with *West Side Story* (1961). While a standard musical might open with a memorable number, he had in mind something cinematically stunning, sticking a camera in a helicopter and sending it racing up a mountain to meet the star at the top, spinning round singing the title song. Nobody had thought to bring that verve, that cinematic chutzpah to a musical, not since, oh, *West Side Story*. Both films began in similar fashion with aerial footage, the music soft while the scene was being set, waiting until the camera targets characters before voice(s) are in full flow.

It would have been a different story had original director William Wyler continued at the helm.[1230] His previous film *The Children's Hour* (1961) had flopped but he was still flush with cash from *Ben-Hur*. *The Sound of Music* was not the biggest musical in the Rodgers and Hammerstein canon, fourth among the Broadway long-runners with 1443 performances behind the duo's champs *South Pacific* (1925 performances) and *Oklahoma* (2212) and trailing Lerner and Loewe's *My Fair Lady* (2717). At 47, Mary Martin, who had originated the part of Maria on Broadway, was too old. Although *Mary Poppins* had not been released, Walt Disney showed Wyler the rushes and, aware of Julie Andrews' potential from the Broadway hit *Camelot*, she was signed.[1231] Writer Ernest Lehman (*North by Northwest*, 1959) had been hired by Fox[1232] but Wyler wanted to emphasize the darker aspects of the story, the Nazi background, with tanks breaking through walls.[1233] However, he was diverted by the prospect of filming the unpublished John Fowles novel *The Collector*. Robert Wise had originally turned down *Sound of Music* in favor of *The Sand Pebbles* and Fox had then approached Stanley Donen, George Roy Hill and Gene Kelly.[1234] When Wyler quit, Wise became available when *The Sand Pebbles* stalled. The $7.1 million budget went up about $1 million largely due to bad weather in the Alps.[1235]

Considered for the role of Captain von Trapp were Yul Brynner, Richard Burton and Sean Connery.[1236] Christopher Plummer turned the part down several times. A Who's Who of future talent was in the running for the children: Kurt Russell, Mia Farrow, Geraldine Chaplin.[1237] The Von Trapp Family had been popular postwar performers in America, releasing various albums, public interest boosted by a 1949 memoir and the 1962 release of a dubbed West German picture.[1238] For the film, Rodgers and Hammerstein added two new numbers, "Something Good" and "I Have Confidence."

The wholesome Andrews was ideal casting although in some respects repeating her *Mary Poppins* nanny role, minus the magical powers. This time, however, she was permitted to fall in love with the stern father. The growing Nazi threat forms the background and the flight is every bit as well contrived as escapes in other war pictures. From the first frames of her appearance, Andrews just bursts out of the screen. Plummer is excellent in a constrained role and the kids, while cute enough, are never Disney cute. Being filmed largely on location, the musical is opened up and in the best 70mm style the idyllic landscape is both fresh and refreshing. Like *My Fair Lady*, it is about a character finding herself but, with responsibility towards her charges, never relieved of a maternal burden.

The strength of the songs makes the picture fly. There is hardly a weak song. A few ("Edelweiss" and "Climb Ev'ry Mountain") are among the most touching ever written, another couple ("Do-Re-Mi" and "My Favorite Things") imaginatively evocative, and that's not counting the title song or "So Long, Farewell," "Maria," "Something Good," "I Have Confidence" and "Sixteen Going on Seventeen." It was a jukebox musical before such a thing was ever invented. As a film, it was almost the last hurrah of innocence.

The audience response was unlike any film since *Gone with the Wind*.[1239] It would not have reached such starry box office heights without people seeing it two, three, four, five times. Even people who had never been to the cinema in years were tempted back. At the Oscars, it was named Best Picture with Wise taking the directing accolade and three other gongs besides. Among five more nominations, there were mentions for Andrews and Peggy Wood (Mother Abbess).

Critical reception: "Ideal family entertainment" (*Box Office*); "romantic nonsense and sentiment" (*New York Times*); "three hours of visual and vocal brilliance" (*Los Angeles Times*); "self-indulgent and cheap" (*McCall's*); "more embarrassing than most" (*Vogue*).[1240]

Rentals: $72 million[1241] ($513 million equivalent)

Conclusion

The public got it right, most of the time, regardless of the yea or nay of critics. Not that we are keeping score, but the vast majority of the films featured in this volume clearly fall into the category of "good" films with many guaranteed a tilt at greatness. However, this is a book about public approval rather than what appealed to the critic. The public seemed perfectly capable of recognizing quality and/or supporting those pictures that attempted to say something new, broke down barriers, took a tougher stance against racism, or introduced new concepts of filmmaking, whether it be technical such as split-screen, or editing *à la Bonnie and Clyde*, or "cinema of sensation" trips like the all-embracing sound of *Grand Prix* or the car chase in *Bullitt*. Public acceptance of new levels of sexuality and/or violence permitted the production of more pictures pushing these boundaries, since films that flop have little impact on the way Hollywood turns next.

There was considerable alignment (see Appendix) between what the public favored and the choices made by the Academy of Motion Pictures Arts and Sciences in handing out the annual Oscars. Every year during the decade, the Best Picture was commercially successful enough to be included in this book, with a similar success rate for those cited for Best Director. Perhaps somewhat surprisingly, the picture receiving the accolade for Best Color Cinematography every year also came from the ranks of the Top 100 movies. I was intrigued by how often commercially successful films struck gold in the technical departments: 90 percent of the winners of the Film Editing category feature in this book. For costume design in color, it was 80 percent, the same ratio for art direction in color and best use of sound. And it made me rethink my preconceptions about what qualified a film for nomination as Best Picture. A couple of movies, most notably *The Alamo* and *Doctor Dolittle*, were derided by journalists for their inclusion in the Best Picture nominations in their particular years. But it appears to me now quite obvious that Oscar voters judge a film as much on its technical proficiency as overall emotional impact and central performances. No film has won the Oscar for Best Picture with just a nomination in that category; generally they have five or six nominations, often in the technical categories, giving the impression that Academy members are looking for all-around distinction.

While the decade may be remembered as the one that broke the Production Code, the films that inflicted the most damage, with the exception of *I Am Curious (Yellow)*, will be remembered more for their dramatic involvement rather than those elements which flouted the existing censorship system. *The Fox* and *Who's Afraid of Virginia Woolf?*, shot at different ends of the budgetary divide, for example, remain absorbing pictures. The Vietnam War and issues of race were given a foothold, although it would take later decades before either would be explored more seriously. But you will still laugh at *The Odd Couple*, *That Touch of Mink* and *It's a Mad Mad Mad Mad World* and you cannot fail to be thrilled by *Bullitt* and *Where Eagles Dare*. The bulk of the commercially successful 70mm roadshow vehicles have enjoyed continued popularity, *The Sound of Music* and *Doctor Zhivago* the clear leaders in that department courtesy of successive reissues.

Stardom provided a generational mix. The decade was particularly notable for the rise of new stars such as Julie Andrews, Sean Connery, Hayley Mills, Faye Dunaway, Jane Fonda, Barbra Streisand, Julie Christie, Mia Farrow, Dustin Hoffman, Lee Marvin, Peter O'Toole, Steve McQueen, Omar Sharif and a hint of what was to come from Robert Redford and Clint Eastwood. Many of the previous generation who had been expected to step up to the plate did so with aplomb, in most cases extending their range or altering their screen persona, including Paul Newman, Peter Sellers, Dean Martin, Rock Hudson and Richard Burton. There was still room at the top table for stars who had emerged in the 1940s: Burt Lancaster, Gregory Peck, Frank Sinatra and Elizabeth Taylor took on roles with greater maturity and scope. That Hollywood could provide considerable career longevity was demonstrated in the ongoing box office traction of Cary Grant, Spencer Tracy, Katharine Hepburn, John Wayne, James Stewart and Rex Harrison, who had all first come to public attention in the 1930s. And there was no question that the star of the decade, as far as this excursion through the decade's top movies makes apparent, was Sidney Poitier, whose box office potential was clearly, and inexcusably, for most of the decade ignored by the studios. Julie Andrews, exuding innocent appeal in controversial times, ran him close.

Experience was, however, the watchword when it came to directors. Although the likes of Mike Nichols, George Roy Hill, Arthur Penn and Peter Yates gate-crashed the commercial party, the industry still relied on elder statesmen; only a quarter of the top 20 pictures were helmed by the younger brigade. Traditional methods of filmmaking were certainly challenged. While avoiding the sin of putting off the audience, techniques introduced by the new breed, whether fast cutting, musical interludes, freeze frame, balletic spaceships or disaffection with normality, were welcomed by the moviegoer. On the production side, the story of the decade, arguably, was United Artists, which pulled out a massive commercial plum with its investment in the James Bond pictures at the same time as besting all other studios in the race for the Best Picture accolade. However, the decade's other studio miracle was the Disney reincarnation through the Udult model, investment in *Mary Poppins* and the return to animation top form with the "cool" *The Jungle Book*.

While the decade proved the high-water mark for big-budget roadshows, it was equally memorable for the "little films that could" breaking out of expected exhibition confines, particularly the arthouse, to take a wider commercial bow, and especially for the introduction of the spy genre, epitomized, of course, by the Bond films, the impulse towards this type of sexy thriller also picked by the Matt Helm and Derek Flint imitators. The Bond series is as strong today, as well as inspiring new rivals like Jason Bourne and, to some extent, the *Fast and Furious* franchise. Several of the 1960s pictures have been remade, some from the Disney brand: *The Love Bug*, *The Parent Trap*, *101 Dalmatians,* etc.—but also *Planet of the Apes*, which not only had its own series of sequels in the 1970s but was re-imagined twice since. Of course, there have also been a variety of ill-judged sequels and prequels: *Force Ten from Navarone* (1978), *Butch and Sundance: The Early Days* (1979), *2010* (1984). But mostly the best films of the decade have been excused further dilution or attempts to squeeze more dollars out of a one-time cash cow.

Conclusion 199

The "youthquake" that found temporary support at the end of the 1960s[1] went so completely against the perceived wisdom of what constituted what the pubic really wanted that, on reflection, it was insane that the notion was given any credence in the first place. Had studios been conforming to popular taste, as seen in the end-of-decade box office, they would gone down a different route since all the films boasting rentals above $10 million, with one exception, could be generally classified as family pictures.[2]

It is worth pointing out, however, that spiraling box office in the 2010s that saw success measured in billion-dollar franchises—themselves enhanced by colossal marketing expenditures—cannot genuinely be compared to the top films of the 1960s unless one is able to balance audience attendances across a 50-, 60-year chasm. Research by Robert P. Munafo[3] on that very topic has put in cumulative terms *Gone with the Wind* top of the stack with *The Sound of Music* fourth, *Doctor Zhivago* ninth, *Ben-Hur* twelfth and *Mary Poppins* eighteenth. But, even so, cinematic sensation brings its own inflation and the top movies from other decades that sparked massive queues attracted in many cases greater cumulative figures.

While Hollywood was battered by missteps towards the end of the decade that resulted in full-scale financial disaster, the roadshow format, which took the brunt of the blame for such decline, surprisingly came back into favor the following decade, but in a slightly different form. Rather than two-a-day separate performances, wide general release fast became the preferred option, but it would be hard to argue that *The Godfather* (1972) and *The Towering Inferno* (1974) were not roadshows in all but name.

It's a pretty dispiriting experience to view this decade's best performing pictures through the eyes of critics. You would not have to look far to find negative notices for every movie chosen by the public. And if often appeared that critics were completely out of touch with their readers. Interestingly, a couple—Joan Didion and Pauline Kael, reportedly—were bounced for their antagonistic stances towards popular pictures while the opposite held true for *The New York Times*' Bosley Crowther, relieved of duties for his opposition to the violence in the New Wave of American movies, most notably *Bonnie and Clyde*. If you were compiling a book on smart remarks or stinging reviews, movie critics of the period would be your first port of call. Of course, it comes with the territory that anyone engaged in public performance in whatever capacity will endure negativity, but sometimes it must have felt as if the critics were building a gargantuan black hole in which to dump virtually 99 percent of Hollywood filmmakers. If the critics had been in agreement as to what excellence actually constituted, that would have been helpful, but they appeared as much to be taking potshots at each other as the movies which came into range. Popularity in this instance appeared to breed contempt.

If this is a period in which you are interested, then you are in luck. The revival business has focused in recent times on the exploitation of various anniversaries. Initially, it had been imagined that such anniversaries had to be spaced out in 25-year segments but that has proved far from the case. The popularity of the sixtieth anniversary reissue or reappearance in a 4K format means that many of the best films of the decade will appear as a brief cinematic prelude to DVD/streaming release. So, if you are interested, you may be able to follow the development of the 1960s as the decade of the 2020s progresses. Park Circus Films, which has the licensing rights to a number of older pictures for picture house exhibition, has, for example, *West Side Story*, *The Graduate* and *Bonnie and Clyde* among their suggestions for Valentine's Day screenings.

Appendix
Oscar Alignment

Best Picture

Winner: *The Apartment, West Side Story, Lawrence of Arabia, Tom Jones, My Fair Lady, The Sound of Music, A Man for All Seasons, In the Heat of the Night, Oliver!, Midnight Cowboy.* (The Top 100 Pictures had a 100 percent success rate in this category.)

Nominees: *The Alamo, The Guns of Navarone, The Longest Day, To Kill a Mockingbird, Mutiny on the Bounty, Cleopatra, How the West Was Won, Mary Poppins, Doctor Zhivago, Alfie, The Russians Are Coming, The Russians Are Coming, The Sand Pebbles, Who's Afraid of Virginia Woolf?, Bonnie and Clyde, The Graduate, Guess Who's Coming to Dinner, Funny Girl, Romeo and Juliet, Butch Cassidy and the Sundance Kid.* (The Top 100 accounted for just under half of the nominees in this category.)

Best Director

Winner: *The Apartment, West Side Story, Lawrence of Arabia, Tom Jones, My Fair Lady, The Sound of Music, A Man for All Seasons, The Graduate, Oliver!, Midnight Cowboy.* (The Top 100 Pictures had a 100 percent success rate in this category.)

Nominees: *Psycho, The Guns of Navarone, La Dolce Vita, To Kill a Mockingbird, Doctor Zhivago, The Professionals, A Man for All Seasons, Who's Afraid of Virginia Woolf?, Bonnie and Clyde, Guess Who's Coming to Dinner, In the Heat of the Night, Romeo and Juliet, 2001: A Space Odyssey, Butch Cassidy and the Sundance Kid.* (The Top 100 accounted for 35 percent of the nominees in this category.)

Best Actor

Winner: *To Kill a Mockingbird, My Fair Lady, Cat Ballou, A Man for All Seasons, In the Heat of the Night, Charly, True Grit.* (The Top 100 had a 70 percent success rate in this category.)

Nominees: *The Apartment, Lawrence of Arabia, Tom Jones, Cleopatra, The Russians Are Coming, The Russians Are Coming, Who's Afraid of Virginia Woolf?, Alfie, The Sand Pebbles, Bonnie and Clyde, The Graduate, Cool Hand Luke, Guess Who's Coming to Dinner, Oliver!, Midnight Cowboy* (two nominations). (The Top 100 accounted for 37.5 percent of the nominees in this category.)

Best Actress

Winner: *BUtterfield 8, Mary Poppins, Who's Afraid of Virginia Woolf?, Guess Who's Coming to Dinner, Funny Girl.* (Half the winners appeared in movies in the Top 100.)

Nominees: *The Apartment, Irma La Douce, The Sound of Music, A Patch of Blue, Georgy Girl, The Graduate, Bonnie and Clyde, Wait Until Dark.* (The Top 100 accounted for 20 percent of the nominees in this category.)

Best Supporting Actor

Winner: *Spartacus, Cool Hand Like.* (Only 20 percent of the winners appeared in movies in the Top 100.)

Nominees: *The Apartment, Exodus, The Alamo, West Side Story, Lawrence of Arabia, Tom Jones, My Fair Lady, Doctor Zhivago, The Sand Pebbles, Georgy Girl, Who's Afraid of Virginia Woolf?, A Man for All Seasons, The Dirty Dozen, Bonnie and Clyde* (two nominations), *Guess Who's Coming to Dinner, Oliver!, Easy Rider.* (The Top 100 accounted for 45 percent of the nominees in this category.)

Best Supporting Actress

Winner: *West Side Story, A Patch of Blue, Bonnie and Clyde, Rosemary's Baby.* (Forty percent of the winners appeared in Top 100 pictures.)

Nominees: *Psycho, To Kill a Mockingbird, Tom Jones* (three nominees), *My Fair Lady, The Sound of Music, Who's Afraid of Virginia Woolf?, A Man for All Seasons, Alfie, Thoroughly Modern Millie, Barefoot in the Park, Guess Who's Coming to Dinner, The Graduate, Funny Girl, Midnight Cowboy.* (The Top 100 accounted for 40 percent of the nominees in this category.)

Best Screenplay

Winner: *The Apartment, How the West Was Won, Guess Who's Coming to Dinner, Butch Cassidy and the Sundance Kid.* (Forty percent of the winners appeared in films in the Top 100).

Nominees: *La Dolce Vita, Lover Come Back, That Touch of Mink, Those Magnificent Men in Their Flying Machines, Bonnie and Clyde, 2001: A Space Odyssey, Easy Rider, The Wild Bunch.* (The Top 100 accounted for 20 percent of the nominees in this category.)

Best Adapted Screenplay

Winner: *To Kill a Mockingbird, Tom Jones, Doctor Zhivago, A Man for All Seasons, In the Heat of the Night, Midnight Cowboy.* (Sixty percent of the winners came from Top 100 movies.)

Nominees: *The Guns of Navarone, West Side Story, Lawrence of Arabia, Mary Poppins, My Fair Lady, Cat Ballou, Alfie, The Professionals, The Russians Are Coming, The Russians Are Coming, Who's Afraid of Virginia Woolf?, Cool Hand Luke, The Graduate, The Odd Couple, Oliver!, Rosemary's Baby, Goodbye, Columbus.* (The Top 100 accounted for 40 percent of the nominees in this category.)

Best Cinematography (Color)

Winner: *Spartacus, West Side Story, Lawrence of Arabia, Cleopatra, My Fair Lady, Doctor Zhivago, A Man for All Seasons, Bonnie and Clyde, Romeo and Juliet, Butch Cassidy and the Sundance Kid.* (The Top 100 pictures had a 100 percent success rate in this category.)

Nominees: *The Alamo, BUtterfield 8, Exodus, Hatari!, Mutiny on the Bounty, How the West Was Won, Irma La Douce, It's a Mad Mad Mad Mad World, Mary Poppins, The Great Race, The Greatest Story Ever Told, The Sound of Music, Hawaii, The Professionals, The Sand Pebbles, Camelot, The Graduate, Funny Girl, Oliver!* (The Top 100 accounted for 47.5 percent of the nominees in this category.)

Best Cinematography (Black-and-White)*

Winner: *The Longest Day, Who's Afraid of Virginia Woolf?* (Films from the Top 100 had a near-30 percent success rate here—see explanatory note below.)

Nominees: *The Apartment, Psycho, The Absent Minded Professor, To Kill a Mockingbird, A Patch of Blue, Georgy Girl.* (The Top 100 accounted for just over 21 percent of the nominees in this category—see explanatory note below.)

Best Art Direction-Set Decoration (Color)

Winner: *Spartacus, West Side Story, Lawrence of Arabia, Cleopatra, My Fair Lady, Doctor Zhivago, Camelot, Oliver!* (The Top 100 had an 80 percent success rate.)

Nominees: *El Cid, Mutiny on the Bounty, That Touch of Mink, How the West Was Won, Tom Jones, Mary Poppins, The Greatest Story Ever Told, The Sound of Music, The Sand Pebbles, Guess Who's Coming to Dinner, Thoroughly Modern Millie, 2001: A Space Odyssey.* (The Top 100 accounted for 30 percent of the nominees in this category.)

Best Art Direction-Set Decoration (Black-and-White)*

Winner: *The Apartment, To Kill a Mockingbird, Who's Afraid of Virginia Woolf?* (Films from the Top 100 made up just over 40 percent of these winners—see explanatory note below.)

Nominees: *Psycho, The Absent Minded Professor, La Dolce Vita, The Longest Day, A Patch of Blue.* (The Top 100 accounted for about 17 percent of the nominees in this category—see explanatory note below.)

Best Sound

Winner: *The Alamo, West Side Story, Lawrence of Arabia, How the West Was Won, The Sound of Music, Grand Prix, In the Heat of the Night, Oliver!* (The Top 100 had an 80 percent success rate.)

Nominees: *The Apartment, The Guns of Navarone, The Parent Trap, That Touch of Mink, Cleopatra, It's a Mad Mad Mad Mad World, Doctor Zhivago, The Great Race, Shenandoah, Hawaii, The Sand Pebbles, Who's Afraid of Virginia Woolf?, Camelot, The Dirty Dozen, Thoroughly Modern Millie, Bullitt, Funny Girl, Butch Cassidy and the Sundance Kid.* (The Top 100 accounted for 45 percent of the nominees in this category.)

Best Song

Winner: *Mary Poppins, Butch Cassidy and the Sundance Kid.* (Only 20 percent of the films in the Top 100 were successful in this category.)

Nominees: *The Alamo, El Cid, Mutiny on the Bounty, It's a Mad Mad Mad Mad World, Cat Ballou, The Great Race, What's New Pussycat?, Alfie, Georgy Girl, Hawaii, The Jungle Book, Casino Royale, Thoroughly Modern Millie, Chitty Chitty Bang Bang, Funny Girl, True Grit.* (The Top 100 accounted for 40 percent of the nominees in this category.)

Best Score[1]

Winner: *Exodus, Lawrence of Arabia, Tom Jones, Mary Poppins, Doctor Zhivago, Thoroughly Modern Millie, Butch Cassidy and the Sundance Kid.* (Seventy percent of the films in the Top 100 were successful in this category.)

Nominees: *The Alamo, Spartacus, El Cid, The Guns of Navarone, Mutiny on the Bounty, To Kill a Mockingbird, Cleopatra, How the West was Won, It's a Mad Mad Mad Mad World, The Greatest Story Ever Told, A Patch of Blue, The Bible, Hawaii, The Sand Pebbles, Who's Afraid of Virginia Woolf?, Cool Hand Luke, The Fox, Planet of the Apes, The Wild Bunch.* (The Top 100 accounted for 47.5 percent of the nominees in this category.)

Best Scoring Of Music[†]

Winner: *West Side Story, Irma La Douce, My Fair Lady, The Sound of Music, Cat Ballou, Camelot, Oliver!* (Seventy percent of the winners in this category belonged to Top 100 movies.)

Nominees: *Mary Poppins, Guess Who's Coming to Dinner, Thoroughly Modern Millie, Valley of the Dolls, Funny Girl.* (The Top 100 accounted for 12.5 percent of the nominees in this category.)

Best Film Editing

Winner: *The Apartment, West Side Story, Lawrence of Arabia, Tom Jones, Mary Poppins, The Sound of Music, Grand Prix, In the Heat of the Night, Bullitt.* (The Top 100 had a 90 percent success rate in this category.)

Nominees: *The Alamo, Spartacus, The Guns of Navarone, The Parent Trap, The Longest Day, Mutiny on the Bounty, Cleopatra, It's a Mad Mad Mad Mad World, My Fair Lady, Cat Ballou, Doctor Zhivago, The Great Race, The Russians Are Coming, The Russians Are Coming, The Sand Pebbles, Who's Afraid of Virginia Woolf?, The Dirty Dozen, Guess Who's Coming to Dinner, Funny Girl, The Odd Couple, Oliver!, Midnight Cowboy.* (The Top 100 accounted for 52.5 percent of the nominees in this category.)

Best Sound Effects

Winner: *It's a Mad Mad Mad Mad World, Goldfinger, The Great Race, Grand Prix, The Dirty Dozen.* (This award was introduced at the 1964 ceremony. Over 70 percent of these awards were taken by films in the Top 100.)

Nominees: *Von Ryan's Express, In the Heat of the Night.* (There were fewer films nominated in this category and films from the Top 100 accounted for just under 30 percent of the nominees.)

Best Special Effects†

Winner: *The Guns of Navarone, The Longest Day, Cleopatra, Mary Poppins, Thunderball, 2001: A Space Odyssey.* (Films in the Top 100 took 60 percent of these awards.)

Nominees: *The Absent Minded Professor, Mutiny on the Bounty, The Greatest Story Ever Told.* (There were fewer nominees than the usual four in this category and films from the Top 100 accounted for 30 percent of the nominees.)

Best Costume Design (Color)

Winner: *Spartacus, West Side Story, Cleopatra, My Fair Lady, Doctor Zhivago, A Man for All Seasons, Camelot, Romeo and Juliet.* (Eighty percent of the winners in this category came from Top 100 pictures.)

Nominees: *How the West Was Won, Mary Poppins, The Greatest Story Ever Told, The Sound of Music, Hawaii, Bonnie and Clyde, Thoroughly Modern Millie, Oliver!, Planet of the Apes.* (The Top 100 accounted for 22.5 percent of the nominees in this category.)

Best Costume Design (Black-and-White)*

Winner: *La Dolce Vita, Who's Afraid of Virginia Woolf?* (Top 100 films accounted for 35 percent of the winners—see explanatory note below.)

Nominees: None

---

*The separate Black-and-White categories were ended after the awards for films released in 1966.
†These categories changed their name or definition during the decade: Best Score (Drama or Comedy) changed to Music Score—Substantially Original; Best Score (Musical) changed to Best Scoring of Music—Adaptation or Treatment; Best Special Effects changed to Best Visual Effects.

Chapter Notes

Preface

1. Andrew Sarris popularized the French notion, as espoused in French magazine *Cahiers du Cinéma* by François Truffaut ("Une certain tendance du cinéma français") in 1954, that a director should be considered on the same artistic plane as a painter or sculptor rather than merely an excellent technician who put together the various elements of a movie. His article ("Notes on the Auteur Theory in 1962," *Film Culture* No 27 Winter 1962–1963) introduced the theory to American readers and his book *The American Cinema: Directors and Direction, 1929–1968* (1968) categorised the top directors according to his perception of their worth. Highest-ranked were those in the "pantheon"—John Ford, D.W. Griffiths, documentary film-maker Robert Flaherty, Howard Hawks, Buster Keaton and Orson Welles plus British directors Charlie Chaplin and Alfred Hitchcock and five Europeans. Many directors hitherto considered at the top of the profession were either ridiculed or reduced to the category of also-rans—including David Lean, Billy Wilder, Elia Kazan, Stanley Kramer and Stanley Kubrick. Sarris reviewed movies for *Village Voice*. Not every leading critic agreed with this perspective. Pauline Kael of the *New Yorker* attacked the auteur theory in an article "Circles and Squares" in the Spring 1963 edition of *Film Quarterly* (Vol. 16 No. 3, 12–26). However, Kael took the auteur theory one step further (or sideways) when she credited screenwriter Herman Mankiewicz ("Raising Kane," *New Yorker*, February 20, 1971, 43–89) and not Orson Welles as being the creative force behind *Citizen Kane* (1941)

2. Baker, Peter, "The Screen Answers Back," *Films and Filming*, May 1962, 11–18, 45. In an examination of the power of the critics and how they were considered by the people they wrote about, the prestigious British monthly ran a lengthy article. There were more than 100 film critics in the U.K., some extremely powerful, the *Daily Mirror*, for example, boasting 4.5 million readers. Many of the critics were not particularly influential, those in local newspapers rarely wrote anything studios could object to, being kept in line by the threat of advertising being withdrawn. Such potential action did not deter the national dailies, however. "The big circulation papers can afford to ignore film company tantrums," wrote Baker, "Some years ago there was a hot war between Wardour Street and the Beaverbrook Press. The film men withdrew all their advertising. The Beaverbrook Press (mainly the *Daily Express* and *London Evening Standard*) was unperturbed; it knew it could hold out longer than the film men could afford to do so." Baker also pointed out that the dailies were unlikely to write about little-known pictures. "The critic writing for a big circulation paper will find it difficult to persuade an editor that he should write about films unlikely to be seen in more than half a dozen cinemas." And he was also sanguine about the impact of a critic on the general populace. "Although unanimous in their condemnation of *King of Kings*, the British critics have not deterred a large proportion of their readers from going to see it." The most important British critics of the time, by dint of circulation or reputation, were: Felix Barker (*London Evening News*), Peter Burnup (*News of the World*), Penelope Gilliatt (*Observer*), Penelope Houston (*Sight & Sound*), Leonard Mosely (*Daily Express*), James Monahan (*Guardian*), Dilys Powell (*Sunday Times*), and Alexander Walker (*London Evening Standard*). Baker's article included a survey of those involved in the movies. Dirk Bogarde commented: "Far too many critics write to please themselves and a small band of chums." Jose Ferrer said, "The public will always have the last word." John Huston argued, "Criticism has been getting worse and consequently its influence has been diminishing." Otto Preminger noted, "I never complain about bad notices and never thank them for good ones." Peter Sellers was of the opinion that "good criticism is getting better," but Sam Speigel disagreed— "Film criticism is getting worse. Much criticism seems to give the personal view of the writer rather than a balanced view for the particular readership." Federico Fellini made the salient point that "critics are always more generous judging films from countries other than their own."

3. Astria, Bill "Long Shots," *Kine Weekly*, April 25, 1970, 4. "It is a popular game to regard the circuit bookers...to be knocked down every time that a film which takes the fancy of the critics is

Notes—Introduction

not immediately shown on one or the other of the major circuits, irrespective of whether it is a commercial proposition for national release."

4. Wollen's book, written while working the education department of the British Film Institute, was in three parts: an exploration of the work of Sergei Eisenstein, a comparison of John Ford and Howard Hawks, and more importantly for future film scholars the development of a semiology system for cinema.

5. Movie criticism had almost moved backward from the cultured critiques of the 1950s delivered by the likes of James Agee in *Time* to the days of Dorothy Parker describing Katharine Hepburn in *Christopher Strong* going through the "gamut of emotions from A to B." Critics in the 1960s had a tendency to demolish films in crisp one-liners. Manny Farber in *New Republic* was notorious for such literary demolition derbies. Pauline Kael (*New Yorker*) and Frank Rich (*Time*) could be equally acerbic. Other notable critics of the decade included Vincent Canby (*New York Times*), Rex Reed (*New York Observer*), Gene Siskel (*Chicago Tribune*) and Richard Schickel (*Time*). Critics felt they were in a no-holds-barred profession, that culminated in an infamous meeting with David Lean following the launch of *Ryan's Daughter* (1970) where he was abused so badly verbally that he gave up directing temporarily. Studios had a love-hate relationship with critics but did not hesitate to plaster favourable quotes on movie advertising. This practice helped to popularize the names of some critics who worked for magazines with small circulations such as *Village Voice* and *New Republic*.

Introduction

1. Total box office receipts which had sunk to a low of $903 million in 1962 jumped to $1,099 million by 1969.

2. Movie budgets rose faster during the 1950s and 1960s than ever before, mostly driven by historical epics and by the industry's need to develop unique product to woo viewers from television. While *Gone with the Wind* (1939) cost $4.25 million and *Forever Amber* (1947) $6.35 million, the difference between *Quo Vadis* in 1951 and *The Ten Commandments* in 1956 was much more pronounced, the former costing $7.6 million, the latter $13.2 million. *Ben Hur* (1959) was made for $15.1 million. But *Mutiny on the Bounty* (1962) raised the ante much further, costing $19 million and *Cleopatra* the following year $31 million; both, it has to be said, well above the original budget estimates. Even so, the $10 million-plus movie was a regular occurrence in the 1960s, thanks to the splurge of historical epics and musicals. Although ancillary revenue was still in its infancy, producers expected to reap extra financial benefits from reissues and from television sales (these were leased rather than an outright sale so a movie could be sold to television two or three times in a decade) and also from programs sold on the night to roadshow audiences as well as a growing income from original soundtrack albums and singles.

3. Elizabeth Taylor was the highest-paid star of the decade, pocketing $2 million for *Cleopatra*, and nearly as much, including her share percentage, for *The Sandpiper* (1965) but more commonly her basic rate was $1 million per picture. Although Marlon Brando earned $1 million for *The Fugitive Kind* (1959), his earnings dropped sharply throughout the decade. But John Wayne, Paul Newman, Steve McQueen and Julie Andrews were in the $750,000 per-picture class. Salaries increased at a comparative rate. The minute one big star received a bigger salary, the others with similar box office marquee appeal demanded the same.

4. Although the auteur theory helped put directors on a critical pedestal, the commercial appeal of some directors was already widely recognised, the possessive credit written into the contracts of Alfred Hitchcock, John Ford, Otto Preminger, Stanley Kramer and William Wyler, for example, but by the end of the decade it was common for unknown directors to receive a similar "film by" credit.

5. The number of films produced by the top seven studios in 1960—184—was the peak for the decade. In 1964, only 144 appeared; in 1966 only 149. Output from individual studios varied enormously. In 1960 Columbia made 35 pictures but by 1968 that was down to 20. On the other hand, MGM, which had only 18 films on release in 1960, was up to 27 in 1968. Paramount went from 22 in 1960 to 33 in 1968; Twentieth Century-Fox from 49 in 1960 to 21 in 1968; United Artists produced the same number—23—in both 1960 and 1968; Universal leapt from 20 in 1960 to 30 in 1968 and Warner Brothers from 17 in 1960 to 23 in 1968. (Source: Christopher H. Sterling and Timothy R. Haight, *The Mass Media: Aspen Institute Guide to Communication Industry Trends* (New York: Praeger, 1978).

6. As I discovered in writing two previous books, *Coming Back to a Theater Near You: A History of Hollywood Reissues, 1914–2014* (McFarland, 2016) and *In Theaters Everywhere: A History of the Hollywood Wide Release, 1913–2017* (McFarland, 2019), this was a decade of seismic change in the way films were released. Reissues underwent their biggest-ever boom while, as a method of getting films out to the public via the quickest route, studios invested heavily in what became known then as "saturation" or "showcase" release—what today would be termed "wide release"—although the numbers of theaters involved in these release strategies were considerably smaller than 4,000-plus screens we might see today.

7. The term "superstar"—into which bracket many fell—did not come into play until the next decade.

8. Clark Gable died in November 1960 and Gary Cooper passed in May 1961. Even posthumously, Gable remained an enormous star as the reissues of *Gone with the Wind* in 1961 and 1967 can testify.

Notes—Introduction

9. "All-Industry Plans to Sell New Stars Are Disclosed," *Box Office*, November 13, 1961, 5. "Crusade to accelerate public acceptance of new stars will include a tour to tout the new personalities and their films. Newcomers include Karen Balkin, Peter Brown, Madlyn Rhue, Annette Funicello, Ken Scott, Joyce Taylor and Darlene Tompkins." This plan was not particularly successful with only Funicello achieving low-key success, and possibly only because she was already the best-known of the bunch. Occasionally studios such as MGM would make a "commitment" to new talent, but such ventures were rarely successful as actors in whom the public showed the slightest bit of interest were inclined to dump, as quickly as possible, the company or producer who had given them their big break.

10. While road shows dated back to the silent era when films would go round the country, city by city, in just one theater, in the manner of touring stage shows, the modern boom was generally attributed to *Ben-Hur* (1959). Over 70 were released in the 1960s, the peak years being 1966 and 1968 which each saw 11 movies released in that format. Although the bulk were big-budget 70mm pictures, the roadshow was also used as a glorified arthouse, the separate program technique bringing a certain amount of kudos to a movie. Among the curiosities slipped into the mix were travelogue *Scent of Mystery* (1960) in 70mm Smell-O-Vision, the controversial *Ulysses* (1967), the six-hour Russian *War and Peace* (1968 U.S. release), and the French *Marry Me! Marry Me!* (1969). Ordinary first run theaters would screen single-billed regular movies five or six times a day—30–40 shows a week—while a roadshow would restrict attendance to 10–12 programs a week. The roadshow hoped that hiked ticket prices and long runs would make up for fewer screenings.

11. The roadshow was designed to be an event on a par with going to see a musical or play on stage. As with the stage, the idea of booking in advance was a commitment, a kind of futures market for movies; you could not just turn up on a whim. Unlike the standard first run picture, the movie would stay put, running in the one theater for a "season" lasting 13 weeks, and then longer if successful.

12. Holston, Kim R. *Movie Roadshows: A History and Filmography of Reserved-Seat Limited Showings, 1911–1973* (McFarland, 2013) 222.

13. Hannan, Brian, *In Theaters Everywhere*, 148, 156.

14. Hannan, Brian, *Coming Back to a Theater Near You*, 117–123.

15. "An operation boasting two, three, four, or even six theaters in the same building created unprecedented opportunity for longer runs." (Hannan, *In Theaters*, 163); "In August 1960, *Variety* reported that 25 cinemas were operating as shopping center hardtops nationwide." (Monaco, *The Sixties*, 48). "Indianapolis Circuit Plans Shopping Center Theater," *Motion Picture Herald*, March 31,

1965, 13; "Gulf States Circuit Planning to Build 8 Twin Drive-Ins and Shop Centers," *Box Office*, November 22, 1965, 4; "Multi Theatres for B'Way, Dallas," *International Motion Picture Exhibitor*, August 7, 1968, 3. Durwood planned a six-theater complex in Dallas while RKO-Stanley-Warner opened a Broadway triplex in New York in the former Warner Theatre. "First Tri-Level Multiple Theatre Planned Forman Hawaii Circuit," *Motion Picture Exhibitor*, April 24, 1968, 6. Each theater had its own parking level and could in total accommodate 1,000 patrons. By the end of the decade the most famous name—AMC—in the multiplex business came into being. ("Durwood Circuit Becomes American Multi-Cinema Inc," *International Motion Picture Exhibitor*, May 7, 1969, 7).

16. In fact, there were very few mainstream sequels of any kind. You had to go back to *Father of the Bride* (1950) and *Father's Little Dividend* (1950)—both with Spencer Tracy and Elizabeth Taylor—to find a decent example.

17. There were also three films in the United Artists Harry Palmer series starring Michael Caine, three films made from John Le Carre novels and four pictures in the Italian Eurospy *OSS 117* series. Eight times movies were made out of twinning episodes of *The Man from U.N.C.L.E.* television series though these were largely for foreign exposure. Two movies were made from Bulldog Drummond adventures. A pair of Alfred Hitchcock thrillers—*Torn Curtain* (1966) and *Topaz* (1969)—fitted into the genre. The French reinvented Nick Carter with Eddie Constantine in the lead. And there were endless others.

18. Studios and exhibitors had bet big on reviving *The Glenn Miller Story* (1954), *Friendly Persuasion* (1956) and *The King and I* (1956) with markedly poor results (Hannan, *Coming Back*, 113–124).

19. *Sons and Lovers* (1960) and *Saturday Night and Sunday Morning* (1960) were the prime examples.

20. "*Pawnbroker* Granted Seal by MPAA Review Board," *Motion Picture Herald*, March 31, 1965, 5.

21. "Valenti Launches Campaign to Promote Code and Seal," *Box Office*, March 20, 1967, 3. *Blow-Up* was released through an MGM subsidiary called Premier Films which was not a member of the MPAA. Jack Valenti commented that members were free to do this. "No sanctions are put on our members," he said.

22. *The Learning Tree* (1969).

23. "Women Biggest Picture-Goers, So U Laces *Midnight* Campaign with Fashions," *Variety*, Sep 7, 1960, 16.

24. "Advertisement, *Doctor Zhivago*," *Variety*, January 4, 1967, 37; "Paris Fashions—1967," *Variety*, February 15, 1967, 2; "H'wood Fashions Boom Year," *Variety*, Oct 4, 1967, 5.

25. Pressbook, *Seven Days in May*; Pressbook, *Point Blank*.

26. Some studios—Paramount, United Artists—were takeover targets because they were

making money, others such as MGM and Twentieth Century-Fox because they were losing money. Gulf & Western—a conglomerate with interests in automobile accessories and supplies—had begun to specialize in what would later be termed the leveraged buyout and acquired Paramount in 1966. Gulf & Western then bought, among other enterprises, television production company Desilu, Madison Square Garden, International Holiday on Ice, *Esquire* magazine and two publishing companies and in 1969 formed Cinema International Corporation with Universal to distribute the studios' movies in parts of Europe including Britain. Trans-America Corporation took over United Artists in 1967. The same year Warner Brothers merged with Seven Arts and then two years later that company was acquired by Kinney National Services Corporation, which, among other businesses, owned funeral homes. Kirk Kerkorian took control of MGM in 1969. Joe Levine's operation Embassy, far from being a major, was bought by Avco in 1968. But where Gulf & Western chief Charles Bludhorn became involved in Paramount and supported its film-making, Kerkorian made MGM subsidiary to the company's hotel business. Columbia avoided a takeover by a European consortium because the proposed deal fell foul of antitrust laws. Twentieth Century-Fox, which had weathered a financial storm in the early 1960s, recovered to boost record profits after the success of *The Sound of Music* only to post staggering losses in 1969 of $36.8 million and leave the company open to takeover. All the 1960s takeover had come from outside the entertainment business but the acquisition in 1959 of Universal by talent agency MCA went against that particular grain. That resulted in Universal becoming a major producer of television programs and changing its business dynamic. "By mixing production for television with production of feature films for theatrical release," author Paul Monaco pointed out, "Universal's losses on less successful productions could be covered by hits, costs could be spread to cover high overhead and Universal's facilities could be kept in constant use." (Source: Monaco, Paul, *The Sixties*, University of California Press, 2001, 30–39).

27. Based on the U.S. Inflation Calculator for the year 1969 which projected a cumulative rate of inflation of 612.8 percent.

28. Monaco, *The Sixties*, 1.

29. "Rental Potential of 1960 (When Fully Played Off)," *Variety*, January 4, 1961, 3; "Rentals & Potential," *Variety*, January 10, 1962, 13; "Big Rental Pictures of 1962," *Variety*, January 9, 1963, 13; "Top Rental Films of 1963," *Variety*, January 8, 1964, 37; "Big Rental Pictures of 1964," *Variety*, January 6, 1965, 39; "Big Rental Pictures of 1965," *Variety*, January 5, 1966, 6; "Big Rental Pictures of 1966," *Variety*, January 4, 1967, 8; "Big Rental Films of 1967," *Variety*, January 3, 1968, 25; "Big Rental Films of 1968," *Variety*, January 8, 1969; "Big Rental Films of 1969," *Variety*, January 7, 1969, 15; "All-Time Box Office Champs," *Variety*, January 7,

1970, 25; "All-Time Film Rental Champs," *Variety*, January 9, 1980, 24; "Top 100 All-Time Film Rental Champs," *Variety*, January 24, 1990, 46.

30. Cohn, Lawrence, "Alphabetical All-Time Film Rental Champs," *Variety*, May 10, 1993, C-76. A number of movies which would have qualified for the Top 100 according to figures supplied by the year-end annual rental charts were found later on to have over-stated their results. These included *The Unsinkable Molly Brown* (1964) and *The VIPs* (1963).

31. Other figures have been the source of debate. For example, *Hatari!* (1962) was credited with $7 million in domestic rentals by *Variety* in its annual chart, enough for a position in the top 100 for the decade, but the figure quoted in Todd McCarthy's biography of Howard Hawks put the numbers lower but with no reference as to how that lower figure came from, so in that case I have stuck with the original Paramount figure.

32. "All-Time Film Rental Champs" *Variety*, January 9, 1980, 24. *Butch Cassidy and the Sundance Kid* earned another $31 million in the 1970s and *Easy Rider* another $11.9 million. Others adding to their 1960s pot included *Mary Poppins* with an additional $10 million, *Funny Girl* ($9.8 million), *2001: A Space Odyssey* ($9.6 million), *Midnight Cowboy* ($9.3 million), *Doctor Zhivago* ($8.3 million), *The Sound of Music* ($7 million), *The Graduate* and *The Love Bug* (both $6 million) and *Swiss Family Robinson* ($5.9 million). Some properties such as *The Sound of Music, Lawrence of Arabia* and Disney animated classics continued to earn substantial rental sums throughout the century and beyond as classics underwent another series of reissues

The Films

1. The world premiere at the Empire, Leicester Sq, in London was a 70mm roadshow. In the U.S. it went straight into general release in the 35mm format. MGM probably shied away from roadshow in the U.S. because the box office for another MacLean thriller *Ice Station Zebra* (1968), a 70mm Cinerama production, fell below expectations. Elsewhere in Europe it was released first as a roadshow. In Britain it ran in roadshow until the end of 1969. In some countries where showings of films on television were more limited, it was revived again and again. According to Stefan Adler ("Projection Dare," *Cinema Retro Movie Classics Special Edition* on *Where Eagles Dare*, 2012, 99), after opening in 1969 at the Draken in Stockholm, for example, it was reissued, still in 70mm, in 1972, 1974, 1975, 1978, 1980, 1982 and 1984 with runs that always lasted at least eight weeks.

2. With another former agent Jerry Gershwin, he formed Winkast Film Productions and they made 11 films together. These included *Where Eagles Dare* where Winkast was credited but Kastner received the sole producer credit. Kastner

Notes—The Films

parlayed securing a big star like Richard Burton into a big studio deal. "When word got out that I had Richard Burton, the studios started calling, which is how I liked it. They were chasing me, which is the way I like it. If you go to them first, you end up with a different kind of deal," he said. ("Calling Kastner," *Cinema Retro* Special, 57).

3. From *On the Waterfront* (1954) to *Nicholas and Alexandra* (1971), Spiegel's productions were released by Columbia.

4. *Kaleidoscope* (1966), *The Bobo* (1967) and *Sweet November* (1968) were also made for Warner Brothers. While the first was a Winkast film, the two others were credited to Gina Production.

5. MacLean's original title was *Castle of the Eagles*. Kastner changed this to *Where Eagles Dare*, drawing on a line from Shakespeare's *Richard III*— "Where eagles dare not perch."

6. UK Pressbook. Later, Kastner would plunder MacLean's work to film *When Eight Bells Toll* (1971), *Fear Is the Key* (1972), and *Breakheart Pass* (1975). He would hire—and then fire—Richard Burton from *Laughter in the Dark* (1969).

7. *Cinema Retro* Special, 102.

8. This was worth $5.3 million at today's prices. But there is really no comparison between what top actors earned in the 1960s and fees paid out today. A different sort of inflation escalated star salaries in the 1970s and 1980s and beyond so that were *Where Eagles Dare* being remade today the salary for the Burton part would be more in the region of $20 million. The top male stars earned $500,000-$750,000 during this decade.

9. Eastwood's fee was $300,000.

10. *Cinema Retro* Special, 102.

11. "Casting Clint—The Untold Story," *Cinema Retro* Special, 38.

12. He had been nominated in successive years for *Becket* (1964), *The Spy Who Came in from the Cold* (1965) and *Who's Afraid of Virginia Woolf* (1966).

13. Hutton went on to work twice with Burton's then-wife Elizabeth Taylor in the dramas *X, Y and Zee* (1972) and *Night Watch* (1973) and was Eastwood's choice for a further war adventure *Kelly's Heroes* (1971).

14. Polish-born Pitt would later become Hammer's scream queen as the vampire picture segued into a brief lesbian cycle with *The Vampire Lovers* (1970) and *Countess Dracula* (1971).

15. Canby, Vincent, "In the War Tradition, *Where Eagles Dare*," *New York Times*, March 13, 1969; Robe, Review, *Variety*, December 11, 1968, 6; Feature Reviews, *Box Office*, December 23, 1968.

16. "All-Time Rentals," *Variety*, 1993. It was downgraded from $6.8 million to $6.56 million for the 1960s but the 1970s brought in a little more revenue so its lifetime rentals were $7.15 million. This was considered a disappointing result for a movie costing $6.2 million but its overseas box office—exploiting demand for roadshow—more than made up.

17. Before his breakthrough in *Bridge on the River Kwai* (1957), Alec Guinness's Ealing comedies had followed much the same release strategy. But arthouse never translated into true commercial appreciation. Although the cognoscenti were appreciative, to the vast majority of American moviegoers, Guinness was an unknown quantity and the same held true for Sellers.

18. Mirisch, Walter, *I Thought We Were Making Movies Not History* (Madison: University of Wisconsin Press, 2008) 163; "Mirisch Co. Sues Ustinov for Performance Failure," *Box Office*, January 14, 1964. Original female lead Ava Gardner had been replaced by Capucine (*North to Alaska*, 1960) and Ustinov refused to act alongside her. When he pulled out prior to the start of filming he was sued for $175,000. Ustinov and Sellers also crossed paths on what was to end up as famous heist picture *Topkapi* (1964). When it was known as *Man in the Middle*, Sellers pulled out of this one, only for the part to go to Ustinov and it became one of his most famous roles ("Out of One Cast, Into Another for Sellers," *Variety*, April 10, 1963, 4).

19. "Edwards, Jurow Form New Production Unit," *Box Office*, June 18, 1962, 9. Edwards and former agent Martin Jurow formed G&E Productions with five films lined up. First out was *Soldier in the Rain* co-written by Edwards but directed by Ralph Nelson, then *The Pink Panther* which was to be followed by *The Great Race*, *The Fabulous Showman* and *The Working Girls*. The last two were never made and after *The Great Race* the partnership was dissolved and Jurow did not make another film for nearly a decade although he was co-producer of Oscar-winner *Terms of Endearment* (1983).

20. Mirisch, *I Thought*, 163.

21. On the back of this trio, *The World of Henry Orient* (1964) received a greater level of bookings than had originally appeared likely and after a quiet start gathered steam after the opening of *A Shot in the Dark*.

22. Although *The Pink Panther* is known as a 1963 picture, that was courtesy of a world premiere in Italy in December 1963. It didn't open in the U.S. until March 1964. United Artists wanted to launch it as Radio City Music Hall in New York and you had to wait in line for a slot there. It would be the first Mirisch picture to open there and the first from UA since *The Men* (1950).

23. Hawkins, Robert F., "Salary with Fringe on top," *Variety*, November 28, 1963, 3. Ava Gardner had been dumped on account of her excessive demands. In addition to her $400,000 salary she had demanded a secretary and personal hairdresser flown in from abroad, likewise for make-up and wardrobe, and other extras that totaled $60,000.

24. Mirisch, *I Thought*, 163–164. Loren did not like the script.

25. "Walter Matthau to Star in *Shot in the Dark*," *Box Office*. August 26, 1963. Matthau had won a Tony for his performance in the original Broadway production.

26. "Blake Edwards Makes Like Dynamic

Type," *Variety*, October 9, 1963, 4. Litvak had fallen ill before filming was due to begin.

27. The Broadway version kept much of the French origins, for example, in France an investigation is led by an examining magistrate, and that element was retained in the American adaptation. The magistrate, played on stage by William Shatner, was, however, incompetent and, therefore, it was easy to see how this would fit the Clouseau persona. The show ran for 389 performances and there was a touring version. It was also presented in London, whose audiences were particularly amenable to farces, and Australia.

28. "Tailor *Shot in Dark* for Sellers," *Variety*, November 20, 1963, 3. In the original play the female lead had a bigger role than the male lead. With Sellers in the frame, that would all change. Clouseau would dominate at the expense of everyone else.

29. Moviegoers are more inclined to associate William Peter Blatty with the bestselling novel *The Exorcist*, published in 1971. He was better known in the 1960s as a screenwriter for *The Man from the Diners Club* (1963), *John Goldfarb, Please Come Home* (1965), Warren Beatty vehicle *Promise Her Anything* (1966), *What Did You Do in the War, Daddy* (1966), *Gunn* (1967) and western *The Great Bank Robbery* (1969) with Kim Novak.

30. Mirisch, *I Thought*, 163–169.

31. *Ibid.*

32. Gross, Mike, "Pics and Labels Tie Closer," *Billboard*, February 29, 1964, 1; Tiegel, Eliot, "Showcase for Recording Talent," *Billboard*, December 26, 1964, 24; "Top LPs," *Billboard*, December 26, 1964, 24. *The Pink Panther*, composed by Henry Mancini, was one of the great theme tunes of the 1960s and instantly recognizable from the first few bars. Mancini was considered the "king of instrumental composers" after his success with "Moon River" from *Breakfast at Tiffany's* (1961) and "Baby Elephant Walk" from *Hatari* (1962). Eight singles and two albums were recorded for *The Pink Panther*. Records were best-selling properties in their own right, the variety of performers covering every potential market, but also "key exploitation tools" by attracting radio airplay and retail window displays. It worked both ways, of course, movie exposure vastly assisting record sales, the outcome being "evidence of the mutual benefits that films and disks are giving each other." By Xmas 1964, Mancini's original soundtrack to *The Pink Panther* had spent 38 weeks in the charts. *A Shot in the Dark* utilized the same theme to a large extent so that the original tune being a hit helped spur on the sequel.

33. Mirisch, *I Thought*, 163–165. Almost as much revenue was generated from the stand-alone cartoons that were created for the main title sequence for *The Pink Panther* by a new company Freleng-DePatie. Friz Freleng had made his name, along with Chuck Jones, on the Warner Bros *Bugs Bunny* and *Roadrunner* cartoon series. Animated titles had been done before but not with such

panache or humor. Mirisch and Freleng-DePatie then collaborated on a six-minute cartoon *The Pink Phink* which won an Oscar, cost only $30,000, and went out as a successful short to other films, leading to a contract for another 11, again for theatrical distribution. In the 1990s, the team turned to television and made 120 12-minute cartoons. The cartoon character also spawned a merchandising bonanza in its own right. In the 1980s ABC TV launched *The Pink Panther and Sons* while *The Pink Panther and Pals* went out in the 2000s. To fill out a complete 30-minute program for television syndication, the cartoonists invented *Roland and the Rat Fink* and *The Ant and the Aardvark*.

34. Whit, *Variety*, June 24, 1964, 6; Scheuer, Philip K., "*Zulu* Carries on in *Geste* Tradition," *Los Angeles Times*, July 16, 1964; Coe, Richard L., "Peter Sellers Stars at Town," *Washington Post*, July 31, 1964: McCarten, John, Review, *New Yorker*, July 4, 1964, 58–59.

35. Swedish release—October 1967.

36. "Valenti Launches Campaign to Promote Code and Seal," *Box Office*, March 20, 1967, 3. Of 400 films released in the previous three years only 16 had gone out without a Seal of Approval.

37. "Test U.S. Customs as Censor," *Variety*, November 24, 1965, 1. The Tariff Act had authorized customs to seize obscene films. The last one seized that had brought about a lawsuit and been tested in court had been *Ecstasy* 30 years before. Customs had seized *491* as obscene and that decision had been backed up by the New York Federal Court.

38. "High Court Turns Down Pa. Censorship Appeal," *Box Office*, November 13, 1961, 6; "A Tougher Classification Law Sought in Chicago," *Box Office*, December 25, 1961, 4; "Chicago Passes Stiff Under-17 Censorship," *Box Office*, January 1, 1962, 13; "Catholic Bishops Urge Classification Law," *Box Office*, December 3, 1962, 8; "If N.Y. Assembly Says Yes Again, Will Senate Kill Classification?" *Motion Picture Herald*, March 6, 1963, 14; "Uneasy Truce Continues in Classification Fight," *Motion Picture Herald*, April 24, 1963, 7; "Texas Exhibs Face Censor Problems," *Motion Picture Herald*, April 24, 1963, 10; "N.Y. Committee Plans June Hearings On Film Licensing, Classification," *Motion Picture Herald*, May 22, 1963, 7; "N.C. Studies New Ways to Battle Obscenity in Films, Reading Matter," *Motion Picture Herald*, March 31, 1965, 11; "Judge Vetoes Banning *Ulysses* in Chicago," *Box Office*, March 20, 1967.

39. "Burgeoning Burlesque Outstripping Other Attractions; New B.O. Bonanza," *Variety*, November 24, 1965, 1. There were nude shows in Las Vegas and now three new theaters had opened in New York and two in Boston.

40. "Valenti Launches Campaign," *Box Office*.

41. "Valenti Asks Industry, Press, Public to Work Together for Common Goal," *Box Office*, November 17, 1969, 6.

42. "Valenti Explains Ratings System on TV Stations," *Box Office*, September 15, 1969, 10. He

Notes—The Films

appeared on *The Mike Douglas Show* and *The David Frost Show*.

43. "Broadcasting Code Deadline Aug. 15 for MPAA Ratings on Ads for Films," *Box Office*, July 7, 1969, 6.

44. "Swedish Nudies Now Mild as Italo Bruties Currently Bothering the Germans," May 8, 1968, 30; "Sex Film Wave Still Rolling in German Market," *Variety*, July 17, 1968, 30. *I Am Curious, Yellow* was top of the most screened pictures in West Germany

45. "Stiffer Censoring Shatters Myth Re: French Liberalism," *Variety*, October 16, 1968, 5.

46. Sicha, Choire, "All the Young Dudes, a posthumous memoir that goes behind the scenes of Burroughs, Miller and Malcolm X," January 9, 2012, *Slate* online magazine. Its legal efforts drained the company. In 1962, on sales of $2 million, it lost $400,000.

47. "Grove Press Blocks Run of *Curious* in Boston," *Box Office*, May 26, 1969.

48. "Swede Pic Vs. U.S. Customs," *Variety*, May 15, 1968, 13. Grove Press also argued on a technicality, that there had been unreasonable delay on bringing the case.

49. Verrill, Addison, "Changing Pattern in Course of Foreign-Language Films," *Box Office Barometer 68/69*, 56.

50. "Jury Upholds U.S. Customs on *Curious*; Grove Press Now to Further Appeal," *Variety*, May 29, 1968, 12. To support its defense, Grove Press had recruited a team of critics like Hollis Alpert of *Saturday Review* and Paul Zimmerman of *Newsweek*, novelist Norman Mailer and psychologists.

51. "Swedish Sex Film Ruled Not Obscene," *Box Office*, December 9, 1968.

52. "*Curious, Yellow* to have U.S. Debut in New York," *Box Office*, February 17, 1968.

53. Advert, *Variety*, April 2, 1969, 25. The gross of $79,000 beat the theater's previous record of $60,000 for *Goldfinger*.

54. "L.A. Zingy, *Curious* Record 63G in 2 Sites," *Variety*, May 28, 1969, 8; "New Films Boost Chi; *Curious* Record 45G," *Variety*, September 24, 1969, 8.

55. "Maryland First State Banning *Curious*," *Box Office*, July 14, 1969, 7.

56. "Grove Press Blocks," *Box Office*. The film barely lasted a few hours before being seized. Playing at Boston's Symphony One and Symphony Two theaters, the first program on opening day started at noon and five complete and incomplete showings had been achieved before, at 5:15pm, it was removed from the premises. "Exhibitors View Seizure of 2 Films as Renewal of Censorship Efforts," *Box Office*, June 16, 1969. The Symphony pair had expected to gross $50,000 in the first seven days. Tickets cost $3 each and 2,600 had already been sold in 36 hours.

57. "*I Am Curious, Yellow* Obscene in Houston," *Box Office*, May 26, 1969. Hoping at least to make a quick buck before the authorities swooped, the Art Cinema, which was holding the South West Area Premiere, had programmed in six shows a day.

58. "Appeal Kansas Ruling," *Variety*, September 24, 1969, 22.

59. "What Price All That Erotica?" *Variety*, April 9, 1969, 5. The state had re-enacted old obscenity laws.

60. "Youngstown Bans *Curious Yellow*," *Variety*, October 1, 1969, 28.

61. "Court Allows *Curious* Run Continue in Michigan," *Box Office*, September 15, 1969, 10.

62. "Kansas Obscenity Laws Used to Halt Two Films," *Box Office*, June 30, 1969; "Bills on Anti-Obscenity Pend in Several States," *Box Office*, July 7, 1969, 4.

63. "Grove Press Distrib Buys Mpls Theater for *Curious* Booking," *Variety*, September 24, 1963, 22; "*Curious* Giant $22,500 in Mpls," *Variety*, September 24, 1969, 22. A local distributor of Grove Press publications, realizing that no theater in the city would show the film, bought the 620-seat Rialto with the express purpose of showing it. The ploy worked, as the box office figures attest.

64. "Exhibitors View Seizure," *Box Office*. This was at the State.

65. "Pittsburgh Jury Trial Re Lesbian Theme in *Therese and Isabelle*," *Variety*, December 4, 1968, 7. This French film had been given an "X" rating by the new Production Code which should have made it available to anyone over 18, but the district attorney wanted to ban it entirely.

66. "$100 Fee on X Films Set Pawtucket Council," *Box Office*, December 22, 1969, 10; "X and R Films Would Draw $10,000 Licensing Charge," *Box Office*, December 22, 1969, 10. Pawtucket in Rhode Island proposed its charge for each exhibition and planned to act as a review board with the powers to declare movies obscene. In Savannah the plan was to charge theaters showing G-rated films $300 a year, those with M-rated films $500 and those screening R-rated and X-rated features $10,000.

67. "N.Y. Customs Seizes *Pattern of Evil*," *Variety*, May 28, 1969, 4. It was released in 1971 as *Fornicon*. Under the title *Blue Perfume*, hard-core elements were added.

68. "Chevron Looks to 'R' For Explicit Sex," *Box Office*, September 15, 1969, 12. *Venus in Furs* had a name star in Laura Antonelli but due to its sado-masochistic content was denied release in the U.S. until 1975.

69. "You Name It...Russ Meyer's *Vixen* Outgrossed It," advert, *Box Office*, March 10, 1969; "What Price," *Variety*; advert, *Box Office*, September 1, 1969. *Vixen* had been screened informally for the Illinois state attorney in an attempt to bypass legal action. The advert claimed it was heading for a $6 million gross.

70. "Sex and N.Y. Showcase Dollar," *Variety*, October 22, 1969, 5. *Inga* starring Swedish sensation Marie Liljedahl had already grossed $1.5 million. It was directed by American Joe Sarno who had made his name in adult-oriented features earlier in the decade before progressing to the more explicit. Sarno's reputation as an artist grew in the 1970s when Andrew Sarris backed his cause, and

his work has been shown at various film festivals and the British Film Institute. "Everybody Loves *Inga*," *Box Office*, February 24, 1969, 15. It had broken house records in Connecticut, and Portland, Maine, was in its fourteenth week in New York and photos from the film had been published in a three-page spread in *Playboy*. "The girl with the million-dollar legs," advert, *Box Office*, July 7, 1969. A New York two-week showcase release in 20 theaters had generated $266,000 and it boasted a six-week run in Portland, four weeks in Tampa and three in San Diego.

71. Advert, *Box Office*, October 6, 1969. This Italian sex comedy had a decent cast in Catherine Spaak and Jean-Louis Trintignant. It was released through Audubon Films, fast becoming a specialist in this field. It had run for seven weeks in Boston, four in Cleveland, and three in Washington.

72. Advert, *Box Office*, October 6, 1969, 15. *Karla* was also directed by Joe Sarno but with an American setting. It broke the record at the 230-seat Avon at the Love Theater in New York with a gross of $25,703 and claimed it was the biggest take in any cinema of this size.

73. Advert, *Box Office*, February 24, 1969 (back page). Distributor Time Film Corporation claimed a New York record and was also promoting the double bill of *Lollipop* and *Naked World* that had been booked on various circuits.

74. "Sex and N.Y.," *Variety*. Diana Kjaer took the title role in this Swedish venture. It had opened in New York at the prestigious Astor. It was being booked into 22–30 theaters in the Loews chain, the first sexploitation picture to go into a showcase release.

75. "How Sexy Is N.Y. Film Fare," *Variety*, March 19, 1969, 7. This was an in-house survey, the trade magazine merely examining the films tabulated in its weekly box office section.

76. "Sex and N.Y.," *Variety*. It was showing at the United Artists Theater Circuit.

77. Canby, Vincent, "*I Am Curious—Yellow* from Sweden," *New York Times*, March 11, 1969; Ebert, Roger, Review, www.rogerebert.com; Review, *Box Office*, March 10, 1969; Fred, Review, *Variety*, November 1, 1967, 7.

78. "Grove Press Blocks," *Box Office*.

79. "*Curious*: Sexy, Dull Shocker," *Variety*, March 19, 1969, 7.

80. "All-Time Rentals," *Variety*, 1993. Further bookings in the 1970s increased rentals to $8.5 million; Carroll, Kent E., "Grove Asks Cash, Ahead," *Variety*, April 9, 1969, 5. One of the reasons why the movie's rental is so high is not so much from people queuing up to see it but from the exceptionally high rental deal cut in Grove's favor. Grove demanded 90 percent of the gross—unprecedented for an arthouse picture—as well as a cash guarantee paid in advance in case the movie was banned in a particular city.

81. Lemmon, Jack, "Such Fun to Be Funny," *Films and Filming*, November 1960, 7.

82. *Ibid*. Only the "I." in the writer's name was

real. Because he was a reporter originally, the byline "I. Diamond" was odd. The "A.L." had no meaning at all.

83. It was the first time anyone had won three Oscars in an evening.

84. Ron, Review, *Variety*, May 18, 1960, 6; Crowther, Bosley, "Busy *Apartment* Jack Lemmon Scores in Billy Wilder's Film," *New York Times*, June 16, 1960; Cutts, John, *Films and Filming*, September 1960, 21–22.

85. "All-Time Champs," *Variety*, 1993. Downgraded from $9.3 million to $6.65 million. This was one of the most significant downgrades.

86. "*Musa Dagh* Nearer," *Variety*, July 7, 1965, 9. Proof of the director's increased standing in MGM circles was that he had been handed one of the studio's longest-running projects. *Forty Days at Musa Dagh* by Franz Werfel had been an American bestseller in the mid-1930s. Clark Gable and William Powell were set for the film under the direction of William Wellman. The idea was revived again by Walter Wanger in the 1950s and again by Carl Foreman at the start of the 1960s. MGM allocated the film a budget of $7.5 million and by the time Guy Green became involved it had attracted the interest of Omar Sharif. But nothing happened. Interest revived in the mid-1970s and in 1979 it was set to star Charles Bronson on a $10 million budget. That, too, fell by the wayside. On a much smaller budget with a cast of unknowns it was finally made in 1982 and sank without trace at the box office. *The Promise* (2016) with Christian Bale covered similar ground

87. Pandro Berman was a legendary twice-Oscar-nominated Hollywood producer, firstly at RKO then from 1940 at MGM where he oversaw the production of *Father of the Bride* (1950), *Ivanhoe* (1952) and *BUtterfield 8* (1960). This was his first film as an independent producer.

88. Harris, Mark, *Scenes from a Revolution: The Birth of the New Hollywood* (New York: Penguin, 2008 and Edinburgh: Canongate, 2008—all quotes from the Canongate paperback) 59.

89. "In 1964, black Americans were still virtually invisible in filmed entertainment," wrote Mark Harris (*Scenes*, 56). Winning the Oscar did not give Poitier a magic wand. The National Association for the Advancement of Colored People (NAACP) forced a meeting with producers to ensure Hollywood committed to the idea of using more African-Americans in movies (*Scenes*, 57).

90. "Redstone Keynote; Unseen Hartman 'Star of the Future,'" *Variety*, October 6, 1965, 19. The Theater Association of America (TOA) presented her with this award at its annual conference despite the fact that she had not been seen in any picture yet.

91. "Liz Hartman Buys Out of Warner Contract," *Variety*, November 2, 1965, 5. She had a two-picture deal with WB but never made one. She had instead signed up for one film a year with MGM while *You're a Big Boy Now* was for Seven-Arts and *The Group* for *United Artists*.

92. Shelley Winters won the Best Supporting

Actress Oscar for *The Diary of Anne Frank* (1959) and had been nominated in the Best Actress category for *A Place in the Sun* (1951).

93. "Ahead of Schedule, Under Budget; Berman-Green Tout H'wood Crews," *Variety*, May 5, 1965, 16.

94. "Best Oscar B.O. Payoff: Poitier's," *Variety*, August 19, 1964, 1.

95. In order to qualify for Oscar consideration, a film had to be shown in one theater in Los Angeles before the end of the year.

96. "MGM Prints Special Brochure for *Patch* Promotion," *Box Office*, February 7, 1966. The studio printed a 96-page brochure for its field sales team, promoting the rave reviews and suggesting ways of promoting the picture.

97. "Books *Patch*," *Box Office*, September 27, 1965. It was set for the 760-seat Crest Westwood in Los Angeles. The original date was December 24. But it was eventually brought forward a fortnight, possibly to sneak in ahead of Poitier's other picture *The Slender Thread*.

98. "Oscar Shadow Seen," *Variety*, September 15, 1965, 5.

99. "Aspen Pic Conference Moves to L.A. Campus," *Variety*, September 8, 1965, 18.

100. "MGM Uses Special College Sell for *Patch of Blue*," *Box Office*, December 13, 1965, 13. Targeting the 26,000 students attending U.C.L.A., MGM distributed 10,000 bookmarks, took adverts in the student newspaper and promoted the film through display cards. "*17* Magazine Award to *Patch*," *Box Office*, December 13, 1965, 13. *Seventeen* magazine awarded it "picture of the month" status three months before national release.

101. Fessier Jr., Michael, "U.S. Films Shun Racial T.N.T; It's Poitier Or It's Nothing," *Variety*, March, 17, 1965, 1. He argued, "The Hollywood film colony is frankly afraid of racial strife in Mississippi and Alabama as subject matter for releases" and for that reason held back from making films that would either struggle to find a market in territories in the South or face open hostility, thus jeopardizing potential box office. He stated that this "will carry a soft-sell pitch of varying degrees of directness" although he was inclined to believe that the "subtle treatment of inter-racial relationships is infinitely more effective than soapbox techniques."

102. Until Isabelle Adjani.

103. "Inrush of Productions at Year-End with Some Oscar-casting," *Variety*, November 24, 1965, 1. This also opened in Los Angeles to qualify for Oscar consideration and based its marketing on the combination of Oscar-winners Anne Bancroft and Sidney Poitier.

104. "KKK, Freshly Laundered Pickets *Patch of Blue*," *Variety*, May 11, 1965, 1. This was in Memphis where it had been scheduled for a six-week run.

105. "Gold-Hued *Blue*, Cost at $1,050,000, Heads for $6-Mil," *Variety*, March 9, 1966, 3. Records were broken or nearly broken in the first

40 houses it played and it developed "legs"—20 weeks in Philadelphia, for example. When it went wide in New York it proved amazingly consistent, grossing $160,000 from 27 theaters in its opening week, $150,000 from 27 in the second week and $149,000 from 27 in the fifth ("New York Showcases," *Variety*, March 23, March 30, April 20).

106. Feature Review, *Box Office*, December 13, 1965; Murf, Review, *Variety*, December 8, 1965, 6.

107. Reviews from advert, *Variety*, January 19, 1966, 17; Philip K. Scheuer, *Los Angeles Times*, and Archer Winston, *New York Post*.

108. While it had been common for stars to run production shingles in the silent era—Mary Pickford, Buster Keaton and Charlie Chaplin come to mind—the concept had died out with the rise of the studio system. Orson Welles and Laurence Olivier had acted and directed on *Citizen Kane* (1941) and *Henry V* (1944), respectively. Joan Bennett, Ingrid Bergman and Hedy Lamarr were briefly involved in production in the late 1940s (Hannan, Brian, *When Women Ruled Hollywood*, Baroliant 2020, 209–210.) Marlon Brando's directorial debut *One-Eyed Jacks* (1961) was a disaster. Comedian Jerry Lewis was the most successful of the actor-directors in the 1960s, helming eight films including *The Bellboy* (1960) and *The Nutty Professor* (1963), the latter providing a massive pension fund when it was remade as an Eddie Murphy vehicle.

109. "Fonda on Fonda," *Films and Filming*, February 1963, 8. "I set up my own company for *Twelve Angry Men* for the reason most actors do," said Henry Fonda. "If a picture is profitable, the profits go to a corporation and it pays corporate taxes rather than income taxes. I didn't produce any more films after *Twelve Angry Men* because it didn't take much money and it took three years for me to get my deferred salary back."

110. Douglas acted as producer on only one other picture during the decade—*The Brotherhood* (1968), but through his partnership with Edward Lewis he was involved in films in which he starred, like *Seven Days in May* (1964) and *Cast a Giant Shadow* (1966) as well as films where he took no acting role, such as *Seconds* (1966) starring Rock Hudson and *Grand Prix* (1967), both directed by John Frankenheimer, who had helmed *Seven Days in May*.

111. Initially known as Jodell, it soon changed its name to Salem Productions (Levy, Shawn, *Paul Newman, A Life*, New York: Harmony Books, 2009, 150). By the time of *Cool Hand Luke*, it had folded and Newman was on the point of entering into a partnership with former agent John Foreman—they would work together on *Butch Cassidy and the Sundance Kid* (1969).

112. Lemmon, Jack, "Such Fun to Be Funny," *Films and Filming*, November 1960, 7. Lemmon said, "Having my own company helps in two ways. The reasons I formed a company are purely economic. In other words, on personal income and taxes it wouldn't be possible to have enough money to buy a property; but with a company, being under

less tax, then the company can slowly begin to get money into it that isn't completely taxed."

113. O'Brien, Daniel, *Paul Newman* (London: Faber & Faber, 2004), 129.

114. Bette Davis had been approached for a cameo role as Luke's mother (Levy, *Paul Newman*, 204).

115. The first of four films he would make with Newman, the others being *WUSA* (1970), *Pocket Money* (1972) and *The Drowning Pool* (1975).

116. Mahoney, John, "Rosenberg's Megging on Pic *Cool Hand Luke* Excellent, *Hollywood Reporter*, May 31, 1967; Ebert, Roger, "The Gospel According to *Luke*," a re-review (July 10, 2008) based on his original review and found on www.rogerebert.com; Murf, Review in *Variety*, May 31, 1967. It was chosen as one of the top ten films of the year by the *NY Times*, *NY Post*, *Newsday*, *Saturday Review*, *Chicago Sun-Times*, *Cleveland Press*, *St Louis Post-Dispatch*, *Charlotte News* and *Tulsa Oklahoman* ("Year-End Best Picture Pick," *Variety*, January 10, 1968.)

117. "All-Time Rentals," *Variety*, 1993. Slightly downgraded from original $6.9 million.

118. Henry Denker and Foulton Oursler had collaborated on a 30-minute radio show called *The Greatest Story Ever Told* that started a decade-long run in 1947. Oursler produced a novelization in 1949. The rights were sold to Twentieth Century-Fox for $110,000. ("Denker, Original Author, Feared Crisis Now Facing *Greatest Story*," *Variety*, Jun 29, 1960, 4). Fox had sold the rights to UA in 1961 for $1.18 million ("Profit Horizon on *Greatest Story*," *Variety*, Oct 28, 1964, 5).

119. As well as drawing on various episodes such as *Samson and Delilah* (1949) and *The Ten Commandments* (1956), aspects of the Bible had supplied material for books like Henryk Sienkiewicz's *Quo Vadis* (filmed in 1951 by MGM), Lloyd C. Douglas's bestseller *The Robe* (Twentieth Century-Fox's first Cinemascope venture in 1953) and General Lew Wallace's *A Tale of Christ,* filmed as *Ben-Hur* by MGM in 1959.

120. He had also been nominated as Best Director for *The More the Merrier* (1943), *Shane* (1953) and *The Diary of Anne Frank* (1959).

121. Only the original cut approached that length. The most commonly shown version is around the three-hour mark.

122. It was his penultimate picture. Twentieth Century-Fox handed him a $10 million budget for *The Only Game in Town* (1970) starring Elizabeth Taylor and Warren Beatty.

123. This proved a breakthrough for von Sydow, who would later command one of the leading roles in *Hawaii* (1966) and go on to have a long Hollywood career.

124. The German Emil Jannings and Hungarian pair Peter Lorre and Paul Lukas were less significant box office attractions.

125. Cook, Peter, "The Greatest Story Ever Told" article in "Roadshow Epics of the '60s," *Cinema Retro Special Edition*, 57.

126. Stang, Joanne, "*The Greatest Story* in One Man's View," *New York Times*, 14 February 1965.

127. These two quotes are taken from an advertisement placed by UA in *Variety* (Mar 3, 1965, 16) so you would expect the reviews to be favourable.

128. Land, Review, *Variety*, February 17, 1965, 6.

129. *Tribune* and *NY Times* reviews taken from review round-up in "N.Y. News Four-Stars *Greatest Story*; Cameo Star Angle Widely Panned," *Variety*, February 17, 1965, 7.

130. "All-Time Rentals," *Variety*, 1993. Slightly downgraded from original $7 million.

131. Uncredited, Hawks also hired Frank and Tom Waldman to work on the movie separately from Brackett (McCarthy, Todd, *Howard Hawks: The Grey Fox of Hollywood*, New York: Grove Press, 572).

132. At a time when foreign directors—Bergman, Fellini, Godard etc.—were all the vogue, Andrew Sarris, Eugene Archer and future director Peter Bogdanovich persuaded the New Yorker cinema in New York to run a two-week series in January 1961 called "The Forgotten Film." Of the 28 films featured, 11 were by Hawks. The following year Bogdanovich persuaded the Museum of Modern Art in New York to launch a three-month Hawks retrospective. Paramount, with *Hatari!* coming up, paid for it. Bogdanovich produced an influential monograph *The Cinema of Howard Hawks* and Sarris contributed a two-part article to the British *Films & Filming* magazine, these combined activities cementing Hawks reputation as a leading auteur. (McCarthy, *Howard Hawks*, 592–593), In 1968 Robin Wood wrote the seminal critical biography *Howard Hawks*, London: Secker and Warburg/BFI, 1968. One curiosity was that where John Ford, of equal interest to the new wave critics, had been acclaimed by his peers with four Oscars and two nominations, Hawks had but one Best Director nomination.

133. McCarthy, *Howard Hawks*, 574–576.

134. Martinelli was a well-known model for the Eileen Ford agency and had appeared three times in *Life* magazine. (Schaefli, Roland, "*Cinema Retro* Interviews Elsa Martinelli," www.cinemaretro.com).

135. MacAdam, Henry and Cooper, Duncan, *The Gladiators vs. Spartacus, Dueling Productions in Blacklist Hollywood, Vol. 1* (Cambridge Scholars, 2021) 35–36. Martinelli was due to co-star in a Douglas production, being prepped by Lewis Milestone, called *Queen Kelly*.

136. Martinelli believed her career had been held back because she was tall and skinny rather than statuesque as were so many of her compatriots. "When I started in Italy, it was quite difficult for me to get roles. It was five years ago, the time of very bosomy girls…Now it's changed. If people like the picture, they'll like the girl." However, she exempted Loren and Lollobrigida from criticism. ("Elsa Martinelli Can't See Italian Actresses for Their Big Bosoms," *Variety*, May 23, 1962, 1).

137. Shaefli, "*Cinema Retro* Interviews."

Notes—The Films

138. "You can't sit in an office and write what a rhino or any other animal is going to do," said Hawks, explaining that much of the picture was improvised day to day. ("In Own Program Notes," *Variety*, August 22, 1962, 12.)

139. Eyman, Scott, *John Wayne: The Life and Legend* (New York: Simon & Schuster, 2015) 352.

140. "Wholesome Back in Fashion?" *Variety*, May 23, 1962, 5.

141. Crowther, Bosley, "*Hatari* Captures the Drama of Tanganyika Wildlife," *New York Times*, July 12, 1962; Tube, Review, *Variety*, May 23, 1962, 5; Cutts, John *Films and Filming*, January 1963, 46.

142. Hilliers, *Cahiers du Cinéma Vol 2*, 328–334—this was the highest ranking any American picture achieved during the entire decade.

143. In *Howard Hawks* (593) Todd McCarthy claimed that *Hatari!* only made $4.3 million in domestic rentals without specifying where he came by this information. Generally speaking, studios did not lie to *Variety* about overall rentals, in part because the principals often received their percentage based on rentals rather than gross, so inflating such amounts put them needlessly in debt to stars or directors, in part because the magazine had a firm grasp of the essentials of release—and had called out Twentieth Century-Fox, for example, over inflating rentals for *Can Can* (1960) and would often revise figures in its all-time box office chart—and in part because there was an unspoken accord between studio and magazine. So I trusted *Variety* in this instance and the amount was not downgraded in later reports as had been the fate of other big pictures.

144. Field, Matthew, "Fantasmagorical: The Making of *Chitty Chitty Bang Bang*" (*Cinema Retro*, Vol. 5 Issue 13, 27). Field credited this tale to an interview of the usually reticent Hughes by Cliff Carson in *SPFX* magazine in 1998.

145. Field, "Fantasmagorical," 28. Field attributed the Hill angle to the book *Saucy Boy: The Revealing story of Benny Hill* by Leonard Hill (London: Grafton, 1990).

146. Field, "Fantasmagorical," 28.

147. *Ibid.*, 29.

148. *Ibid.*

149. *Ibid.*, 31.

150. "Feature Reviews," *Box Office*, December 9, 1968; "Chug-Chug, Mug-Mug," *Time*, December 27, 1968; Adler, Renata, "*Chitty Chitty Bang Bang*, Fast Friendly Musical for Children, Bows," *New York Times*, December 19, 1968; Ebert, Roger, Review, *Chicago Sun-Times*, December 24, 1968.

151. "All-Time Rentals," *Variety*, 1993. Originally showing as $7.5 million for the 1960s it was downgraded to $7 million.

152. Disney movies were slotted into tiny release windows around holiday periods. Its films attracted larger audiences at matinees at reduced prices for children than in evening shows at normal prices.

153. "Secret Fear of Family Films," *Variety*, February 24, 1960, 3. "Most theater-men are secretly afraid of these entries especially if they are of the sort that will not attract adults during evening hours."

154. Crisp, Donald, "We Lost So Much Dignity as We Came of Age," *Films and Filming*, December 1960, 7. The Scots actor was aged 79 at this point and had appeared in 419 silent and sound pictures "The first we made were mutascopes, where you put a penny in the slot and turned a handle. My first one of these was *The New French Maids*," he recalled. "The full Biograph films of that period were only 800ft long and perhaps you had two or three hundred hours to make the whole thing." He was with the original Biograph company when it started with D.W. Griffith. "We were both actors at that time, there was no such thing as a director them. The director was merely a man that shouted the instructions to you through a megaphone, almost someone bawling what to do." Of *Birth of a Nation* (1915), he said, "We used to work on it for a while and then go back and make the other little pictures in between."

155. *Pollyanna* was probably the best example of Disney's unique casting approach. Although Hayley Mills was the star she was supported by one of the biggest contingent of Oscar winners and nominees, some of whom still had or were remembered as having considerable box office pedigree. Jane Wyman had won the Oscar for *Johnny Belinda* (1948) and been nominated another three times; Karl Malden had achieved fame as Best Supporting Actor in *A Streetcar Named Desire* (1951) and another nomination for *On the Waterfront* (1954). Three-time Oscar nominee Agnes Moorehead had appeared in *The Magnificent Ambersons* (1942), Frenchman Adolphe Menjou had been nominated for *The Front Page* (1931) during a decade when he was a big box office attraction, and silent film star and director Donald Crisp was an Oscar-winner for *How Green Was My Valley* (1942). There could not have been a more obvious marketing ploy than employing actors who went back three or four generations who would be remembered not just by parents but grandparents. Crisp also starred in *Greyfriars Bobby*.

156. Hannan, Brian, *When Women Ruled Hollywood* (Glasgow: Baroliant Press, 2019), 200–202,

157. She was the female lead opposite William Holden in *Union Station* (1950), *Submarine Command* (1951) and *Force of Arms* (1951) and John Wayne in *Big Jim McLain* (1952).

158. Crowther, Bosley, "Reinflation," *New York Times*, February 9, 1963; Review, *Variety*, January 16, 1962, 6; "Feature Reviews," *Box Office*, January 21, 1963.

159. "All-Time Rentals," *Variety* 1993.

160. In a few theaters in Los Angeles to qualify for Oscar consideration.

161. Respectively written by A.J. Cronin, Marjorie Kinnan Rawlings, Laura Z. Hobson, C.S. Forester, Ernest Hemingway, Mark Twain, H.E. Bates, Sloan Wilson and Herman Melville.

162. Written respectively by Brigadier-General

S.L.A. Marshall, Sheilah Graham, Nevil Shute, Alistair MacLean, and John D. MacDonald.

163. Fishgall, Gary, *Gregory Peck: A Biography* (New York: Scribner, 2002) 234–235.

164. Tube, Review, *Variety*, December 12, 1962; Sarris, Andrew, "A Negro Is Not a Mockingbird," *Village Voice*, March 7, 1963; Ebert, Roger, Review, *Chicago Sun-Times*, retrieved November 11, 2001 on www.rogerebert.com; "Feature Reviews," *Box Office*, December 17, 1962.

165. Farber, Manny, *Movies* (New York: Stonehill Publishing, 1971) 151.

166. "All-time Rentals," *Variety*, 1993. Slightly downgraded from original $7.2 million.

167. Based on the Len Deighton bestseller featuring an anonymous hero. It was the film that christened him Harry Palmer. There would be two more in the series starring Michael Caine.

168. The television pilot was turned into *To Trap a Spy* (1964) and two episodes were edited to make *The Spy with My Face* (1965).

169. Solomon, Aubrey, Twentieth Century-Fox, *A Corporate and Financial History* (Lanham and London: Scarecrow Press, 1998), Appendix B, Production Costs, 254. *Modesty Blaise* only returned rentals of $2 million and *Batman* $1.8 million (Appendix A, Domestic Rentals, 230).

170. "Unfair" was attributed to Agents 004 and 005, "mucho sexy" to Fidel Castro; "competition!" to the director of the C.I.A.—these spoof quotes ran in the advert, "Introducing *Our Man Flint* for January," *Box Office*, January 17, 1966

171. Whit, *Variety*, January 12, 1966, 6; Crowther, Bosley, "Inferior Burlesque of Bond," *New York Times*, January 26, 1966; Feature Reviews, *Box Office*, January 10, 1966.

172. Biskind, Peter, *Easy Riders, Raging Bulls* (London: Simon & Schuster, 1998; quotes from Bloomsbury paperback edition, 2007) 68. Southern claimed he wrote the entire script. He also said Fonda and Hopper wanted a completely different ending to the one he wrote—which was filmed.

173. Biskind, *Easy Riders*, 74. The initial budget was projected at $360,000 (Biskind, *Easy* Riders, 61).

174. AIP was the initial potential backer (Biskind, *Easy* Riders, 61)

175. When told about the new film by Jane Fonda, Bruce Dern, who had made 11 biker movies, told her, "It's over for biker movies" (Biskind, *Easy Riders*, 73).

176. This was a version of wide release, not the 3,000–4,000 theaters these days that would book a picture on its first week but either a sequential wide release, prints of the movie moving from region to region over a period of weeks, or a nationwide release with upwards of 500 prints in circulation. This kind of movie did not normally take up residence in a major city center theater but would go out directly to a circuit or play simultaneously in a number of neighborhood theaters in one area, so the picture would have a freshness of release not attached to that category of distribution.

177. MacDougal, Dennis, *Five Easy Decades* (New Jersey: John Wiley, 2008), 104. True to their rebellious natures, stars Peter Fonda and Dennis Hopper courted controversy by turning up for official evening functions in war uniforms.

178. "*If...*Big Winner at Cannes," *International Motion Picture Exhibitor*, May 28, 1969, 2. In a 500-word op-ed piece the magazine congratulated the winner of the top award. At the very bottom of the article mention was made of the other winners, of which there were six; *Easy Rider* was not mentioned until the final three lines. So, in a sense, giving praise where praise was truly due and not responding to hype. (The "international" in the magazine title was a device to expand interest in the magazine—the bulk of the coverage concerned the American film industry).

179. Advertisements tended to blur the distinction as to what Cannes prize it had actually won, the film being generally promoted as "Cannes Prize Winner."

180. "The management of the Beekman had never seen people like this on the East Side. They were sitting on the sidewalk, no shoes. They had to take the doors off in the men's room because people were in there smoking pot" (Biskind, *Easy Riders*, 73–74).

181. The trick was to find a theater where you could break the box office record, thus giving producers something to market, running advertisements extolling its success in the trade press and exhorting journalists to take the bait and write about another little picture that defied the odds. So producers targeted theaters with low seating capacities on the grounds that it would be easier for a film even with a moderate appeal to generate queues and break an existing record. Then the picture would sit in one or two locations for several weeks or months, allowing word-of-mouth and critical response to build, before attempting to reach a wider marketplace.

182. Advertisements: *Variety*, July 16, 1969, 20; *Box Office*, August 4, 1969. It opened with $40,422.

183. Advertisement, *Variety*, August 6, 1969, 23; "*Easy Rider* Smashes Record in L.A. Area Run," *Box Office*, September 22, 1969; "*Easy Rider* Breaks Two House Records," *Box Office*, October 6, 1969.

184. Fonda and Hopper each had an 11 percent share of profits (Biskind, *Easy* Riders, 62).

185. Advert, "Film buffs," *International Motion Picture Exhibitor*, May 7, 1969, 15. Paramount repeated an advert in the trade magazine that had run in the *New York Times* on Sunday, April 27, 1969. Showing a photo of two young people and headlined "Film buffs," the text ran as follows: "Young people and thousands like them are doing their movie thing. They are all seeing three motion pictures that have made their world more meaningful. And many are seeing these films again and again. *Goodbye, Columbus, Romeo and Juliet* and *If...* express everything that young people feel strongly about...like life and the establishment. You should see them, too, if you want to see the great change that is happening."

186. "Feature Reviews," *Box Office*, July 21, 1969; Elsa, Review, *International Motion Picture Exhibitor*, July 9, 1969, 6; other reviews culled from advertisement in *Variety* (July 23, 1969, 10).

187. "All-Time Rentals," *Variety*, 1993; Hannan, *Coming Back*, 232. *Easy* Rider made the bulk of its earnings in the 1970s, which included a reissue in 1972. Lifetime rentals totalled $19.1 million.

188. Original budget of $3 million soon soared to $5 million.

189. It was launched in that format at the Sutton theater in New York, and although that served as a useful marketing tool the public showed little appetite for it as a roadshow and it was quickly rolled out in general release. Length (just over 150 minutes) was one factor in the roadshow launch, the other being the success of previous aviation adventure *Those Magnificent Men in Their Flying Machines* (1965).

190. Murphy, Arthur D., Review, *Variety*, June 22, 1966, 6; Scheuer, Philip L. "Aerial Dogfighters, Ursula Fly High in *Blue Max*," *Los Angeles Times*, June 29, 1966; Coe, Richard L., Review, *Washington Post*, July 1, 1966; Eyles, Allen, *Films and Filming*, September 1966, 8.

191. "All-Time Rentals," *Variety*, 1993. Downgraded from the original $8.4 million. Although Solomon (*Twentieth Century-Fox*, 230) also gives the rentals as $8.4 million, that book was written in 1988 before this revision.

192. Hannan, Brian, *The Gunslingers of '69: Western Movies' Greatest Year* (Jefferson, NC: McFarland, 2019), 17–20. As a consequence of the Consent Decree of 1948, studios had been banned from acting as exhibitors. A natural consequence of this, you would have thought, was that exhibitors were prevented from entering the movie-making business. But that turned out not to be the case for in the early 1960s there was such a dearth of new movies that the government was inclined to encourage rather than place limitations on anybody who could throw hard-pressed exhibitors a lifeline. First into the field was National General which had 217 theaters. By 1968 it was making films of the caliber of western *The Stalking Moon* starring Gregory Peck. Assuming barriers to production had been effectively lifted, CBS Television set up a movie-making arm called Cinema Center and ABC Television set up Cinerama Releasing Corporation.

193. Goldman had written the screenplay for *Masquerade* (1965) which had starred Robertson.

194. Pfeiffer, Lee, "Candidly Cliff," *Cinema Retro*, Vol. 2, Issue 4, 22. Goldman maintained he had been unfairly fired, but Robertson saw it as an amicable parting of the ways. Goldman was paid $30,000.

195. *Ibid.*

196. *Ibid.* Interestingly, at a time when the auteur theory was riding high and every director under the sun was receiving the possessive credit, Robertson turned down Nelson's request for one. "I don't think it's anybody's *Charly* except maybe mine," said Robertson.

197. *Ibid.*

198. *Ibid.*, 23. So low were his prospects that Robertson did not attend the ceremony. He was filming *Too Late the Hero* (1970) in the jungle near Manila. Imelda Marco was so impressed at having such a famous movie star in the country that she threw a big party in his honour. There was a Hollywood backlash against his award, believing he had won because of the campaign for his award rather than for the performance itself. Robertson tried to set up a sequel but without success.

199. "Medical Menace," *Time*, October 18, 1968; Canby, Vincent, "Cliff Robertson in Title Role of *Charly*," *New York Times*, September 24, 1968; Rapf, Maurice, "Is *Charly* Cuter than Necessary?" *Life*, November 1, 1968; Ebert, Roger, Review, *Chicago Sun-Times*, December 31, 1968.

200. "All-time Rentals," *Variety*, 1993. Downgraded from original $8 million.

201. The leading lady in the other films in the series would be as well-known as Stella Stevens, Ann-Margret in *Murderer's Row* (1966), Senta Berger in *The Ambushers* (1967) and Elke Sommer in *The Wrecking Crew* (1968).

202. Both *Our Man Flint* and *The Silencers* were released within a couple of months of Bond juggernaut *Thunderball* (1965). Both series also benefitted from the 19-month gap between *Thunderball* and *You Only Live Twice*. In between the Bonds came *Murderer's Row* in December 1966 and *In Like Flint* in March 1967.

203. Whit, Review, *Variety*, February 9, 1966, 6; "Dean Martin and (Shapely) Company Arrive in *The Silencers*," *New York Times*, March 17, 1966; "Feature Reviews," *Box Office*, February 14, 1966.

204. Taking *Ben-Hur* as the starting point of the roadshow boom only 15 more movies had appeared in this format excluding those which used this distribution device as an arthouse exhibition ploy such as *La Dolce Vita*.

205. As production was given the greenlight, the movie faced the prospect of competition from a potential rival *The Mutineers* to be directed by James Clavell. (Pfeiffer, Lee, and Worrall, Dave, *Mutiny on the Bounty*, "Roadshow Epics of the '60s," *Cinema Retro* Special Edition, 10.)

206. Kanfer, Stefan, *Somebody: The Reckless Life and Career of Marlon Brando* (New York: Alfred A. Knopf, 2008; quotes from British paperback, Faber & Faber, 2011), 169–170.

207. *Ibid.*, 171.

208. *Ibid.*, 173. Borden Chase, William Driscoll and Howard Clewes were among the others involved (Schumach, Murray, "Hollywood at Sea, Director Blames a Timorous Management for Tumultuous Saga," *New York Times*, March 25, 1962). There was also input from the producer and MGM bosses Sol Siegel and Joseph Vogel (Higham, *Brando: An Unauthorized Biography*, 193).

209. Unlike Paul Newman on *Exodus*, Brando's suggestions found their way into the script (Cook, *Cinema Retro*, 12).

210. Peter Finch had been first choice (Hopper,

Hedda, "*Restless Night* Set for Niven," *Los Angeles Times*, July 1, 1960, 24.

211. *Ibid.* Firing Reed cost MGM $250,000 (Pfeiffer and Worrall, *Cinema Retro*, 12).

212. *Ibid.*, 176. George Seaton also shot a few scenes uncredited.

213. Cook, Peter, "Recreating the Bounty," *Cinema Retro* Special Edition, 13.

214. Below deck scenes—and those above deck considered too difficult to shoot on the ship—were filmed at MGM studios in Culver City. Portsmouth Harbor was built on Lot 3 of the huge backlot. MGM adapted an existing set known as Dutch Street with cobblestones, a bridge and harbor walls to resemble an English port. For this scene a replica ship was used. (Pfeiffer and Worrall, *Cinema Retro* Special Edition, 12)

215. Pfeiffer and Worrall, *Cinema Retro*, 12.

216. Kanfer, *Somebody*, 172. Five thousand temporary dentures were flown over for the local women hired as extras whose teeth were stained brown from chewing betel nuts.

217. Kanfer, *Somebody*, 174–175.

218. Coe, Richard L, "*Bounty* Sets Freudian Sail," *Washington Post*, November 21, 1962; Review, *Variety*, November 14, 1962, 6; Crowther, Bosley, "New Version of *Mutiny on the Bounty* Seen at Loew's State," *New York Times*, November 9, 1962, 31.

219. "All-Time Rentals," *Variety*, 1993. Downgraded from the original $9.8 million, this was one of the biggest differences between the original rentals announced and later reassessment.

220. Pfeiffer, Lee, "The World of Nancy Kwan," *Cinema Retro*, Vol. 10, Issue 29, 39. First choice director Jean Negulesco (*Three Coins in the Fountain*, 1954) was fired.

221. Holden, William, "I'm Old-Fashioned—and This is Why," *Films and Filming*, January 1961, 37- 39. "It's the new-fashioned thing to break away from the large studios, to form one's own production company and be one's own boss, complete with artistic freedom and potential profits. While I don't want to become my own boss, equally I don't want to be bossed by other people...This was the cause of my trial-by-strength with Paramount. They lent me out to do films of my own choosing...*Love Is a Many Splendored Thing* at Fox, *Kwai* at Columbia. Then after I had done *The Key*, they wanted to put me in a film which I knew was not right...So I dug in my heels...A legal battle was waged. And I won...Paramount and I remain good friends, but from now until my contract expires in 1964 I pick the films."

222. Brando had received $1 million for *The Fugitive Kind* (1959). Holden and John Wayne were joint-second, both receiving $750,000 for *The Horse Soldiers* (1959).

223. Pfeiffer, "The World of Nancy Kwan," *Cinema Retro*, 39. Kwan had screen-tested for the role but it was given to Nuyen. When that did not work out, she was summoned from America, where she was acting in a touring Broadway show.

224. In Mason's book, the hero is younger, but in the film made closer to Holden's real age of 41.

225. Hayakawa, Sessue, "Nazis and Japs," *Films and Filming*, February 1962, 21, 45. In his autobiography *Zen Showed Me the Way* (London: George Allen and Unwin, 1960) he explained how after the Second World War he made *Tokyo Joe* (1949) with Bogart and *Three Came Home* (1950) with Claudette Colbert and initially turned down *Bridge on the River Kwai* (1957) for the same reason as co-star Alec Guinness—it was not interesting enough.

226. The Hays Code had an anti-miscegenation policy which prevented Wong playing the wife of Paul Muni in *The Good Earth* (1935) but she became the first Chinese American actress to star in a television series *The Gallery of Madame Liu-Tsong* which premiered in 1951.

227. Nancy Kwan was just outside the top 20 in a poll to find "The All-American Favorites of '61," (*Box Office*, Mar 26, 1962) and was among the top dozen "Most Popular Young Players of '62," (*Box Office*, April 16, 1963, 46–47).

228. She won the Golden Globe for Most Promising Newcomer for *The World of Suzie Wong* and was nominated for a Golden Globe in the Drama category for the same film.

229. Tube, Review, *Variety*, November 16, 1960, 6; others culled from an advertisement in *Variety*, November 16, 1960, 18–19.

230. It is worth pointing out that although all these foreign pictures entered America under the guise of arthouse pictures, they had actually been huge box office hits in their country of origin—which would not have occurred had their release been confined to arthouses. *La Dolce Vita* had been the year's top film in Italy, outgrossing *Some Like It Hot*, *Rio Bravo* and *North by Northwest* ("Probable Top Earners, All Sources, 1959–60, in Italian Playoff," *Variety*, April 20, 1960, 65).

231. Fellini, Federico, "The Bitter Life—Of Money," *Films and Filming*, January 1961, 13, 38 "I had to try fifteen producers before I found one willing to make *La Strada*. After *Cabiria* and a second Oscar, I still had difficulty finding a producer for *La Dolce Vita*." Nor did he profit from the success of *La Dolce Vita*. "I didn't have a percentage on the profits it is making all over the world. And my salary went to pay back the producer who had first backed the film but wanted an American actor to play Marcello! My new company, Federiz, might be called a gift, or bonus, from Angelo Rizzoli who put up the money for *La Dolce Vita*." He added, "In Italy nobody quite understands how I can refuse the fabulous sums that are offered me...I had turned down a quarter of a million dollars offered me by an American company to make a film about horses with an Italian star."

232. "Sweet Life: Road Show If," *Variety*, January 25, 1961, 5. So many rumors had swirled around regarding the rights that the makers took out a full-page ad in *Variety* (December 14, 1960, 12) to announce that nobody had yet secured a deal.

233. "Legion Decides Shocks Are Moral in *Dolce Vita*," *Variety*, May 17, 1961, 5.

234. Lane, John Francis, "La (The) Dolce (Sweet) Vita (Life)," *Films and Filming*, June 1961, 30. Lane dubbed this film and explained the process and its importance to Italian filmmaking. "Certainly it is the first time that such an enormous amount of time, care and money has been devoted to an English-language version of a film that has already been a box-office success in its own country." He said it was a "creative rather than a mechanical operation...in other aspects *La Dolce Vita* was an ideal film to dub into English. Some of the original dialog on the original soundtrack was already in English anyway; so the voice of Anita Ekberg, Lex Barker and other characters in the film star episode are from the original sound track." "He added, "All Italian films are dubbed. In the case of a director such as Fellini, half the creative work is done post-synchronization. The actors give their performances in the dubbing theater not in front of the cameras."

235. Advertisement, *Variety*, March 22, 1961, 10.

236. Hawk, Review, *Variety*, February 17, 1960, 6; Ebert was too young to review this on its first appearance so this review is dated January 5, 1997 (www.rogerebert.com).

237. These three adverts were re-used to support the promotional material for the "uncut" reissue (Pressbook).

238. Hilliers, *Cahiers du Cinéma Vol. 2*, 328–334.

239. "All-Time Rentals," *Variety*, 1993. Later reissue carried it to $8 million

240. Hannan, Brian, *The Making of Butterfield 8* (Glasgow: Baroliant Press, 2016) 4. Taylor thought she would be playing "little more than a prostitute" (Mann, *How to Be a Movie Star*, 274).

241. "It's a terrible thing they are doing to me. They have the power to keep me off the screen for the next two years unless I do *Butterfield 8*," complained Taylor. (Hannan, *Making of*, 5).

242. Reid, John Howard, "Portraying Life with Dignity," *Films and Filming*, March 1962, 19–20, 44. In this analysis of the work of Daniel Mann—and an article of this length in a prestigious magazine indicated that the director was highly regarded—Reid argued, "BUtterfield 8 is essentially a cameraman's film. Charles Harten assisted Joe Ruttenberg to obtain some brilliant deep-focus effects and imbued many of the night-time scenes with a dazzling array of flickering color and iridescent neon. For the most part, Mann is content to aid this photographic display by shooting static or unobtrusive angles."

243. Taylor and Fisher went on holiday, but Laurence Harvey was broke because of the limitations imposed by the British government on the amount of money that could be taken into the country. (Hannan, *Making of*, 9–10)

244. Hannan, *Making of*, 17.

245. Crowther, Bosley, "Elizabeth Taylor at *Butterfield 8*," *New York Times*, November 17, 1960;

Scott, John L., "Taylor Role Torrid in *Butterfield 8*," *Los Angeles Times*, November 4, 1968; Coe, Richard L., "*Butterfield 8* Made for Liz," *Washington Post*, November 10, 1960.

246. "All-Time Rentals," *Variety*, 1993. Downgraded from original $8.2 million.

247. On the back of *Who's Afraid of Virginia Woolf* (1966), *BUtterfield 8* was reissued in 1966 in a double bill with *Cat on a Hot Tin Roof*.

248. *Vogue* and *Newsweek* quotes from advertisement, *Variety*, Oct 26, 1966, 11.

249. Eyles, Allen, Review, *Films and Filming*, November 1966, 16–18; McVeigh, Linda G., Review, *The Harvard Crimson*, November 30, 1966.

250. When starting he had made an occasional comedy like *Here Come the Nelsons* (1950) and *Has Anybody Seen My Gal?* (1952) but it was not a genre he was known for.

251. Gill, Brendan, Review, *New Yorker*, February 24, 1962, 110; Crowther, Bosley, "*Lover Come Back* Opens at Music Hall," *New York Times*, February 9, 1962, 21; Scheuer, Philip K., "*Lover Come Back* Brisk, Gay Farce," *Los Angeles Times*, December 25, 1961; Coe, Richard L., "A Lovely Spoof of the Ad Man," *Washington Post*, February 16, 1962.

252. "All-Time Rentals," *Variety*, 1993. Downgraded from original $8.5 million.

253. Kaplan, James, *Sinatra: The Chairman* (New York: First Anchor Books, 2016) 599.

254. Hopper, Hedda, "*Von Ryan's Express* Will Star Sinatra, Robson to Produce War Story," *Los Angeles Times*, April 16, 1964.

255. Pfeiffer, Lee, "*Von Ryan's Express*" in "World War II Movies of the Sixties," *Cinema Retro* Special Edition, 40.

256. *Ibid.*, 37.

257. Kaplan, *Sinatra*, 600.

258. Pfeiffer, *Cinema Retro* Special Edition, 41.

259. *Ibid.*, 37.

260. Kaplan, *Sinatra*, 600–601.

261. *Ibid.* 605–606

262. *Ibid.*, 601.

263. Pfeiffer, *Cinema Retro* Special Edition, 40.

264. Solomon, *Twentieth Century–Fox*, Appendix B: Production Costs, 254.

265. *Variety*, Review, May 19, 1965, 6; Gow, Gordon, *Films and Filming*, August 1965, 24; Feature Reviews, *Box Office*, May 31, 1965.

266. Munn, Michael, *James Stewart: The Truth Behind the Legend* (London: Robson Books, 2005), 260.

267. First performed in 1974 at the Goodspeed Opera House in East Haddam, Connecticut, it transferred the following year to the Alvin Theatre in Broadway where it logged up 1,050 performances, closing in 1977. It was nominated for six Tony awards including Best Musical.

268. Sullivan, Leo, "*Shenandoah* Abets a Welcome Trend," *Washington Post*, July 29, 1965; Howard Thomson, "Civil War Drama," *New York Times*, July 29, 1965; Scheuer, Philip K., "*Shenandoah*, Full of Homely Virtues," *Los Angeles Times*, July 22, 1965; Review, *Variety*, April 14, 1965, 6.

269. Shlyen, Ben, "Disney Points the Way," *Box Office*, November 22, 1965, 2. "While other filmmakers and many exhibitors have shunned so-called 'family' pictures because they were not doing any business, Walt Disney continued making them. In fact, he never made any other kind," wrote Shlyen, "The Disney name has substantial draw in itself...Not every Disney film is an outstanding success, but few are failures."

270. Pfeiffer, Lee, "The World of Nancy Kwan," *Cinema Retro*, 41. Kwan recalled an idyllic shoot in Hawaii. "I had fun making that...after lunch every day I used to fall asleep on the beach...they would wake me up to do a scene and then I'd go back and fall asleep."

271. Thomson, Howard, "Local Houses Offer a Disney Twin Bill," *New York Times*, July 14, 1966; Kevin Thomas, "*Lt. Crusoe* Fine Family Film Fare," *Los Angeles Times*, Jun 29, 1966; Coe, Richard L. "Van Dyke Is Highly Comic as Downed Pilot," *Washington Post*, June 30, 1966; Davis, Richard, *Films and Filming*, September 1966, 12–1

272. "All-Time Rentals," *Variety*, 1993. A 1970s reissue pushed rentals up to $10 million.

273. Her absence from the screen was mainly due to domestic reasons rather than a sudden fall in popularity.

274. Woodward, Ian, *Audrey Hepburn* (London: W.H. Allen, 1984; revised edition Virgin, 1993) 286.

275. Hannan, Brian, *Coming Back to a Theater Near You: A History of Hollywood Reissues, 1914–2014* (Jefferson, NC: McFarland, 2016), 178.

276. Austin, David, "After Alan Arkin," (*Films and Filming*, November 1967, 4–7). Arkin said, "I feel very embarrassed about it although I'm not sure why, perhaps because I've never played a villain before...I thought it would be fascinating to play a heavy...but I don't want to make a career out of doing heavies, for me I think it's limiting."

277. Robert Redford, George C. Scott and Rod Steiger had been considered for these roles.

278. Woodward, Ian, *Audrey Hepburn*, 286, 289, 291.

279. Crowther, Bosley, "Audrey Hepburn Stars in *Wait Until Dark*," *New York Times*, October 27, 1967; "Return of the Helpless Girl," *Time*, November 3, 1967; Ebert, Roger, Review, *Chicago Sun-Times*, February 26, 1968; Rider, David, Films *and Filming*, November 1966, 8.

280. "All-Time Rentals," *Variety*, 1993. Upgraded from original $7.6 million.

281. Eyman, *John Wayne*, 215–217.

282. *Ibid.*, 309.

283. *Ibid.*, 316.

284. *Ibid.*, 309–310.

285. *Ibid.*, 317. Widmark was paid $200,000 and Harvey $100,000. Wayne deferred his own salary, taking the Directors Guild minimum of $13,000 for his work behind the camera. He was gambling on hefty profits—he would earn 7.5 percent of the gross (*Ibid.*, 319). And towards the end of filming had to add in another $400,000 of his own money to finish the film (*Ibid.*, 329). The 27

stuntmen earned $1,000 a week (*Ibid.*, 323). Composer Dmitri Tiomkin earned $117,000 for writing and recording his mammoth score (*Ibid.*, 332).

286. *Ibid.*, 320.

287. *Ibid.*, 322.

288. *Ibid.*, 330.

289. *Ibid.*, 344.

290. Crowther, Bosley, "John Wayne's 3-Hour Remembrance of *The Alamo*; He Produces and Stars in Film at Rivoli," *New York Times*, October 27, 1960; Tube, Review, *Variety*, October 26, 1960, 6.

291. "All-Time Rentals," *Variety*, 1993. Slightly downgraded from original $8 million. .

292. Crowther, Bosley, "Doris Day vs. Cary Grant: *That Touch of Mink* Seen at Music Hall," *New York Times*, June 15, 1962; Review, *Variety*, May 9, 1962, 6.

293. "All-Time Rentals," *Variety*, 1993. Downgraded from original $8.5 million.

294. Beaupre, Lee, "Rising Skepticism on Stars," *Variety*, May 15, 1968, 1. The last four Curtis films had produced an average $1.77 million at the U.S. box office.

295. He was not top billed in either.

296. Curtis, Tony, with Golenbrook, Peter, *Tony Curtis, American Prince: My Autobiography* (London: Virgin Books, 2008), 269.

297. Dunne, John Gregory, *The Studio* (1969) 23–24.

298. Solomon, *Twentieth Century-Fox*, 255.

299. Although his guilt was doubted at the time, in 2013 DNA connected him to a victim.

300. Ebert, Roger, Review, *Chicago Sun-Times*, October 22, 1968; Adler, Renata, Review, *New York Times*, October 17, 1968.

301. "All-time Rentals," *Variety*, 1993; Solomon, *Twentieth Century-Fox*, 230.

302. It was revived for two weeks at the New York City Center in 1965 and for three weeks in 1980. A production by New York City Opera ran between February and April 1988. Opening on April 27, 2000, it ran for 699 performances at the Neil Simon Theater. A new Broadway revival starring Hugh Jackman, originally set for October 2020, opened in 2022.

303. Crowther, Bosley, "Preston Stars in *Music Man*, Film Version of Stage Comedy," *New York Times*, August 24, 1962; Review, *Variety*, December 31, 1961, 6.

304. Daniel, Douglass K., *Tough as Nails: The Life and Films of Richard Brooks* (Madison: The University of Wisconsin Press, 2011), 164. Cardinale was no more Mexican than several others in the cast. Although considered Italian, she was born in Tunisia. Jack Palance was Ukrainian American, Marie Gomez half-French and half-Spanish.

305. Brooks extensively changed the novel. The opening sequence is all him. There were five mercenaries in the book, he cut it to four and turned one of them into a dynamiter. He added in that the kidnapped woman was Raza's lover (Douglass, *Tough as Nails*, 161–163).

Notes—The Films

306. Douglass, *Tough as Nails,* 161.

307. Buford, Kate, *Burt Lancaster: An American Life* (London: Aurum Press, 2000), 241. He had been a partner in Hill-Hecht-Lancaster and even when it split up left considerable debts which were paid off by United Artists.

308. Lancaster, Burt, "Hollywood Drove Me to a Double Life," *Films and Filming,* January 1962, 10, 35. "The basic reason for an actor getting himself involved in production on his own pictures is not simply a question of ego or any performer believing he can make pictures as good as or better than anyone else. The reason involves questions of career survival and of simple economics... In the thirties and forties..the burden of production rested quite naturally with the studios...After the war...the top-named stars faced some of Hollywood's newer realities, chief among which was the fact that somehow they would have to find productions for themselves." He explained, "The necessity of getting into the business of making pictures, not only for the possible profits, but because of the sheer need to keep busy." He also pointed out that "the independent producer-star has one other factor in his favor which studios could not afford—time ... (On *Elmer Gantry* that involved) "a seven month incubation period for a script..as a producer-star I can afford this luxury. A studio with its tremendous overheads cannot."

309. Lane, John Francis, "C.C.," *Films and Filming,* January 1963, 19–20. "Claudia Cardinale has become a sex symbol without a story ever appearing in a newspaper about her private life. No scandals, no dolce vita, no public boyfriends, not even a fixed fiancé. Not since Garbo has there been such an image of mystery about a star's private life." Her reputation as an actress rather than just a star or sex symbol was indicated by her work with Italy's top two directors, Visconti (*The Leopard,* 1963) and Fellini (8½, 1963). She commented, "I don't mind being sexy but it's not the most important thing." Buford, *Tough as Nails,* 167, 168 explained that the script called for Cardinale "to offer her body" to Lancaster but she refused to do a nude scene and instead was robed in a flesh-coloured strapless top. However, when it came time to film for Marie Gomez's nude scene Brooks cleared the set.

310. Buford, *Tough as Nails,* 165–167.

311. Although filmed in 1964, *A Fistful of Dollars* did not reach the U.S. until 1967, its release stimulated in part by the public's acceptance of the violence in *The Professionals.*

312. Adams, David, *Films and Filming,* July 1967, 25; Crowther, Bosley, "Burt Lancaster in *The Professionals:* Noisy Western Opens at 2 Local Theaters," *New York Times,* November 3, 1966; Murf, Review, *Variety,* November 2, 1966, 6; Feature Reviews, *Box Office,* November 7, 1966.

313. Fujiwara, Chris, The *World and Its Double: The Life and Work of Otto Preminger* (London: Faber & Faber, 2008) 255.

314. O'Brien, *Paul Newman,* 71.

315. Fujiwara, *The World and,* 255.

316. *Ibid.,* 257.

317. O'Brien, *Paul Newman,* 71

318. Levy, *Paul Newman,* 148

319. Fujiwara, *The World and,* 259. Despite Preminger's supposed truculence, Trumbo said, "I had more pleasure working with Otto than anyone in my life."

320. Fujiwara, *The World and,* 260.

321. *Ibid.,* 261–262.

322. Newman started rewriting his part, but Preminger refused to look at what he had written, explaining that, if he accepted the new lines, the actor would come in every day with new material (Levy, *Paul Newman,* 163). Saint more readily accepted the director's right to ignore suggestions from the cast without being upset about it (Fujiwara, *The World and,* 258).

323. Fujiwara, *The World and,* 257.

324. *Ibid.,* 271. This is based on a memo from Arthur Krim in the United Artists files at the Wisconsin Center for Film and Theater Research. However, Tino Balio puts the figure at $4.5 million in his book (*United Artists: The Company That Changed the Film Industry* (Madison: University of Wisconsin Press, 1987) 133.

325. Fujiwara, *The World and,* 257. The profit share was later increased to 85 percent, but in 1962 Preminger sold his share of the profits for a straight $1 million.

326. United Artists made the bulk of its revenue from distribution. Typically, a studio took 30 percent of receipts for distribution. That meant UA would make a good chunk of money whether a film went into profit or not. If the film generated $10 million in rentals, UA would take home a straight $3 million for distribution, plus its original $4.5 million investment. That left $1.25 million once Preminger had his initial slice. Of the remaining $1.25 million, UA took another 25 percent, not to mention income from a television sale. So it was not quite the sweetheart deal it would appear for the director. In addition, UA never did one-off deals. The studio tied directors down to three-picture deals, losses on one picture being offset by profits on others.

327. *Ibid.,* 267.

328. Angeli, Roger, Review, *New Yorker,* December 17, 1960, 136; Coe, Richard L. "Fact Helps Fiction on Current Screen," *Washington Post,* March 5, 1961; Scheuer, Philip K., "*Exodus* Stirring But Uneven Epic," *Los Angeles Times,* December 22, 1960; Crowther, Bosley, "A Long *Exodus,*" *New York Times,* December 16, 1960, 44.

329. Hilliers, *Cahiers du Cinéma Vol. 2,* 329.

330. "All-Time Rentals," *Variety,* 1993. Downgraded from original $8.7 million.

331. Biskind, *Easy Riders,* 25.

332. *Ibid.* Allen wanted $40,000 and dropped his price when offered the part.

333. *Ibid.*

334. Harris, Mark, *Scenes from a Revolution: The Birth of the New Hollywood* (Edinburgh: Canongate Books, 2008) 86.

222   Notes—The Films

335. When Beatty was still on the scene he stipulated that Capucine, girlfriend of producer Feldman, would not be in the picture (*Ibid.*) .

336. *Ibid.*, 26.

337. Sarris Andrew, Review, *Village Voice*, August 5, 1965; Crowther, Bosley, "*What's New Pussycat* Wild Comedy Arrives at Two Theaters," *New York Times*, June 23, 1965; Durgnat, Raymond, *Films and Filming*, October 1965; Schickel, Richard in Byron and Weir, *National Society of Film Critics*, 145.

338. "All-Time Rentals," *Variety*, 1993. Downgraded from original $8.7 million.

339. There was a sequel *Alfie Darling* (1975) with pop star Alan Price in the title role. Jude Law starred in a remake in 2004.

340. Despite a big marketing push by marketing king Joe Levine.

341. He had also lost out on the stage play. Caine, Michael, *What's It All About?: His Autobiography* (London: Century, 1992; reissued Arrow paperback, 2010) 193.

342. Gilbert, Lewis, *All My Flashbacks* (Richmond: Reynolds & Hearn, 2010) 240.

343. *Ibid.*, 242.

344. *Ibid.*, 243–244.

345. Austen, David, "Making It or Breaking It," *Films and Filming*, May 1969, 15–18. Caine said, "What was argued for a long time by the companies, which Lewis and I fought, was to cut the abortion. The rows we had over this, and part of the sequence was cut from the picture anyway because when we showed it to the secretaries five of them fainted." He added, "When it got to the girls who were being done and treated badly and loved and left, un-wined, un-dined, and undone, one realized that practically every girl in the audience was in sympathy with the girls in that position in the film."

346. *Ibid.*, 252.

347. *Ibid.*, 252–253. It was the first film to receive the classification "suggested for mature audiences" which later evolved into the PG.

348. *Ibid.*, 255.

349. Caine, *What's It*, 219.

350. Lewis, *All My*, 255.

351. *Ibid.*, 256. Added Caine, "*Alfie...* had been such a big success that it was going to be put on general release throughout the country—an almost unheard-of event at that time for a small British picture. Not only had that happened but *The Ipcress File*, which was already on show in small art-house-type cinemas, where you would normally see foreign-language films, had been bought by Universal and that was going on general release as well" (Caine, *What's It*, 232). Caine also said: "I never thought of *Alfie* as being anything other than a parochial British movie with no market 'abroad'" (*Ibid.*, 217).

352. All the quotes are taken from the Pressbook. Many European pictures used quotes as the prime means of hooking audiences, but it was unusual for a British film to go down the same route. Some of the adverts in the Pressbook showed only the title character surrounded by quotes, others interspersed the quotes with scenes from the film.

353. In 1950.

354. Signed to British film production company Rank on a standard seven-year contract.

355. Ebert, Roger, *Chicago Sun-Times*, found on www.rogerebert.com; Adler, Renata, "*The Fox* Opens: Lawrence's Novella Is Intelligently Treated," *New York Times*, February 8, 1968; Durgnat, Raymond, *Films and Filming*, July 1968, 34.

356. This has been listed as a 1960s film for the simple reason that it made the vast bulk of its income in 1960 (plus later reissue in that decade). While it opened on December 3, 1959, that was only in one theater—the Radio City Music Hall in New York. It did not open anywhere unless until Xmas Day. According to Universal (Advert, *Variety*, December 30, 1959, 17) it played a total of 24 theaters in the Xmas week. The grosses for 11 of those theaters were covered by the box office reports in *Variety* for that week. Theaters that appeared in *Variety's* box office reports were from the biggest cities so we can assume they delivered the biggest individual results. The four-week gross (*Variety*, December 9, December 16 and, December 23, December 30) at Radio City Music Hall was $783,000. Gross for the other 10 theaters mentioned in *Variety* contributed another $252,000. Assuming the remaining 14 houses were in lesser cities and possibly smaller theaters, I have made a calculation that these would have brought in another $250,000 gross. However, all entrants in this Top 100 are measured by rentals rather than gross. Since studios were desperate to get their product into the Radio City Music Hall, that exhibitor was able to dictate terms so I am assuming that would be a 50/50 split averaged out over the four weeks. That would mean a rental of $391,100. For theaters in the other cities, it would be a different situation. Those theaters would concede ground to the studio in order to get a major movie for Xmas. So I am assuming the studio would be able to negotiate a 70 percent rental share for the opening week. That would mean the total rental for the houses in all the other cities would come to $351,000. So the overall rental made in 1959 amounted to $742,000. The total lifetime rental for *Operation Petticoat* was put at $9.5 million. So I have subtracted the 1959 rental from that figure which accounts for the $8.75 million allocated to the film for the purposes of this book.

357. Curtis, *American Prince*, 218.

358. Grant, Cary, "What it Means to be a Star," *Films and Filming*, July 1961, 12–13 "I've often been called the longest lasting young man about town...It took time to be accepted, almost twenty years until I got to be like a well-advertised brand of tea. Housewives buy that kind rather than take a chance on a brand they are not familiar with. The cinemagoer is the same. He'll see one of my

Notes—The Films

223

pictures because he's pretty sure of getting a certain quality."

359. Morecambe, Gary and Sterling, Martin, *Cary Grant: In Name Only* (London: Robson Books, 2001), xviii; Higham, Charles and Moseley, Roy, *Cary Grant: The Lonely Heart* (New York: Avon Books, 1990), 152. Following his retirement, he joined the board of Faberge and later was a director of MGM.

360. "Grant Asks $8.8 Million for Sale of Films to TV," *Box Office*, August 18, 1969, 4. Companies mentioned here were: Grandstand Co., Grandstand Productions, Granley Co. and Granex Co. Stanley Donen.

361. Powe, Review, *Variety*, September 30, 1959, 6; Crowther, Bosley, "*Operation Petticoat*, Submarine Movie Is at the Musical Hall," *New York Times*, December 4, 1959.

362. "All-Time Rentals," *Variety*, 1993. Adding in the sums taken in December 1959 gave the film a tally of $9.5 million. This included a 1960s reissue.

363. "Person of Promise: Jane Fonda," *Films and Filming*, July 1960, 17. "I thought that a girl who wanted to be happily married should not become an actress," she said.

364. "WB Sues Para re *Barefoot in the Park*, Claims Unfair Inducement," *Variety*, April 24, 1963, 7.

365. "No 1 Playwright," *Variety*, Mar 16, 1966, 1.

366. It ran on Broadway from 1963 to 1967.

367. "No 1 Playwright," *Variety*. He was earning $20,000 a week from royalties from three plays currently showing on Broadway—*Barefoot in the Park*, *The Odd Couple* and *Sweet Charity*.

368. "Pictures," *Variety*, October 27, 1965, 15.

369. On Broadway, he had directed *Mame* and *Half a Sixpence*.

370. Previous films that had begun as stage productions were *Tall Story*, *Period of Adjustment*, *Sunday in New York*, *Any Wednesday* and *La Ronde*.

371. Gill, Brendan, Review, *New Yorker*, June 10, 1967, 72; Sullivan, Leo, "Going *Barefoot in the Park* Is Fun," *Washington Post*, June 16, 1967; Champlin, Charles, "*Barefoot in the Park* Moves to the Screen," *Los Angeles Times*, June 30, 1967; Crowther, Bosley, Review, *New York Times*, May 26, 1957, 51.

372. *Dr. No* had earned $2 million and *From Russia with Love* $4 million.

373. Hannan, Brian, *Coming Back to a Theater Near You: A History of Hollywood Reissues, 1914–2104* (Jefferson, NC: McFarland, 2016) 147–151.

374. On last reissue, in 1961, *Gone with the Wind* had made $6.5 million in rentals. It had made $7 million in 1954, $5 million in 1947 and $4 million in 1941.

375. Hannan, *Coming Back*, 142–147.

376. *Ibid.*, 176.

377. *Ibid.*, 188.

378. *Ibid.*, 188.

379. *Ibid.*, 172.

380. *Ibid.*, 188–189.

381. *Ibid.*, 193–197.

382. *Ibid.*, 197–200.

383. "Once More unto the Breach," *Time*, April 10, 1964; Crowther, Bosley, "James Bond Travels the Orient Express," *New York Times*, April 9, 1964; Roud, Richard, Review, *The Guardian*, October 11, 1963, 11; Farber, Manny, *Movies* (New York: Stonehill Publishing, 1971), 181.

384. "All-Time Rentals," *Variety*, 1993; Hannan, *Coming Back*, 227. Reissue in 1972 bumped the rentals total up to $9.85 million.

385. At that point, the Marvin parts were to be played as rival brothers by Burt Lancaster and Tony Curtis. Natalie Wood would have essayed the Jane Fonda part.

386. Kael, Pauline, Review, *Film Quarterly*, Fall 1965; Coe, Richard L., "*Cat Ballou* Is Zingy Spoof," *Washington Post*, June 24, 1965; Crowther, Bosley, Review, *New York Times*, June 25, 1965, 36; Gow, Gordon, *Films and Filming*, October 1965, 26–27; Crist, Judith in Byron and Weir, *National Society of Film Critics*, 110–111.

387. Originally the script was to be written by Lewis John Carlino ("Frankenheimer's *Grand Prix* in Cinerama," *Box Office*, December 7, 1964, 8).

388. Jarre had won the Oscar for *Doctor Zhivago* and its theme had sold by the millions so for *Grand Prix* MGM put a huge marketing effort behind the original soundtrack album, which was a glossy production number, appearing in a double-fold style with a brochure containing photos of the film and cast (Advert, "Racing Excitement Sets New Sound Track Record," *Variety*, December 21, 1966, 64). The studio undertook some unusual marketing projects, sending, for example, three Formula One racing cars on a nationwide tour ("Cars Go in Tour," *Box Office*, November 21, 1966, b2) and participating in an exhibition at the Museum of Modern Art in New York ("MGM Stills Displayed at Modern Museum," *Box Office*, October 31, 1966).

389. Post-production was undertaken at a record speed, just over seven months from end of production to the world premiere, but meeting the deadline involved hiring nine different editing crews working on two shifts ("Nine Cutting Teams Speed *Grand Prix* to Dec. 21 Preem," *Variety*, November 16, 1966, 7).

390. Cinerama was in dire financial trouble, having made a $17.9 million loss the previous year, and was in the market for a merger. As a result, it was withdrawing from any future financial investment in movies using its process, although now demanding a daily licensing fee from exhibitors using its projection equipment of $250 a day—instead of a five-cents royalty per theater seat—and demanding cash advances plus a ten percent share of rentals from all future movies ("Cinerama Dowry: Tax Loss," *Variety*, July 7, 1965, 9). Oddly enough, MGM was no better off, carrying a debt of $57 million which it expected to pay in three years ("MGM's, Hopefully, Final Loan," *Variety*, September 14, 1966, 3).

391. Pfeiffer Lee, "Film in Focus, *Grand Prix*," *Cinema Retro*, Vol. 2, Issue 4. 28.

392. Both did later make racing movies—Newman in *Winning* (1969) and McQueen with *Le Mans* (1971)

393. "Sturges-McQueen Gas Up in Europe for *Champion*," *Variety*, June 23, 1965, 24. They were shooting racing footage for *Day of the Champion* at Nuremberg on August 1, 1965. The movie itself was scheduled for 1966. The footage they shot became the subject of a lawsuit when MGM tried to prevent its use ("Sturges Recovers Film Footage of *Grand Prix* Tied Up by Frankenheimer," *Variety*, February 9, 1966, 4) although the film was ultimately postponed altogether.

394. "Frankenheimer Talks Up His Next One," *Variety*, November 3, 1965, 19.

395. "MGM Productions Showcase New Talent," *Box Office*, December 5, 1966, 12–13.

396. Mifune earned his highest-ever fee for the film and at the time had been set for another two big blockbusters, both of which failed to get off the ground, *The Day Custer Fell* and *Will Adams* ("Toshiro Mifune Wonders," *Variety*, October 5, 1966, 14).

397. After *Grand Prix*, like Paul Newman and Jack Lemmon before him, he planned to move into the production business to help develop his career ("James Garner Moves from Actor Towards Production Status," *Variety*, October 5, 1966, 5).

398. This had some followers. Robin Bean gave it a three-star review (the magazine's highest accolade and rarely awarded)—"first time I've come out of a cinema numb and, just…frightened." (*Films and Filming*, January 1967, 28–29).

399. The producers tied down all the European racing circuits—including Monte Carlo, Monza and Brands Hatch—in a two-year deal permitting filming of any of the racetracks ("MGM to Finance, Handle, *Grand Prix* in Cinerama," *Box Office*, September 27, 1965, 16). Frankenheimer also staged his own race at Claremont-Ferrand in France (Pfeiffer, *Cinema Retro*, 28).

400. Pfeiffer, *Cinema Retro*, 32. A 200mph Ford GT 40 and the Cobra were rigged with cameras to film the action at top speed. A device called a 'spinner' was used to film stars behind the wheel to make it look as though the car was going out of control

401. The cameras comprised handheld and 18 Panavision cameras as well as, in Monaco, one rigged up in a low-flying helicopter to film the entire race (Advert, *Variety*, June 1, 1966, 16). A dozen cameras were connected by a new electronic system that the director could easily control while shooting race footage ("Electronic Rig Controls 12 Cameras Shooting Races for *Grand Prix*," April 13, 1966, 7).

402. "Feature Review," *Box Office*, January 9, 1967, 12; Review, *Variety*, December 28, 1966, 6; Sullivan, Leon, "*Grand Prix* Is Exciting Spectacle," *Washington Post*, May 25, 1967; Scheuer, Philip K., "*Grand Prix* in Driver's Seat," *Los Angeles Times*, December 23, 1966.

403. "All-Time Rentals," *Variety*, 1993. Upgraded from original $9.1 million to $9.5 million.

404. Janssen and co-star Jim Hutton were opposed to the Vietnam War as was George Takei (*Star Trek* television series) who played a South Vietnamese officer (Eyman, *John Wayne*, 432–433).

405. It was produced by Wayne's production company Batjac, now run by son Michael.

406. Eyman, *John Wayne*, 432.

407. *Ibid.*

408. *Ibid.*

409. *Ibid.*, 436.

410. *Ibid.*, 433. His current deal was $200,000 a picture plus a percentage.

411. *Ibid.*, 434. Most people believed his role more associate producer rather than director.

412. *Ibid.*, 436.

413. *Ibid.*, 435.

414. *Ibid.*, 438.

415. *Ibid.*

416. *Ibid.*, 440.

417. Wayne's presence guaranteed at least $4 million in rentals but the last four, including *The Green Berets*, did considerably better. His films were comparatively inexpensive by the standards of the other top actors and he had a big following overseas. Other stars—Paul Newman (*The Secret War of Harry Frigg*, 1968)—had flops, but not him.

418. Korda, Michael, Review, *Glamour*, October 1968; Elsa, Review, *Motion Picture Exhibitor*, June 19, 1968, 14; Mahoney, John, Review, *Hollywood Reporter*, June 17, 1968; Adler, Renata, "The Absolute End of the 'Romance of War,'" *New York Times*, Jun 30, 1968.

419. "All-Time Champs," *Variety*, 1993. A small later uptick at the box office increased this to $9.75 million.

420. Although Jodie Foster and Brooke Shields played young characters in *Taxi Driver* (1976) and *The Blue Lagoon* (1980), they were hardly child stars in the Disney mold. And while Ricky Schroeder (*The Champ*, 1979) and Henry Thomas and Drew Barrymore (both *E.T.*, 1982) appeared as children they did not have extensive child-star careers. Culkin's appearance in *Uncle Buck* (1989) encouraged John Hughes to write *Home Alone* for him.

421. This trend towards animals had also been reflected in the animated features department where the studio mixed the retelling of classic fairytales with fare like *Lady and the Tramp* (1955) and *One Hundred and One Dalmatians* (1961).

422. While Disney still could not afford to employ big stars, all the animal-oriented pictures still had actors with some box office recognition: Oscar-nominated Dorothy Maguire in *Old Yeller*, Oscar-winner Donald Crisp in *Greyfriars Bobby*, Brian Keith, who had starred in *The Parent Trap*, in *Savage Sam*, and imported British actors Patrick McGoohan and Susan Hampshire for *The Three Lives of Thomasina* (1963).

423. Gill, Brendan, Review, *New Yorker*, December 11, 1965, 232; Review, *New York Times*, December 3, 1965; Coe, Richard L., "Disney's *Cat* Fuel for Yule," *Washington Post*, December 25, 1965;

Scheuer, Philip K., "D.C. Will Take Juveniles' Fantasy," *Los Angeles Times*, December 30, 1965.

424. "All-Time Champs," *Variety*, 1993; Hannan, *Coming Back*, 231. One reissue in the 1970s brought lifetime rentals up to $12.5 million.

425. Replacing Sam Peckinpah who was fired.

426. Mirisch, Walter, *I Thought We Were Making Movies Not History* (Madison: University of Wisconsin Press, 2008) 240–241. The original location was New England but this was switched to Northern California, in the Fort Bragg area in Mendocino County.

427. The production rented a 165ft replica that had appeared in *Morituri* (1965)

428. *Ibid.*, 242. Farr was pregnant.

429. Coe, Richard L. "A Perceptive Witty Comedy," *Washington Post*, June 22, 1966; Scheuer, Philip K., "Marxmanship, Comedy Meet in *Russians*," *Los Angeles Times*, June 5, 1966, 3; Alden, Robert, Review, *New York Times*, May 26, 1966, 55; Gill, Brendan, Review, *New Yorker*, June 4, 1966, 87.

430. "All-Time Champs," *Variety*, 1993. Marginally downgraded from $10 million.

431. The book had been filmed for CBS television in the U.S. in 1954 starring Barry Nelson and Linda Christian. It was filmed again in 2006.

432. Blake Edwards and Clive Donner would have been added to the list, but Feldman would not pay Edwards what he wanted and Sellers rejected Donner (Owen, Gareth, *Casino Royale, Cinema Retro*, Vol. 2, Issue 6, 26).

433. Fleming had sold the film rights to actor-producer Gregory Ratoff in 1955 for $6,000 which amounts to over $60,000 now (Raymond Benson, *The James Bond Companion*, Boxtree, 1988, 11) and Feldman purchased them from Ratoff's widow (Barnes, Alan and Hearn, Marcus, *Kiss! Kiss! Bang! Bang!, The Unofficial James Bond Film Companion*, Batsford Books, 200, 56). Howard Hawks showed an interest in developing the project with Cary Grant (McCarthy, *The Grey Fox*, 595, 629).

434. Theme song "The Look of Love" sung by Dusty Springfield was the big hit by Burt Bacharach and Hal David. An instrumental version by Herb Alpert and the Tijuana Brass topped the Easy Listening chart. Mireille Matthieu sang the theme song in French and German.

435. Second unit director Richard Talmadge was uncredited though he directed the final scene.

436. Sophia Loren was Sellers' first choice for a leading lady and Shirley MacLaine and Trevor Howard were also approached (*Ibid.*, 25).

437. Cooper was Feldman's original pick—before the screenplay was jam-packed with Bonds—to play the lead character and had tied him down to a two-year contract ("Watts, Stephen, "An 0071 Movie Without Connery? Get Headquarters," *New York Times*, May 22, 1966, 129).

438. Bouchet had been released from a seven-year contract with Otto Preminger after appearing in *In Harm's Way* (1965) without—see Paul Newman—having to buy her way out. In London to meet Michelangelo Antonioni, she bumped into Feldman and following up his interest landed a role in the picture and another seven-year deal. (Owen, Gareth, "Remembering Miss Moneypenny," *Cinema Retro*, Vol. 2, Issue 6, 33).

439. Andress was under contract to Feldman who paid her $250 a week (Owen, Gareth, *Cinema Retro*, 28).

440. Caroline Munro, British horror star, also made her debut as an extra wearing a costume designed by Paco Rabanne (Owen, Gareth, "Caroline Munro, How *Casino Royale* Changed My Life," *Cinema Retro*, Vol. 2, Issue 6, 29).

441. Owen, Gareth, *Cinema Retro*, 25–26.

442. Pfeiffer, Lee, "*Casino Royale*—The Missing Scenes," *Cinema Retro*, Vol 2, Issue 6, 32.

443. Owen, Gareth, *Cinema Retro*, 25.

444. Other writers pitching in included Woody Allen, Sellers, director Val Guest, novelist Joseph Heller of *Catch-22* fame and Billy Wilder (Canby, Vincent, "007 to Multiply in *Casino Royale*, A Half-Dozen James Bonds Cast in Film by Feldman," *New York Times*, October 5, 1966, 38.

445. Ken Hughes was assigned the Berlin scenes, John Huston directed those at the Scottish castle and the house of Sir James Bond, Joseph McGrath responsible for scenes involving Sellers, Andress and Welles, Robert Parrish some casino scenes and Val Guest worked with Woody Allen and David Niven (Barnes and Hearn, *Kiss! Kiss!*, 63).

446. Huston contributed the most to the final cut (38 minutes) then Guest (26 minutes), Hughes (25 minutes), and McGrath and Parrish each had 20 minutes (Canby, "007 to Multiply," *New York Times*).

447. Crowther, Bosley, Review, *New York Times*, April 29, 1967; "Keystone Cop-Out," *Time*, May 12, 1967; Ebert, Roger, Review, *Chicago Sun-Times*, May 1, 1967.

448. The budget was small—$2.5 million—by Hollywood standards according to Alexander Walker in *Hollywood, England* (London: Michael Joseph, 1974 and Orion paperback 2005) 394.

449. It ran for 2,618 performances. A movie was not permitted until 18 months after the West End closure to allow for touring companies ("*Oliver!* Pic to Roll 7yrs after Legit," *Variety*, January 25. 1967, 23).

450. *My Fair Lady* ran on Broadway for 2,717 performances, *The Sound of Music* for 1,443 performances and *Oliver!* for 774 performances.

451. Gilbert, *All My Flashbacks*, 283.

452. *Ibid.*, 285.

453. Columbia pinned high hopes on Shani Wallis, taking out a full-page advert in *Variety* (January 25, 1967, 23) convinced that she "will rank as one of the world's finest musical stars." Georgia Brown had played the role on the London stage. Wallis, while a British singer, was working in America. But a Columbia executive had taken a shine to her (Gilbert, *All My Flashbacks*, 287).

226   Notes—The Films

454. Gilbert, *All My Flashbacks*, 281–286.

455. *Ibid.*, 296. *The Adventurers* did not appear until 1970, four years after publication, a long enough interval for Gilbert to have directed both *Oliver!* and this.

456. *Ibid.*, 288.

457. Ebert, Roger, Review, *Chicago Sun-Times*, December 22, 1968; Elsa, *International Motion Picture Exhibitor*, December 4, 1968, 11; other quotes taken from an advert in *International Motion Picture Exhibitor*, December 4, 1968, 8–9—these are all from British newspapers since the movie opened there first.

458. "All-Time Champs," *Variety*, 1993. The movie ended up with lifetime rentals of $16.8 million.

459. Budget estimated at $1.5 million (Solomon, *Twentieth Century-Fox*, 163).

460. Canby, Vincent, Review, *New York Times*, April 4, 1969; Review, *Variety*, Apr 3, 1969; Buckley, Peter, *Films and Filming*, November 1969, 42.

461. The relationship between director and star grew so difficult that the *Pink Panther* series was put on an indefinite hold (Mirisch, *I Thought We Were*, 167). It took a decade for reconciliation.

462. Mirisch, *I Thought We Were*, 144.

463. *Ibid.*, 239.

464. Curtis, *American Prince*, 252–254.

465. "Lemmon for Chemistry," *Variety*, May 27, 1964, 5. These were: *Some Like It Hot, The Apartment, Irma La Douce, Days of Wine and Roses* and *Under the Yum Yum Tree*.

466. *Ibid.* Lemmon, Edwards and director Richard Quine had formed Artists Productions Associates.

467. "Liz into Albee's *Woolf*," *Variety*, October 7, 1964, 4. Prior to Elizabeth Taylor being signed for *Who's Afraid of Virginia Woolf*, Natalie Wood had been under consideration for the role, which would indeed have been a major dramatic departure.

468. Finstad, Suzanne, *Natasha: The Biography of Natalie Wood* (New York: Random House, 2009) 297.

469. "Tony Curtis: A Yank Production in a Foreign Land Certain to Be Swindled or Conned," *Variety*, October 14, 1964, 4. The trigger for this outburst was that the producers of *The Great Race* had been denied promised access to the Schonbrun Palace in Vienna.

470. "Mr Laurel and Mr Hardy Salute Precedes All Else as *Great Race* Opener," *Variety*, March 17, 1965, 19.

471. Curtis, *American Prince*, 251–252.

472. Schickel, Richard, "A $12 Million Romp in Hollywood's Attic," *Life*, September 17, 1965, 8; Review, *Variety*, June 30, 1965, 6; Feature Reviews, *Box Office*, July 5, 1965, 9.

473. "All-Time Champs," *Variety*, 1993. Extra dates in the 1970s increased the rentals to $11.4 million.

474. Ball's novel took four years to get published.

475. "Sid Poitier's Role Range," *Variety*, November 25, 1964, 3. This was *To Sir, with Love*.

476. Mirisch, *I Thought We Were*, 246. Mirisch had met Poitier when he was filming *Porgy and Bess*. "He is an extraordinary man," wrote Mirisch (*I Thought*, 247)," who has built his life and career by overcoming the tremendous handicaps of poverty and prejudice while remaining a man of great intelligence and charm."

477. Walter Mirisch was one-third of the Mirisch Brothers company which almost operated like a mini-major. He started out in the late 1940s-early 1950s working on low-budget B-pictures like the *Bomba, The Jungle Boy* series for Poverty Row outfit Monogram before moving on to the more upscale Allied Artists. With brothers Harold and Marvin, he set up Mirisch Brothers and the production company set up an exclusive deal with United Artists. They produced *Some Like It Hot, The Magnificent Seven* (1960), *West Side Story* (1961), *The Great Escape* (1963), *The Pink Panther* (1964), *The Russians Are Coming, The Russians Are Coming* and *Hawaii* (1966), collecting two Best Picture awards in seven years.

478. *Ibid.*, 252.

479. *Ibid.*, 249.

480. *Ibid.*, 250. The percentage Poitier was offered for *In the Heat of the Night* was double the going rate for the likes of Paul Newman and John Wayne. Low budgets worked in Poitier's favor. If the film pulled in a decent box office, then Poitier would be rewarded from a low profit base whereas for Newman and Wayne, whose movies were far more expensive in part because of their salaries, their projects had to make a lot more money before they saw any benefit from a percentage. However, he had done well from previous percentage deals, especially the low-budget *A Patch of Blue*.

481. *Ibid.*, 249.

482. Despite Oscar nomination for *The Pawnbroker*, his next job was in Europe for *The Girl and the General*. This was far from the glossy big-budget affairs afforded the likes of Audrey Hepburn, who filmed *How to Steal a Million* (1965) in Paris, or Gregory Peck, shooting *Arabesque* (1966) in London.

483. *Ibid.*, 247–248.

484. Harris, *Scenes*, 138–139. After *Village of The Damned* in 1960, Silliphant had not written a movie in five years until *The Slender Thread*. He had no time. He was too busy making a fortune in television. He earned $10,000 an hour for television drama and was exceptionally prolific. For the first season of 30-minute *The Naked City*, which he conceived, he wrote 32 of the 39 episodes, and he also wrote for another of his creations *Route 66*. His annual income was far higher than that of any screenwriter.

485. Although Oscar-nominated in the supporting category for her debut in *The Detective* (1951), being blacklisted as a result of the McCarthy Communist hearings meant she did not work again in Hollywood, though she was acceptable to

Notes—The Films

television and had won an Emmy for *Peyton Place* in 1964.

486. Harris, *Scenes*, 83.

487. *Ibid.*, 177–180.

488. Mirisch, *I Thought*, 250–251. This was luck. The producers found a town of this name in Illinois. That meant, to save money, for example, they did not have to paint the name of the town on any building. The movie was shot here apart from a short visit to cotton fields in Tennessee and some scenes filmed elsewhere.

489. Suiting George C. Scott down to the ground.

490. For example, there was no scene of Tibbs entering a whites-only hotel,

491. Mirisch, *I Thought*, 248.

492. Harris, *Scenes*, 180.

493. The final draft was 26 pages shorter than the first draft (Harris, *Scenes*, 80).

494. Morgenstern, Joseph, "Redneck and Scapegoat," *Newsweek*, Aug 14, 1967; Sarris, Andrew, "Inoffensive Hero," *Film*, 1967–1968, 214–215, repeat of *Village Voice* review; Gilliatt, Penelope, "Heated Bandwagon," *New Yorker*, August 5; Murphy, A.D., Review, *Variety*, June 21, 1967, 6.

495. "All-Time Champs," *Variety*, 1993. Marginally downgraded from $11 million.

496. "Album Bestsellers," *Variety*, December 24, 1969, 40. The *Midnight Cowboy* original soundtrack was fifteenth in the chart, having been there for 15 weeks, making steady progression upwards. (In those days albums did not hit the number one spot in the first week and go down, like today, they usually started lower down and crept up.) Although Harry Nilsson had a hit in the singles chart with *Everybody's Talkin'* earlier in the year, Ferrante and Teicher were currently in the singles chart ("Single Record T.I.P.S.," *Variety*, December 24, 1969, 40) at number nine with the theme from the film. In the same week in the album chart *Easy Rider* was at number ten (after 11 weeks in the chart), *Alice's Restaurant* seventeenth, *Romeo and Juliet* twenty-fourth, *Paint Your Wagon* twenty-sixth, and *Oliver* forty-ninth.

497. Known as the MPAA Code and Rating Administration. Geoffrey Shurlock, who had run the Production Code since 1954, retired at the start of 1969 and Eugene G. Dougherty took over.

498. "Generally Favorable Reaction Greets Industry's Film Rating System," *International Motion Picture Exhibitor*, October 20, 1968, 3; November 20, 1968, 8 "Rating System Principal Topic at NATO's San Francisco Meet," *International Motion Picture Exhibitor*, November 20, 1968, 8. The industry was quick to respond to the new system.

499. Bear in mind that pornography in those days did not for the most part comprise the graphic sex pictures to be found routinely on the Internet. Fitting that category on screens at the same time, some in the notorious Times Square grind-houses, were movies like *The Lustful Turk* (1968). Colin Heard in "Underground U.S.A. and

the Sexploitation Market" (*Films and Filming*, August 1969, 24–29) reported on the kind of films being shown in America—compilations of shorts (known as "loops") presented with titles like *Bang Up Beaver Bust Out*, *Call Girls of Frankfurt* (1966) and bondage-themed flicks like *All the Way Down* (1968). Already obscenity laws were being invoked to prevent, for example, British film *Pattern of Evil* (retitled *Fornicon* in 1971) being shown anywhere. Since it was Italian, sex comedy *The Libertine* (1968) with Catherine Spaak was not required to apply for a certificate from the MPAA. Even so, for marketing purposes, it plastered an X-certificate over all its posters.

500. Coincidental with *Midnight Cowboy's* release, Swedish film *Inga*, for example, was prevented from opening in Pittsburgh. On the other hand, some states found ways round the restrictive X-certificate. In Omaha, the certificate was bypassed since doing so did not violate provisions relating to the 18-age sections of local law ("*Midnight Cowboy* Given Plus by Catholic Paper, *Box Office*, August 25, 1969).

501. "Ban on X-film Ads Brings Criticism," *Box Office*, December 15, 1969. This was in Oklahoma where a newspaper chain refused to accept advertising for X-rated pictures. "Sell Around No-X Dailies, UA *Cowboy* Big in San Diego," *Variety*, August 20, 1969, 20. Despite being unable to publicise the picture in local newspapers, the film opened to record business at the Cinema 21.

502. "New Film Ratings," *International Motion Picture Exhibitor*, December 25, 1968, 12.

503. "N.C. Prosecutor Cites Difficulties in Determining What Is Obscene," *International Motion Picture Exhibitor*, May 9, 1969, 7. Local censors in North Carolina cut out the controversial sex scene.

504. British film *If...* being considered at the same time was threatened with an X-certificate unless it edited out two shots. The producers obliged and received an "R."

505. "Motion Pictures Rated the Code and Ratings Administration," *Box Office*, May 26, 1969, 13. In the same week as an "X" was slapped on *Midnight Cowboy*, *Easy Rider* and *The Picasso Summer* were also rated "R," *The Chairman* and *Once Upon a Time in the West* were each given the "M" rating while *The Last Escape* was granted the "G" rating. *Winning* starring Paul Newman was reclassified upwards, form "G" to "M" after complaints about the subject matter which included adultery. And *The Moon Is Blue* (1953) which had been banned in its day was reissued in the "M" category.

506. "UA's *Midnight Cowboy* Most Costly Film to Be Marked "X" for Youth," *Variety*, May 21, 1969, 25. "Although such classification was included on preview prints, the distributor was apparently hoping for a less restrictive tag and last week told members of the press the film would receive an R." It was also noted that UA had been hoping to tap into the audience that had made *The Graduate* such a big success, which was in the main a younger crowd.

507. All except *Tom Jones* had been produced by Mirisch, but were financed by United Artists, which, therefore, took a possessive credit as powerful as that of any callow director.

508. "Self-Regulation—More Than a Label," *International Motion Picture Exhibitor*, May 21, July 16, 1969, 4.

509. Advert, *Variety*, June 4, 1969, 8–9. It turned into the "biggest grossing film in history in the New York East Side" with an all-time weekly record at the Coronet of $61,503.

510. "*Midnight Cowboy* Holding Saddle as Box Office Bronco," *Variety*, July 30, 1969, 5. "Industryites…questioned whether less sophisticated or more provincial filmgoers outside Gotham would buy this offbeat boy prostitute tale."

511. "Bum from Texas, Puerto Rican Hero Restore United Artists to Rapture," *Variety*, June 4, 1969, 7.

512. "*Midnight Cowboy*, 49 Dates, $3.4-Mil," *Variety*, August 29, 1969, 3. In the Coronet it had earned $637,000 over 12 weeks, a phenomenal average.

513. "*Midnight Cowboy* Rides Wide Range on Type Ratings," *Variety*, June 18, 1969, 4. Usually, the National Catholic Office agreed with the Code. But in this case, it rated the film A-4— "morally unobjectionable for adults." Other Catholic organisations fell into line, the newspaper *True Call* in Omaha giving it a pass ("*Midnight Cowboy* Given Plus by Catholic Paper," *Box Office*, August 25, 1969).

514. "Two Sets of Raves from N.Y. Critics; One for Sordid Saga, Other for Folksy," *Variety*, June 4, 1969, 24. *Midnight Cowboy* received seven favorable reviews out of eight, the only dissenter being the *New Yorker*. The "folksy" picture was *Popi* with Alan Arkin.

515. Based on the book by Thomas Hardy.

516. "Dust Off Old Hoffman Film," *Variety*, June 25, 1969, 7. AIP had bought up the rights and was bringing it out capitalize on the success of *Midnight Cowboy*.

517. "Honest Ad Angle," *Variety*, July 16, 1969, 5. This did not remain unreleased for long. UA had bought it to keep it out of the way while arranging the release of *Midnight Cowboy*. In bringing it out, the adverts intended to convey that it had been made before *Midnight Cowboy*, in order to forewarn audiences.

518. His play *Blue Denim* was filmed in 1959 and previous novel *All Fall Down* in 1962 starred Eva Marie Saint.

519. Gow, Gordon, "A Buck for Joe," *Films and Filming*, November 1969, 4–8. Explained Schlesinger: "We used our week's advance rehearsal rather than plotting everything accurately…just finding out how far beyond the scripted material the actors could go…We had a tape-recorder.and by working with the two actors in this manner, we expanded both the film and their performances. We took the tape and examined what areas were missing from the script and reshaped it accordingly."

520. Eddy, *International Motion Picture Exhibitor*, May 21, 1969, 6.

521. Review of *Times* and *Post* quoted from "Two Sets of Raves from N.Y. Critics; One for Sordid Saga, Other for Folksy," *Variety*, June 4, 1969, 24.

522. "All-Time Champs," *Variety*, 1993. The Oscar win, which came in 1970, continued its box office pace and it ended up with $20.4 million.

523. Disney, Walt, "Humour: My Sixth Sense," *Films and Filming*, November 1966, 8

524. Feature Review, *Box Office*, February 27, 1961; Durgnat, Raymond, *Films and Filming*, August 1961, 26.

525. Giblin, Gary, "We All Go a Little Mad Sometimes," *Cinema Retro*, Vol. 6 Issue 18, 27. Bidding anonymously, Hitchcock bought the rights for just $5,000.

526. In London there was no press preview which critics took to mean that it was a turkey.

527. Giblin, "We All," 25–26. The movie was based on the real-life murders of Ed Gein, overly attached to her mother, so much so that since her death in 1945, he started killing and skinning "matronly" women. If the public were shocked by Hitchcock, they would have been completely turned off if the director had delved further into Gein's life.

528. *Ibid.*, 26–27.

529. *Ibid.*, 33.

530. *Ibid.*, 27. Cavanaugh had worked on the April 1957 *Alfred Hitchcock Presents* episode "One More Mile to Go," which Hitchcock himself had directed. This script proved "too talky and preachy."

531. *Ibid.*, 27.

532. *Ibid.*, 31.

533. *Ibid.*

534. "In *Psycho* the princess is killed by the ogre." Wollen, Peter, *Readings and Writings: Semiotic Counter-Strategies* (London: Verso Editions and NLB, 1982) 34. Just one of the many theories surrounding the picture.

535. Gene, Review, *Variety*, June 20, 1966, 6; Baker, Peter, *Films and Filming*, September 1960, 21.

536. Hilliers, *Cahiers du Cinéma Vol 2*, 329–334.

537. Hannan, *Coming Back*, 197–200.

538. Hopper, Hedda, "Hayley Mills to Play (Both) Twins in Film," *Chicago Daily Tribune*, March 9, 1960. It went through a number of other titles including *Petticoats and Blue Jeans* and *We Belong Together*.

539. "Now Sophistication on Disney Slate," *Variety*, January 18, 1961, 24. This "would seem like a departure" for the studio, commented the trade paper.

540. "$16,500,000 Invested in Disney Line for 1961," *Variety*, January 18, 1961, 3. *Pollyanna*, while profitable, produced only $3.75 million in rentals, below the $5 million originally anticipated.

541. O'Hara, Maureen and Nicoletti, John, '*Tis Herself: A Memoir* (New York: Simon and Schuster, 2005—reference from Thorndike Press edition)

418. Assuming she was desperate for work, Disney offered her only $25,000 but she held out for her usual $75,000 fee.

542. Crowther, Bosley, "Hayley Mills Plays 2 Roles in comedy," *New York Times*, June 22, 1961, 23; Stimson, Charles, "*Parent Trap* Fun for the Entire Family," *Los Angeles Times*, June 26, 1961; Coe, Richard L., "Truly Plural Is Hayley Mills," *Washington Post*, July 11, 1961.

543. "All-Time Champs," *Variety*, 1993. Marginally upgraded from $11.2 million.

544. Schickel, Richard, "Walt's Good—and Bad—Goodbye," *Life*, January 5, 1968; Review, *Time*, January 19, 1968, 90; Champlin, Charles, "Disney Craft Flavor for *Jungle Book*," *Los Angeles Times*, October 18, 1967.

545. "All-Time Champs," *Variety*, 1993; Hannan, Coming Back, 219, 232, 273, 283. *The Jungle Book's* reissues in 1970, 1978 and 1984 saw rentals soar to $27 million.

546. Austen, David, "Following No Formula" *Films and Filming*, December 1969, 4–9. In an interview Hal Wallis said, "I've always tried to get a streak of realism into my pictures. I think it's a very necessary ingredient, if it's a western… (Rooster Cogburn is) the very antithesis of the handsome swashbuckling character. But it's a kind of reality that accounts for a great deal." The novel "was practically a screenplay already." As regards violence, he added, "There is a very violent moment in *True Grit* but the whole thing is reflex action and we cut it very fast."

547. Hannan, Brian, *The Gunslingers of '69: Western Movies' Greatest Year* (Jefferson, NC: McFarland, 2019) 123.

548. Quotes taken from adverts in *International Motion Picture Exhibitor*, July 16, 1969, 2–3 and June 18, 1969, 2–3.

549. "All-Time Rentals," *Variety*, 1993 Hannan, *Coming Back*, 214. John Wayne was furious to discover Paramount had prematurely sold *True Grit* off to television which reduced its reissue prospects. Even so, it added another couple of million, pushing lifetime rentals to $14.25 million.

550. She spent $125,000 on buying the property and developing the script (Murf, Review, *Variety*, April 24, 1968, 6).

551. $150,000 of her salary was deferred, so if a flop she would only earn $100,000. Her share of the profits was split between her company and herself (Murf, Review, *Variety*, April 24, 1968, 6).

552. Adler, Renata, "Lucille Ball and Henry Fonda Star in a Comedy: *Yours, Mine and Ours* Opens at 2 Theaters 2 Westerns Also Bow—Chabrol Returns," *Variety*, April 25, 1968; Feature reviews, *Box Office*, April 22, 1967; Murf, Review, *Variety*, April 24, 1968, 6.

553. "All-Time Rentals," *Variety*, 1993. Marginally upgraded from $11.5 million.

554. Callan, *Richard Harris*, 166. The actor bombarded Joshua Logan with telegrams and even impersonated a waiter to deliver a note in person to the director saying "Harris for Arthur!"

555. Kennedy, Matthew, *Roadshow! The Rise and Fall of Film Musicals in the 1960s* (Oxford: Oxford University Press, 2014) 27–28.

556. In the original Broadway production the role was taken by Richard Burton who was not particularly qualified either but it worked out fine. So it seemed fair enough for the film version that Richard Harris with an equally growly voice could play the part.

557. Holston, *Movie Roadshows*, 207. "The casting was considered unusual: three non-singers in the lead roles…director Joshua Logan explained his casting choices in his autobiography. He'd not been impressed with the Broadway cast, noting in particular that Julie Andrews was too sweet to be Guenevere. He wanted someone dangerous."

558. Warner Brothers, in any case, believed they had uncovered a new singing star and went to considerable lengths to persuade the public. "He also carries a fine strong song in his heart and world film audiences will be struck by the splendid quality of his singing voice. The Lerner and Loewe songs could have been written for him…the pride and joy in "Camelot," the heart-breaking tenderness of "How to Handle a Woman." (*Camelot* Souvenir Program, 1967, 16)

559. Ironically, David Hemmings, playing Mordred, and a trained singer, was not given a tune. The singing of Franco Nero, as Lancelot, was dubbed.

560. The British title was *Morgan, A Suitable Case for Treatment*.

561. Although she took top-billing in *Morgan!* even though David Warner had the bigger part of the title character, in *Blow Up* she was second-billed to David Hemmings.

562. He chose *Star!* instead.

563. Holston, *Movie Roadshows*, 207.

564. Gow, Gordon, "Gold Diggers of 1969," *Films and Filming*, December 1969, 8. Joshua Logan adopted Vanessa Redgrave's suggestion for the staging of her song involving three different knights by placing each in a separate location. Said Logan, "I took her idea and had new costumes made and postponed the shooting of that number until new sets were built for those three different areas where she would sing to each of the knights in turn."

565. Review, *Variety*, October 215, 1967, 6; Coe, Richard L, "*Camelot* Tommyrot," *Washington Post*, November 9, 1969; Champlin, Charles, "*Camelot* Opens at Cinerama Dome," *Los Angeles Times*, November 3, 1967.

566. "All-Time Rentals," *Variety*, 1993; Hannan, Coming Back, 231–232. One reissue lifted *Camelot* to $14 million.

567. Martin, *The Magnificent Showman*, 73. "On the credits, the writers are listed as Philip Yordan and Frederick M. Frank. Neither wrote a word for the finished film. It was not until 1999 that Barzman's name was properly put back in the credits."

568. Baker, Peter, "And now the greatest picture since…" *Films and Filming*, June 1961, 14–15,

230 Notes—The Films

36. On location with the picture, Baker describes how the finale was filmed in Peniscola 200km from Valencia, not a set but an active fishing village. The scene involved 348 technicians, a dozen caravans for stars and portable tents for others. Among the extras were local orange pickers paid 125 pesetas a day. "Women held up production for the best part of a day when they insisted on hanging out their washing to dry as usual.

569. "Egos: Watch My Line," *Time*, January 5, 1962. However, in effect, they shared top billing. When the designers of a 600ft billboard over Times Square in New York inadvertently positioned Heston's name above that of Loren, she sued.

570. Martin, *The Magnificent Showman*, 69. It is worth pointing out that only one man in the 1960s received $1 million for a film—Marlon Brando in *The Fugitive* Kind (1960)—but in addition to Loren, Audrey Hepburn hit the million-dollar mark and Elizabeth Taylor surpassed it for *Cleopatra*.

571. Canutt was a second-unit director famed for *Stagecoach* (1939) and *Ben-Hur* (1959).

572. Martin, *The Magnificent Showman*, 69. Lom replaced original choice Orson Welles.

573. *Ibid.*, 75, 76. "Heston came to resent Loren having what Heston perceived as her own writer."

574. *Ibid.*, 79.

575. *Ibid.*, 77.

576. "A Round Table of One," *Time*, December 22, 1961; Strick, Philip, *Films and Filming*, February 1962, 30–31; Review, *Variety*, December 6, 1961; Scheuer, Philip K., "*El Cid* Flexes Its Muscles—to the Glory of Moviemaking," *Los Angeles Times*, December 10, 1961, 3; "How to Lose Friends," *Newsweek*, December 18, 1961, 98.

577. Bean, Robin, "The Two Faces of Shirley," *Films and Filming*, February 1962, 11–12. Even the stars did not know how it was going to turn out. In this interview, she told Bean, "As of now it's going to be a musical." "Excise the Music for Film Version of *Irma La Douce*," *Variety*, June 27, 1962, 3. The musical had run for three years in London. "*Irma* Profit Tops 100G Thus Far on 190G Ante," *Variety*, March 7, 1962, 57. It ran for 66 weeks in New York and embarked on two-year road tour. Whereas not in the long-running league of *My Fair Lady* or *The Sound of* Music, it was hardly a flop.

578. Mirisch, *I Thought We Were*, 155.

579. "*Irma La Douce* Is Split Four Ways from Start," *Box Office*, June 11, 1962, W-2.

580. *Ibid.*

581. Balio, *United Artists*, 171.

582. Bean, "Two Faces. "I may do pictures for my own company," said MacLaine, "When you work for your company you can take less salary. If you make a big gross on a film the money is much better than a salary."

583. Hannan, *When Women Ruled Hollywood*, 38–40, 42–47, 60–61, 64–66, 69, 86–99, 136–140, 146–150, 196, 209–210.

584. "Excise the Music," *Variety*.

585. Mirisch, *I Thought We Were*, 156.

586. "*Irma La Douce* Not Showcased 'Till Later," *Variety*, May 1, 1963, 5.

587. Advert, *Variety*, July 24, 19643, 14. It set the record for the best fifth week at both the DeMille and Baronet in New York where it had first opened.

588. "Excise the Music."

589. "Cap Adds Lemmon," *Variety*, March 27, 1963, 56. He cut an album at Capitol Records with him playing the piano.

590. Feature Reviews, *Box Office*, June 17, 1963; Review, *Variety*, June 5, 1963, 6; Crowther, Bosley, "Wilder's *Irma La Douce*," *New York Times*, June 6, 1963, 37; Code, Richard L. "Now *Irma's* Not So Sweet," *Washington Post*, June 22, 1963.

591. Hilliers, *Cahiers du Cinéma Vol 2*, 329–334.

592. He also wrote the screenplay for *Lawrence of Arabia* (1962) and *Doctor Zhivago* (1965).

593. "English Weather Obliged *All Seasons*; Zinnemann Came in under $2-Mil," *Variety*, December 21, 1966, 16. The budget would probably have been higher—possibly much higher—if the movie had been hit by bad weather. Later, *Doctor Dolittle's* budget expanded considerably when bad weather hit filming in England.

594. "English Weather," *Variety*. "Everyone involved took a pay cut."

595. Redgrave took an uncredited smaller part as Anne Boleyn, one of the king's six wives.

596. "*Man for All Seasons* to Realty Equities," *Box Office*, January 15, 1968, 10; "Columbia Reasserts Control Over *Seasons* Rights," *Box Office*, January 15, 1968, 10. While Zinnemann's percentage was never disclosed to the media, it must have been considerable for a private company to buy out his share of the picture through his Highland Films vehicle. Judging from the story regarding Columbia, it looked like the studio had provided financing in return for distribution rights and television licensing. It would not be unusual for a director-producer to take a percentage that was bigger or equal to that enjoyed by the studio—Billy Wilder on *Irma La Douce* had a quarter of the film, the same share as three other major contributors. Studios often made the bulk of their revenue from distribution for which they normally charged a company 30 percent of the gross.

597. "Columbia Special Play Off Strategy For Zinnemann's New *All Seasons*," *Variety*, September 28, 1966, 4. "Columbia's angle on roadshow was to market 'class' rather than bigness." Twentieth Century Fox had used arthouses to launch the roadshow engagements for *The Blue Max* (1965) and *Those Magnificent Men in Their Flying Machines* (1965) at East Side arthouses the Sutton and the DeMille respectively.

598. "Columbia *Seasons* Set For Roadshow Release," *Box Office*, October 10, 1966.

599. "New York Advance For *Seasons*," *Box Office*, November 16, 1966; "*Man For All Seasons*" At Capacity Since Its December 12 Premiere," *Box Office*, January 2, 1967. Following one single-page advert in the *New York Times* on October 16, the Fine Arts recorded 38 sold-out performances from

Notes—The Films

231

December 12 to February 19. The actual theater box office for people to go there and buy tickets in advance did not open till November 21, so the sell-outs all came from postal applications. From the start of its run until the end of the year the theater "never had a vacant seat."

600. Advert, "What the Critics Are Saying," *Motion Picture Herald* supplement, January 11, 1967,

601. Hannan, Brian, *The Making of The Guns of Navarone* (Glasgow: Baroliant Press, 2013; revised edition 2019) 17. This was Foreman's share of the production company he had set up with Stanley Kramer.

602. *Ibid.*, 33–35.

603. *Ibid.*, 33. 39.

604. *Ibid.*, 33.

605. *Ibid.*, 69.

606. *Ibid.*, 38.

607. *Ibid.*, 62–63

608. *Ibid.*, 37, 39. Trevor Howard was involved in her screen test.

609. *Ibid.*, 66–67.

610. *Ibid.*, 70–72.

611. *Ibid.*, 74–76. Mackendrick withdrew either because of a back injury or a falling-out with the producer. He later worked with Anthony Quinn in *A High Wind in Jamaica* (1965).

612. *Ibid.*, 77–78.

613. *Ibid.*, 63–64.

614. He was Best Supporting Actor for *Viva Zapata* (1952) and *Lust for Life* (1956)

615. Anthony Quayle's credit status varied, top-billed in British drama *Serious Charge* (1959), leading man to Jayne Mansfield in *It Takes Thief* (1960) but taking second place to Gordon Scott in *Tarzan's Greatest Adventure* (1959). Stanley Baker starred in British film *The Concrete Jungle* (1960). Teen idol James Darren had moved from fluff like *Gidget* (1959) to war picture *All the Young Men* (1960), Greek actress Irene Papas starred in *The Lake of Sighs* (1959) and biopic *Bouboulina* (1959) and English-born Gia Scala had the female lead in *The Angry Hills* (1959), also featuring Stanley Baker.

616. Hannan, *Making of The Guns of Navarone*, 120–127.

617. *Ibid.*, 85.

618. *Ibid.*, 85–86.

619. *Ibid.*, 88–90.

620. *Ibid.*, 102. Tiomkin also received a share of publishing and performance rights.

621. Manvell, Roger, *Films and Filming*, June 1961, 22; Scott, John L., "*Guns of Navarone* Booming Film Hit," *Los Angeles Times*, June 30, 1961; Gill, Brendan, Review, *New Yorker*, July 1, 1961, 41–42; Coe, Richard L., "Oscars Loom in *Guns* Boom," *Washington Post*, July 12, 1961.

622. Spiegel, *Steve McQueen*, 192.

623. Sandford, *McQueen*, 180, 183, 190. Sandford reported $350,000 plus his profit share of $200,000. That was in addition to his location requirements of luxury home, gym and Triumph TR6 bike. Spiegel, *Steve McQueen*, 196, countered with $650,000.

624. She was the author of *Emmanuelle*, later turned into an infamous soft-porn picture.

625. Sandford, *McQueen*, 184. It rained solid for four weeks, never mind issues with snakes, disease and drinking water.

626. Spiegel, *Steve McQueen*, 197.

627. Annakin, Ken, *So You Wanna Be a Director* (Sheffield: Tomahawk Press, 2001) 147–151.

628. *Ibid.*, 154. Sellers pulled out in favor of *The Pink Panther*.

629. *Ibid.*, 150, 159. Van Dyke's agent never informed him of the offer.

630. *Ibid.*, 150–151. United Artists at that point was involved in *The Great Race* so turned it down.

631. *Ibid.*, 154. The original estimate for the Rank/UA collaboration was a more modest $3 million.

632. Julie Christie had an early role.

633. *Ibid.* 155. She was slotted in at the behest of Darryl F. Zanuck, then head of Fox, mainly because she was his girlfriend but he justified her inclusion by explaining, "You need more female interest than the Limey girl."

634. *Ibid.*, 155. 158.

635. *Ibid.*, 158. Christie wanted to move away from comedy after the consecutive *The Fast Lady* (1962) and *Billy Liar* (1963).

636. *Ibid.*, 155. "We all agreed Michael was very talented with probably a great future," commented Annakin. This was just after *Zulu* in which Caine had played an upper class British officer, but before *Alfie* and *The Ipcress File*. But "he could not hold a candle to the genuine public schoolboy, James Fox."

637. *Ibid.*, 155.

638. *Ibid.*, 167. The lyrics were written first by Lorraine Williams, wife of Elmo William, a noted director and now head of the studio's European operation. "The most perfect theme tune I have ever been given," was the Annakin verdict.

639. Bean, Robin, *Films and Filming*, August 1965, 31.

640. Annakin, *So You Wanna*, 109. When Walt Disney first broached Annakin about the subject, he encouraged the director to imagine any level of experience that the family could undergo.

641. *Ibid.*, 110–112. The menageries also included macaws, a baby elephant, tiger, Rhesus monkeys, anacondas, pigs, ducks, sheep and geese.

642. And its sequel *Davy Crockett and the River Pirates* (1956).

643. *Ibid.*, 115. Hayakawa, who was 63, was challenged by the considerably younger members of the stunt team to a judo competition. "He threw all twenty stunt boys, one after the other."

644. As well as *The Sword and the Rose* (1953).

645. Annakin, Ken, "In the Vast Outdoors," *Films and Filming*, July 1960, 15, 34.

646. Exteriors for *20,000 Leagues under the Sea* were shot in Jamaica.

647. Annakin, Ken, "In the Vast Outdoors.

648. Annakin, *So You Wanna*, 112.

649. Annakin, "In the Vast Outdoors." As regards

232   **Notes—The Films**

lighting, Annakin explained: "The shooting days are short and the light too overhead for easy photography. The interesting fact is that with an overhead sun you often get a smaller exposure than you have when shooting in northern latitudes because the sun rarely slants on the object being photographed. A great portion of the picture was made under trees and foliage which meant we were struggling to get any exposure at all." In addition, weather disrupted shooting. "Three times the storms changed the course of a small river running into the sea and three times for the sake of continuity we had to put it back."

650. Annakin, *So You Wanna*, 112–115.

651. *Ibid.*, 118.

652. Annakin, "In the Vast Outdoors."

653. "$16,500,000 Invested," *Variety*. The 1954 film had generated $6.6 million in rentals on its initial box office and Disney hoped the new film would clear that figure and then some. *20,000 Leagues under the Sea* would add more revenue from a 1960s reissue. Ken Annakin put the cost at $4 million (*So You Wanna*, 122).

654. Annakin, "In the Vast Outdoors."

655. "Times Square Embassy for *Family Robinson*," *Variety*, November 30, 1960, 22. How far removed from what might constitute the mainstream operation Disney would have preferred can be gauged from the picture currently screening— Brigitte Bardot sex film *Come Dance with Me* (1959). At one point the cinema was an all-newsreel operation. Perhaps it was Disney who other studios copied in placing their movies in low-capacity theaters as a means of generating lines round the block. In London, Disney movies were usually launched in the small Studio One just off Leicester Square where *Swiss Family Robinson* ran for nearly two years.

656. Thompson, Howard, "New Version of *Swiss Family Robinson*," *New York Times*, December 24, 1960; Tube, Review, *Variety*, November 9, 1960, 6.; Bean, Robin, *Films and Filming*, January 1961,33.

657. "All-Time Champs," *Variety*, 1993. *Swiss Family Robinson's* third reissue pushed lifetime earnings to $20.1 milion.

658. Kashner and Schoenberger, *Furious Love*, 139. Extras included complete suites for dressing rooms, for their arrival on set three bottles of Dom Perignon, a pound of caviar, case of scotch and gin, and bottles of brandy (Mann, *How to Be a Movie Star*, 345).

659. In the original play, the character of Martha is 52.

660. Mann, *How To*, 355.

661. *Ibid.*, 346.

662. Kashner and Schoenberger, *Furious Love*, 138

663. *Ibid.*, 139

664. Kashner and Schoenberger, *Furious Love*, 138.

665. *Ibid.*, 139. Zinnemann was already committed to *A Man for All Seasons*. Clouzot was a wild card suggested by Burton and Frankenheimer ultimately rejected the picture because he wanted his name above the title.

666. "Sandy Dennis Film Debut," *Variety*, April 7, 1965, 24.

667. "Liz's Voice Okay, *Woolf* on Time," *Variety*, Aug 11, 1965, 23.

668. Advert, "Why the Secrecy About the Burtons' New Movie?" *Variety*, September 29, 1965, 8.

669. Mann, *How To*, 367. Said Nichols, "Elizabeth can keep in her mind fourteen dialog changes, twelve floor marks and ten pauses."

670. *Ibid.*, 354.

671. Mann, *How To*, 347. John Schlesinger would take a similar approach a couple of years later with *Midnight Cowboy*.

672. *Ibid.*, 349.

673. "WB Sets Adults Only Policy for *Woolf*," *Box Office*, Jun 6, 1966, 5. Nobody under 18 could be allowed in unless accompanied by an adult.

674. "PCA Board Approves Seal for *Virginia Woolf*," *Box Office*, June 20, 1966, 6. This film and *Blow Up* (1966) led to the revision of the Code with a new system in place for November 1968.

675. "Two Phrases Cut from Soundtrack of *Who's Afraid of Virginia Woolf*," *Variety*, July 13, 1966, 1. WB had insisted no cuts were made so when this story emerged it was front page news in the trade papers.

676. "The Code Is Dead," *Motion Picture Daily*, June 27, 1966. Many theaters, however, barred under-18s from attending.

677. "*Life's* Exhaustive Pictorial-Critical Slant on *Afraid of Woolf*," *Variety*, June 15, 1966, 20; Farber, *Movies*, 178; Gow, Gordon, *Films and Filming*, September 1966, 6; Feature Reviews, *Box Office*, July 4, 1966.

678. For the Royal Command Film Performance. The previous year it had been *The Taming of the Shrew*.

679. "*Romeo and Juliet* Plays 75 Metropolitan Houses," *Box Office*, February 6, 1967. A filmed version of the British Royal Ballet performance played two days in each theater in New York on a separate showings basis.

680. "WB-7A Plans a Musical on Shakespeare's Life," *Box Office*, December 18, 1967, 12. To be produced by Kenneth Hyman (*The Dirty Dozen*, 1967).

681. Advert, *Variety*, July 31, 1968, 21. Another Italian version directed by Ricardo Freda that attempted to beat the Zeffirelli film to the box office was promoted as "filmed in romantic color." Reviews were diametrically opposed. *Variety* said it was a "spare, beautiful adaptation" (September 4, 1968, 6) but *Box Office* (September 9, 1968) considered it "totally incompetent."

682. "Often Are Thou, Romeo," *Variety*, January 24, 1968, 22. The first was in 1908.

683. Vanessa Redgrave played the charismatic teacher.

684. "Romeo, 16, Juliet, 15; Way Bard Wrote 'Em," *Variety*, May 31, 1967, 1. Over 300 actors were considered for the two roles and filming was postponed for three months when they could not be immediately found.

685. Du Noyer, Paul, *Conversations with*

McCartney (New York: The Overlook Press, 2015) 138–139.

686. He was in Rome anyway working on *The Shoes of the Fisherman*.

687. "Check of Youth Puts Them in Par's Corner on *Romeo and Juliet*," *Variety*, March 20, 1968, 5.

688. "Clutch of Roadshows in Offing; Detail Par's Marketing Plans for Its Youth-Oriented *Romeo and Juliet*," *Variety*, August 14, 1968, 5.

689. "Zeffirelli in N.Y.; Paramount's Grind Policy on *Romeo* Reflects His View," *Variety*, October 9, 1968, 24.

690. Ebert, Roger, Review, *Chicago Sun-Times*, October 15, 1968; Rich, Review, *Variety*, March 13, 1968, 6; Armstrong, Michael, *Films and Filming*, July 1968, 34; Feature Reviews, *Box Office*, September 16, 1968.

691. "All-Time Champs," *Variety*, 1993; Hannan, Coming Back, 232, 249. A big reissue in 1973 and a smaller one in 1976 saw *Romeo and Juliet's* rentals increase to $17.4 million.

692. Hannan, *Coming Back*, 177–188. *Bonnie and Clyde* took more in the first month of 1968 than in its entire run in 1967.

693. "Beaucoup Secrecy (Not Just Publicity) on Kubrick's *2001*, Even from Metro," *Variety*, April 8, 1968, 7.

694. Kubrick's *2001* For Easter 1968," *Variety* Jun 7, 1967, 3.

695. "Special, Not Star, Billing in Suit of E.G. Marshall," *Variety*, April 26, 1967, 5. Marshall, best known for television series *The Defenders*, claimed he had an oral contract worth $85,000 to play Dr. Floyd (the part later taken by William Sylvester). He was to receive star billing but when Keir Dullea came on board this credit was reduced to special billing, forcing Marshall to bail.

696. "Beacucoup Secrecy," *Variety*.

697. *Ibid.*

698. It was never made once MGM gave *2001* the greenlight.

699. "Late-Starting and Uniquely-Motivating Selling Campaign for MGM's *2001*; See Kubrick Calling Promo Shots," *Variety*, February 1968, 7. Kubrick instigated a major mail-order campaign minus stills from the movie, instead using paintings by Bob McCall. Mail order was the standard method of drumming up advance sales. Advance bookings were seen as the key to a movie's anticipated box office.

700. "Kubrick's $205,000 Buy of MGM Shares; Ticket Orders for *2001* Perky," *Variety*, March 6, 1968, 4. Advance orders, based on the mail order campaign, were, purportedly, running 25 percent ahead of *Doctor Zhivago*.

701. "*2001* Draws Repeat and Recant Notices, Also Quasi-Hippie Public," *Variety*, May 15, 1968, 20. "The quasi-hippie plunks money down at the box office (for that immediate performance) but is unlikely to buy ducats three or six weeks in advance."

702. "Kubrick Gathers a Famous Fans File; Reviews Except in N.Y. Good," *Variety*, June 19, 1968, 28.

703. "Kubrick Trims *2001* By 19 Mins; Adds Titles to Frame Sequences," *Variety*, April 17, 1968, 7. It was not unusual to edit films after first showing, *Lawrence of Arabia*, *The Greatest Story Ever Told* and *Doctor Zhivago* all did the same. Kubrick tightened scenes rather than eliminating any.

704. "2001 Draws Repeat and Recant Notices," *Variety*.

705. Konecoff, *International Motion Picture Exhibitor*, April 10, 1968, 6.

706. Kael, Pauline, "Trash, Art and the Movies," *Harpers*, February 1969.

707. Reviews taken from advert in *International Motion Picture Exhibitor*, April 17, 1968, 3.

708. Hilliers, *Cahiers du Cinéma Vol 2*, 329–334.

709. "All-Time Champs," *Variety*, 1993; Hannan, *Coming Back*, 232, 240, 243, 244. Sci-fi adventure *2001: A Space Odyssey* was reissued in 1971, 1972 and 1976 and further beyond to rack up a lifetime rentals universe of $25.5 million.

710. Hannan, Brian, *The Making of The Magnificent Seven* (Jefferson, NC: McFarland, 2015) 32.

711. *Ibid.*, 34.

712. *Ibid.*, 34–35, 313.

713. *Ibid.*, 33. United Artists chief Arthur Krim cabled Douglas: "Yul Bryner has agreed in the interests of good will to your use of title *Spartacus*."

714. Douglas, *The Ragman's Son*, 307.

715. *Ibid.*, 310.

716. *Ibid.*, 311.

717. For the complete story on the battle to become the first production to feature Spartacus, refer to MacAdam, Henry and Cooper, Duncan, *The Gladiators vs. Spartacus: Dueling Productions in Blacklist Hollywood, Vol 1: The Race to the Screen* (Cambridge Scholars, 2021).

718. *Ibid.*, 326. It cost $750,000 more to make the movie than build an entire movie studio for Universal.

719. *Ibid.*, 313. Douglas did not think Curtis "was right for the picture" but created the role of Antoninus for him.

720. Munn, *Tony Curtis*, 163–164. Curtis did not see it as a big role, more of a cameo, just 12 days' work. Mann argued that Universal saw Curtis still as teen magnet and as insurance at the box office.

721. *Ibid.* 314–315.

722. *Ibid.*, 315.

723. *Ibid.*, 317–318. Bethmann earned $35,000. She never became a big star but had supporting roles in movies until 1971.

724. *Ibid.*, 307–310, 323.

725. *Ibid.*, 316. Douglas did not want Mann.

726. *Ibid.*

727. Crowther, Bosley, "*Spartacus* Enters the Arena," *New York Times*, October 7, 1960, 28; Cutts, John, *Films and Filming*, January 1961, 32–33; Pryor, Thomas, Review, *Variety*, October 12, 1960, 6; Coe, Richard L., "Vividly Alive Is *Spartacus*," *Washington Post*, January 19, 1961.

728. The songs were arranged by Andre Previn.

729. Lee, Norma, "Three Cheers for Ross

Hunter," *Chicago Tribune*, April 28, 1968, 40. Hunter wanted to film *The Boyfriend* but did not want to shell out $400,000 for the rights.

730. Champlin, Charles, "*Millie* Mirrors Hectic Pace of Roaring 20s," *Los Angeles Times*, April 17, 1967; Crowther, Bosley, "Pleasant Spoof of 20s Opens at Criterion," *New York Times*, March 23, 1967; Land, Review, *Variety*, March 29, 1967, 6.

731. "All-Time Champs," *Variety*, 1993. Rentals marginally increased to $15.55 million.

732. "Bill Castle's Low Budgeter Ballyhoo Takes on $5-Mil Sophisticated Look," *Variety*, September 6, 1967, 15. He bought the rights for $150,000. Castle was an independent producer specialising in horror films costing between $300,000 and $750,000 and including *The Tingler* (1959), *13 Ghosts* (1960) and *Straitjacket* (1964) with Joan Crawford. For *Rosemary's Baby*, he tied up a marketing deal with Yamaha motorbikes ("Paramount Sets National *Rosemary's Baby* Tie-Up," *Box Office*, December 11, 1967).

733. "National Screen Service Now Distributing Movie Books," *Box Office*, March 29, 1965, 11. Bestsellers were linked so automatically to movie theaters that they were sold in foyers.

734. Made into a film three years later.

735. Filmed as *The Haunting* (1960).

736. "Publishing Company Boosts *Rosemary's Baby* Film," *Box Office*, April 15, 1968. The publishers sent a four-page color brochure to 1,200 booksellers urging them to take advantage of Paramount's advertising campaign in 32 newspapers.

737. "Paramount Hits Production Peak; 24 Films Shooting and Editing," *Box Office*, August 7, 1967, 8; "Paramount Hits Production Peak with Over 125 Films in the Offing," *Box Office*, December 11, 1967, 8. Since the take-over by Gulf & Western, Paramount had become "a company with a new urgency and a new dynamism."

738. Wasson, Sam, *The Big Goodbye: Chinatown and the Last Years of Hollywood* (New York: Flatiron Books, 2020) 21–22; "Gutowski-Polanski Prep 4-Pic Slate," *Variety*, April 9, 1967, 67. *Downhill Racer* was planned as the second film in the deal with a script by James Salter and Robert Redford considering the lead.

739. Sandford, Christopher, *Polanski: A Biography* (New York: Macmillan, 2009) 111.

740. *Ibid.*, 112.

741. *Ibid.* Jack Nicholson briefly came into the frame. He would later play the Devil in *The Witches of Eastwick* (1987) and a werewolf in Mike Nichols' *Wolf* (1994).

742. "Condemned Rating NCO to *Rosemary's Baby*," *Box Office*, Jun 24, 1968, 16. The National Catholic Office gave it a "C" rating, despite being passed "R" by the MPAA's censorship board.

743. Gow, Gordon, *Films and Filming*, March 1969, 38–39. The magazine's critic may well have been kicking himself after the award was announced for his review had contained this patronizing classic: "I revere Ruth Gordon...but, bless her heart, she's all wrong here."

744. Adler, Renata, "*Rosemary's Baby*, a Story of Fantasy and Horror, John Cassavettes Stars with Mia Farrow," *New York Times*, June 13, 1968; Feature Reviews, *Box Office*, June 3, 1968; Murf, Review, *Variety*, May 29, 1968, 6.

745. Reviews excerpted from an advert, *Variety*, June 19, 1968, 9.

746. Hilliers, *Cahiers du Cinéma Vol 2*, 329–334.

747. Hannan, *The Making of The Guns of Navarone*, 187. Thompson owned the rights and had developed the movie before being forced to drop out.

748. "*Planet of Apes* Off for Present," *Variety*, March 10, 1965, 26. This was to have been Edwards's last outside film before committing exclusively to Mirisch.

749. Unusually, the two films were not cross-collaterized, a standard studio device whereby the losses on one film were played against the profits in the other, which would have almost certainly resulted in no profit payments to Jacobs.

750. "MacDonald Novels Cue Major Pictures Corp.," *Variety*, May 17, 1967, 5. Schaffner also made an abortive attempt to film the private eye novels of John D. MacDonald, whose total sales exceeded 14 million.

751. Austen, David, "It's All a Matter Of Size," *Films and Filming*, April 1968, 5. "In my view I haven't made a commercial film since *Ben-Hur*," said Heston (clearly ignoring the success of *El Cid*, 1961).

752. "Warners *Ape* World," *Variety*, March 18, 1964, 4; "High Costs Impress Capital," *Variety*, March 23, 1964, 3; "*Planet of Apes* Off for Present," *Variety*, March 10, 1965. Warner Brothers had been involved in the project when Blake Edwards was to direct. The movie was cancelled due to cost—it was budgeted at $3–$3.5 million—and production problems.

753. "Fox's Talent School," *Variety*, June 26, 1968, 13. Harrison was a graduate of the studio's program of investment in young talent. Others included Jacqueline Bissett (*The Detective*, 1968) and Edy Williams (*The Secret Life of An American Wife*, 1968).

754. "Michael Wilson Under His Own Name for A.P. Jacobs," *Variety*, December 14, 1966, 7. He had won an Oscar for *A Place in the Sun* (1951) and another one for *Friendly Persuasion* (1956) although that was actually awarded to Jessamyn West since Wilson's involvement was kept secret.

755. Russo, Joe, Landsman, Larry, and Gross, Edward, *Planet of the Apes Revisited: The Behind the Scenes Story of the Classic Science Fiction Saga* (New York: Thomas Dunne Books/St Martin Griffin, 2001)

756. "A million dollars' worth of make-up," *Life*, August 18, 1967, 82. Chambers had previously been a surgical technician repairing the faces of wounded soldiers. He had a team of 78 make-up artists.

757. "Film Locations for *Planet of the Apes*," www.film-locations.com

758. Austen, "It's All a Matter," *Films and Filming.* "If Frank (Schaffner) and I have done our jobs well," said Heston, "then the bitter social comment implicit in Boulle's novel will also work."

759. Murf, Review, *Variety*, February 7, 1968, 6; Adler, Renata, "She Reads *Playboy*, He Reads *Cosmopolitan*: Ritual Roles Reversed in *Sweet November*, *Planet of the Apes* and *Winter* Also Open," *New York Times*, February 9, 1968; Thomas, Kevin, "*Planet of the Apes* Out of This World," *Los Angeles Times*, March 24, 1968; Coe, Richard L., "The Simians Take a *Planet*," *Washington Post*, April 12, 1968.

760. Hannan, Brian, *The Making of Lawrence of Arabia* (Glasgow: Baroliant Publishing, 2103) 7.

761. Turner, Adrian, *The Making of David Lean's Lawrence of Arabia* (London: Dragon's World, 1994) 27–30.

762. Hannan, *Making*, 11.

763. Turner, *Making*, 23, 32–33.

764. *Ibid.*, 35–36.

765. *Ibid.*, 41.

766. *Ibid.*, 51–54, 65–68, 76–77. Turner's book showed how much of the film was Wilson's contribution.

767. *Ibid.*, 42.

768. Hannan, *Making*, 47.

769. *Ibid.*, 53.

770. Lean, David, "Out of the Wilderness," *Films and Filming*, January 1963, 12–15. The director explained the screenplay process. "We have short-circuited certain incidents and run six characters into one. It would be impossible to include them all in the screenplay so we have one (played by Anthony Quayle) who represents them as 'an English military character' complementary to the role Jack Hawkins has as General Allenby...There were several political officers out there at the time and we have created one, a mixture suggested by various other characters, who we call Dryden, but who never really existed. Similarly, on the Arab side, we've used one young Arab character who is called Ali. He appears in *The Seven Pillars of Wisdom* quite a bit but not in the way we have used him."

771. Turner, *Making*, 85.

772. Brownlow, *David Lean*, 452.

773. Lean, David, "Out of the Wilderness." Said Lean, "I shall never forget it; a terrible place. The production office was in a building that was once occupied by the Foreign Legion. During July and August when we were there they were sending legionnaires there as a punishment. The heat was tremendous."

774. Brownlow, *David Lean*, 468.

775. Hannan, *Making*, 78–80.

776. *Ibid.*, 91.

777. Brownlow, *David Lean*, 483.

778. The movie opened during a newspaper strike so there were a limited number of reviews.

779. Review, *Variety*, December 18, 1962; Crowther, Bosley, "A Desert Warfare Spectacle: *Lawrence of Arabia* Opens in New York," *New York Times*, December 17, 1962; Walker, Alexander, Review, *London Evening Standard*, December 13, 1962; Review, Sarris, Andrew, Review, *Village Voice*, December 20, 1962.

780. All-Time Champs," *Variety*, 1993; Hannan, *Coming Back*, 232, 284–286. *Lawrence of Arabia* was reissued in 1971 and, more famously, in the first of a trendsetting series of revivals, as a "Director's Cut" in 1988, nudging the lifetime rentals up to $20.3 million.

781. The previous record was $300,000 to William Rose for *It's a Mad, Mad, Mad, Mad World* (1963). Before that it was $150,000. In 1960 the average income was $15,000 a year. Moreover, William Goldman was a freelance, a term that was anathema a decade before. Columbia's executive story editor William Fadiman wrote an article ("The Typewriter Jungle," *Films and Filming*, December 1960, 8) explaining that the 1,800 writers in the Writers Guild of America (later the Screen Writers Guild) earned between them an annual $27 million which broke down into $15,000 each. "In fact, these 1,800-odd writers never write except for money," he commented. "There is a stern clause in their contracts that expressly forbids anything more than speculative than an exchange of ideas across a conference table with a prospective employer-producer. They assume no financial risk; they do not gamble with their time and talent the way as a playwright or novelist does. Even a rejection slip is alien to their way of life. Their scripts may well be rejected ("shelved" is the more picturesque Hollywood term) but this can only happen after they have been paid. Only when a writer is temporarily off the payroll does he ever attempt to write a story in the hope of selling it to a studio. But the quantity of such freelance submission is small. A Hollywood writer prefers the less hazardous procedure of being on salary."

782. He benefitted from the paperback boom of the 1960s, when big fat novels like his own *Boys and Girls Together* (1966)—movie rights purchased for $100,000—became "beach" and "airport" reads.

783. Opening sentence of *Adventures in the Screen Trade* by William Goldman (New York: Abacus, 2003).

784. Solomon, *Twentieth Century-Fox*, 255. *The Undefeated* (1969) cost $7.1 million, George Cukor's *Justine* (1969) $7.8 million.

785. Flynn, Bob, "A Slice of Lemmon for Extra Character," *Canberra Times*, August 15, 1998, 7. Jack Lemmon also turned it down.

786. It was completed before *Butch Cassidy and the Sundance*, but Universal sat on it for a year and then only brought it out months after *Butch Cassidy* had opened.

787. And a Best Director Oscar nomination for *Rachel, Rachel* (1968) starring his wife, Joanne Woodward.

788. Burt Bacharach was the composer in the Bacharach-David partnership responsible for hits like "Make it Easy on Yourself," "What's New

Pussycat," and "This Guy's in Love." He had also written the scores for *What's New Pussycat*, *After the Fox* (1966) and *Casino Royale*, but mostly was called upon to supply theme tunes like *Alfie*. As a stop-gap, Hill had used Simon and Garfunkel's "Fifty-Ninth Street Bridge Song (Feeling Groovy)," but was taken with Bacharach's "Raindrops Keep Falling on My Head" for the bicycle sequence. Despite that song's title, it was shot in bright sunlight and over the objections of the studio board of directors.

789. All-Time Champs," *Variety*, 1993; Hannan, *Coming Back*, 213–214, 232, 237–240, 249. Until television swooped, *Butch Cassidy and Sundance Kid* was barely off the screens in the 1970s and tripled its 1960s account, ending up with $45.9 million.

790. "Embassy to Release 23 in '63, Staff Told," *Box Office*, February 11, 1963. 6.

791. Sova, Dawn B., *Literature Suppressed on Sexual Grounds* (Infobase Publishing, 2006) 39. The book had "sex and/or sadism every 17 pages."

792. "That Money Writer Harold Robbins Sells Third (Unwritten) to Levine," *Variety*, September 18, 963, 3. Robbins was the first million-dollar novelist, earning a $1 million advance including movie rights for this book, *The Adventurers*. It was a premature investment since the film was not filmed till 1970.

793. "Pre-Sold A Dangerous Illusion," *Variety*, June 24, 1964, 11.

794. *Ibid.*

795. Advert, *Variety*, March 11, 1964, 17.

796. "Famed Plane to Appear in *The Carpetbaggers*," *Box Office*, August 26, 1963. The fashion show included a $40,000 sable coat worn by Elizabeth Ashley. The airplane mentioned in the title of this article was a pioneering Lockheed Vega being brought out of retirement to feature in the picture.

797. "Tie in for *Carpetbaggers*," *Box Office*, May 11, 1964. Carroll Baker was modelling the suntan lotion in adverts appearing in a variety of magazines.

798. It was banned from bookshops in Bridgeport ("Bridgeport Bans *Carpetbaggers*," *Variety*, March 21, 1962, 69) and faced an obscenity action in Albany ("*Carpetbaggers* Lawyers Act," *Variety*, December 26, 1962, 44).

799. "Set Top Female Roles for *Carpetbaggers*," *Box Office*, June 3, 1963, 15. Director Dymytryk spent seven days, 15 hours a day, working his way through 385 aspirants for the top female roles, in the end choosing Baker, Martha Hyer and Elizabeth Ashley. These talent hunts always produced acres of publicity.

800. "*Carpetbaggers* Seal Still Core of Verbiage," *Box Office*, October 28, 1963. Although Shurlock had approved the script, he demanded the removal of a semi-nude scene and some dialog.

801. Hannan, Brian, *In Theaters Everywhere: A History of Hollywood Wide Releases, 1913–2017* (Jefferson, NC: McFarland, 2019) 153. *The Carpetbaggers* took the top two weekly slots for the year.

802. Feature Reviews, *Box Office*, April 20, 1964; Crowther, Bosley, "*The Carpetbaggers* Opens," *New York Times*, July 2, 1964, 24; Scheuer, Philip K., "*Carpetbaggers* in Bad Taste as Film," *Los Angeles Times*, June 5, 1964; Coe, Richard L., "*Carpetbaggers* Safe on Base," *Washington Post*, June 13, 1964; Tube, Review, *Variety*, April 15, 1964, 6.

803. Mirisch, *I Thought We Were*, 218–219.

804. *Ibid.*, 220.

805. *Ibid.*, 221.

806. *Ibid.*, 222.

807. *Ibid.*, 223.

808. *Ibid.*, 227–228.

809. *Ibid.*, 228–229.

810. *Ibid.*, 229.

811. *Hawaii* Souvenir Program (hardback version). The first phase took place 150 miles above the Arctic Circle where sequences were filmed showing the ship *Thetis* sailing through the Magellan Straits, which, of course, was at the other end of the world. The second phases took place in Massachusetts. Seven weeks were spent in Hollywood sound stages during the third phase filming interiors and shipboard scenes using a full-sized replica of *Thetis*. Finally, in June 1965, the crew headed for Hawaii for four months. A village consisting of 107 buildings was constructed and a former Navy warehouse was converted into a sound stage.

812. Gill, Brendan, Review, *New Yorker*, October 29, 1966, 152; Sheuer, Philip K., "*Hawaii*—Poi in the Sky," *Los Angeles Times*, October 9, 1966; Canby, Vincent, "Big, Long Film Has Its Premiere," *New York Times*, October 11, 1966, 54.

813. All-Time Champs," *Variety*, 1993. Marginally downgraded from $16 million to $15.5 million.

814. *The Thomas Crown Affair* was his first screenplay.

815. D'Antoni would later produce *The French Connection* (1971) itself containing an epic car chase.

816. *Girl on a Motorcycle* (1968) was more of an erotic drama.

817. *Robbery* was inspired by the real Great Train Robbery in Britain a few years previously.

818. Day, Peter, "The Suggestive Experience," *Films and Filming*, August 1969, 4. Peter Yates said, "I wanted to make several changes to the script and also that I thought the only way to make this picture was to do it entirely on location. I felt that kind of picture had come back into popularity through the *Late, Late Show*, the James Cagney thriller, that kind of thing. What I tried to do was use that format to a) say something about America and b) bring it up to date by taking it out on the streets and making it on location."

819. Valdes-Dapena, Peter, *CNN*, January 10, 2020. "$3.7 million Ford Mustang driven in the movie *Bullitt* sells for record price." This was lent to the picture for promotional purposes.

820. Myers, Marc, "Chasing the Ghosts of *Bullitt*," *Wall St Journal*, January 26, 21011.

821. He played one of the hitmen in the film.

822. Monaco, *The Sixties*, 99.

Notes—The Films   237

823. Adler, Renata, Review, *New York Times*, October 18, 1968; Elsa, Review, *International Motion Picture Exhibitor*, October 30, 1968, 4; Austen, David, *Films and Filming*, November 1966, 39–40—despite what sounded like a negative tone the movie still got a three-star rating, the magazine's highest accolade.

824. All-Time Champs," *Variety*, 1993. *Bullitt* still had some gas left in the tank in the 1970s and went up to $19 million lifetime rentals.

825. She had also won a Tony in musical *I Can Get It for You Wholesale* on Broadway.

826. Herman, Jan, *William Wyler, A Talent for Trouble* (New York: Da Capo Press, 1997, 442). The project actually began as a straightforward biography, a book he commissioned called *The Fabulous Fanny*, but it never saw the light of day. Stark did not like the result and bought up the printer's plates for $50,000 to prevent publication.

827. *Ibid.* Ben Hecht had first crack at the screenplay and so did ten others. Isobel Lennart was the eleventh. She penned a musical entitled *My Man* that gave Stark enough of a basis for a stage show.

828. Garson Kanin directed from a book by Isobel Lennart with lyrics by Bob Merrill and music by Jule Styne.

829. "N.Y. Box Scores," *Billboard*, April 11, 1964, 10. Mike Gross of *Billboard* was a naysayer, describing the musical as a "routine backstage yarn that plods along unimaginatively." The score by Jule Styne was judged by the *New York Daily News* and the *New York Times* as "not one of his best." But later reviews put a different slant on things. An advert in *Billboard* (April 18, 1964, 7) showed *Time* commenting that "Barbra Streisand sets the theater ablaze." *Variety* called it "a gem of a show" and the *New York World-Telegram* deemed it "just this side of paradise."

830. It was nominated in every category.

831. It ran for over three years on Broadway and Streisand headed up the cast for the London transfer. The cast album hit the number two spot on the *Billboard* chart.

832. "*Girl* Caster Goes Up, Up," *Billboard*, July 11, 1964, 32.

833. "Barbra Streisand Pacing Field with Five Gold Disk Albums," *Billboard*, February 6, 1965, 12. Commented the music trade magazine, "Prime excitement stemming from Miss Streisand's extraordinary success is the fact that when a girl has a hit in the record market the pattern has been that she's rarely able to follow up that success let alone parlay it into a string of even greater successes."

834. "Barbra's Star Glow Brightly," *Billboard*, July 11, 1964, 20. Her annual earnings had gone from $23,000 in 1962 to $225,000 in 1963 to $500,000 in 1964 and with her television deal could easily surpass $1 million in 1965.

835. "Barbra Lands Whale of a Deal," *Billboard*, July 11, 1964, 20. She signed a 10-year deal guaranteeing her a minimum $5 million.

836. He also made comedy *Drop Dead Darling* (1966) with Tony Curtis and the offbeat *Oh Dad, Poor Dad, Mamma's Hung You in the Closet and I'm Feeling So Sad* (1967).

837. Herman, *William Wyler,* 442. Stark turned down $400,000 from Columbia for the musical, preferring to retain control.

838. *Ibid.*

839. "*Funny Girl* Looking for Director and Studio After Lumet-Stark Split," *Variety*, January 18, 1967, 13. "Artistic" differences were the cause of the split between director and producer. Stark was reported as also switching the musical over to Warner Brothers.

840. "Wm. Wyler First Tuner, Co-Producer with Stark on Columbia's *Funny Girl*," *Variety*, March 22, 1967, 4. Columbia was sticking with Stark. The dispute had been over the budget.

841. By Francis Ford Coppola.

842. Herman, *William Wyler,* 441.

843. *Ibid.*, 442. Wyler had been invited to see the stage musical with a view to directing but claimed he was too hard of hearing and turned the project down.

844. Merger, Crowther, "*Funny Girl* Profits—It's a Big Week for Col." *International Motion Picture Exhibitor*, September 25, 1968, 6.

845. Herman, *William Wyler,* 445.

846. *Ibid.*

847. *Ibid.*, 444.

848. Advert, *Billboard*, April 18, 1964, 7. The idea of carrying an image over from one medium to the next, most usually from book cover to film poster, was generally seen as having originated in the 1970s with films like *The Godfather* (1972) and *Jaws* (1975). Clearly, it did not.

849. The budget, as Columbia had predicted, had gone up.

850. Advert, *Variety*, July 11. 1967, 11. Since a total of 44 performances were already sold out ahead of the film's launch on September 11, 1968, "even before any advert appeared," Columbia was now inviting the public to put their names down to go on a "first choice" mailing list. The sold-out shows were, presumably, groups, and the mailing list would allow individuals to get ahead of the pack in buying tickets.

851. Advert, *Box Office*, May 6, 1968. Months ahead of opening, the film had already broken advance booking records set by the likes of *My Fair Lady*.

852. Elsa, *International Motion Picture Exhibitor*, September 25, 1968, 6; Coe, Richard L, "*Funny Girl* at The Ontario," *Washington Post*, October 24, 1968; Abel, Review, *Variety*, September 25, 1968, 6; Ebert, Roger, Review, *Chicago Sun-Times*, October 18, 1968.

853. All-Time Champs," *Variety*, 1993; Hannan, *Coming Back*, 231–231. *Funny Girl* continued to sell well in the 1970s and hit the top scales with $26.3 million.

854. "UA Cuts in on *Jones* Import Kudos," *Variety*, October 16, 1963, 5. It had been traditional for

Notes—The Films

big Hollywood studios to put a firewall between themselves and the fall-out from any sexy pictures they might import, United Artists did this through a company it owned called Lopert. But after the movie's sensational New York opening and talk already beginning of Oscars the "big company wants a piece of the action" and almost immediately United Artists put its brand on the picture.

855. Petrie, Duncan, *Bryanston Films: An Experiment in Cooperative Independent Film Production and Distribution* (Historical Journal of Film, Radio and Television, Volume 38, 2018, Issue 1) 95–115. The black-and-white *Saturday Night and Sunday Morning* cost $406,000 and *The Loneliness of the Long Distance Runner* $455,000, budgets that even Hollywood B-picture specialists would find on the low side.

856. Woodfall was set up by future Bond producer Harry Saltzman, director Tony Richardson and playwright John Osborne initially to make a cinematic version of his stage success *Look Back in Anger* (1959).

857. *Ibid.*

858. *Tom Jones* Pressbook. A special "motion picture" unabridged paperback edition of the book was published by Signet with the movie artwork on the cover surrounded by film reviews. The soundtrack was also being heavily promoted. "The windfall of rave notices," exhibitors were reminded, provided the opportunity for a 40"×60" free-standing lobby poster to be situated in a shopping center "and other places where it will get big crowd exposure."

859. Eyles, Allen, *Odeon Cinemas 2: From J. Arthur Rank to the Multiplex* (London: Cinema Theatre Association, 2005) 210. It was ranked in the top 12 films of the year at the box office by the British Odeon chain.

860. "Four New Bills Boost Uneven B'Way," *Variety*, October 16, 1963, 9–10. The movie took $35,500 at the 700-seat Cinema One. The theater put on extra shows. The total was more than Cinema One and Cinema Two had ever taken together.

861. Advert, *Variety*, December 4, 1963, 12. It rolled out in San Francisco on December 17, Boston and Chicago a day later, and Washington on Xmas Day.

862. Pressbook. *Women's Wear Daily* was promoting fashions inspired by the film—a male nightshirt and a "Tom Jones Girl" look.

863. *Ibid.* Since a bed was the focus of all the advertising, exhibitors were pointed in the direction of furniture stores for cross-promotion activities.

864. A separate Pressbook was created to promote the film's success to exhibitors.

865. "Finney's % on *Tom Jones* Goes Over $1 Million," *Variety*, October 21, 1964, 1.

866. "John Bull in his Barnyard," *Time*, October 18, 1963; Rich, Review, *Variety*, July 13, 1963,12; Knight, Arthur in Byron and Weir, *National Society of Film Critics*, 143–144.

867. These reviews were splashed all over the movie's Pressbook.

868. Hilliers, *Cahiers du Cinéma Vol 2*, 329–334.

869. All-Time Champs," *Variety*, 1993. Marginally downgraded from the original $17.2 million.

870. Lee had originated the part on the Broadway production.

871. "Promotion Meeting for *Love Bug* Held in New York Buena Vista," *Box Office*, November 4, 1968.

872. "Volkswagen Tie-in for *Love Bug*," *Box Office*, February 10, 1969, 2.

873. Listed in the opening credits as well as Hickman and Ekins were another 20 speedsters including Formula One driver Bob Drake.

874. *Midnight Cowboy* and *Easy Rider* continued to play into the 1970s and *The Love Bug*, as per standard Disney modus operandi, was reissued several years after initial opening. Taking this into account, *The Love Bug* was the overall top rental earner with $23.1 million, then came *Midnight Cowboy* with $20.4 million and *Easy Rider* on $19.1 million. It never occurred to any other studio to invest in adult-friendly family pictures rather than those just aimed at youth.

875. Whit, Review, *Variety*, December 11, 1968, 6; Feature Reviews, *Box Office*, January 6, 1969; Davis, Richard *Films and Filming*, August 1969, 40; Canby, Vincent, "And Now a Word From...," *New York Times*, March 14, 1969, 50.

876. All-Time Champs," *Variety*, 1993; Hannan, *Coming Back*, 232, 249. Disney fired out *The Love Bug* in a double bill with *The Jungle Book* in 1970 and then solo six years later and, surprisingly, it was the latter program that did better. In total rentals were boosted to $23.1 million.

877. Dunne, John Gregory, *The Studio* (New York: Farrar, Straus & Giroux, 1969; reprinted in Vintage paperback 1998) 4. In the previous three years it had lost an additional $48.5 million and had to sell most of its backlot for $43 million to stay afloat.

878. Eyman, *John Wayne*, 363.

879. *Ibid.*

880. *Lawrence of Arabia* was in production at the same time and with two unknowns—Peter O'Toole and Omar Sharif—in the leads had bolstered the film with Oscar-winners Alec Guinness and Anthony Quinn.

881. "A Cheque for the Real Thing," *Films and Filming*, November 1962, 10–11 Unlike the chaotic multi-directorial approach of *Casino Royale* (1967), this was a highly-coordinated exercise. He said, "From the very beginning I had two units shooting simultaneously and at times there were four… everything had been worked out in advance, in great detail and I used a helicopter to drop in on my directors and supervise the work being done."

882. *Ibid.* Said Zanuck, "This is the first time I have directed so substantial a portion of one of my own films."

883. *Dr. No* and *The Longest Day* were launched about the same time in Britain. To British audiences, revelling in James Bond, his appearance was

Notes—The Films

greeted with recognition. Connery did not have the same impact on American audiences. But by the time of the film's reissue in 1969, he was the biggest star, outside of John Wayne, in the picture.

884. Annakin, *So You Wanna*, 137.

885. *Ibid.*, 139.

886. *Ibid.*, 139–140.

887. "A Cheque for the Real Thing," *Films and Filming*.

888. Review, *Variety*, October 3, 1962, 6; Gill, Brendan, Review, *New Yorker*, October 14, 1962, 188; Coe, Richard L., "*Longest Day* Is Battle Epic," *Washington Post*, October 12, 1962,

889. Hannan, *Coming Back*, 144, 157. 172. The 1964 reissue turned out to be an exercise in hubris rather than anything else. Zanuck had decided that the 20th anniversary of D-Day was too good an opportunity to miss so he yanked the film out of theaters when it still had decent mileage and relaunched it with marketing hullabaloo—and it sank like a stone. The 1969 reissue—25th anniversary of D-Day—did much better since the film had been out of circulation for several years.

890. That had originally been planned as the fifth Bond but shelved due to location costs.

891. Field, Matthew and Chowdhury, Ajay, "He's a Bit Quirky, Isn't He?" *Cinema Retro*, Vol 13, Issue 39, 22. He wrote a treatment closely based on the book.

892. He received an Additional Story Material credit and was responsible for Bond's fake death and the ninja attack.

893. Hannan, *The Making of The Guns of Navarone*, 196. This was his actual movie debut because he had previously written *The Bells of Hell Go Ting-a-Ling-a-Ling* starring Gregory Peck that had been cancelled mid-shoot.

894. Gilbert, *All My Flashbacks*, 269–270.

895. Dahl, Roald, "007's Oriental Playfuls," *Playboy*, June 1967, 86–87.

896. *Ibid.*, 267. The Japanese authorities had stipulated that the actresses be genuinely Japanese not American Japanese.

897. Filmed as *International Secret Police: Key of Keys*, it had been re-edited and dubbed by Woody Allen and turned into a comedy.

898. *Ibid.*, 270–271.

899. Field, Matthew and Chowdhury, Ajay, "What's A Nice Girl Like You Doping in a Place Like This?" *Cinema Retro*, Vol 13, Issue 39, 36.

900. *Ibid.*, 277.

901. *Ibid.*, 274–275.

902. Ebert, Roger, Review, *Chicago Sun-Times*, June 19, 1967; Crowther, Bosley, "Sayonara 007," *New York Times*, June 14, 1967, 40; Review, *Variety*, June 14, 1967.

903. "All-Time Champs," *Variety* 1993. The film only added a small extra amount in the 1970s bringing the lifetime rentals to $19.4 million.

904. Hannan, *Coming Back*, 175. It was the first Bond reissue not to be coupled with another 007 picture. Instead it went out on a double bill with *The Good, the Bad and the Ugly*, kicking off a

pattern of United Artists pairing the Connery pictures with those of Clint Eastwood.

905. In *The Long Ships* (1964) and *The Bedford Incident* (1965) he was given second billing behind Richard Widmark, hardly a huge star, and in *Duel at Diablo* (1966) it was the same again below James Garner.

906. "Sammy Davis to Produce *The Man* with Poitier," *Box Office*, March 29, 1965, 17; "Seven More Para. Films on Production Line-Up," *Box Office*, May 31, 1965, 15. *The Man* based on the Irving Wallace bestseller was about the first African American president. The other film was *Down Will Come the Sky* to be directed by Sydney Pollack, who had directed Poitier in *The Slender Thread* (1965). He was also lined up ("Poitier as Crown Prince," *Variety*, December 22, 1965, 2) for *Doctor Dolittle* (1967) behind Rex Harrison but did not participate.

907. Filmed in 1965 by Bryan Forbes who also wrote the screenplay.

908. "Clavell's *Tai Pan* Goes to Ransohoff?" *Variety*, January 29, 1966, 3. It had, indeed, and for an asking price of $750,000. The book had been a massive bestseller. MGM had come on board as financier. Martin Ransohoff was a top independent producer and had made *The Sandpiper* (1965) with Elizabeth Taylor and Richard Burton and *The Cincinnati Kid* (1965) with Steve McQueen.

909. "Col of Canada Finally Releases Clavell Pic," *Variety*, August 31, 1966, 14. It had been held up due to litigation. It had been shot in Vancouver and Clavell had acted in a triple-hyphenate capacity—writer, producer and director. But it disappeared without trace at the box office.

910. It was published in 1959.

911. Beaupre, Lee, "Deferred Pay as Key to Quality," *Variety*, September 20, 1967, 5.

912. Five weeks at Pinewood studios and three weeks exteriors, although this was limited to shots of red double-decker buses, dockland areas, landmark tourist sites and the scene at the museum.

913. *Ibid.*; "Some Talent Stars Share in Risk," *Variety*, May 18, 1966, 5. The profit shares were significantly different. Poitier got his share off the top, out of the gross, while Clavell had to wait until the film went into profit. If the film flopped, they would earn nothing. It was a decent enough gamble—no Poitier film grossed less than the $2 million required to break even. So even if it just did that Poitier would earn his normal fee of around $200,000. As this book has shown, small British films had achieved success in America—but that was with British stars, so it was no guarantee that Poitier's fans would take to the star in a film located so far from home. *The Long Ships*, for example, had not exactly set the box office alight. Poitier's deal was 10 percent, Clavell's 30 percent.

914. This trend, a bid to capture the youth market, explained the appearance of John Lennon in *How I Won the War* (1967) and Paul Jones in *Privilege* (1967). Even so, her presence defeated the purpose. She would sing the theme song, but it would

240   **Notes—The Films**

not attract any attention since it was put out on the B-side of "The Boat That I Row."

915. Suzy Kendall (*Circus of Fear*, 1966) had her biggest role so far making an appearance as a sympathetic teacher with romantic leanings towards Poitier which are not reciprocated.

916. Murf, Review, *Variety*, June 14, 1967, 6. The trade paper noted that Columbia's treatment of the film's release was "bizarre." Basic promotional material had been put out six months before, and it had been screened to exhibitors in May ("Congrats Col on *To Sir with Love*," *Box Office*, May 22, 1967). The paper commented, "(This) policy is usually a manifestation of fear on the part of a distributor who either has a dud on its hands or does not know what to do with the film." British expectations were no higher, the release held back until after the American opening, when a standard marketing ploy might have seen the studio open it in London, hope to build an audience and use those box office figures to attract the attention of American exhibitors.

917. "Poitier Redhot in TV Ratings," *Variety*, April 19, 1967, 1; "*Lilies* Top Pic of Season," *Variety*, April 26, 1967, 168; "Poitier Drops Out of NBC's *Othello*," *Variety*, August 31, 1966, 25. The first story here, which also mentioned him hosting a television special *A Time for Laughter*, was front-page news in the trade paper, and the public response to the *Lilies* screening demonstrated Poitier had enormous, untapped, pull. CBS had been first to try to attract Poitier to playing *Othello*, NBC picking up the project when it dropped out, the concept eventually collapsing because both networks could not contemplate running the play at its proper length. In fact, it would be a television studio which was the first to recognise his potential as a top-billed star. ABC, through its movie-making arm, lined up Poitier in *For Love of Ivy* ("ABC Makes Feature Deals with David, Nelson, Maybe Poitier," *Variety*, June 14, 1967, 3).

918. Ironically, even as Columbia continued to sit on *To Sir with Love*, he was hired to make another film for the studio, *Guess Who's Coming to Dinner*, but, in reality, that was nothing to do with Columbia since the movie was being made by independent producer Stanley Kramer, over whom Columbia had no power of veto regarding his casting choices.

919. Murf, Review, *Variety*, June 14, 1967, 6. Trade paper reviews differed from consumer magazine reviews because they always attempted to estimate where a movie's appeal might lie and its potential box office. In this instance, the reviewer, "Murf," reckoned the film's best way forward was through "youth appeal."

920. The movie needed some kind of magic because it opened in New York the same week as *You Only Live Twice* and *The Dirty Dozen*.

921. Advert, *Variety*, June 21, 1967, 21. The movie broke the five-day record.

922. "*Sir* Looms Big; Ditto Staircase; Pedagog Cycle," *Variety*, July 12, 1967, 4. In Boston it broke records in two arthouses.

923. From British Guiana.

924. Poitier had already been on the other end of the teacher-pupil divide after playing the rebellious student challenging Glenn Ford in *Blackboard Jungle* (1955).

925. This is never explained since corporal punishment was endemic at the time.

926. Crowther, Bosley, "Poitier Meets the Cockneys: He Plays Teacher Who Wins Pupils Over," *New York Times*, June 15, 1967; Murf, Review, *Variety*, June 14, 1967, 6; Feature Reviews, *Box Office*, Jun 19, 1967.

927. All-Time Champs," *Variety* 1993. The film was done by the end of the decade in terms of reaping more rentals and its lifetime rental figure did not stray from this figure. However, it was by far, Poitier's biggest payday. The rental translated into at least a $40 million gross, so Poitier would taken home $4 million, making him, by a long margin, the top-earning actor in Hollywood. He might have even earned more than Clavell, whose percentage was based on the rentals, but who would have been subject to whatever other costs the studio applied to the picture before it was deemed "profitable."

928. Hannan, *Coming Back*, 188–189. Poitier's success turned him into a reissue star and his movies tumbled out in various double bills.

929. "The reason for this humorlessness," writes Donald Spoto in *Stanley Kramer Film Maker* (London: Samuel French edition, 1990, 20) "is probably the insistent gravity with which Kramer has viewed the world and himself."

930. As producer (the Best Picture award is for the producer) he was nominated for *High Noon*, *The Caine Mutiny* (1954), *The Defiant Ones*, *Judgment at Nuremberg* and *Ship of Fools* (1965); as director it was for *The Defiant Ones* and *Judgment at Nuremberg*.

931. Kramer, Stanley, with Coffey, Thomas M., *A Mad Mad Mad Mad World: A Life in Hollywood* (New York: Harcourt Brace and Company, 1997) 193.

932. Canby, Vincent, "*Mad World's* $280,000 Junket," *Variety*, Nov 6, 1963, 4.

933. Pressbook.

934. "Angle on Stage Auto Accident," *Variety*, July 11, 1962, 15.

935. Pressbook.

936. "UA Going Cinerama with Steven's *Greatest Story* & Kramer's *World*," *Variety*, August 15, 1962, 3.

937. "Big, *Mad, Mad Sign*," *Box Office*, June 24, 1963. Getting the new theater built cost a fortune in overtime. To ensure everyone knew it was there, the biggest movie sign in the world—265ft × 8ft— was erected above the theater.

938. "Kramer Touts His One-Eye Cinerama and Vexes Metro, Reisini and Stevens," *Variety*, November 6, 1963, 4. There was only one problem promoting the single-strip Cinerama—and that was you reminded the public that MGM's current Cinerama picture *How the West Was Won* was

Notes—The Films

241

filmed in the older three-strip process which, on projection, showed up as vertical lines on the screen.

939. "Kramer Puts Spotlight on Hollywood," *Motion Picture Herald*, April 24, 1963, 6. Biggest press launch ever with over $400,000 spent on bringing in global journalists.

940. Feature Reviews, *Box Office*, November 18, 1963; Tube, Review, *Variety*, November 6, 1963, 6; Bean, Robin, *Films and Filming*, January 1964, 25.

941. All-Time Champs," *Variety* 1993; Hannan, *Coming Back*, 216, 232. As the result of a reissue in 1970, the movie's lifetime rental increased to $20.8 million.

942. Mirisch, *I Thought We Were*, 124. Their ages by the time the film appeared.

943. Woodward, Ian, *Audrey Hepburn* (London: W.H. Allen, [1984] 2007) 231, 239.

944. *Ibid.*

945. When the movie appeared.

946. Clayton, Dick and Heard, James, *Elvis: By Those Who Knew Him Best* (New York: Virgin Publishing, 2003) 226.

947. Long, Robert Emmet, *Broadway, The Golden Years: Jerome Robbins and the Great Choreographer-Directors* (New York: Continuum International Publishing Group, 2003) 96.

948. Laurents, Arthur, *Original Story By: A Memoir of Broadway and Hollywood* (New York: Knopf, 2000) 354.

949. It won for choreography and scenic design but lost out in the Best Musical category to *The Music Man*.

950. "Race Against Raze," *Variety*, August 24, 1961, 16. General Demolition which was clearing away a section of Lincoln Square had agreed to leave intact one street between Amsterdam and West End Ave. However, the interiors of the buildings had already been gutted as well as windows removed and all markings. This part of the shoot lasted 22 days and cost $200,000.

951. Mirisch, *I Thought We Were*, 125–6. Initially, Wise had maintained there was "no conflict" with Robbins ("Wise Softens Stereo on *West Side Story*; Tandem Direction Okay, Not Easy," *Variety*, March 8, 1961, 3).

952. Mirisch, *I Thought We Were*, 126. Costs did not include a substantial sum being spent on marketing ("Up to $4,000,000 Budget to Promote 3 UA Films," *Box Office*, August 7, 1961, 11). However, fears about the escalating costs were offset by advance sales ("*West Side Story* Racks Up Record Advance Sales," *Box Office*, October 23, 1961, 5) of $215,000 for launch venue, the Rivoli in New York.

953. "Top LPs," *Billboard*, November 20, 1961. At this stage, about a month before the film was launched, the original cast album had spent 59 weeks on the *Billboard* chart and currently stood at No. 20. Stan Kenton had his interpretation of the show's music at No. 41 after five weeks. The original movie soundtrack had been released ahead of launch and after five weeks in the chart stood at No. 48. However, sales of the cast album paled

into insignificance against *South Pacific* at No. 35 after 389 weeks, *My Fair Lady* at No. 37 (294 weeks) and *The Sound of Music* at No. 7 (101 weeks). Original movie soundtracks had undergone a public re-evaluation and Ernest Gold's *Exodus* themes, now at No. 13, had spent 45 weeks in the chart while *Never on Sunday*, after 44 weeks, was currently at No. 28 and a compilation "Great Motion Picture Themes"—including *The Alamo*, *Exodus*, *The Magnificent Seven* and *Never on Sunday*—stood at No. 19 after 43 weeks.

954. The only category it lost out in was Best Screenplay.

955. Reviews taken from advert in *Billboard*, November 6, 1961, 5.

956. Reviews taken from advert in *Variety*, November 1, 1961, 10–11.

957. Hilliers, *Cahiers du Cinéma Vol 2*, 239–334.

958. All-Time Champs," *Variety* 1993. *West Side Story* was one of several movies whose rental was downgraded. Initially, it had been reported as $25 million for the end of this decade, but that was later re-assessed to produce this current figure.

959. Nunnally Johnson had been Oscar-nominated for John Ford's *The Grapes of Wrath* (1940) and *Holy Matrimony* (1943) and wrote *The Desert Fox* (1951) and *Mr. Hobbs Takes a Vacation* (1962), starring James Stewart. He was also a director—*The Man in the Grey Flannel Suit* (1956) and *The Angel Wore Red* (1960) among others. Prior to his involvement, Henry Denker who had written *Twilight of Honor* for Perlberg-Seaton was lined up for the screenplay.

960. "Up *Dirty Dozen* for Widescreen," *Variety*, April 19, 1967, 4. Aldrich battled for *The Dirty Dozen* to be a roadshow picture, but MGM already had too many of those. The compromise was a 70mm launch (35mm blown up with six-track stereophonic sound) for its premiere booking (and overseas) but everywhere else ordinary general release.

961. Eyman, *John Wayne*, 496.

962. Producer William Perlberg and director George Seaton were most famous for *The Country Girl* (1954).

963. In November 1963—18 months before publication. Novels were always being purchased while still in the galley stage but this must have set some kind of record.

964. Hannan, Brian, "*The Dirty Dozen*," *Cinema Retro*, Vol 13, Issue 38, 24,

965. After Perlberg and Seaton split up.

966. A producer most famous for *The Hill* (1965) starring Sean Connery.

967. "Aldrich Sells Shares of *Dozen* to MGM," *Box Office*, January 15, 1968. He had been promised 15 percent of the profits and now he cashed in, to the tune of $1.4 million. This was a huge sum for a director, but he needed the money to build his own studio. If Aldrich had held on, he would have received more cash.

968. Both starred Burt Lancaster. He had also received artistic acclaim for *The Big Knife* (1955),

winner of the Silver Lion at the Venice Film Festival, and *Autumn Leaves* (1956), Silver Bear at the Berlin equivalent.

969. Hannan, *Cinema Retro*.

970. *Ibid.*, 25. Other actors considered for roles were George Chakiris while Jack Palance turned down $125,000 for the Savalas role.

971. "Jim Brown's Two Jobs; Football, Pic Conflict," *Variety*, June 29, 1966, 11 "*Dirty Dozen* Reaps Ballyhoo on Jim Brown Case," *Variety*, July 20, 1966, 28. While filming, it somehow (I wonder how) got into the newspapers that Brown was considering retirement after he finished the picture. This created a torrent of newspaper interest and at least kept sports fans extremely well informed about the film.

972. Walker had been top-billed in the low-budget *Maya* (1966).

973. George Kennedy and Ernest Borgnine had been in The *Flight of the Phoenix*, and Charles Bronson and Richard Jaeckel in *4 for Texas* (1964). Borgnine had won the Oscar for *Marty* (1955) and had a few swings at being a leading man but usually in lower-budgeted pictures. Bronson had starred as *Machine Gun Kelly* (1958). Kennedy would win Best Supporting Actor for *Cool Hand Luke* (1967). Cassavettes was an acclaimed independent low-budget director of *Shadows* (1958).

974. He was working in London with bit parts in British television series *Gideon's Way* and *The Saint*. You might have spotted him in the British-filmed *The Bedford Incident* (1965) and *Interlude* (1968).

975. "3 Yank Films Stalled: Erratic Weather in Europe This Summer," *Variety*, August 24, 1966; "Cheaper by *The Dozen*," *Variety*, September 20, 1966, 27. The picture had to dip into its contingency fund of $500,000 pushing the budget up to $4 million. In addition, a fire at the set of the chateau had cost $80,000 and extra time for rebuilding. Although the film would not benefit from the Eady Levy—the tax cash-back system operated by the British government for American pictures made in Britain—since there were too many Americans involved, the country had been deliberately chosen for the locations. Continuity could get out of whack if a sequence that started off with bright blue skies was suddenly interrupted by grey skies or rain.

976. "Some MGM European Features Burst Budgets but O'Brien Holds Boxoffice Potential Justified," *Variety*, September 14, 966, 3. O'Brien was the MGM boss. At this stage, the budget was now up to $5 million—$1.5 million ahead of the original plan. He blamed delays for putting the movie behind schedule. That forced Trini Lopez to quit to fulfill other commitments, explaining why he is missing from the attack on the chateau. "Aldrich Sells Shares of *Dozen* to MGM," *Box Office*, January 15, 1968—now that the film was a huge success MGM could afford to admit that the final budget was $5.6 million.

977. Eyles, Allen, "The Private War of Robert Aldrich," *Films and Filming*, September 1967, 4–9.

Apart from the obvious prestige, one of the reasons Aldrich was keen to go roadshow (see note above) was length. His experience with *The Flight of the Phoenix* had instilled in him the notion that the ideal running time for a film in general release was 140 minutes. *The Flight of the Phoenix* had come in at 142 minutes. He explained, "You said 2 hours and 22 minutes to a distributor, he'll tell you without seeing it it's two minutes too long. It has nothing to do with whether the picture is too long. Every picture has its own length but that bit of wisdom is not shared by the distribution companies." By that standard, at 150 minutes, *The Dirty Dozen* was ten minutes too long.

978. Feature Reviews, *Box Office*, June 26, 1967; Durgnat, Raymond, *Films and Filming*, October 1967, 21.

979. Murf, Review, *Variety*, June 21, 1967, 6. This sounded as though *Variety* was trying to do MGM's promotional job for them because a long action movie with no women was considered a risky prospect, ignoring the exception of *Lawrence of Arabia*. In fact, MGM was conscious of this problem and the Pressbook offered suggestions to "interest the ladies" (sexist as that sounds now) by offering a free ticket to the movie to anyone who brings 12 bags of wash in one day to a Laundromat ("Dirty Dozen Day"). Exhibitors were prompted to organize a nursery in the lobby or see if a local fashion shop would promote a "military look."

980. All-Time Champs," *Variety* 1993; Hannan, *Coming Back*, 172. *The Dirty Dozen* had been quickly reissued before the end of the decade and did not earn any more.

981. "Deutsch (*The Unsinkable Molly Brown*, 1964) and Kingsley (*Pal Joey*, 1957) were veterans but only came onto the project after Harlan Ellison (*The Oscar*, 1966) who demanded his name be removed from the credits when the ending was altered.

982. "Seven Premieres on Cruise Ship Set to Launch *Dolls*," *Box Office*, September 18, 196; "*Dolls* Debut Set For December 15," *Box Office*, October 30, 1967. There was some confusion as to what actually constituted a world premiere. Fox had hired the *MS Princess Italia* for a series of charity premieres. The first took place in Genoa, so conceivably that counted as the world premiere. But the movie's launch at the upscale Criterion in New York was also promoted as the world premiere.

983. Its status as the worst (or best) film in this category was guaranteed after the publication of *Bad Movies We Love*, by Stephen Rebello and Edward Margulies who placed it as the top of this particular pantheon.

984. Susann was already 30 when, after small parts on stage, she made her first appearance on television, a running bit part in *The Moray Amsterdam Show* at the end of the 1940s. She had small roles in episodes of three television series but no luck with the movies though not for want of trying and she channeled her disappointing acting career into fuel for *Valley of the Dolls*.

985. "A Real Lively *Doll*," *Variety*, September 21, 1966, 68. By this time it had spent 20 weeks atop the *New York Times* hardback bestseller list (21 weeks if you went by the *Time* chart) with 354,000 copies sold. There had been no book club sales, either, which was usually what helped drive big books to big numbers. She was already the bestselling female author of all time in hardback, outranking Grace Metalious (*Peyton Place*), Mary McCarthy (*The Group*), Katherine Anne Porter (*Ship of Fools*) and even Margaret Mitchell (*Gone with the Wind*).

986. Only 22 percent of the titles in the annual Top Ten charts of the 1960s and 24 percent of the 1950s were by female writers, according to a survey I undertook based on the *Publishers Weekly* figures. In those 20 years only two books by female authors topped the annual chart, *Ship of Fools* by Katherine Anne Porter and *Valley of the Dolls*. The two authors had this much in common: very little in the way of formal education and careers that initially skirted the edges of the movie business.

987. Only *The Group* (1966) with five top female roles and *Little Women* (1949) with four could offer anything comparable.

988. "*Valley of the Dolls* as Dialog Dilly in Screen Form," *Variety*, September 7, 1966, 3. It was described as a "high priority item" for the studio. Fox wanted to make a film quickly to capitalize on expected high sales and, not expecting it to reach the phenomenal status, wanted a movie out before it dropped out of the bestseller charts. But that never happened. "Sexy Novel Tops the Magellan Bit, *Dolls* Rolls Home," *Variety*, November 29, 1967, 5. Fox had bought the book pre-publication for $200,000. Susann had received $75,000 as a down payment and then 75c per hardback copy sold until the figure reached the $200,000. "Runaway Paperback," *Variety*, August 9, 1967, 70. Bantam had sold 5.3 million copies in less than a month. The paperback cost $1.25 per copy, of which Susann received a royalty of 13 cents, and had already pocketed $72,000. By the time the film appeared sales had topped 8.65 million.

989. Rebello, Stephen, *Dolls! Dolls! Dolls! Deep Inside Valley of the Dolls* (New York: Random House, 2020) 98.

990. "Candice Bergen's Nix," *Variety*, February 15, 1967, 5.

991. Rebello, *Dolls! Dolls! Dolls!*, 105–114.

992. *Ibid.*, 128.

993. "They Only Had to Ask Me Once," *Variety*, March 8, 1967, 5.

994. Best Supporting Actress Oscar for *The Miracle Worker* (1962).

995. "Barb Parkins Back, No *Peyton* Shutdown," *Variety*, May 10, 1967, 48. She returned to the television show once filming on *Valley of the Dolls* was complete.

996. Discounting a bit part in low-budget *20,000 Eyes* (1961).

997. "Records For *Dolls* Songs in France, Italy and Germany," *Box Office*, December 4, 1967. Tony Scotti cut an album of songs from the film

including the theme "Come Live with Me" and then sang the songs in three other languages apart from English which were released abroad.

998. *Ibid.*, 52–53. Mark Robson had dropped out of another Fox project, *The Detective* (1968), in itself a surprising choice because he had fallen out with its star Frank Sinatra while filming *Von Ryan's Express*. Robson's initial remuneration was low, just $82,500, until you took in his profit share which pushed his total package closer to $300,000.

999. "*Valley of the Dolls* as Dialog Dilly in Screen Form," *Variety*, September 7, 1966, 3; "Dorothy Kinglsey Adapts *Valley of Dolls*; Its Filming Problematic," *Variety*, December 14, 1966, 4. Helen Deutsch complained that she was "struggling with the lingo" of the book and to stay "in the bounds of good taste."

1000. "H'wood Fashions Boom Year," *Variety*, October 4, 1967, 5. Although overshadowed by the $1 million spent on *Doctor Dolittle* and the $750,000 for *Star!* given musicals always had hefty costume budgets, it was a significant sum for a straightforward drama. Travilla designed a $17,000 dress for Judy Garland and then the studio had to commission another one for $20,000 for her replacement Susan Hayward because the women were different sizes.

1001. *Ibid.* Made-to-measure outfits from Travilla's retailing operation cost $400-$4,000, well out of the pocketbook of the ordinary woman, but many of his designs were sold to manufacturers for retail in fashion stores all over the country.

1002. *Ibid.*

1003. Rebello, *Dolls! Dolls! Dolls!*, 147.

1004. *Ibid.*, 166, 171, 173, 175,

1005. "David Wiesbart Dies; Prominent Producer," *Box Office*, July 31, 1967, 9.

1006. "20th-Fox Ballyhoo Film Before Production Starts," Box Office, March 21, 1966. The novel had been published on February 10. Fox launched a three-stage mail shot to all the country's media. Stage one was a document containing a prescription, stage two was an imitation "doll" (the pills of the title) and stage three was a copy of the book.

1007. "*Valley of the Dolls* Outfits in New York Exhibition," *Box Office*, June 19, 1967; "National Fashion Shows for *Valley of Dolls*," *Box Office*, October 2, 1967; advert, *Box Office*, December 4, 1967, 4–5. These consisted either of fashion shows aimed at fashion editors or to the public at department stores across the country. Over 60 of the outfits designed by Travilla had found their way into retail.

1008. "Guess-Who Angles of Fox *Dolls* Bringing Back Legal Disclosure Increasingly Omitted Nowadays," *Variety*, December 6, 1967, 5. Studios had by and large done away with this concept.

1009. *Ibid.*, 98. Production Code supremo Geoffrey Shurlock sent the producers a long list of words, lines and actions to be removed from the film.

1010. Review, *Variety*, December 20, 1967, 6; Feature Reviews, *Box Office*, December 18, 1967.

1011. Durgnat, Raymond, Review, *Films and Filming*, March 1968, 31–32. This was the only review I came across that seemed to get the picture. The magazine rated it two-stars (the same as *Will Penny* and above *Point Blank* in the same issue) and its top rating was three-stars (it was actually a four-level rating system because often films got no stars at all). "This is the best split-level show...He has set out to out-Hunter Ross, to out-Sirk Douglas... And the result! Dada lives. This is Hollywood's first auto-satirical soap-opera."

1012. The film was done and dusted in terms of extra revenue by the time the decade ended.

1013. "Paramount Gets Screen Rights to Another Simon Play," *Box Office*, December 18, 1967, 6. After the success of *Barefoot in the Park*, Paramount struck a seven-year first-look deal with the playwright. *The Odd Couple* and *Star-Spangled Girl* were the first two plays in the deal, *Plaza Suite* the third

1014. "Koch's Contract Amended at Paramount Studio," *Box Office*, November 10, 1966, 10. Koch was head of the studio and was relinquishing the post to go independent. His departure paved the way for wunderkind Robert Evans to take over.

1015. Advert, *Box Office*, July 22, 1968, 12–13. The movie opened at Radio City Music Hall in New York. By its tenth week it was grossing $258,000—more than the opening week. It subsequently took the record for length of run and total gross from *Barefoot in the Park*.

1016. "*Couple, Funny* Profits," *Variety*, July 12, 1967, 59. The play cost $150,000 to set up and earned just over $1 million after costs (turnover was over $3 million).

1017. "*Odd Couple* Tie-in," *Box Office*, June 26, 1967; "Paramount Schedules *Odd Couple* Party," *Box Office*, May 20, 1968; "IBM Computer Selects Town's *Odd Couple*," *Box Office*, September 9, 1968; "Paramount *Odd Couple* in Nationwide Campaign," *Box Office*, May 13, 1968; "Paramount's Mammoth Five Page Ad," *Independent Film Journal*, August 6, 1968, 14. The "tie-in" with New York's WHN radio was a competition to find "New York's Most Courteous Cab Driver," (a side element of the picture). The notion was almost a challenge—courtesy in a cab? In New York? The "party" was another competition, this time looking for the oddest couples ever to appear on *The Merv Griffin Show*. IBM was involved in finding the oddest couple in El Paso. In the nationwide campaign, adverts for the film were plastered all over Pepsi Cola trucks and promoted in Bohack supermarkets and through Diners Club and Schlitz in a series of cross-promotional marketing deals. As a result of the success of *The Odd Couple* and *Rosemary's Baby* and other films and television shows, Paramount claimed, in the "mammoth ad," that it was the "entertainment champion of the year." The advert ran over five pages of the *New York Times*, the biggest-ever by a studio in any newspaper,

1018. Champlin, Charles in Byron and Weir, *National Society of Film Critics*, 174; Eyles, Allen,

Films and Filming, August 1966, 24; Bill, Review, *International Motion Picture Exhibitor*, April 24, 1968, 10; Review, *Independent Film Journal*, April 27, 1968, 23.

1019. *The Odd Couple* was played out by the end of the decade. It would occasionally turn up as the supporting feature to a newer film or in a double bill with something like *True Grit* (Hannan, *Coming Back*, 214) but in neither situation did it make enough money to alter its rentals position.

1020. Harris, *Scenes from a Revolution*, 12–14. Newman and Benton had started writing the film several years before and attracted the interest of French director François Truffaut. Biskind, *Easy Riders, Raging Bulls*, 32–33. Robert Towne also did some work on the script.

1021. In the 1930s Warner Brothers had virtually invented the gangster picture with the likes of *Little Caesar* (1931) and *Public Enemy* (1931). Beatty appealed to the vanity of current studio boss Jack Warner, who had also been running the studio in those days, to win funding.

1022. Showing at the Montreal Film Festival stated to everyone that it was an art film. It was also a marketing ploy that backfired. Opening at a festival as with *Easy Rider* was a way of getting advance reviews prior to a film opening. It worked very well for *Easy Rider* which arrived with a French seal of approval. For *Bonnie and Clyde* it just meant that the questions asked—about the violence and the film itself—were asked sooner.

1023. Hannan, *Coming Back*, 178. *Bonnie and Clyde* cost $2.9 million, *Wait until Dark* $3 million and *Cool Hand Luke* $3.2 million.

1024. One of the great fears of studios was that while New York audiences might be sophisticated enough to applaud an *Alfie* or a *Charly*, launched in a low capacity venue to increase the chance of breaking box office records, that in the sticks it would sink like a stone. That's exactly what happened to *Bonnie and Clyde* on its first nationwide go-round. If there was a critical division in America, it was a provincial distrust of the big newspaper and magazine critics who had a tendency to laud films that the general public ignored.

1025. *Ibid.*, 178–180.

1026. "*Newsweek* Reverses *Bonnie* Stand: Calls First Review Grossly Unfair," *Variety*, August 30, 1967, 5. He had originally deemed it "a squalid shoot-em-up for the moron trade." Pauline Kael claimed to have waged a campaign to rehabilitate the film (*New Yorker*, October 21) but that article came three months after the film had opened so probably had little direct effect.

1027. *Ibid.*, 183–184. Eliot Hyman had succeeded Jack Warner as WB boss. Hyman had built his fortune on the acquisition of film libraries, so he knew the value of squeezing the last ounce of revenue out of reissuing pictures.

1028. Hannan, *Coming Back*, 184–186.

1029. Toubiana, Serge and de Baecque, Antoine, *Truffaut: A Biography* (New York: Knopf, 1999).

1030. Harris, *Scenes from a Revolution*, 66–67.

Notes—The Films

1031. Cook, David A., "Auteur Cinema and the Film Generation in 1970s Hollywood" in Lewis, Jon, editor, *The New American Cinema* (Durham: Duke University Press, 1998) 11–12. "In popular terms, authorship became associated with the work of New American cinema announced in 1967 by Arthur Penn's *Bonnie and Clyde*. This sensational film—heavily influenced by the *Cahiers*-inspired French New Wave...took both critics and industry by surprise in its revolutionary mixing of genres and styles and unprecedented violence."

1032. Harris, *Scenes from a Revolution*. Harris, for example, picked out the scene where Bonnie first sees Clyde's pistol. "A series of disembodied shots of her moist lips and flashing eyes, his gun at his waist, her lips parting in excitement as her mouth plays over the rim of a Coca-Cola bottle, her hand tentatively reaching over to fondle his gun" suggests a far greater connection between sexuality and violence.

1033. Farber, *Movies*, 159. Manny Farber of the *Saturday Review* begged to differ. "Faye Dunaway glides, drifts like a vertical sashay...leaving a graceful, faint, unengaged wake behind her."

1034. "Too Much Sex, Violence in Films May Bring Back Censor—Crowther," *Motion Picture Exhibitor*, May 22, 1968, 15. The *New York Times* critic started a campaign against violence. He wrote three negative reviews of the film. "I strongly rejected *Bonnie and Clyde* and I still do," he said, nearly a year after the film first opened.

1035. "Warren Beatty *Bonnie* Share May Hit $6,300,000," *Variety*, August 7, 1968, 1. He had given Penn 10 percent of his share.

1036. Reviews taken from the Pressbook.

1037. Ebert, Roger, *Chicago Sun-Times*, September 25, 1967; Crowther, Bosley, "*Bonnie and Clyde* Arrives," *New York Times*, August 14, 1967.

1038. Hilliers, *Cahiers du Cinéma Vol 2* 239–334.

1039. All-Time Champs," *Variety* 1993. There was too much violence for *Bonnie and Clyde* to be an easy sell to television, so it hung around in the reissue market for some time in the 1970s and topped up its lifetime rentals to $22.7 million.

1040. This was not true of fiction pieces in magazines, a source for a wide range of movies for decades. Many producers were first alerted to a prospect by its appearance as a short story or novel serialization in one of the many top-drawer magazines. Robert J. Landry ("Magazines a Prime Screen Source," *Variety*, May 30, 1962, 11) pointed to *Cosmopolitan* as the original publication vehicle for *To Catch a Thief* by David Dodge in 1951 and Fannie Hurst's *Back Street*, serialized over six months from September 1930. Frank Rooney's *The Cyclist's Raid*—later filmed as *The Wild One* (1953) first appeared in *Harper's* magazine. Edna Ferber's *Ice Palace* and *The Executioners* by John D. MacDonald, later filmed as *Cape Fear* (1962) were initially published in *Ladies Home Journal*. The *Saturday Evening Post* published Alan Le May's *The Avenging Texan*, renamed *The Searchers* (1956),

and Donald Hamilton's *Ambush at Blanco Canyon*, renamed *The Big Country* (1958) as well as Christopher Landon's *Escape in the Desert* which was picturized under the more imaginative *Ice Cold in Alex* (1958).

1041. Frayling, Sir Christopher, *How the West was Won*, Cinema Retro, Vol 8, Issue 22, 25. This was recorded in July 1959, two months after the *Life* series ended.

1042. *Ibid.*, 25–26.

1043. *Ibid.*, 26.

1044. *Ibid.*, 28. Gary Cooper, also initially considered, died before the film got underway.

1045. *Ibid.*, 28–29. When projected, the picture was twice the size of 65mm and before the invention of the single-camera lens led to vertical lines running down the screen. Trees were built into compositions to hide these lines.

1046. Crowther, Bosley, "Western Cliches; *How West Was Won* Opens in New York," *New York Times*, March 28, 1963; Review, *Variety*, November 7, 1962, 6; Feature Reviews, *Box Office*, November 26, 1962.

1047. All-Time Champs, *Variety*, 1993. There appeared to be several doubts about what *How the West Was Won* had actually earned. Originally put down as producing $23 million by the end of the 1960s, it was later downgraded to just over $12 million before being reinstated at $20.93 million.

1048. Pressbook.

1049. *Ibid.*

1050. "Knocking Off Fort Knox," *Time*, December 18, 1964; Feature Reviews, *Box Office*, November 16, 1964; Review, *Variety*, September 23, 1964, 6.

1051. All-Time Champs, *Variety*, 1993; Hannan, *Coming Back*, 227. Like all the Bond films throughout the next decade *Goldfinger* was available to be summoned up for a speedy reissue. Prior to its television premiere in 1972, it returned with a variety of double-bill partners and at one point was a constituent of a "Spend the Night with James Bond" triple bill. But most of its high-earning days were over and it only added a small amount to its original earnings for the 1960s bringing its lifetime total up to $22.9 million.

1052. Cowie, Peter, "The Defiant One" *Films and Filming*, March 1963, 18 "*The Defiant Ones* nearly went to the Berlin Festival in 1958 but was considered unsuitable by the authorities."

1053. Kramer, *It's a Mad*, 218. "The film industry taboo against even the implication of sex between blacks and whites was still in force."

1054. "Exhibitors Fear White Harem of Poitier Tho Only Story," *Variety*, June 17, 1964, 1. Southern exhibitors demanded Columbia excise the 12–13 minutes which showed Poitier having Rosanna Schiaffino as his wife and Bebe Loncar as a member of his harem. Columbia refused.

1055. *Ibid.* Rose's initial concept was to set the film in South Africa

1056. *Ibid.*, 219–220. Kramer had been set to make *Andersonville*, based on the MacKinlay

246 — Notes—The Films

Cantor best-seller about the Civil War. Sets had already been built when Columbia pulled the plug on the basis of expense. But he still had a contract that allowed him carte blanche to make a picture under the $3 million budget.

1057. Tracy, Spencer, "An Actor's Director," *Films and Filming*, January 1962, 10. Tracy admired Kramer. In this interview, Tracy said, "Kramer takes the view that an actor thinks, reflects, reacts and has a feeling about the part he's playing...It establishes something strong and warm between an actor and his director." Tracy had worked with Kramer three times—*Inherit the Wind* (1960), *Judgement at Nuremberg* and *It's a Mad, Mad, Mad, World* (1963).

1058. *Ibid.*, 220. Kramer told the Columbia executives "it had to do with a proposed marriage but I didn't say it would be a marriage between a Black man and a white woman. I explained that I didn't want to go into details."

1059. *Ibid.*, 222–223.

1060. *Ibid.*

1061. *Ibid.*, 223. "These were businessmen," recollected Kramer, "what they saw was money flying out and no money coming back in." Since Columbia had already agreed to finance the film, they would have to at least pay the director. And the budget was low by anybody's standards especially with such a sterling cast.

1062. Harris, Mark, *Scenes from a Revolution*, 233–234. Harris takes issue with Kramer's version. In the first place, Kramer had the most to lose. His salary was far greater than any of the three principals—Tracy on $200,000 but not paid until the film was completed, Hepburn $100,000 and Poitier $225,000 plus 9 percent of the profits. Argues Harris, "It's hardly likely that Mike Frankovich or Columbia's board of directors, looking at the millions of dollars that had been earned by MGM's interracial drama *A Patch of Blue* (also starring Poitier in 1965) would suddenly have been stricken with terror at the subject matter of a Stanley Kramer movie." Interestingly, while Harris questioned Kramer's version of events in the same book he accepted Warren Beatty's self-aggrandizing story of how he "saved" *Bonnie and Clyde*.

1063. *Ibid.*, 224. Tracy was on $750,000, Hepburn $250,000. If the film was unfinished, nobody would be paid. Columbia's loss would be minimal especially when set against the prospect of having to pay Kramer his fee whatever happened.

1064. Curtis, James, *Spencer Tracy: A Biography* (London: Hutchinson, 2011), 806, 818, 822. Illness had forced Tracy to pull out of *Cheyenne Autumn* (1964) and *The Cincinnati Kid* (1965).

1065. *Ibid.*, 225. Poitier "could hardly speak his lines in that first rehearsal," said Kramer.

1066. "A Recipe for Greatness" *Films and Filming*, March 1968, 5–7 A few days before principal shooting completed, Tracy said to Kramer, "I read the script again last night. If I was to die tonight, you have enough to realize the film." Tracy died 17 days after the film finished shooting.

1067. Andersen, Christopher, *An Affair to Remember: The Remarkable Love Story of Katharine Hepburn and Spencer Tracy* (New York: William Morrow and Company Inc, 1997) 306.

1068. Harris, Mark, *Scenes from a Revolution*, 371–372. The movie reaped an unexpected publicity bounty when in the run-up to release, Dean Rusk, U.S. Secretary of State, planning to walk his daughter up the aisle, offered to resign if his daughter's wedding to an African American embarrassed the LBJ administration. LBJ, himself a supporter of civil rights, refused to countenance such action but the story made newspaper headlines and the wedding made the cover of *Time*.

1069. And television viewers since the Tracy-Hepburn collaborations had been endlessly programmed on the small screen. Their last film together had been *Desk Set* a decade before. Many of the younger moviegoers would never have seen the couple on the big screen.

1070. Spoto, *Stanley Kramer*, 277–278. "What the critics didn't know," said Poitier, "and what blinded them to the great merit of the film was that Hollywood was incapable of anything more drastic in 1967."

1071. She would win again the following year for *The Lion in Winter* (1968) in a tie with Barbra Streisand for *Funny Girl* (1968).

1072. I have to confess a personal problem with the film in that it was ever proposed as a project in the first place to a very sick man, knowing that exertion of the kind required on a film set could possibly kill him. I never once saw Kramer or anybody else apologize for putting Tracy in this situation. I understand the whole sentimental Hollywood notion. I accept that it's a great film and that Tracy would be happy for it to be seen as his acting eulogy, but I can't help feeling sorry for the family he left behind and wondering if they would rather have had him not working and enjoying his company for a few more years.

1073. Schickel, Richard, "Sorry Stage for Tracy's Last Bow," *Life*, December 15, 1967; Morgenstern, Joseph, "Spence and Supergirl," *Newsweek*, December 25, 1967; Review, *Variety*, December 6, 1967, 6; Feature Reviews, *Box Office*, December 11, 1967.

1074. This film did not add to its 1960s earnings.

1075. A tribe of screenwriters preceded these two. First up was a notion of devising a screenplay out of *The Life of Cleopatra* by Charles Franzero (Wanger's 20th *Cleopatra*, *Variety*, October 22, 1958, 24). Then actress-turned-television-writer Ludi Claire was brought in ("Ludi Claire's Pair for 20th," *Variety*, February 25, 1959, 7) only to be replaced by another television writer Dale Wasserman ("New-Style *Cleopatra*," *Variety*, December 2, 1959, 7) who was instructed to avoid basing the tale on the work of George Bernard Shaw or Shakespeare and to focus on historical research. He was quickly eschewed in favor of British novelist Nigel Balchin ("*Cleopatra* Starts April 4, Probably Todd AO," *Variety*, December 9, 1959, 20; advert, *Variety*, January 6, 1960, 16) at a time when the movie

Notes—The Films 247

was intended as a Christmas 1960 release. When Mamoulian took over he installed Nunnally Johnson (Solomon, *Twentieth Century-Fox*, 141) who wrote nothing except "two words—his name on a contract" even though paid $140,000. When Mankiewicz became involved it was turned over to another British novelist Lawrence Durrell, whose *Alexandria Quartet*, the first of which was *Justine*, the director was setting up when the call came from Fox ("Unexplained Decamp of Mamoulian; *Cleopatra* May Go to Mankiewicz," *Variety*, January 25, 1961, 5).

1076. Wanger had a long production history, responsible for *Joan of Arc* (1948) but was most famous in Hollywood for shooting agent Jennings Lang whom he suspected of an affair with his wife Joan Bennett. He was jailed for four months.

1077. "Hi-Ho, It's Lone Wanger," *Variety*, January 5, 1963, 5. Producer Walter Wanger had written a book, *My Life with Cleopatra*, which provided this figure.

1078. The actual cost has been much queried. Aubrey Solomon (Solomon, *Twentieth Century-Fox*, 141–142) said the first budget set was $4 million and that had risen by $1 million when the film shut down. For the second attempt the budget was set at $15.2 million excluding the studio overhead which would add another $5.3 million. He put the final figures at $30 million. Sheldon and Neale (*Epics, Spectacles and Blockbusters: A Hollywood History*, Wayne State University Press, 2010, 196) put it slightly higher at $31.15 million with another $13 million or so spent on distribution, print and advertising which took the film to $44 million. But that sum excluded the $5.6 million that Fox had written off ("20th-Fox Write-Offs Amounted to $13,922,000," *Box Office*, May 7, 1962) after the first film folded including $2 million from a Lloyds insurance payout ("Lloyds Payoff on *Cleopatra* Near $2,000,000," *Variety*, October 25, 1961, 1). So really the entire production had come in at around $50 million.

1079. Advert, "Galatea," *Variety*, November 25, 1959, 23; "Guarding Liz Taylor, 20th Buys Rival Cleopatra," *Variety*, December 23, 1959, 20. Italian producer Galatea was already promoting in the U.S. *The Legend of Cleopatra* starring Linda Cristal forcing Fox to step in a buy it outright to prevent any clash with its major production.

1080. The studio was already heading for trouble before the premature death of studio production chief Buddy Adler ("Buddy Adler, 51, Dies of Cancer; Zanuck Return?" *Variety*, July 13, 1960, 3). To save on costs, the studio had heavily invested in British films, both the finished product ("20th-Fox Pays $2,000,000 for 7 Rank Films," *Variety*, December 16, 1959, 3) and new pictures ("20th-Fox Set British Product at 21 Films," *Variety*, July 13, 1960, 13), both cheaper options than Hollywood films, around $250,000 each for the U.S. distribution rights to the Rank pictures and $2.5 million per picture for the new ones. In 1961 Fox lost $22.5 million ("*Cleopatra*: Staggering Costs," *Variety*,

April 11, 1962, 7) and it was selling off real estate to prevent bankruptcy. Former studio boss Darryl F. Zanuck stepped in to save the day.

1081. "Unexplained Decamp of Mamoulian," *Variety*.

1082. "*Cleopatra* Interior Shots to Be in Hollywood," *Box Office*, May 1, 1961, 20. At this point after the shutdown when the movie was planned to re-start in Hollywood it was expected Finch and Boyd would be used "if available." As it turned out, by the time shooting re-commenced they had other commitments.

1083. "Adler Agrees Shooting *Cleopatra* in British studios," *Variety*, May 25, 1960, 24.

1084. "Hollywood Report," *Variety*, September 4, 1961, 11.

1085. "Richard Burton to Net $250,000 in *Cleopatra*," *Variety*, September 6, 1961, 2. Burton was paid $300,000 but had to pay $50,000 to get out his contract with Broadway musical *Camelot*.

1086. "Another *Karenina* Launches Eddie Fisher as a Film Producer," *Variety*, October 5, 1960, 5; "WB Call Off Projected 4-Film Deal," *Box Office*, January 22, 1962. Taylor's affair with Burton spelled the end of Eddie Fisher's dreams of moving into production. Mirisch/UA was funding *Anna Karenina* which was to follow *Cleopatra* and a previous commitment by Taylor to Billy Wilder's *Irma La Douce*. Of the four pictures for Warner Brothers, Taylor was to have starred in two.

1087. Solomon, *Twentieth Century-Fox*, 141.

1088. Woodward, *Audrey Hepburn*, 228.

1089. She ended up being paid $2 million after the extensive delays. But she also benefitted from the film being shot in Todd-AO, her deceased husband Mike Todd having been involved in developing that process and Taylor, as his widow, his beneficiary. She also set up a company with then-husband Eddie Fisher called Cleopatra Enterprises ("Liz Has Cut on 20th's *Cleo* Tie-in Loot," *Variety*, February 7, 1962, 2) to control what would be called these days "image rights," the merchandising of her face for the marketing of jewelry and fashion.

1090. Technically, Marlon Brando was first to be paid $1 million for *The Fugitive Kind* (1960) since Taylor's deal was made in 1959 prior to the Brando film commencing. But *Cleopatra* did not begin shooting until after the Brando so Taylor was not "paid" her million first. Her previous fee was $500,000.

1091. "To Shift Site of *Cleopatra* from Hollywood to Rome," *Box Office*, July 10, 1961, 10.

1092. "Adler Agrees Shoot," *Variety*.

1093. "*Cleopatra* Is Now Before Todd-AO Cameras in Rome," *Box Office*, October 2, 1961, 10.

1094. "Inside Stuff—Pictures," *Variety*, October 21, 1959, 17.

1095. "Wanger Off Payroll," *Variety*, June 13, 1962, 13 "The Last Time I Saw *Cleo*," *Variety*, October 31, 1962, 5. Mankiewicz had the right to a "preview cut" not "final cut" but he had filmed the picture in such a way minus the usual covering

248   Notes—The Films

shots that it was impossible to reduce the colossal running time. Zanuck fired him before realizing that the director was the best person to carry out post-production.

1096. "More *Cleo* Scenes Add $2-Mil Cost," *Variety*, December 5, 1962, 4. One battle and four other scenes were added to clarify the narrative.

1097. Adverts, "Before a word of advertising breaks," *Variety*, January 23, 1963, 23 and January 30, 1963, 13. The first ad trumpeted the fact that, despite no advertising, the movie had received 2,616 enquiries at the Rivoli box office plus 3,185 telephone calls and 43 requests from groups. As a result by the time the next advert ran a week later the first 19 nights after the June 12 launch at the Rivoli were sold out.

1098. Canby, Vincent, "Is *Cleo* Cheap at the Price?" *Variety*, May 23, 1962, 3.

1099. "70% of Window-and-Mail Advance on *Cleo* Goes to 20th Fox," *Variety*, June 5, 1963, 1. In order to recoup the money as soon as possible and pay off a debt that was accruing at the rate of $2.55 million a year ("The Last Time I Saw Cleo," *Variety*) Fox played hardball with exhibitors demanding that cash advances paid over by moviegoers go straight to the studio rather than being placed in an escrow account as had occurred with *Exodus*. On the other hand, unlike most roadshows, the studio did not hold the movie back by rolling it out slowly and instead had over 40 venues lined up to play the picture within a month of launch. Although that incurred a print cost of $500,000 it meant Fox was able to demand hefty guarantees totaling $18 million from so many cinemas planning to screen it.

1100. Primarily proof of where the money went, for art direction, costume design, special effects plus Leon Shamroy's cinematography. He had previously won for swashbuckler *The Black Swan* (1942), biopic *Wilson* (1944) and drama *Leave Her to Heaven* (1945).

1101. Anby, Review, *Variety*, June 19, 1963, 6; Review, *Hollywood Reporter*, Jun 13, 1963; Crowther, Bosley, "*Cleopatra* Has Premiere at Rivoli: 4-Hour Epic Is Tribute to Its Artists' Skills," *New York Times*, June 13, 1963; *Journal-American* review by Rose Pelswick taken from advert, *Variety*, June 19, 1963, 14.

1102. Hilliers, *Cahiers du Cinéma Vol 2*, 329–334.

1103. "All-Time Champs, *Variety*, 1993; Hannan, *Coming Back*, 217–218, 254. The *Cleopatra* reissue in the early 1970s was a last-ditch attempt to claw in more cash before the picture made its television debut on ABC. Occasionally, it resurfaced for a 70mm revival festival but in neither instance did it make enough to increase its original tally significantly. Despite many protestations to the contrary, primarily from journalists arguing that it was the worst example of a bloated budget, the movie made a fortune. By 1966, thanks to foreign rentals and a $5 million sale to television—a record fee at the time (TV *Cleo* Price $5-Mil,"

Variety, September 28, 1966, 3) it was safely into profit—though it was not shown on television until the early 1970s. From then, thanks to massive ancillary sales from television, cable, VHS, DVD, Blue-Ray, and streaming, it has probably made three or four times its original budget.

1104. "Production Notes for *Thunderball*"—www.MI6.co.uk.

1105. Scheuer, Philip K., "Action Galore in *Thunderball*, But Cinematically It's a Dud," *Los Angeles Times*, December 20, 1965; "Subaqueous Spy," *Time*, December 24, 1965; Bean, Robin, *Films and Filming*, March 1966, 56; Farber, *Movies*, 161.

1106. All-Time Champs, *Variety*, 1993; Hannan, *Coming Back*, 227. As with all the Bonds, this came back again and again—in 1972, for example, doubled with *You Only Live Twice*—to bring its lifetime total to $28.6 million.

1107. "*MFL* Champ Musical Ends 7 Years on B'way: $20,257,000 and 2,717 Performances," *Variety*, September 26, 1962, 2. *Oklahoma* now came second with 2,212 performances and *South Pacific* a distant third with 1,693.

1108. "Grosses of *My Fair Lady*," *Variety*, September 26, 1962, 2. It took $20 million in New York, $18 million from the touring company and $8 million each in London and Australia.

1109. "Warners Pays Record $5,500,000 for Film Rights to *My Fair Lady*," *Box Office*, February 12, 1962, 6.

1110. Woodward, *Audrey Hepburn*, 257. Julie Andrews and Rex Harrison had not been first choices for the stage production. Preferred females were Mary Martin, 1940s movie box office star Deanna Durbin and Dolores Gray. On the male side, Noel Coward, Michael Redgrave and George Sanders were considered ahead of Harrison.

1111. *Ibid*.

1112. *Ibid*., 254–255.

1113. *Ibid*., 257

1114. *Ibid*., 256.

1115. "Film Musicals Make Comeback Bid," *Box Office*, May 21, 1962, 14–15. *West Side Story* kickstarted U.S. production with 13 musicals slated for 1962 including *The Music Man* and *The Flower Drum Song* but that still did not overcome the problem of foreign disinterest.

1116. The others were *The Reluctant Debutant* (1958) and *The Happy Thieves* (1961). And *Cleopatra* was nine months away from release.

1117. "Return Sexy Rexy as *Fair Lady* Prof," *Variety*, October 31, 1962, 3.

1118. *Ibid*., 259.

1119. It Looks Luverly for *Fair Lady* Again," *Billboard*, September 5, 1964, 1; advert, "The Excitement's About to Begin," *Billboard*, September 26, 1964, 17. As well as immediate revenues from movie box offices, the picture also expected to cash in on album sales. The cast recording of the original show had sold five million copies. *West Side Story's* cast album had sold two million, but the original soundtrack from the movie twice that.

1120. Feature Review, *Box Office*, October 26,

1964; Crowther, Bosley, "Lots of Chocolates for Miss Eliza Dolittle," *New York Times*, October 22, 1964, 41; Scheuer, Philip K., "*Fair Lady* Movie Is a Total Triumph," *Los Angeles Times*, October 22, 1964.

1121. Hilliers, *Cahiers du Cinéma Vol 2*, 329–334.

1122. "All-Time Champs," *Variety*, 1993; Hannan, *Coming Back*, 217, 218, 232. *My Fair Lady* was reissued in 1971 and again in 1973, lifting lifetime earnings to $34 million. But, like *How the West was Won*, doubts had been cast on the validity of its initial success and at one point was downgraded to just $22 million in rentals before it was accepted that the original figures were correct.

1123. "Julie Andrews Remembers *Mary Poppins*," *Vanity Fair*, October 7, 2019.

1124. *Ibid.*

1125. It had been developed at RKO.

1126. In *The Boyfriend*, *My Fair Lady* and *Camelot*.

1127. "Julie Andrews Remembers." The actress had to quickly come to terms with the difference between a close-up and a waist-shot and to understand the nature of the establishing shot and the need for a reverse shot. At the same time, because songs were pre-recorded she had no idea of the context of the words she was singing.

1128. "Julie Andrews Remembers." You might be able to blame J. Pat O'Malley, who voiced some of the animated characters in the film, for that. O'Malley, as you might guess, was an Irishman. So the idea of an Irishman trying to teach an American how to speak Cockney was probably asking for trouble.

1129. Crowther, Bosley, Review, *New York Times*, September 25, 1964, 34; Guerin, Ann, "*Poppins* with Snap and Crackle," *Life*, September 25, 1964, 28; "Have Umbrella, Will Travel," *Time*, September 18, 1964, 114.

1130. "All-Time Champs," *Variety*, 1993; Hannan, *Coming Back*, 230–232. Unlike United Artists with its Bonds, Disney was not indiscriminate in the reissue marketplace and for its major successes would leave up to seven or eight years before a revival. In this case, *Mary Poppins* returned in 1973 to earn around $10 million in rentals and reappeared later to hoist lifetime rentals to $45 million.

1131. "Big *Ben-Hur* Sell for Haya Harareet," *Variety*, August 19, 1959, 2. MGM turned on the publicity taps for the Israeli actress, commissioning Helen Rose to design an entire wardrobe that would see the actress through the month of interviews which had been lined up.

1132. The book was published in 1880 but was a slow burner. However, by 1885, sales topped 50,000 a year and reached 500,000 within a decade. It was turned into a stage show in 1899 that took New York by storm, the actors most closely associated with the role, William S. Hart and William Farnum, going on to greater fame as silent screen cowboys. Wallace earned a million dollars from the stage show.

1133. There was a curious—and accepted—by-product of the roadshow. The 1948 Consent Decree which had forcibly detached studios from the exhibition business also set down new regulations regarding the manner of release and clearances (that being the period between a film going from first run to second run and second run to third run and so on), contracting the time that films could remain in first run. Whereas before the roadshow era, a movie might remain in first run for a couple of months in what was called a "pre-release" before going into general release, now reserved-seat roadshow might remain on the one site for a year and then go into a prolonged first-run-at-normal-prices release before entering general release and there was no sign whatsoever of an exhibitor outcry. If anything, "many theaters were forced to make structural alterations to accommodate wider and larger screens" (Hall and Neale, *Epics*, 156).

1134. Herman, *William Wyler*, 393. "I felt this picture would make a lot of money and I would get some it—which I did," said Wyler. Even if the movie had been less successful, his points-share would have been worthwhile. Had it grossed a mere $12 million, he would have earned $1 million. As it was, he took home the best part of $3 million, the kind of remuneration only stars could hope for and even then, at that time, only William Holden for *Bridge on the River Kwai* had come close. It was the biggest amount anyone, star or director, had ever been paid.

1135. *Ibid.*, 394. He earned the "scorn of the intellectuals." The avant-garde—the *Cahiers du Cinéma* mob—which had considered him a "favorite for years" cut him loose

1136. "MGM Net (Aug 31) Near $8,000,000," *Variety*, Nov 18, 1959, 86. Its projected profit of around $8 million for the year was a sharp increase on the $774,000 of the previous year but the profit had only been achieved by cutting $17 million overhead in the previous two years. Without it, the studio would have gone bust. It had little other overhead to cut so if movies did not bring in real profits, it would go under.

1137. Herman, *William Wyler*, 394.

1138. "Unknown *Ben-Hur*, If He's Uncovered," *Variety*, May 29, 1957. 3.

1139. "*Ben-Hur* Rolls on Camera 65," *Variety*, May 21, 1958, 22. The terms 65mm and 70mm are interchangeable, as are 65m and 70m, the latter being the American usage, the former the British, and the numerical difference being accounted for by the sound strip. This was the second time MGM had filmed in 70mm, but the first time, for *Raintree County* (1957), the movie was released in ordinary 35mm. The cost of 70mm equipment was $500,000.

1140. "Metro and the 1924 *Ben-Hur*," *Variety*, November 18, 1959, 3. Originally budgeted at $750,000, it was mostly filmed in Rome but the chariot race took place in Hollywood. However, most of the profit went to investors and it was surmised that the studio was left with a $1 million loss

250   Notes—The Films

rather than any profit. A previous silent version had been filmed in 1907, a one-reeler with a chariot race.

1141. Herman, *William Wyler*, 395.

1142. *Ibid.*, 395–396.

1143. "Unknown *Ben-Hur*," *Variety*. Wyler's contract allowed him to pick an unknown.

1144. *Ibid.*, 396.

1145. Brownlow, *David Lean*, 392. The credit would read "Chariot Race directed by David Lean."

1146. Cole, Clayton, "Fry, Wyler and the Row Over *Ben Hur*," (*Films and Filming*, January 1960, 26). The Screen Writers Guild (SWG) refused Fry a credit despite Wyler's objections. Gore Vidal, who had also done work on project, also wanted a credit equal to Fry. "The chronology of the *Ben-Hur* script reaches back to 1953 when Tunberg was first engaged…at that time Sidney Franklin was to direct the film and he and Tunberg conferred on changes which Tunberg says he subsequently made. Later, according to studio advice, the script was given to S.N. Berman for polishing and he spent 3½ or 4 weeks working on it." The SWG decided Fry had not contributed one-third to the script, so did not fulfill the guidelines for receiving a credit. Just how much Vidal wrote is also open to dispute (Herman, *William Wyler*, 400–401).

1147. "Zimbalist of *Quo Vadis* Dies at 57 on Eve of Winding M-G *Ben*," *Variety*, November 12, 1958, 5. He died of a heart attack with two months filming to go.

1148. "*Ben-Hur* Whips in," *Variety*, November 18, 1959, 86.

1149. Herman, *William Wyler*, 398.

1150. *Ibid.*, 405–407.

1151. "*Ben-Hur* Cost Metro Over $13-Mil but It'll Still Make Money, Vogel," *Variety*, October 29, 1958, 5. The biggest-budgeted movie to date had been Paramount's *The Ten Commandments* (1956) at $13.5 million, which *Ben-Hur* would soon surpass. MGM's biggest previous outlay had been $7 million for *Quo Vadis*.

1152. "Metro on a $3,000,000 Ad-Pub Binge to Keep *Ben-Hur* Chariots Greased," *Variety*, August 26, 1959, 2. Around $1.75 million went on newspaper advertising including $200,000 on the New York premiere. However, public awareness was extremely high, a survey by Sindlinger and Co. putting that at 53 percent.

1153. "*Ben-Hur* Whips in"; "Metro on a $3,000,000 Ad-Pub Binge; "11 Different Kinds of Books," *Variety*, July 8, 1959, 23; "MGM on Chariot for *Ben-Hur* Albums," *Variety*, April 15, 1959, 138; "Millionth *Ben-Hur* Patron," *Box Office*, October 2, 1961; "Egyptian Run of *Ben-Hur* Claimed World Record," *Box Office*, Jun 19, 1961. There were over 100 merchandizing tie-ins including toy chariots and weaponry, board games, beach towels, painting-by-numbers kits, candy packages, jigsaw puzzles, postcards, bookends, sweatshirts and jewellery. The number of retail companies desperate to become involved and, by their presence adding extra marketing heft, set the template for future movies during the decade. As well as 11 versions of the novel, MGM put out an expensive album alongside a cheaper edition.

1154. Holl, *Variety*, November 18, 1959, 6; Crowther, Bosley, "*Ben-Hur*, a Blockbuster," *New York Times*, November 19, 1959; Scheuer, Philip K., "Magnificent *Ben-Hur* Inspiring in Premiere," *Los Angeles Times*, November 25, 1959.

1155. "All-Time Champs," *Variety*, 1993. *Ben-Hur* had been downgraded, its original estimate of $39.1 million dropped to the current mark, including the subtraction mentioned in my introduction to the film.

1156. Hannan, *Coming Back*, 123–124, 143–144. *Bridge on the River Kwai* had been revived as a roadshow in London, but Columbia decided against that method of presentation in America.

1157. "Metro Rejects $10,000,000 for One TV Exposure of *Gone with the Wind*," *Variety*, February 15, 1967, 1.

1158. "Metro's 6th *Wind* Round Goes 70mm, $6,000 for Print," *Variety*, February 22, 1967, 3.

1159. "*GWTW* Advance Sales to Million Mark," *Box Office*, October 16, 1967, 8.

1160. Hannan, *Coming Back*, 169–170.

1161. Schickel, Richard, "Glossy, Sentimental, Chuckle-Headed," *Atlantic Monthly*, March 1973.

1162. Sarris, Andrew, "The Moviest of All Movies," *Atlantic Monthly*, March 1973.

1163. "The 80 Best-Directed Films," *Directors Guild of America*, Spring 2016.

1164. Murphy, A.D., "Still Powerful *Gone with the Wind*," *Variety*, October 18, 1967, 6; Feature Review, *Box Office*, October 16, 1967, 14.

1165. "All-Time Champs," *Variety*, 1993; Hannan, *Coming Back*, 216, 229, 232, 240, 243, 244. Until its 1976 television premiere *Gone with the Wind* was a regular in the reissue market and earned an extra $5.9 million in rentals.

1166. Pasternak had been awarded the 1958 Nobel Prize for Literature.

1167. Pressbook, 2. Ponti bought the rights in 1962 from Italian publisher Feltrinelli.

1168. Brownlow, *David Lean*, 499.

1169. *Ibid.*, 510.

1170. *Ibid.*, 512. Whether O'Toole actually turned it down is open to question. Sam Spiegel, to whom O'Toole was contracted, refused to release him from current commitments. O'Toole was apparently keen and was sent a script, but not the final one, and turned it down.

1171. *Ibid.*, 513

1172. *Ibid.*, 509–510.

1173. *Ibid.*, 509.

1174. *Ibid.*, 510.

1175. *Ibid.*, 509. She was the wife of producer Carlo Ponti, who had a natural tendency to want to put her in all his films.

1176. *Ibid.*, 510–511.

1177. *Ibid.*, 513.

1178. "Metro Plots Two Features for Geraldine Chaplin," *Variety*, February 24, 1965, 5; "Geraldine Chaplin Not Seen Yet, Booked Solid," *Variety*, July

21, 1965, 1. Contrary to the general build-up of the actress, this was not her debut. She had appeared in French film *Lovely Summer Morning* (1965, U.S. title *Crime on a Summer Morning*), a thriller with Jean-Paul Belmondo. MGM had her lined up for *Anne of a Thousand Days* before that Hal Wallis project shifted to Universal. Prior to that she was due to appear in Nicholas Ray's *The Doctor and the Devil*, followed by *We Will Go to the City*—neither made—and Wallis's *Barefoot in the Park*. In the end, her next movie was her father's *A Countess from Hong Kong* (1967) then *Stranger in the House* (1967).

1179. Brownlow, *David Lean*, 519–520.

1180. Pressbook, 4. Finland was used for the scenes showing Zhivago escaping across the Russian steppes. Finnish Railways provided two traditional wood-burning engines that simulated Russians trains of 50 years before. For extras, the filmmakers turned to Lapland gypsies.

1181. Brownlow, *David Lean*, 528.

1182. *Ibid.*, 530.

1183. Pressbook, 5.

1184. Brownlow, *David Lean*, 528.

1185. Fowlie, Eddie, *David Lean's Dedicated Maniac, Memoir of a Film Specialist* (London: Austin & Macauley, 2010) 181,183, 184–185

1186. *Ibid.*, 532. Lean's instruction to Sharif to achieve the requisite look in his eyes was to imagine the moment just before orgasm when making love.

1187. "*Zhivago* an O'Brien Project," *Variety*, September 1, 1965, 5.

1188. "National Board of Review," *Variety*, January 12, 1966, 24. Her name received more public attention when she was named Best Actress for *Darling* by the NBR which also placed *Doctor Zhivago* third in its year's ten best list. But this came after the film's opening.

1189. Pressbook, 5. Dalton forecast that "not many women in the audience will be able to resist" the furs nor Sharif's greatcoats—"the ladies will want to confiscate them for their own." "MGM Sets Tour of Costumes for *Zhivago* Campaign," *Variety*, November 15, 1965, *Box Office*. One thousand costumes out of the 5,000 made for the picture were heading out on a nationwide tour of 200 cities.

1190. "Two-Page Ad on *Zhivago* Opening Big Response," *Box Office*, October 4, 1965; "National Diners Club Tie in For *Zhivago* Promotion," *Box Office*, November 22, 1965; "*Doctor Zhivago* Advance," *Variety*, December 1, 1965, 13; "Groups Increase to Aid *Zhivago* Ticket Sales," *Box Office*, December 6, 9. MGM did its best to whip up public interest, response to the advert in the New York Times on September 12 reported as "overwhelming" with more ticket requests than any other movie in the studio's history. It also recruited as ticket-sellers companies that did not usually sell movie tickets, i.e., Diners Club, which sent a mail-shot to its 262,000 members, and the four biggest New York theater group agencies which primarily sold tickets for Broadway shows. Despite these efforts the results were "only a fairish advance by

contemporary roadshow standards," according to *Variety*. The figures quoted are for advance bookings for the New York openings. Even *The Agony and the Ecstasy* (1965) had pulled in more—$240,000—and that was destined to be a flop.

1191. *Ibid.*, 538. "MGM was paying to keep the film on," claimed Lean. Biographer Brownlow said this chimed in with his own experience (Brownlow, *David Lean*, 774 n12).

1192. "*Zhivago* LP Soars Over 600,000 Mark," *Variety*, August 17, 1966, 43. It was MGM's biggest-selling soundtrack.

1193. "Winner of Six Academy Awards" was quickly added to the advertising.

1194. Review, *Variety*, December 29, 1965, 6; other reviews taken from "*Doctor Zhivago* Splits New York Critics," *Variety*, December 29, 1965, 2. Judith Crist delivered the *New York Herald-Tribune* verdict, Kate Cameron wrote for the *New York Daily News* and Bosley Crowther for the *New York Times*. Six years later, at an infamous gathering of the New York Critics Circle, Lean, a guest of honor, and expecting a gentle discussion about his movie career, was verbally slaughtered for *Ryan's Daughter* (1970).

1195. "All-Time Champs," *Variety*, 1993. One of the most enduring of the 1960s big-budget hits *Doctor Zhivago* has brought its lifetime rentals up to $60.9 million.

1196. Harris, *Scenes from a Revolution*, 29.

1197. *Ibid.*, 26.

1198. With another $20,000 if the film was made.

1199. He had also produced medical drama *The Young Doctors* (1961) and about to get involved in political drama *The Best Man* (1964) starring Henry Fonda, none of which were particularly successful.

1200. *Ibid.*, 29, 50. Hanley later wrote *The Gypsy Moths* (1969).

1201. "Mike Nichols Will Direct Larry Turman *Graduate* for Embassy Release," *Variety*, October 7, 1964, 4.

1202. "Nichols Schedule: Mayhem," *Variety*, September 23, 1964, 4. His debut was to be *The Public Eye* for Universal

1203. "Mike Nichols Will Direct," *Variety*.

1204. Harris, *Scenes from a Revolution*, 69, 71. Embassy owner Joe Levine was a marketing genius who had brought those skills to bear on films as diverse as *Hercules* (1958) and *The Carpetbaggers* (1964).

1205. *Ibid.*, 97, 98, 119, 121. Henry also took out sections of the book—a fire-fighting episode, dalliance with hookers—that did not seem to fit the overall frame. He also brought the movie, period-wise, up to date rather than setting it in the early sixties of the book.

1206. Bergan, Ronald, *Dustin Hoffman* (London: Virgin Books, 1991, 57). Nichols had worked with Redford on stage for *Barefoot in the Park*.

1207. Biskind, *Easy Riders*, 34

1208. *Ibid.* Day told Nichols the part "offended" her values.

252 Notes—The Films

1209. *Ibid.*, 237–238.

1210. To keep up some publicity momentum Turman announced a nationwide hunt for an unknown to play Benjamin Braddock.

1211. Day, Barry, "It Depends on How You Look at It," *Films and Filming*, November 1968, 4–8. Mike Nichols said he rejected that idea because it would represent "old Europe and young America."

1212. Day, Barry, "It Depends," *Films and Filming*. Said Nichols, "She had been at the same point as Benjamin and had come to where she is presently with full knowledge. She is a very intelligent and cynical woman. She knows what's happening to her."

1213. Harris, *Scenes from a Revolution*, 271–272.

1214. The two off-Broadway plays in which he had a leading role, *Harry Noon and Night* and *Journey of the Fifth* ran for no time at all, three weeks and ten days, respectively, even though the latter won him an Obie.

1215. Bergan, *Dustin Hoffman*, 56. Nichols already knew Hoffman from auditioning him for Broadway musical *The Apple Tree*.

1216. Harris, *Scenes from a Revolution*, 273. Their tests had not been with Hoffman.

1217. Bergan, *Dustin Hoffman*, 58. In order to take on the part Hoffman had to turn down a role in what would be later known as *The Producers*, directed by Bancroft's husband Mel Brooks.

1218. Bergan, *Dustin Hoffman*, 62.

1219. Harris, *Scenes from a Revolution*, 318

1220. *Ibid.*, 359.

1221. *Ibid.*, 365.

1222. Crowther, Bosley, "Graduating with Honors," *New York Times*, December 31, 1967. This was Crowther's last review as the critic of the august newspaper and he bowed out with a positive review.

1223. Day, Barry, "It Depends," *Films and Filming*. "I had no awareness of, or concern with, any generation gap," said Mike Nichols. "I'm, to this day, startled and inarticulate when people consider it a picture about the generation gap. What interested me was the idea of people acquiring products ... whatever is in the picture about living your life and making certain choices applies to more people of a certain age." He added, "I think it's about someone who is trying to become (1) active instead of passive and (2) not to be used as an object because of being surrounded by objects and things ... He's a thing, he's a status symbol."

1224. It would not be too long a shot to suggest that it was the success of *The Graduate* that encouraged audiences to give *Bonnie and Clyde* a second hearing when it was reissued.

1225. Murf, Review, *Variety*, December 20, 1967, 6; Kael, Pauline (*New Yorker*) Byron and Weir, National Society of Film Critics, 166–167; Review, *Time*, December 29, 1967; Farber, *Movies*, 197.

1226. "All-Time Champs," *Variety*, 1993; Hannan, *Coming Back*, 232. Until snapped up by television *The Graduate* was a reissue regular in the 1970s lifting the overall rentals total to $44 million.

1227. "Fox Studios to Reactivate with *Sound of Music*," *Box Office*, December 1962, 8. The movie was expected to start shooting, with exteriors in the Alps, in summer 1963, but that proved premature.

1228. "20th $1,250,000 Films Rights Buy Gives *Sound of Music* 100% Net," *Variety*, July 6, 1960, 65. The musical had cost under $500,000 to stage on Broadway so the sale of the rights put it immediately into profit.

1229. "U.S. Can't Say No to R&H; $65-Mil in Albums Since '43," *Variety*, February 24, 1960, 1. Putting album prices at an average $5, that amounted to 13 million sales. *Oklahoma*, the pair's first show, was the standout with 2.5 million copies shifted for the stage cast album and 1 million for the movie. *South Pacific* accounted for 2.2 million for the stage version and 1.5 million for the movie, for the *King and I* it was one million and two million while the total from both formats for *Carousel* was two million plus sales from smaller enterprises. Before Fox announced the film, the cast album from *The Sound of Music* had sold a million ("*Sound of Music* Gold Disk Swap," *Variety*, September 27, 1961, 55).

1230. Herman, *William Wyler*, 419.

1231. *Ibid.*, 420.

1232. "Fox Studios to Reactivate," *Box Office*.

1233. Hirsch, Julia Antopol, *The Sound of Music: The Making of America's Favorite Movie* (Chicago: Contemporary Bos, 1993) 421.

1234. Baer, William, *Classic American Films: Conversations with Filmmakers* (Westport: Praeger Publishers, 2008) 113.

1235. "Mountain Dew (Rubber Boot Kind) Slows *Sound of Music* at Salzburg," *Variety*, July 1, 1964, 24. Three weeks of inclement weather added $500,000 to the budget.

1236. Hirsch, *The Sound of Music*, 51–53.

1237. *Ibid.*, 61–63; Pressbook. Of the children selected only Angela Cartwright (Brigitta) was a "real pro," having been a regular on the *Danny Thomas Show* for some years. Duane Chase (Kurt) was found while Wise was leafing through a magazine and saw him in a cereal advert. Charmian Carr (Liesl, the eldest) was cast courtesy of a photo that had been sent in, her only prior work some modelling. Heather Menzies (Louisa) was spotted in an amateur television program *Teen Age Trials*. Debbie Turner (Marta) had appeared in a few commercials, Nicholas Hammond (Friedrich) some stage work and Kym Karath (Gretl) had previously been in *The Thrill of It All*. They all had to stick to California law and undertake school lessons four hours a day.

1238. Hannan, *In Theaters Everywhere*, 125.

1239. "*Sound of Music* to Get 5-Yr. Rest after $68M," *International Motion Picture Exhibitor*, July 16, 1969, 9. It had played 9,500 dates. In roadshow it ran for a year in several locations and when towards the end of the decade Fox announced it was withdrawing the film from circulation there was a rush to see it again.

1240. Feature Review, *Box Office*, March 15,

Notes—Conclusion

1965; Crowther, Bosley, "*The Sound of Music* Opens at Rivoli," *New York Times*, March 3, 1965. *McCall's* reviewer was Pauline Kael and for *Vogue* it was Joan Didiom. An article by Justine Smith in *Little White Lies* ("Joan Didiom vs. Pauline Kael vs. The *Sound of Music*," May 23, 2018) asked whether negative reviews by both critics cost them their jobs.

1241. "All-Time Champs," *Variety*; Hannan. *Coming Back*, 232, 303. As promised Twentieth Century-Fox brought back its box office champ in the 1970s and its total reached $79.9 million but in the current century it has also generated, one would expect, substantial extra revenue from the "Singalong" presentation phenomenon, but those revenues are not included here.

Conclusion

1. Landry, Robert J, "Generation-Bridging Pics," *Variety*, July 17, 1968, 5. "The most parroted catchphrase in the film trade today runs: 'No film can succeed without youth appeal.' But, in fact, the most successful movies at that time, halfway through 1968, were *The Sound of Music*, *The Thomas Crown Affair*, *Wait until Dark* and *To Sir, With Love*. "People do not separate into arbitrary age brackets. The best entertainment cuts across all generations." Although this article appeared almost a year before *Easy Rider*, the issues raised pre-empt that picture's impact. What primarily went wrong with Hollywood at the end of the decade was loss of confidence and although the industry went through a difficult period the ship righted itself within a few years.

2. Frederick, Robert F., "Year's Surprise: Family Films Did Best," *Variety*, January 7, 1970, 15.

3. "All-Time Top 232 Movies U.S. Theater Attendance." mrob.com/pub/film-video/topadj.html

Bibliography

Sources and Books for Further Reading

Trade Press

Box Office
Hollywood Reporter
Independent Film Journal
Kine Weekly
Variety

Books and Articles

Allvine, Glendon. *The Greatest Fox of Them All.* New York: Lyle Stuart, 1969.

Andrews, Julie. *Home Work: A Memoir of My Hollywood Years.* London: W&N, 2019.

Annakin, Ken. *So You Wanna Be a Director?* Sheffield: Tomahawk Press, 2001.

Armstrong, Stephen B. *Andrew V. McLaglen: The Life and Hollywood Career.* Jefferson, NC: McFarland, 2011.

Babington, Bruce, and Evans, Peter William. *Biblical Epics: Sacred Narrative in the Hollywood Cinema.* Manchester: Manchester University Press, 1993.

Bacharach, Burt. *Anyone Who Had a Heart.* New York: Harper, 2013.

Balio, Tino. *United Artists: The Company That Changed the Film Industry.* Madison: University of Wisconsin Press, 1987.

Balio, Tino (ed). *The American Film Industry,* 2nd revised edition. Madison: University of Wisconsin Press, 1985.

Basinger, Jeanine. *Anthony Mann.* Boston: Twayne, 1979.

Baxter, John. *The Cinema of John Ford.* London: A. Zwemmer, 1972.

Baxter, John. *Stanley Kubrick: A Biography.* New York: Carroll & Graf, 1997.

Bergan, Ronald. *Dustin Hoffman.* London: Virgin Books, 1991.

Bergan, Ronald. *The United Artists Story.* London: Octopus, 1986.

Bernstein, Matthew. *Controlling Hollywood: Censorship and Regulation in the Studio Era.* New Brunswick: Rutgers University Press, 1999.

Biskind, Peter. *Easy Riders, Raging Bulls.* New York: Simon & Schuster, 1998.

Biskind, Peter. *Star: The Life and Wild Times of Warren Beatty.* New York: Simon & Schuster, 2011.

Bizony, Piers. *The Making of Stanley Kubrick's 2001: A Space Odyssey.* Cologne: Taschen, 2020.

Bogdanovich, Peter. *John Ford.* Berkeley: University of California Press, 1967.

Borgnine, Ernest. *My Autobiography.* London: J.R. Books, 2009.

Bragg, Mervyn. *Rich: The Life of Richard Burton.* London: Hodder and Stoughton, 1988.

Brownlow, Kevin. *David Lean.* London: Faber & Faber, 1997.

Buford, Kate. *Burt Lancaster: An American Life.* London: Aurum Press, 2008.

Byron, Stuart, and Weis, Elizabeth. *The National Society of Film Critics on Movie Comedy.* New York: Grossman, 1977.

Caine, Michael. *What's it All About?* London: Arrow Books, 2010.

Callan, Michael Feeney. *Robert Redford: The Biography,* New York: Simon & Schuster, 2012.

Cameron, Ian, and Pye, Douglas (eds). *The Movie Book of the Western.* London: Studio Vista, 1996.

Caspar, Drew. *Post-War Hollywood 1946–1962.* Hoboken: Wiley-Blackwell, 2007.

Caughie, John (ed). *Theories of Authorship.* London: Routledge and Kegan Paul, 1981.

Cripps, Thomas. *Making Movies Black: The Hollywood Message Movie from World War II to the Civil Rights Era.* New York: Oxford University Press, 1993.

Cronin, Paul (ed). *George Stevens Interviews.* Jackson: University of Mississippi Press, 2004.

Curtis, Tony, and Golenbock, Peter. *American Prince: My Autobiography.* London: Virgin Books, 2009.

Daniel, Douglass K. *Tough as Nails: The Life and Times of Richard Brooks.* Madison: University of Wisconsin Press, 2011.

Davis, Ronald L. *John Ford: Hollywood's Old Master.* Norman: University of Oklahoma Press, 1995.

Bibliography

Dick, Bernard F. *Engulfed: The Death of Paramount and the Birth of Corporate Hollywood.* Lexington: The University Press of Kentucky, 2001.

Douglas, Kirk. *I Am Spartacus: Making a Film, Breaking the Blacklist.* New York: Open Road, 2012.

Douglas, Kirk. *The Ragman's Son.* London: Simon & Schuster, 2012.

Dunne, John Gregory. *The Studio*, vintage edition. New York: Farrar, Strauss & Giroux, 1998.

Durgnat, Raymond. *Sexual Alienation in the Cinema.* London: Studio Vista, 1972.

Edwards, Anne. *Streisand: A Biography.* Lanham: Taylor Trade, 2016.

Epstein, Dwayne. *Lee Marvin: Point Blank.* Tucson: Schaffner Press, 2014.

Everson, William K. *The Hollywood Western.* New York: Citadel Press, 1992.

Eyman, Scott. *Cary Grant: A Brilliant Disguise.* New York: Simon & Schuster, 2020.

Eyman, Scott. *John Wayne: The Life and Legend.* New York: Simon & Schuster, 2014.

Farber, Manny. *Movies.* New York: Stonehill, 1971.

Farkis, John. *Not Thinkin'... Just Remberin'... The Making of John Wayne's The Alamo.* Albany: Bear Manor Media, 2015.

Fenin, George N., and Everson, William K. *The Western: From Silents to Cinerama.* New York: The Orion Press, 1962.

Fishgall, Gary. *Gregory Peck: A Biography.* New York: Scribner's, 2002.

Fonda, Jane. "Fonda on Fonda," *Films and Filming.* London: Hansom Books, February 1963.

Fonda, Jane. *My Life So Far.* London: Ebury Press, 2006.

Fowlie, Eddie, and Torne, Richard. *David Lean's Dedicated Maniac: Memoirs of a Film Specialist.* London: Austin & Macauley, 2010.

Fraser-Cavassoni, Natasha. *Sam Spiegel: The Biography of a Hollywood Legend.* London: Little, Brown, 2003.

Frayling, Sir Christopher. "How the West Was Won." *Cinema Retro*, Vol. 8, Issue 22, 2012.

Freedland, Michael. *Some Like It Cool: The Charmed Life of Jack Lemmon*, revised edition. London: Robson Books, September 2002.

French, Philip. *Westerns: Aspects of a Genre*, revised edition. Manchester: Carcanet Press, 2001.

Fujiwara, Chris. *The World and Its Double: The Life and Work of Otto Preminger.* New York: Faber & Faber, 2008.

Gabler, Neil. *Walt Disney: The Biography.* London: Aurum Press, 2011.

Garfield, Brian. *Western Films: A Complete Guide.* New York: Da Capo Press, 1982.

Garner, Simmons. *Peckinpah: A Portrait in Montage.* Austin: University of Texas Press, 1982.

Gilbert, Lewis. *All My Flashbacks: The Autobiography of Lewis Gilbert, Sixty Years a Film Director.* London: Reynolds and Hearn, 2010.

Goudsouzian, Adam. *Sidney Poitier: Man, Actor, Icon.* Chapel Hill: University of North Carolina Press, 2011.

Grant, Barry Keith (ed). *American Cinema of the 1960s: Themes and Variations.* New Brunswick: Rutgers University Press, 2008.

Hannan, Brian. *Coming Back to a Theater Near You: A History of Hollywood Reissues, 1914–2014.* Jefferson, NC: McFarland, 2016.

Hannan, Brian. *In Theaters Everywhere: A History of the Hollywood Wide Release, 1913–2017.* Jefferson, NC: McFarland, 2019.

Hannan, Brian. *The Making of Lawrence of Arabia.* Glasgow: Baroliant, 2013.

Hannan, Brian. *The Making of The Guns of Navarone.* Glasgow: Baroliant, 2013.

Hannan, Brian. *The Making of* The Magnificent Seven: *Behind the Scenes of the Pivotal Western.* Jefferson, NC: McFarland, 2015.

Hannan, Brian. *Paisley at the Pictures 1950.* Glasgow: Baroliant, 2019.

Hannan, Brian. *When Women Ruled Hollywood: The Untold Story of How Actresses Took on the Hollywood Hierarchy—and Won.* Glasgow: Baroliant, 2020.

Harris, Mark. *Scenes from a Revolution: The Birth of the New Hollywood.* New York: Penguin, 2008.

Henderson, Brian. *A Critique of Film Theory.* New York: E.F. Dutton, 1980.

Herman, Jan. *William Wyler: A Talent for Trouble.* New York: Da Capo Press, 1997.

Hilliers, Jim. *Cahiers du Cinéma Vol. 2: The 1960s.* London: Routledge and Kegan Paul, 1986.

Hirsch, Julia Antopol. *The Sound of Music: The Making of America's Favorite Movie.* Chicago Review Press, 2018.

Hoberman, James. *The Dream Life: Movies, Media and the Mythology of the Sixties.* New York: The New Press, 2005.

Holston, Kim R. *Movie Roadshows: A History and Filmography of Reserved-Seat Limited Showings, 1911–1973.* Jefferson, NC: McFarland, 2013.

Horton, Andrew. *The Films of George Roy Hill*, revised edition. Jefferson, NC: McFarland, 2009.

Izod, John. *Hollywood and the Box Office.* New York: Columbia University Press, 1992.

Jackson, Kevin. *Lawrence of Arabia.* London: British Film Institute, 2007.

Jewison, Norman. *This Terrible Business Has Been Good to Me.* Toronto: Key Porter Books, 2006.

Jordan, J.R. *Robert Wise: The Motion Pictures*, revised edition. Albany: Bear Manor Media, 2020.

Kael, Pauline. "Circles and Squares." *Film Quarterly.* Vol. 16, No. 3, 1963.

Kanfer, Stefan. *Ball of Fire: The Tumultuous Life and Comic Art of Lucille Ball.* London: Faber & Faber, 2005.

Kanfer, Stefan. *Somebody: The Reckless Life and Remarkable Career of Marlon Brando.* New York: Knopf, 2008.

Kaplan, James. *Sinatra, The Chairman.* New York: First Anchor Books, 2016.

Kashner, Sam, and Schoenberger, Nancy. *Furious Love: Elizabeth Taylor, Richard Burton, the Marriage of the Century.* London: J.R. Books, 2010.

Bibliography

Kezich, Tullio. *Federico Fellini: His Life and Work*. London: I.B. Tauris, 2007.

Kitses, Jim. *Horizons West*. Bloomington: Indiana University Press, 1969.

Kramer, Stanley, and Coffey, Thomas M. *A Mad Mad Mad Mad World: A Life in Hollywood*. New York: Harcourt, Brace, 1997.

Lemmon, Jack. "Such Fun to Be Funny." *Films and Filming*. London: Hansom Books, November 1960.

Lev, Peter. *The Fifties: Transforming the Screen 1950–1959*. New York: Charles Scribner's Sons, 2003.

Levy, Shawn. *Paul Newman, A Life*. New York: Harmony Books, 2009.

Lewis, Jon (ed). *The New American Cinema*. Durham: Duke University Press, 1998.

Lovell, Glenn. *Escape Artist: John Sturges*. Madison: University of Wisconsin Press, 2008.

Loy, R. Philip. *Westerns in a Changing America, 1955–2000*. Jefferson, NC: McFarland, 2004.

Lucas, George, Block, Alex Ben ,and Wilson, Lucy Autry (eds). *Blockbusting*. New York: I.T. Books, 2010.

MacAdam, Henry, and Cooper, Duncan. *The Gladiators vs. Spartacus: Dueling Productions in Blacklist Hollywood*. Newcastle-upon-Tyne: Cambridge Scholars, 2021.

MacLaine, Shirley. *My Lucky Stars: A Hollywood Memoir*. New York: Bantam, 2001.

Madsen, Axel. *The New Hollywood*. New York: Crowell, 1975.

Mann, Denise. *Hollywood Independents: The Postwar Talent Takeover*. Minneapolis: University of Minnesota Press, 2007.

Mann, William J. *Edge of Midnight: The Life of John Schlesinger*. London: Hutchinson, 2004.

Mann, William J. *How to Be a Movie Star: Elizabeth Taylor in Hollywood*. London: Faber & Faber, 2009.

Martin, Mel. *The Magnificent Showman: The Epic Films of Samuel Bronston*. Albany: BearManor Media, 2007.

McBride, Joseph. *Searching for John Ford*. New York: St. Martin's Press, 2001.

McCarthy, Todd. *Howard Hawks: The Grey Fox of Hollywood*. New York: Grove Press, 1997.

McDougal, Dennis. *Five Easy Decades: How Jack Nicholson Became the Biggest Movie Star in Modern Times*. Hoboken: John Wiley & Sons, 2008.

McGilligan, Patrick. *Alfred Hitchcock: A Life in Darkness and Light*. New York: Regan Books, 2003.

McGilligan, Patrick. *George Cukor: A Double Life*. Minneapolis: University of Minnesota Press, 2013.

Mirisch, Walter. *I Thought We Were Making Movies, Not History*. Madison: University of Wisconsin Press, 2008.

Monaco, James. *American Film Now: The People, the Power, the Money, the Movies*. New York: Oxford University Press, 1979.

Monaco, James. *Media Culture*. New York: Delta, 1978.

Monaco, Paul. *The Sixties: 1960–1969*. New York: Scribner's, 2001.

Morris, Robert L., and Raskin, Lawrence. *Lawrence of Arabia*. New York: Anchor Books, 1992.

Munn, Michael. *Clint Eastwood: Hollywood's Loner*. London: Robson Books, 1992.

Munn, Michael. *Jimmy Stewart: The Truth Behind the Legend*. London: Robson Books, 2005.

Munn, Michael. *Tony Curtis: Nobody's Perfect*. London: J.R. Books, 2011.

Murphy, Robert. *Sixties British Cinema*. London: BFI, 1992.

O'Brien, Daniel. *Paul Newman*. London: Faber & Faber, 2004.

Pfeiffer, Lee, and Worrall, Dave (eds). *Roadshow Epics of the '60s: Cinema Retro Special Edition*, Issue No. 5, 2018.

Pfeiffer, Lee, and Worrall, Dave (eds). *Where Eagles Dare: Cinema Retro Movie Classics Special Edition*, Issue No. 1, 2009.

Pfeiffer, Lee, and Worrall, Dave (eds). *World War II Movies of the Sixties: Cinema Retro Special Edition*, Issue No. 6, 2017.

Pomainville, Harold N. *Henry Hathaway: The Lives of a Hollywood Director*. Lanham: Rowman & Littlefield, 2016.

Prince, Stephen. *Savage Cinema: Sam Peckinpah and the Rise of Ultraviolent Movies*. Austin: University of Texas Press, 1998.

Rebello, Stephen. *Alfred Hitchcock and the Making of Psycho*. London: Marion Boyars, 2013.

Rebello, Stephen. *Dolls! Dolls! Dolls! Deep Inside the Valley of the Dolls*. New York: Penguin, 2020.

Roberts, Randy, and Olson, James S. *John Wayne: American*. New York: The Free Press, 1995.

Sackett, Susan. *The Hollywood Reporter Book of Box Office Hits*. New York: Billboard Books, 1990.

Sandford, Christopher. *McQueen: The Biography*. London: HarperCollins, 2001.

Santopietro, Tom. *Considering Doris Day: A Biography*. New York: Griffin, 2008.

Sarris, Andrew. *American Cinema—Directors and Directions 1929–1968*. New York: E.P. Dutton, 1968.

Sarris, Andrew. "Notes on the Auteur Theory in 1962." *Film Culture* No. 27, 1962–1963.

Sikov, Ed. *On Sunset Boulevard: The Life and Times of Billy Wilder*. Jackson: University Press of Mississippi, 2017.

Silver, Alain, and Ursini, James. *Whatever Happened to Robert Aldrich? His Life and Films*. Brisbane: Limelight Editions, 2004.

Sinclair, Andrew. *John Ford: A Biography*. New York: Dial Press 1979.

Solomon, Aubrey. *Twentieth Century Fox: A Corporate and Financial History*. Lanham, MD: The Scarecrow Press, 1998.

Spiegel, Penina. *Steve McQueen: The Untold Story of a Bad Boy in Hollywood*. London: Collins, 1986.

Spoto, Donald. *The Dark Side of Genius: The Life of Alfred Hitchcock.* New York: Little, Brown, 1983.

Spoto, Donald. *Stanley Kramer, Film Maker.* London: Samuel French Edition, 1990.

Steinberg, Cobbett. *Reel Facts.* New York: Vintage Books, 1978.

Sterling, Christopher H., and Haight, Timothy R. *The Mass Media: Aspen Institute Guide to Communication Industry Trends.* New York: Praeger, 1978.

Stowell, Peter. *John Ford.* Boston: Twayne, 1986.

Truffaut, Francois. "Une certain tendance du cinema francais." *Cahiers du Cinéma,* 1954.

Turner, Adrian. *The Making of David Lean's Lawrence of Arabia.* Limpsfield, Surrey: Dragon's World, 1994.

Wallis, Hal B. *Starmaker: The Autobiography of Hal Wallis.* London: Macmillan, 1980.

Wapshott, Nicholas. *Carol Reed: A Biography.* New York: Knopf, 1994, reprint.

Wasson, Sam. *The Big Goodbye, Chinatown and the Last Years of Hollywood.* New York: Flatiron Books, 2020.

Weddle, David. *If They Move ... Kill 'Em: The Life and Times of Sam Peckinpah.* New York: Grove Press, 1994.

Williams, Charles (ed). *The Richard Burton Diaries.* New Haven: Yale University Press, 2012.

Wollen, Peter. *Readings and Writings: Semiotic Counter-Strategies.* London: Verso Editions, 1982.

Wollen, Peter. *Signs and Meaning in the Cinema.* London: BFI, 1969.

Woods, Robin. *Howard Hawks,* revised edition. London: BFI, 1981.

Woodward, Ian. *Audrey Hepburn.* London: W.H. Allen, 1984.

Zinnemann, Fred. *Fred Zinnemann: An Autobiography: A Life in the Movies.* New York: Scribner's, 1992.

Index

Numbers in **bold italics** indicate pages with illustrations

ABC 10
ABC/Cinerama Releasing 39
ABC TV 39
abortion 49, 72
The Absent Minded Professor 30, 99–101, **100**, 103, 104, 149, 181
Ace in the Hole 30
Adam, Ken 28, 154
Adams, Nick 160
Addison, John 146
advance bookings 169, 176, 186, 180
African American 8, 20, 21, 31, 173, 174, 188
The African Lion 84, 119
The African Queen 89
After the Fox 77
The Agony and the Ecstasy 130, 131, 190
Aimeé, Anouk 45, 47
AIP 6, 35, 47
The Alamo (1960) 9, 22, 42, 56, 59–62, **60**, 83, 115
Albee, Edward 120, 121
Aldrich, Robert 4, 97, 160–162; *The Dirty Dozen* 160–162; *see also* violence
Alfie (1965) 7, 35, 70–72, **71**, 73, 89
All About Eve 105
All Fall Down 82
All Quiet on the Western Front 65
Allen, Irving 41
Allen, Woody 69, 87
Allied Artists 8, 10, 109
Allison, Mark 15
Alwyn, William 119
Ambler, Eric 114
American Film Institute 188
The Americanization of Emily 143
The Amorous Adventures of Moll Flanders 178
And God Created Woman (1956) 7, 45, 50, 114
Anderson, Lindsay 5
Anderson, Robert Woodruff 115
Andersson, Harriet 81
Andress, Ursula 37, 38, 69, 70, 79, 88, 154
Andrews, Julie 27, 28, 29, 66, 89, 108, 127, 129, 142, 143, 179, 181, 182, 183, 192, 193, 195, 198; *The Americanization of Emily* 143; *Hawaii* 25, 52, 94, 108, 113, 129, 130, 138, 142–143; *Mary Poppins* 5, 27, 28, 29, 56, 57, 105, 127, 149, 181–183, **182**, 194, 198, 199; *The Sound of Music* 3, 5, 89, 91, 108, 115, 127, 190, 192–195, **193**, 198, 199; *Star!* 138; *Thoroughly Modern Millie* 127–129, **128**, 138, 146; *Torn Curtain* 22, 56, 129
Angel Face 68, 126
Anhalt, Edward 63, 65

animation 104–105, 181, 183; *Fantasia* 99; *The Jungle Book* (1967) 104–105; *Mary Poppins* 181–183; *One Hundred and One Dalmatians* (1961) 30, 198; *The Sleeping Beauty* 104; *Snow White and the Seven Dwarfs* 99; *The Sword in the Stone* 104, 105
Annakin, Ken 117–119, 151–142
Anne of the Thousand Days 106
Annie Get Your Gun 108
annual box office rankings 85, 88
Antonioni, Michelangelo 5
The Apartment 18–19, 49, 98, 101, 111, 112, 157, 164
Apocalypse Now 84; *see also* Vietnam
Arkin, Alan 16, 40, 57, 59, 85–87
The Art of Love 87
arthouse 7, 16, 18, 36, 46, 146, 148, 155, 166, 190, 198
Ashby, Hal 96
Asher, Jane 72
Aspen Film Festival 21
Astor 10, 45–47; *La Dolce Vita* 45–47
Atlanta, Georgia 186
Attenborough, Richard 115, 117
Auger, Claudine 176–178
Auntie Mame 66
Aurthur, Robert Alan 81, 95
Australia 155
auteur 1, 25, 26
Avalon, Frankie 61

Baby Doll 25, 142
Bacharach, Burt 69, 70, 71, 72, 87, 138, 140
Back Street (1961) 129
The Bad Seed 13
Badham, Mary 31
Bahamas 178
Baker, Carroll 25, 140–142, 169, 170
Baker, Stanley 114
Balin, Ina 114
Ball, John 94, 96
Ball, Lucille 57, 106–107
Bancroft, Anne 39, 190–192
Bandolero 55
Barabbas 114, 136
Barbarella 125
Bardot, Brigitte 7, 45, 50, 109, 185
Barefoot in the Park 76–78, **77**, 105, 112, 121, 164
Barnes, Jane 104
Barrett, James Lee 23, 54, 83
Barry, John 9, 96, 152, 154, 170, 178
Bart, Lionel 89
Barzman, Ben 109, 110
Bass, Saul 68

259

260 Index

Bates, Alan 40, 49, 50, 73
Batjac 22, 59
Batman (1966) 34
Battle of the Bulge 13, 56, 107
The Battle of the Villa Fiorita 122
Beatles 65, 145, 146
Beaton, Cecil 9, 179
Beatty, Warren 3, 39, 69, 70, 125, 166–168, 191, 192
Becket 65, 105, 112, 121
Bedford, Brian 82, 83
The Bedford Incident 21, 95
Behold a Pale Horse 113
Belmondo, Jean-Paul 88
Beloved Infidel 32
Ben-Hur (1959) 5, 11, 23, 25, 27, 42, 109, 110, 111, 133, 145, 151, 170, 174, 183–185, *184*, 186, 194, 199
Ben-Hur: A Tale of the Christ 185
Benjamin, Richard 91–92
Benton, Robert 166, 167
Bergen, Candice 115, 117, 163, 181
Berger, Senta 154
Bergman, Ingmar 7, 25
Bergman, Ingrid 126
Bergryd, Ulla 136
Berle, Milton 157
Berlin Film Festival 39
Berman, Pandro S. 48
Bermuda 62
Bernstein, Elmer 31, 40, 105, 127, 140, 142
Bernstein, Leonard 158
The Best Years of Our Lives 185
bestseller 9, 13, 31, 39, 52, 63, 68, 91, 105, 115, 130, 141, 142, 143, 155, 163
Beswick, Martine 126
Bethmann, Sabina 126
Beymer, Richard 158, 160
Bianchi, Daniella 79, 80
The Bible 23, 136–138, *137*
Biblical: *Barabbas* 114, 136; 105, 112, 121; *Ben-Hur* (1959) 5, 11, 23, 25, 27, 42, 109, 110, 110, 111, 133, 145, 151, 170, 174, 183–185, *184*, 186, 194, 199; *Ben-Hur: A Tale of the Christ* 185; *The Bible* 23, 136–138, *137*; *The Greatest Story Ever Told* 23–26, *24*, 55, 143; *King of Kings* (1961) 109; *The Robe* 126; *Sodom and Gomorrah* 23; *Solomon and Sheba* 23; *The Ten Commandments* (1956) 136
The Big Country 126, 169
The Big Sleep 27
biker 6, 35, 36
Billy Liar 98
Billy Rose's Jumbo 63
Biskind, Peter 70
Bisset, Jacqueline 88, 144
Bitter Rice 45, 136
Black, Cilla 71, 72
Black Orchid 101
Blackbeard's Ghost 149
blacklist 98, 106, 114, 126, 135, 141
Blackman, Honor 170, 171
Blatty, William Peter 15, 16
Bloch, Robert 101, 130
Blondie 78
Blood and Roses 26
Bloom, Claire 39–40
Blow-Up 5, 8, 36, 108
The Blue Max 37–38, 49, 117
The Bobo 59
Boehm, Sydney 154

The Bofors Gun 13
Bolt, Robert 112, 133, 135, 188, 190
Bond, James 6, 7, 9, 11, 27, 34, 40, 41, 42, 50, 59, 78–80, 87, 88, 146, 152–154, 170–172, 176–178, 190, 198; *see also* spy films
Bonnie and Clyde 8, 9, 63, 78, 122, 123, 145, 162, 166–168, *167*, 192, 197, 199
Boone, Richard 13
Borg, Veda Ann 61
Borgnine, Ernest 160
Boston 155, 184
Boston Globe 18
The Boston Strangler 63–65, *64*
Bouchet, Barbara 88
Boulle, Pierre 131
Bourne, Jason 198
Box Office magazine 15, 21, 24, 29, 31, 32, 33, 34, 37, 41, 42, 54, 64, 68, 75, 79, 83, 94, 99, 101, 107, 112, 121, 123, 131, 139, 142, 151, 156, 158, 162, 164, 165, 169, 170, 172, 174, 181, 184, 188, 189, 192, 195
Boyd, Stephen 174, 183, 185
Boyer, Charles 77, 88
Brackett, Leigh 26
Bracketville 61
Braithwaite, E.R. 155
Brando, Marlon 13, 42–44, 108, 113, 122, 126, 135, 146, 185, 188
Breakfast at Tiffany's 9, 38, 58, 142, 181
Brice, Fanny 145
Bridge on the River Kwai 44, 45, 78, 119, 126, 132, 135, 186, 188
Bringing Up Baby 27
British/Britain 3, 6, 7, 8, 15, 16, 18, 28, 31, 35, 46, 49, 50, 52, 54, 70, 71, 78, 89, 113, 114, 118, 122, 123, 134, 135, 141, 146, 147, 148, 152, 155, 160, 167, 174, 181, 188
Broadway 39, 95, 138, 143; musical 9, 56, 65, 66, 89, 145, 158, 179, 194; play 59, 70, 76, 77, 164
Broccoli, Albert R. 27, 48, 41, 78, 152, 170, 177
Bronson, Charles 160–162; *Battle of the Bulge* 13, 56, 107; *The Dirty Dozen* 160–162; *The Great Escape* 34, 52, 57, 115, 144, 161; *The Magnificent Seven* (1960) 1, 34, 78, 80, 115, 126, 144, 158, 161; *The Sandpiper* 78, 82, 87, 120
Bronston, Samuel 109–110; *El Cid* 109–110
Brooks, Richard 48, 66–68
Brown, Jim 8, 160, 161
Brunner, Bob 56
Brunner, Robert F. 84
Bruns, George 99, 104, 149
Bryanston 147
Brynner, Yul 3, 108, 126, 194
Buchman, Sidney 174
buddy movie 138, 164
budget 11, 42, 53, 59, 60, 65, 69, 71, 83, 89, 92, 93, 98, 101, 105, 107, 109, 112, 117, 118, 120, 123, 126, 138, 141, 143, 145, 146, 148, 151, 154, 155, 157, 160, 163, 172, 173, 174, 179, 181, 185, 186, 188, 190, 191, 194
Bullitt 8, 78, 144–145, 149, 198
Burton, Richard 3, 7, 13–15, 34, 53, 80, 89, 106, 108, 112, 114, 117, 120–121, 126, 137, 151, 174–176, 194, 198; *Becket* 65, 105, 112, 121; *Cleopatra* 174–176; *The Longest Day* 5, 13, 32, 112, 118, 151–152; *Look Back in Anger* 13; *Night of the Iguana* 121, 136, 145; *The Robe* 126; *The Sandpiper* 78, 82, 87, 120; *The Spy Who Came In from the Cold* 34, 39, 80, 121; *The Taming of the Shrew* 122; *The VIPs* 65, 120; *Where Eagles Dare* 13–15; *Who's Afraid of Virginia Woolf?* 120–121; *see also* Taylor, Elizabeth

Index 261

Bus Riley's Back in Town 13
Busati, Franco 121
Butch and Sundance: The Early Days 198
Butch Cassidy and the Sundance Kid 11, 74, 77, 138–140, *139*, 164
BUtterfield 8 8, 34, 48–49, 61, 111, 120, 174
Buttons, Red 26–27
Bye, Bye, Birdie 57
The Byrds 37

Cactus Flower 11
Caesar, Sid 157
Cahiers du Cinéma 27, 47, 69, 103, 112, 126, 131, 149, 160, 168, 176, 181
Cahn, Sammy 128, 129
Caine, Michael 3, 13, 70, 118; *Alfie* (1965) 7, 35, 70–72, *71*, 73, 89; *Funeral in Berlin* 154; *Hurry Sundown* 76, 173; *The Ipcress File* 34, 70, 72; *The Wrong Box* 70; *Zulu* 7, 70, 141
Calamity Jane 51
Callas, Maria 114, 137
Camelot 107–109
Campbell, Glen 105–106
Canada/Canadian 73, 85, 141
Cannes Film Festival 4, 34, 36, 47
Canutt, Yakima 109, 119, 185
Cape Fear (1962) 32
Capucine 69, 70
The Cardinal 16
Cardinale, Claudia 26, 66–68
Carlino, Lewis John 73
Carmen Jones 68
Carney, Art 164
Caron, Leslie 13
Carousel 66
The Carpetbaggers 38, 140–142, *141*, 143
Carve Her Name with Pride 112
Casablanca 105
Casino Royale (1967) 87–88, 154
Cassavetes, John 130, 131, 161, 162
Castle, William 130
Cat Ballou 22, 67, 76, 80–81
Catholic Church 46, 47, 121; *see also* Production Code
CBS 39
Celi, Adolfo 81, 178
censor 7, 8, 17, 45, 72, 197; *see also* Production Code; sexuality
Chakiris, George 158, 160
The Chalk Garden 84
Champion 52, 126
Chandler, Jeff 75
Channing, Carol 129
Chaplin, Geraldine 77, 188, 190, 194
Charade 34, 59, 164
Charly 3, 9, 39–40, 65, 138
The Chase 76, 167
Cher 72
Cheyenne (television) 160
Cheyenne Autumn 54, 66
Chicago Sun-Times 18, 29, 32, 40, 59, 65, 74, 88, 91, 123, 140, 154, 168
The Children's Hour 58, 73, 145, 194
Chitty Chitty Bang Bang 27–29
Christie, Julie 3, 108, 118, 163, 178, 188, 190, 198; *Billy Liar* 98; *Darling* 50, 98, 190; *Doctor Zhivago* 188–190; *Far from the Madding Crowd* 98
Chubasco 13

Cimarron (1960) 109, 158
The Cincinnati Kid 77, 85, 115, 144
Cinecittà, Rome 45
cinema (London) 174, 179, 181, 185, 186; Carlton 139; Casino 169; Classic Piccadilly Circus 35; Empire 187; Leics Sq Theatre 182; Odeon Haymarket 182; Pavilion 97
cinema (New York): Capitol 96, 190; Cinema One 148, 155; Coronet 98; DeMille 118; Embassy 120; Fine Arts 113; Henry Miller Theater 47; Paris 122; Radio City Music Hall 106
Cinerama 25, 36, 81, 124, 134, 157, 169, 170
Cinerama Dome 157
Circus World 67
cities: Berlin 39, 158; Boston 144, 184; Dublin 38; Florence 52; Hanoi 115; Hong Kong 44; London 13, 21, 27, 49, 7, 78, 79, 87, 89, 98, 114, 122, 133, 139, 146, 152, 155, 157, 168, 170, 171, 182, 187; Montreal 166; Naples 109; New York 17, 18, 21, 96, 97, 125, 184, 189, 192; Paris 16, 20, 22, 31, 157; Philadelphia 184; Pittsburgh 18, 155; Rome 45, 47, 53, 174, 181; Seville 111; Tokyo 178; Venice 79
Citizen Kane 159
Civil Rights 17; *see also* racism
Civil War 54
Clarke, Arthur C. 123, 125
Clavell, James 155, 156
Cleopatra 5, 15, 48, 120, 151, 174–176, *175*, 190
Clouzot, Henri-Georges 120
Cobb, Lee J. 32, 33, 68, 170
Coburn, James 32–34, 152; *The Great Escape* 34, 52, 57, 115, 144, 161; *A High Wind in Jamaica* 34; *The Magnificent Seven* (1960) 1, 34, 78, 80, 115, 126, 144, 158, 161; *Our Man Flint* 32–24
Cold War 85
Cole, Nat King 80
The Collector 70, 145, 194
Collins, Joan 174
Columbia 6, 10, 34, 35, 40, 46, 49, 66, 67, 78, 87, 89, 112, 114, 115, 133, 135, 148, 155, 156, 172, 173
Come Blow Your Horn 164
Come September 31
comedy 6, 8, 18, 19, 31, 51, 54, 56, 62, 69, 70, 74, 76, 80, 84, 87, 92, 93, 99, 100, 103, 104, 111, 112, 130, 149, 164; *The Absent Minded Professor* 99–101; *The Apartment* 18–19; *Barefoot in the Park* 76–78; *Blackbeard's Ghost* 149; *The Bobo* 59; *Bringing Up Baby* 27; *Cactus Flower* 11; *Casino Royale* (1967) 87–88, 154; *Come Blow Your Horn* 164; *Come September* 31; *Days of Thrills and Laughter* 157; *The Dick Van Dyke Show* 57, 87, 129; *Dr. Strangelove* 16, 123, 136; *The Facts of Life* 107; *Father Goose* 13; *The Fortune Cookie* 164; *Genevieve* 157; *The Glass Bottom Boat* 63; *The Graduate* 190–192; *The Great Race* 92–94; *A Guide for the Married Man* 164; *Heavens Above* 16; *Inspector Clouseau* 16; *Irma La Douce* 111–112; *It's a Mad Mad Mad Mad World* 156–158; *Lt. Robin Crusoe U.S.N.* 56–57; *Love Bug* (1968) 149–151; *Lover Come Back* 51; *The Millionairess* 16; *Mr. Hobbs Takes a Vacation* 54; *No Time for Sergeants* 19, 130; *The Odd Couple* 164–166; *Operation Petticoat* 74–76; *The Parent Trap* (1961) 103–104; *Pillow Talk* 19, 51, 63; *The Pink Panther* 16, 67, 70, 92; *Please Don't Eat the Daisies* 19, 114; *Promise Her Anything* 167; *The Russians Are Coming, the Russians Are Coming* 85–87; *The Seven Year Itch* 18, 112; *The Shaggy Dog* 19, 30; *A Shot in the Dark* 15–16; *Some Like It Hot* 18, 30,

262   Index

74, 92, 101, 112, 148, 157, 164; *Son of Flubber* 29–31; *That Darn Cat!* 84–85; *That Touch of Mink* 62–63; *Those Magnificent Men in Their Flying Machines* 117–119; *Tom Jones* 146–149; *What's New Pussycat* 69–70; *When Comedy Was King* 157; *With Six You Get Eggroll* 63; *The World of Henry Orient* 16; *The Wrong Arm of the Law* 16; *The Wrong Box* 70; *Yours, Mine and Ours* (1968) 21, 106–107

The Commancheros 67

composer (film composer): Addison, John 146; Alwyn, William 119; Bacharach, Burt 69, 70, 71, 72, 87, 138, 140; Barry, John 9, 96, 152, 154, 170, 178, Bart, Lionel 189; Bernstein, Elmer 31, 40, 105, 127, 140, 142; Brunner, Bob 56; Bruns, George 99, 104, 149; Delerue, George 112; De Vol Frank 51, 80, 160, 172; Fox, Charles 91; Goldsmith, Jerry 20, 32, 37, 52, 115, 117, 131; Grusin, Dave 191; Hefti, Neal 76, 164; Jarre, Maurice 9, 66, 81, 135, 151, 188, 190; Karlin, Fred 106; Komeda, Krystof 130; Mancini, Henry 15, 26, 27, 58, 92; Mandel, Johnny 85; Mayzumi, Toshiro 136; Newman, Alfred 168, 170; North, Alex 117, 120, 123, 126, 174; Previn, Andre 111, 129, 162; Rollins, Sonny 70; Rosza, Miklos 83, 109, 110, 183; Rota, Nino 122; Schifrin, Lalo 22, 23, 73, 74, 144; Smith, Paul 103; Soloff, Maurice 135; Steiner, Max 186; Strouse, Charles 166; Tiomkin, Dmitri 59, 61, 114, 115; Williams, John 162

Connery, Sean 3, 4, 34, 78, 79, 80, 148, 151, 152–154, 170–172, 176–178, 194, 198; *From Russia with Love* 152–154; *Goldfinger* 170–172; *The Longest Day* 151–152; *Thunderball* 176–178; *see also* spy film

Cook, David A. 10

Cool Hand Luke **20**, 22–23, 59, 78, 138, 166, 192

Cooper, Gary 3

Cosmopolitan 168

Costa-Gavras 4, 5

costume 163, 179, 183, 190

countries: Australia 155; Bahamas 178; Bermuda 62; Canada 4, 34, 36, 37; Cyprus 68; Denmark 17; Egypt 174; Eire 38; Finland 188; France 16, 25, 36, 70, 76, 81, 118, 143, 151, 152, 161, 162, 167; Germany 17, 25, 38, 52, 54, 118, 152, 161, 162, 194; Greece 174; Jamaica 34, 79; Japan 31, 51, 118; Mexico 61, 66, 157; Norway 17; Poland 53, 130; Polynesia 42, 143; Puerto Rico 31, 158; Scotland 79; Spain 52, 109–111, 135, 174, 188; Sweden 7, 17; Taiwan 116; Turkey 179; Wales 79; West Indies 31

Courtenay, Tom 143

Crawford, Joan 3

Creature from the Black Lagoon 92

Crenna, Richard 58, 59, 117

crime 8, 59, 63, 166

Crisp, Donald 29

Crist, Judith 36

critical reviews 9, 15, 16, 18, 19, 21, 23, 26, 27, 29, 31, 32, 34, 36, 37, 38, 40, 42, 44, 45, 47, 49, 50, 51, 54, 56, 57, 59, 62, 63, 65, 66, 68, 69, 70, 72, 74, 76, 77, 80, 81, 83, 84, 85, 87, 88, 91, 92, 94, 96, 99, 101, 103, 104, 105, 106, 107, 109, 111, 112, 113, 115, 117, 119, 120, 121, 123, 127, 129, 131, 133, 136, 138, 140, 142, 143, 145, 146, 149, 151, 152, 156, 158, 160, 164, 166, 168, 170, 172, 174, 176, 178, 181, 183, 185, 188, 190, 192, 195

Crosby, Bing 108, 169

Crowther, Bosley 47

Cukor, George 66, 109, 179

Curtis, Tony 3, 19, 63, 74, 75, 76, 92, 93, 94, 126; *The Boston Strangler* 63–65; *The Defiant Ones* 20, 156, 173; *The Great Race* 92–94; *Operation Petticoat*

74–76; *The Perfect Furlough* 74; *Sex and the Single Girl* 92; *Some Like it Hot* 18, 30, 74, 92, 101, 112, 148, 157, 164; *Spartacus* 22, 109, 117, 123, 126–127, 129, 135; *The Vikings* 22, 126

Custer of the West 13

Cyprus 68

Da Costa, Morton 65

Da Gradi, Dom 181

Dahl, Roald 27, 28, 152, 154

Daily Mail 91

Daily Mirror 91

Darby, Kim 105, 191

Darby O'Gill and the Little People 119

Dark of the Sun 13

Darling 50, 98, 190

Darling Lili 130

Darren, James 114, 115

David, Saul 32, 52

Davis, Bette 3, 120, 163

Day, Doris 3, 6, 19, 51, 62–63, 85, 111, 120, 148, 179, 191; *Billy Rose's Jumbo* 63; *Calamity Jane* 51; *The Glass Bottom Boat* 63; *Lover Come Back* 51; *Pillow Talk* 19, 51, 63; *Midnight Lace* 9, 63, 179; *Move Over Darling* 51; *Please Don't Eat the Daisies* 19, 114; *Send Me No Flowers* 85; *That Touch of Mink* 62–63; *The Thrill of It All* 51, 63, 85; *With Six You Get Eggroll* 63

Days of Thrills and Laughter 157

Days of Wine and Roses 22, 32, 39, 92, 111, 164

The Deadly Companions 105

Dear Brigitte 54

Decca 55

The Deer Hunter 84; *see also* Vietnam

The Defiant Ones 20, 156, 173; *see also* racism

Dehn, Paul 170

De Laurentiis, Dino 10, 136

Delerue, George 112

Delon, Alain 25, 135

Demick, Irina 118, 152

DeMille, Cecil B. 66, 136, 190

Denmark 17

Dennis, Sandy 73, 74, 120, 121

The Desert Fox 38

Desilu Productions 107

The Detective (1968) 63, 144

Deutsch, Helen 162

The Devil's Brigade 39

De Vol, Frank 51, 80, 160, 172

Dexter, Brad 52

Les Diaboliques 101

Dial M for Murder 59

Diamond, I.A.L. 18, 19, 111, 112

The Diary of Anne Frank 25

The Dick Van Dyke Show 57, 87, 129

Dietrich, Marlene 9

Dior 9

Directors Guild of America 188

The Dirty Dozen 13, 22, 78, 88, 130, 160–162, *161*

Disney 10, 27, 29–31, 56–57, 84–85, 89, 99, 103–104, 104–105, 111, 119–120, 148, 149–151, 181–183, 194; *see also* Udult

Disney, Walt 84, 99, 100, 103, 105, 119

distribution 140

Dmytryk, Edward 140, 141, 142

Doctor Dolittle (1967) 63, 89, 95, 127, 138

Dr. Goldfoot and the Bikini Machine 34

Dr. No 6, 34, 38, 59, 70, 78, 79, 151, 154, 172; *see also* Bond, James

Index · 263

Dr. Strangelove 16, 123, 136
Doctor Zhivago 9, 37, 77, 95, 136, 186, 188–190, **189**, 198, 199
La Dolce Vita 5, 7, 36, 45–47, 46, 50, 146
Donen, Stanley 194
Donner, Clive 69, 70
Donovan's Reef 67
Dor, Karin 154
Dotrice, Karen 183
Double Indemnity 18, 29
Douglas, Kirk 22, 26, 83, 94, 126, 127, 185; *Spartacus* 126–127
Downhill Racer 130
Dublin 38
Duel at Diablo 94
Duke, Patty 130, 162, 163
Dullea, Keir 73, 123
Dunaway, Faye 3, 166, 167, 168, 198
Dyer, Geoff 15

Eastwood, Clint 3, 13, 15, 57, 198; *Where Eagles Dare* 13–15
Easy Rider 7, 9, 10, 11, 34–37, 35, 92, 106, 151, 172
Eaton, Shirley 172
Ebert, Roger 23, 47
The Ed Sullivan Show 65
Edwards, Blake 15, 16, 62, 74, 92, 131; *Operation Petticoat* 74–76; *A Shot in the Dark* 15–16
Egan, Richard 13
Egypt 174
Eire 38
Ekberg, Anita 45, 47
El Cid 5, 109–111, **110**, 126, 127
El Dorado (1967) 83
Elmer Gantry 66
Embassy Pictures 191
Emmy 22, 57, 67
Esquire 168
Evans, Robert 91, 130
Evening Standard (London) 136
exhibitor 6, 78
Exodus 5, 9, 68, 82, 84, 109, 135, 151, 190
Eyman, Scott 62, 83

The Facts of Life 107
Fahrenheit 451 123
Fail Safe 164
Falk, Peter 94
family films 27, 29, 56, 84 89, 99, 104, 117, 119, 119, 156, 181; *The Absent Minded Professor* 99–101; *The African Lion* 84, 119; *Blackbeard's Ghost* 149; *Chitty Chitty Bang Bang* 27–29; *Darby O'Gill and the Little People* 119; *Doctor Dolittle* (1967) 63, 89, 95, 127, 138; *Genevieve* 157; *The Great Race* 92–94; *Half a Sixpence* 89, 127; *The Happiest Millionaire* 89, 127; *Hatari!* 26–27; *How the West Was Won* 168–170; *In Search of the Castaways* 57, 84, 181, 183; *The Incredible Journey* 85; *Inspector Clouseau* 16; *It's a Mad Mad Mad Mad World* 156–158; *The Jungle Book* (1967) 104–105; *Lt. Robin Crusoe U.S.N.* 56–57; *The Love Bug* (1968) 149–151; *Mary Poppins* 181–183; *The Moon-Spinners* 84; *Old Yeller* 29, 50, 85, 119; *Oliver!* 89–91; *One Hundred and One Dalmatians* (1961) 30, 198; *The Parent Trap* (1961) 103–104; *The Pink Panther* 16, 67, 70, 92; *The Shaggy Dog* 19, 30; *A Shot in the Dark* 15–16; *Sleeping Beauty* 104; *Snow White and the Seven Dwarfs* 99; *Son of Flubber* 29–31; *The Sound of Music* 192–195; *The Story of Robin Hood and His Merrie Men* 29, 119; *Swiss Family Robinson* 119–120; *The Sword in the Stone* 104, 105; *Tarzan Goes to India* 38; *Tarzan the Ape Man* (1959) 104; *Tarzan's Greatest Adventure* 37; *Tarzan's Three Challenges* 172; *That Darn Cat!* 84–85; *Those Magnificent Men in Their Flying Machines* 117–119; *The Truth About Spring* 84; *The Valley of Gwangi* 33; *When Comedy Was King* 157; *Yours, Mine and Ours* (1968) 106–107
The Family Way 84
Fantasia 99
Fantastic Voyage 123, 133
Far from the Madding Crowd 98
Farrow, Mia 52, 130, 131, 194, 198
fashion 9, 50, 72; *see also* costume
Fast, Howard 126
Father Goose 13
Faye, Alice 105
Fearless Frank 98
The Fearless Vampire Killers 130
Fellini, Federico 5, 7, 45, 46, 136
Ferrer, José 25, 135
Ferrer, Mel 58
Fiddler on the Roof 85
Field, Sally 105
Film Comment 178, 192
Film Quarterly 81
Films and Filming 4, 19, 27, 38, 50, 54, 57, 68, 70, 74, 81, 92, 101, 103, 111, 115, 117, 119, 120, 121, 123, 127, 138, 145, 151, 158, 162, 164, 166, 169, 171, 177, 178
Finch, Peter 174
Finland 188
Finney, Albert 59, 135, 146, 147, 148
Firecreek 107
First Amendment 17
Fisher, Eddie 174
A Fistful of Dollars 67
Five Card Stud 105
Five Gates to Hell 155
Flame in the Streets 31
Fleischer, Richard 63, 65
Fleming, Ian 27, 130, 152, 170, 177; *see also* Bond, James
Fleming, Victor 186
Flight of the Phoenix 160
Flint, Derek 6, 32–34, 87, 88, 198; *Our Man Flint* 32–34
Florence 52
Florida 75, 172
The Flower Drum Song 129
Flowers for Algernon 39; *see also* Charly
The Fly 155
Foch, Nina 126
Fonda, Henry 3, 36, 47, 63, 76, 106, 107, 136, 151, 169; *Battle of the Bulge* 13, 56, 107; *The Boston Strangler* 63–65; *Fail Safe* 164; *Firecreek* 107; *How the West Was Won* 168–170; *In Harm's Way* 13, 52; *The Longest Day* 151–152; *Madigan* 63, 107; *Sex and the Single Girl* 92; *Yours, Mine and Ours* (1968) 21, 106–107
Fonda, Jane 3, 36, 76, 77, 80, 125, 163, 198; *Barbarella* 125; *Barefoot in the Park* 76–78; *Cat Ballou* 80–81; *The Chase* 76, 167; *Hurry Sundown* 76, 173; *Joy House* 76; *La Ronde* 76; *Sunday in New York* 76, 80
Fonda, Peter 34, 35, 36, 37
Foote, Horton 31, 32
For the Love of Ivy 39; *see also* Poitier, Sidney
Force Ten from Navarone 198

264 Index

Ford, Glenn 19, 40, 120, 160, 170
Ford, John 4, 26, 38, 55, 60, 61, 66, 67, 103, 106, 168, 169, 188; *The Alamo* (1960) 9, 22, 42, 56, 59–62, **60**, 83, 115; *Cheyenne Autumn* 54, 66; *The Horse Soldiers* 26; *How the West Was Won* 5, 8, 38, 42, 54, 168–170, **169**; *The Man Who Shot Liberty Valance* 54, 67; *The Quiet Man* 60, 103; *Rio Grande* 60; *The Searchers* 158, 169; *Sergeant Rutledge* 31; *Stagecoach* (1939) 67; *Two Rode Together* 66; *Young Cassidy* 188
Foreman, Carl 114, 115, 157
Forsyth, Rosemary 54
The Fortune Cookie 164
Four for Texas 38, 40
Fowlie, Eddie 189
The Fox 8, 73–74, 197
Fox, Charles 91
Fox, James 117, 127, 129
France/French 16, 25, 36, 70, 76, 81, 118, 143, 151, 152, 161, 162, 167
franchise 199
Frank, Frederic M. 109, 110
Frankenheimer, John 4, 73, 81, 82, 83, 112, 120
Frazetta, Frank 70
Friendly Persuasion 56, 67, 119
Frobe, Gert 28, 118, 157, 171
From Here to Eternity 113, 143, 152
From Russia with Love 6, 34, 78–80, **79**, 112, 154, 172, 178
From the Terrace 52, 68, 163
Fry, Christopher 136
Fuller, Sam 39
Fun in Acapulco 38
Funeral in Berlin 154
Funny Girl 129, 145–146

Gable, Clark 3, 26, 42, 51, 75, 109, 134, 186–188; *Gone with the Wind* 186–188; *It Happened in Naples* 109
gangster 166, 168
Garbo, Greta 9
Gardner, Ava 16, 136, 191
Garland, Judy 163
Garner, James 3, 28, 51, 57, 81, 83, 85, 94, 163
Garson, Greer 49
Gavin, John 102, 126, 129
Geeson, Judy 155, 156
generation gap 192
Genevieve 157
Gentleman's Agreement 25, 31, 119
Georgy Girl 7, 49–50, 70, 73
Gerber, Matthew 183
Germany/German 17, 25, 38, 52, 54, 118, 152, 161, 162, 194
Giant 23, 48, 51
Gigi 66
Gilbert, Lewis 70, 71, 89, 154
Gingold, Hermione 66
The Glass Bottom Boat 63
Glenn, Roy 173
The Glory Stompers 35
Godard, Jean-Luc 167
The Godfather 199
Golan, Gila 32, 33
Gold, Ernest 68, 156
Golden Globe 65, 74, 92, 123
Goldfinger 6, 15, 28, 34, 78, 170–172, **171**, 178
Goldman, William 39, 138, 140, 191
Goldsmith, Jerry 20, 32, 37, 52, 115, 117, 131

Gone with the Wind 3, 68, 78, 170, 176, 184, 186–188, **187**, 195, 199
Good Housekeeping 26
The Good, the Bad and the Ugly 186
Goodbye, Columbus 37, 91–92, 106
Goodbye, Mr. Chips (1969) 106
Goodwin, Ron 13, 15, 117, 118
Gordon, Ruth 130, 131
The Graduate 8, 9, 37, 91, 98, 107, 122, 123, 186, 190–192, 199
Grand Prix 65, 78, 81–83, **82**, 95, 117, 124, 144, 149, 197
Grant, Cary 19, 59, 62–63, 74–76, 94, 109, 114, 179, 198; *Charade* 34, 59, 164; *North by Northwest* 30, 62, 68, 74, 87, 101, 159, 194; *Operation Petticoat* 74–76; *That Touch of Mink* 62–63
Grant, James Edward 59, 60
Grant, Lee 95
The Great Escape 34, 52, 57, 115, 144, 161
Great Expectations (1946) 7
The Great Race 63, 192–94, **93**, 118, 129, 144, 164
The Greatest Story Ever Told 23–26, **24**, 55, 143
Greece 174
Green, Guy 20
The Green Berets 83–84, 105, 106
Grodin, Charles 191
The Group 21, 117, 145
Grove Press 10, 17
Grusin, Dave 191
Guardian newspaper 15, 80, 91
Guess Who's Coming to Dinner 8, 94, 172–174
Guest, Val 87
A Guide for the Married Man 164
Guillermin, John 37
Guinness, Alec 133, 143, 188
Gulf & Western 10
Gunga Din 23
Guns at Batasi 38, 117, 130
The Guns of Navarone 13, 15, 32, 42, 114–115, 131, 151
Guys and Dolls 126
Gypsy 93

Hackett, Buddy 66, 149
Hackman, Gene 143, 167, 168, 191
Half a Sixpence 89, 127
Hall, Conrad 23
The Hallelujah Trail 66
Hammerstein, Oscar II 192
Hancock, Tony 118
Hanks, Tom 181
Hanley, William 191
Hanoi 115
The Happiest Millionaire 89, 127
Harareet, Haya 183, 185
Hardy, Françoise 82, 83
Harper 9, 13, 22, 56
Harpers 125
Harris, Mark 95
Harris, Phil 104, 105
Harris, Richard 42, 44, 107, 108, 109, 136, 142, 143, 148; *The Agony and the Ecstasy* 130, 131, 190; *The Bible* 136–138; *Camelot* 107–109; *Hawaii* 142–143; *Major Dundee* 32, 34, 66, 131, 136; *Mutiny on the Bounty* 42–44
Harrison, Linda 131
Harrison, Rex 39, 108, 174, 176, 179, 181, 198; *The Agony and the Ecstasy* 130, 131, 190; *Cleopatra* 174–176; *Doctor Dolittle* (1967) 63, 89, 95, 127, 138; *My Fair Lady* 179–181; *Midnight Lace* 9, 63, 179

Index

265

Hartman, Elizabeth 20, 21
Harvard Crimson 50
Harvey, Laurence 48, 59, 61, 70
Hatari! 26–27
Hathaway, Henry 4, 105, 106, 117, 168, 169
Hawaii 25, 52, 94, 108, 113, 129, 130, 138, 142–143
Hawks, Howard 4, 26, 56, 138
Hawley, Lowell S. 119
Hawn, Goldie 130
Haworth, Jill 69
Hayakawa, Sessue 45, 119
Hayes, John Michael 48, 140
Hayward, Susan 48, 163, 174
Heavens Above 16
Hecht, Ben 88
Hecht, Harold 80, 81
Hecht-Hill-Lancaster 22, 81
Hefti, Neal 76, 164
Heller in Pink Tights 109
Hellfighters 105, 138
Hellman, Jerome 96
Hellman, Monte 36
Hell's Angels on Wheels 35
Helm, Matt 6, 40, 78, 87, 88, 198
Helpmann, Robert 28
Hemmings, David 109
Hendrix, Jimi 37
Henry, Buck 190, 191
Henry V (1944) 122, 147
Hepburn, Audrey 3, 9, 38, 57–59, 66, 73, 136, 143, 158, 174, 179–181, 183, 188; *Breakfast at Tiffany's* 9, 38, 58, 142, 181; *Charade* 34, 59, 164; *The Children's Hour* 58, 73, 145, 194; *How to Steal a Million* 59, 145; *My Fair Lady* 179–181; *Wait Until Dark* 57–59
Hepburn, Katharine 3, 39, 146, 172, 174, 198
Hercules (1958) 46, 141
Herlihy, James Leo 96–98
Hermann, Bernard 101, 102
The Heroes of Telemark 143
Hershey, Barbara 191
Heston, Charlton 3, 25, 109, 110, 133, 151, 183, 185; *Ben-Hur* 183–185; *Major Dundee* 32, 34, 66, 131, 136; *Planet of the Apes* 131–133; *The War Lord* 131; *Will Penny* 131
Heywood, Anne 73
High Noon 67, 113, 114, 138, 157
High Society 108
A High Wind in Jamaica 34
Hill, Benny 28, 118
Hill, George Roy 4, 74, 127, 129, 138, 142–143, 146, 194, 198; *Butch Cassidy and the Sundance Kid* 138–140; *Hawaii* 142–143; *Thoroughly Modern Millie* 127–129; *Toys in the Attic* 138, 143; *The World of Henry Orient* 16
Hiller, Arthur 143
historical films 5, 8, 198, 112, 136, 146; *The Agony and the Ecstasy* 130, 131, 190; *The Amorous Adventures of Moll Flanders* 178; *Anne of the Thousand Days* 106; *Barabbas* 114, 136; *Becket* 65, 105, 112, 121; *Ben-Hur* (1959) 5, 11, 23, 25, 27, 42, 109, 110, 110, 111, 133, 145, 151, 170, 174, 183–185, **184**, 186, 194, 199; *Ben-Hur: A Tale of the Christ* 185; *The Bible* 23, 136–138, **137**; *Cleopatra* 5, 15, 48, 120, 151, 174–176, **175**, 190; *Doctor Zhivago* 9, 37, 77, 95, 136, 186, 188–190, **189**, 198, 199; *El Cid* 5, 109–111, **110**, 126, 127; *Far from the Madding Crowd* 98; *Gone with the Wind* 3, 68, 78, 170, 176, 184, 186–188, **187**, 195, 199; *Great Expectations* (1946) 7; *The Greatest Story Ever Told* 23–26, **24**, 55, 143;

Gunga Din 23; *Hercules* (1958) 46, 141; *Ivanhoe* (1952) 106; *Jamaica Inn* 103; *Khartoum* 15, 131; *King of Kings* (1961) 109; *Land of the Pharaohs* 26; *Lawrence of Arabia* 3, 5, 10, 13, 32, 42, 81, 132–136, 134, 148, 163, 188, 190; *The Lion in Winter* 40, 146; *The Long Ships* 21; *Lord Jim* 40, 49, 66, 190; *Lust for Life* 126; *Moby Dick* (1956) 32; *Mutiny on the Bounty* (1962) 32, 42–44; *Raintree County* 142; *Reap the Wild Wind* 66; *The Robe* 126; *Romeo and Juliet* (1968) 9, 37, 121–123, 158; *The Sand Pebbles* 115–117, **116**, 144, 194; *Seven Samurai* 81; *The Seventh Seal* 25; *She* 38; *Sodom and Gomorrah* 23; *Solomon and Sheba* 23; *Spartacus* 22, 109, 117, 123, 126–127, 129, 135; *Swiss Family Robinson* (1961) 30, 57, 118, 119–120, 151; *The Taming of the Shrew* 122; *The Ten Commandments* (1956) 136; *Tom Jones* 7, 98, 146–149, **147**; *The Vikings* 22, 126; *War and Peace* (1956) 136; *The War Lord* 131; *The Wrong Box* 70; *Zulu* 7, 70, 141; *see also* westerns
History of the American Cinema 10
Hitchcock, Alfred 36, 51, 56, 62, 68, 78, 101–103, 114, 190; *Dial M for Murder* 59; *Jamaica Inn* 103; *The Man Who Knew Too Much* (1956) 51; *North by Northwest* 30, 62, 68, 74, 87, 101, 159, 194; *Psycho* (1960) 8, 101–103, 130; *Rear Window* 48; *Spellbound* 114; *Torn Curtain* 22, 56, 129; *Vertigo* 36, 102
Hoffman, Dustin 3, 92, 96–99, 106, 190–192, 198; *The Graduate* 190–192; *Midnight Cowboy* 96–99
Holden, William 39, 44, 45, 52, 59, 72, 88, 114, 135
A Hole in the Head 19
Hollywood Reporter 23, 84, 176
Hombre 13, 22, 138
Home of the Brave 52
Hong Kong 44
Hopalong Cassidy 78
Hope, Bob 70
Hopkins, John 176
Hopper, Dennis 22, 34–37
Hordern, Michael 15
horror 6, 8, 101, 130; *Blood and Roses* 26; *Hush... Hush, Sweet Charlotte* 160; *Psycho* (1960) 8, 101–103, 130; *Repulsion* 130; *Rosemary's Baby* 5, 8, 130–131
The Horse Soldiers 26
Houghton, Katharine 173
Hour of the Gun 98
Houseboat 19, 62, 74, 109
Houston, Donald 15
How the West Was Won 5, 8, 38, 42, 54, 168–170, **169**
How to Steal a Million 59, 145
Howard, Sidney 186
Howard, Trevor 42, 44, 52, 54, 174
Howes, Sally Ann 27–29
Hud 22, 73
Hudson, Rock 3, 19, 23, 31, 48, 51, 62, 73, 81, 82, 85, 179, 185, 198; *Come September* 31; *Giant* 23, 48, 51; *Lover Come Back* 51; *Pillow Talk* 19, 51, 63; *Seconds* 73, 82; *Send Me No Flowers* 85
Hughes, Ken 27, 28, 87
Hunter, Kim 131
Hunter, Ross 127
Hurry Sundown 76, 173; *see also* racism
Hush...Hush, Sweet Charlotte 160
Hussey, Olivia 121–122
The Hustler 22, 23
Huston, John 87, 136
Hutton, Brian G. 13–15

I Am Curious (Yellow) 17–18, 97, 197
I Could Go on Singing 191

266　　　　　　　　　　　　　　　　　　　**Index**

I Love Lucy 107
Ice Cold in Alex 114, 119
If... 36, 37
In Harm's Way 13, 52
In Like Flint 34, 78, 152; *see also* spy films
In Search of the Castaways 57, 84, 181, 183
In the Heat of the Night 8, 63, 85, 94–96, **95**, 98, 155, 173
In Theaters Everywhere 141
The Incident 92
The Incredible Journey 85
Independent Film Journal 166
The Indian Fighter 26
Inga 18
Inherit the Wind 156, 157
Inside Daisy Clover 76, 93
Inspector Clouseau 16
Interlude 9
International Motion Picture Exhibitor 37, 84, 91, 99, 125, 140, 145, 166
The Intruder 31
The Ipcress File 34, 70, 72
Irma La Douce 31, 111–112, 148
It Happened in Naples 109
Italy/Italian 25, 46, 47, 52, 54, 81, 118, 122, 136
It's a Mad Mad Mad Mad World 87, 92, 118, 144, 149, 156–158, 173, 198
Ivanhoe (1952) 106

Jacobi, Lou 112
Jailhouse Rock 50, 192
Jamaica 79
Jamaica Inn 103
Janssen, David 83
Janus Films 10, 17
Japan 31, 81, 118
Jarre, Maurice 9, 66, 81, 135, 151, 188, 190
Jewison, Norman 4, 85, 94, 115
Johnson, Nunnally 160
Jones, Dean 29, 76, 84, 85, 149, 150
Jones, James 151, 152
Jones, Quincy 94, 95
Jones, Shirley 65, 66
Jones, Tom 70
Jourdan, Louis 114
Joy House 76
Judgment at Nuremberg 156, 157
The Jungle Book (1967) 104–105, 186, 198

Kaleidoscope 167
Kaper, Bronislau 42, 48
Karlin, Fred 106
Karlson, Phil 40
Kastner, Elliott 13
Kaye, Stubby 80
Kazan, Elia 158
Keaton, Buster 157
Keith, Brian 103, 104
Kelly, Gene 135, 194
Kennedy, Arthur 135
Kennedy, George 22, 23, 55, 160
Kerr, Deborah 7, 49, 88, 108
Keyes, Daniel 39
The Keys of the Kingdom 31
Khartoum 15, 131
Kidnapped (1960) 119
The Killers (1964) 67
The Killing of Sister George 97

A Kind of Loving 98
Kine Weekly 35, 43, 58, 90, 97, 139, 167
The King and I 108, 158, 186
King of Kings (1961) 109
Kingsley, Dorothy 162
Kipling, Rudyard 104
Kiss Me Kate 122
Knott, Frederick 58, 59
Koch, Howard 73
Komeda, Krysztof 130
Kovacs, Laszlo 36
Kramer, Stanley 4, 36, 92, 156–158, 172–174; *The Defiant Ones* 20, 156, 173; *Guess Who's Coming to Dinner* 172–174; *Inherit the Wind* 156, 157; *Judgement at Nuremberg* 156, 157; *It's a Mad, Mad, Mad, Mad World* 156–158; *Judgement at Nuremberg* 156, 157; *Ship of Fools* 33, 67, 80, 130, 173
Krim, Arthur 111
Kruger, Hardy 26, 27
Kubrick, Stanley 4, 123–126
Kwan, Nancy 44, 45, 56, 57
Kwouk, Burt 16

Ladd, Alan 140–142
Lady Chatterley's Lover 73
The Ladykillers 114
LaGarde, Jocelyn 143
Lancaster, Burt 3, 9, 22, 32, 36, 47, 54, 66–68, 81, 82, 94, 112, 113, 143, 152, 156, 157, 160, 167, 170, 185, 188, 198; *From Here to Eternity* 113, 143, 152; *The Hallelujah Trail* 66; Hecht-Hill-Lancaster 22, 81; *Judgement at Nuremberg* 156, 157; *The Leopard* 36, 67; *The Professionals* 66–68; *Seven Days in May* 9, 82; *The Train* 54, 66, 82, 112, 167
Lanchester, Elsa 183
Land of the Pharaohs 26
Las Vegas Story 181
Last Command 60
Last Summer 37, 106
Laughton, Charles 42, 112, 126, 127
Laurel and Hardy 92
Laurents, Arthur 158
Lavi, Daliah 40, 88, 154
Law, John Philip 87
Lawford. Peter 152
Lawrence, D.H. 73
Lawrence of Arabia 3, 5, 10, 13, 32, 42, 81, 132–136, 134, 148, 163, 188, 190
LGBT depictions 8, 73
Lean, David 4, 32, 37, 72, 126, 133–136, 188–190; *Bridge on the River Kwai* 44, 45, 78, 119, 126, 132, 135, 186, 188; *Doctor Zhivago* 9, 37, 77, 95, 136, 186, 188–190, **189**, 198, 199; *Great Expectations* (1946) 7; *Lawrence of Arabia* 3, 5, 10, 13, 32, 42, 81, 132–136, 134, 148, 163, 188, 190
le Carré, John 34, 130; *see also* spy films
Lederer, Charles 42
Lee, Harper 31
Lee, Michele 149
The Left Handed Gun 167
Lehman, Ernest 120, 158, 159, 192, 194
Leigh, Janet 101–103
Leigh, Vivien 186–188
Lemmon, Jack 18–19, 22, 32, 51, 63, 86, 87, 92–94, 111–112, 120, 164–166; *The Apartment* 18–19; 92–94; *Days of Wine and Roses* 22, 32, 39, 92, 111, 164; *The Great Race* 92–94; *Irma la Douce* 111–112; *The Odd Couple* 164–166

Index

267

Lenya, Lotte 80
The Leopard 36, 67
Lerner, Alan Jay 107, 108, 179
LeRoy, Melvyn 83
Lester, Mark 89
Let's Make Love 114
Levin, Ira 19, 114
Levine, Joseph E. 7, 46, 140–142, 190–192; *The Carpetbaggers* 140–142; *The Graduate* 190–192; *Hercules* (1958) 46, 141
Lewis, Edward 81
Lewis, Jerry 33
The Libertine 18
Lt. Robin Crusoe U.S.N. 45, 56–57
Life 36, 37, 40, 72, 94, 105, 121, 125, 149, 160, 168, 174, 183
Lili 7
Lilies of the Field 3, 7, 9, 20, 21, 25, 39, 94, 155; *see also* Poitier, Sidney
Lilith 39, 69, 166
The Lion in Winter 40, 146
The Liquidator 34
Little Caesar 83
The "little film that could" 59, 73, 81, 146, 155, 170, 198
Little White Lies 15
Litvak, Anatole 16
Lloyd, Harold 92
Lockwood, Gary 123
Loewe, Frederick 107, 108, 179
Logan, Joshua 107–109
Lolita 16, 49, 123
Lollobrigida, Gina 23, 26, 31, 45, 164; *Come September* 31; *Mirage* 164; *Solomon and Sheba* 23
Lom, Herbert 16, 110, 126
London 13, 27, 49, 72, 78, 79, 87, 89, 98, 114, 122, 133, 139, 146, 152, 155, 168, 170, 171, 182, 187; *see also* cinemas (London)
The Long, Hot Summer 22
The Long Ships 21
The Longest Day 5, 13, 32, 112, 118, 151–152
Look Back in Anger 13
Lopez, Trini 160
Lord Jim 40, 49, 66, 190
Loren, Sophia 3, 7, 16, 19, 26, 38, 45, 62, 109, 110, 188; *El Cid* 109–111; *Heller in Pink Tights* 109; *Operation Crossbow* 13, 15, 38; *Two Women* 109
Los Angeles 21, 157
Los Angeles Times 16, 21, 38, 49, 51, 56, 57, 69, 77, 83, 85, 87, 105, 106, 109, 111, 115, 126, 129, 133, 138, 142, 143, 166, 178, 181, 185, 195
The Lost Weekend 18
The Love Bug (1968) 149–151, **150**, 198
Love with the Proper Stranger 93, 115
Lover Come Back 51
low-budget 3, 6, 7, 11, 20, 21, 35, 40, 49, 50, 55, 71, 73, 92, 94, 101, 102, 146, 147, 155
Lulu 156
Lumet, Sidney 4, 145
Lust for Life 126

MacArthur, James 119, 120
MacDougall, Ranald 174
MacGraw, Ali 91–92
Mackendrick, Alexander 114
Mackenna's Gold 131
MacLaine, Shirley 18, 19, 49, 73, 111–112, 166; *The Apartment* 18–19; *The Children's Hour* 58, 73, 145, 194; *Irma La Douce* 111–112

MacLean, Alistair 13, 114
MacMurray, Fred 29–31, 99–101, 107, 149; *The Absent Minded Professor* 99–101; *Son of Flubber* 29–31
The Macomber Affair 66
Madigan 63, 107
Madigan's Millions 98
The Magnificent Seven (1960) 1, 34, 78, 80, 115, 126, 144, 158, 161
Maibaum, Richard 170, 178
Major Dundee 32, 34, 66, 131, 136
Mamoulian, Reuben 174
A Man for All Seasons 8, 112–1113, 122
The Man from U.N.C.L.E. television series 34, 144
The Man Who Knew Too Much (1956) 51
The Man Who Shot Liberty Valance 54, 67
The Man with the Golden Arm 68
The Manchurian Candidate 52, 54, 82
Mancini, Henry 15, 26, 27, 58, 92
Mandel, Johnny 85
Mankiewicz, Joseph L. 174–176
Mankovitz, Wolf 87
Mann, Anthony 55, 56, 109, 126
Mann, Daniel 32, 34, 48
Mann, Delbert 51, 62
Mantle, Mickey 62
Mardi Gras 36
marketing 21, 64, 71, 91, 132, 163, 185
Marshall, George 168, 169
The Martian Chronicles 123
Martin, Dean 40–42, 83, 114, 152, 198; Meadway-Claude Productions 41; *Murderers Row* 152; *Ocean's 11* (1960) 40, 42, 128; *Rio Bravo* 26, 27, 30, 40; *Robin and the 7 Hoods* 128; *The Sons of Katie Elder* 83, 105; *The Wrecking Crew* 40
Martin, Mary 66, 108, 194
Martin, Strother 22
Martinelli, Elsa 26–27, 126
Marton, Andrew 151, 185
Marty 7, 50, 147
Marvin, Lee 3, 66–68, 80, 160–162, 198
Marx Brothers 70
Mary Poppins 5, 27, 28, 29, 56, 57, 105, 127, 149, 181–183, **182**, 194, 198, 199
Mason, James 37–38, 49, 120, 188
Masquerade 39, 138
Mast, Gerald 10
Mastroianni, Marcello 45, 47
masturbation 73
Matthau, Walter 16, 164–166
Maugham, Somerset 44
Mayes, Wendell 52
Mayzumi, Toshiro 136
McCalls 195
McCartney, Paul 72, 122
McClory, Kevin 176–178
McClure, Douglas 54
McDowell, Roddy 131
McGrath, Joe 87, 88
McGuire, Dorothy 25, 119
McLaglen, Andrew V. 54–55
McLintock 55
McQueen, Steve 3, 34, 56, 57, 81, 85, 93, 94, 115–117, 120, 138, 142, 144–145, 170, 198; *Bullitt* 144–145; *The Cincinnati Kid* 77, 85, 115, 144; *The Great Escape* 34, 52, 57, 115, 144, 161; *Love with the Proper Stranger* 93, 115; *The Magnificent Seven* (1960) 1, 34, 78, 80, 115, 126, 144, 158, 161; *The Sand Pebbles* 115–117; *The Thomas Crown Affair* 85, 144

268   Index

merchandising 153, 171
Merchant, Vivien 72, 73
merger 10
Merman, Ethel 157
Merrill, Dina 74, 76
methodology 11
Mexico 61, 66, 157
Meyer, Russ 18
MGM 5, 9, 10, 13, 14, 21, 32, 34, 42, 48, 56, 68, 74, 78, 81, 82, 117, 123, 124, 134, 160, 168, 169, 174, 179, 183, 186, 188
Michener, James 142
Mickey One 166
Midnight Cowboy 8, 37, 96–99, **97**, 106, 151
Midnight Lace 9, 63, 179
Mifune, Toshiro 81
Miles, Sarah 117, 188
Miles, Sylvia 99
Miles, Vera 101
Milestone, Lewis 42, 44
The Millionairess 16
Mills, Hayley 29, 84–85, 103–104, 119, 198; *The Chalk Garden* 84; *The Family Way* 84; *In Search of the Castaways* 57, 84, 181, 183; *The Moon-Spinners* 84; *The Parent Trap* 103–104; *Pollyanna* (1960) 30, 84, 103; *That Darn Cat!* 84–85; *The Truth About Spring* 84
Mills, John 114, 119, 120
Mimieux, Yvette 77, 188
Mineo, Sal 68
The Miracle Worker 39, 167
Mirage 164
Mirisch, Walter 85, 94, 96, 112, 142, 143, 158, 159
Mirisch Brothers 16, 111
Mission Impossible (television) 107
Mr. Hobbs Takes a Vacation 54
Mitchum, Robert 66, 73, 83, 151
Moby Dick (1956) 32
Modesty Blaise 34, 152
Moment to Moment 83
Monroe, Marilyn 111, 114, 163; *Let's Make Love* 114; *The Seven Year Itch* 18, 112; *Some Like It Hot* 18, 30, 74, 92, 101, 112, 148, 157, 164
Montand, Yves 4, 25, 26, 81, 83
Montreal 166
Moody, Ron 89
The Moon-Spinners 84
Moore, Mary Tyler 129
Moore, Robin 83
Moreau, Jeanne 188, 191
Moreno, Rita 158, 160
Morgenstern, Joseph 166
Morocco 135
Motion Picture Association of America (MPAA) 17, 121, 126
Move Over Darling 51
Mulligan, Robert 4, 31–32, 115, 123
Munafo, Robert P. 199
Munro, Janet 119, 120
Murchison, Clint 60
murder 31, 36
Murderers Row 152
The Music Man 32, 65–66
musicals 3, 5, 8, 28, 32, 51, 63, 65, 68, 89, 93, 107, 108, 111, 127, 145, 158, 181, 194; *Annie Get Your Gun* 108; *Billy Rose's Jumbo* 63; *Bye, Bye, Birdie* 57; *Calamity Jane* 51; *Camelot* 107–109; *Carmen Jones* 68; *Carousel* 66; *Chitty Chitty Bang Bang* 27–29;

Darling Lili 130; *Doctor Dolittle* (1967) 63, 89, 95, 127, 138; *Fiddler on the Roof* 85; *The Flower Drum Song* 129; *Fun in Acapulco* 38; *Funny Girl* 129, 145–146; *Gigi* 66; *Goodbye, Mr. Chips* (1969) 106; *Guys and Dolls* 126; *Gypsy* 93; *Half a Sixpence* 89, 127; *The Happiest Millionaire* 89, 127; *Jailhouse Rock* 50, 192; *The Jungle Book* (1967) 104–105, 186, 198; *The King and I* 108, 158, 186; *Kiss Me Kate* 122; *Mary Poppins* 5, 27, 28, 29, 56, 57, 105, 127, 149, 181–183, **182**, 194, 198, 199; *The Music Man* 32, 65–66; *My Fair Lady* 5, 9, 28, 58, 66, 89, 108, 127, 138, 179–181, 180, **183**, 194; *Oklahoma* 66, 194; *Paint Your Wagon* 108; *Porgy and Bess* 20, 68; *Robin and the 7 Hoods* 128; *The Sound of Music* 3, 5, 89, 91, 108, 115, 127, 190, 192–195, **193**, 198, 199; *South Pacific* 66, 108, 194; *Thoroughly Modern Millie* 127–129, **128**, 138, 146; *The Unsinkable Molly Brown* 65; *West Side Story* (1961) 31, 42, 93, 98, 108, 122, 158–160, **159**, 194, 199
Mutiny on the Bounty (1935) 42
Mutiny on the Bounty (1962) 32, 42–44, **43**, 89, 108, 141
My Fair Lady 5, 9, 28, 58, 66, 89, 108, 127, 138, 179–181, 180, **183**, 194
My Forbidden Past 181
My Geisha 111

The Naked Runner 15
The Naked Spur 109
The Name of the Game 22
Narrizano, Silvio 49, 50
Nathanson, E.M. 160
National Catholic Office for Motion Pictures 98; *see also* Catholic Church
Naughton, Bill 70
Neal, Patricia 73, 191
Nelson, Peter 191
Nelson, Ralph 39
Nero, Franco 108, 109, 136
Nesbitt, Derren 15
Nevada Smith 56, 105, 117, 142, 143; *see also* Hathaway, Henry
Never on Sunday 9, 49, 111
Never Say Never Again 177
New Jersey 192
New Republic 32, 80
New Wave 4, 5, 7
New York 17, 18, 21, 96, 97, 125, 184, 189, 192
New York Daily News 18, 26, 47, 106, 113, 190
New York Film Critics Award 95
New York Herald Tribune 26, 47, 81, 113, 160, 190
New York Journal American 45, 160, 176
New York Post 72, 99, 113, 136
New York Times 15, 18, 19, 21, 24, 26, 27, 31, 34, 40, 42, 44, 45, 47, 49, 51, 56, 57, 59, 62, 63, 65, 66, 68, 70, 72, 74, 76, 77, 81, 84, 85, 87, 88, 92, 99, 104, 106, 107, 112, 113, 117, 119, 120, 125, 127, 129, 131, 133, 136, 142, 142, 145, 149, 151, 154, 156, 160, 168, 170, 176, 181, 183, 185, 190, 195
New Yorker 16, 51, 69, 77, 85, 87, 96, 115, 117, 143, 152, 192
Newman, Alfred 23, 168, 170
Newman, David 166–167
Newman, Lionel 63
Newman, Paul 8, 20, 22–23, 47, 52, 56, 63, 68–69, 81, 115, 120, 125, 137, 138–140, 151, 170, 185, 188, 192, 198; *Butch Cassidy and the Sundance Kid* 138–140; *Cool Hand Luke* 22–23; *Exodus* 68–69; *Harper* 9, 13, 22,

56; *Hombre* 13, 22, 138; *Hud* 22, 73; *The Hustler* 22, 23; *The Prize* 16, 52, 163; *Torn Curtain* 22, 56, 129
Newman, Walter 80
Newsday 131, 168
Newsweek 37, 50, 96, 111, 125, 149, 166, 174
Nichols, Mike 77, 92, 98, 120, 121, 125, 190, 191, 192, 198; *Barefoot in the Park* 76–78; *The Graduate* 190–192; *Who's Afraid of Virginia Woolf* 120–121
Nichols, Peter 49
Nicholson, Jack 34–37, 73
The Night Fighters 73
Night of the Iguana 121, 136, 145
Niven, David 16, 19, 87, 88, 114, 115
Nixon, Marni 108, 179
No Time for Sergeants 19, 130
None But the Brave 52
North by Northwest 30, 62, 68, 74, 87, 101, 159, 194
North, Alex 117, 120, 123, 126, 174
North to Alaska 69, 105, 169
Norway 17
Novak, Kim 163, 178
nudity 8, 16, 17, 73, 91; obscene 17; *see also* Production Code; X-certificate; sexuality
Nuyen, France 44, 45
Nyman, Lena 17

Oates, Warren 95
O'Brien, Joan 74, 76
obscene 17
Ocean's 11 (1960) 40, 42, 128
The Odd Couple 8, 106, 164–166, **165**, 198
Odeon 35, 171, 177, 182
Of Human Bondage (1964) 28, 44
O'Hara, Maureen 29, 48, 103–104
Oklahoma 66, 194
Old Yeller 29, 50, 85, 119
Oliver! 40, 89–91, **90**
Olivier, Laurence 80, 122, 126, 127, 174
Olson, Nancy 29, 30, 99
On Her Majesty's Secret Service 154
On the Beach 156
On the Waterfront 68
One Hundred and One Dalmatians (1961) 30, 198
One Hundred Rifles 8
One, Two, Three 158
Operation Crossbow 13, 15, 38
Operation Petticoat 62, 74–76, **75**, 92
Oscar 4, 7, 9, 18, 19, 20, 21, 23, 25, 28, 32, 37, 40, 44, 46, 47, 48, 49, 56, 59, 61, 65, 66, 67, 68, 69, 71, 72, 73, 80, 85, 90, 91, 96, 98, 99, 103, 105, 106, 112, 113, 115, 117, 119, 121, 123, 126, 127, 131, 135, 138, 140, 145, 146, 147, 148, 149, 152, 156, 159, 160, 163, 164, 166, 167, 168, 170, 174, 176, 178, 181, 183, 185, 190, 191, 195, 197, 198
Othello (1965) 80
O'Toole, Peter 3, 32, 40, 59, 69–70, 106, 112, 133–136, 136–138, 148, 179, 188, 198; *Becket* 65, 105, 112, 121; *The Bible* 136–138; *How to Steal a Million* 59, 145; *Lawrence of Arabia* 133–136; *The Lion in Winter* 40, 146; *Lord Jim* 40, 49, 66, 190; *What's New Pussycat* 69–70
Our Man Flint 32–34, **33**, 40, 56, 78, 85, 152
Our Man in Havana 104
Out of It 98
The Outrage 22

The Pad 13
Page, Genevieve 110
Paint Your Wagon 108

Pakula, Alan J. 31–32
Palance, Jack 67, 114
Paluzzi, Luciana 178
Panavision 25, 42, 157
Papas, Irene 114
Paramount 9, 10, 26, 44, 70, 71, 76, 77, 89, 91, 101, 122, 125, 130, 140, 164, 165
The Parent Trap (1961) 30, 84, 103–104, 105, 149, 198
Paris 16; see also *Paris Blues*; *Paris When It Sizzles*
Paris Blues 20, 22, 31
Paris When It Sizzles 59
Park Circus Films 199
Parkins, Barbara 162, 163
Parks, Gordon 8
Parks, Michael 136
Parrish, Robert 87
Parsons, Estelle 167
Pasternak, Boris 188
A Patch of Blue 20–21, 72, 94, 95
Paths of Glory 22
Patton 145
Paul, Byron 56
The Pawnbroker 7, 8, 17, 32, 80, 95, 190
Pearce, Donn 22
Peck, Gregory 31–32, 66, 108, 113, 114–115, 123, 126, 135, 146, 151, 168–170, 198; *Behold a Pale Horse* 113; *Beloved Infidel* 32; *The Big Country* 126, 169; *Cape Fear* (1962) 32; *The Guns of Navarone* 114–115; *How the West Was Won* 168–170; *Mirage* 164; *On the Beach* 156; *The Stalking Moon* 140; *To Kill a Mockingbird* 31–32
Peckinpah, Sam 4, 104
Peerce, Larry 91, 92
Penn, Arthur 4, 166–168, 197
Peppard, George 37–38, 140–142, 170
The Perfect Furlough 74
Perkins, Anthony 101–103
Peter Gunn (television series) 74
Peters, Brock 31
Pettet, Joanna 88
Peyton Place (1957) 52, 163
Peyton Place (television) 52, 130, 163
Philadelphia 184
Phillippines 76
Pierson, Frank 22, 80
Pillow Talk 19, 51, 63
The Pink Panther 16, 67, 70, 92
Pitt, Ingrid 15
Pittsburgh 18, 155
A Place in the Sun 23
Planet of the Apes 8, 123, 125, 131–133, **132**, 198
Pleasance, Donald 154
Please Don't Eat the Daisies 19, 114
Plummer, Christopher 163, 192–195
Point Blank 9
Poitier, Sidney 3, 8, 20–21, 24–25, 39, 78, 94–96, 155–156, 172–174, 198; *The Bedford Incident* 21, 95; *The Defiant Ones* 20, 156, 173; *Duel at Diablo* 94; *For the Love of Ivy* 39; *The Greatest Story Ever Told* 23–26; *Guess Who's Coming to Dinner* 172–174; *In the Heat of the Night* 94–96; *Lilies of the Field* 3, 7, 9, 20, 21, 25, 39, 94, 155; *The Long Ships* 21; *Paris Blues* 20, 22, 31; *A Patch of Blue* 20–21; *Porgy and Bess* 20, 68; *Pressure Point* 20, 173; *A Raisin in the Sun* 20, 155; *The Slender Thread* 21, 95; *To Sir, with Love* 155–156; *see also* racism
Poland 33, 130
Polanski, Roman 5, 130

270 Index

Pollack, Sydney 4
Pollard, Michael J. 167–168
Pollyanna (1960) 30, 84, 103
Polynesia 42, 143
Ponti, Carlo 136, 188
Porgy and Bess 20, 68
pornography 17, 48, 97
Portis, Charles 105
Portnoy's Complaint 91
Posta, Adrienne 155, 156
Preminger, Otto 68–69, 109, 126, 130
Prentiss, Paula 91
Presley, Elvis 38, 40, 50, 158
Pressbook 161, 180
Pressure Point 20, 173
Preston, Robert 65–66
Previn, Andre 111, 129, 162
Prima, Louis 105
private eye 8
The Prize 16, 52, 163
Production Code 7, 11, 17, 19, 45, 46, 47, 73, 91, 96, 121, 142, 148, 172, 197; *see also* sex
The Professionals 66–68, 72
Promise Her Anything 167
Psycho (1960) 8, 101–103, 130
pubic hair 8
Puerto Rico/Puerto Ricans 31, 158; *see also* racism
Purple Noon 135

Quayle, Anthony 114
The Quiet Man 60, 103
The Quiller Memorandum 105
Quine, Richard 44
Quinn, Anthony 113, 114, 133, 135

racism 3, 8, 10, 17, 20, 31, 32, 45, 94, 96, 156, 158, 172, 173, 174, 197; *The Bedford Incident* 21, 95; *The Chase* 76, 167; Civil Rights 17; *Dark of the Sun* 13; *The Defiant Ones* 20, 156, 173; *Duel at Diablo* 94; *Flame in the Streets* 31; *For the Love of Ivy* 39; *Gentleman's Agreement* 25, 31, 119; *Gone with the Wind* 186–188; *Guess Who's Coming to Dinner* 172–174; *Home of the Brave* 52; *Hurry Sundown* 76, 173; *In the Heat of the Night* 94–96; *The Incident* 92; *Lilies of the Field* 3, 7, 9, 20, 21, 25, 39, 94, 155; *The Long Ships* 21; *Nevada Smith* 56, 105, 117, 142, 143; *A Patch of Blue* 20–21; *Porgy and Bess* 20, 68; *Pressure Point* 20, 173; *A Raisin in the Sun* 20, 155; *The Searchers* 158, 169; *Sergeant Rutledge* 31; *The Seventh Dawn* 72; *The Slender Thread* 21, 95; *The Stalking Moon* 140; *To Kill a Mockingbird* 31–32, 112, 135; *To Sir, with Love* 155–156; *West Side Story* (1961) 158–160; *The World of Suzie Wong* 44–45
Raintree County 142
A Raisin in the Sun 20, 155
Rampling, Charlotte 49, 50
Rank 73, 118, 134
rape 31, 21, 22, 31, 37, 55, 63–65, 60, 76, 109, 188–190; *Bandolero* 55; *The Boston Strangler* 63–65; *Cape Fear* (1962) 32; *The Collector* (1965) 70, 145, 194; *The Detective* (1968) 63, 144; *Doctor Zhivago* 188–190; *Hurry Sundown* 76, 173; *Last Summer* 37, 106; *The Outrage* 22; *Sergeant Rutledge* 31; *Two Women* 109
The Rat Race 31
ratings board 99
Rattigan, Terence 65
Reap the Wild Wind 66
Rear Window 48

Rebel Without a Cause 158
Red River 27, 48, 138
The Red Shoes 7, 50
Redford, Robert 76–78, 121, 130, 138, 167, 191, 198; *Barefoot in the Park* 76–78; *Butch Cassidy and the Sundance Kid* 138–140; *The Chase* 76, 167; *Downhill Racer* 130; *Tell Them Willie Boy Is Here* 138; *This Property Is Condemned* 76
Redgrave, Lynn 39, 49–50
Redgrave, Vanessa 49, 107–109, 113
Reed, Carol 4, 42, 72, 89–91; *The Agony and the Ecstasy* 130, 131, 190; *Mutiny on the Bounty* (1962) 42–44; *Oliver!* 89–91; *Our Man in Havana* 104; *The Third Man* 7, 42
Reed, Oliver 89–91
Reiner, Carl 85–87
reissue 6, 11, 19, 42, 47, 49, 59, 62, 78, 80, 101, 103, 104, 119, 120, 127, 145, 149, 152, 154, 156, 157, 160, 166, 172, 178, 185, 186, 188, 190, 198, 199
Reisz, Karel 4
Reitherman, Wolfgang 104
release strategy 98, 102, 113, 122, 125, 140, 148, 155, 166
Relyea, Robert 61
remake 42, 198
Remick, Lee 59, 163
rentals 9, 15, 16, 18, 19, 21, 23, 26, 27, 29, 31, 32, 34, 36, 37, 38, 40, 42, 44, 45, 47, 49, 50, 51, 54, 56, 57, 59, 62, 63, 65, 66, 68, 69, 70, 72, 74, 76, 77, 80, 81, 83, 84, 85, 87, 88, 91, 92, 94, 96, 99, 101, 103, 104, 105, 106, 107, 109, 111, 112, 113, 115, 117, 119, 120, 121, 123, 127, 129, 131, 133, 136, 138, 140, 142, 120, 121, 123, 127, 129, 131, 133, 136, 138, 140, 142, 143, 145, 146, 149, 151, 152, 156, 158, 160, 164, 166, 168, 170, 172, 174, 176, 178, 181, 183, 185, 188, 190, 192, 195
Republic 60
Repulsion 130
research 9, 18
Return to Peyton Place 78
Reynolds, Debbie 65, 163, 168–170
Rhodes 114
Rice Girl 26
Richards, Beah 173
Richardson, Ralph 68
Richardson, Tony 4, 146, 148
Ride the Whirlwind 36
Rio Bravo 26, 27, 30, 40
Rio Conchos 118
Rio Grande 60
Ritt, Martin 22, 36
RKO 10
roadshow 5, 6, 8, 23, 27, 37, 42, 59, 68, 69, 81, 89, 92, 108, 112, 113, 115, 116, 117, 118, 122, 123, 125, 126, 127, 128, 129, 133, 135, 136, 142, 143, 145, 151, 156, 158, 174, 179, 183, 184, 186, 188, 192, 198, 199
robbery 144
Robbins, Harold 141
Robbins, Jerome 158–160
The Robe 126
Roberts, Christian 155–156
Roberts, Marguerite 105
Robertson, Cliff 39–40
Robin and the 7 Hoods 128
Robson, Mark 52–54, 162–164; *Valley of the Dolls* 162–164; *Von Ryan's Express* 52–54
Rocco and His Brothers 135
Rodgers and Hammerstein 108, 192–195
Rollins, Sonny 70, 72
romance 9, 91, 106

Index 271

Rome 45, 47, 53, 174, 181
Romeo and Juliet (1968) 9, 37, 121–123, 158
La Ronde 76
Room at the Top 70, 89, 146
Rose, Tania 156–157
Rose, William 85, 87, 156–157, 172–174
Rosemary's Baby 5, 8, 130–131
Rosenberg, Aaron 42
Rosenberg, Stuart 22
Ross, Arthur A. 92
Ross, Herbert 146
Ross, Katharine 54, 92, 138, 190–192
Rosza, Mikloz 83, 109, 110, 183
Rota, Nino 122
Roth, Philip 91
Russell, Kurt 194
The Russians Are Coming, the Russians Are Coming 82, 85–87, **86**, 94
Ryan, Cornelius 151, 152
Ryan, Robert 67, 160
Rydell, Mark 73, 74, 123

Sabato, Antonio 81–83
The Sad Sack 19
Saint, Eva Marie 68, 81–83, 85–87; *Exodus* 81–83; *North by Northwest* 30, 62, 68, 74, 87, 101, 159, 194; *Raintree County* 142; *The Russians Are Coming, the Russians Are Coming* 85–87; *The Sandpiper* 78, 82, 87, 120; *The Stalking Moon* 140
St. Laurent, Yves 9
The St. Valentine's Day Massacre 166
Saks, Gene 76–77, 164
salary 59, 69, 93, 94, 95, 107, 111, 115, 120, 121, 135, 145, 149, 151, 174, 179, 184, 185
Salt, Waldo 96, 98, 99
Saltzman, Harry 78, 152, 170, 177
San Francisco 145
The Sand Pebbles 115–117, **116**, 144, 194
Sanders, George 104–105
The Sandpiper 78, 82, 87, 120
Sanford, Isabel 173
Sarris, Andrew 1, 36, 125, 188
Satan Never Sleeps 45
Saturday Night and Sunday Morning 148
Saturday Review 106, 121, 125, 149
Saul, Oscar 40
Savalas, Telly 22, 160, 162
Saving Mr. Banks 181
Scala, Gia 19, 114
Scenes from a Revolution 95
Schaffner, Franklin J. 4, 131
Schatz, Thomas 10
Scheider, Romy 70
Schickel, Richard 36, 188
Schifrin, Lalo 22, 23, 73, 74, 144
Schlesinger, John 4, 96–99, 125
Schnee, Charles 48
Schneider, Romy 16
Schofield, Paul 112, 117
Schulman, Arnold 91, 92
science fiction: 8, 123, 131; *Barbarella* 125; *Charly* 3, 9, 39–40, 65, 138; *Creature from the Black Lagoon* 92; *Dr. Goldfoot and the Bikini Machine* 34; *Fahrenheit 451* 123; *Fantastic Voyage* 123, 133; *The Fly* 155; *The Martian Chronicles* 123; *Planet of the Apes* 8, 123, 125, 131–133, **132**, 198; *Two Thousand and One: A Space Odyssey* 8, 9, 36, 123–126, **124**, 133; *The Valley of Gwangi* 33

Scotland 79
Scott, George C. 95, 136
The Searchers 158, 169
The Second Best Secret Agent in the World 34
Seconds 73, 82
Segal, George 120, 121, 151
Sellers, Peter 3, 15–16, 26, 59, 67, 69–70, 77, 87–88, 94, 118, 186, 198; *After the Fox* 77; *The Bobo* 59; *Casino Royale* (1967) 87–88, 154; *Dr. Strangelove* 16, 123, 136; *Heavens Above* 16; *The Millionairess* 16; *The Pink Panther* 16, 67, 70, 92; *A Shot in the Dark* 15–16; *Two-Way Stretch* 16; *What's New Pussycat* 69–70; *The World of Henry Orient* 16; *The Wrong Arm of the Law* 16; *The Wrong Box* 70
Selznick, David O. 186
Send Me No Flowers 85
Sennett, Mack 158
Separate Tables 114
sequel 178, 198
Sergeant Rutledge 31
series film 78
Serling, Rod 131
The Servant 118
Seven Arts 21, 83, 108, 145, 148
Seven Days in May 9, 82
Seven Samurai 81
The Seven Year Itch 18, 112
The Seventh Dawn 72
The Seventh Seal 25
70mm 5, 8, 37, 61, 68, 89, 109, 118, 123, 186, 188, 198
Seville 111
Sex and the Single Girl 92
sexuality 3, 4, 7, 8, 10, 19, 47, 70, 72, 73, 91, 106, 107, 111, 148, 174, 186; abortion 70–72; censor 7, 8, 17, 45, 72, 197; LGBT (*The Children's Hour* 58, 73, 145, 194; *The Detective* [1968] 63, 144; *The Fox* 73–74; *The Killing of Sister George* 97; *Psycho* [1960] 101–103; *Therese and Isabelle* 18; *The Trials of Oscar Wilde* 28); masturbation (*The Fox* 73–74; *Portnoy's Complaint* 91); nudity 8, 16, 17, 73, 91; Production Code 7, 11, 17, 19, 45, 46, 47, 73, 91, 96, 121, 142, 148, 172, 197; rape (*Bandolero* 55; *The Boston Strangler* 63–65, **64**; *Cape Fear* [1962] 32; *The Collector* [1965] 70, 145, 194; *The Detective* [1968] 63, 144; *Doctor Zhivago* 188–190; *Hurry Sundown* 76, 173; *Last Summer* 37, 106; *The Outrage* 22; *Sergeant Rutledge* 31; *Two Women* 109); sex (*Alfie* [1965] 70–72, **71**; *The Americanization of Emily* 143; *The Apartment* 18–19; *Baby Doll* 25, 142; *Barbarella* 125; *Bitter Rice* 45, 136; *Blow-Up* 5, 8, 36, 108; *BUtterfield* 48–49, *The Carpetbaggers* 140–142, **141**; *Darling* 50, 98, 190; *Easy Rider* 34–37; *The Fox* 73–74; *Goodbye, Columbus* 91–92; *The Graduate* 190–92; *A Guide for the Married Man* 164; *I Am Curious (Yellow)* 17–18; *Irma La Douce* 111–112; *La Dolce Vita* 45–47; *The Libertine* 18; Meyer, Russ 18; *Midnight Cowboy* 96–99; *Of Human Bondage* [1964] 28, 44; *One Hundred Rifles* 8; *Rice Girl* 26; *Romeo and Juliet* [1968] 121–123; *Sex and the Single Girl* 92; *The Sweet Ride* 144; *Tom Jones* 146–149; *Valley of the Dolls* 162–164; *Venus in Furs* [1969] 18; X-certificate 17, 18, 97, 98)
The Shaggy Dog 19, 30
Shakespeare, William 121
Shane 56, 67, 142
Shapiro, Stanley 62, 74
Sharif, Omar 3, 133–136, 145–146, 188–190, 198; *Doctor Zhivago* 188–190; *Funny Girl* 145–146; *Lawrence of Arabia* 133–136

272 Index

Shavelson, Melville 106
Shaw, George Bernard 179
Shaw, Robert 78, 80, 112
She 38
The Sheepman 169
Shenandoah 8, 54–56, *55*, 66, 78
Shepperton Studios 115
Sherlock Holmes 6; *Sherlock Holmes and the Deadly Necklace* 172
Sherlock Holmes and the Deadly Necklace 172
Sherman, Richard M. 27–28, 181–183
Sherman, Robert B. 27–28, 181–183
Ship of Fools 33, 67, 80, 130, 173
A Shot in the Dark 15–16, 92
Showboat (1951) 108
Shurlock, Geoffrey 17, 72, 121, 142; *see also* Production Code
Siegel, Don 163
Signoret, Simone 22
The Silencers 40–42, *41*, 56, 85, 152
Silliphant, Stirling 39, 94, 95
Silver, Phil 156
Silverstein, Elliott 80
Simmons, Jean 7, 126, 127
Simon, Neil 76–77, 164–166
Simon and Garfunkel 191
Sinatra, Frank 3, 9, 19, 51–53, 61, 66, 68, 108, 130, 146, 198; *Come Blow Your Horn* 164; *The Detective* (1968) 63, 144; *From Here to Eternity* 113, 143, 152; *The Manchurian Candidate* 52, 54, 82; *The Naked Runner* 15; *None But the Brave* 52; *Ocean's 11* (1960) 40, 42, 128; *Robin and the 7 Hoods* 128; *Tony Rome* 9, 63, 70; *Von Ryan's Express* 52–54
Sinatra, Nancy 154
Sink the Bismarck! 72
Six Three Three Squadron 15, 39
Sjoman, Vilgot 17
Skidoo 130
Sleeping Beauty 104
The Slender Thread 21, 95
A Small Rebellion 22
Smashing Time 39
Smith, Paul 103
Snow White and the Seven Dwarfs 99
Sodom and Gomorrah 23
Sol Madrid 13
Soloff, Maurice 135
Solomon, Aubrey 11
Solomon and Sheba 23
Some Like It Hot 18, 30, 74, 92, 101, 112, 148, 157, 164
Sommer, Elke 15, 16
Son of Flubber 27, 29–31, 181
Sondheim, Stephen 158
The Sons of Katie Elder 83, 105
Sordi, Alberto 118
The Sound of Music 3, 5, 89, 91, 108, 115, 127, 190, 192–195, *193*, 198, 199
South Pacific 66, 108, 194
Southern, Terry 34, 88
Spain 52, 109–111, 135, 174, 188
Spartacus 22, 109, 117, 123, 126–127, 129, 135
Spartacus and the Gladiators 126
Spellbound 114
Spiegel, Sam 13, 133–136, 188
Splendor in the Grass 8, 93, 121, 158, 166
split screen 65, 81
spy films 6, 32, 34, 40, 87, 152, 170, 176; Bond, James 6, 7, 9, 11, 27, 34, 40, 41, 42, 50, 59, 78–80, 87, 88,

146, 152–154, 170–172, 176–178, 190, 198; Connery, Sean 3, 4, 34, 78, 79, 80, 148, 151, 152–154, 170–172, 176–178, 194, 198; Fleming, Ian 27, 130, 152, 170, 177; Flint, Derek 6, 32–34, 87, 88, 198; *From Russia with Love* 152–154; *Funeral in Berlin* 154: Goldfinger 170–172; Helm, Matt 6, 40, 78, 87, 88, 198; *In Like Flint* 34, 78, 152; *The Ipcress File* 34, 70, 72; Le Carre, John 34, 130; *The Liquidator* 34; Martin, Dean 40–42, 83, 114, 152, 198; *Modesty Blaise* 34, 152; *Murderers Row* 152; *Never Say Never Again* 177; *On Her Majesty's Secret Service* 154; *Our Man Flint* 32–34, *33*, 40, 56, 78, 85, 152; *Our Man in Havana* 104; *The Quiller Memorandum* 105; *The Second Best Secret Agent in the World* 34; *The Silencers* 40–42, *41*, 56, 85, 152; *The Spy Who Came In from the Cold* 34, 39, 80, 121; *Thunderball* 6, 81, 154, 176–178, *177*, 190; *Torn Curtain* 22, 56, 129; *The Wrecking Crew* 40; *You Only Live Twice* 28, 82, 152–154, 153, 188
The Spy Who Came in from the Cold 34, 39, 80, 121
Stagecoach (1939) 67
Stalag 17 18, 44
The Stalking Moon 140
Stamp, Terence 70
Stanwyck, Barbara 47
Star! 138
Star Trek (television) 107
Stark, Ray 145, 148
Stefano, Joseph 101
Steiger, Rod 80, 94, 95, 96, 188
Steiner, Max 186
Steppenwolf 37
Stevens, George 23–26, 56, 67
Stevens, Stella 40
Stevenson, Robert 29–31, 84–85, 99–101, 181–183; *The Absent Minded Professor* 99–101; *Blackbeard's Ghost* 149; *In Search of the Castaways* 57, 84, 181, 183; *The Love Bug* 149–151; *Mary Poppins* 181–183; *Old Yeller* 29, 50, 85, 119; *Son of Flubber* 29–31; *That Darn Cat* 84–85
Stewart, James 51, 54–56, 107, 168–170, 198; *Bandolero* 55; *Cheyenne Autumn* 54, 66; *Firecreek* 107; *Flight of the Phoenix* 107; *How the West Was Won* 168–170; *The Man Who Shot Liberty Valance* 54, 67; *Mr. Hobbs Takes a Vacation* 54; *Rear Window* 48; *Shenandoah* 54–56; *Two Rode Together* 66; *Vertigo* 36, 102
The Story of Robin Hood and His Merrie Men 29, 119
La Strada 46, 136
Streisand, Barbra 145–146, 198
Strode, Woody 67, 126, 127
Strouse, Charles 166
Stroyberg, Annette 114
Sturges, John 61
Suddenly, Last Summer 48, 173
Sunday in New York 76, 80
Sunset Blvd. 18
Surtees, Robert 42
Susann, Jacqueline 130, 162
Sutherland, Donald 160, 162
Sweden 7, 17
The Sweet Ride 144
Swift, David 103
Swiss Family Robinson (1961) 30, 57, 118, 119–120, 151
Switzerland 44, 172
The Sword in the Stone 104, 105
Sylbert, Richard 131
Syms, Sylvia 45

Index

273

Tahiti 42
Taiwan 116
takeover 10
The Tall Story 76, 80
Tamahine 45
Tamblyn, Russ 158
The Taming of the Shrew 122
Tammy and the Bachelor 78
Taradash, Daniel 142, 143
Tarantino, Quentin 37
Tarzan 6, 78
Tarzan Goes to India 38
Tarzan the Ape Man (1959) 104
Tarzan's Greatest Adventure 37
Tarzan's Three Challenges 172
Tate, Sharon 40, 130, 162–163
tax 44
Taylor, Elizabeth 3, 48, 58, 78, 89, 120–121, 143, 158, 174–176, 179, 198; *Butterfield 8* 120–121; *Cleopatra* 174–176; *Ivanhoe* (1952) 106; *A Place in the Sun* 23; *Raintree County* 142; *The Sandpiper* 78, 82, 87, 120; *Suddenly, Last Summer* 48, 173; *The Taming of the Shrew* 122; *The VIPs* 65, 120; *Who's Afraid of Virginia Woolf?* 120–121
Taylor, Rod 13, 51
television 5, 32, 39, 51, 55, 57, 62, 66, 67, 78, 80, 85, 91, 92, 95, 100, 101, 104, 105, 107, 119, 138, 155, 157, 160, 164, 169, 181, 183, 191
Tell Them Willie Boy Is Here 138
The Ten Commandments (1956) 136
Texas 61
That Darn Cat! 84–85, 149
That Touch of Mink 8, 62–63, 198
Therese and Isabelle 18
These Three 73
The Thin Red Line 73
The Third Day 38
The Third Man 7, 42
Thirty Six Hours 28, 82
This Property Is Condemned 76
The Thomas Crown Affair 85, 144
Thompson, J. Lee 114, 131
Thoroughly Modern Millie 127–129, **128**, 138, 146
Thorpe, Richard 169
Those Magnificent Men in Their Flying Machines 94, 117–119, 129
The Three Stooges 157
The Thrill of It All 51, 63, 85
Thunderball 6, 81, 154, 176–178, **177**, 190
Time 29, 40, 59, 62, 70, 72, 80, 88, 105, 106, 111, 131, 140, 145, 149, 172, 178, 192
Tiomkin, Dmitri 59, 61, 114, 115
To Kill a Mockingbird 31–32, 112, 135
To Sir, with Love 35, 94, 155–156
Tobago 119
Tokyo 178
Tom Jones 7, 98, 146–149, **147**
Tomlinson, David 149
Tony Rome 9, 63, 70
Torn Curtain 22, 56, 129
The Towering Inferno 199
Toys in the Attic 138, 143
Tracy, Spencer 156–158, 169, 172–174, 198; *Guess Who's Coming to Dinner* 172–174; *Inherit the Wind* 156, 157; *It's a Mad, Mad, Mad, Mad World* 156–158; *Judgement at Nuremberg* 156, 157
The Train 54, 66, 82, 112, 167
Trauner, Alex 112

Travers, P.L. 181
Travilla, William 163
Trevelyan, John 72
The Trials of Oscar Wilde 28
The Trip 22, 36
True Grit (1969) 8, 36, 105–106
Truffaut, François 167
Trumbo, Dalton 68, 126, 142, 143; *see also* blacklist
The Truth About Spring 84
Turkey 79
Turman, Lawrence 191
Turnberg, Karl 183
Turner, Lana 9, 39
Twentieth Century-Fox 5, 6, 10, 11, 24, 32, 34, 37, 38, 48, 52, 56, 63, 68, 78, 89, 115, 117, 118, 123, 125, 131, 133, 136, 138, 145, 151, 162, 163, 174, 192, 194
Two for the Road 59
Two Rode Together 66
Two Thousand and One: A Space Odyssey 8, 9, 36, 123–126, **124**, 133
Two-Way Stretch 16
Two Women 109

Udult 29, 30, 31, 57, 99, 103, 149, 198; *see also* Disney
The Undefeated 56, 138
Underworld U.S.A. 39
United Artists 10, 11, 15, 18, 23, 24, 25, 27, 34, 59, 68, 69, 78, 92, 94, 96, 97, 98, 106, 111, 112, 118, 126, 142, 146, 148, 152, 155, 156, 157, 158, 170, 178, 198
U.S. Circuit Court of Appeal 17
US Supreme Court 173
Universal 9, 10, 13, 26, 31, 51, 54, 62, 74, 83, 123, 126, 127, 129
University of Wisconsin 11
The Unsinkable Molly Brown 65
The Untouchables (television) 107
Up the Down Staircase 73
Ure, Mary 13, 15
Uris, Leon 68
Ustinov, Peter 16, 26, 126, 127, 149

Vadim, Roger 26, 76, 114
Valenti, Jack 17, 121
The Valley of Gwangi 33
Valley of the Dolls 107, 130, 162–164, 186
Vallone, Raf 110
Van Dyke, Dick 27–29, 56–57, 118, 181–183
Van Heusen, Jimmy 128, 129
Variety 11, 15, 16, 18, 19, 21, 23, 24, 26, 27, 31, 32, 34, 38, 42, 44, 45, 47, 54, 56, 62, 63, 66, 68, 76, 83, 92, 94, 96, 101, 103, 107, 109, 111, 112, 119, 120, 123, 127, 129, 131, 133, 136, 142, 151, 152, 154, 155, 156, 158, 162, 164, 165, 170, 172, 174, 176, 182, 183, 185, 188, 190, 192
Vaughn, Robert 34, 144
Venice 79
Venus in Furs (1969) 18
Vertigo 36, 102
The Victors 38
Vietnam 17, 83, 84, 117, 168, 197
The Vikings 22, 126
Village Voice 32, 36, 37, 70, 96, 136
violence 3, 8, 10, 34, 36, 67, 102, 162, 168, 174, 186; *The Boston Strangler* 63–65; *The Dirty Dozen* 160–162; *A Fistful of Dollars* 67; *The Good, the Bad and the Ugly* 186; *One Hundred Rifles* 8; *The Professionals* 66–68; *Psycho* 101–103; *Where Eagles Dare* 13–15; *The Wild Bunch* 44, 105, 140, 162
The VIPs 65, 120

274   **Index**

The Virginian 55
Vitti, Monica 82, 152
Vogue 50, 168, 195
Voigt, Jon 96–99
Von Ryan's Express 52–54, **53**, 78, 163
von Sydow, Max 23, 25, 142, 188

Wages of Fear (1953) 81, 120
Wagner, Robert 158
Wait Until Dark 57–59, **58**, 78, 166, 186
Wakabayashi, Akiko 154
Wales 79
Walker, Clint 160, 161
Wallace, Edgar 78
Wallace, Lew 183
Wallach, Eli 170
Wallis, Hal B. 76, 105
Walsh, Bill 29, 56, 84, 99, 149, 181
Walters, Jessica 82, 83
Walton, Tony 183
Wanger, Walter 174, 176
war 5, 13, 54, 84, 160, 162; Africa (*Dark of the Sun* 13; *Guns at Batasi* 38, 117, 130; *Khartoum* 15, 131; *Last Command* 60; *Zulu* 7, 70, 141); China (*The Sand Pebbles* 115–117, **116**, 144, 194); Civil War (*Gone with the Wind* 3, 68, 78, 170, 176, 184, 186–188, **187**, 195, 199; *Raintree County* 142); Russia (*Doctor Zhivago* 9, 37, 77, 95, 136, 186, 188–190, **189**, 198, 199; *War and Peace* [1956] 136); Vietnam (*Apocalypse Now* 84; *The Deer Hunter* 84; *The Green Berets* 83–84, 105, 106); World War I (*All Quiet on the Western Front* 65; *The Blue Max* 37–38, 49, 117; *Paths of Glory* 22); World War II (*The Americanization of Emily* 143; *Battle of the Bulge* 13, 56, 107; *Bridge on the River Kwai* 44, 45, 78, 119, 126, 132, 135, 186, 188; *Carve Her Name with Pride* 112; *Casablanca* 105; *The Desert Fox* 38; *The Devil's Brigade* 39; *The Dirty Dozen* 13, 22, 78, 88, 130, 160–162, **161**; *Force Ten from Navarone* 198; *From Here to Eternity* 113, 143, 152; *The Great Escape* 34, 52, 57, 115, 144, 161; *The Guns of Navarone* 13, 15, 32, 42, 114–115, 131; *The Heroes of Telemark* 143; *Home of the Brave* 52; *Ice Cold in Alex* 114, 119; *In Harm's Way* 13, 52; *Judgement at Nuremberg* 156, 157; *The Longest Day* 5, 13, 32, 112, 118, 151–152; *None But the Brave* 52; *Operation Crossbow* 13, 15, 38; *Sink the Bismarck!* 72; *Six Three Three Squadron* 15, 39; *Stalag 17* 18, 44; *The Thin Red Line* 73; *The Train* 54, 66, 82, 112, 167; *The Victors* 38; *Von Ryan's Express* 52–54, **53**, 78, 163; *Where Eagles Dare* 13–15, **14**, 198)
War and Peace (1956) 136
The War Lord 131
The War Wagon 83
Warner, Jack L. 10, 108, 179, 183
Warner Brothers 10, 13, 21, 22, 58, 65, 66, 73, 77, 78, 83, 92, 108, 118, 120, 121, 131, 166, 179, 191
Washington Post 16, 38, 44, 49, 51, 56, 57, 69, 77, 81, 83, 85, 87, 104, 109, 112, 115, 117, 127, 133, 138, 152, 155
Watusi 155
Wayne, John 3, 6, 22, 24, 25, 26–27, 55, 56, 59, 61, 62, 67, 83–84, 105–106, 120, 134, 151, 160, 168–170, 198; *The Alamo* (1960) 59–62; *Circus World* 67; *The Commancheros* 67; *El Dorado* (1967) 83; *The Green Berets* 83–84; *Hatari!* 26–27; *Hellfighters* 105, 138; *The Horse Soldiers* 26; *How the West Was Won* 5, 8, 38, 42, 54, 168–170, **169**; *In Harm's Way* 13, 52; *The Man Who Shot Liberty Valance* 54, 67; *McLintock* 55; *North to Alaska* 69, 105, 169; *The Quiet Man* 60,

103; *Red River* 27, 48, 138; *Rio Bravo* 26, 27, 30, 40; *Rio Grande* 60; *The Searchers* 158, 169; *The Sons of Katie Elder* 83, 105; *Stagecoach* (1939) 67; *True Grit* (1969) 8, 36, 105–106; *The Undefeated* 56, 138; *The War Wagon* 83
weather 160, 194
Webb, Charles 190
Webb, James 168, 169
Webber, Robert 13
Welch, Raquel 3, 163, 178
Welcome to Hard Times 107
Weld, Tuesday 77, 130
Welles, Orson 87, 88, 112
Werner, Oskar 80
West India 31
West Side Story (1961) 31, 42, 93, 98, 108, 122, 158–160, **159**, 194, 199
western 1, 5, 6, 8, 15, 32, 34, 36, 38, 51, 54, 66, 67, 68, 80, 105, 106, 138, 140, 169, 186; *The Alamo* (1960) 9, 22, 42, 56, 59–62, **60**, 83, 115; *Bandolero* 55; *The Big Country* 126, 169; *Butch and Sundance: The Early Days* 198; *Butch Cassidy and the Sundance Kid* 11, 74, 77, 138–140, **139**, 164; *Calamity Jane* 51; *Cat Ballou* 22, 67, 76, 80–81; *Cheyenne* (television) 160; *Cheyenne Autumn* 54, 66; *Cimarron* (1960) 109, 158; *The Commancheros* 67; *Custer of the West* 13; *The Deadly Companions* 105; *Duel at Diablo* 94; *El Dorado* (1967) 83; *Firecreek* 107; *A Fistful of Dollars* 67; *Five Card Stud* 105; *Four for Texas* 38, 40; *Friendly Persuasion* 56, 67, 119; *The Good, the Bad and the Ugly* 186; *The Hallelujah Trail* 66; *High Noon* 67, 113, 114, 138, 157; *Hombre* 13, 22, 138; *The Horse Soldiers* 26; *Hour of the Gun* 98; *How the West Was Won* 5, 8, 38, 42, 54, 168–170, **169**; *The Indian Fighter* 26; *The Left Handed Gun* 167; *Mackenna's Gold* 131; *The Magnificent Seven* (1960) 1, 34, 78, 80, 115, 126, 144, 158, 161; *Major Dundee* 32, 34, 66, 131, 136; *The Man Who Shot Liberty Valance* 54, 67; *McLintock* 55; *The Naked Spur* 109; *Nevada Smith* 56, 105, 117, 142, 143; *North to Alaska* 69, 105, 169; *One Hundred Rifles* 8; *The Outrage* 22; *Paint Your Wagon* 108; *The Professionals* 66–68, 72; *Red River* 27, 48, 138; *Ride the Whirlwind* 36; *Rio Bravo* 26, 27, 30, 40; *Rio Conchos* 118; *Rio Grande* 60; *The Searchers* 158, 169; *Sergeant Rutledge* 31; *Shane* 56, 67, 142; *The Sheepman* 169; *Shenandoah* 8, 54–56, **55**, 66, 78; *The Sons of Katie Elder* 83, 105; *Stagecoach* (1939) 67; *The Stalking Moon* 140; *Tell Them Willie Boy Is Here* 138; *True Grit* (1969) 8, 36, 105–106; *Two Rode Together* 66; *The Undefeated* 56, 138; *The Virginian* 55; *The War Wagon* 83; *Welcome to Hard Times* 107; *The Wild Bunch* 44, 105, 140, 162; *Will Penny* 131
Wexler, Haskell 121
What's New Pussycat 69–70, 78, 87
When Comedy Was King 157
Where Eagles Dare 13–15, **14,** 198
Whiting, Leonard 121
Whitman, Stuart 117, 151
Whittingham, Jack 176, 178
Who's Afraid of Virginia Woolf? 17, 73, 117, 120–121, 131, 191, 197
Wicki, Bernard 151
Widmark, Richard 21, 59, 61, 107, 169
The Wild Angels 35, 36
The Wild Bunch 44, 105, 140, 162
The Wild One 192
Wilder, Billy 4, 18–19, 42, 44, 111–112, 135, 158; *The*

Index

275

Apartment 18–19; *The Fortune Cookie* 164; *Irma La Douce* 111–112; *Some Like It Hot* 18, 30, 74, 92, 101, 112, 148, 157, 164
Wilder, Gene 167
Will Penny 131
Williams, John 162
Williamson, Nicol 13
Willingham, Calder 191
Willson, Meredith 65
Wilson, Michael 131, 132, 133, 135
Winters, Shelley 20, 21, 25, 70, 72
Wise, Robert 4, 66, 108, 115–119, 158–160, 192–195
With Six You Get Eggroll 63
Wollen, Peter 1
Wood, Ed 1
Wood, Natalie 3, 76, 77, 92–94, 115, 158, 160, 163
Woodfall 147, 148
Woolf, John 70, 89
The World of Henry Orient 16
The World of Suzie Wong 44–45, 111
world premiere 169, 171, 177, 186, 190
World Telegraph and Sun 45
World War I 37, 134
World War II 9, 13, 52, 58, 74, 151, 161, 181, 186, 194
The Wrecking Crew 40
The Wrong Arm of the Law 16
The Wrong Box 70
Wyler, William 4, 56, 58, 61, 67, 70, 73, 145–146, 183–185, 194; *Ben-Hur* 183–185; *The Best Years of Our Lives* 185; *The Big Country* 126, 169; *The Children's*
Hour 58, 73, 145, 194; *The Collector* 70, 145, 194; *Friendly Persuasion* 56, 67, 119; *Funny Girl* 145–146; *How to Steal a Million* 59, 145
Wymark, Partrick 15

X-certificate 17, 18, 97, 98; *see also* Production Code

Yankee Stadium 62
Yates, Peter 144, 198
Yordan, Philip 198, 110
York, Michael 122
York, Susannah 113, 118, 146, 148
You Only Live Twice 28, 82, 152–154, 153, 188
Young, Terence 57–59, 78–80, 152, 170–172, 176–178; *Goldfinger* 170–172; *Thunderball* 176–178; *Wait Until Dark* 57–59; *You're a Big Boy Now* 21
Young Cassidy 188
Yours, Mine and Ours (1968) 21, 106–107
youth 10, 37, 122, 125, 151, 199
Yugoslavia 188

Z 4, 5, 36
Zanuck, Darryl F. 10, 38, 118, 131, 151–152
Zanuck, Richard 63
Zeffirelli, Franco 121–123, 125, 158
Zimbalist, Sam, Jr. 183, 185
Zinnemann, Fred 25, 67, 112–113, 135, 138, 143
Zorba the Greek 50
Zulu 7, 70, 141